T0189876

Lecture Notes in Computer Science 14031

Founding Editors

Gerhard Goos
Juris Hartmanis

The series Lecture Notes in Computer Science (LNCS), including its subseries Lecture Notes in Artificial Intelligence (LNAI) and Lecture Notes in Bioinformatics (LNBI), has established itself as a medium for the publication of new developments in computer science and information technology research, teaching, and education.

LNCS enjoys close cooperation with the computer science R & D community, the series counts many renowned academics among its volume editors and paper authors, and collaborates with prestigious societies. Its mission is to serve this international community by providing an invaluable service, mainly focused on the publication of conference and workshop proceedings and postproceedings. LNCS commenced publication in 1973.

Aaron Marcus · Elizabeth Rosenzweig ·
Marcelo M. Soares
Editors

Design, User Experience, and Usability

12th International Conference, DUXU 2023
Held as Part of the 25th HCI International Conference, HCII 2023
Copenhagen, Denmark, July 23–28, 2023
Proceedings, Part II

 Springer

Editors
Aaron Marcus
Aaron Marcus and Associates
Berkeley, CA, USA

Elizabeth Rosenzweig
World Usability Day and Bubble Mountain
Consulting
Newton Center, MA, USA

Marcelo M. Soares
Southern University of Science
and Technology – SUSTech
Shenzhen, China

ISSN 0302-9743   ISSN 1611-3349 (electronic)
Lecture Notes in Computer Science
ISBN 978-3-031-35695-7   ISBN 978-3-031-35696-4 (eBook)
https://doi.org/10.1007/978-3-031-35696-4

This Springer imprint is published by the registered company Springer Nature Switzerland AG
The registered company address is: Gewerbestrasse 11, 6330 Cham, Switzerland

Foreword

Human-computer interaction (HCI) is acquiring an ever-increasing scientific and industrial importance, as well as having more impact on people's everyday lives, as an ever-growing number of human activities are progressively moving from the physical to the digital world. This process, which has been ongoing for some time now, was further accelerated during the acute period of the COVID-19 pandemic. The HCI International (HCII) conference series, held annually, aims to respond to the compelling need to advance the exchange of knowledge and research and development efforts on the human aspects of design and use of computing systems.

The 25th International Conference on Human-Computer Interaction, HCI International 2023 (HCII 2023), was held in the emerging post-pandemic era as a 'hybrid' event at the AC Bella Sky Hotel and Bella Center, Copenhagen, Denmark, during July 23–28, 2023. It incorporated the 21 thematic areas and affiliated conferences listed below.

A total of 7472 individuals from academia, research institutes, industry, and government agencies from 85 countries submitted contributions, and 1578 papers and 396 posters were included in the volumes of the proceedings that were published just before the start of the conference, these are listed below. The contributions thoroughly cover the entire field of human-computer interaction, addressing major advances in knowledge and effective use of computers in a variety of application areas. These papers provide academics, researchers, engineers, scientists, practitioners and students with state-of-the-art information on the most recent advances in HCI.

The HCI International (HCII) conference also offers the option of presenting 'Late Breaking Work', and this applies both for papers and posters, with corresponding volumes of proceedings that will be published after the conference. Full papers will be included in the 'HCII 2023 - Late Breaking Work - Papers' volumes of the proceedings to be published in the Springer LNCS series, while 'Poster Extended Abstracts' will be included as short research papers in the 'HCII 2023 - Late Breaking Work - Posters' volumes to be published in the Springer CCIS series.

I would like to thank the Program Board Chairs and the members of the Program Boards of all thematic areas and affiliated conferences for their contribution towards the high scientific quality and overall success of the HCI International 2023 conference. Their manifold support in terms of paper reviewing (single-blind review process, with a minimum of two reviews per submission), session organization and their willingness to act as goodwill ambassadors for the conference is most highly appreciated.

This conference would not have been possible without the continuous and unwavering support and advice of Gavriel Salvendy, founder, General Chair Emeritus, and Scientific Advisor. For his outstanding efforts, I would like to express my sincere appreciation to Abbas Moallem, Communications Chair and Editor of HCI International News.

July 2023   Constantine Stephanidis

HCI International 2023 Thematic Areas
and Affiliated Conferences

Thematic Areas

- HCI: Human-Computer Interaction
- HIMI: Human Interface and the Management of Information

Affiliated Conferences

- EPCE: 20th International Conference on Engineering Psychology and Cognitive Ergonomics
- AC: 17th International Conference on Augmented Cognition
- UAHCI: 17th International Conference on Universal Access in Human-Computer Interaction
- CCD: 15th International Conference on Cross-Cultural Design
- SCSM: 15th International Conference on Social Computing and Social Media
- VAMR: 15th International Conference on Virtual, Augmented and Mixed Reality
- DHM: 14th International Conference on Digital Human Modeling and Applications in Health, Safety, Ergonomics and Risk Management
- DUXU: 12th International Conference on Design, User Experience and Usability
- C&C: 11th International Conference on Culture and Computing
- DAPI: 11th International Conference on Distributed, Ambient and Pervasive Interactions
- HCIBGO: 10th International Conference on HCI in Business, Government and Organizations
- LCT: 10th International Conference on Learning and Collaboration Technologies
- ITAP: 9th International Conference on Human Aspects of IT for the Aged Population
- AIS: 5th International Conference on Adaptive Instructional Systems
- HCI-CPT: 5th International Conference on HCI for Cybersecurity, Privacy and Trust
- HCI-Games: 5th International Conference on HCI in Games
- MobiTAS: 5th International Conference on HCI in Mobility, Transport and Automotive Systems
- AI-HCI: 4th International Conference on Artificial Intelligence in HCI
- MOBILE: 4th International Conference on Design, Operation and Evaluation of Mobile Communications

List of Conference Proceedings Volumes Appearing Before the Conference

47. CCIS 1836, HCI International 2023 Posters - Part V, edited by Constantine Stephanidis, Margherita Antona, Stavroula Ntoa and Gavriel Salvendy

https://2023.hci.international/proceedings

Preface

User experience (UX) refers to a person's thoughts, feelings, and behavior when using interactive systems. UX design becomes fundamentally important for new and emerging mobile, ubiquitous, and omnipresent computer-based contexts. The scope of design, user experience, and usability (DUXU) extends to all aspects of the user's interaction with a product or service, how it is perceived, learned, and used. DUXU also addresses design knowledge, methods, and practices, with a focus on deeply human-centered processes. Usability, usefulness, and appeal are fundamental requirements for effective user-experience design.

The 12th Design, User Experience, and Usability Conference (DUXU 2023), an affiliated conference of the HCI International conference, encouraged papers from professionals, academics, and researchers that report results and cover a broad range of research and development activities on a variety of related topics. Professionals include designers, software engineers, scientists, marketers, business leaders, and practitioners in fields such as AI, architecture, financial and wealth management, game design, graphic design, finance, healthcare, industrial design, mobile, psychology, travel, and vehicles.

This year's submissions covered a wide range of content across the spectrum of design, user-experience, and usability. The latest trends and technologies are represented, as well as contributions from professionals, academics, and researchers across the globe. The breadth of their work is indicated in the following topics covered in the proceedings.

Five volumes of the HCII 2023 proceedings are dedicated to this year's edition of the DUXU Conference:

- Part I addresses topics related to design methods, tools and practices, as well as emotional and persuasive design.
- Part II addresses topics related to design case studies, as well as creativity and design education.
- Part III addresses topics related to evaluation methods and techniques, as well as usability, user experience, and technology acceptance studies.
- Part IV addresses topics related to designing learning experiences, as well as design and user experience of chatbots, conversational agents, and robots.
- Part V addresses topics related to DUXU for cultural heritage, as well as DUXU for health and wellbeing.

The papers in these volumes were included for publication after a minimum of two single–blind reviews from the members of the DUXU Program Board or, in some cases, from Preface members of the Program Boards of other affiliated conferences. We would like to thank all of them for their invaluable contribution, support, and efforts.

July 2023

Aaron Marcus
Elizabeth Rosenzweig
Marcelo M. Soares

12th International Conference on Design, User Experience and Usability (DUXU 2023)

Program Board Chairs: **Aaron Marcus**, *Aaron Marcus and Associates, USA,* **Elizabeth Rosenzweig,** *World Usability Day and Bubble Mountain Consulting, USA,* and **Marcelo M. Soares**, *Southern University of Science and Technology – SUSTech, P.R. China*

Program Board:

- Sisira Adikari, *University of Canberra, Australia*
- Claire Ancient, *University of Winchester, UK*
- Eric Brangier, *Université de Lorraine, France*
- Tian Cao, *Nanjing University of Science & Technology, P.R. China*
- Silvia de los Ríos, *Indra, Spain*
- Romi Dey, *Lowe's India Pvt Ltd, India*
- Cristina Pires Dos Santos, *Polytechnic Institute of Beja, Portugal*
- Marc Fabri, *Leeds Beckett University, UK*
- Guneet Ghotra, *Wayne State University, USA*
- Michael Gibson, *University of North Texas, USA*
- Hao He, *Central Academy of Fine Arts, P.R. China*
- Wei Liu, *Beijing Normal University, P.R. China*
- Zhen Liu, *South China University of Technology, P.R. China*
- Keith Owens, *University of North Texas, USA*
- Gunther Paul, *James Cook University, Australia*
- Francisco Rebelo, *University of Lisbon, Portugal*
- Christine Riedmann-Streitz, *MarkenFactory GmbH, Germany*
- Patricia Search, *Rensselaer Polytechnic Institute, USA*
- Dorothy Shamonsky, *Brandeis University, USA*
- David Sless, *Communication Research Institute, Australia*
- Maksym Tkachuk, *service.so, Ukraine*
- Elisângela Vilar, *Universidade de Lisboa, Portugal*
- Wei Wang, *Hunan University, P.R. China*
- Haining Wang, *Hunan University, P.R. China*

The full list with the Program Board Chairs and the members of the Program Boards of all thematic areas and affiliated conferences of HCII2023 is available online at:

http://www.hci.international/board-members-2023.php

HCI International 2024 Conference

The 26th International Conference on Human-Computer Interaction, HCI International 2024, will be held jointly with the affiliated conferences at the Washington Hilton Hotel, Washington, DC, USA, June 29 – July 4, 2024. It will cover a broad spectrum of themes related to Human-Computer Interaction, including theoretical issues, methods, tools, processes, and case studies in HCI design, as well as novel interaction techniques, interfaces, and applications. The proceedings will be published by Springer. More information will be made available on the conference website: http://2024.hci.international/.

General Chair
Prof. Constantine Stephanidis
University of Crete and ICS-FORTH
Heraklion, Crete, Greece
Email: general_chair@hcii2024.org

https://2024.hci.international/

Contents – Part II

Creativity and Design Education

Design Case Studies

Design Specifications for Bidirectional Feedback on Indoor Environmental Quality

Eli Alston-Stepnitz[1,2]([✉]) [iD], Angela Sanguinetti[1,2] [iD], and Sarah Outcault[1] [iD]

[1] Energy and Efficiency Institute, University of California, Davis, CA 95616, USA
ecalstonstepnitz@ucdavis.edu
[2] Consumer Energy Interfaces Lab, University of California, Davis, CA 95616, USA

Abstract. Recent scientific research and the COVID-19 pandemic have underscored the impact that indoor environmental quality (IEQ) has on human health. Technological developments have made low-cost air quality sensors widely available, and that has given rise to many products that aim to monitor and report IEQ. A wide range of environmental conditions impact occupant health and comfort, leaving product developers with critical decisions about what information to collect and report, as well as how to display it. This paper reviews the user interfaces of 19 IEQ products by examining the parameter, data, spatial, and temporal granularity of information presented, an approach informed by the Eco-feedback Design Behavior (EFDB) framework. Common tendencies and patterns are identified. The findings and the EFDB framework are used to identify best practices for IEQ user interfaces, explaining how and when to utilize high and low granularity data to provide salient, meaningful and motivating information to both building occupants and building managers.

Keywords: indoor environmental quality (IEQ) · air quality · user interface · eco-feedback

1 Introduction

Over the last decade, scientific research has increasingly shown the impact of indoor environmental quality (IEQ) on human health. The World Health Organization (WHO) has identified several indoor air pollutants - including benzene, carbon monoxide, formaldehyde, radon, and nitrogen dioxide - as the most common and most frequently linked to negative health effects (WHO 2010). In addition, recent global events such as large-scale wildfires and the COVID-19 pandemic have affirmed the importance of indoor air quality (IAQ) and other factors that determine indoor environmental quality (IEQ).

Industry standards reflect this pattern. The fourth version of "Standards on Indoor Air Quality Assessment" issued by Leadership in Energy and Environmental Design (LEED), the most popular building rating system, places caps on particulate matter (PM2.5 and 10), ozone, carbon monoxide (CO), total volatile organic compounds (TVOCs), formaldehyde (HCHO), and a group of target volatile compounds made up of 35 different compounds including the same substances identified by the WHO (U.S.

A. Marcus et al. (Eds.): HCII 2023, LNCS 14031, pp. 3–18, 2023.
https://doi.org/10.1007/978-3-031-35696-4_1

Green Building Council 2019). RESET Air for Commercial Interiors, a performance-based standard whose intent is to monitor, track, and report IAQ uses six key performance targets: PM2.5, TVOC, CO, CO2, temperature, and relative humidity (RH).

Also reflected in contemporary standards are the new and continually expanding definitions and parameters of building wellness. The International WELL Building Institute (IWBI) recently released WELL v2, the first building standard that focuses exclusively on human health and wellness and uses measures from eleven main categories: air, water, nourishment, light, movement, thermal comfort, sound, materials, mind, community, innovation (IWBI 2018). Parameters related to air, light, thermal comfort, and sound include: Air: PM2.5, PM10, HCHO, CO, CO2, radon, ventilation; Light: illuminance, light levels, glare, color rendering, flicker; Thermal Comfort: temperature, relative humidity, air speed; and Sound: background noise level and acoustical privacy (IWBI 2018).

In parallel with the evolution of building standards, there have been recent technological developments in sensors that have enabled a proliferation of indoor air and environmental quality monitoring tools. However, the effectiveness of such tools relies on the accuracy of the underlying sensors, as well as the presentation of the information they gather. This paper applies a framework for designing effective eco-feedback to assess 19 existing IEQ monitoring products and identify best practices for the user interface design of such products[1]. The focus is on the topic of granularity of information displayed and considering the potential user experience of residential and commercial consumers (i.e., building occupants and managers).

2   Literature Review and Theoretical Framework

This paper draws on the Eco-feedback Design-Behavior (EFDB) Framework (Sanguinetti et al. 2018), which was developed to help guide the design of effective eco-feedback. Eco-feedback typically refers to the provision of information related to energy or other resource use and associated environmental impacts to consumers with the aim of encouraging more sustainable behavior (Froelich et al. 2010). This research adapts and applies the EFDB Framework to the topic of IEQ monitoring and display.

The EFDB Framework includes a typology of design dimensions (related to the information provided, display style, and timing of feedback interfaces) that influence the degree to which the interface can draw users' attention to important information, communicate that information in a meaningful way, and motivate appropriate actions. This framework is highly relevant to IEQ monitoring and display devices which are designed to inform occupants or building managers (or both) of the indoor conditions in a building, and potentially act in response to the information provided. The present research focuses on the design dimension of information granularity. Figure 1 illustrates our adaptation to the framework to fit the context of IEQ monitoring and display; adapted section outlined. The following sections define the sub-dimensions of information granularity considered in this research and describe relevant literature on IEQ monitoring and display.

---

[1] We gratefully acknowledge this work was funded in part by a research contract with arbnco.

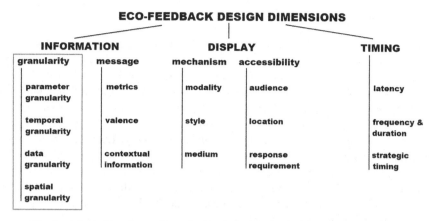

Fig. 1. Adapted typology of eco-feedback design dimensions for IEQ feedback.

2.1 Parameter Granularity

Information granularity originally includes three sub-dimensions: behavioral, temporal, and data granularity (Sanguinetti et al. 2018). Behavioral granularity refers to the magnitude of behavior reflected in eco-feedback (e.g., how many different energy-using behaviors are captured by the data). For example, whole-home energy feedback reflects a wider range of behaviors than appliance-specific feedback. Sanguinetti et al. (2018) summarized the value of both high and low behavioral granularity: High behavioral granularity provides precision to support learning connections between relevant actions and monitored environmental consequences, whereas low behavioral granularity can provide summary information useful for goal-setting and tracking.

Behavioral granularity is not particularly relevant to the context of IEQ displays; however, it inspired us to consider another sub-dimension, "parameter granularity," which refers to the potential to display specific IEQ parameters (e.g., TVOCs, relative humidity) or an aggregate of multiple parameters (e.g., air quality). Because IEQ encompasses myriad aspects of the ambient environment that can affect human health, categories (i.e., aggregate parameters) are often used (Heinzerling et al. 2013). Wei et al. (2019) reviewed fourteen Green Building classification schemes, identifying 90 parameters, and found that the most frequently used IEQ categories for assessment are: thermal environment, IAQ, visual environment (e.g., lighting), and acoustic environment. For the thermal environment, the most commonly used specific parameters were predicted mean vote (PMV), predicted percentage of dissatisfied (PPD), room operative temperature, room air temperature, room air relative humidity, and air speed. For IAQ, the most commonly used specific parameters were ventilation rate (outdoor air supply rate), TVOC, HCHO, CO_2, CO, PM10, PM2.5, ozone, benzene, and radon. For the visual environment, the most commonly used parameters were illuminance level, daylight factor, and spatial daylight autonomy. The acoustic environment is most commonly captured by ambient noise and reverberation time. Additional categories found in the literature but less frequently used include office layout, office furnishings, cleanliness, and maintenance (Altomonte and Schiavon 2013).

2.2 Temporal Granularity

Temporal granularity refers to the length of time the displayed information reflects (e.g., instantaneous, reflecting a single moment in time, or accumulated throughout the day). Sanguinetti et al. (2018) summarized the value of both high and low temporal granularity in the context of eco-feedback: Similar to high behavioral granularity, high temporal granularity provides precision to support learning connections between relevant actions and monitored environmental consequences, whereas low temporal granularity can provide summary information useful for goal-setting and tracking. Temporal granularity is an important consideration for IEQ parameters because some can have negative health impacts immediately while others cause damage from prolonged exposure; for example, CO and HCHO and their associated health impacts are dependent on concentration and frequency and length of exposure (Abdul-Wahab et al. 2015). Therefore, more complex levels of temporal granularity may be warranted.

2.3 Data Granularity

Data granularity refers to the resolution of information conveyed and is often a function of the visualization mode. For example, numeric data, which has many levels, can have very high granularity, whereas the same data conveyed via a red-amber-green light scheme (only three levels) is low granularity. Once again, high data granularity provides precision to support learning connections between relevant actions and monitored environmental consequences, whereas low data granularity can provide summary information (Sanguinetti et al. 2018).

Ambient displays (of IEQ as well as eco-feedback) are intended to convey important information at a glance, which can be accomplished with low data granularity (e.g., green or red light). When presented in a salient manner, low data granularity information is useful for attracting attention, at which point a user should be able to engage further for more details.

Higher granularity information (in terms of all sub-dimensions) is often provided as users drill down. In an approach the UI literature calls progressive disclosure, advanced information and explanations are provided only when the user requests it (Springer and Whittaker 2019). This allows users to drive exactly when and how information is provided, removing confusion and avoiding the inefficiencies that arise from spurious, unwanted information (Springer and Whittaker 2019).

2.4 Spatial Granularity

Researchers identified a fourth sub-dimension relevant for IEQ feedback: spatial granularity, defined as the size of the space reflected in the data (e.g., building, floor, specific office). With regard to IEQ, space matters immensely. Complex indoor structures and dynamic environments result in heterogeneous IEQ performance, or spatial variations in thermal comfort and air quality (Jin et al. 2018). Indoor air pollutant distribution, in particular, can vary substantially within a building. Usage of personalized heating and cooling devices can also create variation in thermal conditions (Jin et al.). LEED and WELL also disaggregate physical spaces within buildings into smaller areas with different space conditioning or lighting requirements. Thus, aggregating IEQ information across a large space (i.e., low spatial granularity) may obscure issues. Pritoni et al. (2017) demonstrated the benefits of monitoring thermal comfort data with high spatial granularity across a large campus to identify problematic rooms, which can be linked to building automation system zones to guide troubleshooting.

Similar to the benefits of high and low granularity across the other sub-dimensions, high spatial granularity offers precision to ensure all spaces are safe, whereas low spatial granularity can be useful for tracking goals at higher levels (e.g., whole building or campus). Furthermore, similar to temporal granularity in the context of IEQ, there can be greater complexity to spatial granularity considerations. For example, studies on occupant satisfaction (e.g., Hua et al. 2014) have found that occupants who have perimeter workspaces (windows) in buildings tend to be more satisfied with their environment than occupants in interior workspaces (no windows). More specifically, they found that satisfaction levels across multiple IEQ parameters (e.g., relative humidity, air movement, and lighting conditions) were significantly different between occupants working in perimeter and interior zones during both winter and summer. Since IEQ issues may be localized in particular ways, monitoring devices should be strategically distributed

Table 1. Commercially available IEQ monitoring systems.

Tool	Year	Company Location	Setting
AirBeam	2006	United States	Personal/Wearable
Airthings	2008	Norway	Commercial/Residential
Airthinx	2017	United States	Commercial/Residential
Arbnwell	2012	United Kingdom	Commercial
Awair	2013	United States	Commercial/Residential
CITI-SENSE	2016	Europe	Personal/Wearable
CleanSpace	2009	United Kingdom	Personal/Wearable
Comfy	2012	United States	Commercial
Foobot	2015	United Kingdom	Residential
iBiosys: RubiXpod	2010	United Kingdom	Commercial
Iota	2018	United States	Commercial
IQAir- AirVisual Pro	2017	Switzerland/United States	Personal/Wearable
Kaiterra	2014	United States/ Asia-Pacific	Commercial/Residential
NATEDE	2016	Italy	Residential
netatmo	2012	France	Residential
Purple Air	2015	United States	Commercial/Residential
QLEAR	2013	China	Commercial
uHoo	2014	Asia-Pacific	Commercial/Residential
Vaisala	1973	Finland	Commercial

throughout a space and displays should provide information at corresponding levels of spatial granularity (i.e., to pinpoint specific locations) for certain IEQ parameters.

3 Method

3.1 Product Review

In June of 2020, the researchers conducted a product review of 19 commercially-available IEQ monitoring and feedback products (Table 1). Product reviews involved collecting data from product websites, sales materials, user guides, and tutorials, and carefully examining descriptions and images of the products to better understand the range of available features and functionalities. The data collected was organized into tables summarizing key attributes related to the sub-dimensions of granularity outlined above and then analyzed to identify common themes and effective strategies.

4 Results

4.1 Parameter Granularity

Across the 18 products reviewed, the most commonly monitored IEQ parameters are temperature, humidity, carbon dioxide (CO_2), particulate matter (PM2.5 and/or PM10), and volatile organic compounds (VOCs) (Table 2). The second most frequently included IEQ parameters are carbon monoxide (CO) and air pressure. Tools more focused on overall IEQ/wellness as opposed only to IAQ (e.g., iBiosys RubiXpod) also display information about lighting and sound (e.g., acoustics, noise, vibration).

With regard to labeling parameters, most products use the exact (scientific) name (e.g., humidity, CO_2, radon). Just over a quarter ($n = 5$) of products employ some more colloquial, user friendly terms. For example, VOCs are labeled as "chemicals" (Awair), "airborne chemicals" (uHoo), and "chemical pollutants" (Foobot), while PM is referred to as "dust" (Awair, NATEDE) and "particles" (iBiosys RubiXpod).

In addition to displaying specific IEQ parameters, almost all tools present an aggregate parameter that summarizes multiple individual parameters (see Table 2). This aggregate parameter is typically an air quality index, such as the United States Air Quality Index (AQI), a numerical value from 0–500 derived from the levels of ozone, nitrogen dioxide, sulfur dioxide, carbon monoxide, and particulate matter (Environmental Protection Agency 2023) (Figs. 2 and 3). IAQ Air Visual Pro dashboard is unique in also providing an outdoor air quality index (Fig. 3). uHoo and Awair display a more general aggregate score, with the latter allowing users to select the combination of specific parameters that contribute to the aggregate score (Figs. 4 and 5). uHoo's aggregate score appears to include temperature, humidity and air pressure in addition to those parameters used in the US AQI index. It is also important to note that based on the interface alone, it is often unclear whether the aggregate index is a standard one (and which standard, such as the US AQI) or which specific parameters are incorporated (e.g., Figs. 6 and 7).

Table 2. Parameters displayed in reviewed products.

Tool	Aggregate			Specific						
	IAQ	OAQ	Other	Temp	Hum	Light	CO2	PM	VOC	Other
AirBeam	X	X						X		
Airthinx	X			X	X		X	X	X	CH_2O, air pressure
Airthings	X			X	X		X		X	Radon, air pressure
Arbnwell	X			X	X		X	X	X	
Awair			X	X	X		X	X	X	
CITI-SENSE	X	X		X	X			X		NO, NO_2, O_3
CleanSpace		X								CO
Comfy	X			X		X				
Foobot	X	X		X	X		X	X	X	
iBiosys: RubiXpod	X	X		X	X	X	X	X		NH_3, CO, H_2S, FA, odor, noise, vibration, air pressure
iota				X	X		X	X	X	CO, methane
IQAir - AirVisual Pro	X	X		X	X		X	X		
Kaiterra	X	X		X	X		X	X	X	
NATEDE	X	X		X	X			X	X	CO
netatmo	X			X	X		X			noise
Purple Air	X	X		X	X			X		Air pressure
QLEAR	X	X		X	X		X	X	X	
uHoo	X			X	X		X	X	X	NO2, ozone, air pressure
Vaisala	X	X		X	X		X			

4.2 Data Granularity

Most IEQ displays include both low and high data granularity information for each parameter. Aggregate parameters (i.e., low granularity parameters), such as air quality indices, are most often communicated via low data granularity, with a few levels denoted by red-amber-green colors and/or normative labels such as "good", "moderate", and "poor". Such low granularity indices are often the most salient aspect of interfaces, particularly on home screens. However, many products pair these low data granularity indicators (colors and normative labels) with higher granularity numeric data, such as scores and percentages (Figs. 2 and 4, 5, 6, 7).

Fig. 2. Kaiterra kiosk view displays aggregate AQI and individual parameter breakdowns. Retrieved from: kaiterra.com.

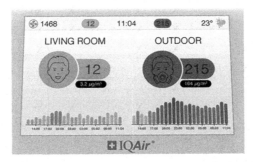

Fig. 3. IQ Air Visual Pro dashboard allows users to compare AQI for both indoors and outdoors. Retrieved from: iqair.com.

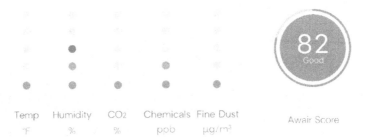

Fig. 4. Aggregated Awair score and individual IEQ parameters. Retrieved from: getawair.com.

In app home screens and desktop dashboards, specific IEQ parameters are sometimes conveyed with low data granularity only (Figs. 4 and 5 use a color-coded scale), and sometimes with both low and high data granularity (Figs. 2 and 6, 7). In Airthings and Airthinx displays (Figs. 6 and 7), the high granularity numeric levels are always present, and a low granularity (amber and red light) indicator only appears when a parameter is outside the healthy range.

Fig. 5. uHoo dashboard with aggregated IEQ score and individual parameters. Retrieved from: getuhoo.com.

Fig. 6. Airthings aggregate score and individual parameters. Retrieved from: airthings.com.

4.3 Spatial Granularity

Most IEQ feedback tools provide a breakdown of IEQ data by space (higher spatial granularity) in addition to indices that summarize IEQ across the whole space (lower spatial granularity). For example, Awair and Kaiterra allow users to view data from all of their sensors in one place (Figs. 8 and 9), while also providing the option to filter which spaces to monitor and drill down for more detailed information (e.g., high granularity parameters). Airthinx, Iota, foobot, IQAir, NATEDE, and uHoo all have a similar process. Again, Awair is unique in allowing users to customize an aggregate score based on user-selected spaces.

Fig. 7. Airthinx aggregate score and individual parameters. Retrieved from: airthinx.io.

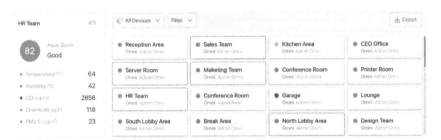

Fig. 8. Awair dashboard displays real-time aggregate score and breakdown by location. Retrieved from: awair.com.

Fig. 9. Kaiterra dashboard displays real-time levels from different sensors in multiple locations. Retrieved from: kaiterra.com.

4.4 Temporal Granularity

All the products reviewed offer the ability to monitor IEQ in real-time, i.e., display instantaneous data that immediately reflect changes. Many tools also offer historical graphs of instantaneous data or other strategies to break down accumulated data into meaningful summaries (Figs. 10, 11, 12 and 13). Awair uses weekly averages to compare current conditions to past records (Fig. 11). QLEAR and Airthinx report the percentage of time that conditions were within particular ranges or thresholds over user-specified time

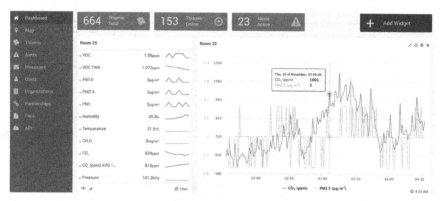

Fig. 10. Airthinx website dashboard allows users to see historical data. Retrieved from: <u>airthi nx.io</u>.

<u>DASHBOARD</u>   **WEEKLY REPORT**

Awair Dashboard   📅 5 March - 12 March   ⌄

SUMMARY

Average Score of the Week   ● **89.9**   Compared to the previous week, your score **decreased** by   **-1.3%**

Weekly Average
Your Aggregated Dust has the most room for improvement.

Temperature	Humidity	CO₂	Chemicals	Aggregated Dust	PM 2.5
● Good	● Good	● Good	● Fair	● Fair	● Good
23.4 ·c	43.2 %	624.0 ppm	396.6 ppb	19.8 µg/m³	2.0 µg/m³
+ 3.1%	+ 3.3%	+ 12.6%	+ 24.0%	- 8.0%	+ 105.7%

Fig. 11. Awair dashboard provides users with comparative feedback about weekly averages. Retrieved from: <u>getawair.com</u>.

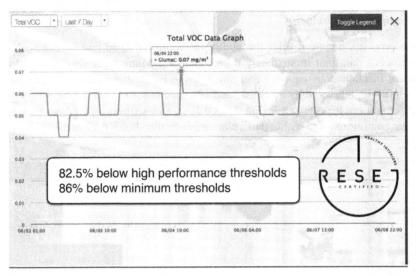

Fig. 12. QLEAR dashboard displays historical data and offers performance summaries. Retrieved from: qlear.io.

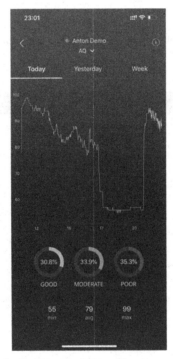

Fig. 13. Airthinx dashboard displays historical data with aggregate scores. Retrieved from: airthi nx.io.

intervals (e.g., day, week; Figs. 12 and 13); Airthinx also provides summary statistics (min, max and mean; Fig. 13).

5 Discussion

The following sections suggest best practices for information granularity in IEQ displays based on the product review, literature review, and consideration of potential user experience.

5.1 Best Practices for Parameter Granularity

IEQ displays should include both low and high granularity parameters (aggregate and specific). Aggregate parameters support easy, quick interpretation and prioritization, whereas specific parameters are required to pinpoint IEQ issues. Aggregate parameters should be emphasized at highest notification levels (e.g., home screens). Specific IEQ parameters should include those with the greatest impact on occupant well-being and those utilized in the most common IEQ standards (LEED, WELL, and RESET). Including IEQ parameters across all four WELL v2 categories (i.e., air, light, thermal comfort, and sound), rather than narrowly focusing on air quality, can offer a holistic picture of IEQ to support wellness and support user requirements related to IEQ building certifications.

Aggregate parameters should reflect meaningful constructs. They should draw attention to why the data are important for human well-being (e.g., comfort, air quality). This is particularly important for users who do not already recognize the value of IEQ data or are not familiar with some of the specific parameters. For example, separate air quality and thermal comfort categories may offer opportunities for user education (e.g., understanding the specific parameters that contribute to each, and learning to associate perceived conditions with objective IEQ data).

Another way to create meaningful categories is to use concepts that are important to users for other reasons. For example, using categories and labeling consistent with WELL standards may make the tool more appealing to users who are familiar with or already use those standards. Users familiar with the standard US or other country's AQI may find that to be a meaningful high data granularity index. Enabling users to create or choose some categories, as well as parameter and category labels, might be a useful strategy. Future user research should explore which specific parameters and categorizations (and their labeling) resonate most with different user groups, and if there are other reasons particular users may prefer concepts to be framed a certain way.

5.2 Best Practices for Data Granularity

IEQ displays should include both low and high data granularity. Similar to low granularity parameters (aggregate indices), low data granularity supports easy, quick interpretation and prioritization, whereas high data granularity provides precision. By providing different levels of granularity in response to different levels of user engagement, IEQ monitoring devices strike a balance, employing the advantages of both levels of detail.

Aggregate Parameters. IEQ displays should include a low data granularity index for aggregate parameters, e.g., Comfort Level: High, Air Quality: Fair. These low data granularity highest notification levels should be salient on an interface main screen; for example, if a building management team has the dashboard up to monitor IEQ data, they can notice issues with a passing glance. For occupants, the salient low granularity info should be on the app main screen or standalone display they can passively observe (e.g., a red-amber-green color scheme can evoke injunctive norms, telling the user that levels are good or bad). Further research is needed to determine whether adding a high granularity (numeric) score to a salient low data granularity indicator for an air quality index at a high notification level (e.g., home screen) adds significantly to the display when higher granularity data are available for specific parameters and/or upon further engagement.

Specific Parameters. Specific parameters (e.g., CO2, PM2.5, temperature) should be communicated in both low and high data granularity. Low granularity data for specific parameters is important for both building managers and occupants to allow them to easily identify whether they are within or outside acceptable standards. Thus, the levels (e.g., below minimum threshold) for these low data granularity indicators should map directly on to those standards for each parameter. Allowing building managers, or even occupants, to set those standards for particular parameters where appropriate could make the data much more meaningful.

High granularity data for specific parameters is especially important for building managers, to enable them to analyze precise data for patterns and for more sensitive feedback on changes they make, e.g., to building automation systems. However, pairing precise measurements (high data granularity) with normative low granularity cues (red, amber, green lights) might also benefit occupants by building literacy regarding acceptable levels for specific IEQ parameters. Additionally, communicating familiar parameters (e.g., temperature) in low granularity only may frustrate the user if they are used to seeing the high granularity measure. Usability research is needed to further explore these issues.

5.3 Best Practices for Spatial Granularity

IEQ displays should provide high and low spatial granularity information. Low spatial granularity is useful to summarize across (all sensors installed in) a whole building or campus (e.g., sick buildings, well buildings), whereas high spatial granularity provides precision, enabling the user to hone in on a problem or assess a particular issue that might be obscured in low spatial granularity data. IEQ tool interfaces could also allow users to aggregate across spaces in a way that suits their needs (e.g., across office spaces that may be spread across multiple floors and mixed with other space types that don't require the same type of monitoring).

Important considerations for spatial granularity are which spatial levels are most meaningful for the measured parameters (e.g., perimeter versus interior spaces), as well as how and where to present that information. Heat maps could be a powerful data visualization style that the researchers did not see in the reviewed tools. Future research should consider ways user experience and understandings may be enhanced through data visualizations.

5.4 Best Practices for Temporal Granularity

IEQ displays should include both low and high temporal granularity information. Real-time, instantaneous data is typically presented at the highest notification levels, which allows identification of immediate conditions and concerns. Accumulated data is typically provided at lower notification levels, enabling facilities managers and building occupants to see temporal patterns, e.g., to determine the severity of a problem (i.e., high VOCs due to new carpet installation versus a gas leak).

However, IEQ display designers should carefully consider the importance of frequency and duration of exposure when determining what temporal granularity will provide the most meaningful feedback for a given parameter. This should be the level at which the data are provided for that parameter at the highest motivation level. For example, thermal comfort parameters are likely most relevant in real-time (though they can also have a cumulative impact on occupant comfort and satisfaction). Real-time feedback of contaminant levels such as CO_2 is necessary to ensure real-time safety for occupants. However, for some parameters the risk lies in prolonged exposure (e.g., VOCs, PM2.5). If real-time, instantaneous levels are not as meaningful for a certain parameter, they should not be highlighted with greater salience or ease of access compared to the more important information of levels accumulated over a meaningful duration and/or frequency. The researchers did not observe this kind of complexity in the reviewed products and it could be challenging to display data for different parameters at different levels of temporal granularity. This is an area ripe for further study.

Users could also be allowed to specify the periods of time over which data are summarized, e.g., if they want to capture specific intervals such as before and after a retrofit. Historical (accumulated) data and the ability to summarize levels over multiple user-specified time periods would enable this use case.

6   Conclusion

Drawing on the product review of 19 commercially available IEQ monitoring and display tools, through the lens of the EFDB Framework (Sanguinetti et al. 2018), this research identified best practices for IEQ information granularity in the user interface. High and low granularity information - over the parameter, data, spatial, and temporal domains - serve distinct and important roles. Overall, low granularity data is useful at high notification levels and for goal-setting and tracking, whereas high granularity data is required to pinpoint problems and test solutions. The optimal level of granularity depends both on the user (i.e., occupant versus building manager), and the notification level (e.g., home screen versus three levels in). Providing users with the right level of detail is a balancing act. Display too much and you risk overwhelming the user, while too little may fail to adequately inform them. Existing products at the time of this research included a variety of useful low and high granularity IEQ information. Identified opportunities for further development include elaborated levels of temporal granularity for IEQ parameters for which frequency and duration of exposure are critical. Future research is needed to empirically determine the most effective IEQ feedback user interface designs in applied settings, and the suggested best practices herein can serve as hypotheses.

Policymakers establish standards and guidelines for various aspects of IEQ to protect occupants from the potential harms of indoor pollutants. Ensuring those standards are met requires IEQ monitoring, and corrective action when needed. Unlike the IEQ parameters themselves, IEQ monitoring devices are not subject to stringent requirements. The onus is on product developers to create products that display relevant, understandable, and actionable information in a manner that captures occupants' attention and provides building managers with the information they require to address problems.

References

Abdul-Wahab, S.A., En, S.C.F., Elkamel, A., Ahmadi, L., Yetilmezsoy, K.: A review of standards and guidelines set by international bodies for the parameters of indoor air quality. Atmos. Pollut. Res. **6**(5), 751–767 (2015)

Altomonte, S., Schiavon, S.: Occupant satisfaction in LEED and non-LEED certified buildings. Build. Environ. **68**, 66–76 (2013)

Carroll, J.M., Carrithers, C.: Training wheels in a user interface. Commun. ACM **27**(8), 800–806 (1984)

Environmental Protection Agency. Air Quality Index (AQI) Basics (n.d.). https://www.airnow.gov/aqi/aqi-basics/. Retrieved 10 Feb 2023

Froehlich, J., Findlater, L., Landay, J.: The design of eco-feedback technology. In: Proceedings of the SIGCHI Conference on Human Factors in Computing Systems, pp. 1999–2008, April 2010

Heinzerling, D., Schiavon, S., Webster, T., Arens, E.: Indoor environmental quality assessment models: a literature review and a proposed weighting and classification scheme. Build. Environ. **70**, 210–222 (2013)

Hua, Y., Göçer, Ö., Göçer, K.: Spatial mapping of occupant satisfaction and indoor environment quality in a LEED platinum campus building. Build. Environ. **79**, 124–137 (2014)

International WELL Building Institute. WELL Building Standard version 2 pilot ("WELL v2") (2018). https://v2.wellcertified.com/v/en/overview

Jin, M., Liu, S., Schiavon, S., Spanos, C.: Automated mobile sensing: towards high-granularity agile indoor environmental quality monitoring. Build. Environ. **127**, 268–276 (2018)

Sanguinetti, A., Dombrovski, K., Sikand, S.: Information, timing, and display: a design-behavior framework for improving the effectiveness of eco-feedback. Energy Res. Soc. Sci. **39**, 55–68 (2018)

Springer, A., Whittaker, S.: Progressive disclosure: empirically motivated approaches to designing effective transparency. In: Proceedings of the 24th International Conference on Intelligent User Interfaces, pp. 107–120, March 2019

World Health Organization. WHO guidelines for indoor air quality: selected pollutants. World Health Organization. Regional Office for Europe (2010)

Digital Fabrication in the Industrial Sector in Middle East, General Overview

Lindita Bande[✉], Jose Berengueres, Anwar Ahmad, Entesar Alawthali,
and Hala Ajiba

Architectural Engineering Department, College of Engineering,
Abu Dhabi, United Arab Emirates
{lindita.bande,jose}@uaeu.ac.ae

Abstract. Digital fabrication is a technology that is being applied in various sectors of the industry in the middle east. The application in laboratories is done with the aim to contribute to the modelling of buildings and structure in the field of Architectural Engineering, Mechanics, Biotechnology and more. Companies apply this technology to projects of different complexity.

The methodology to be followed in this study is as per the below steps:

1. Literature review on current application of Digital Fabrication in the Industrial Sector in Middle East

2. Current application of digital fabrication in UAE

3. Digital fabrication of complex structures, material overview

4. Findings and results

The aim is to analyze the current application of digital fabrication in academic environment such as UAE for a particular project of complex structures. Based of the literature review baselines are drawn. The analysis of the current application of the digital fabrication in UAEU creates the base for the focus of this research: 3D printing of Complex structures. The findings of this research can be of great use to the industrial sector but also to the Academic of Engineering College in UAEU.

Keywords: Digital Fabrication · Complex Structures · Middle East

1 Introduction

Digital fabrication is computer-controlled manufacturing. Digital design can be realized directly from design data using digital fabrication techniques. It enables architects to design and create at the same time. This facilitates prototyping [1]. Traditional fabrication techniques depend on molds and mechanical equipment that can only perform a few limited functions. They make exact duplicates of a particular product. While Digital fabrication machines enable the rewriting of command line and functions digitally. Instead of producing a single identical piece, they can generate multiple original designs as they fit within the constraints of the specific machine. These constraints can include size, material, and achievable multidimensionality.

© The Author(s), under exclusive license to Springer Nature Switzerland AG 2023
A. Marcus et al. (Eds.): HCII 2023, LNCS 14031, pp. 19–31, 2023.
https://doi.org/10.1007/978-3-031-35696-4_2

Internationally There are two types of digital fabrication: additive fabrication and subtractive fabrication. The end result of additive fabrication is achieved by adding material. Meanwhile, subtractive fabrication achieves the end result by removing material. The 3D printer and Computer Numerical Control mill are two of the most common examples of these fabrication methods [2]. Subtractive and additive fabrication can be classified to 2-Dimensional (2D) and 3-Dimensional (3D). For subtractive fabrication 2D includes plasma cutter, laser cutter and waterjet cutter. However, 3D includes Computerized Numerical Control (CNC) milling and hot water cutters [3, 4]. On the other hand, for Additive fabrication 2D includes traditional printers and 3D includes all Kinds of 3D printers [3, 4] such as, MX3D-Metal printer [5] and glass printer by Neri Oxman at MIT [6]. Formative fabrication can be considered as one of the digital fabrication methods. It includes bending, melting and stretching process normally applied on the elastic kind of materials [2]. Robotic arms can work utilizing one or more of the previously mentioned methods due to the different tools that can be attached to the robot arms [7]. Drones are adaptable in the same way that robotic arms are, but they are only now being investigated for fabrication requirement. They have the potential to do everything that robotic arms can, but they are not restricted to a single position. Drones and robotic arms could potentially work together in the future [8].

Digital fabrication has so far been used to I create topologically optimized structures and introduce novel architectural elements, produce furniture or sculptures, and print walls for comparably small houses [9].

In a collaborative study between several 3D printing laboratories and a research center in Zürich, Switzerland, they printed a 3D staircase with characteristics that maintain the structural stability of the staircase and reduce the materials used. The staircases optimized using computational design and fabricated using 3D printers, the staircase printed using concrete materials [10] (Fig. 1).

Fig. 1. Optimized stair string and slaps structure [10]

Other project under the name of "Flight Assembled Architecture." (Fig. 2) By Gramazio & Kohler and Raffaello D'Andrea in cooperation with ETH Zurich, the project contains of more 1.500 blocks which are installed by a swarm of robot helicopters, cooperating as per mathematical algorithms which translate digital design parameters to flying machine behavior [8].

Figure 3 depicts the KnitCandela concrete shell project, which was digitally fabricated. "It has a 5-ton concrete shell that was built with a 55 kg flexible cable net and knitted-fabric formwork tensioned into a timber and steel scaffolding frame".

Fig. 2. "Flight Assembled Architecture." Project [8]

Fig. 3. KnitCandela concrete shell project [11]

Other project depended on additive fabrication utilizing 3d printing technology is Star Lounge project which aimed to demonstrate the potential of small 3D printers on an architectural scale, by printing 3d printing for small objects and join them to gather to create human scale structure [12]. Figure 4 When considering the entire scale of architecture, current innovative projects remain relatively small scale.

Fig. 4. Star lounge by Emerging objects. [12]

2 Methodology

2.1 Literature Review on Current Application of Digital Fabrication in the Industrial Sector in Middle East

In response to the global climate change catastrophe and to promote more sustainably environment-friendly practices we must consume sustainable and affordable local building materials in the region, which is exactly what the paper focuses on.

This essay investigates the use of regional materials in building in the Middle East and North Africa. This consists of vegetal and earthen materials, rammed earth, municipal solid waste incineration ash (MSWIA), gypsum and phosphogypsum (PG), and construction and demolition waste (CDW).

It was conducted that the earth-based materials for 3D printing could be favorable in the region due to its climate. The usage of natural fibers can as well enhance the properties of printed materials. Additionally, it reprocesses eco-friendly materials and offers good thermal comfort. There are several different trends in the region for recycling these materials. Furthermore, the levels of development are extremely uneven between countries in the region [1].

The study examines the syllabus of two architectural programs in the Middle East and compares the findings with award-winning architectural firms in international competent practice from a digital design perspective. It was a two-step process, the first step started with an investigation into cutting-edge technology-driven firms and ended with selecting three award-winning firms subsequently and studying them using a deliberate review.

Phase two examined the curriculum of each architecture school and the responsible and interviewed the responsible instructors through a qualitative approach of in-depth interviews. The perceptions and recommendations were recorded when interviewing the staff members from both schools, four from each school, this helped evaluate the state of integrated digital design techniques in the architecture education of the intended schools. As a result of the study, it was clearly discussed how the current structures of architecture education curricula cannot keep up with the novel demands and societal requirements of architecture in the digital age. The significance of curriculum review and various methods for incorporating digital design applications are also recommended [2].

According to the study's findings that the maker movement sustains significant momentum in Egypt, Tunisia, and Morocco. The movement has gained traction quickly, in tandem with the changes in the area set off by the Arab Spring from 2011 forwards. Based on the 10 maker spaces studied, it is clear that dynamic methods of knowledge-sharing, innovation, and scaling, all of which foretell well for strengthening the public of practice in the spaces. This article is based on findings from research exploring approaches to revolution at makerspaces in Egypt, Tunisia and Morocco.

Relying on interviews, with individuals involved in makerspaces in each country-seven spaces in Egypt, two in Tunisia and one in Morocco, the article shows findings on both the origins and typical characteristics of the spaces, in addition to findings on five core themes that came up from the interviews: "knowledge-sharing; innovation and product development; openness, cooperation, and innovation ownership; attitudes in the direction of intellectual property (IP); and scaling [3].

Digital fabrication technologies have newly been adopted in architectural applications and constructions; however, the environmental influences of such approaches have been completely uninvestigated.

In this study, the environmental impact of constructing walls using 3D printing construction methods was compared to the impact of conventional construction methods. "A total of four types of materials were examined: conventional concrete, conventional cob, 3D printed (3DP) concrete, and 3DP cob." The study, later on, indicates that the utilization of renewable energy resources and innovative materials science can significantly enhance the abilities of both 3DP cob and 3DP concrete respectively for the following construction [4].

A reasonably economical method of preserving imperiled, lost, or damaged cultural artifacts is using 3D scanners and printers. The paper reviews recent creative projects adopting digital reproduction technology (which now increasingly results in physical replicas) for 3D scans of charged artifacts from the Middle East. Through the unconstitutional and open dissemination of this data, these works critically intervene in cultural heritage discourses [5].

The study describes three-dimensional printing as "a smart instrumental tool created to produce three-dimensional objects by imposing a semi-liquid material layer by layer to form the object." An approach of mixed methods was used in this study. Two steps were taken into consideration to analyze the efficiency of printed shelter cost, time, and energy performances against timber and steel shelters. First is to apply quantitative methods in a set of questions with ME engineers, Secondly, by having semi structured interviews with aid organizations. The outcomes can be used to regularize the architectural requirements, financial constraints, and construction schedules for 3DP shelters in refugee camps [6].

2.2 Current Application of Digital Fabrication in UAE/MATERIALS

Although digital fabrication of concrete has been hailed as a path to more environmentally friendly building through more resource-efficient design, the materials it has produced have larger carbon footprints and are likely to be less durable than those used in conventional construction. In this brief article, a relationship to help understand how a structure affects the environment is introduced, and it is underlined that the only distinctive environmental benefit that digital concrete offers is shape efficiency. Yet, efforts should still be made to bring digital concrete closer to normal concrete, particularly by adding big aggregates and more accurately describing the durability [7].

In order to explicitly establish the boundaries of the process and identify the class or sub-class to which a given technology belongs, it is critical that the work clearly defines the materials, application environment, and product to be manufactured. The RILEM MAPP qualities for characterizing DFC technology are what were given this moniker. In order to establish the effect (if any) on classification and to visually communicate the nature of the operation of the process, whether this is in series, simultaneously, or concurrently, the identification of subprocesses that are indispensable to the operation of the process need to be identified and mapped in time and synchronicity.

The research has led to a change in terminology and the meaning of "Binder Jetting," with Binder Jetting now falling under the umbrella term "Particle-bed Binding."

For the sake of process classification, the approach taken here does not refer to cement-based mortars and concretes as composite. When discretely positioned reinforcement is applied, resulting in the associated advantages in mechanical properties, a composite material is formed. When more than one separate material is utilized, the phrase "multi-material" is employed [8].

2.3 Digital Fabrication of Complex Structures, Material Overview

Current Applications. Currently the complex structures in the design environment are advancing with high velocity. Tools such rhino/grasshopper allows user to enter in the scripting language such as python and improve the building design by adding parameters corresponding to the geographical location, architectural style ad so on. However more work is needed in the3D printing technology in order to bring such complex design into life for a better environment thru an advanced technology where the time and cost are drastically reduced.

The research laboratories, the technology companies, and construction companies can improve the time and cost of construction. Trials in laboratories and architectural exhibitions are avatars of such an innovative approach to this dynamic. Machine learning based on available data can give the best available scenarios of specific structures (buildings) in terms of design, performance, stability, application to reality. The parametric design, 3D Printing, Digital Fabrication, innovative materials are all variables in a hybrid connection to the AI. Figures 5 and 6 show early formation of complex design starting from nonlinear elements. Figure 7 Shows how such complex design can be adapted in the urban environment. The future step would be to have an advanced technology for this structures to be built [9].

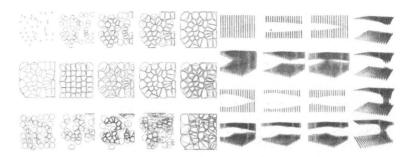

Fig. 5. Examples of non-linear architecture workshop, 2D concepts. [14]

There are many fields of application can be used such as digital bio fabrication where bioplastic is integrated in complex shapes in order to help plants improve the root system and the process of growth with the help of the biologically and digitally designed materials [10].

Reinforced concrete is a challenging material to be used in 3D printers. However, trials for various projects are ongoing and the results are promising. This with the aim of improving the current construction industry. This new way of building shall save time, save material waste, be more productive in terms of labor use [11, 12].

Moreover, the 3D printing technology can help improve the interior and exterior design of houses into more interesting design and shape. Where architects can experiment with their design in order to improve the indoor comfort and quality [13] (Figs. 8, 9, 10, 11, 13 and Table 1).

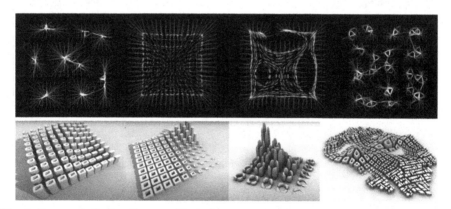

Fig. 6. Parametric Design Concepts liked with music, from Patrik Schimacher and Rosey Chan [15]

Fig. 7. Exhibition of the AI Parametric Design in Pavilion l'Arsenal in Paris [16].

Table 1. 3D examples of non-linear architecture workshop. [21]

3D Examples of Non-linear Architecture Parametric Workshop

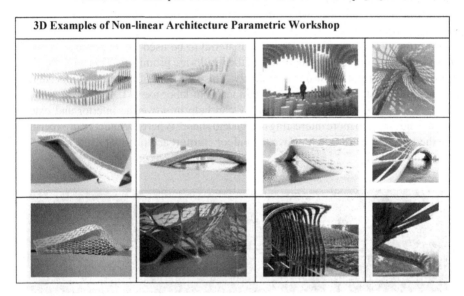

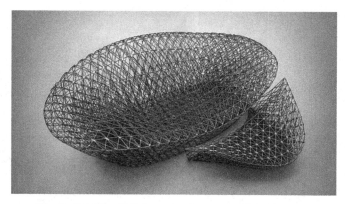

Fig. 8. 3D Printed Sofa made of cooper and chrome [17].

Fig. 9. 3D Printed Artwork by Zaha Hadid [18]

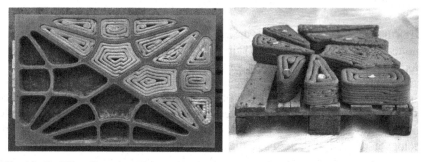

Fig. 10. Building Complex Elements in Concrete with 3D Printed Foam Formworks. [19]

Fig. 11. Complex design of Concrete 3D printed wall. [13]

Fig. 12. 3D printing of concrete in Netherland from BAM and Saint Gobbain. [20]

3 Results

Based on the analysis of the literature, the applications of the digital fabrications currently are limited. Even though it is a futuristic path, our current technology allows a faster development of this industry. The main developments are in the complex design of structures, although limited to commercial elements of art. An improvement in the 3D printing technology is done in the filed of the concrete 3D printing mainly for offices and housing projects. This is promising result for a future application to more complex shapes. Figure 12 shows how the complex design can have infinite forms, as the printing technology in terms of robotics used, materials applied, resistance of materials, cost of materials is in a developing process (Fig. 13).

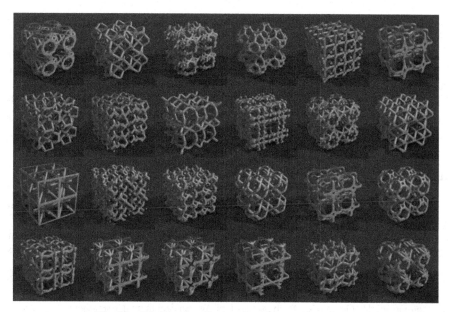

Fig. 13. 3D Complex Geometries for 3D printing [21].

4 Conclusions and Discussion

The literature review presented in this paper highlights the current state of digital fabrication in the Middle East and its potential for future applications in the construction industry. The discussion section aims to provide further analysis and evaluation of the findings, as well as to identify gaps in the existing research and suggest future directions for investigation.

One of the main findings of the literature review is the potential of regional and eco-friendly materials for 3D printing in the Middle East. The use of vegetal and earthen materials, as well as construction and demolition waste, can offer sustainable and affordable solutions for building in the region. However, it is worth noting that the levels of development are extremely uneven between countries in the region, which may affect the availability and accessibility of these materials for construction.

Another key finding is the lack of integration of digital design techniques in the architecture education curricula in the Middle East. The study showed that the current structures of architecture education cannot keep up with the novel demands and societal requirements of architecture in the digital age. This suggests the need for a curriculum review and various methods for incorporating digital design applications in the education system.

The potential of digital fabrication technologies in preserving cultural artifacts and building shelters in refugee camps was also explored in the literature review. The use of 3D scanners and printers can offer a reasonably economical method for preserving imperiled, lost, or damaged cultural artifacts. Furthermore, the study on the efficiency of printed shelter cost, time, and energy performances against timber and steel shelters provides valuable insights into the potential of 3D printing for building in refugee camps. Hence we note the potential of 3D digital fabrication technologies to address humanitarian crises.

In conclusion, the literature review highlighted the current state of digital fabrication in the Middle East. The use of locally available materials in building has been investigated, and it was concluded that the earth-based materials for 3D printing have potential to realize sustainable architecture. The study also showed that the regional curricula is not keeping up with the fast-paced advances digital fabrication. The potential for preserving cultural artifacts and building shelters in refugee camps was also explored.

References

1. Sonebi, M., et al.: Trends and opportunities of using local sustainable building materials in the Middle East and North Africa region. RILEM Tech. Lett. **7**, 127–138 (2022)
2. Abdullah, H.K., Hassanpour, B.: Digital design implications: a comparative study of architecture education curriculum and practices in leading architecture firms. Int. J. Technol. Des. Educ. **31**(2), 401–420 (2021)
3. Elhoussamy, N., Rizk, N.: Innovation practices at makerspaces in Egypt, Tunisia and Morocco. African J. Inf. Commun. **26**, 1–25 (2020)
4. Alhumayani, H., Gomaa, M., Soebarto, V., Jabi, W.: Environmental assessment of large-scale 3D printing in construction: a comparative study between cob and concrete. J. Clean. Prod. **270**, 122463 (2020)
5. Elias, C.: Whose digital heritage? **33**(6), 687–707 (2019). https://doi.org/10.1080/09528822.2019.1667629
6. Akeila, M.: Evaluating the feasibility of building refugee shelters with 3D printing technology in the Middle East, through BIM design & simulation platform (2019)
7. Flatt, R.J., Wangler, T.: On sustainability and digital fabrication with concrete. Cem. Concr. Res. **158**, 106837 (2022)
8. Buswell, R.A., et al.: A process classification framework for defining and describing Digital Fabrication with Concrete. Cem. Concr. Res. **134**, 106068 (2020)
9. Vilar, E., Filgueiras, E., Rebelo, F.: Virtual and Augmented Reality for Architecture and Design (2022)
10. Zhou, J., Barati, B., Wu, J., Scherer, D., Karana, E.: Digital biofabrication to realize the potentials of plant roots for product design. Bio-Design Manuf. **4**(1), 111–122 (2020). https://doi.org/10.1007/s42242-020-00088-2
11. Lloret, E., et al.: Complex concrete structures: merging existing casting techniques with digital fabrication. Comput. Des. **60**, 40–49 (2015)
12. Popescu, M., et al.: Structural design, digital fabrication and construction of the cable-net and knitted formwork of the KnitCandela concrete shell. Structures **31**, 1287–1299 (2021)
13. (14) (PDF) 3D Construction Printing – A Review with Contemporary Method of Decarbonisation and Cost Benefit Analysis. https://www.researchgate.net/publication/335464720_3D_Construction_Printing_-_A_Review_with_Contemporary_Method_of_Decarbonisation_and_Cost_Benefit_Analysis. Accessed 9 Feb 2023
14. Non-Linear Architecture Parametrics Workshop 2010 at Tsinghua University | ArchDaily. https://www.archdaily.com/85603/non-linear-architecture-parametrics-workshop-2010-at-tsinghua-university?ad_source=search&ad_medium=search_result_all. Accessed 21 July 2020
15. Parametricism movie by Patrik Schumacher and Rosey Chan|Dezeen. https://www.dezeen.com/2020/05/15/rosey-chan-patrik-schumacher-vdf/. Accessed 21 July 2020

16. Von Richthofen, A.: Aurel von Richthofen, on tools, technology and society around the future of AI and architecture. arq: Archit. Res. Q. **24**(4), 379–381 (2020)
17. A Complex, 3D Printed Sofa by Janne Kyttanen. https://design-milk.com/complex-3d-pri nted-sofa-janne-kyttanen/. Accessed 9 Feb 2023
18. Top 8 of the best 3D printed art projects (2021 Update). https://www.sculpteo.com/blog/2018/ 05/29/top-6-of-the-best-3d-printed-art-projects/. Accessed 9 Feb 2023
19. Building Complex Elements in Concrete with 3D Printed Foam Formworks|ArchDaily. https://www.archdaily.com/973893/generating-complex-elements-in-concrete-with-3d-pri nted-foam-formwork?ad_medium=gallery. Accessed 9 Feb 2023
20. 3D Printing in Construction: Growth, Benefits, and Challenges. https://constructionblog.aut odesk.com/3d-printing-construction/. Accessed 9 Feb 2023
21. 3D Printing News Briefs, September 8, 2022: Boosting Startups, Expansion in the Middle East, and More - 3DPrint.com|The Voice of 3D Printing/Additive Manufacturing. https://3dp rint.com/293938/3d-printing-news-briefs-9-8-2022/. Accessed 9 Feb 2023

Colour Accuracy in Fashion E-tail

Carolina Bozzi[1]([⊠]) [iD], Marco Neves[1,3] [iD], Claudia Mont'Alvão[2] [iD],
and João Nuno Pernão[1] [iD]

[1] Centro de Investigação em Arquitetura, Urbanismo e Design, Faculdade de Arquitetura,
Universidade de Lisboa, Lisboa, Portugal
carolinamarianna@campus.ul.pt
[2] PUC-Rio | LEUI, Rio de Janeiro, Brazil
[3] ITI/LARSyS, University of Lisbon, Lisbon, Portugal

Abstract. Clothing possesses characteristics that are considered non-digital in the sense that they are difficult to be communicated over the Internet. Consumers feel the need for multisensorial contact with these products before purchasing them to carry out a thorough inspection. Attributes such as fabric texture and fit, are poorly communicated through text or photos as are the colours of objects. This paper aims to raise some issues related to the colours of clothing products when viewed on e-commerce websites, frequently, photographs do not represent accurately the colour of clothing items. The existing literature mostly addresses the use of colour psychology and the colour of web design elements, there is little work discussing the importance of colour accuracy in product representation in e-commerce. Through a narrative literature review and a preliminary systematic literature review, we will discuss the importance of colour accuracy to the user experience when buying clothes online. To conclude, we consider that the lighting; the texture of the materials; the skin colour of the models, and the backgrounds used to photograph products should be selected carefully so that consumers have a more reliable perception of the colours.

Keywords: E-commerce · Women's clothing · Lighting · Colour accuracy

1 Introduction

Users of apparel e-commerce websites feel unsure about some of the products' information, especially those considered non-digital attributes. Fabrics, for example, have varying textures and physical properties, such as elasticity and thickness, and weight that directly influence how they fit the body [1]. These qualities are difficult to convey digitally, via a screen [2], as is colour. In e-commerce, there is an information asymmetry [3, 4] generated by the lack of physical contact with the product that is seen as a factor that hinders or prevents its purchase online.

E-commerce websites must ensure at least the same level of security that a consumer has when buying in a physical store [5], providing users with enough information in a clear way to support their purchase decision-making process.

A. Marcus et al. (Eds.): HCII 2023, LNCS 14031, pp. 32–46, 2023.
https://doi.org/10.1007/978-3-031-35696-4_3

This article will address some issues related to lighting, colour, and the material used to make a garment that should be considered when photographing an item. These considerations can mitigate some of the problems related to the lack of physical contact prior to purchase.

2 Theoretical Background

2.1 Fashion E-tail

This mismatch between depicted and real products may lead to dissatisfied consumers and returns. Almost half of the products bought online are returned, 25% of these products are sent to landfills [6], and represent 5 Bn lb. of waste only in the US [7]. In fact, according to [8], 45% of clothing items were returned because the size, fit, or colour was wrong.

These concerns are directly related to the sustainability performance of companies and Corporate Responsibility and should be incorporated into the core of fashion businesses [9]. Being sustainable not only comprehends supply chains but the whole business. How products are communicated and represented in online media impacts directly the number of returned products and waste generation, not to mention logistics. It is estimated that the fashion industry contributes to 4% [10] of all greenhouse gas emissions worldwide and generates around 92 million tons of waste every year [11].

Fashion was the largest segment of the global e-commerce market in 2020 with a revenue of 666 billion U.S. dollars [12] making it the category with the most returned items. In the U.S., for example, 26% of all returned items of online purchases, were clothes [13].

This behaviour possibly occurs from the fact that garments are products with more non-digital attributes than digital ones and can be classified as experience goods. In the sense that consumers must experience them before purchasing to gather all the information necessary to have an informed opinion [14].

Regarding product attributes, there are two categories: digital and non-digital [15]. Digital ones are easily communicated over the internet; they are the price or the dimensions of a book, and there is no loss of information when communicated on a website. These attributes can also include information previously acquired by users when they have direct contact with the product during a visit to the physical store.

The category of non-digital attributes includes characteristics that can only be assessed through physical contact with the product. In the field of clothing, texture, and fit, key characteristics for the evaluation of the product by the consumer, can only be verified through tactile contact and, therefore, physical contact. Note that the fit of a shirt, for example, when presented or described online, can raise significant uncertainties for certain consumers. Therefore, depending on the channel used, consumers may not have complete information before making a purchase. Maybe, for the reasons above, consumers still feel the need for multi-sensory contact with clothing items before purchasing them.

From a user-centred design perspective, when a product does not meet expectations, it contributes to a negative user experience [UX]. The lack of information and the physical interaction with the product are some of the main barriers to online shopping [16]. In the case of garments, that might require multisensory contact, it is found that this lack of direct interaction can lead to lower consumer satisfaction in the shopping process and a higher perception of risk [17].

2.2   Interaction Design as a Means to Improve UX

In a time when human-human interactions are gradually being replaced by human-computer interactions, design has been contributing in a significant way to more intuitive and user-friendly digital projects. Buying online, among other tasks, is becoming the norm. In this realm, executing a wrong command or buying the wrong product can result in frustrating experiences with consequences that can be difficult to reverse especially for novice users [18].

Design acts as the mediator of the relationship between people and their activities to interact with the environment [19]. According to [20], the development of design practice is becoming more complex and focusing on the experience and behaviour resulting from this interaction [20]. This paradigm shift, of the focal point of the design process, from object to experience, demands a new body of knowledge as well as new methodologies to support the decision-making process within the field. The scope of investigation expands beyond the immediate interaction of users with artifacts to include the influence of design within more complex social, physical, economic, and technological systems, and our research strategies must go beyond tests performed in ergonomics laboratories, and focus groups that separate people from environments where research-relevant behaviour can be observed [20].

Hereof, the main goal of interaction design is to reduce negative aspects of the user experience and enhance its positive ones. It is about developing user-centred interactive products that are easy, effective, and enjoyable [18]. With this in mind, this paper intends to discuss how this interaction with e-commerce websites can be improved when it comes to the colour perception users have of products.

2.3   Light and Colour

Colour is not an immutable attribute of objects, it varies according to light, texture, surface, or context. Our brain enables us to interpret colours through the light waves captured by our eyes, without light there is no colour. [21] explains that what we see when we look at a colour is the action and reaction of light. White light, or the visible spectrum, is composed of wavelength, amplitude, and saturation. Shorter wavelengths include x-rays and the visual spectrum of colour and white light; longer wavelengths include infrared. Different wavelengths are also associated with different hues. The shorter wavelengths indicate violet and blue, and the longer wavelengths indicate yellows, oranges, and reds [21].

There are two colour systems, subtractive and additive. The subtractive colour system includes all pigments. As light strikes an object of varying or different hues, the wavelengths are subtracted or removed, and we see what is left: the reflected colour [21].

The additive system, on the other hand, is the basis of digital colour, such as those displayed in photographs on e-commerce websites. There are many variables when working with digital colour, the type of monitor, for example, can affect the colour that is perceived and produced. When working with digital colours, we are dealing with additive colours or light itself [21].

In the additive system the primary colours change from red, yellow, and blue (red, yellow, and blue [RYB]) to red, green, and blue (red, green, and blue [RGB]). Only when printing an image do we go back to dealing with subtractive colours, and even then, the primary system will change from RYB to cyan, magenta, yellow and black (cyan, magenta, yellow and black [CMYK], the 'k' is used to represent black so that it is not mistaken with the 'b' for blue) [21].

3 Metamerism

The light used in a photo shoot, the colour and characteristics of the background, the device used for viewing, and the material, are factors that can directly influence how colours are perceived by us when interacting with digital interfaces. There are two main features in light perception: the colour temperature of the light (warmer or cooler) and the characteristic of the electromagnetic spectrum of light (with different importance on blue, green, yellow, or red).

Since there are many different types of light bulbs and light sources, it is essential to understand their effect on colour perception. Tungsten, or incandescent bulbs, tend to emit a warm light and highlight the warmest range of tones, including yellows, oranges, and reds. Fluorescent lights, on the other hand, are much cooler and highlight a wider range of green, blue, and violet tones. LED lighting enhances blue tones and reduces the perception of warm tones. Therefore, an object can appear to have one colour tone under one type of lamp and look drastically different when viewed with another light source. This occurrence is called metamerism [21].

Seemingly identical colours can also be metameric pairs. For instance, two items that are the same colour under one light may appear different under another light [22]. This equation, the type of light, and its effect on the colour of surfaces must be considered when photographing products for websites. The colours in digital photographs must be as close as possible to the original not to frustrate the consumer when receiving their products. Besides, there are also other issues concerning light and perception, such as the number of light sources, their position, direction, and intensity.

Colours are also affected by adjacent colours, the perception of one colour will change depending on those surrounding it [22]. Chevreul [23] described three situations where this effect can be observed. First, is the simultaneous contrast, when two colours are side by side. The successive contrast is the afterimage produced after looking at a colour for a certain time; and finally, the mixed contrast: when two colours are viewed one after the other, the second colour is mixed with the negative afterimage of the first - an effect that Chevreul [23] observed in the distorted colour judgments of textile buyers who had examined many fabrics of one colour, then another [24].

Chevreul [23] claimed to predict the visual effect of simultaneous contrast in all such situations with a single rule: if two areas of colour are seen together in space or time, each will change hue and value as if the neighbour's visual complementary colour or preceding colour were mixed with it. So that if a dark red and a light yellow are seen side by side, the red will change as if mixed with the visual complement of light yellow (dark blue-violet), while the yellow will change as if mixed with the complement of the dark. Red (light blue-green): the red will appear shifted to violet and the yellow to green. (Similar effects are noticed if any colour is seen after the other).

Chevreul [23] noted that these apparent colour shifts are more noticeable when the colour areas are viewed side by side rather than far apart, are equal in size and not too large, and are viewed in soft light [24], as happens in product photos on e-commerce websites.

Like Chvereul [23], Johannes Itten [25] also studied the effects that colours exert on each other. According to Itten [25], colour can be divided into two aspects; the chromatic agent corresponds to the part of the colour of physical-chemical nature, i.e., the studies of paints, pigments, and dyes. The chromatic effect is the psychophysiological effect, that is, optical illusions generated mainly by contrasts, when the brain constructs colours that are not present as pure pigment, in contrast to white.

Itten [25] defined there are seven contrasts obtained in unfolding the chromatic wheel, listed below:

- Contrast of pure and saturated colours: it occurs between the hues of the chromatic wheel and stands out mainly when they present white or black between them.
- Light and dark (Fig. 1): is the contrast between shades of colours related to the presence of white and black.
- Warm-cold contrast: it happens between warm and cold colours which are opposite each other in the chromatic wheel. There is the possible relativity of colours by contrast, in which a cold colour can appear warm, and vice-versa.
- Contrast between complementary colours.
- Simultaneous contrast (Fig. 1): when a colour "requires" its complementary to achieve harmony, and when we associate two contiguous colours, one will interfere with the other, either enhancing it or diminishing it.
- Saturation: a pure, saturated colour (hue) associated with the same desaturated one. The colour can be desaturated with the addition of white, black or its complementary.
- Quantity/extent/surface: this type of contrast relates to Goethe's proportion, where colours occupy spaces and dimensions according to their intensity. A more intense colour occupies less space than a less intense one, to seek harmony. Warm colours tend to expand and, consequently, require less space, while cold colours, more passive, tend to occupy more space.

Fig. 1. Examples of Johannes Itten's contrasts: Left: Light and dark Right: Cold-Warm. Source: Based on Itten [25].

Nitse et al. [22] discuss some issues regarding the colours of clothing products when displayed in different media, websites, catalogues, and even when displayed in-store. The authors explain that each device can display certain colour ranges; monitors can display colours that printers cannot print; cameras and scanner sensors can register colours that neither monitors nor printers can produce. This happens because different devices use distinct colour models; a colour model is simply a mathematical way of representing them. When different devices use different colour models, they need to translate colours from one model to another, which often presents errors. These factors indicate that the adverse effects of inaccurate colour representation affect not only online shopping websites but also the more traditional means of shopping for apparel products, such as retail stores and printed catalogues. It is more an issue regarding perception than representation, and this gives rise to the difficulty of accurately depicting colours to consumers. Colour is a sensory perception related to the frequency of light waves being reflected from the item being viewed and not an intrinsic property of that item. Therefore, it is entirely possible that two items viewed in a retail store, say under fluorescent lighting, may appear to be the same colour, but when viewed outside, in sunlight, may appear to be different [22].

Nitse et al. [22] explain that printed catalogues present yet another set of lighting factors that affect a consumer's perception of the colour of a fashion product. An image of the item appearing in the catalogue is created under one set of lighting conditions but may be viewed under an entirely distinct set of lighting conditions. Even if the image is carefully corrected to match the original item, it is not possible to have control over the lighting conditions under which that image will be seen by the consumer. An additional problem associated with catalogues is that the colours represented in the printing process are an approximation produced by colour compositions. Printers use the CMYK colour model, which approximates colours in terms of the amounts of each ink colour - cyan, magenta, yellow and black. The range of colours that a printer is capable of representing is much smaller than the full range of colours that the human eye can perceive, so the approximation is often lacking in accuracy. Digitally rendered images of fashion products are subject to the same lighting issues as catalogue images during their creation and viewing, as well as a number of hardware and software factors. Some of these factors include the graphics file format in which the image is stored, the type, brand, and age of the monitor on which the image is viewed, the graphics card to which the monitor is connected, the operating system settings for the number of images, colours to be displayed, and screen resolution. Consumer-owned personal computers vary in their image presentation because of differences in graphics cards and monitor resolution capabilities [22].

4 Light, Colour, and Matter

However, lighting is not the only issue that influences the perceived colour of clothing. Materials absorb a specific frequency of light, depending on the colour [23]. White fabrics refract a wide frequency range of light. Therefore, the spectrum indicates a characteristic similar to the spectrum of LED whites in lighting. On the other hand, the characteristics of the spectra on blue and green fabric are different from the original lighting.

The texture of the fabric also influences, depending on its thickness, lightness, and how it was manufactured [26]. The yarns used in fabrics are arranged in basically two forms. The first uses two groups of yarns, one vertically (warp yarns) and the other horizontally (weft yarns), forming an angle of 90° (Fig. 2), called woven fabrics. Some examples of commercial names of woven fabrics are poplin, Tricoline, cambric, organza, denim, gabardine, satin, and sateen, velvet, terry fabrics such as bath towels, among others [27].

Fig. 2. Woven (right) and knitted (left) structures of fabrics. Source: Freepik.com

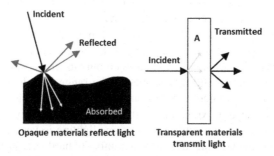

Fig. 3. Some ways in which a certain type of material can change light trajectory. Source: Adapted from Lopes, 2009, p. 26.

The second form is the knitted fabrics. These differ from woven fabrics because the yarns are interwoven (Fig. 2), and the way the yarns are connected defines the characteristics of knitwear. The knits formed across the width of the fabric are called weft knits and the knits formed along the length of the fabric are warp knits [28].

The loop is the fundamental element of knitted fabrics. Its rounded shape ensures the excess of yarn, which provides the elasticity, the good fit, and the feeling of comfort that usually characterizes knitted fabrics [27]. In weft knitting, one thread is enough to feed the loom, the machine in which tubular knit fabrics, such as the ones used in t-shirts, and rectilinear knit fabrics (e.g.: woollen knits) are produced. In warp knitting, each needle on the loom is fed by yarn placed side by side to produce lace and fabrics used to manufacture lingerie, for example [29]. The loop will not only determine the fit of the fabric but also how light will be reflected, absorbed, or transmitted (if the material is transparent) (Fig. 3).

5 Systematic Review

Besides a narrative literature review that we used for our theoretical background, we carried out a preliminary systematic literature review to search for papers we might have missed on the topic. Surprisingly, our review revealed a lack of studies carried out addressing colour inaccuracy, not only in e-commerce but in retail in general.

This shows us there is much room for exploring this topic; the relevance of the use of colour in e-commerce has become of great importance as the numbers of sales increase and the returns due to issues related to colour inaccuracy.

We used three databases to conduct our systematic review, namely, Google Scholar, ACM, and B-On. In Table 1, we list the number of references found for each keyword in each of the selected databases.

5.1 Carrying Out the Systematic Literature Review

A systematic review, like other types of review studies, is a form of research that uses literature on a given topic as a source of data. This type of research provides a summary of the evidence related to a specific intervention strategy by applying explicit and systematized methods of searching, critically assessing, and synthesizing the selected information [30]. A systematic review includes a comprehensive, exhaustive search for studies on a focused question, selection of studies using clear and reproducible eligibility criteria, critical appraisal of studies for quality, and synthesis of results according to a pre-determined and explicit method [31].

Before starting a systematic review, three steps must be considered, which are: defining the objective of the review, identifying the literature, and selecting possible studies to be included. These preliminary steps are important since they help researchers to tailor the guiding question of the review based on available information on the topic of interest.

The following steps are necessary to conduct a systematic review [30, 31]:

- Step 1: Defining the question.
- Step 2: Searching for evidence.
- Step 3: Revising and selecting studies.
- Step 4: Analysing the methodological quality of the studies.
- Step 5: Present the results.

To carry out our review we defined our research question as: What is the importance of colour accuracy for fashion e-commerce?

The following step was to make sure that all the important articles or articles that may have some impact on the conclusion of the review are included. Our search for evidence began with the definition of our keywords, followed by search strategies, the definition of databases, and other sources of information to be searched. Our keywords are listed in Table 1, we chose the following databases B-On, Google Scholar, and ACM

Table 1. Searched keywords and number of results per database on 28/10/2022.

Keywords	Google Scholar	ACM	B-On
"Colour in ecommerce" -psychology -ui	0	0	17
"Colour in e-commerce" -psychology -ui - color	0	0	0
"Color in e-commerce" -psychology -ui -"web design"	2	2	9
"Color in ecommerce" -psychology -ui	0	0	1
"Color accuracy in fashion e-commerce"	0	0	0
"Color accuracy in fashion ecommerce"	0	0	0
"Colour accuracy in fashion ecommerce"	0	0	0
"Colour accuracy in fashion e-commerce"	0	0	0
"Colour accuracy" "fashion ecommerce"	0	0	0
"Colour accuracy" "fashion e-commerce"	1	0	0
"Color accuracy" "fashion ecommerce"	0	0	0
"Color accuracy" "fashion e-commerce"	2	0	1
"Colour inaccuracy" "fashion ecommerce"	0	0	0
"Colour inaccuracy" "fashion e-commerce"	0	0	0
"Color inaccuracy" "fashion ecommerce"	0	0	0
"Color inaccuracy" "fashion e-commerce"	0	0	0
colour "fashion ecommerce" -psychology -ui -"web design"	17	0	6
color "fashion ecommerce" -psychology -ui -"web design"	28	0	8
colour "fashion e-commerce" -psychology -ui -"web design"	17	0	11
color "fashion e-commerce" -psychology -ui -"web design"	294	0	81
"Colour accuracy in e-commerce"	0	0	0
"Color accuracy in e-commerce"	0	0	0
"Color accuracy in ecommerce"	0	0	0
"Colour accuracy in ecommerce"	0	0	0
"Color accuracy" "ecommerce"	4	3	1
"Colour accuracy" "ecommerce"	4	3	1
"Colour accuracy" "e-commerce"	16	3	0
"Color accuracy" "e-commerce"	4	3	0
"Color inaccuracy" "ecommerce"	0	0	0
"Colour inaccuracy" "ecommerce"	0	0	0
"Colour inaccuracy" "e-commerce"	1	0	0
"Color inaccuracy" "e-commerce"	5	0	0
Total references	**395**	**14**	**136**

to carry out our search. Also in Table 1, we listed the number of papers we found on each database.

Our search strategies and selection criteria are listed in Table 2.

Table 2. Search strategies and criteria.

Search strategies	Databases	Selection criteria
1. Time period: 2010 - 2022 (12 years) 2. Language: English 3. Source: electronic databases 4. Type: Journal & Conference papers	1. B-On 2. Google Scholar 3. ACM	1. Involving e-commerce 2. Complete studies 3. Q1 and Q2 journals 4. Published studies 5. Relevant to our objectives

Our initial search resulted in 545 papers, from the three chosen databases. We exported all of the references to an Excel spreadsheet and copied the abstracts to facilitate the reviewing process suggest after searching all sources, to keep track of the included and excluded studies, maintain a log of why specific studies were excluded, and eliminate the need to print out hundreds of abstracts for screening as suggests [31].

The accumulated citations were then screened to select those studies appropriate for inclusion in the review. This process lessens the likelihood of missing relevant studies and reduces subjectivity in study selection. We then evaluated and identified the titles and abstracts independently considering our criteria, following the review steps as indicated by Pai et al. (2004). Some papers were excluded based on the title, others on the abstract, and ultimately by reading the entire content when it was not clear.

Finally, we read all the papers that passed through the previous steps and summarized their contents presented in a table with the highlights of their main characteristics such as authors, year of publication, methodological design, etc. The steps of our review are summarized in Fig. 4.

Our systematic review resulted in a group of eight papers. However, when critically reading the papers, surprisingly, only one paper specifically addressed the colour accuracy issue, namely Kim et al. (2015). We did find a thesis addressing the topic (Tang, 2017), but it did not meet our systematic review criteria, which did not include theses, only journals and conference papers.

Through a narrative literature review we managed to find the papers we used to write this paper, they date before 2010, which was our earliest date within the range used for the systematic review. We also used studies that were developed by great colour researchers as [23, 25].

Table 3. Systematic review papers.

Title	Authors (Year)	Object of study
A complete system for garment segmentation and color classification	Manfredi et al. (2014)	Colour-based retrieval & classification
CrowdColor: Crowdsourcing Color Perceptions Using Mobile Devices	Kim et al. (2015)	Collective colour review application input system performed by customers
When to introduce an online channel, and offer money-back guarantees and personalized pricing?	Chen & Chen (2017)	Returns (acknowledges inaccurate colour perception as one of the main causes for returns)
Interactive trial room–A solution to reduce the problem of rampant return of sold merchandise in fashion E-commerce business	Misra & Arivazhagan (2017)	Returns (acknowledges inaccurate colour perception as one of the main causes for returns)
Predicting the return of orders in the e-tail industry accompanying with model interpretation	Imran & Amin (2020)	Returns (acknowledges inaccurate colour perception as one of the main causes for returns)
Color Variants Identification in Fashion e-commerce via Contrastive Self-Supervised Representation Learning	Dutta et al. (2021)	Retrieval of product colour variants on e-commerce websites
A Tale of Color Variants: Representation and Self-Supervised Learning in Fashion E-commerce	Dutta et al. (2022)	Retrieval of product colour variants on e-commerce websites
Fifty Shades of Pink: Understanding Color in e-commerce using Knowledge Graphs	Liang et al. (2022)	Retrieval of product colour variants on e-commerce websites

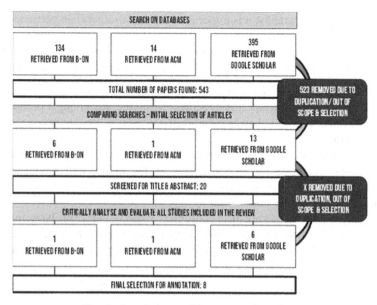

Fig. 4. Step-by-step of the systematic review.

6 Conclusion

Understanding how users interact with digital interfaces and providing ways to improve them and mitigate bottlenecks is one of the main aims of interaction design. By using a human-centred approach it is possible to identify problems that not only happen during and interaction but also before and afterwards can help to create solutions that will tackle the rampant number of returned products that are bought online, for example.

This article aimed to raise some issues related to the colours of apparel products when viewed on e-commerce websites which might lead to dissatisfied consumers and consequently, a return.

The light that was used during the photo shoot, the device used for viewing, and the material are factors that can directly influence how colours are perceived by the human eye. Listed below are some points to consider when producing clothing product images for e-commerce websites:

- Fabric texture: woven fabrics usually have smoother surfaces because of the way they are manufactured, unlike knitted ones. The thickness of the fabric, whether it is transparent or opaque, will also determine the colour perception.
- Skin colour of the models: the colour of the product and the colour of the skin will influence each other, photos of models with different skin colours can help the consumer better perceive the true colour of the product and how it will look with their skin tone. It is important to photograph the item on people so that there is a reference to the skin colour since colours influence each other.
- Neutral and plain backgrounds mitigate the negative effect of the post-image.
- Scale: product photography should communicate the scale, including how it might look when compared to the human body or a familiar object, such as a coin. In the

case of apparel photography, it is important so that consumers can get an idea of the weave of the fabric and thus get a better sense of how it might fit the body. Many websites have a zoom feature, allowing the user to better sees the details of the product. Photographing the products on models' bodies allows you to have a reference.

Our preliminary systematic review revealed that there is an absence of studies on the topic, reinforcing how important it is to address this issue. Receiving a product that is not the same colour as depicted on an e-commerce website is among the top reasons for returning a product.

Most frequently, studies in the marketing field address issues that contribute to improving sales and bettering the experience at the moment of purchase, to our knowledge, there is little literature on how to mitigate the "expectation versus reality conundrum".

Returning products that do not meet consumers' expectations contributes immensely to the emission of greenhouse effect as it doubles, triples the kilometres necessary to fulfil and order. Furthermore, a considerable share of returned or unwanted products are not resold, they are discarded and sent to landfills.

7 Limitations

As a possible development to this study, we could search other databases, use different keywords, and expand our scope to include academic theses and other types of studies to try to find more references on the topic.

Acknowledgements. This work is financed by national funds through FCT - Fundação para a Ciência e a Tecnologia, I.P., under the Strategic Project with the references UIDB/04008/2020 and UIDP/04008/2020.

References

1. Bozzi, C., A experiência do usuário (UX) em sítios de comércio eletrônico de vestuário: um estudo ergonômico. PUC-Rio (2018)
2. Bell, D.: Localização (ainda) é tudo: como vender mais usando a influência do mundo real sobre os hábitos de compra na internet. 1st ed. São Paulo: HSM do Brasil (2016)
3. Akerlof, G.A.: The Market for 'Lemons': Quality Uncertainty and the Market Mechanism. Q. J. Econ. **84**(3), 488–500 (1970). http://links.jstor.org/sici?sici=0033-5533%28197008%2984%3A3%3C488%3ATMF%22QU%3E2.0.CO%3B2-6
4. Mavlanova, T., Benbunan-Fich, R., Koufaris, M.: Signaling theory and information asymmetry in online commerce. Inf. Manag. **49**(5), 240–247 (2012). https://doi.org/10.1016/j.im.2012.05.004
5. Vitor, S., Nery, M.D., Moreira, S.V.: A padronização da modelagem como forma de dinamizar as vendas on-line de calças jeans. In: XXXVI ENCONTRO NACIONAL DE ENGENHARIA DE PRODUCÃO, p. 14 (2016)
6. Reagan, C.: That sweater you don't like is a trillion-dollar problem for retailers. These companies want to fix it. CNBC.com (2019)

7. Optoro. 2018 Optoro Impact Report. Washington D.C. (2018). https://www.optoro.com/2018-impact-report/

8. Narvar. State of Returns: The End of One-Size-Fits-All Returns. San Mateo (2022). https://corp.narvar.com/ty/2022-the-state-of-returns

9. Halme, M., Rintamäki, J., Knudsen, J.S., Lankoski, L., Kuisma, M.: When is there a sustainability case for CSR? pathways to environmental and social performance improvements. Bus. Soc. **59**(6), 1181–1227 (2020)

10. McKinsey and Global Fashion Agenda. FASHION ON CLIMATE. New York (2020). https://www.mckinsey.com/~/media/mckinsey/industries/retail/our%20insights/fashion%20on%20climate/fashion-on-climate-full-report.pdf

11. Dean, C.: Waste – is it 'really' in fashion? (2019). https://www.fashionrevolution.org/waste-is-it-really-in-fashion/. Accessed 15 Nov 2022

12. Statista. E-commerce revenue worldwide from 2017 to 2025, by segment. Statista Digital Market Outlook 2021. https://www.statista.com/forecasts/1223973/e-commerce-revenue-worldwide-by-segment. Accessed 28 Nov 2022

13. Statista Consumer Insights. Returns of online purchases by category in the U.S. in 2022. Global Consumer Survey 2022. https://www.statista.com/forecasts/997235/returns-of-online-purchases-by-category-in-the-us. Accessed 29 Nov 2022

14. Nelson, P.: Information and consumer behavior. J. Polit. Econ. **78**(2), 311–329 (1970). https://doi.org/10.1086/259630

15. Lal, R., Sarvary, M.: When and how is the internet likely to decrease price competition? Mark. Sci. **18**(4), 485–503 (1999). https://doi.org/10.1287/mksc.18.4.485

16. Correios de Portugal. e-commerce Report 2019. Lisboa (2019). https://www.ctt.pt/contentAsset/raw-data/27ebc745-b4e3-436d-b022-a42e91ef9049/ficheiro/export/CTT_ECOMMERCE_2019vers%C3%A3ofinal.pdf

17. Blázquez, M.: Fashion shopping in multichannel retail: the role of technology in enhancing the customer experience. Int. J. Electron. Commer. **18**(4), 97–116 (2014). https://doi.org/10.2753/JEC1086-4415180404

18. Preece, J., Rogers, Y., Sharp, H.: Interaction design: beyond human-computer interaction. 4th ed. West Sussex: John Wileys & Sons (2015)

19. Kaptelinin, V., Nardi, B.: Acting with technology: activity theory and interaction design. First Monday (2007).https://doi.org/10.5210/fm.v12i4.1772

20. Davis, M.: Why do we need doctoral study in design?. Int. J. Des. **2**(3), 71–79 (2008)

21. Bleicher, S.: Contemporary Color Theory & Use, 2nd edn. Cenage Learning, New York (2012)

22. Nitse, P.S., Parker, K.R., Krumwiede, D., Ottaway, T.: The impact of color in the ecommerce marketing of fashions: an exploratory study. Eur. J. Mark. **38**(7), 898–915 (2004). https://doi.org/10.1108/03090560410539311

23. Chevreul, M.E.: The Principles of Harmony and Contrast of Colors and their Applications to the Arts. 2ed., vol. 51, no. 4. London: Longman, Brown, Green, and Longmans (1855)

24. MacEvoy, B.: Michel-Eugène Chevreul's 'principles of color harmony and contrast. Handprint 2015. https://www.handprint.com/HP/WCL/chevreul.html. Accessed 15 Nov 2022

25. Itten, J.: The Art of Color: The subjective experience and objective rationale of color. John Wiley & Sons, New York (1974)

26. Yamashita, S., Mujibiya, A.: Palette: Enhancing E-Commerce Product Description by Leveraging Spectrophotometry to Represent Garment Color and Airiness. In: CHIEA 2015: Proceedings of the 33rd Annual ACM Conference Extended Abstracts on Human Factors in Computing Systems, pp. 1597–1602 (2015). https://doi.org/10.1145/2702613.2732860

27. de S. Martins, A.V., Lopes, L. A.: Modelagem: tecnologia em produção de vestuário. In: Modelagem: tecnologia em produção de vestuário/Organizador Flávio Sabrá. 2nd ed., Rio de Janeiro: SENAI CETIQT, p. 158 (2014)

28. ABIT. Cartilha de costurabilidade, uso e conservação de tecidos para decoração. São Paulo (2011)
29. da Rosa, L.: Vestuário Industrializado: Uso da Ergonomia nas Fases de Gerência de Produto, Criação, Modelagem e Prototipagem. PUC-Rio (2011)
30. Sampaio, R., Mancini, M.: Estudos de revisão sistemática : um guia para síntese. Rev. Bras. Fisioter. **11**, 83–89 (2007)
31. Pai, M., et al.: Clinical research methods systematic reviews and meta-analyses: an illustrated, step-by-step guide. Natl. Med. J. India **17**(2), 86–95 (2004)
32. Kalinosky, S.: How can the e-commerce experience be improved through strategic design?. Sundoginteractive 2012. https://www.sundoginteractive.com/uploads/whitepaper_attachments/Kalinoski_WhitePaper_ecomm.pdf. Accessed 31 May 2019

Ux in Immersive Reality: The Power of the Users

Janaina Ferreira Cavalcanti[✉]

Universitat Politècnica de València, 46022 Valencia, Spain
jaferca@doctor.upv.es

Abstract. Repeated exposure to a sign can generate habits with it and, consequently, less attention to it. In order to prevent this, it is possible to make use of new accessories that make the signage more dynamic. On the other hand, the individual's behavior tends to change when he/she is in a dangerous situation, which makes the same individual behave differently in terms of a warning when there is a stressor load or not. For this purpose, an immersive virtual environment was generated, in which different warning variables can be set, as well as different types of hazard presence to evaluate the user's actions. This paper presents the evaluation of the users of the immersive environment. The results show that most users have different feedback to the signage depending on the degree of risk exposure. This study is of great importance for the prevention of occupational hazards, as well as for the creators and developers of games and extended realities.

Keywords: Virtual Reality · User experience · User-centered methodologies · Signage

1 Introduction

Accidents can generate big financial and social losses with serious, hard, and, sometimes, even irreparable consequences for people and companies. Studies show that every three-and-a-half second an European worker is forced to stay at home for at least three working days due to a labor accident. Due to the magnitude of the problem, any initiative to improve the current situation will be of great interest. In this context, current technological developments such as Internet, "smart" environments, virtual reality (VR), and others affect not only the work, bringing new challenges to the safety of workers [1] and opportunities to improve safety training.

The behaviour of a person is determined by the context in which he/she develops an activity. So, when thinking about behaviour and performance is necessary to consider the interaction between the person and her working environment. In order to investigate human behaviour and its relation to accidents and human errors is important to observe individuals working during critical situations, taking account of performance, emotional and physiological levels [2].

For the other side, over the past decades, there has been a movement in the industry to improve work safety practices based on previous experiences. This happens based on the premise that personal experiences and memories strongly influence the perception of risk. A challenge faced today is to transfer the knowledge gained from past experience to citizens who may not have witnessed serious works incidents and as a result may fail to recognise the potential injury associated with the job.

In this sense, Virtual Reality (VR) can offer us experiences with no limits, but if VR environments and interactions are not designed and implemented properly, users have the risk of feel frustrated and or even sick [3]. For obtaining good results is mandatory provide a Human – Centered design. Immersive virtual reality also offers an environment without distractors. In this context, we conceive safety as a promising domain for virtual reality because we will be able to develop more engaging learning experiences in immersive environments without exposing trainees to risky situations. VR hardware and software can be used to enhance learning processes, being able to activate human senses and feelings and to improve memory performance.

User experience (Ux) and usability are widely used tools for quality testing [4]. They allow obtaining valuable information from the interaction with the user, for a better adjustment, redesign, and/or improvement of the system based on the opinion and typology of the end user [5]. Usability is related to the ease of use of a product by an individual [6] and its measurement should be based on the quality of manipulation, the degree to which a product can be used by specific individuals to achieve specific objectives effectively, efficiently, and satisfactory manner [7]. Usability problems lead to reduced utilization, lower rates of retention, and increase frustration [8]. On the other hand, the term user experience, popularized by Don Norman, includes the feelings and meaningful aspects of user interaction with machines and services. It is related to the product handling experience ("How did I feel using this?"). Usability directly influences the user experience [9].

Following these aspects, this paper presents a gamified immersive virtual environment developed to evaluate human behaviour in risk environments, and to improve safety. It is organized in the following manner: Sect. 2, describes information's about gamification and Usability, the main topics of this project; Sect. 3 presents Game for Safety (GfS); the material and methods are presented in Sect. 4; Sect. 5 presents the results and discussion; and in Sect. 6 conclusions and outline of future works are presented.

2 Gamification and Ux Research

Researchers have recently paid attention to the playability and appeal of gamification techniques for human behavior assessments. Coming from the video games and games, but differing of them by their non-entertainment purpose, these techniques are also becoming an important tool for training because they can be closely aligned with the design of good educational experiences. In addition, they allow players to naturally produce rich sequences of actions while performing complex tasks by drawing on their competencies [10].

A game environment is full of stimuli. Gamification techniques are interactive, which is a key for motivation [11].We could say that features of games are directly associated with human desires: reward, status, success, self-expression, competition and others, but for an appropriate result is necessary to pay attention to the challenges. They couldn't be so easy or so difficult to keep players/learners engaged. In this way, the safety training could be supported with progressive levels and scores [12].

Another strong point of the serious games is that they could help users to build richer cognitive maps. This feature, highlighted by Chittaro [13] allows different types of special knowledge acquisition.

Based on this, VR games could provide a comprehensive training environment.

Ux Research

Ux Research is a process that aims at the optimization of a product or system. Thus, Ux research aims to prevent usability problems. Since usability problems lead to reduce utilization, decrease user retention, and increased user frustration, this is an important and essential tool for product success [14].

When we think of usability, we must consider interactions that are usable, safe, effective, and comfortable interactions, easy to learn and with a low level of error occurrence. To this end, it is necessary to take into account the performance of users while interacting with the product (e.g., measuring the time to perform a task, the level of perception, and others) [15]. It is also necessary to take account the affective responses elicited by a product, which are classified according to the user´s emotional state, which are dynamic and time-dependent.

Thus, taking into account the usability objectives mentioned above, it is important to proceed to key questions to address each objective. That is, when we think about:

- effectiveness - which says how good a system or product is at doing what it is supposed to do;
- efficiency - which refers to the way a system helps users to perform their tasks;
- safety – intended to protect the individual against dangerous conditions and undesirable situations;
- usability - which refers to the extent to which the system provides the right kind of functionality so that users can do what they need or want to do; V. learning - which deals with the extent to which the system provides the right kind of functionality so that users can do what they need or want to do;
- learning - which deals with how easy it is to learn to use a system or product;
- recall - which is related to how easy it is to remember how to use a system once it is learned.

Consequently, we must think about key questions such as, for example:

- Is the system capable of enabling people do their work efficiently, access the information they need, buy the goods they want? When we think of efficiency, for example.
- After they learn to use the system, are they able to sustain high performance in their tasks, if we think about efficiency?
- Is the system or product able to prevent users from making serious errors, and, if they make any errors, is it possible to heal them easily? if thinking about the security objective
- Does the system provide an appropriate set of functions so that users can do what they want? In terms of usability;
- How easy is it and how long does it take for the user to start performing their activities? If we think about learning;

- What help interface does the user have to remember how to perform the tasks they don't have to do often? When thinking about memory

This approach allows us to evaluate the performance of the products.

3 Game for Safety

Game for safety is an immersive environmental virtual game simulating an office setting in which a recent incident occurs, with a single, seamless collection and no choice of routes. This allows decision-making in the environment to focus only on hazard-related tasks, reducing the excess of items and abundance of information that can generate noise in information processing. On the other hand, in relation to cognitive load, the tasks generated in response to the hazard are mandatory.

The environment is adopted by two zones: a training hallway and a main room. These are detailed below.

Training Hallway
The training corridor is located at the beginning of the stage and continues its dual function: to convey a background story and to familiarize the subjects with the environment and its functionalities (controls and keyboards, for example). It has the same floor, ceiling, and walls as in the main room. On it, there are signs informing about an incident that occurred in the office, the necessary commands for navigation, the subject's task to act in connection with the obvious dangers (eliminate fire, dry the floor). In the end of this hallway, a signal offer the possibility to follow and begging the experience or go back and train once more.

The Fig. 1 shows a view of the training hallway.

Fig. 1. Training hallway

Main Room

The main room is a linear path with curves where as the player advances, he is confronted with dangers and elements found in an office as can be seen in the diagram below (Fig. 2). The participant does not know which hazard he will encounter, he only becomes aware of it as he makes the curve and visualizes it in the section where he is. Such a factor serves to maintain engagement with the narrative and increase the element of surprise.

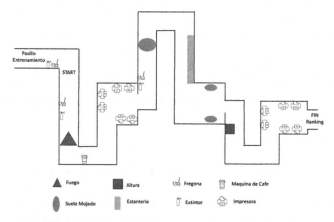

Fig. 2. Diagram with office hazards and equipament

Some hazards occupied the entire width, so that in order to pass through them, users would have to resolve them (extinguish the fire and dry the floor). On the other hand, for decision making, there was in the height hazard a wooden plate (board). The user should choose to pass through the fixed floor (diverting his path a little) or through the board (following the direct path).

Near the hazards that require a task (to cure the problem) there are two tools (one correct for the action and one incorrect), and a sign indicating which tool option requires the hazard that is nearby. In addition to these signs, others are distributed identifying the visible hazards, the risks that may occur (falling objects), and informing of equipment failures.

With the aim of stimulating stress (more proximity to the real scenario of use of the posters) but without general discomfort or harm to the user, we made use of some artifices such as:

- Signs: the blurring of the signs remained, but with less intensity.
- Fire extinguisher: when dropped to the ground, the user could not pick it up again. There were only 3 fire extinguishers in the environment, but only 2 could be used to remove the fire, since the last one was located after the fire flame, and the player would not be allowed to advance the fire without extinguishing it.
- When approaching the wall the user would see everything in the color of the wall, as information that it had collided. This action was given to add a sense of uncertainty.

If that happened, the participant should then look to the opposite side and press the button to advance.

The gamification strategy adopted is the competition between users. In this way we added a leaderboard/ranking among the users was created. The ranking was only presented at the end of the game, but at the beginning of the game the player was aware of it. In addition, as the experience was to be applied within a coexistence network, the ranking table allowed to promote interaction between users, even if they were not all together at the same time.

In terms of interaction, to better fit the user's technological profile, the game allowed the player to choose the speed of movement within the environment. In addition, the user was free to change it when he/she felt necessary, even after being immersed in the environment, choosing to use the left controller (faster and more sensitive, so that if you put your finger up, it moves) or the right one (slower and you need to press).

4 Materials and Methods

Taking into account the principle of subjectivity [17] that comments on the necessary user participation, but with the care that this is guided to avoid deviations from the learning objective, the sample was warned to pay attention to the signal along the way.

From a methodological point of view, we adopted a user-centered design. This study privileged measures of behavior (attention, performance, errors and learnability) and satisfaction (subjective responses after game interaction). The experimental session was divided into 3 stages: (1) pretest survey; (2) immersive simulation session; and (3) per-test survey, in English or Spanish (user's choice).

The pretest survey was designed with some points in mind.

- the questions had to be clear and organized in a cohesive way so that the individual could answer them alone;
- they should be designed in a homogeneous way. Thus, when using a scale, they should all start, for example, from the most assiduous to the least assiduous.

The experimental passes took place in the laboratory with a free area of 2.40 m x 2.0 m for free movement and locomotion of the user and happened from 2022, April until 2022, July (one academic term). Participation was voluntary and participants were free to leave the task whenever they wished. The immersive experience took place seated, in first person and without sound to maintain the user's freedom to express their doubts and opinions at any time. It had an average duration of 15 min. The character movement adopted is lineal character movement. It consists of making the character move forward immediately when the user pushes the forward button.

Components
Regarding the components required for this proposal, we took into account two premises: (a) implementing a device system that allows easy use anywhere and is easily recognized, familiar and affordable; (b) technological devices, tracking and mobile systems with a high degree of accuracy in stimuli reproduction to create a sense of presencea.

Based on this, was used sensor-type HDMs for VR headsets, HTC Vive headset. It consists of a headset with two controllers and two base stations that emit infrared pulses at 60 Hz, providing submillimeter tracking precision to the headset and controllers. The headset has the following characteristics: two OLED panels, each with a display resolution of 1080 × 1200 pixels per eye update at 90 Hz cover a send out horizontal and vertical infrared laser sweeps spanning 120° in each direction, a mass of 470 g, G-sensor, gyroscope, proximity, remote control with a battery with a range of 6 h of play, and SteamVR tracking sensorsb. The differences in time at which the laser hits the various photodiodes allows recovery of the position and orientation of headset a.

HTC Vive has development compatibility with the Unity and Unreal Engine 4 game engines. For this work, we chose Unreal because of its more straightforward coding method (C++ coding allows the possibility of coding through blueprints and Visual Studio). Unreal is developed by Epic Games and is free for use for academic purposes.

5 Results and Discussion

Responses were labeled with all respondents and questionnaire identification numbers. The sample was composed by 50 individuals (30 males and 20 females). The age range was between 41 and 50 years old (36%); 18 to 30 years old and 31 to 40 years old (22% each) and the remaining 20% between 51 and 65 years old.

In terms of education, the level of study ranged from a high school diploma to a completed doctorate.

For the evaluation and analysis of the data we made use of the Welch t-test (also known as "t-test for unequal variances" or "Welch's t-test for unequal variances"), thus, of the difference in the valid sample of the quantity of men ($x = 30$) and women ($y = 20$). In this way we were able to maintain the assumption of normality of the population sample with unequal variances.

The characteristics of the users that can influence the results obtained in the experience are:

- all are smartphone or tablet users, but 54% of the sample never play games on the devices;
- in relation to the use of technology our sample is classified as digitally literate ($x = 100\%$), making daily use of Tablet, computer or Smartphone, but mostly not a user of video games ($x = 78\%$), and not a user of VR technology ($x = 48\%$);
- of gamer profile, although most of our sample is classified as explorers (60%), we have present the 4 types of profiles of the Bartle classification as can be seen in Fig. 3.

Considering the presence, we used the subjective measure through the evaluation of the ITC- SOPI questionnaire. The mean (MD) and standard deviation (SD) of each dimension were calculated, resulting in the following results:

- spatial presence: MD = 3.79 and SD = 0.53;
- engagement: MD = 3.99 and SD = 0.5;
- ecological validity: MD = 3.26 and SD = 0.75;

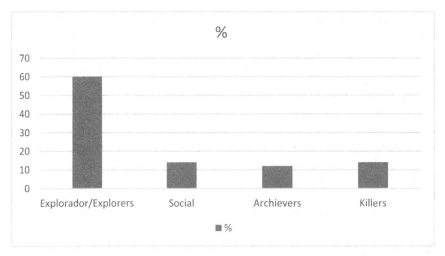

Fig. 3. Perfil Gamer

– negative effects: MD = 2.36 and SD = 0.87.

We also proceed to conduct presence using the count of user response. A total of 218 counts were considered valid. It stands out the fact of a higher perceptual count in actions near the hazards considered perceptible and of higher degree: fire (58%) and height (21.6%).

As for the negative effects, it is worth noting that, at times, the environment had a blurring effect, to encourage the idea of accident. This fact generated a bias in the answers to the question "difficulty to focus", in which a little more than half of the respondents (55.1%) affirmed to have it in a slight way.

The analysis results in the identification of experiences that illustrate satisfaction.

The data obtained showed that learning and memorization of the system was considered by 43% of the sample as sufficiently intuitive and easy to use.

Efficiency was considered good by 57% of the participants, but to improve perfor- mance, it is necessary to fix insignificant problems. The game was also considered safe and effective.

In addition, when evaluating the dates it was possible to realize that the Game for safety was considered "Moderately interesting" for most of the participants, and overall rated as 8–10 recommendable.

In relation to the signs In general, the signs with LEDs (technological variable) were more interesting to the users. In terms of the color of the turn signal used, there was no difference between white, red or yellow light. However, the LED position on the sign was of great relevance to the users. According to the data, users find the sign more interesting with the presence of the LED around the pictogram.

Based on these dates and the opinion expressed by the subjects it was possible to conclude that the Game fos Safety achieves its objective. The environment, in addition to motivating users to participate in the activity, allowed for a good evaluation of the different signage and danger levels.

6   Conclusion and Future Works

VR system enables users to physically walk around objects and touch them as if they were real. The possibility of designing first-person, fully immersive experiences with high-quality visualizations, the advanced interactive capabilities, connectivity and flexibility offered by modern VR solutions can impact in a very positive way in safety education.

The results suggest that the possibility of evaluating cause and effect constitutes a powerful argument for the use of an immersive virtual environment. Additionally, the engagement produced by gamification stimulates training tools. Motivators in a virtual environment consist of better adjusting objectives to user profiles rather than enhancing elements. This happens, for example, because the system requirements of a person with game familiarity differ from those of a person without game familiarity. Game mechanics and the virtual environment therefore provide a level of engagement and interactivity that makes it a promising tool in any phase of the design process.

Immersive virtual reality, in our opinion, is a very adequate and important tool, since makes possible immersive learning, contextualized content, living a more realistic experience, without risks, flexible, at reduced cost if compared to being reproduced in reality. It makes possible build optimized, first person virtual safety training, engaging, personal, and believable.

This work should empower authorities to start pilot projects to introduce this methodology/technology to prevent accidents and safety.

References

1. Smith-Jackson, T., Wolgater, M.S.: Potential uses of technology to communicate risk in manufacturing. Hum. Factors Ergon. Manufact. **14**(1), 1–14 (2004)
2. Olander, J., Ronchi, E., Lovreglio, R., Nilsson, D.: Dissuasive Exit Signage for Building Fire Evacuation. Appl. Ergon. **59**, 84–93 (2017)
3. Cavalcanti, J.F., Duarte, F.C.A., Ayabe, R.C.F., da Silva, A.G.B.: Virtual Reality and Ergonomics: Making the Immersive Experience. In: Soares, M.M., Rosenzweig, E., Marcus, A. (eds.) HCII 2021. LNCS, vol. 12781, pp. 158–170. Springer, Cham (2021). https://doi.org/10.1007/978-3-030-78227-6_12
4. Organización Internacional de Normalización: Ergonomía de la inetracción hombre-sistema. Parte 11:Usabilidad, Definiciones y conceptos (ISO 9241–11:2018) (2018)
5. McNamara, N., Kirakowski, J.: Functionality, usability, and user experience: three areas of concern. Interactions **13**(6), 26–28 (2006)
6. Thies, K., Anderson, D., Cramer, B.: Lack of adoption of a mobile app to support patient self-management of diabetes and hypertension in a federally qualified health center: interview analysis of staff and patients in a failed randomized trial. JMIR Hum. Factors **4**(4), e24 (2017)
7. Norman, D., Miller, J., Henderson, A.: What You See, Some of What's in the Future, And How We Go About Doing It: HI at Apple Computer; Association for Computing Machinery: New York, NY, USA, (1995)
8. Fonseca, D., Redondo, E., Villagrasa, S.: Mixed-methods research: a new approach to evaluating the motivation and satisfaction of university students using advanced visual technologies. In: Stephanidis, C. (ed). Universal Access in the Information Society, vol. 14(3), pp. 311–332, (2015)

9. Quitana, Y., Fahy, D., Abdelfattah, A.M., Henao, J., Safran, C.: The design and methodology of a usability protocol for the management of medications by families for aging older adults. BMC Med. Inform. Decis. Mak. **19**, 181 (2019)

10. Villegas, E., Fonseca, D., Peña, E., Bonet, P., Fernández-guinea, S.: Qualitative assessment of effective gamification design processes using motivators to identify game mechanics. Sensors **21**, 2556 (2021)

11. Connolly, T.M., Boyle, E.A., MacArthur, E., Hainey, T., Boyle, J.M.: A systematic literature review of empirical evidence on computer games and serious games. Comput. Educ. **59**, 661–686 (2012)

12. Lavoué, É., Monterrat, B., Desmarais, M., George, S.: Adaptive gamification for learning environments. IEEE Trans. Learn. Technol. **12**, 16–28 (2019)

13. Chittaro, L., Rannon, R.: Serious games for training occupants of a building in personal fire safety skills. In: Proceedings of the 2009 Conference in Games and Virtual Worlds for Serious Applications, VS-GAMES, pp. 76–83 (2009)

14. Cavalcanti, J., Valls, V., Contero, M., Fonseca, D.: Gamification and hazard communication in virtual reality: a qualitative study. Sensors **21**(14), 4663 (2021)

15. Rebelo, F., Noriega, P., Duarte, E., Soares, M.: Using virtual reality to assess user experience. Hum. Factors **54**(6), 964–982 (2012)

16. Cavalcanti, J.F., Soler, J.L., Alcañiz, M., Contero. M.: Educational application of virtual reality in safety training. In: Inted2017 Proceedings, pp. 9261–9266 (2017)

17. Belikova, N.Y., Vaskov,M.A., Zritneva, E.I., Afanaseva, O.O., Litvinova, E.Y., Azhiba, M.A.: Formation of a developing educational environment as a condition for socio-psychological interaction of subjects in educational and pedagogical space. In: Dilemas contemporáneos: educación, política y valore, 6 (2019)

Applying Service Design Thinking to UX Research: A Case of Smart Campus Dance Experience Design

Lingdi Chen, Minxin Huang, Zhen Liu, Yushu Jiang, and Tong Wu[✉]

School of Design, South China University of Technology, Guangzhou 510006, People's Republic of China
202221055645@mail.scut.edu.cn

Abstract. Smart Campus is an important part of smart city construction, running through the chain of campus education and life services. At present, digital campus services are facing a new challenge that needs to develop from the original B-End business for schools to operation and value-added services for C-End student consumers. However, the current digital solutions ignore the role of user experience (UX) research techniques and tools, lack holistic thinking in the stages of exploration, the definition of user needs, function transformation and service output, and cannot provide a compelling end-user experience. The study proposed a new user experience research process for methodologically integrating service design (SD) thinking into the exploration of users' psychological aspirations through a smart campus design project, as a complement to the existing usability and human-centered design (HCD) paradigms. The study focuses on improving students' dance experience, taking the dance studio of the South China University of Technology as an example. Research has shown that taking and sharing dance videos stimulates generative activity in student dancers and makes them feel happy later. Therefore, the project designed a system combining an app and smart mirror and offered a scenario-based solution for the user group. The design process improved and applied in this study explores best practices in service design thinking and UX research and should be of value to practitioners wishing to design positive user experiences.

Keywords: User Experience · Service Design · Smart Campus · Dance

1 Introduction

1.1 Background

Smart Campus. In 2014, China's National Development and Reform Commission stated: Smart city is a new concept and model that promotes intelligent urban planning, construction, management and services by using advanced information technologies such as IoT technology, cloud computing, big data and artificial intelligence (AI). In addition to solving livelihood problems, smart cities enable people (residents, employees and visitors) to engage with services in the way best suited to their needs. Also, Smart

A. Marcus et al. (Eds.): HCII 2023, LNCS 14031, pp. 57–74, 2023.
https://doi.org/10.1007/978-3-031-35696-4_5

Cities could hold different kinds of positive and unexpected experiences. Smart Campus is an important part of smart city construction, running through the chain of campus education and life services. In China, the digital campus serves multiple scenarios such as campus life, education, culture, sports, and teaching management through advanced information technologies. According to the 2022 smart campus industry report to facilitate the digital transformation of campus services, enterprises and university projects need to reconstruct key business chains, establish intelligent operation and service centers and scenario-based solutions such as smart venues. At present, digital campus services are facing a new challenge that needs to develop from the original B-End business for schools to operation and value-added services for C-End student consumers. However, current digital solutions ignore the role of UX techniques and tools and do not properly define students' needs to improve the user experience. In the specific context of the campus, they lack holistic thinking in the stages of exploration, user requirement definition, functional transformation and service output to deliver a compelling end-user experience.

Dance Experience. As a very popular activity for Generation Z, dance has driven a surge in the creation of online video works, popular on short videos and social platforms. Based on the data of the TikTok platform, the public has a super high desire to share their dance. The TOP2 hot topics related to dance are #Dance Class Snapshots, #Today Dancing Shoot. Insight into user portraits shows that young people aged 18–23 are more passionate about dancing, who learn to dance and shoot videos to record their beautiful life. The Age of Z insight report shows that in the online user scenario, they publish their works through content platforms to satisfy the highest level of Maslow's hierarchy of needs, which is to gain social respect and satisfy the need for self-actualization.

The school SCUT is committed to creating smart services and smart venues, among which the dance studio is frequently used. Currently, through the WeChat applet, the school dance studio only offers an online booking function for students, leaving much room for improvement in positive user experience (See Fig. 1).

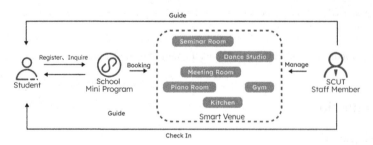

Fig. 1. Venue reservation process in SCUT

1.2 Service Design and UX Design

Service design (SD) is a process that is the design of people rather than the design of products and other things for people. It provides sustainable solutions and optimal experiences in specific contexts, following the five key principles of user-centered, co-creative, sequencing, evidencing, and holistic [1]. User Experience Design (UXD) is the design of things that affect perceptions and responses to a product, system, or service [2]. Both SD and UXD emphasize the end user's experience and gradually intersect in project practice in the trend of transitioning products to digital services in the technological generation. The methods of each other are integrated and used according to the specific situation. UXD focuses more on user value and usability, while SD has a more comprehensive view and systematically focuses on human behavior in the process. Currently, SD is more capable of bringing a human-centered perspective to actual business projects than UXD. An international survey of the overlaps and boundaries of UXD and SD executed by Roto V. revealed that the two practices move towards synergetic interplay and share the same theoretical roots. Holistic and systemic thinking of SD and its strong concern for many different actors in the design process play a positive role in supporting project creation and implementation of design strategies, which help advance UXD work [2]. What remains unclear, is how to properly use UX tools to put users at the center when improving and enhancing positive user experience [3]. Similarly, applying service design thinking can be more rewarding for practitioners when using UX tools to gather and understand user needs and desires. Distinguishing the two practices in the project process into a fuzzy front-end phase and an implementation phase. Aarne argues that the two practices follow the order of precedence. They identify the time and knowledge gaps in the digital service interfacing process and propose the Initial framework for service design handover to agile UX's knowledge transfer framework [4]. While there are several projects integrate SD methods and UXD tools to guide design practice, scholars have less often examined and clarified specific changes in UXD efforts. The way service design thinking could be integrated and applied has not been widely discussed in recent studies. This paper argues that SD and UXD are inextricably linked in digital scenarios and that there is great value in exploring best practices for SD and UXD interactions.

The study aims to propose a new paradigm for methodologically integrating service design thinking into the exploration of users' psychological aspirations through the Smart Campus design project, as a complement to the existing usability and human-centered design (HCD) paradigms, which can be integrated into the design process. The study focuses on improving students' dance experience, taking the dance studio of the Guangzhou International Campus of the South China University of Technology as an example.

2 Design Process and UX Research

2.1 Double Diamond Design Process

Based on the double diamond design process, the study applies service design thinking to conduct contextual user research to gain user needs and insights [12, 13]. Corresponding to different pain points, it highlights process optimization, systematically solves problems to provide holistic experience and services, and is more flexible and applicable to campus service scenarios. Centered on student dance lovers at SCUT, twenty (20) design techniques were adopted and distributed in four (4) phases applied in the double diamond process, as shown in Fig. 2.

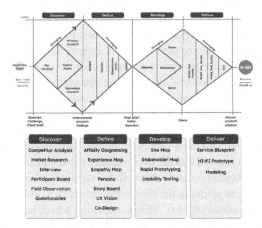

Fig. 2. Design methods and techniques applied in the Double Diamond Process

The UX research is subdivided into four cycles, distributed in the discover, define, and develop phases, as described in Sects. 2.2, 2.3, 2.4 and 2.5. These cycles occurred iteratively and incrementally and adapted to the target needs discovered and refined in each cycle. How to effectively conceptualize the requirements gathered in the contextual user research? The study emphasizes orderliness and goal focus, the project will unpack assumptions and refine hunting statements and insights after each design cycle. The methods and tools used for each cycle are displayed in Fig. 3.

	Method	Discover	Define	Develop
Cycle 1	Interview	O		
	Participant Board	O		
	Affinity Diagram		O	
	Field Observation	O		
Cycle 2	Experience Map		O	
	Empathy Map		O	
	Persona		O	
Cycle 3	Questionaries	O		
	Co-Design		O	
	UX Vision		O	
Cycle 4	Site Map			O
	Story Board		O	
	Stakeholder Map			O

Fig. 3. Methods and techniques applied in each cycle of user research

2.2   Cycle 1: Experience Stories and User Needs

In the first cycle, in addition to secondary research such as competitor analysis, the project used interviews, participant boards and affinity diagramming to explore user stories and needs.

The six semi-structured offline interviews were conducted with students at SCUT, including two high-level dancers and four entry-level dancers. In the pre-interview, the overwhelming majority of interviewees said that the process of learning a new dance once consists mainly of finding a teaching video, following the practice, reviewing and showing it. The interview schedule comprised structured and open questions to identify and explore the activities in the above process, attitudes, experiences and habits regarding dance. Each respondent has one online documentation record.

Based on gaining a thorough and shared understanding of the data, the team distilled the interview transcripts, participant quotes, and observation notes into information points as note cards, which were categorized and summarized to form participant boards. The participant board is divided into seven modules such as featured personal description, dance types and habits, dance attitude and motivation, learning environment, needs and expectations, and frustrations (See Fig. 4).

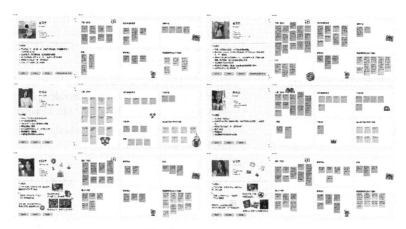

Fig. 4. Participant board

Another tool used is affinity diagramming, which plays a role in locating the common tasks, obstacles and needs of users. The team coded each piece of data with a unique reference to the source material, moved the cards around to synthesize clusters with specific themes, and finally collaborated, sorted and prioritized UX ideas. There are 199 data and 19 themes in the affinity diagram. 9 overarching themes are selected and summarized (See Table 1).

This holistic, organized thinking helps designers to view information points thoroughly, taking into account the characteristics of the individual user experience and the commonality of user needs. Therefore, the team located the user experience to be improved and refined the initial hunting statement. "I like learning KPOP dance but not very high level, and I want to have my cool dance videos."

Table 1. Issues and overarching themes in the affinity diagramming.

Overarching Themes	Issues revealed by clusters
Motivation	Dance to release me (5), Dance to favorite KPOP songs (7), Enjoy dancing with friends (4), Enjoy dancing with friends (4), Dance as sports (2), Practice dance skills to improve (5)
Overarching Themes	Issues revealed by clusters
Gain a sense of accomplishment	Shoot a nice dance video to share (7), Show off (3), Shoot for a record (3)
Dance KPOP songs	Diverse KPOP dance (5), Memory point (2), Popular (5), Discuss with friends (5), Gorgeous and full of energy (7)
Focus on what while learning new dance	Song climax's dance (5), Music (5), Beat (3), Accurate moves (4), Facial expression (4)
Social	Join dance activities (5), Make friends through dance (4), Practice and perform on stage with others (3)
Frustrations	Have trouble shooting and editing (6), Control video progress (10), Select teaching video (4), Remember dance move (3), Review dance (3), Time Conflict (2), Dance the complete song (2)
Teaching Video Requirements	Clear (6), Detailed (4), Short video learning (3), Search video platform (6), Search video platform (6), Own preferred teaching style (4), Detailed (4)
Dance Environment	Bright dance studio (6), Open ground (4), Mirror (5), Dance alone in the dorm (4)

2.3 Cycle 2: Insights and Persona

In the Second cycle, the project carried out field observation, experience map, empathy map and persona to gain insights and generate goals.

After the first cycle, the team targeted interesting and positive user experiences. The purpose of the field trip was to gain insight into the barriers to participants learning the dance and the shooting process and to obtain as many user pain points affecting the experience as possible. The team conducted periodic field observations of three core users during the week. Participants were required to learn a song they like but can't dance to, record a satisfying video of the finished dance and edit it with the designated video editing app. The field trips took place in the dance studio at SCUT and lasted about three hours each. After seeking consent, the team collected information by video recording, observing and asking relevant questions. Of interest was one of the field trips where a team member joined the entire mission process for an in-depth experience and study.

Experience map was applied to the integration of fieldwork information in five stages of preparing, learning the new dance, shooting the dance video, editing and sharing. Information is categorized by emotions, actions, questions and touchpoints, and refined to form the initial design insights (See Fig. 5).

Fig. 5. Initial design insights generated by contextual user research

The team studied the users' empathy in the process to analyze behaviors, thoughts and feelings, which contributes to the understanding of the influence of the pain points on the user's reality (See Fig. 6).

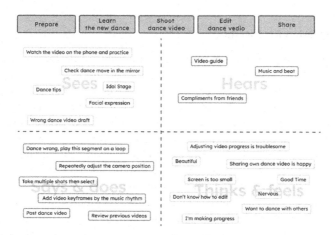

Fig. 6. Empathy map

After analyzing the data from the contextual interviews and the field observation, we further redefined the hunting statement and developed the persona. Considering the wholeness persona will define the core and secondary users, which will become the subsequent design guide. The persona consists of personal information, attitudes, background, task goals, experience goals and frustrations. Based on user-centered and goal-oriented design thinking, it is worth mentioning that the task goals and experience goals respond to the design insights summarized in the previous study and serve as the primary principles to be pursued in the following concept definition.

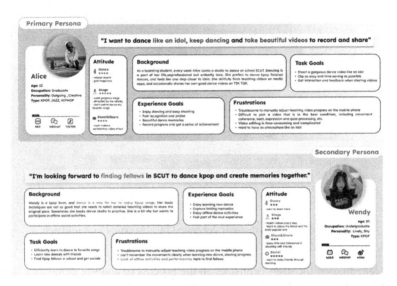

Fig. 7. Persona

2.4 Cycle 3: Design for Insights

In the third cycle, the project conducted a questionnaire, co-design and UX vision to refine insights and ideate promising and attractive solutions.

The questionnaire participants were from the dance hobby group of college students. The analysis of the population characteristics showed that the data trends related to the motivation to dance, frequency and purpose of taking dance videos were consistent with the results of the previous contextual research. Based on the KANO model, the questionnaire provided quantitative data from 37 participants to validate the generated insights. The KANO data shows that 9 of the 12 insights are attractive and 3 are neutral, with respective Better and Worse coefficients attached.

At this point user goals and the design challenge is presented, for which the project will complement insights and propose potential solutions through collaborative design. The design challenge is that respond to the dancers' sharing expectations by easily shooting an idol-like video so that they can get a sense of accomplishment (Table 2).

The co-design workshop member comprised designers, expert video bloggers and dance lovers. They created and discussed future dance experiences, scenario, and digital functions under the design challenge, and finally voted for the most creative and engaging ideas. (See Fig. 8) The feedback observed and collected during the workshop will use as guidance for the subsequent concept development.

Table 2. Design insights for dance experience

Insight	Detail
Easily Shoot	When learning to dance, frequently manipulating the teaching video progress bar will hinder progress
	It is difficult for users to pick a video with the best status, including dance movements, expressions, coherence and eye-tracking
Insight	Detail
Easily Shoot	Shooting and editing high-quality video can take a lot of time, and the steps can be simplified
	Hard to make an idol atmosphere
Share	Dancing is extremely social, and users want to make more friends to dance, share and communicate with each other
	After users share videos, they are eager to interact with dance enthusiasts and gain feedback compared to online comments from strangers
Sense of accomplishment	Users yearn for a gorgeous and energetic stage, and want to dance as the protagonist like an idol to show and satisfy themselves
	The reduction of offline performance opportunities makes users lack the stage to express themselves and the opportunity to gain a sense of accomplishment
	Dance videos become a way for users to document growth and progress, allowing them to capture lasting memories

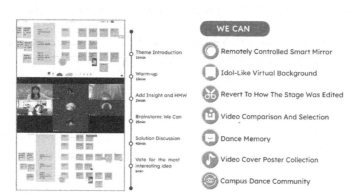

Fig. 8. Co-design workshop

2.5 Cycle 4: Develop Concept

In the fourth cycle, the project proposed the D-ON system, using site map, stakeholder map and storyboard to develop design concepts.

Site map is carried out to define the feature sets and the information architecture of the system. D-ON system includes APP and Smart Mirror design, which will improve user experiences by providing a simplified and linear process (See Fig. 9).

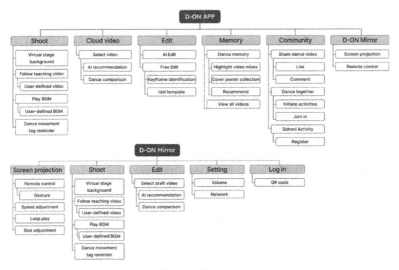

Fig. 9. Site map

In the context of digital campus service for SCUT, the team needs to consider the benefits and incentives of all stakeholders when implementing the system. The stakeholder map effectively assisted in mapping the flow of information, resources and funds. Back to the core user perspective, the team created and iterated on the scenario. Storyboard was used to transform each information point in the scenario, acting as a bridge between the user experience and the framework design (See Fig. 10).

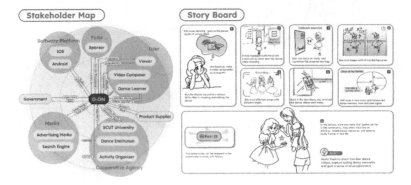

Fig. 10. Stakeholder map and storyboard

3 Usability Testing

3.1 Lo-Fi Prototype

After the UX research, the team started the framework design of the system. Based on the site map and storyboard, the Lo-Fi prototype was made to scheme the flow of tasks and information for each functional module in the D-ON APP and Smart Mirror (Fig. 11).

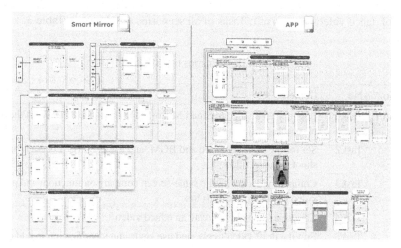

Fig. 11. Lo-Fi prototype

3.2 Usability Testing Process

Process of Experiment. Usability testing can be classified into 2 categories: formative evaluation and summative evaluation. In the low-fidelity stage, formative usability testing was carried out, oriented towards discovering interaction problems and checking whether the functions meet user needs. The testing process included scenario testing, retrospective interviews and a questionnaire.

Participant Sample Description. The participants in the experiment are all dance enthusiasts. Their ages ranged from 21–23 years old. There are 3 females and 1 male, all of whom have experience in video editing.

Scenario Setting. According to the dance activity habits of primary users and secondary users, 3 scenarios and corresponding tasks respectively were designed. Scenarios and tasks are arranged in the order of the user journey, covering learning, shooting, editing, sharing, interaction, participation in activities, memory section, etc. The characters in Scenario 1 and 3 are primary users who love to dance, are willing to share, and hope to have idol dance videos. The characters of Scenario 2 are secondary users who love to participate in various group dance activities offline.

Scenario 1: You are a dance fanatic and love to share. You are appealed by a new Korean dance recently, and you want to learn and make a cool video and share it.

Therefore, you use the D-ON mirror to learn and shoot. After that, you edit the video on the D-ON App and post it in the community to interact with others.

Scenario 2: You are a dance lover and like to hold or participate in various group dance activities offline. Recently, you want to initiate a dance activity to invite more friends to dance together. During the activity, it's heard that SCUT is holding a music event, and you want to sign up for it.

Scenario 3: You are a graduate student and also a dance lover. Recently, you have been busy with your studies and under a lot of pressure, so you want to relax by viewing past cool dance videos of yourself. Tasks of all scenarios are shown in Table 3.

Table 3. Scenarios task sheet

Scenario	No	Content
Scenario 1	Task1	Log in, cast a video to Smart Mirror, adjust the speed to 0.7, set the loop playback
	Task2	Set follow teaching video and BGM, and use the virtual background to shoot a dance video
	Task3	Compare videos with the same-screen comparison function, and pick a video to save to the draft box
	Task4	Choose a template to create an edited video
	Task5	Edit the draft video freely, and use keyframe identification to add effect
	Task6	Post videos to the community and interact with other users
Scenario 2	Task7	Initiate a "Black Pink special" activity
	Task8	Participate in a "random dance" activity in the Community
	Task9	Sign up for an offline dance event organized by the SCUT
Scenario 3	Task10	View the highlight video mixes

Retrospective Interview. After each scenario test, to understand the cause of the problem as comprehensively as possible and to collect users' subjective feelings, we conducted retrospective interviews based on the subjects' operating conditions, and recorded the subjects' answers, as shown in Table 4.

Table 4. Retrospective interview form

Question	Answer
Where do you think the operation made you confused? Why?	
Which tasks do you find difficult to perform? Why?	
Do you think these features meet your needs?	
Do you have any other suggestions?	

Usability Scale. After the scenario test and retrospective interview, the subjects scored the overall system according to their feelings. The usability scale for this test was modified from the System Usability Scale (SUS), which is reliable for small samples [5]. To learn about participants' evaluation relevant to interaction logic, functional requirements and interface layout, Question 11–13 are added to the scale.

The scale scores the system mainly from the aspects of usability, learnability, logicality, and functionality, and quantifies users' evaluation which contributes to our subsequent iterative optimization (See Table 5).

Table 5. Usability scale

Characteristics	Question
Usability	1. I think that I would like to use this system frequently
	2. I found the system unnecessarily complex
	3. I thought the system was easy to use
	5. I found the various functions in this system were well integrated
	6. I thought there was too much inconsistency in this system
	7. I would imagine that most people would learn to use this system very quickly
	8. I found the system very cumbersome to use
	9. I felt very confident using the system
	13. I think the button size and layout of this system are in line with my habits
Learnability	4. I think that I would need the support of a technical person to be able to use this system
	10. I needed to learn a lot of things before I could get going with this system
Logicality	11. I think that the functional organization of this system fits my logic
Functionality	12. I think that the functions provided by this system are very helpful

3.3 Usability Testing Result

Behavioral and Interview Results. The pain points discovered by behavioral observation and user interviews were recorded, as shown in Table 6. These comments provide some guidance for subsequent optimization iterations of the D-ON system.

Usability Results. The calculation formula for the SUS total score is as follows:

$$U = (X + Y) \times 2.5 \tag{1}$$

$$X = (O - 4)/N \tag{2}$$

$$Y = (20 - E)/N \tag{3}$$

Table 6. Pain points sheet

Task	Pain points
1	• Users have to reselect the video every time they project the screen because there is no history record in the screen projection function • Video is played instantly when the loop button is clicked, therefore user can't keep up with the pace
2	• Buttons for confirmation are placed too high
3	• Confuse memory video with cloud video • The entrance of the video comparison function is deeply hidden • Cloud videos are classified on the secondary page of Smart Mirror, which does not conform to user perception The checkmark is too small
4	• Dissatisfied with the effect of AI Edit but unable to edit freely further • Two close buttons appear repeatedly, confusing users • The interface of AI Edit is similar to Free Edit
5	• Can't find the entrance of the musical keyframe identification, the classification is not accurate enough • Unclear semantics of keyframe action buttons
6	• Interactive buttons are too small and difficult to click
7	• Lack of a real-time reminder of the recruitment situation after a successful release
8	• The semantics of the icons involved in the organization are unclear, and there is no feedback after the operation • unable to discuss activities content with other participants in advance • lack of search bar
9	• The semantic of the "participating in the activity" icon is unclear, and there is no feedback
10	• The information structure of the Memory is chaotic
Overall	• Icons in the navigation bar cannot represent the corresponding meaning

U is the average overall score of the SUS. O Sum of the points for all odd-numbered questions. E is the Sum of the points for all even-numbered questions. N is the number of subjects.

The usable score and the learnable score of the system can also be calculated according to the data of SUS [6]. The calculation formula is as follows:

$$S = (X_1 + Y_2 + X_3 + X_5 + Y_6 + X_7 + Y_8) \times 3.125 \qquad (4)$$

$$L = (Y_4 + Y_{10}) \times 12.5 \qquad (5)$$

S is the total usable score of the system, and L is the learnable score of that.

According to the scores of the subjects, the average total SUS score of the D-ON system is 75, which is at GOOD grade [7]. Moreover, the usability score is 63.28 and the learnability score is 81.25. (See Table 7) Combining Table 7 and Table 8, it's found that the scores of question 7, 8 and 11 are low. The main problem of the system can be speculated reasonably that some operations are unnecessarily complicated and part of interactive logic does not conform to user habits.

Table 7. Usability scale statistics (Question 1–10)

Questions No	Liu	Jiang	Yan	Lin	X / Y
1	5	5	5	5	4
2	3	2	2	2	2.75
3	4	4	3	4	2.75
4	1	3	2	1	3.25
5	4	4	4	4	3
6	2	2	3	2	2.75
7	4	4	3	3	2.5
8	2	3	3	2	2.5
9	5	4	4	4	3.25
10	1	3	2	1	3.25
Total score	**82.5**	**70**	**67.5**	**80**	**75**

Usable score: 63.28, Learnable score: 81.25

Table 8. Usability scale statistics (Question 11–13)

Questions No	Liu	Jiang	Yan	Lin	Average score
11	4	3	2	2	2.75
12	5	5	3	3	4
13	3	4	2	3	3

4 System Implement

4.1 Data Actuation

A smart city project generally has certain key components, based on the collection, processing and interpretation of data used to transform different aspects and resources – something that can be called "actuation" [8] (Table 9).

4.2 Service Blueprint

A service blueprint is a map or flowchart that shows all transactions constituting the service delivery process [9]. It can figure out user's behavior, stakeholders and touchpoints

Table 9. Data actuation plan

Data source	Data type
User sourced information	Videos, Digital photos, POI data, Dance Studio Reservation Data, Activity Join Info, Campus Certification, Social Network: Wechat, Weibo
Automated Sensors	Mobile Phone Location, Motion Recognition Data, Gesture interaction recognition data, Smart mirror blue tooth
Data source	Data type
Internet media platform	release songs, Song MVs, Idol stage videos, Top Video Trends, User Portrait Tags
SCUT Venue Management	Staff Arrangement, Venue usage, Venue GPS. School Event Information

throughout the service process, thus helping designers to gain a clear and intuitive insight into what users really want [10]. The whole service process starts from booking a dance studio to the end of attending an offline 'dance together' dance event (See Fig. 12).

Fig. 12. Service blueprint

The front end plans the contact points and interactions with the system at each stage of user behavior. The back end plans the development and maintenance of D-ON systems, technical update requirements and staff organization management to support a range of front-end activities.

4.3 Hi-Fi Prototype

Above all, the design is based on the user-centered model-driven process divided into three main abstract models: a user role model, a task model, and a content mode [11]. The project identified the user role model as student dance lovers (Fig. 7), the task model as learning dance, editing dance videos and sharing them, and the content model as dance memory, and dance activities.

Existing dance apps are mainly concerned with cartoonish and high-saturation color collisions. Such a design style combined with already colorful dance videos will cause users' visual fatigue and make it more difficult for them to operate. The UI design uses a low-saturation, homogenous color scheme to achieve visual harmony and highlight the dance video on display. The dominant color is a gradient pink-purple, with small areas of highly saturated purple used in accented areas. The overall design is in line with the visual aesthetics and operating habits of Generation Z.

Based on UX principles, low-fidelity prototypes and usability testing results, the project developed visual and interaction design specifications and completed the Hi-Fi prototype for the app and smart mirror (See Fig. 13).

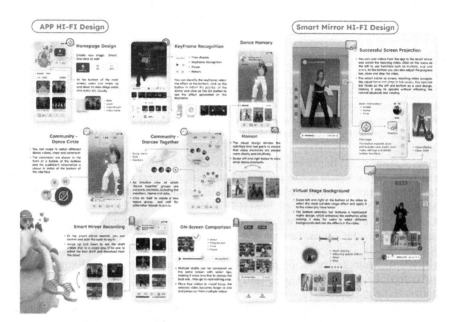

Fig. 13. Hi-Fi prototype

5 Conclusion and Discussion

The study shows that shooting and sharing dance videos stimulates generative activity in student dancers and makes them happy later. Be more specific, student dancers face many obstacles when shooting dance videos. One of the main obstacles is recording and editing high-quality video takes time. Therefore, D-ON gives solutions to the user group through this system combining hardware and software. D-ON includes APP and Smart Mirror design, which improves user experiences by providing a simplified and linear process. Easier, it assists them to shoot 'idol-like' dance videos, capture lasting dance memories and gain a sense of accomplishment. This study explores how students work out their needs in the context of the university and describes a framework for user experience design that is more effective and comprehensive in a campus setting.

The study implies that the D-ON project connects student users, school staff and dance studio resources to create a campus dance community. Users can share videos and interact online, and offline activities drive SCUT dance socialization. Responding to Smart City Calls, in addition to technical innovations, the current project provides references in service and experience design for the proposal of solutions for other life scenarios of smart campus (smart fitness, smart science and education, smart logistics, etc.), which is conducive to continuously expanding service scenarios. The described approach to UX research can contribute to a better understanding of how the methods put the user concretely in the center and what it evokes in the whole system design. The design process improved and applied in this study should, therefore, be of value to practitioners wishing to design positive user experiences.

References

1. Stickdorn, M., Schneider, J., Andrews, K., Lawrence, A.: This is Service Design Thinking: Basics, Tools. Cases. Wiley, Hoboken (2011)
2. Roto, V., Lee, J., Lai-Chong Law, E., Zimmerman, J.: The overlaps and boundaries between service design and user experience design. In: Designing Interactive Systems Conference 2021, pp. 1915–1926 (2021)
3. Fink, V., Langer, H., Burmester, M., Ritter, M., Eibl, M.: Positive user experience: novices can assess psychological needs: psychological needs in context of robot shoppingassistant. In: 9th International Conference on Computational Intelligence and Virtual Environments for Measurement Systems and Applications (CIVEMSA), pp. 1–6. IEEE (2022)
4. Leinonen, A., Roto, V.: Service design handover to user experience design – a systematic literature review. Inf. Softw. Technol. **154**, 107087 (2023)
5. Brooke, J.: SUS-a quick and dirty usability scale. Usability Eval. Ind. **189**(194), 4–7 (1996)
6. Lewis, J.R., Sauro, J.: The factor structure of the system usability scale. In: Kurosu, M. (ed.) HCD 2009. LNCS, vol. 5619, pp. 94–103. Springer, Heidelberg (2009). https://doi.org/10.1007/978-3-642-02806-9_12
7. Bangor, A., Kortum, P., Miller, J.: Determining what individual SUS scores mean: adding an adjective rating scale. J. Usability Stud. **4**(3), 114–123 (2009)
8. World Economic Forum - Global Future Council on Cities and Urbanization: Smart at Scale: Cities to Watch 25 Case Studies. 2020 World Economic Forum, pp. 4–5 (2020)
9. Shostack, G.: Designing services that deliver. Harvard Business Review (1984)
10. Chiu, H., Lin, N.: A service quality measurement derived from the theory of needs. Serv. Ind. J. **24**(1), 187–204 (2004)
11. Constantine, L., Lockwood, L.: Object Modeling and User Interface Design: Designing Interactive Systems. Addison-Wesley Longman, USA (2001)
12. Liu, T., Cai, J.: How service design thinking supports internal brand building within organization: a case study of co-design experiments with medical business domain. In: Stephanidis, C., Antona, M., Ntoa, S., Salvendy, G. (eds.) HCI International 2022 – Late Breaking Posters. HCII 2022, vol. 1654, pp. 444–449. Springer, Cham (2022)
13. Moreno de Oliveira, G., Nascimento Carvalho, A., Lamego, B., Monteiro, I., Gonçalves, E., Basilio, A.: Reporting the application of user experience tools and proxy users in an industrial process based on double diamond. In: Soares, M.M., Rosenzweig, E., Marcus, A. (eds.) Design, User Experience, and Usability: UX Research, Design, and Assessment. HCII 2022, vol. 13321, pp. 57–74. Springer, Cham (2022). https://doi.org/10.1007/978-3-031-05897-4_5

Beyond Car Human-Machine Interface (HMI): Mapping Six Intelligent Modes into Future Cockpit Scenarios

Shuyi Cui[1], Donghan Hou[1], Jiayue Li[1], Yuwei Liu[1], Zi Wang[1], Jiayu Zheng[1], Xueshi Dou[1], Zhanyao Feng[1], Yuxuan Gu[1], Minglan Li[1], Songbo Ni[1], Ziwei Ran[1], Bojuan Ren[1], Jingyi Sun[1], Shenmin Wang[1], Xinyan Xiong[1], Guanzhuo Zhang[1], Wangjun Li[2], Jingpeng Jia[3], and Xin Xin[1(✉)]

[1] Faculty of Psychology, Beijing Normal University, Beijing 100875, China
Xin.Xin@bnu.edu.cn
[2] Faculty of Art Design, Beijing City University, Beijing 101309, China
[3] College of Special Education, Beijing Union University, Beijing 100075, China

Abstract. As an effective means of transportation, automobiles are always considered a necessity in daily life. With the development of electronic devices, information technology is widely engaged in the cockpit human-machine interface (HMI) design. Reflecting on the literature and user studies, this paper narrates a project-based learning (PBL) practice, including six novel contexts, personas, and user experience (UX) design solutions for car HMI design in future cockpit scenarios. The results demonstrate the intelligent modes in a human-centered design (HCD) process.

Keywords: User Experience · Human-Centered Design · Intelligent Mode · Generation Y · Generation Z · Interaction Design

1 Introduction

In recent years, the public pays attention to the market of new energy vehicles (NEVs). By 2025, the competitiveness of China's new energy market will be significantly enhanced, with critical technologies such as power batteries, drive motors, and vehicle operating systems. Highly autonomous vehicles will be commercialized in limited areas and specific scenarios [1]. By 2035, the core technology of NEVs will strive to reach the advanced international level [2]. Electric vehicles will become the mainstream of new sales vehicles, highly autonomous vehicles will achieve large-scale application, and charging and switching service networks will be convenient and efficient [3]. Rich market product supply, high-tech intelligent scene applications, and a safe and suitable use environment will bring more opportunities to the new energy market.

NEVs have subverted the design of traditional oil vehicles in terms of innovation in the cockpit. The interaction styles gradually develop from physical interfaces to digital interfaces [4]. Users can interact with multiple digital interfaces while driving. An intelligent cockpit is equipped with in-vehicle infotainment (IVI) to promote interaction between driver, passenger, road, and even vehicles [5–7]. It is a vital link and critical node in the evolution of the human-vehicle relationship from a transportation tool to a partner. The intelligent cockpit is a new in-vehicle application based on the intelligence and internet of everything, which provides drivers with a convenient and technological driving experience [8–11].

Intelligent cockpit mode is a converged service, which could combine in-car control and online services or content into one service portfolio, bringing an immersive and convenient experience [12]. The innovation of intelligent cockpits in NEVs is an exciting topic. For example, exploring user needs in the cockpit to achieve a better UX which is not only limited to driving and riding, but also re-enabling the cockpit with new value and meaning to achieve intelligence.

With the continuous developing of the economy, culture, and information media, the young generation has a confident culture, they are experiencing multiple growth environments, forming their unique life attitudes and values, and pursuing more needs for family, socialization, respect, and self-fulfillment [13].

Therefore, we have adopted a HCD process [14] to design and develop an intelligent mode to improve the user experience in new NEVs to meet multiple needs, both for the middle age generation and the younger generation [15–17]. The design process needs to consider the usability and aesthetics of the product, as well as the social and cultural background [18, 19].

2   Methodology

In the fall semester of 2022, 31 graduate students of Master of Applied Psychology (MAP) worked in six teams. Regular workshops, review sessions, and company visits took place, ensuring that the results provide the research team with key design and growth opportunities. To achieve this overarching goal, we sought to answer the following research questions.

1. What are the lifestyles and user needs of the target user groups?
2. What are the characteristics of the target user groups?
3. What are the typical user scenarios and journeys?
4. What are the new intelligent modes to enable future cockpit design?

2.1   The UX Foundation Course

The goal of the course was to teach UX research methods and processes. This course offered transdisciplinary projects and focused on the interactions between people and products: How do people understand, use, and experience products in everyday life? How can we design interfaces appropriate to human needs, concerns, and abilities? Students learned to formulate UX visions, create and visualize concepts, and develop and test experiential user interfaces [20]. Regular workshops, review sessions, and company visits took place, ensuring that the results provide usable design and growth opportunities.

2.2 Transdisciplinary Student Team

The participating students came from different backgrounds, including psychology, industrial design, computer science and technology, software engineering, financial engineering, automation, international economics and trade, digital media technology, architecture, etc. All students had competencies in their respective fields, and some had prior PBL [21] experience in academia or industry, as well as experience in automotive design projects and HCD research. Unlike many other academic psychology studies, students had to integrate interdisciplinary knowledge to produce feasible outcomes that can be applied to real-life scenarios.

2.3 The Design Brief Assignment

There were two design briefs assigned by the course instructors. Practical product design flow should be considered, including user interviews, personas, design ideation, prototyping, and mockups.

1. Generation Z [22]. They like to socialize and pay more attention to immersive technology to express their own ways of living. Three student teams explore the lifestyles and user needs of drivers and passengers.
2. Generation Y [23]. They are predominantly male drivers and typically have three family members, some with two children. Three student teams explore the lifestyles and user needs of drivers.

3 Results

The teams defined personas (i.e., target user groups) and contexts through extensive desktop research and user interviews [24–27]. They designed user journey maps and affinity diagrams to analyze user pain points and needs [28, 29]. Then they sorted out the corresponding Jobs-To-Be-Done (JTBD) [30]. Table 1 lists the mappings of the personas, contexts of use, and the key JTBDs applied.

3.1 Team 1: Generation Z

Generation Z usually depends on driving assistance and needs timely feedback. They want driving growth to be appropriately documented and gamified, such as an achievement point badge system. These novice drivers are afraid of traveling alone and need the company of family or friends before they dare to hit the road.

Cui is a novice driver who needs more confidence and used to driving under the guidance of her father. She always has trouble backing up on the side of the road, drives in complicated road conditions, and is often fumbling. She gets very anxious when other drivers honk their horns and is eager to get on the road alone and improve her driving skills.

Team 1 considered a proficiency development system, hoping that as the number of drives, journeys, and hours increases, the proficiency level increases, presenting the information on the screen or glass. When the road trip is over, the system reports a

Table 1. Mapping of the teams, personas, and JTBDs of the results.

Team	Persona	JTBD
1	Novice drivers, 22–27	Drive confidently and safely on his/her own
2	Single ladies with high stress level, 25–30	Relax in the vehicle and have the company of loved ones when they feel lonely
3	Single ladies who care about wellness, 24–27	Enjoy a comfortable and fun driving experience in bad weather and physiological period
4	Male pragmatists, 35–40	Make the in-vehicle environment become a good parent-child communication platform
5	Female designers who care about themselves, 29–35	Adjust air conditioning and seats automatically for a more suitable makeup posture
6	Civil servant, 45–55	Let the dog have a separate and free space

score for that trip for driving operations such as lane changes, straight-line driving, and cornering and broadcasts words of encouragement. At the same time, this mode can record the voice of a loved one or celebrity to provide personalized voice guidance and encouragement. The solution is a guidance system, it could step-by-step guidance and changes the guidance words according to weather conditions, gradually reducing the density of guidance words as proficiency increases.

3.2   Team 2: Generation Z

Generation Z, as network natives, cares more about the emotional value experience provided by the product when they use intelligent products. They also have their own preferences and particular emotional needs in the automotive field. Most Generation Z faces financial anxiety, social pressure, and other problems. The current severe employment environment and high cost of living have intensified their pressure, and they have made some attempts to relieve the stress. One of the most popular ways is to confide in their family or friends. Emotionally, they need more of a "sense of being cared for."

Hou is a single lady from a remote town who has worked for several years after receiving her master's degree and settling in Beijing. However, she is busy, stressed, has little energy, and feels unsafe and tired when driving home alone at night. When she feels worried, she drives around, but she also feels lonely at this time. She is sensitive to air conditions, and the bad mood in the suffocating situation becomes a vicious cycle.

Team 2 targeted to help the user remove the stress, allow her to talk about her anxiety, and meet the necessary social needs. The "way home" mode aims to provide users with an in-vehicle environment that is emotionally safe and secure with a certain level of natural immersion when driving alone. During the trip, the vehicle automatically sends track information to emergency contacts, including location, camera, recorder, and emergency alarm, to alert in critical situations. The emergency contacts can click to check the driving situation at any time. In the case of high-speed driving, the intelligent ventilation function turns on to ensure good air conditions. The system shares cloud space with her phone. The car can automatically play the voice recorded by the user's family for her when this mode is on.

3.3   Team 3: Generation Z

The driving experience can be weakened by the weather, the driver's physical condition, and other factors. For example, getting into the vehicle would become a mess in rainy weather. After entering the vehicle, the temperature and humidity inside are generally uncomfortable and may cause the driver's health problems. In hot weather, it is easy to cause unbearable sweltering heat and continuous exposure to the sun while driving. In addition, during the physiological period, female drivers might lose strength in their feet, fear colds, and other symptoms. They need a warm and comfortable environment and the right amount of throttle and brake force.

Liu is a single lady starting her career, values health and wellness, is more self-disciplined, and wants a healthy body. She sets her routine, buys health products, and goes to the gym regularly. She goes shopping with her friends in her spare time and often takes them with her private car. She has a high pursuit of quality of life and wants a comfortable and fun driving experience.

Team 3 aimed to provide single female users with more attentive services during bad weather and special physical conditions, and intelligently adjust the air conditioning temperature and humidity before they even get into the vehicle. It can alter the ambient lights, music, and fragrance to add a sense of ambiance and interest to the weather and even customize the sun visor or sunroof to add a shade shape. This mode also privately records the physiological cycle after user authorization, adjusts the pedal and steering wheel operation strength, and automatically turns on the seat belt abdominal heating, automatic heating, and insulation in the cupholder.

3.4   Team 4: Generation Y

In recent years, there has been a rise in research on passenger-driver interactions. Positive parent-child communication contributes to the healthy physical and mental development of children. Today, school schedules and reliance on smart devices have decreased intra-family communication. The increased commuting time and longer working hours have left many Generation Y parents to communicate with their children in vehicles. The condition of the relatively confined environment in the vehicle can provide a suitable and stable environment and time for parent-child interaction, which serves as good family time.

Wang is a 40-year-old pragmatist who works in a state-owned enterprise. His children are in elementary school, and his parents usually help him. He drives to take his family but his wife and kids always sleep when he drives. And he can't find anything to talk about with his family. He wishes to create good interactions with his family and build healthy parent-child relationships.

Team 4 designed a mode to: (1) Use windows and passenger screens as interaction carriers to connect passengers to the environment outside the vehicle, and combine current geographic location information and environmental information to provide communication themes using changing outside information. (2) Provide a virtual voice assistant, interior ambient light, fragrance system, and seat vibration function to provide a good atmosphere for family communication.

3.5 Team 5: Generation Y

Generation Y and Generation Z have almost the same percentage of people with makeup habits, but in frequency, Generation Y is significantly higher. This shows that they are more willing to show their positive self. According to the data, ladies aged 25–45 are the leading group who buy NEVs in China. Due to their rush to work, some do their makeup in the vehicle. But they often face problems such as dark light, tricky mirror angles, and insufficient storage space.

Ran is a 35-year-old married and child-bearing designer starting to focus on herself and enjoying life. She drives her children to and from school every day. After dropping off the kids in the morning, she wants to look good and have good spirits for office time, so she chooses to put on beautiful and professional makeup. After work, she occasionally goes out for dinner with her female friends. She has high regard for the quality of life and her image.

Team 5 aimed to provide these ladies with a better in-vehicle make up environment. The user opens the front light shield (which has a mirror and light) and clicks on the "makeup mode" on the center console. The seat has an angle adjustment, including the base's height and the backrest's tilt, allowing the user to take a more comfortable posture. She can choose scenarios with corresponding makeup matches, such as the work scene. The system provides related makeup tutorials when selecting a specific scenario. She can watch the tutorial while putting on makeup in the mirror. She can also use the photo function to record the makeup journey, and share them with friends.

3.6 Team 6: Generation Y

Generation Y groups are very heavily populated by dog lovers. When traveling with (giant) dogs, dog lovers often encounter many problems, such as dogs climbing all over the place to mess up the car, trampling the seats, dropping fur that is not easy to clean, and needing to be carried in the car by their owners when they cannot get in. In addition, dogs often get curious and explore the windows or get into the front row, compromising driving safety and causing motion sickness in passengers.

Sun is a 45-year-old civil servant who loves dogs and has a large golden retriever as a companion. She often drives to the park on her days off and the dog's movements during the drive can interfere with driving safety. She needs to be safe but cannot bear to leave her pet in the trunk when driving.

Team 6 used the considerable area between the trunk and back seat of the vehicle to create a pet area. She needs to set the angle of the back seat according to the dog's height to ensure that the dog can breathe and not escape and assess whether it needs to get on an assistive ladder. Each time the mode is turned on, the rear seat is automatically adjusted to the saved angle, the bottom air cushion in the area starts to inflate, and the ladder pops out of the trunk. It has a tow rope and a hard-wearing washable mat for easy replacement. It also features a side hanging basket for dog treats and water cups. Moreover, a pet camera automatically identifies and alerts the owner on the center console if it detects abnormal situations, such as vomiting.

4 Discussion

4.1 Transdisciplinary Learning

The students had different backgrounds and perspectives on the same research topic. At the beginning of this collaborative study, they had conflicting views based on their specialties and other research methods. They wanted to explore the problem, but these ideas were all valuable. With further collaborative study, they learned to integrate multiple expertise and use various research methods to investigate the problem, resulting in significant innovation in the design. It was important to note that students who were good at one part of the work should not only do the work they were good at but rather learn knowledge and skills they could be better at. Ultimately, all students were able to enrich their knowledge and skills through transdisciplinary learning and were able to deal with problems and difficulties more comfortably in their future studies and work.

4.2 User Needs of Generation Z and Y

The six modes were designed to meet the needs of different people in different scenarios, such as helping novice drivers to become proficient, supporting family members to communicate, and facilitating female drivers to do makeup. These modes would make the cockpit a means of transportation and an essential part of life that carries people's emotions. Therefore, all six modes provided innovative solutions and ideas for studying the user needs of Generation Z and Y.

4.3 Reflection

All students made significant progress during this project and formed fruitful results. However, in retrospect, they had several points to summarize and reflect on.

Understanding background research at the beginning of the project. The desktop research should be the beginning of the project, but as the subsequent iterations went more profound, the students found that the scope set at the beginning might need to be revised. At each milestone, they should go back and see if they needed to update and iterate on the research content and generate new research results.

Fostering a user-centered mind. The students came from various backgrounds and had different ways of thinking, but they all needed to think from user perspectives. For example, they should always keep empathy in the interviews and dig into the underlying demands or values. On the contrary, if they asked direct questions and followed the outline without knowing how to adapt, the results would often be too superficial. This required a certain amount of life experience, communication skills, and user perspectives. The students might be the target users, but it was too subjective to draw conclusions based on their opinions alone. Only conclusions drawn through extensive user research were objective.

Integrating practice and theory. The method learned was a simple theoretical model. After mastering the theoretical knowledge, the students need to use it in combination with practice, make flexible adjustments and applications according to different projects and scenarios, and at the same time, enrich our theoretical knowledge in practice. Only with this combination of theory and practice can they use their knowledge and skills to create meaningful designs that better meet user needs.

Acknowledgment. We would like to thank the students in UX Program of MAP at the Faculty of Psychology at Beijing Normal University.

References

1. Dong, F., Liu, Y.: Policy evolution and effect evaluation of new-energy vehicle industry in China. Resour. Policy **67**, 101655 (2020)
2. Wang, X., Li, Z., Shaikh, R., Ranjha, A.R., Batala, L.K.: Do government subsidies promote financial performance? Fresh evidence from China's new energy vehicle industry. Sustain. Prod. Consumption **28**, 142–153 (2021)
3. Wen, H., Lee, C.C., Zhou, F.: How does fiscal policy uncertainty affect corporate innovation investment? Evidence from China's new energy industry. Energy Economics **105**, 105767 (2022)
4. Jung, S., et al.: Effect of touch button interface on in-vehicle information systems usability. Int. J. Hum. Comput. Interact. **37**(15), 1404–1422 (2021)
5. Wang, R., Sell, R., Rassolkin, A., Otto, T., Malayjerdi, E.: Intelligent functions development on autonomous electric vehicle platform. J. Mach. Eng. **20**(2), 114–125 (2020). https://doi.org/10.36897/jme/117787
6. Olaverri-Monreal, C.: Promoting trust in self-driving vehicles. Nat. Electron. **3**(6), 292–294 (2020)
7. Babic, T., Reiterer, H., Haller, M.: Understanding and creating spatial interactions with distant displays enabled by unmodified off-the-shelf smartphones. Multimodal Technol. Interact. **6**(10), 94 (2022)
8. Tan, H., Zhao, X., Yang, J.: Exploring the influence of anxiety, pleasure and subjective knowledge on public acceptance of fully autonomous vehicles. Comput. Hum. Behav. **131**, 107187 (2022)
9. Zhu, Y., Tang, G., Liu, W., Qi, R.: How post 90's gesture interact with automobile skylight. Int. J. Hum. Comput. Interact. **38**(5), 395–405 (2022)
10. Tan, H., Sun, J., Wenjia, W., Zhu, C.: User experience & usability of driving: a bibliometric analysis of 2000–2019. Int. J. Hum. Comput. Interact. **37**(4), 297–307 (2021)
11. Guerrero-Ibanez, J.A., Zeadally, S., Contreras-Castillo, J.: Integration challenges of intelligent transportation systems with connected vehicle, cloud computing, and internet of things technologies. IEEE Wirel. Commun. **22**(6), 122–128 (2015)
12. Murali, P.K., Kaboli, M., Dahiya, R.: Intelligent in-vehicle interaction technologies. Adv. Intell. Syst. **4**(2), 2100122 (2022)
13. Oana, J., Ona, A.I.: Assertiveness in self-fulfillment and professional success. Interpersonal dynamics in the didactic relation. Psychology **10**(8), 1235–1247 (2019)

14. Norman, D.: The design of everyday things: revised and expanded edition. Basic Books (2013)
15. Zhu, D., Gray, C.M., Toombs, A.L., Liu, C., Liu, W.: Building a cross-cultural UX design dual degree. In: Congress of the International Association of Societies of Design Research, pp. 1128–1134 (2022). https://doi.org/10.1007/978-981-19-4472-7_74
16. Koelle, M., Olsson, T., Mitchell, R., Williamson, J., Boll, S.: What is (un) acceptable? Thoughts on social acceptability in HCI research. Interactions **26**(3), 36–40 (2019)
17. Haritaipan, L., Saijo, M., Mougenot, C.: Impact of technical information in magic-based inspiration tools on novice designers. Int. J. Technol. Des. Educ. **29**(5), 1153–1177 (2018). https://doi.org/10.1007/s10798-018-9476-x
18. Gray, C.M.: Languaging design methods. Design Stud. **78**, 101076 (2022)
19. Desmet, P., Xue, H., Xin, X., Liu, W.: Emotion deep dive for designers: seven propositions that operationalize emotions in design innovation. In: Proceedings of the International Conference on Applied Human Factors and Ergonomics, pp. 24–28 (2022)
20. Liu, W., Lee, K.P., Gray, C.M., Toombs, A.L., Chen, K.H., Leifer, L.: Transdisciplinary teaching and learning in UX design: a program review and AR case studies. Appl. Sci. **11**(22), 10648 (2021)
21. Liu, W., Byler, E., Leifer, L.: Engineering design entrepreneurship and innovation: transdisciplinary teaching and learning in a global context. In: Marcus, A., Rosenzweig, E. (eds.) HCII 2020. LNCS, vol. 12202, pp. 451–460. Springer, Cham (2020). https://doi.org/10.1007/978-3-030-49757-6_33
22. Zhu, Di., Wang, R., Zhang, Z., Wang, D., Meng, X., Liu, W.: Exploring and reflecting on generation Z interaction qualities and selfie scenario designs. In: Markopoulos, E., Goonetilleke, R.S., Ho, A.G., Luximon, Y. (eds.) AHFE 2021. LNNS, vol. 276, pp. 352–357. Springer, Cham (2021). https://doi.org/10.1007/978-3-030-80094-9_42
23. Liu, W.: Designing generation Y interactions: the case of YPhone. Virtual Reality Intell. Hardware **4**(2), 132–152 (2022)
24. Ferreira, B., Silva, W., Oliveira, E., Conte, T.: Designing personas with empathy map. In: SEKE, vol. 152 (2015)
25. Xin, X., et al.: Building up personas by clustering behavior motivation from extreme users. In: International Conference on Human-Computer Interaction, pp. 120–131 (2022). https://doi.org/10.1007/978-3-031-05897-4_9
26. Visser, F.S., Stappers, P.J., Van der Lugt, R., Sanders, E.B.: Contextmapping: experiences from practice. CoDesign **1**(2), 119–149 (2005)
27. Xin, X., Wang, Y., Liu, N., Yang, W., Dong, H., Liu, W.: Research on in-vehicle haptic interactions as crucial resources for driver perceptions. In: Stephanidis, C., Duffy, V.G., Krömker, H., Fui-Hoon Nah, F., Siau, K., Salvendy, G., Wei, J. (eds.) HCII 2021. LNCS, vol. 13097, pp. 373–388. Springer, Cham (2021). https://doi.org/10.1007/978-3-030-90966-6_27
28. Xin, X., Wang, Y., Xiang, G., Yang, W., Liu, W.: Effectiveness of multimodal display in navigation situation. In: The Ninth International Symposium of Chinese CHI, pp. 50–62 (2021)
29. Liu, W., et al.: Designing interactive glazing through an engineering psychology approach: six augmented reality scenarios that envision future car human-machine interface. Virtual Reality Intell. Hardware **5**(5), 1–14 (2022)
30. Lucassen, G., van de Keuken, M., Dalpiaz, F., Brinkkemper, S., Sloof, G.W., Schlingmann, J.: Jobs-to-be-done oriented requirements engineering: a method for defining job stories. In: International Working Conference on Requirements Engineering: Foundation for Software Quality, pp. 227–243 (2018).https://doi.org/10.1007/978-3-319-77243-1_14

Research on Lacquer Display Design in Digital Age

Lin Cui[✉]

Jiangxi Institute of Fashion Technology, Nanchang, China
463848242@qq.com

Abstract. The history of lacquer art can be traced back to 8,000 years ago. The complex production process of lacquer art limited its mass production, and in ancient times it existed mostly in the form of exquisite handicrafts. Since modern times, lacquer art has developed in many directions, gradually moving from arts and crafts to art. However, the public still has a vague understanding of lacquer art, so popularizing and promoting lacquer art culture can make more people understand this niche culture. In the era of digital information, the digital display of artworks has become a trend, presenting a diversified state. As we enter the virtual age of digital information, what would happen if traditional lacquer art were to collide with digital technology? This paper presents this hypothesis, discusses the necessity of digital display of lacquer art products in today's era, and explores the development and application of lacquer art in digital conservation. This paper explores the feasibility of digital display of lacquer art and proposes a feasible solution, combining the change of technological concepts in the context of the digital age, and analyzes the digital conservation of lacquer art, the exploration of the feasibility of virtual and realistic technology of lacquer art, and the digital dissemination of lacquer art culture, in an attempt to expand the diversity of lacquer art cultural heritage, to expand its economic value, and to realize a variety of ways of digital display of diversified lacquer art. In order to promote and publicize lacquer art culture, a new opportunity is established between traditional culture and digital industry culture making lacquer art products rejuvenated in the trend of digital cultural industry development. We discuss the possibility of integrating digital media technology, human-computer interaction technology, and artificial intelligence into the art of lacquer, and propose the possibility of combining digital media with the culture of lacquer to break through the constraints and establish a new mode of displaying lacquer art and pursue a more multifaceted display design experience. Through the digital interactive display, the art of lacquer is inherited and protected.

Keywords: Virtual display · Lacquer art · Preservation of culture

© The Author(s), under exclusive license to Springer Nature Switzerland AG 2023
A. Marcus et al. (Eds.): HCII 2023, LNCS 14031, pp. 84–92, 2023.
https://doi.org/10.1007/978-3-031-35696-4_7

1 Current Status of Lacquer Culture Preservation

1.1 The Heritage and Status of Lacquer Art

Lacquer was used in ancient times as a coating that was both practical and aesthetically pleasing, as well as having a weapon-making function. The ancient ancestors of mankind invented primitive lacquerware when they discovered that the sap flowing from the lacquer tree would form a strong coating when it dried. The ancient lacquer crafts were mostly used by the nobility as vessels, utensils and decorations, and were more precious because of their complicated production process and low production. Lacquer gives a beauty of oriental flavor, with warm and subtle color. The artistic expression of the lacquer medium is an invention in the process of human culture and an integral part of civilizations all over the world. The lacquer art originated in the East, first in East Asia and then spread around the world, continuously absorbing the cultures of the world's peoples and forming an art (Fig. 1).

Fig. 1. Cutting lacquer

Before modern times, lacquer mostly existed in the form of vessels, screens and other crafts with usage functions. After the modern era, some artists tried to combine lacquer with painting and lacquer with installation, and lacquer was not only used as a

Fig. 2. Vietnamese artists Phiphi OANH, Lacquer Installation, The Hall of Mirrors

craft but also as a material for artistic creation, showing many directions of development, gradually moving from the craft market to the art market (Fig. 2).

Contemporary artists use lacquer as a material to express their views and artistic ideas in their works, and some works that cross lacquer and installation have also appeared, such as Vietnamese artist Nguyen Phi Phi's lacquer installation "Mirror Gallery". The artist tries to freely explore the organic material of lacquer, thinking about the Metamorphosis of the material and creating an optical illusion style of the Baroque era. The work creates a space in which a symbolic mirror is represented, creating an illusion compared to a flat lacquer painting. With this work the artist wants to express the therapeutic machine of experiencing the emptiness of the body, a kind of simulation experiment of the movement of the viewer's soul in this cave-like lacquer space. Through the work, the artist tries to trace back to the cave paintings of Atlamira, while at the same time responding to the cave allegory of Plato.

However, whether it is ancient lacquer art or contemporary lacquer installation art, the public vision is not familiar with lacquer material, a natural resin, and the knowledge of lacquer art is relatively unfamiliar. Except for a few artists and craftsmen who are engaged in lacquer-related industries or professions, the cultural circle of lacquer art is small in scope, and the public has insufficient knowledge of traditional lacquer art and less understanding of lacquer ware and lacquer art.

1.2 The Need for Digital Display of Lacquer Art

In ancient times, lacquer art was difficult to escape from the limitations of shape and technical aspects, and handicraft production was slow and could not be produced efficiently. In the modern Japanese lacquer workshop in Wajima, a manufacturing center, electronic equipment has been used to speed up the processing and production of lacquer products, and the complex processes of grinding and painting have been completed with the help of speed-adjustable mechanical equipment, which has improved work efficiency. The new technology creates more possibilities. New technologies create more possibilities, and in recent years, with 3d scanning technology, modeling technology, digital carving technology, etc., have made up for the defects of traditional lacquer handcraft.

In the age of digital information, the digital display of art has become a trend, and it is necessary to collide traditional lacquer art with digital technology and explore the feasibility of digital display of lacquer art, in line with the current digital industry background. With the emphasis on the protection of traditional intangible culture, the protection of traditional lacquer craft skills is also on the agenda, and digital protection is also a good way. Entering the information virtual era, with the emergence of digital museums, digital interaction, and digital collections, lacquer art can appear in a new form to the public. Digital display of lacquer art is also useful and meaningful for the digital conservation of intangible cultural heritage of lacquer craft techniques and the promotion of lacquer art, and it is necessary to explore the development and application of lacquer art digitization.

The change of technological concepts in the context of the digital age, the combination of virtual and realistic technologies of lacquer art, the dissemination of lacquer art in a digital way, the expansion of lacquer culture heritage diversity and economic value, the realization of diversified lacquer art digital display methods become an inevitable trend. This can better promote and publicize lacquer culture, bring into play the application value of lacquer art itself, digital productization of lacquer art, establish a new opportunity between traditional culture and digital industrial culture, and connect the bridge between tradition and contemporary, so that lacquer art works can be revitalized in the trend development of digital cultural industry development. The digital culture preservation and virtual display of contemporary lacquer art should break through the limitations of the physical medium, and involve digital media technology, human-computer interaction technology, and artificial intelligence in the art of lacquer, combining digital display with lacquer art in terms of product, form, content, and theme, exploring the possibility of combining digital media with traditional culture like lacquer in depth, breaking through the constraints and establishing a new model of lacquer art display. The exhibition will explore the possibility of combining digital media with lacquer art, a traditional culture, to break through the constraints and establish a new model of lacquer art display. The combination of digital media and lacquer art will lead to a new display design experience.

2 Database and Technology Development for Digital Preservation of Lacquer Art

In lacquer digitization conservation, workers have to collect, store, apply, and disseminate some data, so as to conduct a full range of digital exploration. Database is the core part of digital conservation, and databases at all levels provide technical support as storage, management, access, information and sharing. By means of digital photography and recording of lacquer artworks, 2D or 3D scanning, virtual reality, and searching, we can better inherit, publicize, and explore the culture of lacquer art and establish a database of lacquer art. At the same time, the Internet and Internet of Things are used as communication carriers to creatively develop and expand the digital propagation and popularization of lacquer art. With the wide application of digital technology in recent years, the digital protection of intangible cultural heritage has gradually become a hot spot, and the digital protection of traditional lacquer craft techniques can also be excavated and digitally protected in depth.

The main steps to realize the digital preservation database of lacquer art are: firstly, collect the data related to lacquer art, classify the techniques and patterns, and digitally collect them according to the graphic characteristics presented by different techniques. Through computerized semantic classification, the meaning of lacquer techniques is summarized and summarized, analyzed independently, and precisely matched with the visual characteristics of lacquer. Through the establishment of the lacquer technique database, it provides an important data base for the digital preservation of lacquer culture.

In the development of digital digital technology, it is important to follow the principle of universality, but also take the different kinds of lacquer art according to the category. There are many kinds of lacquer art developed so far, so it is important to scientifically plan and establish the lacquer art database, and to develop an effective conservation plan through virtual modeling and behavioral interaction technology, knowledge visualization technology, web, etc. for the in-depth digital conservation of different types and regions of lacquer art works, in order to promote the digital conservation of world cultural heritage and promote the digital conservation of world cultural heritage.

3 Exploration of Lacquer Art Digital Display Design Solutions

3.1 Lacquer Art Museum Digital Virtual Experience

Nowadays, museums and art galleries are stepping into the digitalization process. Along with the continuous development of digital technology, digital art museums have become a hot spot, and most museums and art galleries at home and abroad have corresponding digital online museums for users to experience and browse, from the creation process of art to the exhibition layout, with the help of new media technology has become quite common. Listening to the stories of artworks, interacting with artists, and interacting with cultural relics bring users a rich visual and cultural experience through these immersive and innovative ways of experience, and also facilitate the exchange and dissemination of culture and art (Fig. 3).

For example, in the "Patterns" to Carry the Way - The Forbidden City Tencent Immersive Digital Experience Exhibition, which will open in Shenzhen, China in 2021 at the Sea World Culture and Art Center, the exhibition extracts the diverse and meaningful patterns from the Forbidden City's ancient buildings, ceramics, furniture and embroidery, and uses digital technology to give a new application scenario, explore the rich connotations of cultural relics, including the "pattern of nature" interactive heritage plate, interactive area 360° ring curtain including the ground, the inside of the turntable, the outside of four parts, reflecting the theme of "pattern", the The audience can interact with the "patterns" of the artifacts through movement, and the details of the artifacts travel through the dust of history and are revitalized with the support of technology. These examples can also be applied to lacquer digital museum design cases.

Combining digital virtual and lacquer art to achieve the digital virtual reality experience of lacquer art, we can organize lacquer art relics or lacquer-related artworks in

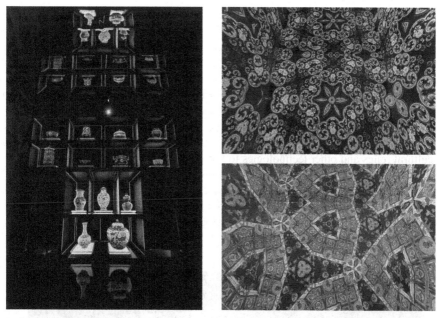

Fig. 3. 2021 "Tattoo" to carry the road - the Forbidden City Tencent immersive digital experience exhibition

physical museums and art galleries around the world, collect and organize these artworks, store them, and build a digital virtual lacquer art museum with both historical and cultural connotations and contemporary. The digital lacquer art museum firstly introduces and experiences lacquer art culture digitally, displays and introduces lacquer art techniques and history, presents lacquer art techniques digitally, and shows lacquer art related process techniques through virtual experience. The interactive design link allows the experiencer to understand lacquer art in a shorter time, perceive the charm of traditional lacquer art, and enrich the digital expression of lacquer art. Different terminals provide a variety of platform services for lacquer digitization, tablet PCs and cell phones can be used for secondary development of software, while virtual design software for lacquer art creations can be developed, experience lacquer art display design mini-games, h5 platform propaganda, etc. The combination of digital lacquer and virtual reality technology has expanded the way of lacquer culture preservation and development.

Lacquer digital virtual reality experience, through virtual reality technology to collect and summarize lacquer visual graphic features, using style migration algorithm and generate lacquer graphics, through the combination of virtual simulation technology and augmented reality technology, to achieve the visual expression of lacquer literature digital products. The virtual information can be applied to the real world through AR technology, where the real environment and virtual objects are superimposed on each other and exist in one dimension, and the actions in the real world are not affected. Taking the lacquer art digital museum guide as an example, we analyze the viewing factors of lacquer art museum visitors and develop an optimization strategy based on research data.

Using the 'petrified socks' as inspiration, artist Max Mollison has sculpted 3D objects that are displayed in a virtual space that can be viewed 360° in the video to provide an immersive way to experience the objects in the digital museum. Immersive experience can also be used as a form of expression for the digitalization of lacquer art. The development of lacquer art digitalization requires more interdisciplinary crossover and cooperation, such as computer graphics data acquisition, artificial network neural algorithm and virtual platform development, etc., all of which require multi-disciplinary interdisciplinary cooperation to realize the digital diversification of lacquer art. The lacquer digital museum can combine cloud structure, scene model, actual roaming, digitization of cultural relics and other technologies to reproduce the history of ancient lacquer art development, production techniques, etc. Through immersive scene experience, virtual replication of the original appearance of ancient cultural relics, combined with AR, VR, etc. and integration of online guided tour, leading users to revisit the birthplace of lacquer culture and experience traditional and current lacquer culture through an interactive way (Fig. 4).

Fig. 4. Artists Max Mollison, Installation art, Petrified socks

3.2 Digital Interactive Experience of Lacquer Art

Heritage interactive, using enhanced technology to move the displayed cultural relics, activate the historical memory of cultural relics, strengthen the interactivity between the audience and cultural relics, and make the ancient cultural relics new vitality in contemporary times, many smart museums are using this technology today. Lacquer art relics interactive, first of all, high-precision digital acquisition and digital restoration of lacquer artworks, display lacquer artworks 720° full view, can zoom in on the details of cultural relics, through the ornamentation, dynamic effects of interactive way to show the history of lacquer art relics story, heritage value, use, etc., and then in an interesting interactive way to make the user vividly understand the past life of lacquer artworks. Here we need to pay attention to the depth of interaction: zoom in, zoom out, and rotate the pictures and lacquer models displayed in augmented reality; set up self-control for voice and video, and drag and drop to achieve forward and backward; set up other interesting ways of interaction, such as in exploration mode, looking for game clues to complete the game interaction. At the same time, the user can interact with the exhibits through the interface in the form of pictures, videos, texts, voices and models; the guide can be customized according to the user's interests and personalized guide routes can be set.

Digital lacquer art creation, the experiencer can choose the existing size model in the database for the creation of lacquer painting techniques, choose the relevant digital body for simulated painting, simulate the style of lacquer art in different historical periods, color matching according to the preferences of the experiencer, and finally present the digital virtual effect with digital graphics. The digital products can also be transformed into virtual digital products at a later stage according to the effects, and the digital products will be presented to the experiencer. The lacquer interactive virtual experience provides users with convenient access to basic information about lacquer art culture and lacquer painting techniques.

3.3 Lacquer Art Digital Collection Display

Digital collection refers to the use of blockchain technology to generate unique digital credentials corresponding to specific works and artworks, and to achieve authentic and credible digital distribution, purchase, collection and use on the basis of protecting their digital copyrights. Digital collections are a new form of digital publications and are divided into two product types: blockchain works copyright and blockchain digital publishing products. Currently many museums have released digital collections based on the treasures in their collections. The core of the lacquer art digital collection is guided by the lacquer culture, with the help of innovative ways to promote and disseminate culture. The lacquer culture digitalization is a digital technology as a means to transform lacquer art works into digital informative expressions, so that more people can understand, experience and spread the medium of lacquer and the culture behind it. The design of the digital lacquer art collection is not only the expression of the visual language, but also the excavation of the cultural layers behind the form.

The design of lacquer art digital collections requires the texture effect of lacquer art, the color and texture effect of the eight types of techniques usually used in traditional lacquer art and modern techniques, which is the key to the design of lacquer art digital collections, and how to emphasize the characteristics of lacquer art and materials in the design of digital collections is the key and difficult point of lacquer art digital collections design. At the same time, the variety of lacquer techniques and the special characteristics of lacquer materials make lacquer digital art full of challenges and possibilities in the production process. At present, lacquer patterns are usually embodied in some ancient lacquerware or recorded in ancient books. In the era of big data, graphic information has to be digitally converted with the times in order to better spread and pass on. The lacquer art digital collection can attract a group of young trendy users, help business, and make the lacquer culture or lacquer art rejuvenate through the sale of the collection, with the play of collection + blind box and collection + physical objects.

4   Conclusion

This paper discusses the possibility of combining lacquer art and digital display into the digital information era, and the development and application of lacquer art in digital display design. Through scanning and virtual reality of lacquer art works, we can better inherit, promote and explore lacquer art culture, scientifically plan and establish lacquer art database, and use virtual modeling and behavioral interaction technology, knowledge visualization technology, web and other technologies to deeply digitally protect different types and regions of lacquer art works. This paper proposes three lacquer art digital display design solutions, namely lacquer art museum digital virtual experience, lacquer art digital display user interactive experience, and lacquer art digital collection display. The feasibility of digital display of lacquer art is explored, combined with the change of technological concepts in the context of the digital era, and the feasibility of digital preservation of lacquer art, virtual and realistic technology of lacquer art, and digital dissemination of lacquer art culture is explored to expand the plurality of lacquer art cultural heritage, to promote and publicize lacquer art culture through diversified lacquer art digital display in many ways, and to bring the more traditional material of lacquer art The project will establish a new opportunity between lacquer art, a traditional material, and digital interactive display.

References

1. Phiphi OANH, F.: 越南当代漆画与漆艺家. 中国生漆 **33**(03) (2014)
2. 刘永亮, F.: 互联网时代工艺美术的产品延伸发展及运作模式探究. 艺术生活(3), 43 (2018)
3. 许聪, F.T.: 新媒体技术在博物馆中的技术应用与开发设计研究, 1st edn. 信息科技, Tianjin (2017)
4. Dyson, F.: Sounding New Media: Immersion and Embodiment in the Arts and Culture. University of California Press, California (2009)
5. Zhou, G.: 数字化保护-非物质文化遗产保护新路向. 文化创新比较研究 **2**(20) (2018)

Pedestrian Presence Detection in Areas of Interest Using Multiple Cameras

Kenedy Felipe dos Santos da Silva[1,2]([✉]) [ID],
João Paulo Silva do Monte Lima[1,2] [ID], and Veronica Teichrieb[2] [ID]

[1] Departamento de Computação, Universidade Federal Rural de Pernambuco,
Recife, Brazil
{kenedy.silva,joao.mlima}@ufrpe.br
[2] Voxar Labs, Centro de Informática, Universidade Federal de Pernambuco,
Recife, Brazil
{kfss,jpsml,vt}@cin.ufpe.br
https://voxarlabs.cin.ufpe.br/

Abstract. Monitoring pedestrians in security scenarios are problems that cover different environments of society. Seeking solutions to this problem, the techniques of detection and tracking of pedestrians can meet the need for constant surveillance. In addition, many solutions involve long training and require much effort, increasing costs. To understand and find techniques that enable the detection of pedestrians in areas of interest, aiming at monitoring the safety of pedestrians, we carried out a comparative evaluation between a pedestrian detection technique and a pedestrian tracking technique, in addition to inserting the validation of pedestrian crossing in areas of interest in the image. We established complementary scenarios that seek a relationship between the pedestrian identification techniques in each scenario, obtaining average results regarding pedestrian detection inside the areas of interest. For the detection technique, we obtained an accuracy of 0.952 and an f-score of 0.970, and for the tracking technique an accuracy of 0.948 and an f-score of 0.967, with a precision of 0.977 and 0.984 for the detection and tracking techniques, respectively. For the number of frames with pedestrian presence in the areas of interest, we obtained the following average results for the pedestrian detection technique: accuracy and f-score of 0.985 and precision of 0.997. For the tracking technique, the accuracy was 0.973, and the f-score was 0.970, and this technique managed to obtain a precision of 1.000.

Keywords: Detection · Tracking · Pedestrian Presence · Areas of Interest · Multiple Cameras

1 Introduction

Pedestrian detection is a problem that covers several contexts in people's daily lives, aiming at security issues and technological evolution. As a result, the

A. Marcus et al. (Eds.): HCII 2023, LNCS 14031, pp. 93–105, 2023.
https://doi.org/10.1007/978-3-031-35696-4_8

community of researchers has been looking for solutions for intelligent cities, monitoring, robotics, behavioral analysis, and actions aimed at safety in environments that can put lives at risk.

In the evolution of detection, many techniques and solutions seek to track pedestrians to know where the same pedestrian passed during the recording and their actions within the scene, which is responsible for solving the same problems mentioned in the detection part. The techniques discussed earlier complement each other, and the complement performed between the detection and tracking of pedestrians leads us to conditions of analysis and validation to meet the contexts mentioned initially.

In the context of security, we can find scenarios that can put people's lives at risk in specific environments, that is, unhealthy environments. With this, we can observe the passages and detections of people in particular places in the image to identify safer and alert areas depending on the scenario. Moreover, the exchange of information can occur in real time, thus allowing taking proactive actions.

Seeking solutions for security scenarios, in this way, we insert in detection and tracking techniques validations of passages in predetermined places, that is, places that we do not want or that we want pedestrians to cross, to identify and alert the detection at that time. The information available for each method makes it possible to compare and analyze which model could be more efficient in generating safety in unhealthy environments. Furthermore, we propose validation of pedestrian crossings in specific scene locations, comparing complementary techniques in which we can obtain information that may go unnoticed by one method and not by the other.

The contributions of this work are:

1. Inclusion in methods for pedestrian detection and tracking with multiple cameras of a pass validation technique in areas of interest (Sect. 3);
2. Demonstration of an algorithm for validating pedestrian crossings at predetermined locations (Sect. 3);
3. Comparison of results and quantitative and qualitative evaluations of both techniques in some areas of interest (Sect. 4);

2   Related Work

Detection of people and objects has become much more accurate with deep learning methods, using data to infer relevant features of the observed domain [6, 15, 26].

Neural network models can learn to extract relevant information about an object in a 3D scene. These can learn about the thing of interest by being trained with images without needing resources or pre-defined cues like traditional approaches. This feature makes deep learning exceptionally well suited for estimating scenarios with little information available, such as simple RGB [18, 19, 29].

However, these RGB deep learning models often need to be trained with many labeled images to supplement the need for more available information (e.g., depth). The effort to obtain, annotate, and maintain data is expensive. The main question arises because acquiring these training sequences and observing their correctness is often complicated, expensive, and time-consuming. Furthermore, there is no guarantee that the annotation will be free of inaccuracies caused by human error or unidentified noise.

And also, each object must have a wide range of views and rotation angles recorded. This recording should also consider the background, foreground, and lighting details [8,10,28]. Even so, generalizing these models to new scenes, lighting, or cameras is a challenge. Still, it is only possible to cover some possible real-world scenarios during training, needing to find other ways to generalize to previously unseen conditions. Being robust in different cameras and environmental conditions is especially relevant for the industry.

Many alternatives have been proposed to deal with data limitations and challenges related to environmental variations, increasing the accuracy of RGBs approaches. Among these methods, we can highlight strategies to transfer and adapt the target domain [23,24,27], to share knowledge for performing continuous learning [11,31], and to perform training with synthetically rendered images [5,12,30].

2.1 Pedestrian Detection

Pedestrian detectors can have both monocular and multi-camera options, and monocular pedestrian detection can get a 3D location using a single camera. They are usually networks trained to acquire a delimitation of the people in the image. Multi-camera detections are performed in the same way as monocular detection models and later integrated for better results, thus being able to deal with occlusion problems, a limitation existing in monocular cases [2].

Multi-camera detection solutions achieve detection goals. However, the information obtained can present problems in identifying the same person in all cameras, increasing the number of people within the same scene. In addition, this imprecision of the estimates may generate ambiguity or doubt in interpretation.

2.2 Pedestrian Tracking

Pedestrian tracking also uses single-camera and multi-camera options, and some solutions discuss the single-camera tracking problem through the multi-object tracking (MOT) problem. Many challenges are seen in this scenario, like stationary, fixed, or moving cameras. There are several tracking methods for single camera tracking created to solve the MOT problem [13,17,20,32].

Other existing tracking solutions, which are the basis for current studies, use video rate surveillance algorithms and real-time monitoring to detect and track multiple people and monitor their activities outdoors, or even moving with cameras [9,21,25].

2.3 Multi-camera Detection and Tracking

The work of Lima et al. [15] performs detection of pedestrians from the multi-camera detections, estimating the point on the ground of each person, which is their location on the ground plane. Subsequently, it merges the data obtaining the 3D coordinates of each person, making it a solution of greater generalization, using deep learning to get the data of the people in the image, estimating a central point between the people's ankles. These points are marked in each camera. This solution does not need to train with a target dataset to estimate the location of pedestrians.

For tracking, pedestrian detection is required. As mentioned above, they can use resources using multiple cameras, and detection must be performed on each of them and then merged on each frame. The detections must be completed at each instant t, and the tracking process manages to track people in the scenes [16].

The process adds re-identification, which is the problem of recognizing individuals who have appeared on different cameras or the same camera but on other occasions. It is a challenging task because of the presence of different points of view, alterations, low or different image resolutions, and lighting modification, among others [33].

A temporal relationship between detections is established, which uses the Kalman filter [14] to predict the location of pedestrians at the next instant in time, then combine the predictions with a distance threshold, and finally update the pedestrian location information.

2.4 Detection of Pedestrian Presence in Areas of Interest

Detecting the presence of pedestrians at predetermined locations is not an approach taken in most pedestrian detection techniques. However, it is usually possible to find information related to pedestrian detection in full images in the literature, identifying their location. In addition, the bounding box is often used to determine the position or location of the pedestrian.

Pedestrian identification techniques for protection or possible threat can be found in the literature. Brogii et al. [3] use a scenario-based model, in which it is necessary to know the pedestrian's location and the vehicle's destination in the scene for validation between information. However, this approach will initially identify the complete scenario, include the vehicle as a detected object, and then detect the pedestrian. In addition, this scenario requires a lot of information and data collection, which makes the technique quite robust and expensive.

The pedestrian detection model used by Pustokhina et al. [22] follows a different identification procedure regarding the presence of pedestrians. It identifies pedestrians with much information for training and uses a pre-process for training neural networks.

The detection of pedestrians in search of their protection is one of the scenarios of great relevance to society when we talk about safety. We could observe many studies in the work of Gandhi & Trivedi [7] that presents pedestrian protection systems. The study shows a vital protection scenario, but in many methods the environment in which the pedestrian is located may have collisions with vehicles. We understand how important it is to protect pedestrians in this environment. Even so, we observe how difficult it is to find studies that cite other environments that may have places of risk for pedestrians. Determining locations can generate a new view of the data, which can bring significant improvements to preventing pedestrian accidents.

The implementation described by Ansarnia et al. [1] shows a scenario that can be compared using deep learning algorithms to identify people and objects in complementary situations. The combination of three algorithms for validating possible collisions between vehicles and pedestrians is mentioned. The segmentation adopted in the experiment shows object detection, pedestrian detection, and detection of the highway on which objects and pedestrians may be. However, only one fixed camera is used, and the design identifies many areas where detections are placed.

3 Method

The methods mentioned are models that complement each other, aiming at new analyses. We compare detection and tracking in predetermined places in the image. They are areas of interest where we can identify the presence of the person in the scene, or even the proximity of a limiting box, thus seeking to determine safety actions or pedestrian crossings in the chosen places.

3.1 Detection in Areas of Interest

For detection of pedestrians in the area of interest, we use a generalizable detection method that calculates the 3D location of pedestrians in the ground plane [15], as described in Subsect. 2.3. The detection performed by the process involves identifying each detected pedestrian, with the marking of the ground plane, seen in Fig. 1.

Fig. 1. Pedestrian detection at the same time instant and view of the ground plane of each pedestrian.

We use the information collected to identify in the areas of interest if there was a pedestrian crossing. If so, we record the moment t when the intersection occurred. This moment is identified for counting and alerting that there was a pedestrian in the defined place, in addition to counting the number of people detected.

3.2   Detection and Tracking in Areas of Interest

For tracking, we have a complement of information using the method described by Lyra et al. [16]. It performs the entire detection process, with the validation of the continuity of the pedestrian movement through a threshold, shown in Fig. 2.

Fig. 2. Pedestrian tracking results seen on multiple cameras at the same time instant t and their trail on the ground plane.

We perform tracking with the method, and then we check if the pedestrian passed through the area of interest determined in the image. At the end we evaluate the number of pedestrians and the time t of the crossings.

The methods perform detection and tracking and save the results containing tracking positions (x, y, z), where $z = 0$ at each instant. We use the data at the end of the detection and tracking process. We calculate presence and validation metrics to define which method would be most effective in identifying people in predetermined locations. Then, it is possible to determine how many moments could have been alerted as a passage of a pedestrian. These two pieces of information are used to evaluate the necessary metrics according to each method and later carry out an evaluation of the two techniques.

3.3   Pedestrian Check in the Area of Interest

We determine the areas of interest by providing two vertices that define the diagonal points of the given area, as seen in Fig. 3. Then, these data are aligned to form a rectangle between the vertices, thus determining the area defined to detect the pedestrian crossing.

We run the detection algorithm or the reading of the saved data containing the pedestrian detections for the detection method. The results obtained have the nomenclature (t, x, y), which are the time instant t, the position x, and the position y.

For tracking, the data of an object are obtained with the following information: the time instant t, the pedestrian identification, and its respective ground-plane position (x, y), with position $z = 0$. However, for tracking a data structure is created that includes all the positioning data from the same person, as the tracking has the ID to identify the same pedestrian in various scenarios.

For both methods, we read the ground truth information to perform the evaluation at the end of the process, thus identifying the successes of each method.

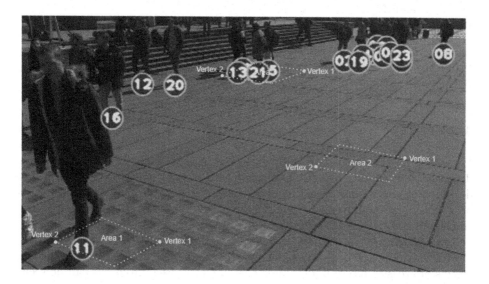

Fig. 3. Example of how to determine the vertices of defined areas of interest.

We create an Algorithm 1 to check the passage in the area of interest. The function checks the pedestrian's (x, y) values, comparing them with the vertices of the area. If the pedestrian is in the area, an alert about the current frame is added at time t.

For the check algorithm to validate the results between detection and tracking, we modify line 4 of the algorithm, which will have the same flow for the other validations, so we change *detection* in *detections* to *track* in *tracks*, where *tracks* is the pedestrian tracking.

Algorithm 1. Pedestrian Check

```
 1: After execute detection method
 2: for area in areas do
 3:     for detection in detecions do
 4:         if detection has in the area then
 5:             Save pedestrian info
 6:             Save frame info (instant t)
 7:         end if
 8:     end for
 9:     Validation Ground Truth info dataset
10:     annotations is Information Real in Ground Truth
11:     for annotation in annotations do
12:         if annotation has in the area then
13:             Save notation info
14:             Save frame info (instant t)
15:         end if
16:     end for
17: end for
18: Validate Ground Truth info and Detection info
19: Create Confusion Matrix
20: Metrics Evaluation
```

4 Results

We evaluated the methods mentioned above in a 3D multi-camera pedestrian detection and tracking scenario to observe the behavior of each technique in the detection of pedestrians in pre-defined locations to use the one that presents the best behaviors, in addition to being possible to identify errors in detection and tracking methods. We present the results obtained in the following subsections and the details about the experiments.

To test some scenarios of passages with the detections, we configured four groups of areas of interest containing three areas in each group, as can be seen in Table 1 that contains the vertices (x,y) of each area in meters.

The points have coordinates in the ground plane, which in the 3D view have the value of $z = 0$.

Table 1. Groups of areas of interest

Runs	Run 1		Run 2		Run 3		Run 4	
Areas	Vertex 1	Vertex 2	Vertex 1	Vertex 2	Vertex 1	Vertex 2	Vertex 1	Vertex 2
Area 1	7.0, 5.0	4.0, 1.0	-5.0, -3.0	0.0, -5.0	-3.0, -3.0	-5.0, -5.0	-3.0, -4.0	0.0, -5.0
Area 2	2.0, 10.0	7.0, 7.0	-3.0, 18.0	0.0, 15.0	-1.0, 21.0	0.0, 18.0	3.0, -5.0	0.0, -8.0
Area 3	1.0, 16.0	4.0, 12.0	10.0, 16.0	6.0, 12.0	5.0, 16.0	8.0, 12.0	2.0, 10.0	6.0, 6.0

4.1 Dataset

We use the same WILDTRACK [4] dataset used by the methods of Lyra et al. [16] and Lima et al. [15] to obtain the same information about the database and thus be able to compare without biasing the result.

The WILDTRACK dataset has seven different cameras from which video frames are extracted, and the scene is captured with many people on the street. The set provides real annotations of each pedestrian for a total of 400 frames in addition to the settings with the camera's intrinsic and extrinsic parameters.

4.2 Metrics

The evaluation consisted of comparing the predictions of the methods with the ground truth for each example. Then, to determine the presence of pedestrians in the areas of interest, note that if only one pedestrian is detected in the predetermined location, the alert will be issued.

Finally, we evaluate the tracking method in the same way as we did for the detection method using the accurate annotations of the WILDTRACK dataset.

From the result obtained, we describe them through a confusion matrix to evaluate the following metrics:

– Accuracy

$$Acc = \frac{TP + TN}{TP + TN + FP + FN} \tag{1}$$

– Precision

$$Prec = \frac{TP}{TP + FP} \tag{2}$$

– Recall

$$Recall = \frac{TP}{TP + FN} \tag{3}$$

– F-Score

$$F_{Score} = 2 \cdot \frac{Accuracy \cdot Recall}{Accuracy + Recall} \tag{4}$$

Where TP is True Positive, TN is True Negative, FP is False Positive, and FN is False Negative.

4.3 Evaluation

According to the results obtained in the prediction, we evaluated the metrics mentioned above. The results obtained for each method are described in Table 2. In the table, we also present other results besides the evaluation metrics. The results are also composed of the number of pedestrians inside the areas of interest detected by each method, the real number of pedestrians inside the areas of interest, that is, with the real information of each pedestrian, and the difference between them, to identify the number of errors.

Table 2. Evaluation metrics of Detection and Tracking methods for each run regarding pedestrians inside the areas of interest

Run	Method	Accuracy	Precision	Recall	F-Score	Detections	Info Real	Diff Total
1	Detection	**0.973**	0.986	**0.984**	**0.985**	1144	1150	6
	Tracking	0.968	**0.992**	0.973	0.982	1104		46
2	Detection	**0.905**	0.942	**0.936**	**0.939**	606	769	163
	Tracking	0.892	**0.956**	0.904	0.930	526		243
3	Detection	0.953	0.987	**0.954**	0.970	720	893	173
	Tracking	**0.955**	**0.994**	0.951	**0.972**	632		261
4	Detection	**0.978**	**0.994**	**0.979**	**0.986**	811	830	19
	Tracking	0.975	0.994	0.976	0.985	799		31
Mean	Detection	**0.952**	0.977	**0.963**	**0.970**	820	910	90
	Tracking	0.948	**0.984**	0.951	0.967	765		145

After the process is completed, we compare the results for the detection method and the tracking method. In direct comparison, we identified that the values obtained by detection are better. We also performed a comparison between the frames that were selected in one method and not in another.

We compared the results to identify why Detection presented better results than Tracking. Finally, with the executions finished, we used the results to compare which time instants t (frames) were incompatible between the methods.

As the Tracking technique uses Detection as the basis for pedestrian detection, we obtained a result of 100% compatibility for three of the four groups of interest between Tracking and Detection. In all frames, the Tracking method generated an alarm, and the Detection method also generated an alarm.

These cases occurred in runs 1, 2, and 4. In run 3, we had two frames in which Tracking generated an alarm, but Detection did not, and five frames in which Tracking did not generate an alarm, but Detection did. However, two of the five frames identified by Detection were false positives, as Tracking output was all correct for these five frames.

We present this comparison in Table 3, which describes the total number of frames that had pedestrians detected in the areas of interest ("Frames Detected" column), the difference between Detection and Tracking, which are the different frames between each of the techniques ("Diff Method" column). Then, in the "Frames Real" column, we have the real number of frames that had pedestrian crossings in the areas of interest.

Finally, in the last column, we have a comparison in the cases where the outputs of both methods were different ("Error Diff" column) to check which ones are correct. This aims to verify if Detection was indeed better than Tracking, because we could have more detections in a method but all False Positives, thus we analyze the number of extra frames detected by Detection and how many of them were correct. The information is based on the total available frames, which are 400 frames for the WILDTRACK dataset.

Table 3. Comparison of frames with pedestrian detection between Detection and Tracking methods

Run Test	Method	Accuracy	Precision	Recall	F-Score	Frames Detected	Diff Method	Frames Real	Error Diff
1	Detection	**0.993**	0.994	**0.997**	**0.995**	363	6	364	2
	Tracking	0.983	**1.000**	0.981	0.982	357	0		0
2	Detection	**0.995**	**1.000**	**0.994**	**0.994**	311	14	313	0
	Tracking	0.960	**1.000**	0.949	0.954	297	0		0
3	Detection	**0.968**	0.994	**0.966**	**0.967**	315	5	326	2
	Tracking	0.965	**1.000**	0.957	0.961	312	2		0
4	Detection	**0.985**	**1.000**	**0.982**	**0.983**	324	0	330	0
	Tracking	**0.985**	**1.000**	**0.082**	**0.983**	324	0		0
Mean	Detection	**0.985**	0.997	**0.985**	**0.985**	**328**	6	333	1
	Tracking	0.973	**1.000**	0.967	0.970	323	1		**0**

Another piece of information about the Tracking method concerns the precision metric being better in all execution scenarios. However, in the other metrics, it was worse.

It makes sense that Tracking was worse than Detection because Tracking sometimes drops the correct detections, causing an increase in false negatives. But on the other hand, Tracking also discards erroneous detections, causing a decrease in false positives.

5   Conclusions

We present in this paper a study about pedestrian presence detection at predetermined locations in the image using multi-camera detection and tracking techniques, performing a comparison between these methods.

As observed, we had greater precision through Tracking. Still, the other metrics were not good, thus showing that the Detection method obtains a better frame-by-frame operation than Tracking, so for the pedestrian crossing problem, or having at least one pedestrian in a area of interest, using Detection is more assertive.

We identified the number of errors for each method. Depending on the purpose of the analysis at a particular location in the image, we can use pedestrian crossing verification in two steps, at the end of Detection and later at the end of Tracking. This analysis can be complementary to identify errors in tracking a pedestrian and also improve pedestrian tracking overall.

For future work, we intend to evaluate the methods on new datasets and also to identify people in risky places, with the goal of improving environment safety.

References

1. Ansarnia, M.S., Tisserand, E., Schweitzer, P., Zidane, M.A., Berviller, Y.: Contextual detection of pedestrians and vehicles in orthophotography by fusion of deep learning algorithms. Sensors **22**(4), 1381 (2022)
2. Baqué, P., Fleuret, F., Fua, P.: Deep occlusion reasoning for multi-camera multi-target detection. In: Proceedings of the IEEE International Conference on Computer Vision, pp. 271–279 (2017)
3. Broggi, A., Cerri, P., Ghidoni, S., Grisleri, P., Jung, H.G.: A new approach to urban pedestrian detection for automatic braking. IEEE Trans. Intell. Transp. Syst. **10**(4), 594–605 (2009)
4. Chavdarova, T., et al.: Wildtrack: A multi-camera hd dataset for dense unscripted pedestrian detection. In: Proceedings of the IEEE Conference on Computer Vision and Pattern Recognition, pp. 5030–5039 (2018)
5. Gaidon, A., Wang, Q., Cabon, Y., Vig, E.: Virtual worlds as proxy for multi-object tracking analysis. In: Proceedings of the IEEE Conference on Computer Vision and Pattern Recognition (CVPR) (June 2016)
6. Gan, Y., Han, R., Yin, L., Feng, W., Wang, S.: Self-supervised multi-view multi-human association and tracking. In: Proceedings of the 29th ACM International Conference on Multimedia. pp. 282–290 (2021)
7. Gandhi, T., Trivedi, M.M.: Pedestrian protection systems: issues, survey, and challenges. IEEE Trans. Intell. Transp. Syst. **8**(3), 413–430 (2007)
8. Garon, M., Laurendeau, D., Lalonde, J.F.: A framework for evaluating 6-dof object trackers. In: Proceedings of the European Conference on Computer Vision (ECCV), pp. 582–597 (2018)
9. Haritaoglu, I., Cutler, R., Harwood, D., Davis, L.S.: Backpack: detection of people carrying objects using silhouettes. Comput. Vis. Image Underst. **81**(3), 385–397 (2001)
10. Hinterstoisser, S., Lepetit, V., Ilic, S., Holzer, S., Bradski, G., Konolige, K., Navab, N.: Model based training, detection and pose estimation of texture-less 3d objects in heavily cluttered scenes. In: Asian conference on computer vision. pp. 548–562. Springer (2012)
11. Hinterstoisser, S., Lepetit, V., Wohlhart, P., Konolige, K.: On pre-trained image features and synthetic images for deep learning. In: Proceedings of the European Conference on Computer Vision (ECCV) Workshops, pp. 0–0 (2018)
12. Hinterstoisser, S., Pauly, O., Heibel, H., Marek, M., Bokeloh, M.: An annotation saved is an annotation earned: Using fully synthetic training for object detection. In: 2019 IEEE/CVF International Conference on Computer Vision Workshops, ICCV Workshops 2019, Seoul, Korea (South), October 27–28, 2019. pp. 2787–2796. IEEE (2019). https://doi.org/10.1109/ICCVW.2019.00340,https://doi.org/10.1109/ICCVW.2019.00340
13. Ize, M.d.C.J.: Multiple pedestrian tracking using geometric and deep features (2019)
14. Kalman, R.E.: A new approach to linear filtering and prediction problems (1960)
15. Lima, J.P., et al.: 3d pedestrian localization using multiple cameras: a generalizable approach. Mach. Vis. Appl. **33**(4), 1–16 (2022)
16. Lyra, V.G.d.M., et al.: Generalizable online 3d pedestrian tracking with multiple cameras. In: VISIGRAPP (5: VISAPP), pp. 820–827 (2022)
17. Papakis, I., Sarkar, A., Karpatne, A.: Gcnnmatch: Graph convolutional neural networks for multi-object tracking via sinkhorn normalization. arXiv preprint arXiv:2010.00067 (2020)

18. Park, K., Patten, T., Vincze, M.: Pix2pose: Pixel-wise coordinate regression of objects for 6d pose estimation. In: Proceedings of the IEEE International Conference on Computer Vision, pp. 7668–7677 (2019)

19. Peng, S., Liu, Y., Huang, Q., Zhou, X., Bao, H.: Pvnet: Pixel-wise voting network for 6dof pose estimation. In: Proceedings of the IEEE Conference on Computer Vision and Pattern Recognition, pp. 4561–4570 (2019)

20. Peng, Z.: Pedestrian tracking by using deep neural networks (2021)

21. Philomin, V., Duraiswami, R., Davis, L.: Pedestrian tracking from a moving vehicle. In: Proceedings of the IEEE Intelligent Vehicles Symposium 2000 (Cat. No. 00TH8511), pp. 350–355. IEEE (2000)

22. Pustokhina, I.V., Pustokhin, D.A., Vaiyapuri, T., Gupta, D., Kumar, S., Shankar, K.: An automated deep learning based anomaly detection in pedestrian walkways for vulnerable road users safety. Saf. Sci. **142**, 105356 (2021)

23. Rozantsev, A., Lepetit, V., Fua, P.: On rendering synthetic images for training an object detector. Comput. Vis. Image Underst. **137**, 24–37 (2015)

24. Rozantsev, A., Salzmann, M., Fua, P.: Beyond sharing weights for deep domain adaptation. IEEE Trans. Pattern Anal. Mach. Intell. **41**(4), 801–814 (2018)

25. Saadat, S., Teknomo, K.: Automation of pedestrian tracking in a crowded situation. In: Pedestrian and Evacuation Dynamics, pp. 231–239. Springer (2011)

26. Song, C., Song, J., Huang, Q.: Hybridpose: 6d object pose estimation under hybrid representations. In: Proceedings of the IEEE/CVF Conference on Computer Vision and Pattern Recognition, pp. 431–440 (2020)

27. Taigman, Y., Polyak, A., Wolf, L.: Unsupervised cross-domain image generation. arXiv preprint arXiv:1611.02200 (2016)

28. Tejani, A., Kouskouridas, R., Doumanoglou, A., Tang, D., Kim, T.K.: Latent-class hough forests for 6-DoF object pose estimation. IEEE Trans. Pattern Anal. Mach. Intell. **40**(1), 119–132 (2018)

29. Tekin, B., Sinha, S.N., Fua, P.: Real-time seamless single shot 6d object pose prediction. In: Proceedings of the IEEE Conference on Computer Vision and Pattern Recognition, pp. 292–301 (2018)

30. Tremblay, J., et al.: Training deep networks with synthetic data: Bridging the reality gap by domain randomization. In: Proceedings of the IEEE Conference on Computer Vision and Pattern Recognition Workshops, pp. 969–977 (2018)

31. Volpi, R., Larlus, D., Rogez, G.: Continual adaptation of visual representations via domain randomization and meta-learning. In: Proceedings of the IEEE/CVF Conference on Computer Vision and Pattern Recognition, pp. 4443–4453 (2021)

32. Wojke, N., Bewley, A., Paulus, D.: Simple online and realtime tracking with a deep association metric. In: 2017 IEEE international conference on image processing (ICIP), pp. 3645–3649. IEEE (2017)

33. Ye, M., Shen, J., Lin, G., Xiang, T., Shao, L., Hoi, S.C.: Deep learning for person re-identification: a survey and outlook. IEEE Trans. Pattern Anal. Mach. Intell. **44**(6), 2872–2893 (2021)

Research on Retail Media Advertisements and Consumer Requirements - Taking E-Commerce Listing Pages as an Example

Shu-Ching Li[✉] and Tseng-Ping Chiu

Institute of Industrial Design, National Cheng Kung University, Tainan, Taiwan, Republic of China
{p36101120,mattchiu}@gs.ncku.edu.tw

Abstract. In the "Cookieless" era, user-oriented privacy awareness highlights the advantages of e-commerce in directly obtaining user information. The era of emphasis on consumer experience has accelerated the development of retail media advertising. Therefore, the goal of this research is to promote the balance between e-commerce, retailers and consumer experience, and to improve digital advertising marketing efficiency and user experience. First of all, this study summarizes the 3 most common page types and 8 types of advertisements for retail advertisements through case studies. Then, a consumer questionnaire survey was conducted through a simulated sample, and the influence of different consumer motivations and search types on the usage status of different pages was also explored. This study found that the list page is the best exposure position for retail media advertisements, and "Top Row ads" is the type of advertisement that attracts the most attention and favor from consumers. On the contrary, it is the type of "Sponsorship Advertising" that is currently the most widely used. It highlights how little e-commerce currently understands about the consumer experience. Finally, 10 key consumer requirements and 8 key design elements are sorted out through focus groups through QFD method.

Keywords: User experience · Consumer requirements · Retail media advertising · E-commerce · Display advertising · Quality function deployment

1 Introduction

The well-known American market research organization eMarketer predicts that by 2025, digital advertising in the United States will account for 77.5% of the total advertising media expenditure, and will exceed 300 billion U.S. dollars (see Fig. 1) [1, 2]. In addition, according to the Google team's webinar on eMarketer, retail media will be the third wave of digital advertising after search advertising and social media advertising [3] (see Fig. 2). Among them, the vast majority of retail media spending will come from e-commerce channels [4]. In recent years, due to the epidemic, a large number of consumers have turned to online shopping, which has also accelerated the vigorous development of e-commerce. In addition, with privacy awareness and consumer-centricity, governments

© The Author(s), under exclusive license to Springer Nature Switzerland AG 2023
A. Marcus et al. (Eds.): HCII 2023, LNCS 14031, pp. 106–122, 2023.
https://doi.org/10.1007/978-3-031-35696-4_9

and technology companies have successively cut back on important digital marketing tools [5]. Actual actions include that Google will disable the data collection and use of third-party browser cookies by 2024. The advent of the "cookieless era" highlights the importance of first-party data [6, 7], and makes it impossible for many website owners or companies to obtain or purchase user data, and cannot provide personalized marketing models through third-party information. Following this trend, retail media ads that can search, integrate, and apply first-party data will become the main channel for advertisers.

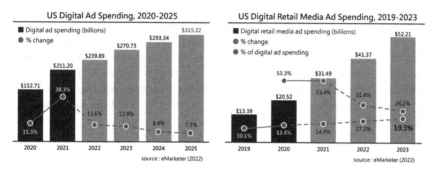

Fig. 1. The U.S. digital advertising market will exceed $300 billion by 2025, accounting for more than three-quarters of all media spending [1, 2]. Image redrawn from this study.

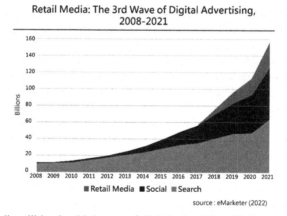

Fig. 2. Retail media will be the third wave of digital advertising [3]. Image redrawn from this study.

This channel allows brand advertisers to use user data collected by retailers to accurately target audiences and provide personalized recommendations [8]. According to a study by eMarketer, 77% of consumer packaged goods (CPGs) brands cooperate with Amazon, 56% cooperate with Walmart Connect, 29% cooperate with eBay, and 27% cooperate with Home Depot [2]. It can be found that the global large-scale e-commerce has already configured a complete advertising delivery system for brand owners. In addition to providing advertising boards to advertisers, the retail media network (RMN) has also been developed. Large retailers will cooperate with advertising technology companies (such as: Carrefour and Criteo, Tesco and Dunnhumby, etc.) to provide advertisers with a complete advertising delivery system [9].

Judging from the above trends, people's emphasis on privacy and the increasing demand for e-commerce in daily life have prompted retail media to provide a good growth environment for digital advertising. However, in the past, when digital advertising was booming, user experience was often ignored, and even led to phenomena such as "banner blindness [10]". Unfriendly interface design prevents information from being delivered to consumers as expected. Therefore, sales-oriented retail media need to pay more attention to the experience of consumers when shopping, so as to prevent consumers from being more repulsed by advertisements. Therefore, the purpose of this study is to determine which advertising display method can best attract consumers' attention and favor, excluding the advertising content that cannot be controlled by the e-commerce platform. This purpose will also help e-commerce operators improve advertising efficiency and advertisers increase exposure efficiency. At the same time, it can also improve the consumer experience.

2 Literature Review

2.1 Display Advertising Dramatically Increases the Profitability of Retail Media

According to the comprehensive research in the field of digital advertising, it can be divided into three major fields: search engine advertising, social media advertising and display advertising [11]. Among them, Internet advertising originated from display advertising, so it is also known as the most classic type of advertising [12]. Display advertising is a form of online advertising [13]. Advertisers or brand operators are provided with advertising spaces on the page by platforms that can publish advertisements, and advertisers purchase these spaces and the display time of advertisements by paying [13–15]. In addition, with the development of mobile phone browsing, social media activities, video advertising and advertising personalized positioning technology, the total amount of display advertising in the United States reached 49.8 billion US dollars in 2018, an increase of about 25% over the previous year [14]. The online display advertising market makes it more difficult for users to ignore by combining visual and audio functions, and has surpassed traditional banner advertisements [16].

As a result, advertisers are starting to use online data about consumers to personalize and target ads, a phenomenon known as online behavioral advertising (OBA) [17, 18]. Its main features are the use of cookies to monitor and track consumers' online behavior and the use of collected data to target advertisements [15, 18, 19] in order to gain insight into their potential interests and communicate personalized advertisements related to user preferences and their online behaviour. This also prompts online advertising to play an important role in e-commerce [15]. Through the interactivity of the Internet, users can interact with advertisements one-on-one. Advertising can use multimedia technology to attract attention and even directly prompt consumers to make purchases [15]. Online retail advertising brings profits and a positive impact on retailers' sales, and its increased revenue can reach more than seven times the advertising cost [20].

2.2   Advertising Models and Advertising Effectiveness Measurement

The first formal marketing model AIDA was proposed by E. St. Elmo Lewis in 1898 as a personal marketing model, and then proposed by Strong as an advertising strategy [21]. AIDA is attention, interest, desire, and action, respectively, which is the effect hierarchy model of the user when receiving the stimulus and making a response. Subsequent scholars have also continued to make many modifications and updates to meet the actual situation of consumers. However, these revisions conform to the basic order of cognition, affect and behavior in terms of hierarchical concepts. These three levels also indicate that after consumers obtain information or knowledge through cognition, they will have a favorable attitude and affect to the stimulus, and finally produce a persuasive state and behavior [22, 23].

Scholars Vakratsas & Ambler (1999) also developed research selection criteria based on a simple framework of how advertising works. Then, through the discussion of theoretical principles and the structure of empirical evidence, it is summarized into seven classifications of advertising operation modes [21]. It can be seen that researchers have continued to transform the advertising model from the original conceptual framework to an empirical study that can be studied and measured, and provided a variety of perspectives and methods for measurement. At present, the main ways to measure advertising effectiveness include advertising recall, advertising attitude, purchase intention,

Table 1. Advertisement-related measurement scales. Organized by this study.

	Type of scale	Scale content	Scholar
1	Advertising Attention Scale	When I saw the ad just now, I thought • The advertisement caught my interest • The advertisement was boring • I paid close attention to the advertisement *Use Likert sentences (nine-step response categories based on "strongly agree" and "strongly disagree")	Duncan & Nelson, 1985 [24]
2	Advertising Value Scale	The web ad that just appeared on the page, I think it • is useful • is valuable • is important *Use Likert sentences (seven-step response categories based on "strongly agree" and "strongly disagree")	Ducoffe, 1996 [25]

(*continued*)

Table 1. (*continued*)

	Type of scale	Scale content	Scholar
3	Inferences of Manipulative Intent Scale	The online advertisement that just appeared on the webpage, I think • The way this ad tries to persuade people seems acceptable to me • The advertiser tried to manipulate the audience in ways that I don't like • I was annoyed by this ad because the advertiser seemed to be trying to inappropriately manage or control the consumer audience • I didn't mind this ad; the advertiser tried to be persuasive without being excessively manipulative • This ad was fair in what was said and shown • I think that this advertisement is unfair fair *Use Likert sentences (seven-step response categories based on "strongly agree" and "strongly disagree")	Campbell, 1995 [26]

eye tracking, etc. In order to understand the current consumers' thoughts on different types of retail media advertisements, this study also chooses three scales as measurement indicators (see Table 1). It includes the Advertising Attention Scale at the cognitive level, the Advertising Value Scale for assessing overall orientation, and the Inferences of Manipulative Intent Scale at the emotional level.

2.3 Quality Function Deployment (QFD)

Quality Function Deployment (hereinafter referred to as QFD) is a Japanese concept in the 1960s, proposed by Professor Yoji Akao (1972) [27]. At that time, Japanese industry got rid of the product development model through imitation and copying, and turned to original product development [28]. Some studies have pointed out that about 35% to 44% of all commodities are considered to be failures [27]. However, QFD is a comprehensive and systematic quality control method that will improve the quality of the product development process itself and meet customer expectations through functional analysis of business process stages [28, 29].

Due to its shape relationship, QFD is often also called "house of quality" [27, 30]. Its concept is different from the concept of "seeking quantity but not quality" during World War II. QFD emphasizes and ensures that "voice of the customer" is included in all stages of product development [29]. Therefore, QFD will explore user needs in the initial stage. Then, the design elements are conceived through the expert group. The third step is the relationship matrix between user needs and design elements, which is used to check whether each design element is related to the needs and whether all the needs can be effectively solved. The fourth step is to explore the relationship between various design elements, whether there are too similar or conflicts. Finally, the key design elements are established through quality group discussion and weighing the weight relationship of each design element.

QFD is mainly to develop higher quality products and products that meet user needs by collecting and analyzing customer voices. Therefore, this method has been extended to other fields, such as design, planning, decision-making, engineering, teamwork, etc. [31], and can also be used in the field of web design [32]. Therefore, this study will explore consumer needs through QFD, and try to develop design elements to enhance consumers' experience in e-commerce.

3   Method

This study will use case studies to understand the current status of retail media advertising, and summarize key pages and types of advertising through status analysis. Then, through consumer surveys, understand consumers' thoughts on each page and various types of advertisements, and collect user needs through questionnaires. Finally, the QFD method is used to collect and measure the weight of requirements, and the design criteria and relationship matrix are developed through focus groups, so as to grasp the key design elements.

3.1   Case Study: Current Status of Retail Media Advertising

In order to broadly understand the current situation of retail media advertising, in addition to domestic e-commerce (such as: Shopee, PChome eBay, MomoShop, PChome24h, etc.), world-renowned e-commerce is also the analysis object of this study (such as: Amazon, Target, Walmart, eBay, Rakuten, etc.). Finally, through the advertising positions that appear on the advertising alliance websites of various e-commerce and the store platform itself, this research analyzes and summarizes 3 common retail advertising pages and 8 types of advertising, as shown in Table 2.

3.2   Consumer Survey

The first point among the main purposes of the consumer questionnaire is to focus on the scope of the research. This research will explore consumers' attitudes towards various types of advertisements, and select the research pages and advertisements with the most

Table 2. 3 common page types and 8 advertisement types for retail advertisements in e-commerce

	page	advertisement type	e-commerce
1	Homepage	Banner ad	Amazon, Target, Walmart, Carrefour, eBay, Rakuten, Mercari, Shopee, PChome eBay, MomoShop, PChome24h, Books.com.tw, Yahoo! Auctions
2		Small ads	Amazon, Target, Walmart, Carrefour, eBay, Rakuten, Shopee, PChome eBay, MomoShop, PChome24h, Books.com.tw, Yahoo! Auctions
3		Sponsorship Advertising	Amazon, Target, Walmart, Carrefour, Rakuten, Shopee, PChome eBay, MomoShop, PChome24h, Books.com.tw, Yahoo! Auctions
4	List Page	Top Row ads	Walmart, Carrefour, Shopee, PChome eBay, Yahoo! Auctions
5		Sponsorship Advertising	Amazon, Target, Walmart, Carrefour, eBay, Etsy, Wish, Shopee, PChome eBay, Yahoo! Auctions
6		Product Block Ads	Amazon, Rakuten, Yahoo! Auctions
7		Banner ad	Walmart, Shopee, PChome eBay
8	Product information page	Associated Ads	Amazon, Target, Walmart, eBay, Etsy, Rakuten, Mercari, Shopee, PChome eBay, MomoShop, PChome24h, Books.com.tw, Yahoo! Auctions

research value. The second point is to understand the current status of consumers' use of e-commerce, including online shopping frequency, consumption behavior, consumption types, etc. Among them, consumer search behavior is divided into goal-oriented and exploratory search. Goal-directed search is the behavior of consumers with a specific purchase plan, while exploratory search is driven by no direction or stimulus [33]. Since different search situations will lead to different page usage, this questionnaire also includes them in the discussion. The third point is to collect consumer demand for current retail media advertisements. Therefore, this questionnaire is divided into two parts. The first part is the e-commerce experience survey, including the current status of consumers using the e-commerce platform and the usage of each page. The second part is the survey on e-commerce advertising experience and attitude. This research will use the scale in Table 1 to inquire consumers' attitudes towards 8 types of advertising. Among them, this study also designed 3 types of webpage simulation diagrams of e-commerce platforms and marked the types of advertisements (see Fig. 3), so that the subjects could clearly understand the types of advertisements.

A total of 96 valid questionnaires were collected in this questionnaire. Judging from the current online shopping frequency of consumers in the past month (see Fig. 4(a)), only 13% of consumers browse less than 3 times in a month, and 28% of consumers browse e-commerce every day. It can be found that e-commerce has become an indispensable part of consumers' daily life. In addition, among the 16 product types, the top six are clothing, household products, accessories (bags, wallets, accessories, etc.), foodstuffs, footwear, 3C products (see Fig. 4(b)).This data will be used as a reference for future experiments.

In addition, we can find from Fig. 4(c) that 72.92% of consumers usually shop online in a goal-oriented state. Therefore, the list page is the first page most consumers want to enter, and they will spend the most time on the product information page (see Fig. 5). Since shopping is goal-oriented, consumers will naturally search for as much information as possible, and the list page will naturally become the primary goal of consumers. In addition, after searching for information, consumers will enter the alternative evaluation stage, including paying attention to product attributes and generating attention to different attributes [34]. Therefore, more time will be spent on product information pages to understand product details to help consumers make purchase decisions. It can be seen from this that if you want to successfully make the product one of the evaluation solutions for consumers, the list page will be a good exposure opportunity for advertisers.

In the questionnaire results of four types of advertisements (Top Row ads, Sponsorship Advertising, Product Block Ads, Banner ad) on the list page (see Fig. 6), it can be found that "Top Row ads" is the type of advertisement that can attract consumers' attention the most, and consumers think that its advertisement value is the highest, followed by "Banner ad". In addition, in the scale results of manipulating intention inference, "Top Row ads" is also the most favorable and acceptable type of advertisement for consumers. In terms of the overall online shopping impression, it is also the most frequently contacted and impressive advertisement for consumers. Therefore, based on the current status of e-commerce listing pages, "Top Row ads" is the advertisement that attracts the most attention and favor from consumers, that is, the type of advertisement that meets the expectations of advertisers and the needs of consumers. In sharp contrast to it is "Sponsorship Advertising", which is the type of advertisement that consumers hate the most. However, although it has the lowest ad attention score, the reason may be that it is not easy for consumers to detect it as an ad. Judging from the responses of the testees, because the advertising sign of "Sponsorship Advertising" is small and difficult to be noticed, it is not found that this product is also an advertisement. As a result, consumers feel disgusted by the idea that it intends to manipulate consumers' minds.

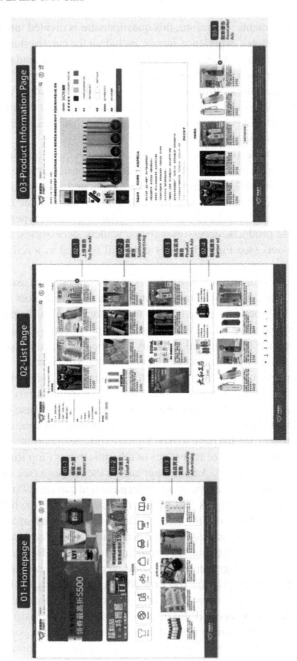

Fig. 3. E-commerce mockup, including 3 pages and 8 types of advertisements.

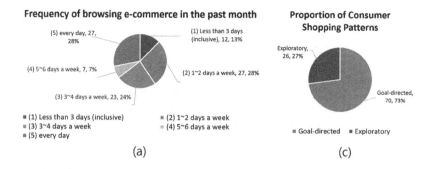

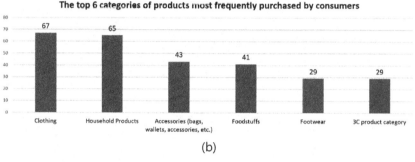

Fig. 4. (a) Frequency of browsing e-commerce in the past month, (b) The top 6 categories of products most frequently purchased by consumers, (c) Proportion of Consumer Shopping Patterns

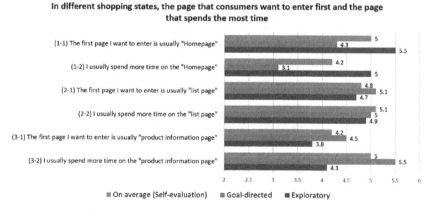

Fig. 5. Usage of different shopping states (self-assessment overall state, goal-oriented and exploratory search) on the homepage, list page, and product information page

In the end, this study collected 95 statements of consumers' stated needs for list page advertisements, including deleting invalid answers and splitting different needs from the same sentence. These data will serve as input for the QFD study.

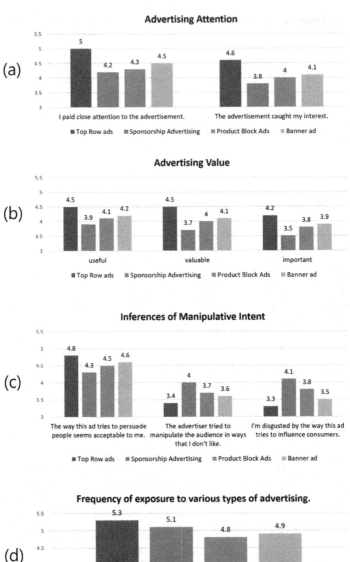

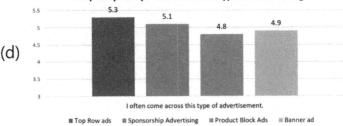

Fig. 6. The data results of the four types of advertisements on the list page. (a) Advertising Attention, (b) Advertising Value, (c) Inferences of Manipulative Intent, (d) Frequency of exposure to various types of advertising.

3.3 Research on Consumer User Needs and Design Criteria Through QFD Method

The QFD of this study is divided into three stages. The first stage is to collect the "voice of users" through consumer survey questionnaires. The second stage is a consumer focus group, with 7 participants who have more than 10 years of online shopping experience. In the early stage of the study, the participants were asked to think about what needs a consumer might have when they browsed the advertisement on the list page and listed

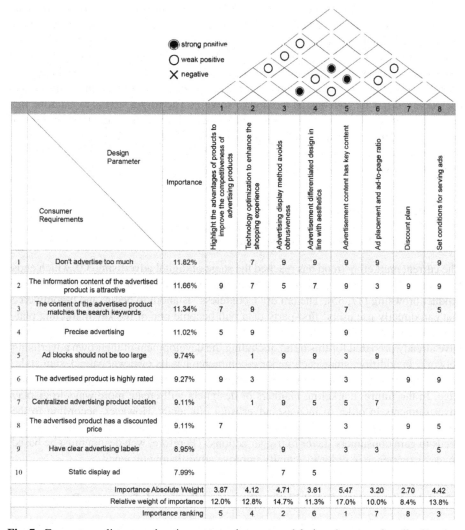

Consumer Requirements	Importance	1 Highlight the advantages of products to improve the competitiveness of advertising products	2 Technology optimization to enhance the shopping experience	3 Advertising display method avoids obtrusiveness	4 Advertisement differentiated design in line with aesthetics	5 Advertisement content has key content	6 Ad placement and ad-to-page ratio	7 Discount plan	8 Set conditions for serving ads
1 Don't advertise too much	11.82%		7	9	9	9	9		9
2 The information content of the advertised product is attractive	11.66%	9	7	5	7	9	3	9	9
3 The content of the advertised product matches the search keywords	11.34%	7	9			7			5
4 Precise advertising	11.02%	5	9			9			
5 Ad blocks should not be too large	9.74%		1	9	9	3	9		
6 The advertised product is highly rated	9.27%	9	3			3		9	9
7 Centralized advertising product location	9.11%		1	9	5	5	7		
8 The advertised product has a discounted price	9.11%	7				3		9	5
9 Have clear advertising labels	8.95%			9		3	3		5
10 Static display ad	7.99%			7	5				
Importance Absolute Weight		3.87	4.12	4.71	3.61	5.47	3.20	2.70	4.42
Relative weight of importance		12.0%	12.8%	14.7%	11.3%	17.0%	10.0%	8.4%	13.8%
Importance ranking		5	4	2	6	1	7	8	3

Fig. 7. E-commerce list page advertisement requirements and design elements of quality function expansion diagram. On the left is consumer needs collected through consumer survey questionnaires, and aggregated into 10 key needs through consumer focus groups. The above list is the 8 key design elements that were developed and compiled through the focus groups of designers.

them in detail. This method is for participants to quickly enter the topic. For research, it is also possible to dig out the needs of consumers through in-depth thinking. Then, according to the needs just sent out and the 95 effective demand statements collected from the questionnaire, the KJ method was compiled. Summarize key requirements through grouping of requirements. Finally, a total of 10 consumer needs were collected and scored for their importance. Among them, the first three items are "Don't advertise too much", "The information content of the advertised product is attractive", "The content of the advertised product matches the search keywords".

The third stage is a focus group for designers, with a total of 10 participants, whose backgrounds include graphic design, website design, multimedia design, UI/UX design, industrial design, website development, software development, etc. First, participants brainstormed about 10 consumer needs to come up with design elements. In the second step, the KJ method is used to integrate the design elements that have been conceived, and 8 key design elements are produced. The third step is to carry out the evaluation of the relationship matrix between consumer needs and design elements, and confirm that each demand has its own design method to solve it. The fourth step is to examine the correlation evaluation among various design elements. Finally, the importance weight of each design element is evaluated through the relationship matrix. Among them, the first three items are "Advertisement content has key content", "Advertising display method avoids obtrusiveness", "Set conditions for serving ads" (see Fig. 7).

4   Discussion

4.1   Diversified Retail Media Advertising

The current marketing trend has reached the stage of digital advertising 3.0, which ends the centering of the product as the operation, and focuses more on the user experience of product browsing [17, 35]. The era of "Cookieless" is about to begin, and e-commerce that can directly use users' first-party data will become one of the key marketing platforms for advertisers [6, 7]. Judging from the case studies, major e-commerce companies have already prepared for this trend, including the development of their own advertising network. In addition, since each major e-commerce has its own webpage design style, various advertisement display methods are produced, especially the design on the homepage. In the future, marketing planners or designers will create more ways to display advertisements in order to increase advertising efficiency. However, according to the three levels of advertising effect [22, 23], while attracting consumers' attention, it still needs to gain consumers' favor to trigger actions. Therefore, web design must be based on user experience in order to actually improve advertising efficiency.

4.2   Advertising Potential of Listing Pages and Product Information Pages

Different motivations of consumers will also lead to differences in search behavior [33], and also affect the usage of different pages. According to consumer surveys, the difference in consumer search behavior obviously leads to differences in the use of the home page, list page, and product information page. From the data point of view, exploratory search consumers will obviously want to go to the home page and spend more time on this page. Consumers with goal-directed searches are more likely to enter listing pages and spend more time on product information pages. In addition, this study found that consumers mainly shop on e-commerce platforms in a goal-oriented state, accounting for 72.92%. Therefore, listing pages and product information pages are more suitable for placing advertisements to attract target-oriented consumers, and it is also easier to increase the probability of purchasing the advertised products.

4.3 Most Potential Ad Type: "TOP ROW Ads"

From the survey data of consumers, this study finds that "Top Row ads" is the most noticeable and accepted advertisement by consumers. According to the respondents' replies, the reasons may include "the advertisement block is clearly marked, consumers can have more control over the advertisement", "the words without advertisement or sponsorship are more comfortable to read", "Not mixed in with common goods (not to be confused with common goods)", "The size of the block is acceptable", etc. Much of it highlights consumer expectations for advertising autonomy. In addition, it can be found from QFD that consumers prefer the appropriate number of advertisements, block size and more concentrated location, and there are clear signs and static presentation of advertisements. The above requirements are in line with the design method of "Top Row ads" in the questionnaire survey, and also echo the types of advertisements that consumers like most in the questionnaire data.

The opposite is "Sponsorship Advertising", which has the same characteristics as the normal commodity style. This type of ad usually has a smaller ad badge appearing in the lower right corner of the image. These characteristics also make consumers think that the advertisement is mixed with ordinary goods, so they feel disgusted and unacceptable. However, based on case studies, this ad type is by far the most widely used display method. This phenomenon shows the current lack of e-commerce understanding of consumer experience.

4.4 Ad Personalization Requirements

Among QFD's advertising requirements, the 2nd to 4th most important rankings are "The information content of the advertised product is attractive", "The content of the advertised product matches the search keywords", and "Precise advertising". It highlights the importance consumers place on personalized advertising. Consumers prefer to obtain products similar to their own goals. Furthermore, in the responses of the respondents to the questionnaire, many of the respondents stated that they often encounter advertisements that do not meet their needs and have a gap with keywords, which also cause them to increase their aversion to advertisements. Among them, the relevant design solutions are related to the search technology of e-commerce itself, and the accuracy of advertising product placement can be improved through technical optimization. The second is related to the information presentation of the advertising content. Regarding this, e-commerce can be improved by setting conditions for placing advertisements, etc.

5   Conclusions and Future Work

The era of "cookieless" and consumer experience has accelerated the development of retail media advertising. In order to improve the effectiveness of retail media advertising and enhance consumer experience, this research uses case studies to understand the current advertising trends and current status of e-commerce, and summarizes the 3 most common page types and 8 types of advertising in retail advertising. Since different consumer motivations will affect their search types and page usage status, this study explores through consumer questionnaires. This study found from the questionnaire data that up to 72.92% of consumers usually shop in e-commerce in a goal-oriented state, focusing on list pages and product information pages. Among them, the list page is the page that consumers most want to enter at the beginning to collect a large amount of information. Therefore, the list page is the best exposure page for retail media advertisements. In addition, through the analysis of advertising types, this study found that "Top Row ads" is the type of advertising that attracts the most attention and favor from consumers. On the contrary, "Sponsorship Advertising" is currently the most widely used type, which highlights the current lack of understanding of consumer experience in e-commerce. Finally, in the QFD experiment, through the consumer demand statement and consumer focus groups collected through the questionnaire, this research summarizes 10 key consumer requirements. Then, 8 key design elements are listed through the focus group of designers.

In order to achieve better advertising efficiency, e-commerce platforms need to think deeply about how to design advertising display methods that can attract consumers' attention and maintain goodwill. In addition to the current type of advertisement, whether there is a more suitable and effective way of displaying advertisements. Among the research results of QFD design elements, "Advertising display method avoids obtrusiveness", "Advertisement differentiated design in line with aesthetics", "Ad placement and ad-to-page ratio" and so on are all points that can be referred to in future advertising design. Through the collection of design criteria, this study will be able to conceive and design advertising display methods based on its principles in the future. Among them, website design, advertising effect and user experience are all research directions that can be further explored in the future.

In addition, this study found that there are significant differences in the design of Western and Eastern websites when conducting case studies. Including the western use of more concise information presentation, fewer block designs, more static presentation methods, etc. In addition, studies have shown that people of different cultures have differences in cognition and perception [36, 37], culture is considered to be one of the key drivers of consumer judgments and decisions [38], and culture can cause differences in advertising strategies [38] and so on. Therefore, the influence of culture between web design and consumers will also be one of the directions for future research.

References

1. eMarketer. Digital Advertising in 2022: Market trends & predictions (2022). https://www.ins iderintelligence.com/insights/digital-advertising-market-trends-predictions/

2. eMarketer. Retail media networks hit their stride in 2021 (2022). https://www.insiderintellig ence.com/content/retail-media-networks-hit-their-stride-2021?fbclid=IwAR0PFsefwASuU r2pAkQ5oEznfDICmmRNXA7MPGfodgkrJ10auVABwJnJydw
3. eMarketer. Retail Media 2022: What's Next for Digital Advertising's Third Big Wave? I Meet the Analyst Webinar I On-Demand (2022)
4. eMarketer. US retail media ad spend will pass $30 billion for the first time this year (2021). https://www.insiderintelligence.com/content/us-retail-media-ad-spend-will-pass-30-billion-first-time-this-year?ecid=NL1001&fbclid=IwAR2v9dpcqn0xQrhj98iZJpfdsOUP8YBf4N Ok0IAfy6wmWkDitKkCIM970Ao
5. Lauren Wiener, L.K., Fisher, S., Abraham, M.: The $100 Billion Media Opportunity for Retailers (2021). https://www.bcg.com/publications/2021/how-to-compete-in-retail-media
6. Dive, M.: Looking ahead: 9 trends that will steer marketing in 2022 (2022). https://www.mar ketingdive.com/news/looking-ahead-9-trends-that-will-steer-marketing-in-2022/616935/
7. eMarketer. A marketer's guide to post-cookie solutions (2023). https://www.insiderintellig ence.com/content/marketer-guide-post-cookie-solutions
8. TenMax. Re-evolution of retail, laying out a big future!2021 US retail media advertising, the market share is estimated to exceed 800 billion Taiwan dollars! (2021). https://www.tenmax. io/tw/archives/30095
9. TenMax. "Market pie, can I eat it?" This article analyzes the 4 major resources necessary for the development of retail media advertising (2022). https://www.tenmax.io/tw/archives/ 31970
10. Benway, J.P.: Banner blindness: the irony of attention grabbing on the World Wide Web. In: Proceedings of the Human Factors and Ergonomics Society Annual Meeting. Sage Publications Sage CA, Los Angeles, CA (1998)
11. Aslam, B., Karjaluoto, H.: Digital advertising around paid spaces, e-advertising industry's revenue engine: a review and research agenda. Telematics Inform. **34**(8), 1650–1662 (2017)
12. Stephen, A.T.: The role of digital and social media marketing in consumer behavior. Current Opinión Psychol. **10**, 17–21 (2016)
13. Chapelle, O., Manavoglu, E., Rosales, R.: Simple and scalable response prediction for display advertising. ACM Trans. Intell. Syst. Technol. (TIST) **5**(4), 1–34 (2014)
14. Choi, H., et al.: Online display advertising markets: a literature review and future directions. Inf. Syst. Res. **31**(2), 556–575 (2020)
15. Turban, E., King, D., Lee, J.K., Liang, T.-P., Turban, D.C.: Marketing and advertising in e-commerce. In: Electronic Commerce. STBE, pp. 403–456. Springer, Cham (2015). https:// doi.org/10.1007/978-3-319-10091-3_9
16. Goldfarb, A., Tucker, C.: Online display advertising: targeting and obtrusiveness. Mark. Sci. **30**(3), 389–404 (2011)
17. Aiolfi, S., Bellini, S., Pellegrini, D.: Data-driven digital advertising: benefits and risks of online behavioral advertising. Int. J. Retail Distrib. Manage. **49**, 1089–1110 (2021)
18. Boerman, S.C., Kruikemeier, S., Zuiderveen Borgesius, F.J.: Online behavioral advertising: a literature review and research agenda. J. Advertising **46**(3), 363–376 (2017)
19. Gertz, O., McGlashan, D.: Consumer-centric programmatic advertising. In: Programmatic Advertising, pp. 55–73. Springer (2016). https://doi.org/10.1007/978-3-319-25023-6_5
20. Lewis, R.A., Reiley, D.H.: Online ads and offline sales: measuring the effect of retail advertising via a controlled experiment on Yahoo! Quant. Mark. Econ. **12**(3), 235–266 (2014). https://doi.org/10.1007/s11129-014-9146-6
21. Vakratsas, D., Ambler, T.: How advertising works: what do we really know? J. Mark. **63**(1), 26–43 (1999)
22. Bendixen, M.T.: Advertising effects and effectiveness. Eur. J. Mark. **27**(10), 19–32 (1993)
23. Lavidge, R.J., Steiner, G.A.: A model for predictive measurements of advertising effectiveness. J. Mark. **25**(6), 59–62 (1961)

24. Duncan, C.P., Nelson, J.E.: Effects of humor in a radio advertising experiment. J. Advert. **14**(2), 33–64 (1985)
25. Ducoffe, R.H.: Advertising value and advertising on the web-Blog@ management. J. Advert. Res. **36**(5), 21–32 (1996)
26. Campbell, M.C.: When attention-getting advertising tactics elicit consumer inferences of manipulative intent: the importance of balancing benefits and investments. J. Consum. Psychol. **4**(3), 225–254 (1995)
27. Bouchereau, V., Rowlands, H.: Methods and techniques to help quality function deployment (QFD). Benchmarking: An International Journal (2000)
28. Akao, Y., Mazur, G.H.: The leading edge in QFD: past, present and future. Int. J. Qual. Reliab. Manage. **20**(1), 20–35 (2003)
29. Cristiano, J.J., Liker, J.K., CC III, W.: Key factors in the successful application of quality function deployment (QFD). IEEE Trans. Eng. Manage. **48**(1), 81–95 (2001)
30. Govers, C.P.: What and how about quality function deployment (QFD). Int. J. Prod. Econ. **46**, 575–585 (1996)
31. Chan, L.-K., Wu, M.-L.: Quality function deployment: a literature review. Eur. J. Oper. Res. **143**(3), 463–497 (2002)
32. Park, H.-S., Noh, S.J.: Enhancement of web design quality through the QFD approach. Total Qual. Manag. **13**(3), 393–401 (2002)
33. Moe, W.W.: Buying, searching, or browsing: differentiating between online shoppers using in-store navigational clickstream. J. Consum. Psychol. **13**(1–2), 29–39 (2003)
34. Hutton, R.J., Klein, G.: Expert decision making. Syst. Eng. J. Int. Counc. Syst. Eng. **2**(1), 32–45 (1999)
35. Mardegan, P., Riva, G., Scatena, S.F.: Digital advertising 3.0. Il futuro della pubblicità digitale. Maggioli Editore (2016)
36. Masuda, T., Nisbett, R.E.: Attending holistically versus analytically: comparing the context sensitivity of Japanese and Americans. J. Pers. Soc. Psychol. **81**(5), 922 (2001)
37. Masuda, T., et al.: Culture and the mind: implications for art, design and advertisement. In: Handbook of Research on International Advertising. Edward Elgar Publishing (2012)
38. Torelli, C.J., Rodas, M.A., Lahoud, P.: Culture and consumer behavior. In: Cross Cultural Issues in Consumer Science and Consumer Psychology, pp. 49–68. Springer (2017). https://doi.org/10.1007/978-3-319-65091-3_4

Research on the Ageing-Friendly Design of Smart Entertainment Products Based on the Perceived Affordances Perspective

Wenrui Li[✉]

Product Design, Department of Design, School of Art, Anhui University, No. 111, Jiulong Road, Hefei 230601, Anhui, China
408434738@qq.com

Abstract. "During the 13th Five-Year Plan period, China's ageing will continue to deepen, with 254 million people aged 60 and above at the end of 2019 [2]. The continued growth of the ageing population has put enormous pressure on the social security and elderly services sectors. The Party Central Committee, with Comrade Xi Jinping at its core, has taken a holistic approach, insisting on combining the response to population ageing with the promotion of economic and social development, and promoting the concerted development of the elderly care industry. It is developing a silver-haired economy, developing age-appropriate technologies and products, solving the difficulties of the elderly in using smart technologies, and fostering a new business model for smart ageing. Smart health, smart ageing and smart entertainment are created through the collaboration of intelligent technologies such as big data, cloud computing, internet and internet of things. Through intelligent, digital services, the traditional elderly care model is deepened. It provides an opportunity for the management of health and mind in old age.

Entertainment is an essential activity in our lives [1], and it is not only for young people, but should also be used throughout the later years of the elderly. Entertainment products are the direction of choice for older people for leisure, but there are very few products designed for older people in the existing market. The size of the product, the layout of the interface and the guidance system can all have an impact on the use of entertainment products by older people, and if they are not designed properly, there are many hidden dangers that can make older people fearful of the product and the development of modern technology. This not only increases the burden on the elderly themselves, but also on the family's children and society [3, 4].

This study first takes into account the physiological, psychological and cognitive characteristics of the elderly group, and constructs the design of elderly entertainment products under the perspective of perceptual schemability. How to truly make the intelligent entertainment system centred on elderly users and provide humane and friendly products and services through the theory of perceptual schemability is the focus of this study. The project will combine questionnaires, interviews, observations and other user research tools and methods to conduct in-depth user research, and carry out user group segmentation, build different types of user role models, and explore the needs of older people for wisdom products and systems in their cognitive environment. In user experience design, perceived schemability is a very important theoretical perspective. When designing products, we should abandon some subjective assumptions and pay full attention to the five dimensions of users' perceived physical performance, perceived cognitive performance, perceived control performance, perceived emotional performance and perceived service performance to build an age-appropriate design framework for smart entertainment in the elderly group. The design of intelligent entertainment is not a single intelligent toy design, but the integration of entertainment behaviour through the synergy of technology, art and technology. It is necessary to classify, summarise, analyse and reorganise information from user research data and the results of stakeholder participation in the design process in a step-by-step manner to complete a theoretical framework for the design of smart entertainment for ageing and its service model from the perspective of perceptual schemability.

It will focus on five key areas, the basic design of wisdom entertainment to enhance the awareness of wisdom entertainment among elderly groups; the optimisation of the application platform of wisdom entertainment linked to home to enhance the cognitive ability of elderly users; the expansion of wisdom entertainment user experience and health services to enhance the confidence satisfaction of elderly users; the enrichment of the beneficial and interesting functions of wisdom entertainment to promote the emotional needs of elderly users; and the upgrading of the all-round service of wisdom entertainment linked to home to promote the harmony of information communication between elderly users and society.

Finally, combining the Kano model, the needs and quality functions of elderly entertainment products are deconstructed using questionnaire survey methods, and the needs of elderly entertainment products in terms of form, function, interaction and other functional quality are qualitatively proposed to derive the charming attribute factors of the products. On the basis of the preliminary analysis, model statistics and interaction design models are established, and the results of the data derived from the analysis are applied to practice to propose a system design scheme suitable for the interaction design elements of intelligent entertainment products for the elderly. It is possible to make the entertainment products for the special group of elderly people well represented in the modern and technological era.

Keywords: Perceived affordances · Interaction design · Entertainment products · Emotional experience

1 Introduction

Since the 19th Party Congress, the construction of socialism with Chinese characteristics has entered a new era, and the report of the 19th Congress mentioned that "without a high degree of cultural self-confidence, without cultural prosperity, there is no great rejuvenation of the Chinese nation". General Secretary Xi also said "four self-confidence" Chinese cultural self-confidence is a more basic, broader and deeper self-confidence, cultural self-confidence is the most fundamental self-confidence. In recent years, with the expansion of urban scale, the rapid development of urban rail transit, the huge volume of urban rail transit vehicles has become an important part of the urban landscape. However, at present, China's urban public transportation system generally lacks overall image planning, connection and integration with urban humanistic environment, and systemic, cultural and regional characteristics. Therefore, how to build and disseminate the regional culture of urban rail transit vehicles becomes a problem that requires designers and engineers to think together [5, 6].

"During the 13th Five-Year Plan period, China's ageing will continue to deepen, with 254 million people aged 60 and above at the end of 2019. The continued growth of an ageing population has put a huge burden on the social security and elderly services sector, which is growing old before it gets rich. The pressure is on. The Party Central Committee, with Comrade Xi Jinping at its core, has taken a holistic approach, insisting on combining the response to population ageing with the promotion of economic and social development, and promoting the concerted development of the elderly care industry. It is developing the silver-haired economy, developing ageing-friendly technologies and products, solving the difficulties of the elderly in using smart technologies, and fostering new forms of smart ageing.

Entertainment such as watching television and playing games has become an important way of daily life, entertainment and access to information about the outside world for elderly people living at home. But technological leaps and artistic achievements in content require humane design to make them more accessible, especially to special groups such as the elderly. Many older people suffer from 'technophobia', fearing that they will not be able to operate the product correctly, that it will be inefficient and that it will be damaged due to incorrect operation, and are therefore 'turned off' by smart entertainment products. In contrast to developed countries where research into the design of entertainment products for the elderly has become increasingly mature, in China [7], the design of entertainment products for the elderly is still in its infancy and there are many problems, with products designed to meet the needs of the elderly not yet being proposed. This study has important theoretical and practical implications for optimising the design and research of intelligent entertainment products for the elderly.

To sum up, with the development of the Internet, digital interactive entertainment will rapidly integrate into people's daily lives and rewrite their lifestyles. The rapid development of emerging media has led to the diversification of leisure and entertainment, and for the elderly, smart entertainment products are their indispensable companions in life. In the era of digital Internet of Things, it is important to study and develop an interactive design strategy for entertainment products that includes the characteristics of the elderly population, so that the elderly can truly experience the benefits of technological advances through humanistic design methods, making entertainment products interactive and friendly, enriching the spiritual life of the elderly in their twilight years and achieving "good care for the elderly".

2 Characteristics of Older Users

2.1 Psychological Characteristics

With physical and psychological changes, older people are a vulnerable group in society, and in today's rapidly developing technology they are the most vulnerable to neglect and impact. Maslow's criteria for psychological health: a full sense of security; a full understanding of oneself; realistic goals in life; maintaining contact with the external environment, keeping one's personality intact and harmonious; having a certain ability to learn; maintaining good interpersonal relationships; being able to express and control one's emotions in a moderate manner; giving limited play to one's abilities and interests without interfering with the interests of the group; and not violating social and moral norms. The basic needs of the individual are met to a certain extent without violating social and moral norms. Old age brings with it different degrees of emotional change [8, 9].

1. A sense of "communicative emptiness"

The reduction of social activities in old age leads to a growing lack of roles to play and less participation in activities. The first role to change is to move from the first line of social work to the second line of family life, which will be easier and more relaxed, but with less interpersonal interaction, children will be busy with work and school, and there will be less communication.

2. "Sense of social dislocation"

This is closely related to changes in physiological characteristics. As physical strength, brain power and memory decline, the sensitivity to new things and the ability to understand and learn gradually decreases, and they often feel more and more disconnected from society, which in turn leads to a sense of loss.

3. Nostalgia for the past"

In their free time, they will reminisce about their past, tell their friends and relatives about their past experiences, and wonder how much time has passed. When they encounter something new, they often compare it to similar experiences in the past and lament the changes in time.

4. "Life is afraid of being alone"

As we enter old age, we recognise the product of a constant need for renewal. After one desire is satisfied, it is often quickly taken over by another, and one is always wishing for something almost all one's life, thus triggering everything.

2.2 Behavioural Cognitive Characteristics

Older people's self-perceptions are tapped into when they participate in social activities, depending on the needs of the different scenarios at the time. The stability of self-perception is derived from the stability of social roles; the clearer the self-perception, the higher the satisfaction with the quality of life. When designing entertainment products, it is important to understand what older people understand by the terms 'entertainment' and 'product'. Older people have a certain level of spending power, but compared to younger people, their spending power is very 'sensible'. Therefore, they habitually believe that consumption should be affordable and reliable, and they look more at the practicality of products when consuming. Older people's consumption behaviour for recreational products is characterised by the following features [10].

(1) Instinctive level-appearance performance of items

For wisdom entertainment products comprehensive cost analysis, in the selection of products, there will be two situations, one is the children buy, think that parents work hard all their lives, in the later years, buy some entertainment products to enrich their parents' later life, after a comprehensive analysis of the product will buy, generally children for entertainment products consumption price is easy to accept; the second is the elderly buy on their own, now the standard of living Nowadays, the standard of living has generally improved, and when purchasing, the elderly will not only consider the price, but also the practicality, quality, style and durability of the product.

(2) Behavioural level - the intrinsic behaviour of the item

Older people are not very sure of what they want and what they want most. Most older people are still very new to entertainment and electronic products and are sometimes unsure of what is essential and what is secondary in the case of exclusive products. This results in confusion when designing entertainment products for older people by taking a portion of the existing popular products and placing it in a senior product.

(3) Level of reflection - the significance of the object's impact on human thinking and emotions

The actual meaning of the product for the individual (social value, status, communication) is the focus of attention. Entertainment products belong to young people and there are few products designed for the specific diagnosis of older people. Some electronic products have fancy interfaces, which affect the visual discrimination of older people in terms of recognition. The content is relatively fast-paced and older people do not respond as well as younger people in terms of physiological or psychological reactions, making it difficult for them to react in a timely manner; cool interfaces, some cumbersome design processes and other factors are a barrier for older people to access entertainment systems; the large amount of text or alphabetic input causes older people to be intimidated by the products. The expression of feelings, self-awareness and emotional control of elderly users when using entertainment products are all design points to be noted in future designs.

3 Perceived Affordances Theory

Gibson coined the term Affordance in 1979 to describe the relationship between the ability to perceive or use other things in the environment [8, 11]. Affordance is a key component of the environment-actor relationship. Greeno further explores the related research on omnipotence, arguing that the properties of omnipotence are relative and that omnipotence does not exist in the absence of other (specific) capabilities. Norman extends the concept of omnipotence into the realm of human-computer interaction and design, extending it to the actor's own capabilities and proposing two types of omnipotence: real omnipotence and perceptible omnipotence. Perceived affordance refers to the user's perception or understanding of the actions that can be taken by a construct, emphasising the user's understanding and expectations of the interaction. Perceived affordance relies on the user's cognitive habits and mental models. Marshall et al. then sorted out the functions of use of demonstrative energetics into seven categories, through which the capabilities of the actors themselves can be extended. Table 1 Function specific mention descriptions.

The introduction of the concept of sensible energetics has had a profound impact on industrial design, human-computer interaction, pedagogy, psychology, information systems and other fields [12, 13]. With the improvement of Internet technology and the extension of scientific research, intelligent entertainment is a theoretical guarantee for the realisation of age-appropriate design in various aspects such as product requirements, interaction design strategies and product components. Therefore, this paper cites the

Table 1. Demonstration of sexual function

Demonstration of sexual function	Concept	Examples
Physical endurance	Initially separates physical and mental capacity and relates only to physical behaviour, hence the description of physical bearing capacity	Body weight bearing
Perceptual ability	Seeking practical availability	Trees that can actually be used
Concealment	The unperceived capacity	Features not found
Design ability	Communicated through design features	User-friendly design with lights on
Tandem ability	Demonstrated ability rarely exists on its own, so multiple functions are applied	Shoes provided for cycling to riding
Social skills (active)	Functions for social interaction	Active dating
Social skills (passive)	Functions for social interaction	Passive dating
Intellectual function	The ability to convey ideas and emotions	Books, media

theoretical framework of perceptual indicativity in order to better provide scientific guidance for the age-appropriate design of intelligent entertainment.

4 Requirements Framework for Smart Entertainment Products Based on Perceived Performance

4.1 Category Requirements

China has paid more attention to the basic needs of the elderly in the direction of information technology products and product services, and less attention to the growth needs of aesthetics, cognition and self-actualisation. The elderly market is not to be ignored, and there is a vast scope for products related to aesthetics, cognition and self-actualisation of the elderly.

4.2 Dimensional Requirements

In the process of using a product, the human-machine-environment is indispensable, and the ultimate goal is the "human". Monotonous forms do not attract attention, and overly complex forms can overload our intuitive systems and stop us from viewing them. In order to be efficient, product form and ergonomics go hand in hand. When designing a product, designers should consider whether the form of the product's operation matches the movements of older people in terms of the psychological, physiological, social and other factors influencing the general environment of the user group; whether the coordination of the movements made by older users when interacting with the product content is regular and whether it will create muscle. The needs of older people for online content are not as extensive as those of younger people, but they need to be targeted. In today's world of rapid technological and productivity development, material needs are no longer dominant, and needs are replaced by spiritual and emotional needs.

Maslow proposed the classic five-level needs theory, but added aesthetic and cognitive needs to this in 1970, forming a seven-level theory that includes physical, security, emotional, respected, aesthetic, cognitive and self-actualisation. Combining these two theories to analyse the needs of different groups of older people for the content of intelligent entertainment products [14, 15] (Table 2).

Table 2. Characteristics of life and recreational needs of older people

Group type	Living Characteristics	Smart product content needs
Group Living	This group of elderly people mainly live separately from their children and live in homes for the elderly for fear of adding to their children's problems	These seniors are actually lonely at heart and are eager to communicate with their children and have an emotional connection
Home	They are less involved in social activities, mainly taking care of their children, and are physically strong	They can independently lead their children in games with good guidance and cooperation; include some information on nutrition matching for meals
Recreational	These elderly people have a cheerful personality, are willing to share with others and actively participate in exercise	They have a wide range of needs for content to facilitate communication, contact and sharing with friends; they are more concerned about the social focus
Intellectual	These elderly people are highly educated, sensitive to all aspects of life and easily accept new things	These seniors do not want to be disconnected from society and love to entertain, make friends and discover new things

4.3 Interaction Needs

Customers don't want to make choices, they just want what they need. The intuition of the elderly user during the use of the product is what determines the success of the product.

(1) Simple styling

Because of physiological changes, older people will not be very sensitive to the various states of using entertainment products to be analysed and easy to grip and carry. In the design of the buttons, focus on the gap, size, shape, texture and material between the buttons, which will affect the choice of the product by elderly users.

(2) Simplicity of the interface

Simplicity does not mean simplicity. The interface is clearly navigated and straightforward to reach with a light touch. Colour categorisation is kept to a minimum and can be understood at a glance, without cumbersome searches. The existing market has a single product interface with text and images that do not match in a friendly way, making it difficult for users to use. Colour can make a design visually appealing and more aesthetically pleasing, and it can enhance the organisation and meaning of the various components of the design.

(3) Communication simplicity

Older people are gradually disconnected from the fast pace of society after retirement and do not receive information from the outside world very quickly, while not wanting to be disconnected from society, they can use entertainment products and the internet as a medium to communicate with their children, interact personally with the internet or share with friends.

5 Interaction Design Strategies for Smart Entertainment Products Based on Perceptual Schemability

5.1 The Proposed Interaction Design of Intelligent Entertainment Product System

Product system design focuses on the user, on the emotional experience of the user, on understanding the target user and their expectations, on understanding the behaviour of the user in interacting with the product, on understanding the psychological and behavioural characteristics of the "human" itself, and on establishing an organic relationship between the product and the user. The seemingly uninfluential conditions are linked in an objective way and are mutually constrained. A unity is created in form, function, state of use and feedback.

Human society is changing from a society based on the manufacture and production of material goods to one based on services or immaterial goods. Material and emotional attributes are one and the same and can be interchanged in states of use, bringing flexibility to the product. If the two existed singularly, the product would be like a fragment and would not express complementarity.

Philip Kotler proposed the theory of the three-tier structure of products, i.e. core products, tangible products and derived products [16, 17]. The core product: the use value or utility that satisfies the user's needs; the tangible product: the core product transformed into a tangible physical object; and the derived product: the services and benefits that the user receives in addition to the tangible product. The three are an integral whole, with use value as the core, and on the basis of meeting the fundamental material attributes of the tangible product, extending the service system to the derived product to meet the emotional needs of the user.

5.2 Interaction Design Elements of Intelligent Entertainment Product Systems

The elements of product interaction system are composed of four parts: People, Activity, Context and Technology. Emphasis is placed on the human-centred approach and the use of reasonable technology in different scenarios, and what actions the user should take to achieve harmony between the product and the user. The design elements are linked to the systematic design of entertainment products for older users: (1) People: what are the mental and emotional needs of elderly users and how should they be addressed to meet the emotional expression and communication of the elderly.

(2) Behaviour: How to interact with the entertainment product, what are the necessary and secondary behaviours in the process of operation, and what are the unnecessary behaviours that should be avoided.

(3) Usage environment: in what kind of environment the entertainment product is used, different usage environments will have an impact on the length of time and frequency of use.

(4) Technology: Technology meets behaviour. The clarity of the images, the size of the text, the multimedia content and some convenient auxiliary functions are the keys to influence the user's usage behaviour.

In summary, all four elements are centred around the "product", emphasising the interdependence and symbiosis between people, products, environment and society, which is an inevitable trend for future social development and a common aspiration of people. What the elderly use is not only the product, a tangible product, but also the emotional experience brought to them by the humanised and intimate functions of the product. Entertainment products are not just about the speed of the fingertips, but also product services that allow older people to communicate with society, communicate with their children, share with their friends and facilitate themselves in a more timely manner.

5.3 Principles of Interaction Design for Intelligent Entertainment Product Systems

(1) Perception of physical demonstrativeness - the principle of home-based services

Families are paying more and more attention to the fulfilment and entertainment needs of the elderly in their old age, and have a certain sense of dependence on the environment in which they live. Combining family needs with their own needs, the humanised service of entertainment products is not only a satisfaction for the user's self in the process of use or a bridge to the outside world. The existing material level of service is extended to the emotional level of service, with targeted design, making the product system closer to the user and society. Product functions and product interface design are in direct contact with the user. When carrying out the design, the design factors are integrated and the core experience is expressed, while attention should be paid to the unnecessary functions for deletion, so that the whole system is simple and easy to operate and information resources are concentrated, reducing the unnecessary memory burden and operational burden of the elderly. At the same time, the content will be effectively and reasonably arranged, with clear functional division; for some unnecessary functions of the elderly can be appropriately hidden. To achieve respect for user experience.

(2) Perception and cognition - the principle of independent interaction

In the information society, interaction is one of the main ways of life for people, and the interaction between the product and the user is an important element of product design. Bringing good emotional sharing to the elderly is the core value of entertainment products. Older people need the help of others when they start to operate wisdom products. Older people do not learn and analyse an unfamiliar system, and appear to be very unfamiliar with the product, from switching on, accessing the interface, operating choices, and program feedback, they will feel overwhelmed. These are to be analysed from the physiological and psychological systems of older people, and to be as simple as possible, not to set up more complicated functions.

The entertainment product itself is interactive, when the elderly are operating the product, it continues the principle of product interactivity, interactivity is not only reflected in the material level of interaction, but also in the emotional experience interaction.

(3) Perception of emotional performance - the principle of emotional communication

The content of intelligent entertainment products can meet the needs of the elderly entertainment spirit, there is also a part of entertainment from the memories of past events, past experiences are valuable, they can share with their families and children, with old friends with similar experiences a moment to recall the past years, through the virtual entertainment content built by the network, can also share the new acquaintance to the community or network friends. This is an intangible asset that not only enriches the life of the elderly but also enriches the spiritual life.

(4) Perceptual control of performance - the principle of sustainability

The principle of sustainability extends from the three principles of homely service, independent interaction and emotional communication, which are centred on sustainability.

The above four design principles, based on the principle of perceptual control of performance, family-oriented services are the basis for the design of the elderly intelligent entertainment product system; multi-level independent development is the core value; emotional communication is the main content, and sustainability is the development direction and goal of the product. The four principles are complementary and cannot exist independently.

6 Different Dimensions of Experience Based on the Perspective of Perceptual Schematic Properties

6.1 Material Functional Properties

Meeting the basic needs of users is essential to the material functional attributes of the product. In the face of elderly users, the design of intelligent entertainment systems for the elderly must first have the function of "entertainment", so that the elderly can place their entertainment emotions on the object and obtain happiness. The physical functional properties must meet the "object" of physical presentation, "object" of property expression and "object" of convenient operation.

(1) Intelligent perception and expression

The product perception system can be expressed in both hardware and software. The use of perception technology to interact with the user is a way of making the product more natural. The user performs actions through the haptic channel and gets realistic feedback information; the dominant role of haptics at this stage is greater than the role of vision. People like to express their positive emotions, for negative emotions on the one hand they are not willing to express them, on the other hand they do not know which way to express them. The elderly in particular are emotionally fragile and do not have as much control over their emotions. The use of an intelligent sensory system to establish interactive communication with the product allows users to use the product without tension and to express their feelings at will through their inner senses, which will make the elderly feel interesting and happy to contact the product.

(2) Humanised scenario setting

The expression of scenarios is the part of the product interface that communicates most with the user. For the setting of scenarios, the user's experience and the acceptable range of modern technology should be analysed, some mechanical designs should be weakened, and more storytelling designs or scenarios that can arouse the deepest memories of the elderly can not only make the user experience more complete, but also let the user's subjectivity be fully experienced.

(3) Minimising operational memory

This electronic photo frame, in terms of appearance, is simple in shape, with a streamlined design blended with geometric forms, and the product's 15° elevation angle design allows users to have a comfortable viewing angle. In terms of functionality, it analyses the fears of the elderly in using electronic products, such as the complexity of the interface operation, the lack of a person to guide them and the difficulty of reading the content. To address these, a one-touch operation was designed the white wireframe area in the diagram (Fig. 1).

Fig. 1. One-touch operating instructions

6.2 Material Functional Properties

"We often think of products as being focused on technology and the functionality they provide, successful products are focused on emotion" The main idea is to integrate emotion into the design of a product so that it is not only usable, but also a rich emotional experience. The biggest difference between physical and emotional attributes is that emotional attributes trigger a desire within the user. The material attribute of a product is to bring visual enjoyment to the user, reflecting the rational value of the product itself. Emotional attributes are enhanced on the basis of satisfying material attributes. Although it is difficult to trigger, it can also bring deeper satisfaction. Emotion adds colour to our experience and, more importantly, to our memory of the body. In the design of elderly game machine entertainment products, the development from material attributes to emotional attributes, so that the user in the product to the emotional experience, service experience, the form of experience to meet.

1. Evoking emotional memories

   Elderly products are not a cold individual, but through communication, meet the needs of users to reflect their own value. Communication is an integrated visual and auditory language that allows users to receive present emotional care and also stimulates emotional nostalgia for the past. Emotions are not only stimulated by sensory intuition, but also by the memory of years and experiences.

2. Communicating and sharing with others

   As older people withdraw from the social work arena, the scope for social interaction becomes smaller. The system design should not only take into account the entertainment of the elderly themselves, but also consider the medium through which the elderly users can communicate and share with the outside world, which on the one hand can expand the social circle of the elderly, and on the other hand meet the information exchange between the elderly and their children, friends and society. Building a platform like this will allow older people to have a stronger sense of presence.

3. Self-customisation

   Self-realisation is the highest level in Maslow's hierarchy theory. In the elderly group, the emotion of wanting to express oneself is stronger compared to younger people. This is why it is important to provide a stage for self-actualisation and to play a positive role under the guidance of the product. In the case of entertainment products, the sense of achievement is achieved and the "emotional experience" and "service experience" of the self is maximised.

7   Analysis and Implementation of the Kano Model from the Perspective of Perceived Performance

7.1   Information Gathering on User Needs

The analysis of user information is a reliable way of carrying out product development. This is directly related to the user's satisfaction with the product when it is user-oriented. The analysis of the original user requirements, the use of filtering and evaluation to determine the weighting of user requirements, the determination of the value of research and development at a later stage, and the improvement of the cost effectiveness of the product. In summary, the product features refined from the user requirements. Table 3 collects product claims in the five dimensions of perceived demonstrativeness.

7.2   User Satisfaction Factor Analysis Table

The main indicator of the Kano model is the analysis of user satisfaction with the factors. Customer satisfaction factor ratio = increase in satisfaction. Coefficient/Dissatisfaction

Table 3. Product Claims

Perceptual energetic dimension	Non-emergent (singularity)	Qualitative (multiplicity)	Quantitative
Perceptual physical energetics	Simple and easy to use system Simple interface, breakpoint operation, simple tasks Easy to press keys		
	Distinctive curves, few keys, raised, not easily dislodged		
Perceptual-Cognitive Schematics	Easy to get started, user-friendly system Auxiliary functions to enhance user understanding		
	Simple intelligence hierarchy with vertical homogenisation Voice guidance available ,	Does not require much data input from the user Has simple options Provides zoom in, zoom out, footprint and other features for easy identification Provides remote assistance for children	Provides a search function for user records Only allow children to upload data bureaus, less selective
Perceptual-emotional schematics	Provide sharing capabilities and meet user interaction needs		
	Provide gamification features to stimulate user engagement Users can customise their own needs and functions Free to play with certain features	Provide sharing functions to meet interactive needs Provide points function	Providing evaluation functions, increasing the viability of data
Perceptual control	Consistent gestures and less rapid page jumps	Self-adjusting background	Provide privacy features, customizable avatars, customize whether information is public or not

coefficient. si denotes the user satisfaction coefficient and Di denotes the user dissatisfaction coefficient. ai, Oi, Mi, Ii represent the percentage of customers choosing that type of quality in the questionnaire. i = 1,…, m, m represents the total number of quality characteristics.

$$S_i = A_i + O_i/A_i + O_i + M_i + I_i$$

$$D_i = -1 \times (M_i + O_i)/A_i + O_i + M_i + I_i$$

Based on the above formula, the user satisfaction coefficients for the attributes were analysed Table 4.

Table 4. Satisfaction factor.

Demand factors	Si	Di	Demand factors	Si	Di	Demand factors	Si	Di
Handle	0.28	−0.58	Light Verification	0.4	−0.52	Easy to identify pictures	0.58	−0.68
Clear curve	0.3	−0.42	Browse the footprint	0.62	−0.46	Few and simple messages	0.68	−0.66
Raised keys	0.28	−0.78	Breathing Lights	0.6	−0.5	Gestures	0.6	−0.46
Not easily dislodged	0.1	−0.66	Memories function	0.62	−0.6	Colourful interface	0.52	−0.66
Number of keys	0.48	−0.74	Music function	0.16	−0.8	Easy to read text	0.46	−0.68
Colour differentiation	0.34	−0.8	Image view	0.24	−0.72	Self-selection	0.62	−0.36
Not fancy	0.44	−0.72	Environment adjustment	0.5	−0.54	Image verification	0.78	−0.52
Easy to operate	0.58	−0.8	Clear interface	0.52	−0.72	Share function	0.66	−0.48
Function notes	0.6	−0.46	Simple icons	0.54	−0.76	Video function	0.46	−0.42
Voice guidance	0.82	−0.28	Breakpoint operation	0.46	−0.54	Recording function	0.64	−0.22
Digital verification	0.78	−0.66	Simple interface hierarchy	0.78	−0.48	Reminder function	0.56	−0.6
Self-selection	0.62	−0.36	Child login	0.56	−0.5			

Based on the above data, the collated design elements have a structured hierarchy. Considering the age-appropriate material attributes of smart entertainment products - appearance, material attributes - operation, emotional attributes - emotion, emotional attributes - service, emotional attributes - form, etc., to explore the hierarchical demand factors that smart entertainment products should have.

8 Conclusions

This paper elaborates on the physiological, psychological and cognitive characteristics of the elderly group, and details the framework of smart entertainment product design, interaction design strategies and different levels of experience based on a perceptual schematic perspective, focusing on perceptual physical schematic, perceptual cognitive schematic, perceptual emotional schematic and perceptual control schematic. Through the Kano model analysis, the charming influencing factors of smart product ageing can be affirmed and the emotional needs of users can be met. To provide theoretical support for the improvement of the ageing-appropriate information needs of wisdom entertainment. To provide useful reference for the human-computer interaction design and information service of ageing wisdom entertainment products. In addition, the author believes that for the characteristics of ageing groups in different cities, how to improve the emotional experience of ageing wisdom entertainment products, health information service mode and enhance the charm of city image will become the focus of future research attention.

Acknowledgements. The authors are very grateful to the Humanities and Social Sciences Research Project of Anhui University, project K220452029, for supporting this research, and to those who contributed to this study.

Research Project on Humanities and Social Sciences in Anhui Universities, Project Approval Number: K220452029.

References

1. Godby, G.: The Leisure of Your Life. Yunnan People's Publishing House, p. 3 (2000)
2. Xinhua: Let the Elderly Heat Experience Smart Technology Products with Dignity
3. Wang, Y.M., Liu, J.B.: A study on the current situation and problems of information technology intervention in the life of the elderly in China, Scientific Research on Aging No. 10 (2014)
4. Cagan, J., Vogel, C.M.: Creating Breakthrough Products: Innovation from Planning Program Approval. FT Press, USA (2001)
5. Gombrich, E.H.: A Sense of Order - A Psychological Study of the Decorative Arts. Hunan Science and Technology Press, Hunan (2009)
6. Joseph Pine II, B., Gilmore, J.H.: Experience economy. Beijing Machinery Industry Press, Beijing, p. 4 (2008)
7. Preece, J., Rogers, Y., Sharp, H.: Interaction Design Beyond Human-Computer Interaction. Wiley, USA (2002)
8. Bauer, M., Gmytrasiewicz, P.J., Vassileva, J. (eds.): UM 2001. LNCS (LNAI), vol. 2109. Springer, Heidelberg (2001). https://doi.org/10.1007/3-540-44566-8
9. Murray, D.M.: Embedded user models. In: Proceedings of INTERACT 1987, Second IFIP Conference on Human-Vomputer Interaction. Elseier, Netherlands (1987)
10. Rich, E.: Users are individuals: individualizing user models. Iint. J. Hum.-Comput. Stud. **51**, 323–338 (1999)
11. Pozzi, G., Pigni, F., Vitari, C., Buonanno, G., Raguseo, E.: Business model in the IS discipline: a review and synthesis of the literature. In: Rossignoli, C., Gatti, M., Agrifoglio, R. (eds.) Organizational Innovation and Change. LNISO, vol. 13, pp. 115–129. Springer, Cham (2016). https://doi.org/10.1007/978-3-319-22921-8_10
12. Antonenko, P.D., Dawson, K., Sahay, S.: A framework for aligning needs, abilities and affordances to inform design and practice of educational technologies: a framework for aligning needs and affordances. Br. J. Edu. Technol. **48**(4), 916–927 (2017)
13. Greenhill, A., Holmes, K., Woodcock, J., et al.: Playing with science: exploring how game activity motivates users participation on an online citizen science platform. Aslib J. Inf. Manag. **68**(3), 306–325 (2016)
14. Simpson, R., Page, K.R., De Roure, D.: Zooniverse: observing the world's largest citizen science platform. In: Proceedings of the 23rd International Conference on World Wide Web, pp. 1049–1054. ACM (2014)

15. Zhao, Y., Zhang, Y., Tang, J., et al.: Affordances for information practices: theorizing engage-ment among people, technology, and sociocultural environments. J. Doc. **77**(1), 229–250 (2021)
16. Gurnell, A.M., England, J., Shuker, L., et al.: The contribution of citizen science vol unteers to river monitoring and management: international and national perspectives and the example of the MoRPh survey. River Res. Appl. **35**(8), 1359–1373 (2019)
17. Horns, J.J., Adler, F.R., şekercioğlu, Ç.H.: Using opportunistic citizen science data to estimate avian population trends. Biol. Conserv. **221,** 151–159 (2018)

Digital Technology and Interactive Experience: Children's Product Design Based on Zhuang Brocade Cultural Elements

Yun Liang[1](✉), Junyi Mo[1,2](✉), Yi Lu[3], and Xing Yuan[4]

[1] School of Design, Guangxi Normal University, Guilin 541006, China
`liangyun0730@me.com`, `1257825091@qq.com`
[2] Guangxi Arts University, Nanning 530022, China
[3] Beijing University Of Technology, Beijing 100124, China
[4] Kyiv National University of Technologies and Design, Kyiv 01011, Ukraine

Abstract. Purpose: The design and dissemination of national cultural products have undergone significant changes with the advent of new technologies such as the Internet of Things, artificial intelligence, and hardware technology. Despite the limitations of traditional design forms in terms of design innovation and cultural heritage, this study explores the redesign of national products by integrating technical means, cultural appeals, and design practice, to bring digital technology and interactive experiences into practical use. Methods: This study takes the Zhuang brocade pattern as its design subject and children's products as the design carrier. The research adopts both qualitative and quantitative methods, including a questionnaire survey and user interviews. By analyzing and summarizing children's learning objectives, environment, cognitive behavior, and needs, the study extracts feasible design opportunities. Results: By using child-oriented products as the design carrier, children can complete the learning of national cultural knowledge in an interesting, interactive, and intellectual manner. The integration of digital technology and rich interactive experiences make the product more innovative, user-friendly, interactive, and culturally significant compared to traditional products. Conclusion: The combination of design means, technological innovation, and cultural intervention will contribute to the innovation of national cultural products. In product design practice, integrating interactive technology, expressing localized culture, and presenting structural design provides new ideas and opportunities for the design, preservation, and dissemination of national culture.

Keywords: Culture and Technology · Brocade Patterns · Cultural Heritage · Children's Products · Teaching Aids Design

1 Instruction

1.1 Background

The emergence of new technologies such as the Internet of Things, artificial intelligence, and hardware technology, has brought about significant changes in the design and dissemination of ethnic cultural products. For instance, the Zhuang and Dong brocade, a representative of ethnic brocades, has mostly been designed for traditional purposes such as clothing, with only simple design innovations in terms of patterns and colors. Even if the brocade pattern symbols are attached to buildings or products for cultural heritage preservation, the presentation remains incomplete, and the meaning becomes unclear, leading to the loss of national culture and connotations during the translation process.

The inheritance of ethnic culture is a delicate process, and there is a significant lack of toys and teaching aids for children to learn about ethnic culture. This is contrary to the state's proposed reforms of aesthetic education and the policy of promoting excellent traditional culture. The design of teaching aids has become a crucial breakthrough and a significant opportunity for ethnic cultural product design. Hence, it is crucial to explore the design of the highly recognizable Zhuang brocade, a national cultural heritage, as an example.

1.2 Current Research on Children's Educational Products

The growth of digital technology has had a substantial impact on society and altered traditional consumption patterns. The rise and popularity of intelligent toys integrated with digital technology are the epitome of this trend. Currently, children's intelligent toys can be classified into the following categories:

(1) Companion toys, such as smart classrooms, vast early education resources, remote chat, etc. The purpose of these toys is to accompany children and impart knowledge, rather than relying on parents. Examples of products in this category include small intelligent screens, Wuling technology, and pudding bean intelligent robots.
(2) Educational toys, such as the highly popular logical thinking training toys and programming knowledge-based toys. Examples of products in this category include HABA, etc.
(3) Creativity toys, such as magnetic modules and programming toys that enable children to assemble unmanned aerial vehicles and hovercraft by themselves. This category of toys is also widely used in primary and secondary school education due to the

Table 1. The average value of user satisfaction evaluation.

Technology	Description
AI intelligent map recognition	Through AR intelligent image recognition technology, the scanned images can be synchronized to the mobile device through the camera
Weight and volume sensing technology	Built-in sensor plate and sensor can be reflected in the intelligent device through the sensor plate according to the size and weight of the volume, so as to know what image is formed
Intelligent sensing chip	The chips built in blocks of different sizes or colors are different. According to the chips that can be detected by the smart backplane, we can know what color is used and what pattern is formed

growth of STEAM education. Examples of products in this category include Lego, Matatalab, Microduino, and Makeblock, etc.

Children's products based on Zhuang brocade cultural elements focus on the cognitive learning of Zhuang brocade patterns (primarily pattern recognition). Hence, the digital technology used in these products (primarily pattern recognition) is analyzed. A summary of the existing technology analysis is presented in Table 1.

2 Analysis of CHildren's Product Demand Based on Zhuang Brocade Cultural Elements

Zhuang brocade is an essential part of daily life in the Zhuang region and has been serving as a spiritual symbol of the Zhuang people throughout the long history of the Zhuang people's development. With changes in lifestyle and the advancement of time, Zhuang brocade has gradually stepped out of daily life scenes and transformed from a Zhuang necessity to a "spiritual necessity" that carries a stronger national cultural significance, taking on the responsibility of promoting and preserving Zhuang culture. As one of the four famous brocades in China, Zhuang brocade boasts unique ethnic cultural characteristics.

2.1 Positioning

Children at different ages differ in terms of physiology and psychology. Thus, it is crucial to consider these differences when designing toys that meet the specific needs and preferences of each age group. In order to effectively design for targeted groups, a comprehensive understanding of the children's psychological and physical development, personality traits, and specific requirements at each stage is necessary. The Table 2 shows the analysis of development characteristics for children between the ages of 2–9.

2.2 User Research and Methodology

The target population of the design is children between the ages of 4 and 7. According to the theories of child psychologist Jean Piaget, children in this age range are in the preoperational stage of cognitive development, where they are able to internalize perceptual actions into symbols, establish symbolic functions, and think using mental symbols. To better understand the needs of these users, a combination of qualitative and quantitative methods was used in the study.

(1) Qualitative analysis: User interviews and a literature review were conducted. Results from visits to kindergartens and educational institutions showed that puzzles and block games help children to practice their flat thinking by combining, decomposing, and recombining graphic patterns. Children as young as 4 years old are able to perform a certain level of fine motor movements, while 6- and 7-year-olds can handle more complex movements. These games can also guide play by setting simple rules, such as using specific patterns or structures to develop children's artistic skills. Additionally, the use of Zhuang brocade pattern recognition in toy design is based on

Table 2. The average value of user satisfaction evaluation.

Age	Development of sports and physical fitness	Development of intelligence and cognitive ability
2–3	The activity ability is at the initial stage; Hasn't had long time attention; They tend to wait, push, pull, fill, fall, touch and other behaviors; Observe the surrounding environment through body senses	Like simple stories; Like humming; Like bright colors; It can distinguish different parts of the body
4–5	Small movements become more delicate; More physical control is needed when playing; The coordination of eyes and hands is enhanced	Have the ability of logical thinking; Understand 8 basic colors; The development of memory; Be interested in scribbling and words
6–7	The skills of large movements have developed rapidly and the balance has been developed; Further master the skills of small movements; Like challenges	Prefer bright and bright colors; Able to read long books; Like to be regular; Like to talk
8–9	Development of exercise muscles and body; Active but need rest time; This stage is beginning to become less active	The further development of reading ability; Learn to try different shades of a color; Further understanding of the more complex concepts of accumulation and deduction; We have a deeper understanding of nature

local ethnic culture and promotes cultural transmission at a young age. Parents and teachers generally agree that block toys exercise children's sense of beauty, spatial ability, and imagination, and have the flexibility and diversity to be combined in various ways.

(2) Quantitative analysis: The data was mainly collected through questionnaire surveys. 93.33% of the respondents showed interest in purchasing educational aids related to ethnic culture and expressed strong interest in Zhuang brocade-related cultural and creative teaching aids. However, 80% of respondents had limited knowledge of Zhuang brocade patterns. When it comes to the design of cultural and creative teaching aids, respondents hoped that the design would promote intelligence, emotional development, and learning ability (93%), have multiple ways to play (93%), be made of high-quality, safe materials (86.67%), and be interactive and participatory (66.67%).

2.3 Characteristics of Zhuang Brocade Design Elements

(1) Abstract and Intuitive Patterns in Zhuang Brocade

The patterns of Zhuang brocade are known for their abstract simplicity, yet they possess a clear graphic outline and rich content. These patterns are created by Zhuang people, who draw inspiration from natural elements such as flowers, birds, insects, and fish, and refine them through a bold and simple process. The resulting abstract yet vivid image is easy to identify, decorative, intriguing, and rich in graphic connotation. Zhuang brocade patterns are not only aesthetically pleasing, but also culturally significant, reflecting the Zhuang people's close relationship with nature.

(2) Repetition of Colors and Shapes in Zhuang Brocade

The surface of Zhuang brocade frequently employs repetition techniques in its composition, making use of geometric patterns characterized by "abstract repetition." The overall brocade surface is mainly monochromatic with simple outlines and embellishments, creating a neat and orderly appearance that offers unlimited imagination and visual interest to viewers. This design technique is a common feature in Zhuang brocade and is evident in both the patterns and color matching (Fig. 1).

Fig. 1. Zhuang brocade

(3) Pixelated Presentation of Weaving and Design in Zhuang Brocade

Zhuang brocade is primarily woven through the warp and weft process, resulting in a thicker surface compared to Shu and Yun brocade. The direction of the weft threads in Zhuang brocade is determined by the weaving process, which can only be horizontal or oblique. Due to these limitations, the pattern presentation is mostly composed of geometric shapes. This structural organization resembles pixel dots, creating a characteristic pixelated presentation in Zhuang brocade. The combination of regular polygonal patterns through repetition, stacking, and interlacing forms various patterns with a multitude of morphological features, each one unique and captivating.

In conclusion, the abstract and intuitive patterns, repetition of colors and shapes, and pixelated presentation of weaving and design make Zhuang brocade a remarkable and distinctive cultural artifact, representing the rich cultural heritage of the Zhuang people. These features not only make Zhuang brocade a beautiful piece of art, but also a symbol of the Zhuang people's wisdom, creativity, and artistic talent. It also provides possibilities for future design development (Fig. 2).

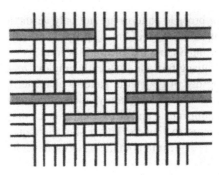

Fig. 2. Zhuang brocade structure (three-shuttle method) [1]

3 Product Design Practice Based on Zhuang Brocade Cultural Elements

3.1 Product Design Methods Based on Zhuang Brocade Cultural Elements

The integration of technology in the design process has transformed the expression of product design from what it used to be in the past. In the context of brocade weaving, the design must balance the refinement of cultural elements with the integration of technology, the allure of ethnic culture, and the innovation of design practices.

(1) Technological Intervention: The integration of the Internet of Things technology and other means has made the process of learning and transmitting ethnic culture more interactive and contemporary. The presence of technology in ethnic culture transmission has grown significantly, from digital presentation to product design forms. To ensure that technology serves the design presentation, designers can adopt a "game + culture" approach that promotes cultural recognition and develops children's aesthetic skills [2].

(2) Cultural Expressions: The repetition of colors and shapes in brocade accurately conveys the meaning of patterns. As proposed by American anthropologist Clifford Geertz: "the concept of culture is essentially a semiotic concept." Cultural symbols are unique carriers that are formed by a nation during its historical development and are important components of the national cultural elements [3]. The connotation of Zhuang brocade cultural elements is embodied in the rich and varied patterns, making it crucial to accurately convey the pattern and its meaning during the design transcription process. The patterns of Zhuang brocade are arranged in a regular repetition, creating a neat visual effect with repeated layers and mostly saturated colors. The repetition of color and shape can be utilized in product design to achieve a high sense of regularity.

(3) Design Practice: By highlighting the characteristics of the weaving process, the structural characteristics of Zhuang brocade are presented. The weaving method of Zhuang brocade is unique and mostly done through the warp and weft method. Before pattern design, designers use a fixed-sized intentional drawing, bringing the possibility of standardized or modular design in product design. In practice, product design based on Zhuang brocade cultural elements can adopt a standardized or

specific modular product structure, presenting the characteristics of Zhuang brocade weaving and enriching the product design form simultaneously (Fig. 3).

Fig. 3. The design process of Zhuang brocade basic body block by pixel grid

The integration of technology has transformed the expression of product design, but it is important to balance this integration with the refinement of cultural elements, the allure of ethnic culture, and the innovation of design practices. In the case of Zhuang brocade, the design must accurately convey the meaning of the patterns and the cultural elements embodied in the rich and varied patterns, while highlighting the characteristics of the weaving process and presenting the structural characteristics of Zhuang brocade.

3.2 Development Framework of CHildren's Product Design Based on Zhuang Brocade Cultural Elements

In view of the characteristics of children aged 4–7 years old who are in the preoperational thinking period, and in response to the findings of user interviews and research, the proposed design development framework for children's product design based on Zhuang brocade cultural elements is shown in Table 3.

(1) Spatial and form cognition: Use of technology incorporation and design integration of STEAM education concepts

　　The product design solution integrates traditional national culture with STEAM education [4]. Advances in technology have made children the natives of the digital age, and some scholars have suggested that a proper integration of children's education with electronic devices can stimulate children's desire for active exploration so that they can participate in learning with a positive attitude [5]. The use of AR technology and electronic devices enhances the vividness and authenticity of the process of using teaching aids in an innovative interactive form that combines games, culture, and technology. The program incorporates AR technology, where the pieced patterns can be recorded and displayed on a linked tablet or mobile app (Fig. 4). In addition, the sense of accomplishment of children using the product is increased by setting motivating behavioral feedback [6]. For example, after completing pattern piecing and color matching design, they can create personal pattern picture cards and customize related derivatives (e.g., generate postcard cards, etc.) (Fig. 5).

(2) Cultural expression and guidance: auxiliary graphic cards for ethnic culture learning

　　The design comes with a comparative illustration of block division and quantity and a Zhuang brocade block quantity awareness question card, which can be used not

Table 3. Design strategy.

Purpose	Design strategy
Develop children's spatial and shape cognitive skills	Technology intervention - AR smart technology is used in the design to scan and shape the finished solid blocks and set up corresponding feedback and reward mechanism in the interaction process to encourage children to learn in a fun way. The blocks are designed according to the ergonomic data, and the blocks are divided according to the structural characteristics of Zhuang brocade patterns, and the squares are divided and pieced together into different geometric shapes, so that children can understand the "sum" relationship between different shapes, and the blocks are used as the basis for children to put together geometric Zhuang brocade patterns
Strengthening cultural guidance and understanding of national culture	Cultural expression - Use Zhuang brocade picture cards to guide children to build patterns, and in the process understand the names and symbolic meanings of pattern patterns to achieve the effect of understanding Zhuang brocade patterns, and in the process implicitly carry out cultural transmission
Training in color perception and aesthetic sense	Design practice - Zhuang brocade is characterized by repetitive colors and shapes, so in the design process, the basic blocks are designed, and gradient colors are used to design the patterns. It is easy for children to accept

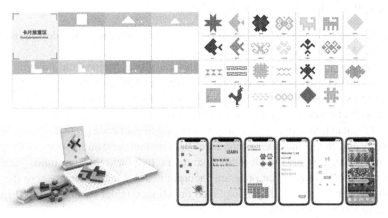

Fig. 4. Product and quantity awareness card and APP design

only to guide children's pattern cognition but also to learn mathematical knowledge through playing. Each Zhuang brocade pattern is made up of different numbers of blocks, so that children can practice the number of blocks used in the corresponding

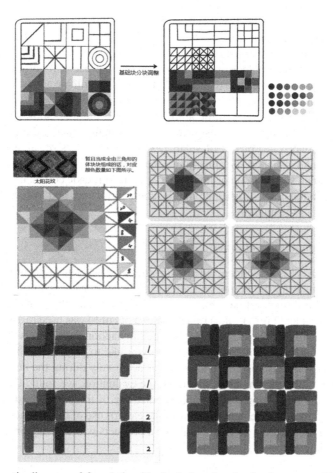

Fig. 5. Schematic diagram of foundation block, design sketch of solar pattern block and fish pattern block

sample cards. The cards can be used as an aid for parents and teachers to test their children's number problems and to practice their ability to understand numbers. The 30 Zhuang brocade pattern cards contain 30 common patterns of Zhuang brocade and 90 color patterns. Children can put together the patterns of Zhuang brocade by comparing with the cards, and they can also use their own creativity to put together their own Zhuang brocade colors.

(3) Color and aesthetic training: design considerations based on blocks and colors

Based on the patterns of Zhuang brocade, 7 basic geometric shapes are refined. The storage tray and the intelligent induction base plate are rectangular and square, plus the seven geometric shapes that are proportionally divided and pieced together by the square, which is conducive to children's understanding of volume and proportional relationships. Different base blocks placed in different ways can form different tapestry patterns, different colors of the base blocks will spell out the effect of the picture will be different. For example, for the sunburst pattern, a sunburst color scheme made of geometric blocks would require a total of 32 large triangular blocks (see Fig. 4). For the fish pattern, four large L-shaped blocks, one small L-shaped block, and one square block are used (Fig. 4). In the process of putting together the pattern, children can enhance their knowledge of body, volume and volume, improve their sense of beauty and imagination and creative ability, and develop and exercise their cognitive and generalization ability of shapes. Figure 4 shows a total of 415 completed basic body blocks designed and placed in three major drawers: 20 pieces of large L-shaped, 20 pieces of small L-shaped, 40 pieces of large I-shaped, 30 pieces of small I-shaped, 125 pieces of square, 120 pieces of large triangle, and 60 pieces of small triangle. According to the extracted brocade colors, they are divided according to the color saturation, and the colors with high and low saturation each take up half of the quantity.

3.3 User Satisfaction Evaluation

The evaluation process was conducted by using the design sketch model trial and demonstration, by comparing the before and after experience of the existing building block products with this design. Fifteen children aged 4–7 years old were invited to participate in the test (Table 4 and Fig. 6), and a Likert scale (5 out of 5) was used to assess the satisfaction level (the higher the score, the higher the satisfaction level). (2) Is there anything you don't like in the building process? (3) Do you like to play with others during the game? (4) Can you learn/recognize the patterns accurately during the building process with reference to the picture cards? Through the evaluation, we found that users were satisfied with the innovation, culture and interactivity of the product, but still felt that there was room for improvement in terms of the ease of use of the product. Overall, the feedback from users on the design of children's products with Zhuang brocade cultural elements is relatively positive.

Table 4. The average value of user satisfaction evaluation

	Innovative	Easy to use	Interactive	Culturally
Traditional building blocks experience satisfaction value	3.98	4.12	4.01	3.70
Zhuang brocade cultural elements of children's products experience satisfaction value	4.73	4.22	4.58	4.48

Fig. 6. The teacher is introducing to children and children are playing

4 Conclusion

The interminable interaction of design, technology and culture helps promote the value of national culture. The children's product design based on Zhuang brocade cultural elements explores feasible design exploration of ethnic cultural heritage in the context of national promotion of aesthetic education reform and dissemination of excellent traditional culture. The main innovation points of the design case are: (1) interactive technology integration. Using existing technologies, the design provides multi-sensory interaction such as sound reminders and visual feedback to increase the interactivity of children's products; (2) localized cultural expression. Taking Zhuang brocade, a representative of local cultural heritage with great recognition, as the design object, on the one hand, while borrowing educational means to revitalize and inherit the national culture, it is also a creative way to inject new vitality into the excellent national culture. On the other hand, the innovative development of ethnic culture-related products can, to a certain extent, alleviate the lack of resources for teaching aids of related themes in primary and secondary schools, and better help children to complete the learning of ethnic culture knowledge in an interesting, interactive and educational learning process; (3) structural design presentation. The design case highlights the characteristics of the weaving process and presents the structural characteristics of Zhuang brocade, achieving organic integration with the product. The changes and iterations of technology have quietly changed the way of design presentation and dissemination of ethnic culture products. By thinking about the integration of design, technology and culture, this case hopes to provide new ideas and useful exploration for the transmission of ethnic culture.

Funding. National Social Science Foundation (China) funded the project, "Research on the Innovative Development Mechanism and Path of Zhuang and Dong Nationality Brocade Special Needs from the Perspective of 'The Belt and Road Initiative'" (Serial number: 17CMZ032).

References

1. Xiaoping, Q.: Chinese Brocade Collection, 1st edn. China Textile Press, Beijing (2014). (in Chinese)

2. Yuanyuan, Y., Tie J., Duoduo, Z.: Design and application of traditional culture in children's educational games: taking the logic Huayao design practice as an example. Decoration (12), 78–81(2018). (in Chinese)
3. Yonglin, H., Mingming, J.: On the creative transformation and innovative development of intangible cultural heritage in cultural industry. J. Cent. China Norm. Univ. (Humanit. Soc. Sci.) **57**(03), 72–80 (2018). (in Chinese)
4. Qun, H., Junzi, L.: The design of children's intelligent toys in the information age. Packag. Eng. **41**(10), 150–156+174 (2020). (in Chinese)
5. Lu, Y., Wang, X., Gong, J., et al.: ChordAR: an educational AR game design for children's music theory learning. Wirel. Commun. Mob. Comput. **2022** (2022)
6. Jihong, Z., Yuechao, Z.: APP interface design for preschool children based on children's cognitive development. Packag. Eng. **41**(10), 42–48 (2020). (in Chinese)

Exploring the Potential Causes of Dormitory Relationship in University Students in Terms of Experiences and Behaviors

Qingyi Liang[✉]

School of Digital Media Arts, Zhujiang College of South China Agricultural University, Guangzhou 510000, People's Republic of China
id_1204199@qq.com

Abstract. In today's social climate, due to the Covid-19 epidemic, most universities have decided to close their schools. Students are forced to be confined to school, and the harmony of interpersonal relationships in dormitories becomes extremely important. Student relationships in college dormitories have a great impact on learning and health. Dormitory relationships are the cornerstone of learning and health, and the cornerstone is stable to make better results. Therefore, it is important to innovate in dormitory relationships and find a new experience in a new context that can affect socialization and personal characteristics as well as academics. Current research on college dormitory relationships have explored some subjective perceptions, emotions and personalities, which are without examining the causes of the universal phenomenon. In addition, the condition of the causes by the phenomenon is missing. For example, the cause of social disorder is a reflection of personal ability; mental problems are a kind of self-deficiency; and school bullying is a way to vent anger or a provocation. Most importantly, there is a lack of a design thinking approach to explore to find the reasons behind the behavior. Therefore, this research is to discover what people are lacking inside through the dormitory problem. A co-design approach was used to obtain information from college students. The main steps included the following: 1) finding an article for each of the 6 students to read; 2) dividing the 6 students into two groups; 3) making each student read the article to get a general idea of the content, underlining the main points, and using personal experience to provide examples for analysis; and4) Discuss how the relationship in their own dorm is, what the specific situation is, and preferably share their own insights about what is good and bad about dorm group life and what to do about the bad ones. The results show that some strange behaviors are to get others' attention, lack of attention and approval, and some aggressive behaviors are to heal their scars and not to be hurt again, which contributes to reveal the underlying etiology of interpersonal behaviors and experiences in college dormitories, which can be used for future experience and service design.

Keywords: Co-design · Mental Models · Interpersonal Relationships · Individual Behavior · College Housemates · Essential Factors

A. Marcus et al. (Eds.): HCII 2023, LNCS 14031, pp. 151–166, 2023.
https://doi.org/10.1007/978-3-031-35696-4_12

1 Introduction

As the world's most populous country, China needs a large amount of grain every year. Many college students, before going to university, do not have the experience of group accommodation, the circle of life is quite closed, do not do anything outside the study, or are arranged by their parents [1]. In addition, modern college students can not deal with their own interpersonal relationships due to their personality self-centeredness, inferiority, pride, jealousy and other psychology in interpersonal communication [2], so when dealing with interpersonal relationships, lack of skills, regardless of each other's emotional experience, go their own way, easy to cause dissatisfaction among other people in the dormitory, and face the confusion of how to deal with different interpersonal relationships [3].

Interpersonal relationship is a direct psychological relationship formed between people through mutual interaction and interaction, which reflects the psychological state of individual or group needs to meet needs. People live in society, inseparable from the interaction and coordination with others, how to deal with all kinds of interpersonal relationships has become a matter that everyone in the world has to encounter, and no one can avoid it [4].

Relationships are very important. It is a new challenge to be away from your parents and to take care of your own studies and life at school on your own. In this environment, it is especially important to build good interpersonal relationships with others [5]. This is not only the guarantee for the normal study and life of college students, but also the deep need for the self-development of college students. However, judging from the many news about college students and the frequent accidents of college students in colleges and universities, the interpersonal relationship situation of contemporary college students is not ideal [6].

The factors that affect college students' interpersonal relationships can be both the cause of interpersonal attraction and the cause of interpersonal disorders. There are also factors that are more direct causes of interpersonal disorders, such as cognitive, emotional, and economic factors, which are discussed below [7].

2 Interpersonal Factors

2.1 Co-design

In my co-creation design, I divided six people into two groups, namely Group1 and Group2 (see Fig. 1). We discussed in groups, and everyone expressed their own views and opinions, and talked about how to face the chaotic relationship and how to improve the bad ones with personal experience. Read the article, get a general understanding of the content, underline the main points, and give examples with personal experience (see Fig. 2). How about discussing their dormitory relationship with each other? The difference between people on the Internet and in reality [8]. Tell me the difference between the good and bad parts of living in a dormitory and living alone.

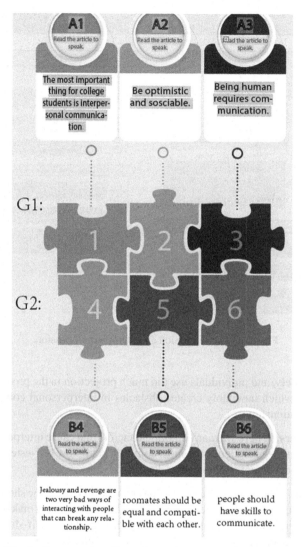

Fig. 1. Group setting discussion on interpersonal relationship.

2.2 Projection

The individual reflects his emotions, will and personality on others, thinks that others are the same, and recognizes others on this basis, that is, projection, that is, the individual inherently expects the other person to be the same. The specific characteristics of college

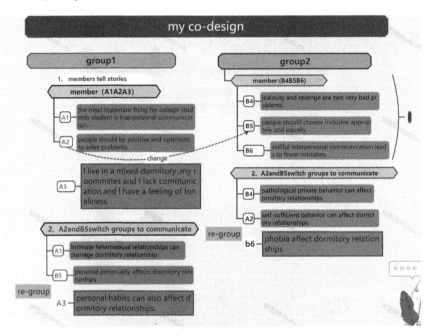

Fig. 2. Group discussion and regroup re-discussion.

students vary widely, and individuals use too much projection in the process of interpersonal cognition, which inevitably creates obstacles in interpersonal communication or interpersonal relationships.

Emotional Factors. There are many emotional factors that cause interpersonal relationship disorders in college students, the most common being low self-esteem and conceit, and its internal mechanism is interpersonal security.

Low Self-esteem. The complex emotions that an individual thinks he should be superior, but does not feel superior and helpless is inferiority. Low self-esteem makes individuals in the process of interpersonal contact show lack of self-confidence, self-shame, withdrawn behavior, sensitive and multi-store, college students with low self-esteem are actually too high expectations for everything, in communication, get along always want to make their own form to hide and protect their inner world (see Fig. 5). That is, his speech, naive and superficial.

Similar to people with low self-esteem, conceited people also expect to have a superior position in communicating and getting along, but the strategy of conceited people to protect themselves is to expand outward, not to adduct as low self-esteem does (see Fig. 6).

2.3 Economic Factors

The financial situation of college students can also affect an individual's interpersonal adjustment. Two extreme cases are discussed here: poverty and affluence.

Poverty. College students with poor family economic conditions experience more depression and distress in school, and it is very easy to have an inferiority complex. Due to financial constraints, these students are disadvantaged in terms of food and clothing, and to avoid embarrassment, they tend to be less sociable with other classmates and more focused on studying hard. Over time, they may develop interpersonal barriers such as interpersonal shyness and interpersonal avoidance (see Fig. 2).

Abundance. The college students with better economic conditions are comfortable with their food and clothing, and can be generous in front of their classmates. In addition, because of their good family circumstances, their life experiences and coping skills are richer, they tend to be happy with others, and there are fewer interpersonal barriers. However, some affluent college students may have certain negative personality traits, such as being egotistical and self-centered in getting along with others, being arrogant and presumptuous in communicating, which may lead to interpersonal barriers.

3 Method

A co-design approach was used to obtain information from students. The main steps included the following: 1) finding an article for each of the 6 students to read; 2) dividing the 6 students into two groups; 3) having each student read the article to get a general idea of the content, underlining the main points and using personal experience to provide examples for analysis; and 4) discussing how the relationship is in their own dormitory, what is the specific situation, and preferably sharing their own insights about what is good and bad about dormitory group life and what to do about the bad ones.

4 Results

4.1 Principle

In dealing with interpersonal relationships, we should respect the following principles:

The Principle of Mutual Respect. Human self-esteem and mutual respect are one of the important foundations for establishing and developing good interpersonal relationships. Only when a person has self-respect can he win the respect of others and develop interpersonal relationships; only through mutual respect can we win mutual trust and consolidate and deepen interpersonal relationships.

The Principle of Mutual Understanding. Understand that trust is another important factor in building and developing good interpersonal relationships. The reason why people can seek common ground while reserving differences and harmony with each other is because people recognize each other and form a tacit understanding. Understanding and believing is the embodiment of identity.

The Principle of Trustworthiness. The emphasis on trust is a virtue of the Chinese nation. It requires people to tell the truth and do practical things in their dealings with each other, so as to "do what they say and do what they do".

The Principle of Compatibility and Adaptation. Interpersonal relationships in university dormitories are a very important part of their interpersonal support system, which directly affects students' mental health, and indirectly affects students' learning and all aspects of university life. Therefore, it is of great importance to study the interpersonal relationships in college dormitories. The once sensational case of Magajue is such a typical negative case, and we must take it as a warning.

In the following, we will summarize some reasons for the tension in the dormitory relationship: 1. Lack of communication is one of the main reasons. Many college students, before going to university, do not have the experience of group accommodation, and the circle of life is quite closed, outside the study, do nothing, or parents do it. Therefore, when managing interpersonal relationships outside, lack of hand skills, regardless of the emotional experience of the other party, go their own way, and easily cause dissatisfaction among other people in the dormitory (see Fig. 3).

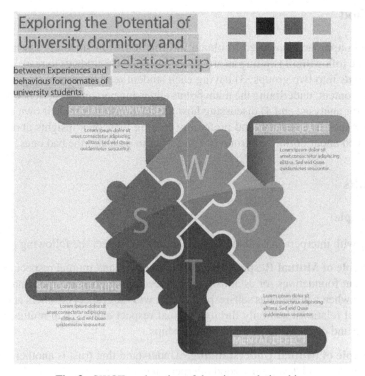

Fig. 3. SWOT explanation of dormitory relationships.

4.2 Economic Factors

The economic background also hinders the normal development of dormitory relations, and the economic and cultural development of different regions and urban and rural areas in China is unbalanced, which causes different dormitory members to have different economic abilities and moral cultivation levels, and different lives.

There are also differences in habits, which is bound to cause many negative psychological reactions.

At the same time, the dormitory is also one of the concentrated outbreaks of various interpersonal tensions among college students, because the dormitory is the main focus of college students' lives, so the interpersonal relationships here will inevitably be reflected (see Fig. 4). So how should we deal with dormitory relationships? First of all, by ourselves. Handling dormitory relationships well involves three major aspects: personality qualities, interpersonal principles, and interpersonal skills and abilities. (1) Personality qualities. The most important personality qualities in handling dormitory relationships well are: tolerance, honesty, generosity, tolerance, respect, care, and help. (2) Use of communication skills. Second, schools should also do a good job in related work and, as far as the school is concerned, establish good interpersonal relationships among college students.

University is one of the most intense and obvious psychological changes in a person's life. If you can't evaluate yourself and others correctly, and can't choose and develop yourself correctly, it will affect your life. College students have a large independent space on campus. They can study vast professional knowledge and roam the vast virtual space of the Internet. Unfortunately, students who are obsessed with games can't get out of the interfaces such as "anti-terrorism" and "legend", and ignore the interpersonal activities among classmates, friends and teachers, because the reality is much less wonderful than the virtual one.

In addition, college students who don't pay attention to the cultivation of interpersonal relationships like to go it alone, tend to be self-contained, and are not good at communicating and cooperating with others to prevent self-denial.

My exposure and loss of competitiveness. Lin is a quiet and introverted student. She was admitted to the university from the countryside with a high score. At first, she was full of passion, but she soon realized that she didn't know how to communicate with others. When she saw others happily chatting and participating in various activities, she felt extremely nervous and didn't even want to appear in crowded places. She had the idea to go home. From the perspective of cognitive psychology, the cognitive image of interpersonal communication comes from experience and feeling. The experience of interacting with others is like inputting information into the brain, and the feelings generated during the interaction are like a software package that, after being processed and implemented at the time, is combined into a file. Like Lin and the children who often stay at home alone, their main task in middle school is learning, and they rarely interact with others. They lack the objective environment and the ability to communicate with people in the process of growing up, so they can't form the experience and realistic feeling of interacting with people, so they can't form the cognitive image of interpersonal communication. As a result, they feel lost and lack confidence in the relatively colorful life of the university campus (see Fig. 6).

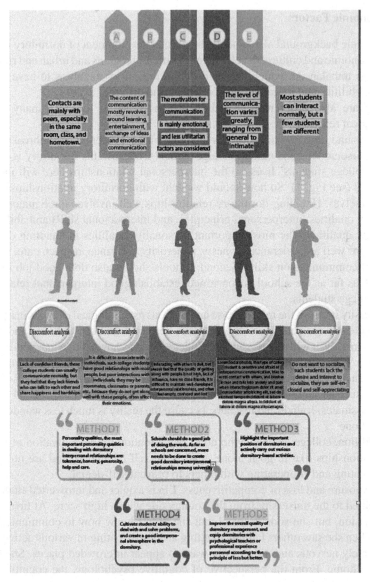

Fig. 4. Analysis of the main content and discount of young people's interactions and solutions.

The dormitory interpersonal relationship is a very important part of the college students' interpersonal support system, and its good or bad directly affects the students' psychological health, and indirectly affects their study and all aspects of college life, so it is very important to discuss the dormitory interpersonal relationship, and the once sensational Magaji case is such a typical negative case that we should be warned.

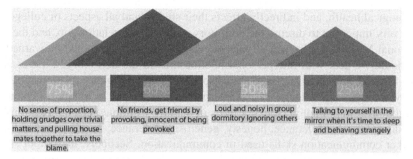

75%	50%	50%	25%
No sense of proportion, holding grudges over trivial matters, and pulling house-mates together to take the blame.	No friends, get friends by provoking, innocent of being provoked	Loud and noisy in group dormitory Ignoring others	Talking to yourself in the mirror when it's time to sleep and behaving strangely

Fig. 5. Reasons for hating others and the degree of hatred.

Fig. 6. Missing communication with parents while growing up.

Here we summarize a few points that cause tension in the dormitory relationship:

1) Lack of communication is the main reason Gu each other's emotional experience, my own way, easy to dry cause dissatisfaction of other people in the dormitory.
2) The economic background also hinders the normal development of dormitory relations, the economic and cultural development of each region, each city and countryside in China is unbalanced, which causes different dormitory members to have different degrees of economic ability and moral cultivation, living > There are also differences in habits, which will inevitably also cause many adverse psychological reactions (see Fig. 7).
3) At the same time, the dormitory is also one of the places where various other interpersonal tensions among college students are concentrated, because the dormitory is the main focus of college students' lives, so the interpersonal relationships here are bound to reflect other aspects of a college student's interpersonal relationships.

The dormitory interpersonal relationship is a very important part of the college students' interpersonal support system, and its good or bad directly affects the students' psychological health, and indirectly affects their studies and all aspects of college life, so it is very important to discuss the dormitory interpersonal relationship, and the once sensational Magaji case is such a typical negative case that we should be warned. So how should we deal with interpersonal relationships in the dormitory? First of all, it comes from us, and there are three main aspects of good dormitory relationships: personality, interpersonal principles, and interpersonal skills and techniques. Personality traits, the most important personality traits in dealing with interpersonal relationships in the dormitory are: tolerance, honesty, generosity, tolerance, respect, care and help, and other communication skills used in communication. Secondly, the school should also do a good job in creating a good interpersonal relationship between students in the university.

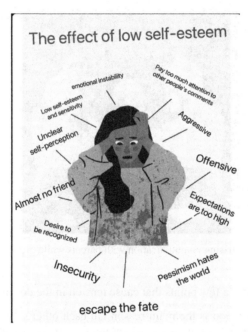

Fig. 7. The effect of low self-esteem.

The school can fill out some forms when students enroll and match them with roommates according to the content of the forms, such as whether they have a smoking habit, whether they have a cleanliness problem, whether they snore in their sleep (see Fig. 8 and Fig. 9).

In the process, the reasons for destroying dormitory relationships and promoting dormitory relationships are summarized (see Fig. 10).

After discussion and summary, the main reasons that affect the dormitory relationship are intimacy and personal character and behavior, which account for 50% and 25%, respectively (see Fig. 11).

Through the discussion, it was found that mutual respect and giving up stereotypes and active concessions would promote the dormitory relationship and also make the

Fig. 8. Individualized needs dormitory assignment.

Fig. 9. Habit preference matching.

relationship closer. Mutual respect accounted for 55%, active concessions accounted for 30%, and giving up stereotypes accounted for 15% (see Fig. 12).

The reason is that each person's personal ability, personal defects and social strategies are different, personal ability accounted for the largest percentage of 75%, the remaining personal defects accounted for 15% and social strategies accounted for 10% (see Fig. 13).

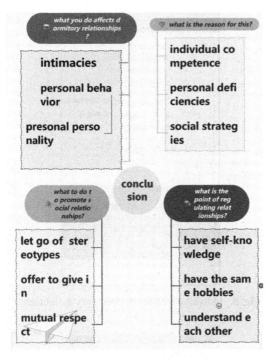

Fig. 10. Major sources of disruption of dormitory relationships.

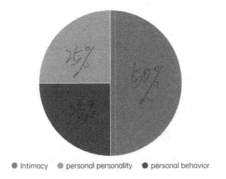

Fig. 11. Percentage of various causes.

The most important point in regulating the relationship is self-awareness, having the same hobbies, and mutual understanding, each accounting for 33.33% (see Fig. 14).

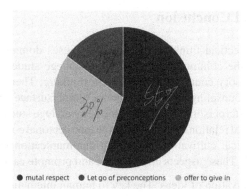

Fig. 12. Percentage of various causes.

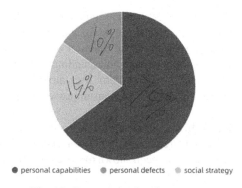

Fig. 13. Percentage of various causes.

Fig. 14. Percentage of various causes.

5   Discussion and Conclusion

According to the dialectical thinking that internal causes dominate external factors, in order to improve the communication ability of college students, it is first necessary to set up compulsory courses to change their thinking; Then develop individual-specific information counseling activities to do so "point, surface" combination. There are ways to improve interpersonal relationships among college students. The basic ways to improve interpersonal relationships and promote interpersonal communication include strengthening ideological cultivation, practicing communication skills and enriching social knowledge, etc. These aspects complement and promote each other [9].

1) Strengthen the cultivation of ideas. The key to human interaction is the exchange of ideas, and some people's lack of interaction is often the result of the quality of ideas, such as suspicion, pride, jealousy, selfishness, and so on. Everyone has an innate need to develop human relations and has the potential to do so, it is important to come out of the closed and selfish world, strengthen moral cultivation, and improve the awareness of ideas [10].

2) Practice social skills. People who are good at socializing are often good at finding and recognizing the value of others, respecting them, and trusting them: they are tolerant of others and do not take into account the faults of others: they are able to express themselves appropriately without being condescending: they try to understand others and do not impose their own views on them: they are good at starting with topics that interest them. Improving these skills can improve the quality of interpersonal communication.

3) Enrich social knowledge. In the process of conversation, pay attention to elegant wording, natural attitude, sincere and moderate conversation, humorous and light. Honesty and truthfulness have been shown to strengthen friendships (see Fig. 15).

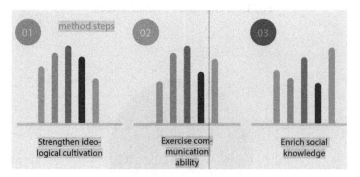

Fig. 15. Ways to change.

4) Establish compulsory professional courses in communication and psychology, carry out open positive publicity and education, everyone has a desire to discover the secrets of others' hearts, generally speaking, only by opening their hearts, they can talk about others.

In my heart, taking the initiative to show favor to others is the first step to achieving ideological communication and emotional harmony. When you encounter disagreement in the process of communication, look at the problem from the perspective of role-swapping, and perhaps you will reach an unprecedented understanding. At the same time, we must understand that everyone has the right to reserve their opinions and live according to their own wishes, not to force others to change, to respect others but not to demand too much of others, and to cooperate with others with an open mind. Visiting roommates' friends, warm welcome, resting time, not making loud noises, good interpersonal relationships start from every little thing around you (see Fig. 16).

5) Develop psychological counseling services and enhance the role of psychological counseling. School psychological counseling is an important way to improve students' mental health and optimize their psychological quality, and it is also an important part of psychological quality education. College students are becoming more mature and stable, their values and world views are basically formed, and they show their own unique views on many issues, but they may also be prone to stubbornness and drilling.

However, there is a certain demand for psychological counseling, they can get explanations and dramas from school psychological counselors, and under the current conditions of "school-to-school" and "house-to-house", it is recommended to set up schools on computer networks.

The use of "no meeting, no name" text and voice synchronous consultation services, so that the work can be loved by the majority of students, will become one of the modern education brands of the school (see Fig. 16).

Fig. 16. Strengthen psychological attention to students.

6) Strengthen the communication between school and family, and form a common educational force of students, parents and teachers. Parents are the first teachers of children, family education is particularly important in a person's educational experience, children's emotions, cognition and values are greatly affected by family education.

College students are mainly boarding school, for the child's performance in school, parents can not understand in time, school and family should strengthen communication through a variety of channels, cooperate with each other to carry out psychological counseling for children, can achieve twice the educational effect with half the effort.

The results show that some strange behaviors are to get others' attention, lack of attention and approval, and some aggressive behaviors are to heal their scars and not to be hurt again, which contributes to reveal the underlying etiology of interpersonal behaviors and experiences in college dormitories, which can be used for future experience and service design.

References

1. Huang, X.: Psychological Characteristics and Education of College Students in Contemporary China. Shanghai Education Press, Shanghai (2001)
2. Han, H.: Introduction to College Student Psychology. Central China Normal University Press, Wuhan (2004)
3. Li, Q.: Current situation and countermeasures of interpersonal relationships among college students. Chin. Sch. Health 23(1), 47–48 (2002)
4. Zhang, X., Fan, F.: Interpersonal conflict behavior of college students and its relationship with mental health. Res. Psychol. Behav. 1, 364–367 (2004)
5. Li, H., Zong, C.M.: Research on interpersonal relationships and loneliness of college students–taking college students of Changzhou university as survey subjects. Mod. Enterp. Educ. 2, 75–76 (2012)
6. She, C.: A brief analysis of the psychological factors affecting interpersonal relationships in college students' dormitories. Adolescence 22, 209 (2012)
7. Wang, T., Xi, B., Wang, C., Xu, L.: Analysis of psychosocial influencing factors of interpersonal relationship distress among college students. Chin. J. Public Health 23(5), 533–534 (2007)
8. Wang, M., Wang, Y.: The impact of network technology on interpersonal communication among human students. Coal High. Educ. 2, 31–33 (2001)
9. Lu, L.: Research on the application of college group work in school social work. China Extramur. Educ. (Second Issue) 4, 1–35 (2012)
10. Liu, X.: Discuss the interpersonal relationships of college students. J. Lincang Educ. 82, 75–78 (2003)

Research on User Experience Design Strategy of Digital Aquarium Based on UTAUT2 Model

Maocong Lin and Yue Huang[✉]

Qingdao University, Qingdao 266000, China
1032184596@qq.com

Abstract. Design comes from the process of solving problems. Under the background of normalization of the epidemic and rapid development of technology, based on the study of the influencing factors of user experience, this paper discusses the suggested strategies for integrating logarithmic intelligent design exhibition into Qingdao Marine Museum. The behavior, experience and service needs of users in Qingdao Underwater World were analyzed. Combined with UTAUT2 model theory, the data research design was carried out, and the user acceptance influencing factor model of Qingdao Underwater World was constructed and described and analyzed. According to the survey, it is found that there are many practical problems, such as dense personnel, weak museum carrying capacity, difficult to link Marine culture and physical display, and weak willingness to develop intelligent museum numbers. In the model architecture, the dependent variable is designed and adjusted, so that the value price is integrated into the promotion factor, and the control variable "education level" is added. The results show that the dependent variables performance expectation, effort expectation, social influence factors, promotion factors, hedonic motivation and control variables all have significant positive effects on users. The control variables age, gender and education level have moderating effects on user behavior and experience. Qingdao Underwater World generates the needs of digital intelligence integration, and puts forward the design strategies of scene model diversification, immersive experience, Marine information visualization, emotional marketing, and online construction of cultural and creative industry.

Keywords: Qingdao Ocean Museum · Digital intelligent design · UTAUT2 model theory · Human-computer symbiosis · The user experience

1 Introduction

The development of Qingdao's Marine cultural characteristics plays a key role in enhancing the city's reputation, accumulating and building recognizable city signs. Looking at the current background of repeated and normalization of the epidemic, the development of tourism and the real economy in various regions has encountered unprecedented obstacles. Design behavior comes from the idea of problem-solving. With the continuous progress of information technology and the rapid development of the digital industry, various new concepts are constantly defining our world. The demand in this background

© The Author(s), under exclusive license to Springer Nature Switzerland AG 2023
A. Marcus et al. (Eds.): HCII 2023, LNCS 14031, pp. 167–188, 2023.
https://doi.org/10.1007/978-3-031-35696-4_13

for cultural tourism has not disappeared, and all parts of the country are actively integrating digital technology into the form of cultural tourism. With the rise of artificial intelligence technology and the rapid development of science and technology, digital data processing methods will also be combined with intelligent algorithms. The new media alliance and balboa park online collaboration released the latest version of the new media alliance horizon report: 2016 museum edition, the digital humanities, intelligent scene space, virtual reality, information visualization technology in education interpretation and the important role of cultural museum, and points out the data based on interactive technology operation, innovative design, personalized experience, content and digital intelligent interaction is the key to accelerate the development trend of museum education technology [1].

The new social background and technology promote the integration of digital intelligence of cultural science popularization exhibition venues, which is not only the objective need of future development, but also the inevitable choice of future strategy. Based on the second generation model theory of UTAUT, this paper constructs the UTAUT user experience model with digital intelligence design integrated into Qingdao Undersea World, puts forward research index design and research assumptions, makes model description and analyzes the influencing factors of user acceptance, and makes discussions and suggestions according to the actual situation. The progress of The Times drives the innovation of tools and carriers, and the waves run horizontally through all vertical fields, making the world a matrix system [2]. Interactive, immersive digital intelligent experience and show the innovation of scientific transmission mode, to enhance the possible factors of reality, so the industry for the number of intelligence into the sea world of Qingdao innovative design strategy to explore, help to guarantee the high quality of the Qingdao Marine culture development, also for the outbreak of normal information data transmission and show the effective transmission innovation way.

2 Digital-Intelligent Design

2.1 The Concept of Digital Intelligence Design

Digital intelligence design (Digital Intelligence Design) is a new form of design in the digital age, which is a form of symbiosis between human and computer in the digital age, is a new relationship between human thinking and digital technology, and is a systematic thinking and method to solve the problems of the physical world and the virtual world [3]. Number intelligence design will we introduced the new digital age, compared with the flattening of the Internet age, is no longer simply based on user thinking experience design, but the digital technology, data statistics, storage, computer algorithm and human general reaction, judgment and even perception, the underlying logic is the computer algorithm of mutual fusion and virtual isomorphism [4].

In this process, the digital intelligence design has two sides of one body. Using digital technology, blockchain data sharing realizes common data communication, experience replication and high-speed and real-time information transmission, which is a unified integration of human experience and data and then calculated according to people's needs. This process overcomes the simplification of human individual knowledge and the limitation and volatility of memory storage. It originates from the whole wisdom of human beings and helps human individuals to expand the boundary of thinking and cognition.

2.2 Digital Intelligent Design into the Cultural Tourism Industry

To foster new forms, promote the Qingdao area tourism economy development, in September 2021, Qingdao tourism industry "difference" planning: construction of text brigade depth fusion development new heights points out: focus on strengthening tourism distribution system, tourism guide system, the construction of wisdom tourism system upgrade and establish the combination of online tourism market supervision mechanism [5]. At the same time, the epidemic has accelerated the process of integrating digital intelligence design, which also makes the cultural tourism industry have to incorporate it into the planning goal, relying on the network to provide the data, services and commodity information digitalization to the two sides for communication and cultivate the development of digital trade.

Qingdao is rich in cultural deposits, especially the deep integration of Marine culture and tourism industry, and is one of the excellent tourism cities in China. In May 2022, a notice was issued for Qingdao to carry out the digital transformation of the whole region, and to carry out the two-year digital transformation of Shinan District, Laoshan District and West Coast New Area [6]. The implementation of this implementation plan also indicates that Qingdao has started the digital transformation. This provides policy support for the integration of digital intelligence in Qingdao Undersea World located in Shinan District, and it is imperative to integrate digital intelligence into the cultural and tourism industry of Qingdao.

From the perspective of industry depth development and long-term development mechanism, Qingdao tourism fully integrated into the number of intellectualization design application development also has the following short board, after on-the-spot investigation and access to information, cultural tourism as a labor-intensive industry, most of the practitioners, including related industry log intellectualization development understanding and matching degree is not high, because involves large-scale changes and personnel structure restructuring and even large-scale transformation, promote the lack of enthusiasm. Also because of the traditional tourism industry mainly by the traditional industry and modern industry, most of the staff is given priority to with maintenance, the lack of emerging talent, for the number of intellectualization services, system development, design strategy, information maintenance work type professional requirements is higher, to some extent, restricted the development of the industry and after the effect of intellectualization design into.

3   Qingdao Underwater World Digital Intelligence Display UTAUT Model Construction

3.1   Unified Technology Adoption and Use Model

The UTAUT model (the unified theory of acceptance and use of technology) is shown in Fig. 1. On the basis of the problem of "factors influencing user cognition", the integrated technology acceptance model is proposed [7]. It is an integrated theory based on the technical acceptance model (TAM), integrating rational behavior theory, motivation model, planned behavior theory, integrated TAM and TPB model, PC utilization model, innovation diffusion theory, social cognition theory and other related theories and models [8]. For the research on the influence and willingness of audience experience preferences. Four of the dependent variables are also the core dimensions of the UTAUT model, including performance expectation, effort expectation, social impact, and facilitative factors.

In 2012, Venkatesh et others modified the UTAUT model structure, see Fig. 2. Three dependent variables, including hedonistic motivation, price value, and habit, were added, and four of the regulatory variables in the original model were adjusted to obtain the UTAUT second-generation extended model [9]. The user's willingness and final use behavior are directly influenced by the core dimensions in the UTAUT model.

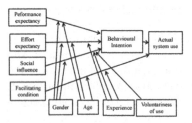
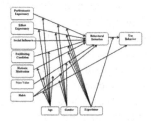

Fig. 1. Unified Technology Adoption and Use Model (UTAUT) Photo source: Baidu

Fig. 2. Second Generation Unified Technology Adoption and Use Model (UTAUT) Photo source: Baidu

4   The Study Hypothesis

4.1   Performance Expectations

Performance expectation variable (Performance Expectancy, PE) refers to the changes caused by the user in the context of work, study and life after visiting and learning. According to Bhattacher jee research, user satisfaction is determined by confirming prior expectations and performance expectations [10]. If the users helps the users in the future, the users' willingness to use the technology will be enhanced.

In this study, in the process of visiting the underwater world, they have produced a pleasant spiritual experience, acquired rich knowledge of Marine culture, and helped their own life, study and work, so that users can more recognize the display scheme of integrating digital intelligent design into the underwater world. If there is a negative direction impact or no impact, the user's willingness to participate in the project will weaken. Based on the above, the study proposes Hypothesis H1: the user performance expectation of Qingdao underwater world digital design presents a significant positive correlation with the viewer's willingness to use.

4.2   Work Expectations

The effort expectation variable (Effort Expectancy, EE) refers to "the degree to which the learner believes that using the system does not require effort [11]." If the underwater world is designed with a digital intelligence system, the influencing factors of the ease of use and complexity of the operation mode in the user experience are evaluated. In this study, if the user can quickly understand the use steps and correctly operate during the use process of using the interactive interface or viewing the interactive device, and believes that the technology or service has strong applicability and is more convenient, then the user's willingness to use the project is enhanced. Based on the above, the study proposes that hypothesis H2: Qingdao underwater world Digital Intelligence design shows users trying to expect a significant positive correlation with the viewer's willingness to use it.

4.3 Social Impact

Social impact variable (Social Influence, SI) refers to the assessment of the impact of the social environment on users 'willingness to use, which is determined by the individual's subjective will and the individual's own code of conduct. In other words, it reflects the degree to which one's attitudes, beliefs, and behaviors are influenced by others' consciousness [12]. In this study, if the classmates and family members have relevant hobbies, or the friends around them recommend the intelligent venue display, the user's willingness to use the project will be enhanced. Based on the above, it is proposed that hypothesis H3: the social influencing factors displayed in the digital intelligence design of Qingdao undersea world show a significant positive correlation on the viewer's willingness to use it.

4.4 Facilitating Factors

Facilitating factor variable (Facilitating Conditions, FC) refers to the degree of support for technology or equipment for the individual. In this study, the promoting factors mainly refer to the policy support and support degree of national and local logarithmic intelligent, digital and intelligent interactive venue construction, the support of the venue itself for exhibition upgrading and resource allocation; the new experience of emerging industries with science and technology progress; the new interpretation and display of good interaction and Marine culture; the high quality content and story, and these factors form the key points to promote users' willingness to use. If the policy is not conducive to the intelligent development of the venue number, the internal acceptance of emerging technologies is low, the positive degree of the staff is low, and the poor quality of the display content will also affect the users' willingness to use it. In this study, combined with the free admission policy welfare of Qingdao, the value price is integrated into the promoting factors, and based on the above, it is proposed that hypothesis H4: the promoting factors of Qingdao underwater world digital intelligence design display show a significant positive correlation on the viewer's willingness to use it.

4.5 Willingness to Use the Behavior

In this study, the willingness to use it is mainly reflected in the users' subjective acceptance of the venue display method of the future digital intelligent underwater world and whether the idea of experiencing the digital intelligent underwater world is generated.

Studies of behavioral willingness to use will further influence whether users will partici-pate in or experience actual activities in the future. Based on the above, it is assumed that H5: behavioral intention has a positive and significant impact on the user's participation in the use of the underwater world.

4.6 Pleasative Motivation (Spiritual Satisfaction)

Pleasic motivation mainly refers to the spiritual level of pleasure or good experience and interest when experiencing the project, which plays an important role in promoting the user's technical acceptance and use [13]. It makes users have emotional preferences to affect their willingness to use them. People with pleasure motivation are different from people with utilitarian motivation, and they pay more attention to happiness, pleasure and playing experience [14]. In this study, the normalization of the epidemic led to the decrease of recreational activities of many local tourists and the demand for the spiritual level. Whether participating in the digital intelligence exhibition of Qingdao Undersea World can enable users to obtain spiritual and emotional relaxation and happy experience has a certain impact on their use behavior. Based on the above, the research hypothesis assumes that H6: hedonic motivation (spiritual satisfaction) has a significant positive correlation effect on the user's acceptance of the digital-intelligent underwater world display.

5   The Study Hypothesis

5.1   Survey Index Design

Based on Venkatesh and Davis (2003) on the basis of the mature scale structure, the Qingdao underwater world in the process of field investigation and the interactive display key questionnaire index design, in the second generation UTAUT six core dimensions as the dependent variable and main factors assessment point, add age, gender and education level as a control variable. The answer assessment is designed to be "very agree", "agree", "general", "disagree" and "very disagree". The main evaluation point lies in the general acceptance of users' logarithmic intelligence design into the underwater world and the initial behavioral intention, which provide support for the later research. Using PE, EE, SI, FC, HM and BI, the specific hypothesis content and indicators are shown in Table 1 below.

5.2   Questionnaire Survey

The questionnaire was put on the questionnaire star platform online, and distributed and recovered in the form of WeChat link and poster scanning. The survey objects are mainly for tourists from all over the country and the intelligent design of the underwater world into the display users. A total of 441 valid questionnaires were collected as the empirical object of this study.

Table 1. Index meaning and index description

Variable	Measurement index	Indicator meaning
Performance expectations	PE1	When I attend the Marine Cultural Center, the digital intelligent and interactive experience can expose me to the experience of cutting-edge scientific and technological achievements and the dissemination of better information and data services
	PE2	The digital intelligent and interactive underwater culture display can make me learn the knowledge of Marine culture more clearly
	PE3	Intelligent and interactive exhibitions can give me a deeper understanding of the culture behind the exhibits
Strive to expect	EE1	Scanning the code to watch or match VR glasses is very simple for me
	EE2	Learning the operation method of electronic devices, I can easily understand the operation guide
Social influence	SI1	If my family and friends recommend the intelligent underwater world exhibition hall
	SI2	When the epidemic becomes normal, I will worry about the crowded personnel and choose the online intelligent underwater world exhibition
	SI3	Participating in the digital intelligent exhibition can get the recognition of my classmates or friends and family
Promoting agent	FC1	The reasonable price will prompt me to visit
	FC2	Quality interactive experience and appreciation of quality content will prompt me to visit
	FC3	National or local policy support will encourage me to visit (free admission for booking)

(*continued*)

Table 1. (*continued*)

Variable	Measurement index	Indicator meaning
Pleasure motivation	HM1	Immersive interactive experience of ocean culture makes me feel fresh and interesting
	HM2	Experience the Smart Marine Life Show with family or friends makes me even happier
	HM3	I am very interested in the presentation of Marine culture and modern digital media technology
Use the will	BI1	I would like to participate in the online or digital intelligent interactive aquarium exhibition
	BI2	If the aquarium exhibition makes me feel good, I will recommend it to my friends and family
	BI3	I am willing to pay attention to the information of the relevant cultural center and may participate again

Table 2. Basic information statistics of survey objects

Variable	Class	Number of people	Percentage (%)
Age	15~20 Years old	19	4.33
	Between 20 and 25 years old	194	44.19
	25~35 Years old	157	35.76
	Over 40 years old	69	15.72
Sex	Man	213	48.52
	Woman	226	51.48
Degree of education	Junior high school and below	44	10.02
	Senior middle school	193	43.96
	Undergraduate course	177	40.32
	Master and doctoral students	25	5.69

5.3 Description of the Statistics

According to Table 2, there are 19 and 194 people aged 15–20,20–25,25 to 35 years old, and over 40, respectively 157 people and 69 people, each accounting for 4.33%, 44.19%, 35.76% and 15.72%. For the gender, there were 213 boys and 226 boys and girls, respectively, accounting for 48.52% and 51.48% respectively. The male to female ratio was basically flat. In the case of education level, there are 44, 193, 177, and 25 doctoral students respectively, accounting for 10.02%, 43.96%, 40.32%, 5.69% respectively.

Table 3. Descriptive statistics and normality test of each measurement item

Project	Sample capacity	Least value	Crest value	Average value	Standard error	Skewness	Kurtosis
PE1	439	1	5	2.61	1.17	0.60	−0.45
PE2	439	1	5	2.62	1.21	0.64	−0.59
PE3	439	1	5	2.60	1.21	0.58	−0.58
EE1	439	1	5	2.42	1.14	0.63	−0.38
EE2	439	1	5	2.40	1.22	0.58	−0.66
SI1	439	1	5	2.52	1.21	0.53	−0.71
SI2	439	1	5	2.44	1.22	0.69	−0.45
SI3	439	1	5	2.50	1.28	0.54	−0.79
FC1	439	1	5	2.43	1.24	0.61	−0.66
FC2	439	1	5	2.40	1.18	0.71	−0.34
FC3	439	1	5	2.32	1.24	0.67	−0.60
HM1	439	1	5	2.47	1.18	0.59	−0.52
HM2	439	1	5	2.59	1.23	0.50	−0.74
HM3	439	1	5	2.37	1.21	0.70	−0.49
BI1	439	1	5	2.49	1.24	0.64	−0.61
BI2	439	1	5	2.50	1.27	0.60	−0.74
BI3	439	1	5	2.49	1.21	0.69	−0.53

As can be seen from Table 3, the measurement items 2.61, 2.62, 2.60, 2.42, 2.40, 2.52, 2.44, 2.50, respectively 2.43, 2.40, 2.32, 2.47, 2.59, 2.37, 2.49, 2.50, 2.49, the score between consent and general, the absolute value of each measurement indicator between 0 and 1, the absolute value of kurtosis between 0 and 1, does not show a serious skewed distribution, indicating that can be considered to follow the approximate normal distribution.

5.4 The Reliability Analysis

The Cronbach's α coefficient is between 0 and 1, where a larger value indicates a higher reliability. When the Cronbach's α coefficient is greater than or equal to 0.9, It indicates that the scale has a very high intrinsic reliability; When the Cronbach's α coefficient is greater than 0.7, Represents that the intrinsic reliability of the scale is acceptable; When the Cronbach's α coefficient is between 0.6 as to 0.7, It shows that the scale also has some reference significance after the adjustment of the project; If the Cronbach's α coefficient is less than 0.6, They think the scale is very problematic, Needs a redesign, This can be explained in combination with the total correlation (CIC) and the α coefficient deleted.

Table 4. Reliability analysis of the scale

project	Scale average after item items	Scale variance after removing the items	Correction Total correlation (CIT)	Item deleted α coefficient	Cronbach α Coefficient
PE1	5.22	5.143	0.771	0.857	0.891
PE2	5.20	4.888	0.793	0.837	
PE3	5.23	4.874	0.793	0.838	
EE1	2.40	1.487	0.734	-	0.846
EE2	2.42	1.304	0.734	-	
SI1	4.94	5.204	0.789	0.795	0.874
SI2	5.02	5.477	0.705	0.868	
SI3	4.95	4.913	0.782	0.800	
FC1	4.72	5.117	0.741	0.856	0.881
FC2	4.75	5.161	0.795	0.808	
FC3	4.83	5.017	0.771	0.829	
HM1	4.96	4.845	0.770	0.772	0.860
HM2	4.85	4.926	0.704	0.834	
HM3	5.06	4.864	0.733	0.806	
BI1	5.00	5.023	0.799	0.779	0.872
BI2	4.98	5.102	0.748	0.826	
BI3	4.99	5.498	0.719	0.851	

Confidence analysis was tested for the reliability of the scale data, as shown in Table 4. Through reliability analysis, the Cronbach's α coefficient of the questionnaire was 0.891, 0.846, 0.874, 0.881, 0.860 and 0.872 respectively, which showed the overall high reliability and good internal consistency, the total correlation (TC) was greater than 0.3, and the α coefficient of the deleted item was not higher than the dimension Cronbach's α coefficient, indicating a high overall reliability.

5.5 Validity Test

The closer the KMO validity coefficient is to 1, the better the validity, the more suitable the factor analysis is suitable for factor analysis; the validity coefficient is appropriate; greater than 0.7 indicates acceptable validity; greater than 0.6 indicates average validity; below 0.6, the validity is inappropriate.

Table 5. KMO and Bartlett tests

KMO price		0.948
Bartlett Sphelicity test	Approximate chi-square	5593.309
	df	136
	p price	0.000

As can be seen in Table 5 above, the approximate chi-square values and KMO values are 5593.309 and 0.948, respectively. The chi-square value test is significant (P = 0.000 < 0.05), and the KMO value is greater than 0.9, indicating very good validity. Next, the validity is illustrated through confirmatory factor analysis, see Fig. 3.

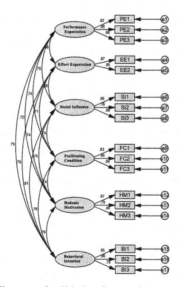

Fig. 3. Model diagram of validation factor of standardized estimation

Table 6. Standardization factor load and Cr, ave value inspection statistics

Subactive variables	Subactive variables	Standard load coefficient	CR	AVE
Performance expectations	PE1	0.824	0.890	0.730
	PE2	0.880		
	PE3	0.859		
Strive to expect	EE1	0.867	0.847	0.735
	EE2	0.847		
Social influence	SI1	0.864	0.876	0.703
	SI2	0.755		
	SI3	0.890		
Promoting agent	FC1	0.829	0.882	0.714
	FC2	0.863		
	FC3	0.842		
Pleasure motivation	HM1	0.869	0.862	0.676
	HM2	0.793		
	HM3	0.803		
Use the will	BI1	0.851	0.873	0.697
	BI2	0.859		
	BI3	0.793		

See Table 6, the confirmatory factor analysis is used to illustrate the convergence validity of the scale, and it is considered good if the observed variables correspond and aggregate well with the latent variables. It is generally considered that the standardized factor load coefficient is greater than 0.7 indicates a good correspondence between the dimension and the item; if the standardized factor load coefficient is less than 0.6, the relationship between the dimension and the project should be weak, and the combined reliability (CR) value is greater than 0.7 and the average extraction variance (AVE) value is greater than 0.5, then the convergence validity meets the requirements.

According to the table above Table 7, the AVE square-root value of performance expectation is 0.855, which is greater than performance expectation and effort expectation, social impact, facilitating factors, and the correlation coefficient of hedonic motivation and willingness to use respectively is 0.590, 0.666, 0.656, 0.629, and 0.691. The AVE square root value of effort expectation is 0.857, which is greater than the correlation coefficient with social influence, facilitating factor, hedonistic motivation and use willingness 0.587, 0.614, 0.628 and 0.653. Similarly, the social influence, facilitating factor, hedonistic motivation and use intention AVE square root value is greater than the maximum correlation coefficient with other dimensions, indicating that the differentiation validity is good. See Fig. 4 for the standardized structure equation model.

Table 7. Discriminant validity: Pearson correlation and ave square root value

	Performance expectations	Strive to expect	social influence	promoting agent	Pleasure motivation	Use the will
Performance expectations	0.855					
Strive to expect	0.590**	0.857				
social influence	0.666**	0.587**	0.838			
promoting agent	0.656**	0.614**	0.653**	0.845		
Pleasure motivation	0.629**	0.628**	0.664**	0.655**	0.822	
Use the will	0.691**	0.653**	0.707**	0.702**	0.684**	0.835

5.6 Structural Equation Model

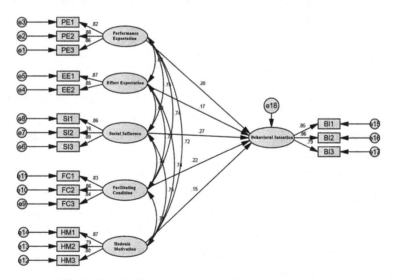

Fig. 4. Standardized structural equation model estimation

Table 8. Fitting index interpretation and numerical evaluation reference

The parameter name	Reference for interpretation and numerical evaluation
CMIN/DF	CMIN/DF is the chi-square degree of freedom ratio, and when its value is less than 3.0, the fit of the model is better. The fit is acceptable at 3–5
GFI	GFI is the fit index, with acceptable values of 0.85–0.9, and values above 0.9 are preferred
AGFI	AGFI is the adjusted fit index, and the value of AGFI is between 0–1, closer to 1, Table The better the fit of the model, the value of 0.8–0.9 is acceptable, and that above 0.9 is better
NFI, TLI, CFI, IFI	The three are the comparative adaptation index The closer the index value is to 1, the better the adaptation degree of the model. 0.9 meets the general requirements, and the model adaptation is perfect when the index is 0.95
RMSEA	RMSEA is the approximate residual root mean square, the smaller the value, the better the fit of the model, when less than 0.05, the model can achieve a good fit, less than 0.08, the model adaptation is accepted

Table 9. Model fitting degree

Model fit	Adaptation standard		Model fit values	fitting degree
	admissibility	good		
Absolute Fit NC (Cmin/df)	3–5	1–3	1.733	good
Goodness of fit index (GFI)	>0.85	>0.9	0.956	good
Adjusted Adapindex (AGFI)	>0.80	>0.9	0.935	good
Approximately residual root (RMSEA)	<0.08	<0.05	0.041	good
Standardized index (NFI)	>0.85	>0.9	0.968	good
Value Adter Index (IFI)	>0.85	>0.9	0.986	good
Unnormalized index (TLI)	>0.85	>0.9	0.982	good
Comparison of the fit index (CFI)	>0.85	>0.9	0.986	good

According to Table 8 and 9 above, overall, GFI, AGFI, RMSEA, NFI, IFI, TLI, and CFI are 1.733, 0.956, 0.935, 0.041, 0.968, 0.986, 0.982, 0.986, respectively, and the whole model is well adapted.

From Table 10, the non-standardized path coefficients are 0.204, 0.173, 0.251, 0.218, and 0.162, and the standardized path coefficients are 0.201, 0.169, 0.271, 0.216, 0.149,

Table 10. Latent variable path coefficient and hypothesis verification

path relationship		Estimate	S.Estimate	S.E.	C.R.	P
Use the will	<---	0.204	0.201	0.062	3.286	0.001
Use the will	<---	0.173	0.169	0.062	2.784	0.005
Use the will	<---	0.251	0.271	0.061	4.123	<0.001
Use the will	<---	0.218	0.216	0.065	3.372	<0.001
Use the will	<---	0.162	0.149	0.075	2.156	0.031

C.R. The values were 3.286, 2.784, 4.123, 3.372, and 2.156, respectively, indicating that the performance expectation, effort expectation, social influence, facilitator factors, and hedonic motivation had a positive and significant influence on the willingness to use the intention.

5.7 Multigroup Regulation Model Test

Table 11. Age adjustment test

path relationship			Under 25 years old (N = 213)			25 years and older (N = 226)		
			Estimate	C.R.	P	Estimate	C.R.	P
Use the will	<---	Performance expectations	0.151	1.693	0.090	0.233	2.632	0.008
Use the will	<---	Strive to expect	0.146	2.087	0.037	0.230	2.120	0.034
Use the will	<---	social influence	0.311	3.913	<0.001	0.153	1.603	0.109
Use the will	<---	promoting agent	0.236	2.878	0.004	0.207	2.053	0.040
Use the will	<---	Pleasure motivation	0.139	1.402	0.161	0.202	1.889	0.059

From the above Table 11, in the influence path of performance expectation on use intention, the P value of those under 25 years old is 0.09, and there is no significant influence. The P value of those 25 years old and above is 0.008, and performance expectation has a significant influence on use intention. This indicates that age has a significant moderating effect between use intention and performance expectation. In the influence path of effort expectation on use intention, s social influence has a significant influence on use intention for those under 25 years old (P < 0.001), and the P value of

182 M. Lin and Y. Huang

Table 12. Gender adjustment test

Path relationship			Male (N = 213)			Female (N = 226)		
			Estimate	C.R.	P	Estimate	C.R.	P
Use the will	<---	Performance expectations	0.202	2.420	0.016	0.233	2.632	0.008
Use the will	<---	Strive to expect	0.234	2.898	0.004	0.230	2.120	0.034
Use the will	<---	social influence	0.284	2.898	0.004	0.153	1.603	0.109
Use the will	<---	promoting agent	0.133	1.589	0.112	0.207	2.053	0.040
Use the will	<---	Pleasure motivation	0.137	1.245	0.213	0.202	1.889	0.059

25 years old and above is 0.109, which does not have a significant influence, indicating that age has a moderating effect on this path.

From Table 12 above, we can see that gender has a moderating effect between performance expectation, effort expectation, social influence, facilitating factors, hedonic motivation and intention to use.

Table 13. Adjustment test of educational level

Path relationship			High school and below (N = 237)			Bachelor degree or above (N = 202)		
			Estimate	C.R.	P	Estimate	C.R.	P
Use the will	<---	Performance expectations	0.254	3.189	0.001	0.138	1.391	0.164
Use the will	<---	Strive to expect	0.189	2.124	0.034	0.166	1.905	0.057
Use the will	<---	Social influence	0.150	1.795	0.073	0.385	4.241	<0.001
Use the will	<---	promoting agent	0.188	2.297	0.022	0.233	2.369	0.018
Use the will	<---	Pleasure motivation	0.143	1.373	0.170	0.195	1.842	0.065

From Table 13 above, It can be seen from the above table that education level has a certain moderating effect on the influence of performance expectation, effort expectation, social influence, and hedonic motivation on the use intention, while there is no significant moderating effect on the influence of promoting factors on the use intention.

6 Proposal and Discussion of Digital Intelligence Design of Qingdao Undersea World

Based on the model analysis results, the performance expectation, effort expectation, social impact, facilitating factors (including price) and hedonic motivation all have significant positive direction factors for users to accept the digital intelligence design into the Qingdao underwater world. According to the field investigation, the author conducted the field investigation in the peak season. On May 30, 2022, Qingdao News Network released A notice that starting from June 1, 2022, some A-level tourist attractions in Qingdao will be allowed to watch the tickets with their identity information. Under the normalization of the epidemic, the real economy and tourism have suffered a huge impact. By the end of 2021, although it remains a large gap from the level of 2019, it has recovered compared with 2020, but according to the latest data on July 15, 2022 and the statistical results of domestic tourism sample survey. In the first half of 2022, the total number of domestic tourists was 1.455 billion, down 22.2% over the previous year, and the domestic tourism revenue (total tourism consumption) was 1.17 trillion yuan, down 28.2% over the previous year [15].

According to the field research, for Qingdao Undersea World, since the free admission, the reservation ticket registration has been welcomed by the majority of domestic and foreign tourists. Due to the dense and closed environment, people wearing masks with poor air circulation will also have the impact of experience. Different areas due to the venue attraction difference, there is obvious audience uneven distribution, venues often appear congestion, which is the most serious tunnel, 2.5 m wide tunnel into half conveyor belt and half fixed viewing area free channel, regardless of the premise of dense crowd, around the full transparent glass let a person can be more clearly watched to all kinds of Marine creatures rich strange dynamic trajectory. From the perspective of cultural science popularization and transmission, as one of the most attractive venues, it is difficult to clearly display the popular science information of Marine organisms under the comprehensive environment. The channel is single, which is only the paper introduction at the bottom of the glass, with small text and short stay time, so it is difficult to effectively distinguish and receive information.

Based on the model analysis results and insight into field investigation, the following strategic suggestions are proposed for the design of Qingdao undersea world.

6.1 Intelligent Multiple Information Transfer Mode Design

The design comes from solving the problems in life. In the process of establishing the digital intelligent design system in Qingdao undersea world, first of all, the large flow of people in the peak season hinders the effective transmission of Marine cultural popular science information. According to the results of the significant positive impact of performance expectations, people attach great importance to the understanding and exploration of the future related technology and Marine culture through the underwater world. In the process of field investigation, the exhibition areas of popular science popularization venues are mostly presented in plane or curved walls, which leads to the fact that, although the exhibition area of some venues is large, the actual viewing area is only 1 or 2 rows of spectators parallel to the wall lines. Reference of Suzhou museum scan code

to watch, can the collection or specimens with electronic image display and voice interpretation mode of information transmission, along with the technology upgrade can also
use the VR or holographic projection specimen collection intelligent stereo playback,
so can make full use of the number of intellectualization data unity accurately passed to
humans, through the data unified to upload processing, can also be combined with artificial intelligence technology, the user voice questions, effective database extraction form
human-computer communion to the completion of human-machine communication,
further form efficient information transmission and intelligent, mass data reflect.

6.2 Suggestions on Bridge Interaction Design for Digital Intelligence Integration

Number intellectualization design into the life, into the development of the travel industry, you need someone machine communion in the middle of the media and channels,
interactive interface as a designer, communication, the bridge between man-machine,
need according to the UTAUT2 model efforts expected factors to provide detailed data
for reference, give full consideration to the participation of different age groups, for the
choice of style. Based on the influencing factors of user experience, the suggestions of
flat style and aging design are put forward. The flat style is not called the minimalist
design style, and the Microsoft company even directly called it the digital design [16]. To
express its high matching to the modern digital presentation mode. Its design principles
by minimizing design elements to achieve clear visual information not only with contemporary aesthetic form, at the same time also can be cut unnecessary factors for the elderly
or children's visual interference, affect the use of operation, its use as far as possible
concise elements will function the concept consistent with the practical requirements of
aging design fit. That is in the process of specific requirements for the overall interaction interface is concise and clear, high fault tolerance, focus function, easy to operate,
beautiful and orderly, intelligent, intelligent expression can be integrated into now has
been very mature voice command function, to achieve the control function, information
data, intelligent processing three dimensions of interactive media construction purpose.

6.3 Visualization of Marine Cultural Information

Qingdao Undersea World has the relevant functions of Marine culture and popular science education. With the advantage of geographical location, the venue shows a vivid
image. Combined with the social influencing factors, people can not only feel the Marine
life dynamics and real life scenes, expand the knowledge of Marine culture, but also
effectively avoid the local gathering of people. Nowadays, under the current situation,
the display of Marine biological information and biological entity dynamics is restricted
by the environment. The traditional information identification card cannot track the corresponding dynamic Marine life. At the same time, if the number of posts is too large, it
will also affect the viewing experience. In the process of integrating the digital intelligent
design into the underwater world display system, the information visualization technology can be applied, so as to better realize the process of effective data mining, feedback
information and receiving information to become more vivid, vivid and accurate, intelligent and accurate information transmission in a short time, and improve the efficiency.
The specific presentation step can be divided into three categories. Basic information

and data are uploaded and stored in the cloud by digital technology; the second step is to match the information images, match the information with the Marine biological images and the basic dynamics, and establish the system identification and classification. The third step is the interactive perception. Through the relevant interactive media, we can match the text data information and the biological visual image information and connect the users simultaneously, so that the audience can receive the targeted, selectively and accurate information. Based on the above requirements, in the process of cultivating intelligent interactive professionals, the cultural and tourism industry can mainly focus on three major parts: data mapping, view transformation and interactive perception [17].

6.4   Immersive Intelligent Experience Mode

The integration of value, price and content experience into promoting factors combined with the current spiritual needs of hedonistic motivation, and the integration of logarithmic intelligence design into the Qingdao undersea world form a significant positive impact, which means that people not only pay attention to the promoting factors of price value, but also put forward requirements for the reception and spiritual experience of high-quality information content. With new media equipment into the public view, holographic projection, dynamic capture, AR, MR and a series of high-tech display media for information presentation is no longer limited to flat network graphics digital transmission, immersive interactive experience is no longer novel, Qingdao underwater world as a national 4 a class tourist scenic spot under the call of policy should also be continuous innovation, combining modern science and technology media and venue core features. The digital age has magnified the importance of emotion in information dissemination and cultural production [18], People are no longer just satisfied with the looking at, based on the design of the five senses, with the new technology and equipment, to create an immersive intelligent interactive underwater world. With the three dimensions of "scene", "role" and "emotion" [19], the concept of digital intelligence is combined with the external model of Marine biology to simulate its dynamics, response and sound, and build a new path for immersive experience to show the wisdom of underwater biology. Let users can not only see, but also "touch" colorful, different kinds of Marine life, play and interact with it. This will more effectively enhance the user's travel experience, and leave a deep impression on it, so as to promote the influencing factors of the willingness to use it, and complete the fission promotion and publicity.

6.5   Build a New Form of Digital and Intelligent Tourism Cultural

Online shopping has provided great convenience for users during the epidemic period, and provided a feasible reference for the online tourism cultural and creative industry model. According to the investigation, the shopping area of Qingdao Undersea World and the cultural and creative area are set up separately. The shopping area is mainly concentrated on edible seafood, and the cultural and creative area is IP image cartoon dolls, folding fans, umbrellas, stationery, etc. Some of which are designed by the author's design team. According to the analysis of real sales data and field research data, people's aquarium IP extended cultural and creative products are generally displayed during the epidemic period. Through the horizontal comparison of IP extension products such as

Shanghai Disneyland and Universal Studios, it is found that the IP background story and users' emotional identity are the main factors influencing the formation of purchase desire. For example, Disney will continue to strengthen the emotional link between IP characters and users through the float tour, animated film and television communication, and doll interaction, and build three streaming media platforms: "Dinsney +", "ESPN +" and "Hulu" [20]. Fusion and promotion. After entering the park, based on high-quality content, enrich the IP matrix to continuously enhance the sense of familiarity and interact in the park, so that users will pay emotionally when they see the relevant derivatives again. However, in the Undersea World of Qingdao, relevant IP images have never appeared in the viewing process of watching the whole route, which makes it difficult for the audience to find the connection between the favorite Marine creatures and IP derivatives, and even feel abrupt and strange. In this context, Qingdao Undersea World also provides the foundation support in the process of integrating the digital intelligence design strategy for the subsequent cultural and creative sales. Can use the fusion of different media for IP promotion, will the sea IP world image "dream ocean group" innovation IP content, with the help of new equipment to establish three-dimensional image architecture and interaction, increase the user impression and emotional contact, in the process, based on large data of intelligence algorithm, for different groups of content, active related derivatives push, even can be combined with the sea world geographical cultural background, the online virtual tourism, namely the combination of Internet services and offline field experience travel [21]. Through network and virtual technology, users in the living environment of IP image and interact and communicate with them. It can not only improve the matching degree between IP image and users' emotions, but also promote the improvement of IP image establishment and communication efficiency in the hearts of users, and can better carry out emotional marketing so as to build a new business form of cultural and tourism derivatives integrated with digital intelligence.

7   Digital Intelligent Design into the Future of Cultural Tourism Industry

In the second generation UTAUT model theory research analysis of user experience and proposed acceptance research, in the Qingdao undersea world into digital intelligent design research simulation of price value into promoting factors, get performance expectations, expectations, social influence factors, promoting factors, pleasure motivation are significant positive direction influence on the user, produced the number of intelligence into the demand. Looking at the world, when the current epidemic is normalized, the tourism industry with people gathering has become an inevitable trend to create a new digital and intelligent tourism mode based on the Internet, combining online and offline, which provides a certain degree of security guarantee for people. The author thinks that for Qingdao underwater world and even the same type of museum, museum, etc., with the help of modern science and technology exhibits digital presentation, into intelligent interaction for human-computer interaction, for cultural collections or cultural information is also a new way of inheritance development, the cloud storage technology to realize the batch data to upload and download extraction, no longer rely on the traditional "word of mouth". And computers also have larger and longer-lasting reserves than the capacity of the human brain.

Human beings build an intelligent database with the intelligence of groups, which is also feeding back human individuals, providing us with convenience and solving problems. In this process, the government's policy support and the professional training of related talents are also needed. While popularizing them vigorously, the differences of individual factors and the psychological distance between man and man-machine should also be considered. The social environment is constantly changing, and the way of design to deal with problems is also constantly innovating. The future of digital intelligence is the man-machine integration and the co-prosperity of man-machine.

References

1. Freeman, A., Adams-Becker, S., Cummings, M., et al.: New Media Alliance Horizon Report: 2016 Museum Edition Open Learning Research, pp. 1–13 (2016)
2. Mochira, D.: The Digital Future, translated by Xue Liang. Modern Press, Beijing, pp. 5–8 (2020)
3. Gu, C., Wang, F.: "Digital intelligence design" - a new form of design in the digital age. Decoration (12), 52–65 (2021)
4. Qi, Y.: Legal regulation of the digital and intelligent society. Soc. Sci. Digest (04), 4–7 (2022)
5. The "14th Five-Year Plan" of Qingdao's tourism industry was released: building a new highland for the deep integration and development of culture and tourism. https://news.qingda onews.com/qingdao/2021-09/02/content_22866361.htm. Accessed 02 Sep 2021
6. Qingdao carries out digital transformation in all regions and fields! The West Coast New Area of Laoshan District, Shinan District was selected as the first batch of pilot projects. https://fin ance.qingdaonews.com/wap/2022-05/23/content_23217045.htm. Accessed 23 May 2022
7. Vencatesh, V., Morris, M.G., Davis, G.B., et al.: User acceptance of information technology: towards a unified vision. Heart Manag. Inf. Syst. Q. 27(3), 425–478 (2003)
8. Li, W., Lu, S.: To construct a theoretical model of the influencing factors that researchers accept the OA knowledge base-intelligence theory and practice 33(2), 73–76 (2010)
9. Yang, L., Liu, G., Zhai, H.: Research on the influencing factors of science museum users accepting intelligent interactive exhibitions designed for user experience. Ind. Eng. Des. 3(06), 10–22 (2021)
10. Bhattacherjee, A.: This paper examines cognitive beliefs and affect influencing one's intention to continue using (continuance) information systems (IS). Expect.-Confirmat 48(2), 162–164 (2010)
11. Chiu, C.-M., Wang, E.T.: Understanding web-based learning continuance intention: the role of subjective task value. Inf. Manag. 45(3), 194–201 (2008)
12. Stone, R.W., Baker-Eveleth, L.: Students' expectation, confirmation, and continuance intention to use electronic textbooks. Comput. Hum. Behav. 29(3), 984–990 (2013)
13. Hong, J.-C., Lin, P.-H., Hsieh, P.-C.: The effect of consumer innovativeness on perceived value and continuance intention to use smartwatch. Comput. Hum. Behav. 67, 264–272 (2017)
14. Hong, S.-J., Thong, J.Y.L., Moon, J.-Y., Tam, K.-Y.: Understanding the behavior of mobile data services consumers. Inf. Syst. Front. 10(4), 431–445 (2008)
15. Ministry of Culture and Tourism: The total number of domestic tourists in the first half of 2022 is 1.455 billion. https://finance.qingdaonews.com/wap/2022-05/23/content_23217045.htm
16. Li, T., Cao, R.: The "honesty" of flat UI design and its expression principles. Packag. Eng. 40(10), 18–21 (2019)
17. Lin, G.: Application of information visualization technology in intelligent interactive talent training. Design (08), 144–145 (2015)

18. Lin, C.: The application of information visualization technology in the cultivation of intelligent interactive talents. Design (08), 144–145 (2015)
19. Zhang, Q.: Three dimensions of immersive experience construction of metaverse movies. Film Lit. (11), 75–79 (2022)
20. Du Xian's opinion on the localized operation of the classic IP industry chain in the era of pan-entertainment, taking Disney as an example, small audio-visual industry (radio and television technology) (05), 120–123 (2018)
21. Zhang, Y.: Market potential evaluation and short-term prediction of online tourism consumption in China—is based on grey system theory (19), 38–40 (2021)

Research on the Strategy of Digital Services in the Adoption Scene of Pet Shelters

Jianan Liu[✉] and Yichen Wu

School of Industrial Design, China Academy of Art, Hangzhou, China
2221351252@caa.edu.cn

Abstract. Shelters are mainly established out of love in the name of individuals or a few people. Due to the limited time, energy, and money of the managers themselves, they cannot effectively maintain the status quo for a long time. In terms of supplies, pets, adoption, etc. The information management experience is not good; on the other hand, most adopters still hold a negative attitude towards the adoption method for reasons such as private security, channel credibility, and pet health. The intervention of digital services can effectively solve their problems in information management, resource allocation, trust building, etc., and improve pet adoption's success rate, indirectly alleviating stray pets' social problems. Therefore, based on the current development dilemma of shelters and the social background of pet adoption, this paper adopts a mixed quantitative and qualitative research method and summarizes the core pain points of pet adoption in the shelter scene at the current stage through relevant tools of service design, and puts forward a discussion on digitalization. The design strategy and principles of the service in the shelter scenario are of great significance to the digital transformation of the shelter.

Keywords: Digital Service · Pet Adoption · Shelter · Design Strategy

1 Introduction

Under the impact of the epidemic (COVID-19), the number of stray pets (mainly cats and dogs) is on the rise globally. According to incomplete statistics, at least 600 million stray pets worldwide exist. Among them, the number of stray pets in China accounts for about 50 million, and the data is still increasing. Its sources are mainly abandoned by breeders and wild breeding. Stray pets have brought a series of problems to society, including aggressive behavior, nuisance, urban sanitation, epidemics, etc. Therefore, alleviating the problem of stray pets is urgent [1, 2].

Currently, the means to control the number of stray pets mainly include: promulgation of laws and regulations, registration of pets and breeders, additional taxes, education and guidance of breeders, promotion of sterilization programs, treatment and rescue of stray pets, etc.; It also includes extreme treatment methods such as euthanasia and shooting [3]. The organizations involved include the government, shelters, pet agencies, etc. Among them, the pet shelter, as a voluntary public welfare organization, has assumed part of its social responsibilities—rescuing and adopting these stray pets and helping them find adopters as much as possible. However, due to the limitations of the person in charge in terms of time, energy, and economic level, it is not easy to effectively maintain the status quo for a long time [4]. At the same time, based on the soundness of China's legal policies and the current development of relief shelters, the lack of professional guarantees and extra support makes it difficult for these spontaneous non-governmental organizations to survive [1]. On the one hand, the shelter has poor experience in managing and disseminating materials and pet information. On the other hand, due to factors such as expected cost deviation, channel reliability, pet health, and breed, most adopters have low acceptance and trust in adoption channels and even give up halfway through the adoption [5–8], which will lead to the saturation of the number of pets in the shelter. Therefore, improving the public's willingness to accept pet adoption, reducing failed adoption experiences, and increasing the retention rate after adoption are essential means to solve the problem of adoption at shelters and are also the research purpose of this paper. This article mainly answers two questions: 1. What are the pain points or needs in the adoption process in the shelter scenario? 2. How to solve these problems or meet these needs?

In the second part, we summarize the concepts related to pet adoption and digital services. The third part introduces the research methods and tools used. The fourth part elaborates on the research process in detail (mainly divided into two parts: user research and case analysis). The fifth part presents the design concept and explains the design strategy in detail. The sixth part conceives the future business model of the shelter and discusses the feasibility of some design strategies. In the end, we highlight the conclusions of the study and its limitations.

2 Introduction

2.1 Pet Adoption

Adoption is usually not the first choice for people. Research shows that the desire for a purebred pet is one of the most common reasons for not adopting from a shelter or rescue [5]. In addition, characteristics such as age, breed, quantity, and neutering status of pets are vital factors affecting adopters' decisions [9]. At the same time, the professional level of the person in charge and the help provided during and after the adoption process are also important influencing factors [6]. Some studies have also investigated the reasons for adoption failures. Although there are many reasons for adoption failure, including pet aggression, poor relationship with children, personality defects, physical diseases, etc., they can all be attributed to poor decision-making before adoption and high expected cost [7, 10]. There is considerable uncertainty about the consequences of pet ownership, which can lead to perceived costs to adopters exceeding real benefits, resulting in animals being abandoned or returned [5]. Suppose adopters obtain more information about pets before adoption. In that case, they can obtain more services and guarantees after adoption (such as: designing some mechanisms to screen adopters, knowing about future responsibilities in advance, providing obedience training guidance, Consulting services after adoption, etc.), some of these problems are likely to be resolved (mainly including adoption acceptance, adoption success rate, and post-adoption retention rate).

2.2 Digital Service

Digital services use the Internet, big data, artificial intelligence, blockchain, and other new-generation information technologies to significantly improve organizations' productivity and efficiency and ensure the overall image and service quality [11]. The current digital services for pet adoption mainly focus on the early and middle stages of the adoption process [12] Wu et al. tried to optimize the current social assistance system for stray animals through technical means (big data, artificial intelligence, etc.) [13]. Allison created an app that allows adopters to match their favorite pets according to their preferences. The purpose is to simplify the adoption process and provide more convenience for stray animals [14]. Da et al. added an AI virtual pet module to the pet adoption application, which allows users to assess the risks and challenges of raising in advance. In addition to paying attention to the service experience before and during adoption, pet retention after adoption and cultivating the breeder's sense of responsibility are equally important [6, 8]. At the same time, digital adoption services usually include the following problems: channels are scattered and lack credibility (mainly attached to small programs or mainstream social platforms for information dissemination), adopters worry about information security and pet health, etc. [2, 14].

3   Methodology

The focus of this article is to take the adoption scene of a pet shelter as an example and propose a design strategy that includes digital services. Before that, it is necessary to obtain honest user feedback in this scenario. First of all, the questionnaire survey is the first step in the research, and the purpose is to understand people's fundamental views on pets. Secondly, this paper uses natural observation and semi-structured interviews as the primary method to conduct in-depth understanding with relevant professionals and extracts keywords from the dialogue, laying the foundation for the subsequent strategy. Then, summarize and integrate the previous quantitative and qualitative research contents and present them through Persona and User Journey Maps. Finally, use the case analysis method to sort out the functions of some representative solutions and provide a reference for strategy research (As shown Table 1).

Table 1. Research steps

Phase	Method	Content
1	Questionnaire Survey	Understanding the basic situation of pet keeping
2	Natural observation	Collecting user needs of shelters and adopters
	Interview	
3	User research	Present pain points and demand in a visual way
4	Case study	Analyze the functions of existing adoption platforms

4 Research Process

4.1 Questionnaire Survey

In this survey, 295 questionnaires were distributed through the online platform, and the number of valid questionnaires was finally determined to be 244 after screening according to the time of filling in the answers and the identity of the breeder. The results show that female breeders account for a large proportion (about 73%), mainly young people aged 18–25 (about 81%), and the average monthly expenditure of pets is between 0–600 yuan (about 92%)). Sickness and nursing care (about 86%) and foster care (about 60%) are the two areas that breeders worry about the most. Disease (about 72%), loss (about 58%), and training (about 52%) are the main factors that annoy breeders. Playing with pets (about 93%), petting pets with friends (about 50%), and sharing pet content on social platforms (about 43%) are the main behaviors that make breeders happy. (As shown in Fig. 1, only the primary data are shown in the figure).

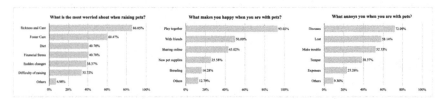

Fig. 1. Some data from the questionnaire

4.2 Field Visit

Naturalistic observations and interviews aim to develop a deep understanding of user needs. We visited eight pet institutions (including two shelters, three pet stores, and three pet hospitals). We conducted a semi-structured interview of about 30 min with each relevant person in charge (from basic personal information, institution operations, breeder/customer situation, and made a brief record (mainly in the form of photography and memorandum) with the prior consent of the interviewee. Only some critical statements are shown in the text (Table 2). The main reasons users hold negative attitudes towards keeping or adopting pets include concerns about pet health, lack of online services, low credibility of the platform, and ambiguity in the adoption process. The existing problems of the shelters include inconvenient information management, troublesome regular return visits, and low adoption success rate. According to the interviewees' point of view, if we want to solve the problem of stray pets, we need to start from the source (such as the improvement of national laws, the attention of the local government, etc.) and rely on the efforts of a few people is not a long-term solution. From a strategic perspective, improving the quality of breeders and doing an excellent job of disease prevention and health protection after pet breeding are essential means to improve the adoption and retention rates.

Table 2. Some oral materials and keyword extraction

Institution	Original oral presentation	Keywords
Corner Pet Store	"Breeders themselves should be highly educated in order for pets to have a healthier living environment"	Quality education for the breeders
April Pet Clinic	"Vaccinations and antibody testing are best done in the early stages"	Good prevention and protection work
Hui Jia Pet Hospital	"There are many categories and brands of food, so breeders don't know how to choose, and some products with good reputation may not be suitable for their pets"	Knowledge of breeding Daily management of pets
Lapin Coco Pet Store	"Since the abandonment rate is getting increasingly high, creating a vicious cycle, I want every pet to have a good home"	Rejection of abandonment
NOVA PETS	"Too many pet stores, imperfect online platform, less services"	Lack of online services
Pet International Animal Hospital	"Some customers abandoned their pets because the cost of disease treatment was too expensive"	Concern for pet health
Simida shelter	"in each platform we have released adoption information, but few people really come to adopt, people's awareness of adoption or breeding awareness is not mature, which is also related to national policy" "To adopt, adopters need to sign an agreement and submit your personal information and part of the deposit, which will be refunded after a few months"	Low credibility of the platform Low adoption success rate (related to the complexity and ambiguity of the adoption process) Information management
Cui's Small Home	"I'm not even too sure about the pets I adopt out, and I return to each pet on a regular interval"	Regular return visits

4.3   User Research and Analysis

We constructed Persona of adopters and shelter leaders using the previous questionnaire survey and field investigation. Persona is an effective tool to outline target users, connect user appeals and design direction, and can represent the primary audience and target group of the product. The adopter is described as a young woman working in the city and living a fast-paced life. Since she lives alone in an apartment, she wants a pet to accompany her to relieve loneliness. The demand is that she does not want to keep pet cubs because it takes more energy to take care of them. She weakly understands adoption channels and does not understand the adoption process, so she thinks it is unreliable. The person in charge is generalized as a middle-aged woman who has her own business and, at the same time, takes care of the stray pets at the shelter. Her motivation for setting up shelters is to wish them all a good home out of compassion and respect. The shelter's daily expenses mainly rely on personal finances, but as the number of pets increases, it often receives material donations from all over the country. The shelter's biggest problem is the difficulty of adoption and the constant adoption of new pets, increasing pressure on the institution.

Based on Persona, we connected the details of the adoption process (including stages, steps, behaviors, touchpoints, emotions, and ideas) through the timeline. We presented them as User Journey Maps (Fig. 2). It is a tool for visualizing an individual's journey or process. It is designed to help designers build consensus and create opportunities for improving the user experience.

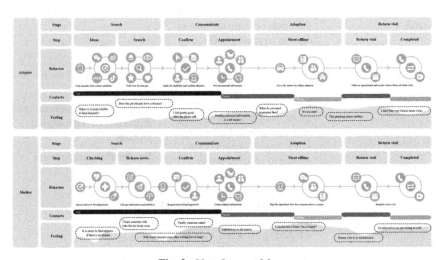

Fig. 2.   User Journey Maps

At the same time, due to the scene's complexity, it will involve the participation of multiple stakeholders, which need to be considered together here. Therefore, we combed through the Stakeholder Maps to sort out the map of interest relationships centered on adopters and shelters to provide a complete perspective for subsequent strategic insights (Fig. 3).

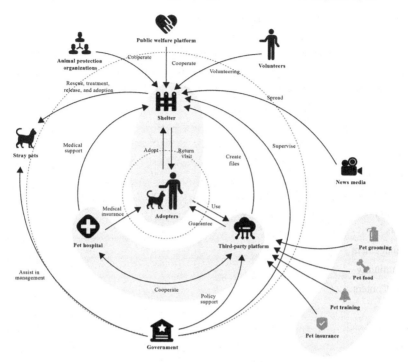

Fig. 3. Stakeholder Maps

4.4 Case Analysis

We conduct functional analysis on four online products related to pet adoption as the basis for follow-up strategy research (Table 3). It is worth learning that. First, some platforms use the method of step donation to convert daily behaviors into real value (pet food, etc.), allowing everyone to participate in it; second, the adoption process is relatively complete, the display of pet information is relatively comprehensive, and it is easy for adopters to understand the situation quickly. At the same time, the following problems are also found: 1. The functions are mainly concentrated before and during adoption, and there are almost no functions after adoption; 2. The user groups after adoption are scattered, leading to a lack of contact and interaction between all parties involved; 3. Lack of incentives Mechanism (currently, there is only photo-taking and clock-in, mainly used for follow-up visits to shelters); 4. The display of pet information is relatively simple, with only the most basic graphic introduction; 5. Shelters cannot efficiently manage pet information and item resources.

Table 3. Case analysis

Case	Pet Help	Apai Adoption	Home for Pets	Zilai Pet
Product Positioning	Adoption + Cloud Raising, Cooperative reselling points	Adopt + Feed, Brand Owned Mall	Adoption, Public Website	Adoption + Knowledge, Public Website
Check-in and Clock-in			√	√
Pet Adoption	√	√	√	√
Pet Delivery	√	√	√	√
Cloud Adoption	√	√		
Find Pets	√			√
Pet Management				
Pet Community				
Graphic Content	√	√	√	√
Short Video				
Topics				√
Knowledge				√
Popularity Ranking		√		
Medal System		√		
Pet Mall	√			√
Blacklist	√		√	√
Public Welfare Activities	√			√
Step Exchange	√	√		
Crowdfunding	√			

5 Solutions

5.1 Concept Description

We envision a service platform that integrates pet adoption and security. The platform is mainly based on mobile applications (Fig. 4). Borrowing digital means, combined with business promotion, public welfare activities, consulting services, joint brand names, etc., to open up the possibility of cooperation between shelters and other pet industries to alleviate the shelter's adoption dilemma. While helping the adopter to become a qualified breeder, it also provides care and protection for pets to prevent secondary wandering.

Fig. 4. Application scenario

5.2 Design Strategy

Based on the previous research content, we refined the problems in the adoption process into 11 phrases (7 related to breeders, four related to shelters) and listed the corresponding design strategies (one question may correspond to multiple strategies, there is no order of these strategies, they only represent the diversity of solutions). A detailed description of the policy content is as follows: (refer to Table 4).

B1. The mismatch between perceived and actual costs is mainly reflected in the fact that adopters, especially novices, have high expectations for adoption and do not regard it as a process that requires patience. In this regard, we provide two strategies for reference. 1. Inform the adopter in advance of the responsibilities, requirements, and risks of raising pets, including but not limited to written agreements, dynamic images, virtual pet raising, etc.; 2. Display as much information about pets as possible, including but not limited to names, Gender, age, breed, body type, personalities, etc.

B2. Most rescue centers are private organizations, so the adoption process is not standardized, making adopters feel unreliable. The solution here is to simplify the process (such as five steps: find your favorite pet, consult the details, make an appointment, confirm the adoption, and accept a return visit) so that the adopter can understand roughly what to do at each stage.

B3. For young people who want to adopt their first pet, the preparation work before raising is difficult. The first strategy is to cooperate with the brand to provide adopters with simple feeding kits (such as small bags of food, traction ropes, food bowls, etc.) to help them transition to the initial stage of adoption and, at the same time, expand brand awareness; the second strategy is to provide training for novices Courses can specifically include both theoretical study and practical operation. For non-novice adopters, they need to complete the course before they can adopt pets smoothly.

B4. Encourage users' enthusiasm for raising pets and guide them to become qualified breeders through growth mechanisms (such as points, achievements, service exchange, etc.).

B5. Disease prevention and health after pet adoption are vital. In this regard, first, we can cooperate with major brands to launch food care, insurance, and other services to ensure the life of pets after adoption; second, update pet knowledge from time to time (released by the official or in cooperation with professionals), and A question and answer library is formed based on big data for subsequent users to find similar questions.

B6. Considering users' needs for daily management of pets, it is recommended to set up related functions in the application (such as: reminding users of key dates, storing beautiful moments with pets, etc.).

B7. Extend the adoption process to a longer period after adoption, relying on the platform to launch some functions and services to meet user needs (refer to B4, B5, B6). The benefits of doing so include: enhancing the communication between users who have something in common, improving users' trust and stickiness to the platform, and being more likely to recommend others for adoption, etc.

R1. Because the shelter is located far away from the city and is usually mostly privately operated, the spread of adoption information is limited. Therefore, we can use brand traffic to carry out commercial cooperation with it, improve the information dissemination efficiency of the shelter, and establish a good image for the brand. Similarly, we can give full play to the dissemination power of adopters, volunteers, and related pet organizations to help spread adoption information,

R2. On the one hand, it is necessary to ensure the standardization and transparency of the adoption process, and on the other hand, it is necessary to strengthen the dissemination and deepen of the concept of adoption in order to increase the success rate of adoption. The "adoption success" here also includes the retention of pets after adoption. At the same time, pet appearance is an important factor affecting adoption (conclusions come from literature research).

R3. Shelters face equipment, materials, pets, and other information management. Therefore, it is recommended to integrate and design these contents through the application program to reduce the management burden of the shelter.

R4. Ensure the ownership of pets by setting the cooling-off period for adoption, identity transfer, and other functions to prevent secondary homelessness. At the same time, leave room for each adopter to consider (for example, it is impossible to continue rising due to actual conditions).

Table 4. Problems and corresponding design strategies

User	No	Problem or Need	Design Strategy
Adopter	B1	Perceive costs do not match the actual cost	Inform the breeding responsibility and requirements in advance
			Detailed display of all identity information about pets
	B2	Cumbersome adoption process	Simplify the process and set the adoption progress display
	B3	Newbie in adoption	Gift for novice adoption sets
			Set up basic training courses
	B4	Quality training and improvement	Guiding users to become qualified breeders through growth mechanism
	B5	Prevention and protection	Cooperate with various brands to introduce privileged services in food, care and clothing etc
			Release general knowledge on breeding from time to time
	B6	Daily management	Remind the key time of vaccination, deworming, washing and care, and manage and supervise various physical indicators of pets; and record and share daily clips of pets
	B7	Few post-adoption services	Establishing a full-chain pet adoption and protection platform
shelter	R1	Low information communication efficiency	Cooperate with mall or brand to promote
			Expand the relationship between adopters and volunteers
	R2	Low adoption success rate	Take care of the appearance of the pet before adopting
			Adoption process is more standardized and transparent through human-pet identity binding and digital agreement
	R3	Management of information and resources	All information and processes are transferred to online
	R4	Worry about the possibility of pets being abandoned again	Set up an adoption adaptation period, identity transfer and other functions to guarantee the belonging of pets

6 Discussion

We found a few points to pay attention to through the discussion and research of these strategies. 1. Some strategies may increase the adoption threshold and the difficulty of adoption. The relationship between the two needs to be balanced in the specific implementation process. 2. We view post-adoption as a more critical stage in the adoption process to ensure pet retention.

Through in-depth research and insight into the pet shelter, we also conceived its future development direction and business model (Fig. 5). The short-term plan is to spread the concept of adoption as the guide, expand the influence of the shelter, and implement the digital transformation of the adoption process (essential functions are prioritized). The long-term plan is to extend the service of shelters to pet hospitals, pet stores, and other industry scenarios, increase the breadth and depth of cooperation, promote win-win results for all parties, and alleviate the social problems of stray pets to a certain extent. During the interview, one person in charge of the shelter mentioned that because the shelter is located in a suburban area, he had thought of developing this place into a team-building activity base or an outdoor activity place and launched a series of pet-related services. This plan is a long-term, high-quality idea, but it still requires the joint efforts of all members of society to realize the excellent vision step by step.

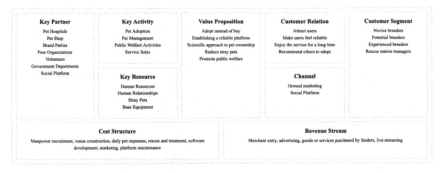

Fig. 5. Business Canvas

7 Conclusion

This research explores the digital transformation strategy of adoption services in the shelter scene. We draw the following conclusions through quantitative and qualitative mixed research methods: 1. Allow users to obtain more information (risks, responsibilities, and requirements) before adopting; 2. Pay attention to pet protection and service support after adoption; 3. Consider the actual needs of shelters; 4. Give full play to the strengths of other pet industries to form a mutually beneficial and win-win situation. Implementing these strategies is still challenging, as they are closely related to complex factors such as local laws, policies, and social concepts. In addition, due to the influence of practical factors, the project still has many deficiencies. For example, there are deviations in the information (age) of the user groups participating in the questionnaire and certain geographical limitations in the selection of cases. The specific design content (function and service) is our future deepening direction.

Acknowledgements. Thanks to everyone who participated in the research.

References

1. Zong, H.: The study of two competitive firms in the online pet industry and a business proposal solving stray pet issue in China. In: 2021 12th International Conference on E-Education, E-Business, E-Management, and E-Learning, pp. 348–354 (2021)
2. Campanilla, B.S., Etcuban, J.O., Maghanoy, A.P., Nacua, P.A.P., Galamiton, N.S.: Pet adoption app to free animal shelters. J. Positive School Psychol. **6**(8), 5993–6006 (2022)
3. Tasker, L.: Stray animal control practices (Europe). WSPA and RSPCA Report, 584 (2007)
4. Hoy-Gerlach, J., Ojha, M., Arkow, P.: Social workers in animal shelters: a strategy toward reducing occupational stress among animal shelter workers. Front. Veterinary Sci. **8**, 734396 (2021)
5. Frank, J.M., Carlisle-Frank, P.: Attitudes and perceptions regarding pet adoption. Found. Interdisciplinary Res. Educ. **1**, 19 (2008)
6. Neidhart, L., Boyd, R.: Companion animal adoption study. J. Appl. Anim. Welfare Sci. **5**(3), 175–192 (2002)
7. Shore, E.R.: Returning a recently adopted companion animal: adopters' reasons for and reactions to the failed adoption experience. J. Appl. Anim. Welfare Sci. **8**(3), 187–198 (2005)
8. Hawes, S.M., Kerrigan, J.M., Hupe, T., Morris, K.N.: Factors informing the return of adopted dogs and cats to an animal shelter. Animals **10**(9), 1573 (2020)
9. Zadeh, A., Combs, K., Burkey, B., Dop, J., Duffy, K., Nosoudi, N.: Pet analytics: predicting adoption speed of pets from their online profiles. Expert Syst. Appl. **204**, 117596 (2022)
10. Applebaum, J.W., Tomlinson, C.A., Matijczak, A., McDonald, S.E., Zsembik, B.A.: The concerns, difficulties, and stressors of caring for pets during COVID-19: results from a large survey of US pet owners. Animals **10**(10), 1882 (2020)
11. Barrett, M., Davidson, E., Prabhu, J., Vargo, S.L.: Service innovation in the digital age. MIS Q. **39**(1), 135–154 (2015)
12. Wu, L., Shao, M., Wei, S., Lu, R., Huang, B.: Widespread of stray animals: design a technological solution to help build a rescue system for stray animals. In: HCI International 2022–Late Breaking Papers: HCI for Today's Community and Economy: 24th International Conference on Human-Computer Interaction, HCII 2022, Virtual Event, June 26–July 1, 2022, Proceedings, pp. 376–396. Cham: Springer Nature Switzerland (2022)
13. Allison, H.: # PawnderAdoption Creating a Public Relations Campaign to Increase Adoption Rates Among Shelters in the United States (2019)
14. Da, W.H.: Design research on AI pet technology applied to pet adoption app. Electron. Test **09**, 115–118 (2022)

A Study on the Service Design of Leisure Campsites in Shanghai Based on Kansei Engineering

Yiyang Mao and Meiyu Zhou[✉]

East China University of Science and Technology, Shanghai, China
y30211539@mail.ecust.edu.cn, zhoutc_2003@163.com

Abstract. As the economy and technology continue to evolve, the era of user-orientation has arrived and designers optimize design outputs by gaining insight into the emotional needs and experiential feelings of users. While Kansei engineering is a science-based approach to user-oriented product development that can be used to model the interaction between emotions and product or service attributes, sustainable service design introduces a new design thinking. Based on an improved Kansei engineering framework, this study assesses satisfaction with existing leisure campsite services, conducts a needs analysis of service design through the Kano model, identifies Kano properties of service attributes and identifies service attributes that need improvement. Finally, an empirical study is conducted in leisure campsite services to test the model and propose sustainable service optimization solutions based on TRIZ theory.

Keywords: service design · Kansei engineering · Kano model · TRIZ · leisure campsite services · sustainable services

1 Introduction

As the economy and technology continue to develop, people's consumer values are undergoing a huge change and user-driven design has arrived. The importance of the user's emotional needs and experience in design has been repeatedly mentioned, making it necessary for today's designers to constantly search for new ways to perceive and satisfy the real needs of users. Service design, as a new interdisciplinary approach to design thinking [1], can achieve the goal of satisfying users' emotional needs and enhancing user experience in this context.

Policy-wise, service design is supported by two guiding opinions, the State Council's Opinions on Promoting the Integrated Development of Design Services of Cultural Creativity and Related Industries (2014) and the Guidance Opinions of the Ministry of Commerce and Other 8 Departments on Accelerating the Transformation and Upgrading of Service Outsourcing (2020), which encourage the model of combining design and services as well as the model of innovative synergistic development.

A. Marcus et al. (Eds.): HCII 2023, LNCS 14031, pp. 202–219, 2023.
https://doi.org/10.1007/978-3-031-35696-4_15

Kansei engineering is a technique that connects perception and engineering to measure, quantify and analyze users' psychological needs, and is applied to model the interaction between emotions and product or service attributes [2, 3]. In product and service experiences, emotions play an important role in increasing customer satisfaction and loyalty [4], and service design based on Kansei engineering has profound implications and research value at a time when consumer needs are constantly changing. In the past decade, Kansei engineering has received rapid attention in the service context.

This study is based on an improved Kansei engineering framework [5] using the KANO model to understand and meet customers' perceptual needs while taking into account social, environmental and economic performance. An empirical study of idle campsites in Shanghai was conducted to further validate the applicability of the model. To highlight the importance of Kansei engineering in sustainable service development with innovative and ground-breaking solutions.

Therefore, the main objectives of this study are twofold. Firstly, this study constructs a Kansei engineering model based on an improved Kansei engineering framework to identify service elements in the service domain that can be improved. Secondly, an empirical study is carried out in the context of leisure campsite services to test the model and propose service optimization solutions.

The paper is structured as follows: Sect. 1 introduces the study, Sect. 2 provides a literature review, Sect. 3 presents the research methods, Sect. 4 presents the empirical study, Sect. 5 analyses and discusses the results, and Sect. 6 concludes.

2 Literature Review

2.1 Service Design based on Kansei Engineering

The beginning of Kansei engineering was proposed as a scientific approach to user-oriented product development, using a Kansei word to relate the user's feelings about a product to its attributes and to provide design directions and ideas for new products. As service design differs from product design, it is possible to analyse the Kansei intentions related to the appearance of the product such as material, form and colour. It is therefore necessary to construct a Kansei intention space by capturing the user's feelings about the service item. Using service design as the object of study and Kansei engineering as an auxiliary tool for the study of user needs, service design that meets user needs can be better carried out [6]. Cai Min et al. (2019) applied the Kansei engineering approach to service design and proposed a comprehensive framework of Kansei engineering assisted by the Kano model to analyse the relationship between customer perception and service attributes by synthesizing the Kansei space and attribute space and establishing a relational model to determine the improvement priority strategy for service attributes [7].

As information technology continues to evolve, a large number of scholars are making breakthroughs in service design research using more user-scale text mining tools for online reviews and Kansei engineering techniques based on artificial intelligence algorithms. The integration of applied Kansei engineering and online content analysis can enable real customer-oriented design needs, providing a complementary role to Kansei design [8].

Online data, which often has complex characteristics such as large volume, unstructured, arbitrary and free expression and covering a wealth of information, can be fully explored in depth through LDA thematic model sentiment analysis techniques for online reviews to identify service elements and calculate customer demand preferences [9]. This leads to the proposal of a model approach for optimal allocation of service elements based on sentiment analysis of online reviews, which provides reference and guidance for solving the service improvement problems of service providers in reality. Combining Kansei engineering in service design, data mining techniques of decision trees are used to quantify the relationship between service attributes, perceived responses and usage intentions, translating users' subjective perceptions into design specifications [10]. Two models with partial least squares (PLS) algorithm and decision tree mining techniques were used to explore the correlation between customer Kansei space and service attribute space and the influence of customer Kansei space and service attribute space on customer usage intention [11].

In addition, some scholars have extended Kansei engineering to the domain of product service systems (PSS) for addressing complex customer experience needs. Based on a systematic review of recent technologies in the field of PSS design, evaluation and operational methods (PSS-DEOM) [12], a new understanding of user-centred SPSS (UC-SPSS) is proposed and provides a conceptual framework and development methodology for UC-SPSS [13], which provides support for realizing intelligent interconnected services is supported.

Finally, exploring and finding hidden and latent needs corresponding to certain service attributes is a challenge for service innovation and sustainability [14]. Hartono, M (2020) [5] offers new ideas for sustainable services, proposing an improved Kansei engineering-based approach for understanding and meeting the emotional needs of customers considering social, environmental and economic performance.

2.2   Leisure Campsite Services

Research on campsites has been conducted abroad for some time, with the establishment of the American Camping Association (ACA), the precursor to the American Campground Management Association, in 1910 marking the emergence of the camping industry. Since the establishment of the World Camping and Camping Federation (FICC) in 1932, theoretical research has been carried out on campsite siting and construction standards and their management, with guidance on campsite siting and construction provided in The Complete Wilderness Travel Handbook (Black Wood, 2000). There has also been research into the development, operation and management of campsites [15]. However, there is also the problem of more practice than theoretical research.

In China, due to the booming development of self-driving tourism and the attention of the State Council, in 2015, GB/T 31710.2–2015 "Code for Construction and Services of Recreational Campsites Part II: Self-driving Campsites" began to receive wide attention from the society and the industry. And with the epidemic since 2020, camping as an emerging track is rapidly becoming popular on social networks due to the large area restricting the development of overseas travel and long-distance tourism [16], relying on attributes such as short-distance, light luxury, outdoor and social. 2022 has become the first year of the camping explosion. The promulgation of the Code of Construction and Services for Leisure Campsites provides consumers with a clear understanding of the facilities and service levels available at campsites, facilitating travel decisions and judging in case of quality disputes, and providing consumers with a reference and basis to protect their legitimate rights and interests [17]. With the development of the camping economy, camping campsites are moving towards a development path of diversified styles to meet users' needs for personalised service experiences. At present, there are "campground + scenic spot" mode, "campground + field" mode, "campground + study" mode, "campground + sports campground + sports" model, "campground + fun" model, "campground + performing arts" model, etc.

Although research on campgrounds in China started late, with the development of camping tourism in recent years, related research has received extensive attention from scholars. Although the development of campgrounds in China is fast, it is still at an early stage, and there is a big gap compared to foreign countries [18], and there are differences between domestic and foreign campground development models.

In the past there have been a large number of studies on Kansei engineering focused on the hotel, airline and logistics service industries [19], and considering the common problems that exist in the services themselves, there are worthwhile lessons from these research methods and theories for leisure campsite services. Josip Mikulić's (2017) study applied relevance decision analysis (RDA) to reveal what is important when choosing a holiday campsite campsite attributes, as well as those that are most decisive for the on-site experience, are informative [20]. However, modern campsites place higher demands on the overall competence of the management team. Unlike hotel management which only solves the supporting function of eating, drinking and living, the core of a leisure campground is the experience function and giving good service to self-driving groups. The campsite covers the hotel, scenic spot and amusement industry, and requires a team with stronger comprehensive ability and compound innovation to meet the management of the campsite.

3 Methods

This paper is based on the general Kansei engineering research framework, the conceptual framework of Kansei engineering first proposed by Schutte [21] (2004), and examines the development of a service design framework integrating Kansei engineering and the Kano model (see Fig. 1), defining the Kansei and attribute spaces related to the service domain early in the research, and measuring the Kansei words through questionnaire design, overall defining the scope of the research, through Kansei engineering tools to identify problems and seek solutions to strategic approaches through TRIZ theory. Prioritizing the important service attributes in this study, more effort will be invested in Kano's Attractive (A) and One-dimensional (O) service attributes as they are the main Kansei stimuli. Drawing on the model of sustainable service application based on Kansei engineering proposed by Hartono, M (2020), the significance of this approach is to propose sustainable innovative service solution strategies through the application of TRIZ theory to find and obtain a single feasible best solution to a well-defined problem [22]. This approach emphasizes logic, speed and accuracy, and focuses on the reapplication of known techniques and information.

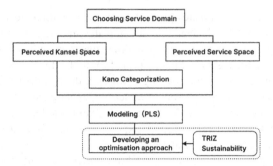

Fig. 1. An application model for sustainable service design based on Kansei engineering

3.1 Service Design

Service design mainly includes two parts: service element design and service delivery process design (see Fig. 2), where service element design is mainly to design the various elements that make up the service and ultimately form a complete service product [23]. Determining the appropriate service area can clarify the main scope of service design and make the research results more reliable.

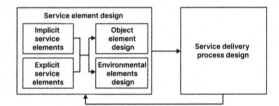

Fig. 2. Key elements of service design

In a service design study based on Kansei engineering, the first step is to select the service domain, i.e. to identify the service design object, including information on the target group, the type of user, the market position, etc., where customer satisfaction and perception play an important role. Once the service domain has been identified, it is necessary to find as many service samples as possible that represent the service domain, including existing services and conceptual ideas. A service domain can be understood as an abstract idea of perfection behind a service, of which representative service providers can be used as samples. The service domain thus comprises three components: existing services, conceptual services and service design solutions.

3.2 Kansei Engineering

In the Kansei engineering study of services, the Kansei lexical space is divided into two parts, the perceptual Kansei space and the service space, and both need to be measured separately. After the service domain has been identified, an extensive desktop study of the service needs to be conducted to collect as completely as possible the Kansei words associated with the service, and the collected Kansei words needs to be analyzed and categorized in terms of affinity diagrams to make the identified service Kansei space more accurate [24]. One can try to use existing algorithmic tools used for semantic analysis, and the collection of Kansei words and Kansei analysis can be achieved more easily by using computer algorithms and machine learning, and establishing the service Kansei space. Wang Xinyu (2016) points out the limitation of the relatively lacking amount of Kansei words in travel reviews [25], and proposes a method that combines a travel Kansei lexicon with machine learning, so that the Kansei in travel online reviews can be tendencies to be judged. All these methods can be used to construct a service Kansei space. The determination of the service attribute space is closely linked to the content involved in the service attributes. It is necessary to fully understand the service content in the service domain, and it is generally possible to draw on the service attributes involved in the service quality evaluation index, or to determine the service attribute space of the research subject by means of expert interviews, for example.

3.3 Kano Model

The KANO model is a tool proposed in 1984 by the renowned Japanese quality management guru Noriaki Kano primarily for classifying and prioritizing user requirements. It is based on an analysis of the impact of user requirements on user satisfaction and demonstrates the relationship between product or service elements and user satisfaction [26]. The KANO model, as a method of service design requirements analysis, assesses users' service requirements at five levels attributes (Fig. 3).

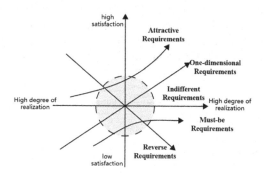

Fig. 3. Overview diagram of the Kano model

The KANO model analysis method, which is mainly researched through a standardized questionnaire, divides user satisfaction into a graded 5 levels, based on users' two-way satisfaction ratings for service provision or not, which can correspond to a two-dimensional demand attribute assessment scale, which can be used like a census to obtain data from users, and which reveals their respective perceptions of the service attributes. As shown in Table 1, A, O, M, I and R are the initials of each of the five categories of demand attributes and Q represents the questionable results. The survey questionnaire was distributed to a certain number of users and by counting the results of the survey, the sum of the number of people for each category of attributes and questionable outcomes in the two-dimensional scale could be calculated separately as a percentage of the total number of people surveyed, and the attribute with the highest score was identified as the final attribute definition for that service.

Table 1. Comparison table of kano evaluation results by category

		Unavailable				
		Dislike	Endurable	Does not matter	Should be so	Satisfaction
Available	**Dislike**	Q	R	R	R	R
	Endurable	M	I	I	I	R
	Does not matter	M	I	I	I	R
	Should be so	M	I	I	I	R
	Satisfaction	O	A	A	A	Q

3.4 TRIZ Theory

Genrich S A et al. [27, 28] proposed a theoretical approach and tool for solving creative problems, TRIZ theory, which consists of 40 innovation principles and is widely used in business and design. TRIZ theory focuses on clarifying and highlighting the contradictions in a system, inventing, solving problems and studying the entire design and development process based on the evolution of technology (Fig. 4).

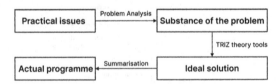

Fig. 4. The basic idea of TRIZ theory problem solving

The TRIZ-based service improvement principles provide new ideas for design innovation in the service design process, and the original principles are modified accordingly in the research. The implementability of models that combine user-generated concepts with innovation is further demonstrated in studies of value co-creation theory, model-based optimization, TRIZ and affective design theory approaches.

4 Application of Kansei Engineering Based Leisure Campsite Service Design

4.1 Identifying Dom of Service for Leisure Campsites

Outdoor camping is special interest tourism that relies on the natural environment and is characterised by the flexible, temporary and mobile nature of the accommodation facilities.

The service area chosen for this paper is a form of camping experience that lies somewhere between fine camping and leisure camping, a form of camping that is more accessible and tried by novice campers, and is also a common market niche for more leisure campsites in China today. There is no shortage of campsites with tents as camping facilities, directly integrated into nature, which are common in national parks in countries such as Europe and the US and have a broader future in China. Given the nature of leisure campsites as described above, in-depth research is needed to explore the quality of service provided by the campsites and its impact on overall user satisfaction. In this case study, the first-tier city of Shanghai leisure campsite was chosen as the service domain. The target customer base was limited to users who had experience with leisure camping services within one year.

4.2 Building Kansei and Attribute Spaces for Leisure Campsite Services

Building a Kansei Space for Leisure Campsite Services. To construct a Kansei space for leisure camp users, a total of 61 Kansei words were first collected through extensive searches on different channels such as relevant websites and mobile apps. After initial screening, the semantically identical Kansei words were grouped using an Affinity Diagram (The KJ method) involving five participants. Subsequently, a dominant word was selected as a representative of each group to develop the Kansei word structure. A total of 10 Kansei words were included in the final Kansei space (K1,K2,... ,K10), as shown in Table 2. The study shows that Kansei perception tends to be more dominant, enhancing the competitive advantage of leisure campsites and user loyalty by satisfying users' emotional needs.

Table 2. Kansei space.

No	Kansei	No	Kansei
K1	Relaxed	K6	Unique
K2	Enthusiastic	K7	Convenient
K3	Sophisticated	K8	Quiet
K4	Interesting	K9	Clean
K5	Reliable	K10	Happy

Building a Space for Leisure Camp Service Attributes. This stage entails the identification of the recreational campsite service elements and the related service attributes. Firstly, the various service attributes (i.e. services provided by leisure campsites) were collected from the leisure campsite service manuals, company websites and relevant literature, containing the various service attributes (i.e. services provided or not and specific content provided) of leisure campsites. In previous studies camping visitors' perceived factors for most leisure campsites were mainly natural environment, supporting facilities, accommodation environment, recreation, management services and perceived value [29].

An online desktop study of Shanghai leisure camps was conducted to further filter and optimize the collected service attributes based on the five dimensions of service quality evaluation, namely tangibility, reliability, responsiveness, assurance and empathy. Ultimately, 19 service attributes containing different service attributes were used in this study to explore service design issues (Table 3) .

Table 3. Service attributes for leisure campsites.

Dimension 1 Tangible		Dimension 3 Responsiveness	
A1	Recreational campsite with good natural beauty	A12	Timely and prompt service from staff, both online and offline
A2	Recreational campsites are clean and hygienic, e.g. toilets	A13	Staff are enthusiastic and willing to help customers
A3	The recreational campsite is well distributed with clear directions to all areas	A14	Service staff respond immediately to customer needs even when busy
A4	Leisure campsites are well equipped	**Dimension 4 Assurance**	
A5	Staff are presentable and tidy	A15	The safety of the leisure campsite is trustworthy, e.g. the accommodation, the car park, etc.
A6	Various forms of publicity and access to consumer information from a variety of media	A16	Friendly and courteous staff
Dimension 2 Reliability		A17	Staff are professional and available to solve problems
A7	Accepting bookings or meeting promises to provide specific services	**Dimension 5 Empathy**	
A8	Staff are caring and helpful when guests encounter difficulties	A18	Staff are proactive in caring for the consumption and needs of different customers
A9	The leisure campsite is committed to providing a wide range of services and meeting the appropriate level of service	A19	Staff are able to provide a variety of services that meet the needs of the client, such as tent construction
A10	Staff keep accurate records, such as lists of materials, menus, bills, etc.		
A11	The leisure campsite offers a variety of payment methods, with easy payment, accurate billing and user convenience		

4.3 Questionnaire Design and Data Collection

The length and wording of the questionnaire was tested and evaluated on urban users who have had experience with recreational camping in the past year (Feb 2022 - Feb 2023), details of the questionnaire can be found on the appendix page. Considering the sample size and validity, this study used both online and face-to-face questionnaires to conduct in-depth interviews, targeting users who have experienced leisure camping in the Shanghai area. In the online questionnaire collection, each user needed approximately 10 min to complete a questionnaire, so questionnaires that took too little time to complete were considered invalid, and a total of 50 questionnaires were collected. This study focused on domestic respondents only, including 46% male and 54% female. The majority were aged between 17–25 (62%) and their occupation was student (52%). Regarding the frequency of undertaking camping activities, more than 54% of the respondents experience camping between 2–12 times per year. Details of the respondent profile are shown in Table 4.

Table 4. Profile of respondents.

Variables	Frequency	% of the total	Variables	Frequency	% of the total
Gender			**Occupation**		
Male	23	46	Student	26	52
Female	27	54	Employee	22	40
Age			Other	4	8
< 17	2	4	**Frequency of camping**		
17–25	31	62	Once a year	19	38
26–35	11	22	2–12 times a year	27	54
36–45	4	8	> 12 times a year	4	8
> 45	2	4			

4.4 Validity Testing and Data Analysis

The study in this paper uses Cronbach α for reliability testing, which is a test of internal consistency between items for a given population at a given time and purpose. All items were reliable in the service attribute and Kansei word space constructs, with Cronbach α values of 0.868 and 0.882 respectively, both greater than 0.6, and therefore all items measured were considered valid and reliable.

Using Kansei word responses as a function of perceived service quality, particularly those with Kano's attractive [A] and one-dimensional [O] categories, the final leisure campsite service with Kano's A and O, and negative customer satisfaction scores were considered to be preferred. Table 5 provides the satisfaction scores and Kano's categories for all service attributes.

Based on the satisfaction scores, it is possible to identify some key leisure campsite service attributes such as A2 cleanliness and hygiene of the leisure campsite, e.g. toilets etc. and A17 prompt and rapid service delivery by staff, both online and offline. The fact that these issues were raised means that we need to focus on these service attributes to make improvements.

Table 5. Leisure campsite service attributes with negative satisfaction score and Kano categories.

Item	Importance	Perception	Exception	Satisfaction [a]	Kano category
A1	4.22	3.60	4.12	-2.1944	Attractive(A)
A2	4.48	3.52	4.44	**-4.1216**	One-dimensional(O)
A3	4.28	3.8	4.16	-1.5408	Indifferent(I)
A4	3.86	3.52	3.66	-0.5404	Indifferent(I)
A5	3.64	3.66	3.72	-0.2184	Indifferent(I)
A6	3.68	3.44	3.70	-0.9568	Indifferent(I)
A7	4.08	3.44	3.98	-2.2032	Must-Be(M)
A8	4.10	3.60	3.94	-1.3940	Attractive(A)
A9	4.14	3.54	3.96	-1.7388	Attractive(A)
A10	3.92	3.56	3.86	-1.1760	Must-Be(M)
A11	4.2	3.98	4.10	-0.5040	Indifferent(I)
A12	4.16	3.60	4.20	-2.4960	Indifferent(I)
A13	4.02	3.52	4.06	-2.1708	Attractive(A)
A14	3.72	3.38	3.54	-0.5952	Attractive(A)
A15	4.38	3.90	4.36	-2.0148	One-dimensional(O)
A16	4.12	3.94	4.14	-0.8240	Indifferent(I)
A17	4.14	3.66	4.32	**-2.7324**	Attractive(A)
A18	3.94	3.14	3.58	-1.7336	Indifferent(I)
A19	4.06	3.58	4.00	-1.7052	Indifferent(I)

[a] Satisfaction Score = [Perception – Expectation] x Importance Rating

Using Kansei engineering as a function of Kano's O and A perceived service quality, the selected leisure campsite service attributes were correlated with refined Kansei words through PLS regression analysis to identify Kansei words that could describe users' emotional satisfaction. The higher the regression coefficient, the more the Kansei word is influenced by the service attributes, with A8 - the staff showing concern and offering help when guests are in difficulty having a greater influence on the perception of several Kansei words, which can be understood as one of the priority factors in leisure camping services. A17 - The staff is professionally qualified and can solve problems is an important service factor that influences the perception of the Kansei terms K2 - Enthusiastic and K4 - Interesting. Rather than improving the entire service attributes with negative user satisfaction scores, it is considered more effective for leisure campsite managers to focus on the key service attributes that have a greater impact on Kansei perceptions.

Table 6. Regression coefficients for the relationship between Kansei words and key service attributes.

	K1	K2	K3	K4	K5	K6	K7	K8	K9	K10
A1	**0.250**	0.073	0.010	-0.023	0.000	-0.096	-0.118	-0.018	-0.007	-0.077
A2	-0.125	-0.264	-0.028	-0.075	0.087	0.174	0.207	-0.107	0.126	-0.031
A8	-0.009	0.403	**0.327**	0.317	0.131	0.179	**0.486**	**0.509**	**0.380**	-0.061
A9	-0.031	-0.318	-0.378	-0.590	-0.160	-0.030	-0.426	-0.011	-0.236	-0.217
A13	-0.042	0.187	0.124	-0.007	-0.040	0.111	0.004	-0.084	-0.136	-0.065
A14	0.091	-0.374	0.092	-0.252	-0.024	**0.257**	0.010	0.003	-0.079	**0.330**
A15	-0.201	-0.037	-0.110	-0.051	-0.091	-0.165	0.020	-0.050	-0.148	0.035
A17	0.058	**0.450**	0.145	**0.336**	-0.019	-0.103	0.019	0.057	0.094	0.048

The specificity of service attribute A2 can also be found in Table 6, which has a weaker perceptual impact on all the Kansei words applied, but is by far the service attribute with the lowest service satisfaction and which is a Kano One-dimensional requirement, while service attribute A17 is also a service attribute with a lower satisfaction level and has an important impact on the Kansei word perception of Enthusiastic and interesting, both of which are service attributes that need to be focused, which are important for the subsequent optimization of services.

4.5 TRIZ Theory-Based Generation of Optimized Service Guidelines

Comprehensive analysis of the two service attributes A2 and A17, combined with the problems and contradictions of the leisure campsite service, using the 39 coefficient Altshuller contradiction matrix table and 40 invention principles provided by TRIZ theory, to compare and extrapolate in order to obtain the best design solution (see in Table 7).

In addition to TRIZ contradiction analysis, service designers should also consider the principle of sustainability of leisure campsite services, and can further develop a sustainable analysis framework for leisure campsite services in three dimensions: environmental, social and economic (Table 8). Taking service element A2 as an example, its optimisation process follows both environmental and social dimensions in sustainability. Reducing waste and fostering good public awareness are also important elements in the design of leisure campsite services, and a quality experience can bring better economic benefits and returns to the leisure campsite.

Table 7. TRIZ-based solutions for service elements.

Service attributes	Contradictions		TRIZ Method	Solutions
	Optimization	Deterioration		
A2 Recreational campsites are clean and hygienic, e.g. toilets	10 Number of substances	36 Ease of maintenance	10 Pre-action Principle	Anticipate the user's experiential behaviour when entering the leisure campsite and install appropriate sanitation facilities and guidelines in advance. Informing users about hygiene before they enter the campsite and raising public awareness
			25 Self-service principle	Use of self-cleaning products for the installation of sanitary facilities, following the principle of sustainability
			32 Colour change principle	Optimize the user's visual experience in the campsite by improving the overall visual appearance of the campsite, thus fostering awareness of the need to keep the campsite clean and hygienic

(continued)

Table 7. (*continued*)

Service attributes	Contradictions		TRIZ Method	Solutions
	Optimization	Deterioration		
A17 Staff are professional and available to solve problems	35 Reliability	46 The complexity of control	1 Splitting principle	A reasonable division of the leisure camp into zones and the matching of different professional staff to provide professional services
			10 Pre-action principle	Users get to know and feel the professionalism of the leisure campsite staff in advance through the online website, so that they can arrange the relevant activities of the camp in advance
			19 Periodic action principle	Leisure campsites regularly invite professionals in the relevant fields to provide professional sharing, a periodic brand activities to drive the activity of the camp
			25 Self-serving principle	Provide guidance on how to experience the leisure camp, users can find solutions to almost all problems in the guide

Table 8. Sustainability dimensions in leisure campsite services (modified from Brown and Legg, 2012 [30])

Environmental	Social	Economic
Water quality	Public awareness and education	Local hiring
Climate change	Stakeholder relationships	Local purchasing
Air quality	Employee practices and procedures	Contribution to community
Land use	Local identity culture and heritage	Contribution to research and development
Biodiversity	Employee well-being	Incentives for sustainable behavior
Waste	Visitor well-being	
Noise and aesthetics		
Green buildings		

5 Discussion

Current research on services incorporating the concept of sustainability is rather limited, especially with regard to perceptual needs in service design. Existing research uses Kansei Engineering (KE) as a pillar of the research methodology, in line with sustainable service content. Service attributes that are most sensitive to Kansei perception are filtered and prioritized through Kansei engineering. Service quality and Kano are first modeled. The Kano model allows the performance of service attributes to be mined and found based on user perceptions and filters the most critical service attributes, called attractive requirements [A]. PLS is then applied to model the Kansei and attribute space of the service. This study focuses only on service attributes where Kano is One-dimensional [O] and attractive [A] with negative satisfaction scores. Finally, the principle of sustainability is promoted by emphasizing more social and human-centred features, as well as more innovative and ground-breaking solutions, reducing contradictions with the proposed solutions and strategies.

Sustainable services, also known as Product-Service Systems (PSS), address the three main components of sustainability, minimizing resource use while increasing the responsibility of suppliers and customers as a means of increasing the profitability of the business.

6 Conclusion

This paper focuses on the camping boom of the past year, but in China there is a lack of policies and research related to camping, and the camping market is blossoming, so studying the services of leisure campsites is currently a relatively new option. At the same time the sustainability highlighted in the framework of this paper is a valuable research topic and direction. This study is limited by its small sample size and the fact that it is a context-based case study. The relationship model was not very smoothly developed and more efficient and appropriate models are needed to construct the relationship between the Kansei and attribute spaces of leisure campsite services. In terms of the next outlook of the study, leisure camping services will receive more attention and its future development will gradually expand to non-first-tier cities, emphasizing the local natural and cultural characteristics of leisure campsites, and the principle of sustainability will remain a key focus in the study in the process of service optimization.

Appendix

Sample questionnaire for leisure campsite services: service quality, Kansei, and Kano.

The purpose of this survey is to collect information on your experience in leisure campsite services. You will take less than 10 min to complete. All information given will be kept strictly confidential.

Section A (omitted)

It is general information on respondent profile.

Section B: Service quality

Based on your experience as a recreational campsite experience, please reflect on the importance of the services provided (importance), indicate the extent to which you think the recreational campsite will have services (expectation) and indicate the extent to which you think the recreational campsite has services (perception). Please tick '1' if you strongly disagree and '5' if you strongly agree.

Service Attributes	Importance	Expectation	Perception
A1 Recreational campsite with good natural beauty	1 2 3 4 5	1 2 3 4 5	1 2 3 4 5
A2 Recreational campsites are clean and hygienic, e.g. toilets	1 2 3 4 5	1 2 3 4 5	1 2 3 4 5
…			
A19 Staff are able to provide a variety of services that meet the needs of the client, such as tent construction	1 2 3 4 5	1 2 3 4 5	1 2 3 4 5

Section C: Kansei

Based on your experience as a recreational campsite experience, please tick 1 (definitely negative perceptive word) to 5 (definitely positive perceptive word) on the Likert scale to rate your Kansei satisfaction.

Code	Negative Kansei	Experience Rating	Positive Kansei
K1	Unrelaxed	1 2 3 4 5	Relaxed
K2	Indifferent	1 2 3 4 5	Enthusiastic
K3	Sketchy	1 2 3 4 5	Sophisticated
K4	Uninteresting	1 2 3 4 5	Interesting
K5	Unreliable	1 2 3 4 5	Reliable

(continued)

(continued)

Code	Negative Kansei	Experience Rating	Positive Kansei
K6	Ordinary	1 2 3 4 5	Unique
K7	Inconvenient	1 2 3 4 5	Convenient
K8	Noisy	1 2 3 4 5	Quiet
K9	Dirty	1 2 3 4 5	Clean
K10	Unhappy	1 2 3 4 5	Happy

Section D: Kano

Based on your experience as a recreational camper, please choose one of the following five options: 5 = I like it; 4 = I wish it were so; 3 = I am neutral; 2 = I don't like it, but I can live with it; 1 = I don't like it and I can't live with it.

Code	Service Attributes	Choices
A1	Recreational campsite with good natural beauty	1 2 3 4 5
A2	Recreational campsites are clean and hygienic, e.g. toilets	1 2 3 4 5
	…	
A19	Staff are able to provide a variety of services that meet the needs of the client, such as tent construction	1 2 3 4 5

References

1. Ying, G.: Research on service design innovation based on the experience value dimension. China Academy of Fine Arts (2017)
2. Nagamachi, M.: Kansei engineering: a new ergonomic consumer-oriented Technology for product development. Int. J. Ind. Ergon. **15**(1), 3–11 (1995)
3. Hartono, M., Tan, K.C.: How the Kano model contributes to Kansei engineering in services. Ergonomics **54**(11), 987–1004 (2011)
4. Hartono, M., Raharjo, H.: Exploring the mediating role of affective and cognitive satisfaction on the effect of service quality on loyalty. Total Qual. Manag. Bus. Excel. **26**(9–10), 971–985 (2015)
5. Hartono, M.: The modified Kansei Engineering-based application for sustainable service design. Int. J. Ind. Ergonomics, 79 (2020)
6. Xue, L.: A study of modular service design based on perceptual engineering. Southwest University of Science and Technology (2022)
7. Min, C., Qianqian, W.: A study of service design methods based on perceptual engineering. Des. Art Studies **9**(06), 60–67 (2019)
8. Hsiao, Y.-H.: Logistics service design for cross-border E-commerce using Kansei engineering with text-mining-based online content analysis. Telematics Inform. **34**(4), 284–302 (2017)
9. Dehua, Z.: Research on service ingredients optimization configuration model based on online review sentiment analysis, Northeast University (2018)
10. Cty, A., Mcc, B.: Applying Kansei Engineering and data mining to design door-to-door delivery service. Comput. Ind. Eng. **120**, 401–417 (2018)

11. Qianqianz, W.: Research on customer perception-driven service design based on perceptual engineering and the Kano model. Hangzhou University of Electronic Science and Technology (2020)
12. Min, Q., Yu, S., Chen, D., et al.: State-of-the-art of design, evaluation, and operation methodologies in product service systems. Comput. Ind. **77**(8), 1–14 (2016)
13. Chang, D., et al.: A user-centric smart product-service system development approach: a case study on medication management for the elderly. Adv. Eng. Inform. **42**, 100979 (2019)
14. Yang, C.-C.: Identification of customer delight for quality attributes and its applications. Total Qual. Manag. Bus. Excel. **22**(1), 83–98 (2011)
15. Loomis, C.W., Wilkins, B.T.A.: Study of campground businesses in New York State. Ithaca: Cornell University (1971)
16. Baogaoservice   Homepage,   https://mp.weixin.qq.com/s/p4ns-qTPHojOZMcq5IatJA. Accessed 10 Feb 2023
17. Lei, F.: Good implementation of the code of practice for the construction and service of recreational campsites series of standards new camping park standards have been developed and submitted for approval process. Standard Living **04**, 18–27 (2022)
18. Lv, N., Xinfang, W.: Research on the development model of campgrounds in China. J. Chongqing Jiaotong Univ. (Soc. Sci. Ed.) **17**(06), 93–100 (2017)
19. Wang, Y.: A study on the optimal allocation of service elements in hotel service design based on online customer reviews. Northeast University (2018)
20. Mikuli, J., et al.: Campsite choice and the camping tourism experience: Investigating decisive campsite attributes using relevance-determinance analysis – Science Direct. Tourism Manage. **59**(Apr.), 226–233 (2017)
21. Simon, T.W., Eklund, J., Axelsson, J.R.C., et al.: Concepts, methods and tools in Kansei engineerin. Theoretical Issues Ergonomics Sci. **5**(3), 214–231 (2004)
22. Cropley, A.: Praise of convergent thinking. Creativ. Res. J. **18**(3), 391–404 (2006)
23. Cianetti, S., Lombardo, G., Lupatelli, E., et al.: Dental fear/anxiety among children and adolescents: a systematic review. Eur. J. Paediatr. Dent. **18**(2), 121–130 (2017)
24. Zhao, X., Cao, Z., Zhang, H.: A service scenario design approach based on perceptual engineering. J. Northeastern Univ. Nat. Sci. Ed. **32**(9), 1360–1363 (2011)
25. Wang, X.: Research on sentiment analysis of tourism network evaluation based on sentiment dictionary and machine learning. Comput. Digital Eng. **44**(04), 578–582+766 (2016)
26. Liang, S.W., Lu, H.P., Kuo, T.K.: A study on using the kano two-dimensional quality model to evaluate the service quality of government websites. J. Internet Technol. **15**(2), 149–162 (2014)
27. Peng, H., Cheng, S., Li, S., et al.: A review of the theoretical system of TRIZ. Mech. Des. Manuf. **10**, 270–272 (2013)
28. Leng, C., Xiang, H., Zhang, Y.: Innovative design optimization of self-cleaning structure of automatic washing machine based on TRIZ ideal solution. Mech. Des. Res. **31**(4), 158–160 (2015)
29. Li, F., Wang, D.:Factors and mechanisms influencing the development of caravan campsites based on visitors' online reviews: the case of Suzhou Taihu caravan camping park. Geography Geograph. Inf. Sci. **0**(2), 135–140 (2019)
30. Brown, C., Legg, S.: Human factors and ergonomics for business sustainability. In: Brown, C., Legg, S. (Eds.) Business and Sustainability: Concepts, Strategies, and Changes Critical Studies on Corporate Responsibility, Governance, and Sustainability. Emerald Group, pp. 59–79 (2012)

Cognitive Mapping for AI-Augmented Interactive Print

Marco Neves[1,2(✉)], João Abrunhosa[1], and Cristina Pires dos Santos[1]

[1] CIAUD, Research Centre for Architecture, Urbanism and Design, Lisbon School of Architecture, Universidade de Lisboa, Rua Sá Nogueira, Polo Universitário Do Alto da Ajuda, 1349-063 Lisboa, Portugal
mneves@fa.ulisboa.pt, cristina.santos@ipbeja.pt
[2] ITI/LARSyS, University of Lisbon, Lisbon, Portugal

Abstract. Interaction design has evolved in recent decades, being improved by artificial intelligence, ubiquitous computing, internet of things and tangible materials. While some research regards combining print media with interaction as an opportunity for development, the quantity of relevant publications is underwhelming, as it can be regarded as a difficult and risky approach. We noted a lack of scientific focus on interactive print probably due to dispersed knowledge of areas that contribute to understanding this phenomenon. To fill this deficit, we propose a first combination of main concepts and their respective connections, to draw a more enlightening framework of understanding and which will aid future research. We intend to know what are the relations between print media, interaction, understood by its materiality and tangibility, HCI and the challenges of AI and ML. How has each wave of HCI affected this set of concepts? How can research regarding interactive print enhanced by AI and ML move forward? Taking on the challenge of articulating concepts and definitions, we produced a cognitive map to better understand interactive print. Our cognitive map reveals the need to deepen research between all areas that surround interaction design and print media that still have social, cultural and educational relevance. The map contributes with a possible network of connections to elaborate theoretical frameworks at the intersection of these areas and opens a space of opportunities for designers to act.

Keywords: Interactive Print · Artificial Intelligence · Machine Learning · Cognitive Map · Interaction Design

1 Introduction

Design of print media has been understood as elaborating visual and static objects, given their tradition related with graphic arts and their expected commercial use. We have been witnessing a decrease in print media use, purchase and circulation [1, 2], as activity sectors focused on printed products have undergone changes leading to a reduction in revenues and employment [3]. Most common recent solution to deal with them is a digital transition of products and services, which generate doubts about cognitive, social and cultural ability of individuals. When not replaced by digital counterparts [4], print

A. Marcus et al. (Eds.): HCII 2023, LNCS 14031, pp. 220–231, 2023.
https://doi.org/10.1007/978-3-031-35696-4_16

media has provide a flat surface for overlapped augmented reality (AR) devices [5–8]. Still, reading on paper seems more effective than reading on screen [9, 10], and most students prefer print over online for tactile aspects, linear progression of text, memory cues, annotations and less fatigue [11]. Digital alternatives bring convenience, speed and, often, lower costs [12], presenting us with opportunities for participation and personalized content. But also, a marked influence on cognition and literacy [13], as paper-based material increase comprehension of texts [14], and help in the development of younger generations and their well-being [15].

We argue that, instead of being limited to transitioning to digital environment, print media can serve as interactive material, improved by technological augmentation. Emergence of terms such as 'embodied interaction' [16, 17], 'material turn' [18], or 'shape-changing interfaces' [19] conditions a reframing of interaction design, away from screen-based interfaces, towards a broader design practice, with a set of diversified artifacts, based on technological qualification of surfaces and information networks that lead us to study interaction in different contexts. Print media are available to be transformed and present potential interaction design initiatives. Material and processes combinations has shown different possibilities of balancing print and interactive features [20–23]. By allowing dynamic information in them through technological augmentation and integrating into digital systems, print media are also subject to the effects of autonomous systems based on artificial intelligence (AI) and machine learning (ML).

Digital systems have been at the forefront of most interaction design devices, given technological advances in the past decades, as smartphones and personal computers are greatly accessible. Alongside this exponential growth in hyperlink media, there has been a concern with exploring the future of interfaces for interaction design, mainly in an ubiquitous computing approach. As AI has fostered promising ML algorithms, inclusion of these autonomous systems in interaction design has been of particular interest recently [24, 25]. The values of Industry 4.0 are very much so in the opportunities available for these approaches, but the output made by researchers has been underwhelming from an interactive perspective. Also called as the Fourth Industrial Revolution, this shift is characterized by advancements in manufacturing through the introduction of "new technologies, including Internet of Things (IoT), cloud computing and analytics, and AI and machine learning into their production facilities and throughout their operations." [26]. As demonstrated by O'Donovan [27], technologies and methods which have had more publications regarding this context were 'Internet', with over 70% of all research documents, followed by 'Enterprise', 'Mobile' and 'Emerging', with around 30%, 10%, and 7% respectively. Finally, 'Interactive' approaches were the least researched about in the Industry 4.0, with around 5% of publications. This outlook on the present state of interaction design context motivated an in-depth assessment of inherent concepts to the field, as well as the relationships between each of them. This task can provide an understanding of the past, present and future tendencies that have characterized the interaction design field and can contribute to evaluate possible opportunities for both practice and research.

For a better organization and representation of the conceptual stages through which interaction design has been through, the categorization of the three waves of HCI [28] overarched the development of this research.

2 Cognitive Mapping

We developed a cognitive map to visualize the network of ideas and concepts associated with this research line and to assist the decision-making process of future research activities. This provides a visual and synthetized output to better understand what are the main concepts related to interactive print media and autonomous systems and what are the existing connections and correlations between them.

Cognitive mapping is a tool that can produce a concise and clear depiction of our research context by visually representing conceptual relations between all identified topics. As our research focused on two main concepts (interactive print and autonomous systems) that are not typically approached together, exploring connections that make for print interaction, and couplings with AI and ML, would provide an insight as how can they complement each other. Print media and autonomous systems might be seen as opposing ends of an interactivity spectrum, that would range from static media, not considered interactive due to the lack of feedback, to dynamic technologies capable of various possibilities of interaction. So, comprehending the connections that exist in the center of that scope, would not only indicate concepts that are simultaneously related to both ends, but would also help define the characteristics that compose them. Additionally, producing a cognitive map on contemporary concepts of interaction design provides a broader scope as to where each research topic is placed in a chronological standpoint, but also to establish a hierarchy of concepts.

2.1 Procedures for an Initial Map on Print Interaction

As per Swan [29]: "In psychology, 'cognitive map' was a term that was developed to describe an individual's internal mental representation of the concepts and relations among concepts" (p. 188). This definition can also apply to domains such as design, as it promotes a broader perspective on the research topics and its context. Not only from a problem-solving point of view, as cognitive mapping can also deepen the understanding of researchers through a dynamic thought process. Kearny and Kaplan, [30] take a psychology-sided approach, in saying that cognitive mapping is an evaluation tool of people's "assumptions, beliefs, 'facts', and misconceptions about the world" (p. 580). This assessment allows for psychologists to evaluate the way that certain concepts are seen and thought of, especially knowledge that is contradictory to someone's depiction of reality, as those tend to ignore or refute it. Relations can go from "proximity (A is close to B), similarity (A is similar to B), cause-effect (A causes B), category (A is a subset to B) and contiguity (A follows B)" [29]. All these sets of relations can prove to be a design challenge, especially in more complex maps, as not all of them can be represented through a line in-between concepts. Ackermann [31] used cognitive mapping as a way to improve information that is gathered in interviews for problem-solving purposes; as the interviewees participate, certain details and recurring phrases allow for the development of a map of relations. Although there are many methods for gathering knowledge to create a cognitive map, mostly through analyzing the mental models of patients or interviewees [29], that was not the case for this particular subject. Our cognitive map comes from a systematic literature review, where we detailed research on print interaction and its connection, existing or estimated, with autonomous systems, in light of technological augmentation of surfaces and materials that allow dynamic information in print media [32]. Even though our processes differed in collected data, the following steps for development were similar to those used in [29, 31, 33]. Lourdel [33], when tackling sustainable development issues with students, firstly produced a simple cognitive map that allowed students to better visualize straight-forward relations between concepts. Ackermann [31] and Lourdel [33] chose to have categories and their definition on the first few steps, as that is going to influence the whole structure of the map, mainly creating hierarchization between words or phrases, even before creating a connection between them. From a representation standpoint, categories can be identified through colors, sizes, and position, therefore creating boundaries for the map to exist in. One of the limitations of this method, when applied to a certain group of people, is that it needs to consider the level of expertise that group possesses about the subject [29, 33]. From the initial categorization of research topics, Ackermann [31], collects a series of phrases that need to be translated from a text format, into mapping content. So, the process in this phase was similar in the development of the cognitive map regarding our systematic literature review, as a number of phrases and words that expressed our research goals and initial findings were gathered into topics:

- Print media understood as communication and knowledge materials, subject to creative action, divided into multiple typologies [34].
- The design of print media, characterized by graphic elements and lacking an approach to behavior and dynamic information.
- Establish a connection between interaction design, as shaping of physical/digital, updatable systems, with print media, regarding tangible interfaces and interactive materials [17, 24, 35, 36].
- Interaction design is dealing with developments allowed by new technology. From GUIs to ubiquitous systems and from programming to AI [24, 37].
- Autonomous systems based on AI and ML introduce dynamic and growing information which may contradict design predictability, offering challenging opportunities for design [38].

Then, more specific terms were gathered from the collection of phrases that would simplify the organization of the map as topics and subtopics. As the main goal of the research is to explore how interactive print can move forward with integration of AI and ML, print media and interaction design were distinctively the main concepts of the map, located on opposite sides. Simultaneously, several other subtopics were introduced on the grid, categorized by proximity with the two aforementioned terms (Fig. 1). Some concepts were inherently connected to their 'parent' concepts, for instance, 'interaction design' and 'technology' had to maintain a close proximity, but others had to be placed in the middle, as they can be influenced by both sides of the map, or not having a particular necessity of being close to any other subtopic, such as 'predictability'.

With the defined initial structure of the map, as Ackermann [31] and Lourdel [33] infer, the next step is to create relations between the terms/phrases. This means that arrows can start to appear between concepts and their hierarchization. For example, an arrow with a large stroke can represent a strong relation, i.e., cause-effect, while a slimmer arrow could merely mean a proximity between ideas (Fig. 2).

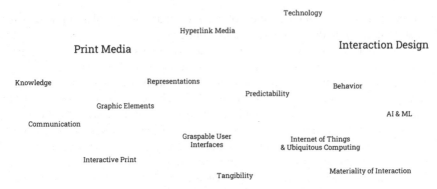

Fig. 1. Initial structure for cognitive map.

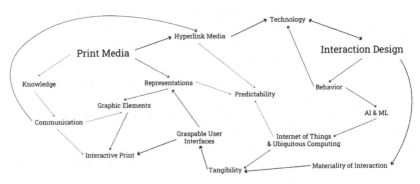

Fig. 2. Linear relations for initial structure.

With the linear affiliations produced, there was still ambiguity with regards as to what the arrows represented. So, the connections between topics had to be better explained and that would allow the whole map to undergo another iterative phase, as some relations would not make sense in a specific location, or there needed to be a stronger connection that better represented the influence of a concept on another (Fig. 3).

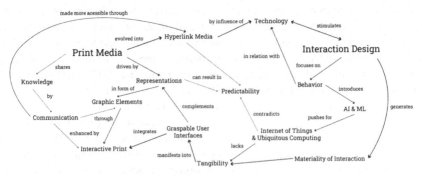

Fig. 3. Addition of labels to relations.

Now that the overall structure and relations of the map were defined, an overhaul of the visual representation of the map was made to better organize the relations in orthogonal directions. This modification improved the appearance of the map as well as better defining the hierarchy in concepts and their respective relations. An additional concern was the introduction of three waves of HCI [28] in complement to the already defined terms and relations, adding a sense of time to the cognitive map. Therefore, simultaneously with the reorganization of the map, three different colored layers were used to represent each wave of HCI, which could work as individual modules when assessing the information. As the literature review matured throughout the development of the map, final additions were made to complement the already existing concepts and relations between them (Fig. 4).

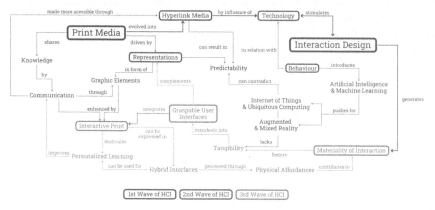

Fig. 4. Final iteration of the cognitive map.

Inclusion of three waves of HCI allows for a better understanding of the main concepts, in light of what each wave means and the relationships that are established between the several topics on the map. For the first wave, the machine was where interaction occurred and people were an external factor of concern [28]. Much as we perceive print media, a material production to convey information which people must reach or obtain without substantial interference in its final shape. Second wave would mark an approach to human cognition and for the 'user' to be a relevant part in interaction, largely considered in adopting technology. Third wave of HCI intends to connect everything in our daily lives aiming for linked devices [39]. Although appealing due to its seemingly efficiency, some challenges arise when focusing on interaction instead of technology (1st wave) or users (2nd wave). Some of those challenges tackle materials, tangible, graspable or hybrid interfaces, where interactive print media through technological augmentation fits.

2.2 Print Interaction and Autonomous Systems: A Novel Concern

Print media is one of the most recognizable media for knowledge sharing over the years, and although there have been great technological advances in recent decades, its characteristics have not changed with it (Fig. 5). Hyperlink media has brought a new dimension to advertisement, social networking and journalism, but static media has not followed in innovation. Tendency for updating static media to an augmented state was to create digital versions of it: books became e-books or printed newspapers became websites [40]. This is mainly corresponding to a very early phase of the second wave of HCI, in which the focus is user-centered design, making such knowledge available to all users, through digital interfaces [28]. This form of communication is also thought of as a representation-driven focused approach, in which the metaphors used represent real world interactions and behaviors. Robles and Wiberg [18] believe that although this was the norm for most digital interfaces created in recent years, it also distanced users from the material world and therefore interaction became devalued as the digital device gained prominence.

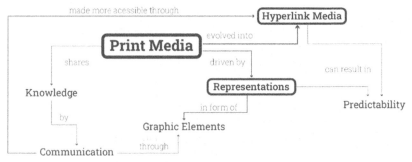

Fig. 5. Cognitive Mapping, 1ˢᵗ wave of HCI.

Although some print formats are in decline, due to drops in sales and circulation, print media still has its advantages, especially when it comes to enhancing education, as the main issue using digital media for education is the cognitive load that comes with that interface [41]. Simultaneous evolution of technology and interaction design has also created a path to enhance traditional print media, by material augmentation [42] or combining AR devices; and an expectable integration into data-driven, Internet of Things ecosystems and AI and ML arrangements (Fig. 6). Advances in AR fostered both educators, engineers, and designers alike to add a new dimension to static media, to express learning subjects [43]. Kazanidis and Pellas [43] also add that AR has proven to be a successful interface when integrated within classrooms, regarding both motivation and participation, and results when it comes to teaching and learning results. Majeed and Ali [44] reinforce this idea as values of interaction design are introduced into an educational environment, mostly user-experience related concepts. Interactive print interfaces are now sought out for various subjects and for different levels of education given its versatility and immersion, as well as its positive impact on the learning experience of students [6]. One other main point for introducing AR in an interactive print media, is personalization, as both students and teachers can access information to their preference and needs [45]. In line with this, the emergence of AI and ML has provided several possibilities when it comes to improving interactive print interfaces. AI can be introduced in this context not just for the improvement of personalization and education, but also to increase the effectiveness of markers that are gradually inconspicuous and accessible. Convergence of both AR and AI advances have made considerable interaction design possibilities seem accessible, either regarding educational systems or any other context when allied with interactive print.

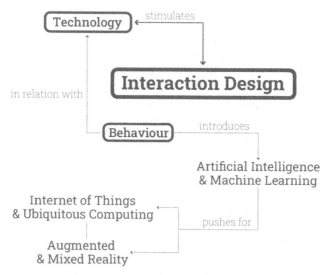

Fig. 6. Cognitive Mapping, 2nd wave of HCI.

Tendency for interaction design devices should be to increasingly add tangibility to interfaces [35], especially because Internet of Things and ubiquitous computing [46] have been regarded as the future of interaction design [47]. This'third wave of HCI' systems expressed in Fig. 7 depend on complex computing devices and are characterized as somewhat intangible, such as cloud services, because although users do not perceive its origin, they still interact with them through material interfaces. This is also in line with what [47] denominates as 'Compositional Material Interaction Design' in which the focus is to add depth to the interaction in relation to already previously design-focused computers (first wave of HCI) and humans (second wave of HCI). This materiality can be expressed by using technologies such as AR and AI as materials in a way to expand the focus in interaction, inside the HCI field. This broadening of an interaction-focused design can also improve the capabilities of integrating print media with a third wave of HCI interface.

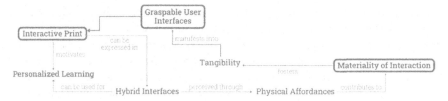

Fig. 7. Cognitive Mapping, third wave of HCI.

3 Conclusions

A presence of interaction in print media is still little considered in design research. This may be due to scarcity of products and services that stand out or are regularly reproduced in our daily lives, but also to the difficulty of framing main concepts that contribute to their understanding. However, as materials that allow printing become able to transmit dynamic information, or participate in integrated systems with other devices that do so, print media start to need an understanding that includes interaction features. Not only that, but they are also subject to transformations and opportunities that arise from autonomous systems based on AI and ML.

The map we are presenting is a first contribution towards exposing the combination of areas that determine and influence the resourcefulness of print media in face of these challenges. It provides and initial visual representation of relevant concepts regarding the connections between print media and autonomous systems in a HCI/interaction design context.

Acknowledgement of the three waves of HCI as the guide for the evolution of the field since its inception can allow researchers to follow a train of thought that justifies and unifies the context that we addressed. Production of the cognitive map and the following definition of concepts that composed the context in which this paper is focused on may provide relevant insights as a first step of research. Separation of the three groups of concepts in the cognitive map allowed for a comparison between the resulting research and practice tendencies of each of them. For example, although AR and AI systems are steadily evolving and providing technological innovations, print media has been overlooked in the interaction design context ever since hyperlink media was introduced. Additionally, the discrepancy of quantity components that relate print media to the second and third wave of HCI is relevant to acknowledge the lack of interest in realizing their potential. One of the ways in which it would be useful to gather more knowledge would be in research through design settings, by notes and records of processes through which materials, definitions of interaction or cognitive aspects are experienced. In particular, it may be interesting to explore the new forms of interaction made possible by the intersection of print media with an understanding of the materiality of interaction, tangibility and hybrid interfaces.

The arrangement of the various concepts, their proximities and distances and the descriptions of dependence or influence can help to situate future research directions, to consider integration of print media in interactive systems, preserving their material and haptic contribution and aid in cognition and distribution of information and knowledge.

Acknowledgements. This Work is Financed by National Funds Through FCT - Fundação Para a Ciência E a Tecnologia, I.P., Under the Strategic Project with the References UIDB/04008/2020 and UIDP/04008/2020.

References

1. Johnson, M., Goidel, K., Climek, M.: The decline of daily newspapers and the third-person effect. Soc. Sci. Q. **95**(5), 1245–1258 (2014)
2. Rose-Wiles, L.M.: Are print books dead? an investigation of book circulation at a mid-sized academic library. Tech. Serv. Q. **30**(2), 129–152 (2013)
3. Franklin, B.: The future of newspapers. Journal. Pract. **2**(3), 306–317 (2008)
4. Twenge, J.M., Martin, G.N., Spitzberg, B.H.: Trends in US Adolescents' media use, 1976–2016: the rise of digital media, the decline of TV, and the (near) demise of print. Psychol. Pop. Media Cult. **8**(4), 329 (2019)
5. Kuru Gönen, S.İ, Zeybek, G.: Using QR code enhanced authentic texts in EFL extensive reading: a qualitative study on student perceptions. Educ. Inf. Technol. **27**(2), 2039–2057 (2021). https://doi.org/10.1007/s10639-021-10695-w
6. Nadolny, L.: Interactive print: the design of cognitive tasks in blended augmented reality and print documents: blended print and augmented reality. Br. J. Edu. Technol. **48**(3), 814–823 (2017)
7. Pellas, N., Fotaris, P., Kazanidis, I., Wells, D.: Augmenting the learning experience in primary and secondary school education: a systematic review of recent trends in augmented reality game-based learning. Virtual Reality **23**(4), 329–346 (2019)
8. Sonderegger, A., Ribes, D., Henchoz, N., Groves, E.: Food talks: visual and interaction principles for representing environmental and nutritional food information in augmented reality. In: 2019 IEEE International Symposium on Mixed and Augmented Reality Adjunct (ISMAR-Adjunct), pp. 98–103. IEEE (2019)
9. Mangen, A., Walgermo, B.R., Brønnick, K.: Reading linear texts on paper versus computer screen: effects on reading comprehension. Int. J. Educ. Res. **58**, 61–68 (2013)
10. Stoop, J., Kreutzer, P., Kircz, J.: Reading and learning from screens versus print: a study in changing habits: Part 1 – reading long information rich texts. New Libr. World **114**(7/8), 284–300 (2013)
11. Mizrachi, D.: Online or print: which do students prefer? In: Kurbanoğlu, S., Špiranec, S., Grassian, E., Mizrachi, D., Catts, R. (eds.) ECIL 2014. CCIS, vol. 492, pp. 733–742. Springer, Cham (2014). https://doi.org/10.1007/978-3-319-14136-7_76
12. Carreiro, E.: Electronic books: how digital devices and supplementary new technologies are changing the face of the publishing industry. Publ. Res. Q. **26**(4), 219–235 (2010)
13. Larson, L.C.: E-books and audiobooks: extending the digital reading experience. Read. Teach. **69**(2), 169–177 (2015)
14. Delgado, P., Vargas, C., Ackerman, R., Salmerón, L.: Don't throw away your printed books: a meta-analysis on the effects of reading media on reading comprehension. Educ. Res. Rev. **25**, 23–38 (2018)
15. Twenge, J.M., Campbell, W.K.: Associations between screen time and lower psychological well-being among children and adolescents: evidence from a population-based study. Preventive Med. Rep. **12**, 271–283 (2018)
16. Dourish, P.: Where the Action Is. MIT Press, Cambridge (2001)
17. Hornecker, E.: The role of physicality in tangible and embodied interactions. Interactions, **18**(2), 19–23 (2011)

18. Robles, E., Wiberg, M.: Texturing the 'material turn' in interaction design. In: Proceedings of the Fourth International Conference on Tangible, Embedded, and Embodied Interaction—TEI '10, 137 (2010)
19. Sturdee, M., Alexander, J.: Analysis and classification of shape-changing interfaces for design and application-based research. ACM Comput. Surv. (CSUR) 51(1), 1–32 (2018)
20. Olberding, S., Soto Ortega, S., Hildebrandt, K., Steimle, J.: Foldio: digital fabrication of interactive and shape-changing objects with foldable printed electronics. In: Proceedings of the 28th Annual ACM Symposium on User Interface Software & Technology, pp. 223–232 (2015)
21. Qi, J., Buechley, L.: Electronic popables: exploring paper-based computing through an interactive pop-up book. In: Proceedings of the Fourth International Conference on Tangible, Embedded, and Embodied Interaction, pp. 121–128 (2010)
22. Ramakers, R., Todi, K., Luyten, K.: PaperPulse: an integrated approach for embedding electronics in paper designs. In: Proceedings of the 33rd Annual ACM Conference on Human Factors in Computing Systems, pp. 2457–2466 (2015)
23. Zheng, C., Gyory, P., Do, E.Y.L.: Tangible interfaces with printed paper markers. In: Proceedings of the 2020 ACM Designing Interactive Systems Conference, pp. 909–923 (2020)
24. Höök, K., Löwgren, J.: Characterizing interaction design by its ideals: a discipline in transition. She Ji: J. Des. Econ. Innov. 7(1), 24–40 (2021)
25. Yang, Q., Banovic, N., Zimmerman, J.: Mapping machine learning advances from HCI research to reveal starting places for design innovation. In: Proceedings of the 2018 CHI Conference on Human Factors in Computing Systems, pp. 1–11 (2018)
26. IBM (n.d.) How Industry 4.0 technologies are changing manufacturing. https://www.ibm.com/topics/industry-4-0#ancho%E2%80%93-1340549465. Accessed 05 Jan 2023
27. O'Donovan, P., Gallagher, C., Leahy, K., O'Sullivan, D.T.J.: A comparison of fog and cloud computing cyber-physical interfaces for Industry 4.0 real-time embedded machine learning engineering applications. Comput. Ind. 110, 12–35 (2019)
28. Bødker, S.: Third-wave HCI, 10 years later—Participation and sharing. Interactions 22(5), 24–31 (2015)
29. Swan, J.: Using cognitive mapping in management research: decisions about technical innovation. Br. J. Manag. 8(2), 183–198 (1997)
30. Kearney, A.R., Kaplan, S.: Toward a methodology for the measurement of knowledge structures of ordinary people: the conceptual content cognitive map (3CM). Environ. Behav. 29(5), 579–617 (1997)
31. Ackermann, F., Eden, C., Cropper, S.: Getting Started with Cognitive Mapping 14 (2004)
32. Neves, M., Bozzi, C., Melo, A., Chasqueira, A., Silva, S.: Print Interaction and Autonomous Systems: First Findings of an Exploratory Systematic Literature Review. Unplished manuscript (2023)
33. Lourdel, N., Gondran, N., Laforest, V., Debray, B., Brodhag, C.: Sustainable development cognitive map: a new method of evaluating student understanding. Int. J. Sustain. High. Educ. 8(2), 170–182 (2007)
34. Kipphan, H. (Ed.): Handbook of Print Media: Technologies and Production Methods. Springer Science & Business Media (2001)
35. Fishkin, K.: A taxonomy for and analysis of tangible interfaces. Personal Ubiquitous Comput. 8(5) (2004)
36. Kirk, D., Sellen, A., Taylor, S., Villar, N., Izadi, S.: Putting the physical into the digital: issues in designing hybrid interactive surfaces. In: In Proceedings of British HCI 2009 (2009)
37. Jung, J., Kleinsmann, M., Snelders, D.: A vision for design in the era of collective computing. J. Eng. Des. 33(4), 305–342 (2022)
38. Yang, Q.: Machine learning as a UX design material: how can we imagine beyond automation, recommenders, and reminders? In: AAAI Spring Symposia, Vol. 1, No. 2.1, pp. 2–6 (2018)

39. Bødker, S., Klokmose, C.N.: Dynamics in artifact ecologies. In: Proceedings of the 7th Nordic Conference on Human-Computer Interaction: Making Sense Through Design, pp. 448–457 (2012)

40. Al-Imamy, S.Y.: Blending printed texts with digital resources through augmented reality interaction. Educ. Inf. Technol. **25**(4), 2561–2576 (2019). https://doi.org/10.1007/s10639-019-10070-w

41. Lai, A.-F., Chen, C.-H., Lee, G.-Y.: An augmented reality-based learning approach to enhancing students' science reading performances from the perspective of the cognitive load theory: augmented reality-based science learning. Br. J. Edu. Technol. **50**(1), 232–247 (2019)

42. Margetis, G., Antona, M., Stephanidis, C.: A framework for supporting natural interaction with printed matter in ambient intelligence environments. In: Proceeding of the Fifth International Conference on Ambient Computing, Applications, Services and Technologies (AMBIENT'15), IARIA, pp. 72–78 (2015)

43. Kazanidis, I., Pellas, N.: Developing and assessing augmented reality applications for mathematics with trainee instructional media designers: an exploratory study on user experience. J. Univers. Comput. Sci. **25**(5), 489–514 (2019)

44. Majeed, Z.H., Ali, H.A.: A review of augmented reality in educational applications. Int. J. Adv. Technol. Eng. Explor. **7**(62), 20–27 (2020)

45. Li, W., Chiu, C.K., Tseng, J.C.: Effects of a personalized navigation support approach on students' context-aware ubiquitous learning performances. J. Educ. Technol. Soc. **22**(2), 56–70 (2019)

46. Weiser, M.: The computer for the 21st century. ACM SIGMOBILE Mobile Comput. Commun. Rev. **3**(3), 3–11 (1991)

47. Wiberg, M.: The Materiality of Interaction: Notes on the Materials of Interaction Design. The MIT Press (2018)

Listening Through Technology: An Interactive Sound Walk for a Suburb in Shenzhen

Marcel Zaes Sagesser$^{(\boxtimes)}$ and Binghuang Xu

School of Design, Southern University of Science and Technology,
Shenzhen, People's Republic of China
msagesser@sustech.edu.cn

Abstract. "Take A Step" is a sound walk that consists of a web-based user interface that the audience opens up on their phone, and with which they control the sound design that they hear on their headphones as they walk through and around the historic "Dawan Shiju" site in the Pingshan suburb of Shenzhen. The sound walk was made by four undergraduate students from the SUSTech School of Design (Shenzhen) in close collaboration with the instructor and co-instructor and was publicly presented at the UABB Biennale in Shenzhen in 2022. With this paper, the authors, who are also the project leaders, analyze specific modalities of interaction with a socio-cultural site through the designing of a digital media experience. They describe this modality as listening through technology and show how it can raise the user's awareness of the social, cultural, and mediatic specifics of the thematized site – not only on this given site, but in any other listening situation in the everyday as users may potentially carry the gained knowledge elsewhere. This paper puts forward the notion of technological listening as a complex modality happening in between reality and fiction, and in between the actual and the virtual. Listening to an environment through technology, the authors argue, is a method that accounts for the always multidimensional social, cultural, as well as sonic characteristics of a given site.

Keywords: Interaction · Sound Technology · Technological Listening · Mobile Media Art · Education

1 Introduction

What happens when we listen to an environment through technology? When we listen to an interactive, mediated stream of sound on our mobile phone while walking outdoors, in a suburb of Shenzhen?

"Our project is a sound walk which represents the conflict of tradition[al] life and modern life" [1], writes Tang Zilu, student in the SUSTech School of Design in Shenzhen, when we asked her to describe their project, "Take a Step." Deng Hexin, another student and co-maker of "Take a Step," states that "Our project is an interesting experiment about sound and interaction based on the cultural heritage of Hakka" [2]. "Take a Step" started in the fall term of 2022 in the core course "Sound Design" in the School of Design. It is a large-scale collaborative project made by four undergraduate students – Tang Zilu,

Deng Hexin, Sheng Yue, and Li Xian – under the guidance of ourselves: Marcel Zaes Sagesser as the instructor of record of the course, and Binghuang Xu as research assistant and co-project leader. All students were tasked, in groups, to create a site-specific sound walk for Pingshan where a part of the 9th Shenzhen/Hong Kong Bi City Biennale Of Urbanism/Architecture (UABB) was going to take place. The UABB invited our School in the first place to produce content for their exhibition, thus we developed the idea of sound walking as a way of responding with interactive technology to the given site. We hence tasked our students to develop interactive sound walks, the best of which would then be publicly presented at the Biennale. "Take a Step" was one of the four chosen projects that was voted for by peer students and project leaders to be publicly presented in December 2022 (see Fig. 1 and 2).

Fig. 1. The "Take a Step" audience walking around the historic monument "Dawan Shiju", guided by student Li Xian (photo courtesy of Profile Visual Art Studio, 2022)

"Take a Step" consists of a web-based user interface designed for mobile phones with Bluetooth headsets along with an interactive, digital sound design. It lets the users – the visitors of the UABB Biennale – get immersed into a hybrid experience when walking through the given environment in Shenzhen. This project hence not only is a *sound walk* – a genre with its own history – but also a piece of *mobile media art*, which Lanson et al. define as "art with diverse forms of mobile media" [3, p. 1], typically closely linked to the "social turn" [4, p. 19] and "social practice" at the beginning of the 21st century, where the digital becomes increasingly prevalent [3, p. 1]. In the sound walk "Take a Step", users interact with a ubiquitous mobile device. Yet, this mobile device also acts as a mediator between the user and the environment. Thus, the user ultimately interacts *with* the environment – *through* their mobile device. They listen to the environment through a digital, technological device.

In this paper, as authors who are also the project leaders, we closely analyze what it means to *listen through technology* with the example of the interactive sound walk

Fig. 2. Team member Li Xian guiding the "Take a Step" audience inside the historic monument "Dawan Shiju" (photo courtesy of Profile Visual Art Studio, 2022)

"Take a Step" that our four students, under our guidance, designed for a suburb in Shenzhen. We will analyze, from an interdisciplinary perspective, the interaction between people and a given site through a technological intervention. "Interaction", in this context, we understand as something much larger than the users tapping on the mobile phone's user interface as in the more typical touch-based and screen-based HCI applications. We are inspired by the methods of human-centered design that typically include all "interactions that occur between people and their environments" [5, p. 73], including social interactions, and interactions mediated through technology. We follow art historian Claire Bishop's notion of "participatory art", which she defines as the "involvement of many people (as opposed to the one-to-one relationship of 'interactivity')" in a process in which "people constitute the central artistic medium or material" [4, p. 2]. More so, we extend our definition of interaction by Lanson et al.'s understanding of *mobile media art* as something in which "social and critical enquiry and intervention becomes heightened" [3, p. 1], since we believe that "Take a Step" is a textbook example for a project emphasizing collaborative, social and critical inquiry. Such a broad understanding of *interaction* as the collaboration among all human and non-human participants – between all project creators, the locals interviewed during fieldwork in the suburb, with the complex cultural history of the chosen site, as well as between the users and the outdoor environment – gives us an opportunity to rethink the role of technology in these manifold interactive relationships. Hence, we understand walking on the site, body movement, and listening – and particularly *technologically mediated listening* – as an interaction device. The particular emphasis on *technological listening* we see as one possible way of interacting with an outdoor site. The case study "Take a Step" helps us outlining some notes toward the notion of technological listening – or *listening through technology* – as a modality that many of us practice every day. We argue that this modality, as an interaction technique performed by humans, can bring us additional knowledge about a particular environment.

2 Sound Walking as a Format

Sound walking – particularly without any technological extension such as headphones – is much older than the use of Walkmans or Bluetooth audio in public space. The famous field recordist Hildegard Westerkamp started in the 1970s to use sound walking as a method to study particular environments, both indoors and outdoors, by way of prioritizing listening over watching. For Westerkamp, sound walking is a practice that one can use, for example, when "walking across a downtown street, through a park, along the beach; ... [when] sitting in a doctor's office, in a hotel lobby, in a bank; ... [or when] shopping in a supermarket, a department store, or a Chinese grocery store" [6, p. 1]. In this sense, Westerkamp uses sound walking as a practice-based method – she refers to it as a method that is "diametrically opposed to the academic context" [7, p. 120] – to investigate the acoustic possibility of a particular place [6]. Sound walking, in Westerkamp and R. Murray Schafer's meaning [6, 8], has been done by many in groups or alone, in natural, rural, or urban environments.

That sound walking is not just fun,[1] but is a navigation method of great importance that may have been lost, has also been shown by Westerkamp. She describes how seafarers and Inuit people have historically relied on sound walking – careful, analytical listening while walking – to navigate the utmost difficult terrains that allow for no visual navigation [6].

But with the advent of mobile computing and battery-driven listening technologies that can be performed outdoors, since the early 2000s, walking in public space while listening to mediated sound has opened up manifold new possibilities for interaction [9, 10]. The new listening modality that emerges, which Bull calls "iPod culture", he describes as being about "the seamless joining together of experience in a flow, unifying the complex, contradictory and contingent nature of the world beyond the user" [9, p. 198]. He thereby suggests that sound walking is deeply temporal as it offers a flow, which unfolds in time, to navigate the environment. The user and the site, via listening technologies, are hence connected in, and through, time.

We, the project leaders, chose the format of the sound walk because it allows us, in teaching and in a creative design project, to emphasize interactive digital technologies, technological listening, and responding to a complex real-world site through sound. Interacting with an environment through technology is a key skill set and a core opportunity for design-related interventions that are foregrounded in the educational approach at the School of Design at Southern University of Science and Technology (SUSTech) in Shenzhen under Dean Thomas Kvan, along with the development of "ethically responsible", "socially engaged" design and "innovative pedagogy" [11]. For feasibility, given the short duration of the intense 4-week studio courses that we teach in the SUSTech School of Design, we simplified the realization of the project as much as possible. "Take

---

[1] "Perhaps soundwalking can be a step towards enhancing our chances of survival ... Or can simply be fun" [6, p. 7].

a Step" is based on an interactive website designed for mobile phones, which uses a map with clickable sound dots at the core of its user interface. Yet, for example, the map and website are not location-aware, as using GPS data would have exceeded what is possible in a teaching context within four weeks. Sound walking, and the creation of an interactive sound walk using digital technology, gave us the opportunity to closely work together with groups of undergraduate students, responding to the site through field-work and creative inquiry, and to foster technical knowledge about sound programming, sound design, and sound interaction. The sound walk as a format can thus be seen as a historic genre which lets itself ad libitum adapt to new media and new technologies. Sound walking, used in our teaching, is informed by the participatory art-making app-roach described by art historian Claire Bishop. She writes, "Today, we can recognise not just speech, but also teaching as an artistic medium" [4, p. 245]. In this sense, sound walk making, especially when working in an educational setting, we understand as a meaningful method to deeply engage a given site.

3 Technological Listening in Public Space

Public space, especially in densely populated urban areas, has become increasingly medi-atized in the past decades – for example with public, ambient, and advertising screens, as is shown by Papastergiadis et al. [12]; with "mobile media" primarily used by teenagers for identity creation and entertainment [13, p. 3563]; with storefront loudspeakers emit-ting music or advertisements to sidewalks or into endless shopping mall corridors; with the proposal to add ambient sound to dangerous public spaces in order to increase the safety of people [14]; or with "rooftop loudspeakers" broadcasting prayers and singing from mosques in Islamic countries [15, p. 190]. In addition to public broadcasting of imagery and sonic content, many of us use their private mobile phones with earbuds as a sound source, or as a sound and video source, when walking through urban spaces. Michael Bull writes, "Technology as a medium of organisation seamlessly mediates urban experience for large numbers of citizens – whether it is through individualising technologies like the iPod, the mobile phone or the automobile or through the multitude of hidden technologies that enable everyday life to function" [9, p. 198]. Elsewhere, Bull argues that it is the "Walkman use" (nowadays this would be the use of Bluetooth headsets along with a mobile phone) through which users "manage" their relationship to the environment, including their *social* relationships [10]. In these spaces, we find ourselves confronted with an increased amount of mediated sonic content – individ-ualized and public. This content at times seamlessly blends, and at times, seamlessly masks, the actual, immediate and non-mediated sonic environment. Sagesser has else-where described this blend of unmediated and mediated content that comes together for the user in one moment of time in one specific place (on their eardrum) as "hybrid auditory realities" [16, p. 87]. That the mediation matters and is audible for the users has been shown [17]; and Kromhout describes that a (mediated) reproduction of sound and its original can, and will, never be the same, and that hence the modernist dream of "perfect fidelity" is proven impossible – the reason for this failing of fidelity primarily being the filtering of any mediatic translation of a signal between sender and receiver, as well as the temporal shift between original and playback that is characteristic for recorded sound [18, p. 40].

Yet, what is crucial, is that the virtual component (the streamed audio from the mobile phone) and the actual component (the environmental sound) reach the user's eardrum both, at the same time, as physical sonic matter; for the user there is no difference on a physical, vibrational level of sound [16, 18]. Sound, mediated or not, ultimately comes to the user through a physical, material reality through which it is transmitted – vibrational matter [19].

Analyzing the experience that a potential user will have is difficult, because the sonic perception amidst this blend of a hybrid auditory reality is individual and contextual, but also, because the actual component of ambient sound in the moment of outdoor listening is arbitrary and ephemeral, and as such escapes our analysis. Sheng Yue, one of the undergraduate team members of "Take a Step", recounts an anecdote from when they guided an audience group on their sound walk, that there was a moment when recorded sounds of cooking were audible in the headphones, and at the same time, they had the group walking through the street kitchen where they were recorded – and a similar cooking procedure was taking place in that moment. She says, "you see the cooking place and you really hear some sounds of cooking" – and hence she posits a certain claim of realness when the actual and the deferred virtual coincide [20]. The described scene however remains a special coincidence within "Take a Step", since otherwise, the makers consciously decided against a one-to-one representation of the actual walking route through sound. Sheng says, "the image and the sound is not connected" and that it is exactly this discrepancy in-between that renders the experience unusual. She continues, "I just think it's fun because it's like 'Fǎn zhíjué' ['counterintuitive', translated by the authors]" [20].

It becomes clear that hybrid auditory realities that are to some extent designed by the project makers and to another extent dependent on an arbitrary, ephemeral public sonic ambience, open up a vast room for play – for creating literal, imaginary, fictive, representational, or, as Sheng says, "fun"[2] experiences that capitalize on the difference between mediated and immediate sound. A first conclusion is thus that listening through technology, or technological extensions, gives us an opportunity – or quite literally a playground on which we can explore, learn, and understand an environment like the chosen public space. This includes, as Sheng points out [20], that it enables us to have fun in a way that otherwise we would not.

4 Brief History of the Site: "Dawan Shiju" and "Hakka"

When working with sounds recorded in an outdoor site, or as it is called in anthropology and sound studies, in the "field", Paul Hegarty asks: "Beyond the sounds to be found in the 'field', how do we hear the field itself? What do we presume when going 'into' the field?" [21, p. 11]. His question acknowledges that interaction does not only take place for the end user who is experiencing the sound walk, but also for the makers of the project when they first go into the "field" with yet another form of technology: with sound recorders. In this sense, technological listening as a way of interacting with the site commences much earlier, even before the first recording is made, as the recordist may be listening

---

[2] Note that also Hildegard Westerkamp uses the term "fun" when relating to the practice of sound walking [6, p. 7].

to the site through the headphones connected to the recorder. Hildegard Westerkamp describes, "I usually monitor my recordings on headphones, which separates me from the environment – even though paradoxically I'm in the middle of it" [7, p. 114]. The students who made "Take a Step" conducted on-site fieldwork. They arrived on a site that already was full of sound, a space far from being "a void to be filled with sounds"; they arrived on a site that has "always been replete with social, cultural, and political meanings", as shows Ouzounian [22, p. 25]. In this already "full" space, they started interviewing locals, capturing sound and video recordings, and they explored the field by way of walking and observing. The way they interacted with the site through technology, such as the field recorder or the interview microphone, informed how they heard, how they listened, and ultimately, what kind of imagination they produced for the found site.

Fig. 3. The front of the historic monument "Dawan Shiju" with the pond in front of it, surrounded by modern residential buildings (photograph by the authors, 2022)

Yet, the site chosen for this interactive sound walk is particular. "Dawan Shiju"[3] is an ancient Hakka residence located in the suburban Pingshan, one of the districts of Shenzhen. "Dawan Shiju" is clearly visible as a historical settlement enclosed by walls and completed by a large pond in front of the main gate (see Fig. 3). Built in 1791 by the Zeng family [23, p. 46], today it is a musealized monument – a tourist site – where no one lives. "Dawan Shiju" is often misleadingly – as we will show later – associated with the so-called "Hakka People" – a descriptive term for an ethnic group historically found

---

[3] "Dawan Shiju" is the literal transcription of the Chinese 大万世居, and it literally means "residence for thousands of generations". There are several translations of the name. The curators of the UABB Biennale translated it as "Dawanshiju"; on site, in the now turned museum, it has been translated as "Wanshi Habitat"; yet on the local government website called "Shenzhen Archives", it is called "Dawan Ancestral Residence". For legibility and consistency, we decided to call it "Dawan Shiju" in this paper.

in Mainland China. One of the most important native writers in Taiwan in the early 20th century, Zhong Lihe,[4] imagined a lot about Hakka culture without ever having visited the homelands associated with Hakka culture. In one of his masterpieces, Yuan Xiang Ren, he wrote: "'Homeland, homeland,' they sighed" [25, p. 56]. The "they" refers to Zhong Lihe's grandmother and father who identified themselves as Hakka people, but none of them was born in that distant "homeland". Zhong's words are representative of the nomadic nature of Hakka people who are today spread across countries and holding on to a term built around a shared imagination for an ethnic group. Nicole Constable argues that the term "Hakka", by a long-term shared common sense, means "guest" or "stranger"; people who historically migrated from Northern China to other areas of China [26, p. 3]. In the beginning, the term has not been chosen by the ethnic group themself, but by others referring to them. Hence, the term remains ambiguous, and has multiple meanings under different historical and cultural contexts, including that the term in some periods was pejoratively used and had a deeply discriminatory dimension [27, pp. 6–8].[5] As nomadic people who have repeatedly been on the move, both within Mainland China and worldwide,[6] "Hakka" people have often been referred to as "guests" that stood in stark opposition to the respective locals. Today's meaning of "Hakka" people and culture is much more positive, which mainly goes back to the academic work in Hakka studies and the pivotal work of Luo Xianglin in 1933 [29, pp. 36–92]. Given the complex and ambiguous history of Hakka culture, it would be too hasty to simply associate the Dawan Shiju monument with Hakka culture, or the other way around.

Especially in a project with an educational component, we have to be very precise about the cultural history of Dawan Shiju and its complex yet not simple relationship with Hakka people. Hence, the given site remains historically ambiguous with its complex history, but it is also today an ambivalent space as it has been turned into a tourist site, only partially shaped by Hakka people. There is no single way of portraying Dawan Shiju and Hakka culture; instead, along with our students, we are therefore, like the Hakka people earlier, turned into *guests*. As such, we remain outsiders who capture the several imaginations that we found on site. The site, today, is part of the modern city of Shenzhen. It combines historical tales and contemporary life.

Deng, one of the makers of "Take a Step", explains how they used walking, as well as talking to locals, as a method to learn about the found culture: "The story was born from our research and understanding of Hakka culture, and most of all, from our own walks in [added by authors: "in", but also "around"] Dawan Shiju" [2]. While doing

---

[4] "Zhong Lihe (1915–60) is arguably Taiwan's most important native writer of the early post-Japanese period. His position on the margins of Chinese culture was determined by his birth and first thirty years of life in Japanese Taiwan and, further, by his membership in the Hakka minority" [24, p. 155].

[5] In 1845, the term "Hakka" for the first time showed up in an official report by the Hong Kong government. Before that, Hakka people have been called differently, for instance, Kih, ka, kea jin people, kheh, Hoklo, Hok-ha, Kheh-kia. Most of these terms were based on different pronunciations of the word "Hakka" [28].

[6] "Since the seventeenth century, and particularly during the eighteenth and nineteenth centuries, Hakka people also emigrated to Taiwan, Malaysia, and other regions of Southeast Asia, and as far as South Asia, Africa, Oceania, Europe, the Caribbean, and North and South America" [26, pp. 4–5].

their fieldwork, the four students put themselves into the real scene and interacted with the actual locals. This process of interaction with the site will later become audible – and experienceable – for the audience, when they also walk around the real scene, in and around Dawan Shiju, while participating in the sound walk "Take a Step". Another team member, Tang Zilu, explains, "'Take a Step' means that you just start to know about other culture[s], life and people no matter where you are originally from" [30]. Deng added, saying that after having realized "Take a Step" she now pays more "attention to the local customs … and take[s] the initiative to talk with the locals" when she goes to a new place. She goes on, "Benefiting from the … course [within which we realized "Take a Step with them], I also pay attention to the different sounds in strange places, such as the sound of people talking, the sound of vehicles on the road, or the sound of nature, all of which can reflect the regional characteristics of a place" [31]. This means that the engagement in fieldwork, along with the technological modality of listening through microphones and headphones that she has learned in this course, has lastingly changed her listening practice beyond this project.

5   The Interactive, Map-Based Sound Design of "Take a Step"

The four students conducted on-site field recordings, processed these in audio editing software, and started to extend their sound archive by adding synthetic sounds that they produced in software synthesizers. The recorded sounds are mainly urban ambi-ent sounds, such as traffic; industrial and construction noise; weather-related ambience, such as wind; domestic sounds, such as cooking; birdsong, a recording of the nearby river, recorded voices, etc.; which they extended by synthetic atmospheres and beats that they produced in software. Sound, in media production, can both represent (depict) an outdoor world in sound (i.e. a field recording of a flowing river), or it can illustrate the atmosphere of it in a more abstract way, including its affective dimension (such as with a synthetic atmosphere as an underlying, organizing element). The makers used both concepts simultaneously, combining representational with illustrative sound elements. Yet, they emphasized, even in the representational elements, the non-literal representa-tion – i.e., the detachment of a specific location on the map with a sound that is recorded there, as Sheng said in an interview [20].

They used a digital audio workstation to arrange their sounds in time and to prototype an interactive sound experience. Their concept was to compose a 15-min long sound design – a single file – that starts running as a background sound once the user opens up the website on their phone. In addition to this background track, they designed a number of 16 shorter location sound clips – each between 2 and 8 s long – which can be triggered by the user when clicking on one of the sound location dots in the user interface (see Fig. 4). "Take a Step" maps the site sonically, it creates a map of the environment with location dots as the user interface. Yet, it is worth noting, as Sheng has pointed out, that this map defeats its purpose in the sense that it is not a literal map, but it is one that mixes the actual geography with a sonic imagination that is invented by the student group. They use technology, and specifically sonic technology, to create an alternative space that could not exist in the real world, in which different places and temporalities coincide, co-exist, and overlap.

Fig. 4. An audience member interacting with the web-based user interface of "Take a Step" (photograph by the authors, 2023)

The emerging sound design is hence non-linear, as it blends a linear background track with short sound impulses on top of it, which are controlled by the user. The user decides on which sound dots they click, how fast, and in which succession or simultaneity (i.e. very fast succession) – thus they decide on the density of the urban soundscape that is produced on their phone, in their headphones. Similar to Westerkamp's analysis of "soundscape composition" (a musical genre), our students also walk a "fine line" to balance "the voice of the recorded environment" with "that of the composer" [7, p. 116]. Through the technological intervention of recording and composing an interactive sound experience, they turn an "unmediated sound world of urban society … where nothing happens" for the listening subject [9, p. 202] into a mediated experience full of imaginations, associations, fragments, and sonic events grounded in their fieldwork (see Fig. 5).

The final sound experience for the user, as discussed earlier, blends the actual environmental ambience with the virtual streamed sound from the mobile phones. Kromhout argues that the technological reproduction of recorded sound at the same time is characterized by a deep feeling of something "past", and a deep feeling of "presence". Past, since the reproduction carries the traces of mediation and time past since it was recorded, and presence, because the playback results in vibrational, physical sound happening in the here and now [18]. In this sense, he explains, "technologically (re)produced sound generates a continuous push and pull between pastness and presence" [18, p. 41]. It is this push and pull that the four makers of "Take a Step" benefit from when juxtaposing field recordings of the site with the actual sonic ambience of the site and with synthetic background sounds. As to emphasize this tension, they used the shutter sound of a photo camera as a feedback sound for user interaction: when the user presses a sound location dot on the user interface, they first hear a camera shutter before the sound clip is playing.

With this shutter, the group emphasizes the mediatic dimension of technological listening. They emphasize the fact that the streamed content was recorded in the first place. Kromhout argues that "The 'click' of the photo camera, the short time between pressing the release and the closing of the shutter, constitutes the cut that defines [the] delay" [18, p. 37] – that is, the delay between the original taken and the copy reproduced.

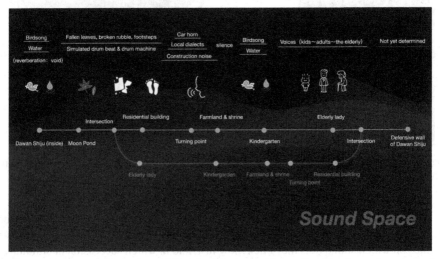

Fig. 5. Conceptual sketch of the sound walk with landmarks, realized by the student team after fieldwork (diagram courtesy of the student team, 2022)

This tension, or simultaneity, of past and presence within "Take a Step" speaks to the technology of memorizing. Sounds have a vast potential to carry memory within them. Student Deng recounts, "During the interview process we built our own unique memories of the place, and at the same time the voices of the people we interviewed appeared in our sound work, and every time we heard them, it was a memory;" and she goes on, "the sound elements we used also have their own 'memory', such as the music of the garbage truck 'Only Mom is Good', which immediately reminds many Chinese people of their childhood" [2]. This means that the interaction of the project makers with the site is also mediated by the technology of memorizing – both with machines when sound is recorded and archived, and with humans, when they recall a memory that they connect to a specific sound. The interaction that "Take a Step" is built on hence emphasizes how *listening through technology* is connected to machinic and human memory of a specific place.

Fig. 6. Team member Li Xian explaining the user interface to the audience (photo courtesy of Profile Visual Art Studio, 2022)

6   Conclusion

Technological listening as in "Take a Step" where we listen to a suburb through a piece of technology, we understand as a device and practice to interact with a site (see Fig. 6). Yet, such *technological listening* is far from simply "adding" a virtual component of sound to an already sonic urban environment. More so, the interaction component extends beyond the obvious pressing and clicking of buttons and icons on a web-based mobile phone user interface. Instead, what is created is a situation that includes the sound walker as a perceiving subject, their mobile phone, their earbuds, streamed sound content, sonic outdoor ambience, and the physical-visual environment that the sound walker moves through – the suburb. This situation is deeply complex, and from the perspective of the sound walker, we could describe it as a modality of perceiving, in which *reality* and *fiction*, *actual* and *virtual*, and *immediate* and *mediated* start to blend. What is created is a "hybrid auditory reality" [16]. It is a situation in which one interacts with the site through listening, through walking or moving, and through controlling the emitted sounds from the phone via the user interface. We argue that such a complex situation of *technological listening* and *interaction* like in "Take a Step" can raise the sound walker's awareness of the specifics of the site they are walking on, including its social, cultural, or historical dimensions. "Take a Step" demonstrates how an interactive technological listening situation can let its users gain additional knowledge about the socio-cultural meaning – and especially about the socio-cultural complexities that we have shown – of Dawan Shiju, the Pingshan suburb that surrounds it, and the interconnectedness with the Hakka people who lived or live there. In sum, "Take a Step" stands for a practice-based, artistic, and interdisciplinary method of responding to a given site through interactive, digital technology. We have shown that if we *listen* to a site *through technology*, we perform a modality of interacting with this site through which we can gain embodied knowledge about the manifold communities, the different histories, the built and natural environments – in short, about the site that will always be a multidimensional social, cultural, and sonic space. "Take a Step" helps us to render the UABB audience aware of this fact. Deng Hexin says, "We hope that the audience of our project can also *take a step* [to] bravely ... explore a new place and a new culture. This is the step that we take them to, towards the local culture" [31]. And Tang Zilu adds, "Everyone takes a step" [30].

Acknowledgments. We want to thank the four students who developed, realized, and presented the sound walk "Take a Step" at the UABB Biennale in Shenzhen in the fall and winter of 2022: Tang Zilu, Deng Hexin, Sheng Yue, and Li Xian. We are also grateful to the curatorial team of the Pingshan UABB Biennale of Shenzhen for inviting us and other SUSTech School of Design members to produce new work for their exhibition. Thanks to members of the SUSTech School of Design for supporting the research and production of the sound walks. Thanks to research assistant Qu Hanyu. Thanks to the residents in Pingshan who were willing to talk to us.

References

1. Tang, Z.: Take a Step - Email Interview (2023)
2. Deng, H.: Take a Step - Email Interview (2023)
3. Lanson, K., Silva, A., Hjorth, L.: Mobile Media Art: An Introduction. In: The Routledge Companion to Mobile Media Art, Routledge (2020)
4. Bishop, C.: Artificial Hells: Participatory Art and the Politics of Spectatorship. (Verso Books, 2012)
5. Rafael, S., Santiago, E., Rebelo, F., Noriega, P., Vilar, E.: Bio-Centred interaction design: a new paradigm for human-system interaction. In: Soares, M.M., Rosenzweig, E., Marcus, A. (eds.) Design, User Experience, and Usability: Design Thinking and Practice in Contemporary and Emerging Technologies, pp. 69–79, Springer International Publishing (2022). https://doi.org/10.1007/978-3-031-05906-3_6
6. Westerkamp, H.: Soundwalking. Sound Heritage **III**, (1974)
7. Lane, C., Carlyle, A.: Hildegard Westerkamp. Interviewed by Cathy Lane. In: In the Field: the Art of Field Recording, pp. 109–121 (Uniforbooks, 2014)
8. Schafer, R.M.: Ear Cleaning. Notes for an Experimental Music Course. (Berandol Music; sole selling agents: Associated Music Publishers, New York, 1969)
9. Bull, M.: The Audio-Visual iPod. In: The Sound Studies Reader (ed. Sterne, J.) (Routledge, 2012)
10. Bull, M.: The world according to sound: investigating the world of walkman users. New Media Soc. **3**, 179–197 (2001)
11. SUSTech School of Design & Kvan, T. SUSTech School of Design. https://designschool.sustech.edu.cn/about (2023)
12. Papastergiadis, N., Barikin, A., McQuire, S., Yue, A.: Ambient Screens and Transnational Public Spaces. Hong Kong University Press (2016)
13. Keeffe, L.O.: Reclaiming Public Space: Sound and Mobile Media Use by Teenagers (2015)
14. Sayin, E., Krishna, A., Ardelet, C., Briand Decré, G., Goudey, A.: Sound and safe: the effect of ambient sound on the perceived safety of public spaces. Int. J. Res. Market. **32**, 343–353 (2015)
15. Eisenberg, A.I.: Islam, Sound and Space: Acoustemology and Muslim Citizenship on the Kenyan Coast (2015)

16. Sagesser, M.Z.: A digital archive of participatory location rhythm performances: listening as a way of attending to the pandemic. In: Agamennone, M., Palma, D., Sarno, G. (eds.) Sounds of the Pandemic: Accounts, Experiences, Perspectives in Times of COVID-19, Focal Press 92022)
17. Bolter, J. D. & Grusin, R. *Remediation: Understanding New Media.* (MIT Press, 1999)
18. Kromhout, M.J.: Hearing pastness and presence: the myth of perfect fidelity and the temporality of recorded sound. Sound Stud. **6**, 29–44 (2020)
19. Eidsheim, N.S.: Sensing Sound: Singing and Listening as Vibrational Practice. Duke University Press (2015)
20. Sheng, Y.: Take a Step - Voice Interview (2023)
21. Hegarty, P.: Annihilating Noise. Bloomsbury Academic (2021)
22. Ouzounian, G.: Stereophonica: Sound and Space in Science, Technology, and the Arts. The MIT Press (2020)
23. Zhang, Y.: (张一兵). Shenzhen Fengwu Zhi [Chuangtong Jianzhu Juan] (*深圳风物志-传统 建筑卷*). (Haitian Publishing House (海天出版社), 2016). Translated by the authors
24. McClellan, T.M.: Home and the Land: the 'Native' Fiction of Zhong Lihe (原鄉與故鄉: 鍾理和小說中的鄉土情結) (2009)
25. Zhong, L.: (钟理和). Yuan Xiang Ren (*原乡人*). (Zhejiang Publishing United Group Digital Media (浙江出版集团数字传媒有限公司), 2013). Translated by the authors
26. Constable, N.: Introduction. What Does It Mean to Be Hakka? In: Guest People: Hakka Identity in China and Abroad (ed. Constable, N.) University of Washington Press (1996)
27. Shih, T.: (施添福) From the "Guest" to the Hakka (3–1): The Label and the Identity of Hakka in Taiwan (從「客家」到客家[三]: 臺灣的客人稱謂和客人認同[上篇]). *Global Hakka Studies* (*全球客家研究*) 3, (2014). Translated by the authors
28. Shih, T.: (施添福). From the "Guest" to the Hakka (2): The Emergence, Transformation, and Spread of the Term Hakka on the Eastern Quangdong (從「客家」到客家[二]: 粵東「Hakka・客家」稱謂的出現、蛻變與傳播). Global Hakka Studies (*全球客家研究*) **2**, (2014). Translated by the authors
29. Luo, X.: (罗香林). An Introduction to the Study of the Hakkas Studies in Its Ethnic, Historical, and Cultural Aspects (*客家研究导论*). (Shi-Shan Library, 1933). Translated by the authors
30. Tang, Z.: Follow-Up Email Interview (2023)
31. Deng, H.: Follow-Up Email Interview (2023)

Designing a Robot for Enhancing Attention of Office Workers with the Heavily Use of Screen

Zhiya Tan, Zhen Liu[✉], Zixin Guo, and Shiqi Gong[✉]

School of Design, South China University of Technology, Guangzhou 510006,
People's Republic of China
liuzjames@scut.edu.cn, 201930091063@mail.scut.edu.cn

Abstract. In the context of the epidemic and the Internet era, the computer screen has become a necessary device for people in the workplace. According to statistics, office workers face the computer for eight hours a day on average. Prolonged gaze at the screen has been shown to be one of the causes of reduced productivity, in addition to workplace loneliness, distraction, lack of motivation, and lack of work planning are the current state of low productivity. Existing work has shown that companion robotics has achieved remarkable success in helping humans and improving human well-being. In this paper, we design a work companion robot to improve worker productivity in the work office in three dimensions: mental, physical, and mental health. To support our study, we conducted a survey of daily computer office workers to understand where the problems lie and to gather information about the possible use of robots to support workers. Then, we proposed the concept of a companion robot to alert workers and suggest next actions by monitoring their pupil status, sight tracking, and blink frequency to determine their concentration and fatigue. To convert between pupil state and concentration level, we collected attention-related eye movement data under task state from a group of computer workers based on the Stroop paradigm and classified and quantified the concentration status using a random forest regression model. Finally, we designed the appearance of the robot, its internal structure, and its interaction. Future work will focus on experimentally verifying the effectiveness of this robot in improving workers' attention and work isolation, and refining more features.

Keywords: Workplace Loneliness · Companion Robot · Gaze Tracking · Feature Selection · Stroop Paradigm · Attention · Pupil Response · Eye Movement Data

1 Background

With the rapid development of technology and the catalyst of the epidemic, the online office has become the trend of enterprise development. The rapid development of information technology has provided important technical support for telecommuting [1]. The evolution of mobile communication technology networks and the upgrading of the functions of computers and smartphones have improved the efficiency of people's interaction and collaboration across time and space. At the same time, the Newcastle pneumonia epidemic has driven and accelerated the popularity of telecommuting, and as a fundamental

A. Marcus et al. (Eds.): HCII 2023, LNCS 14031, pp. 246–261, 2023.
https://doi.org/10.1007/978-3-031-35696-4_18

component of the new digital economy, online working is the main option used by many enterprises to cope with the Newcastle pneumonia epidemic [2]. With the continuous improvement in the level of development of enterprise information technology, office computers have been integrated into every aspect of the modern office of enterprises, becoming a powerful tool for the rapid transmission of information, sharing resources, and improving efficiency and quality. Online office is more inseparable from the support of the computer, and its work mode is mainly based on computer office.

In terms of mental health, it is easy to feel lonely in a solitary workspace. Sometimes, not being able to get an immediate response from a colleague online and not being sure if they are online or if they have received a message not only reduces productivity but often creates a sense of anxiety [3]. As the boundary between life and work becomes blurred in such a working pattern. The work-family balance becomes a problem for employees to solve, and if not properly disposed, this will greatly reduce people's happiness [4].

In terms of physical health, with the shift from offline to online office mode, people are prone to a lack of clear time management, which to a certain extent will disrupt the rhythm of work and teamwork rules, making it easier for people to feel tired in the process of facing the computer for a long time in the office. Employees' wrists, shoulders, and necks may feel sore and even produce dizziness and headaches.

In terms of society, working across time and space allows people to communicate with each other forever separated by screens, which affects employees' social skills to some extent, as people often have difficulty feeling each other's emotions from words [1]. Over time, employees may have difficulty adapting to offline social activities and regulating their emotions in real face-to-face social scenarios.

In this paper, we present the design process of a companion robot for use in office settings to improve their concentration and health during work. A survey of the target group, a young population, was conducted to better understand their needs and to determine the design guidelines for the companion robot. After identifying the needs of the users, we introduced the robot concept by presenting an initial 3D model and a description of its hardware. Finally, we verified the feasibility of our design through Stroop experiments.

2 Literature Review

While robots were originally developed for functional benefits, their role is gradually expanding to include social support and companionship [5]. With the advancement of robotics and artificial intelligence, companion robots started to take shape: these humans or animal-shaped, smaller or bigger mechanic creatures can carry out different tasks and have interactions with humans and their environment. Numerous papers have explored the application scenarios of companion robots, with the main target users being the elderly, children, and patients with special diseases.

As the world's population ages, the mental health, physical health, and quality of life of older adults are in the spotlight, and research has proven that interacting with companion robots can improve engagement, interaction, and stress indicators, and reduce loneliness and substance use in older adults [6]. In elderly care, application scenarios are subdivided and designed mainly for the health of the elderly, such as the care process for the elderly with mild cognitive impairment, health supervision for the elderly living alone, and companionship issues for dementia patients [7–9]. Educational companion robot roles targeting children include improving children's early language education, acting as a social character, interacting with children as peers while understanding each learner's learning status to adjust the child's classroom strategies, and providing after-school assistance [10, 11]. Companion robots play an adjunctive role in the therapeutic care of neurocognitive disorders (autism and dementia), neurophysical injuries (brain injury, cerebral palsy, and Parkinson's disease), and depression [12]. Study finds that using companion robots in animal form can reduce pain and emotional anxiety for patients and their parents [13].

In addition to the elderly, children, and patients, ordinary young people need the companionship of robots. Loneliness and isolation are on the rise, threatening the well-being of all ages globally, and companion robots have the potential to alleviate loneliness [14]. Companion robots that have a wide audience in the market include the Emo emotional companion robot, Panasonic emotional robot, LOVOT intelligent companion robot, and Eilik desktop companion mini robot. All of these robots can provide fun through inter-action with users (e.g., touch, voice, games) and also have small functions to provide convenience to users in their lives (e.g., controlling smart homes, timers). Interaction with a companion robot that provides social support includes utilitarian variables and hedonic variables, where the user wants the robot to be involved in their daily activities, not only useful but also easy to use and able to perform the tasks given by the user with maximum efficiency [15]. The hedonic variables are defined as the pleasure that the robot brings to the user, its appearance and functionality need to be anthropomorphic and pleasing, and interaction needs to be easier and more enjoyable [16]. Existing companion robots focus on hedonic variables more than utilitarian variables, i.e., more to make users feel interesting, novel, and pleasant, instead of giving companion robots more practical uses, resulting in weak user stickiness.

3   Method

3.1   Survey Design

A survey was conducted for this study with the main purpose of understanding the level of concentration during work and their perceptions and expectations of robots. An online survey was conducted with a younger cohort to better understand the context of online working and predict the degree of effectiveness of companion robots, and gather information to support our design definition of robots.

The Participants. Online research participants were all in China. A total of 168 young people participated in this survey, and we obtained 150 valid samples. The participants were between the ages of 20–36 (M = 27.89, SD = 4.04) and included 90 females and 60 males. Participants in the valid sample had work experience at the time of completing the survey.

Questionnaire Content. The survey focused on four aspects: basic information about the young group, frequency of attention loss and regulation, acceptance of robots, and expectations of companion robots. First, the survey collected basic information on the age and gender of the participants. At the same time, we asked the participants about their problems in using computers for office work from three aspects: mental, physical, and social. Second, we asked participants about the frequency of attention loss during work ("never" (-2) to "always" (2)). Fourth, we will ask participants about their acceptance of the robot in terms of how much they like it, how safe it is, and how much they perceive it ("strongly disagree" (-2) to "strongly agree" (2)). To obtain information on the design criteria of the robot, we asked participants about their expectations of the companion robot, which included perceptions of appearance and functionality.

The questionnaire consisted of 16 questions, as shown in Table 1.

Table 1. The question in the questionnaire.

NO	Questions
1	What is your gender?
2	What age group are you in?
3	Which of the following types of jobs do you currently have or have had for the longest time in the past 1 year?
4	How long do you work on the computer at the office?
5	What kind of mental health problems do you have when you use the computer to work?
6	What kind of health problems do you have when you work with computers?
7	What kind of social problems do you have after using the computer for work?
8	How often do you lose your attention when working on your computer?
9	How do you adjust when you can't concentrate?
10	How willing are you to interact with the companion robot when you are working alone?
11	How safe do you feel when a companion robot is working around you?
12	How much do you agree with the statement "I think it's easy to interact with companion robots"?
13	What are your expectations for the look of a companion robot at work?
14	When the companion robot is used as a personal assistant, what functions do you want it to have when working from a computer?
15	When the companion robot is used as a relational companion, what functions would you like it to have when working at the computer?
16	When the companion robot is a close friend, what functions do you want it to have when working on your computer?

3.2 Results and Analysis

According to the results of the questionnaire, we obtained the following information.

Young people use computers for long hours. 36% of them use computers for 7–10 h a day, even 28% use them for 11–13 h, and 4% for 14–16 h. This means that more than half of the respondents use the computer for a long time to work.

Frequency of Attention Loss in Young People and How It is Regulated. Only 6% of people say they never lose focus when working on a computer, while 24% lose focus easily and often. Of these, 60% would choose to take a break to regulate the loss of attention. A close second solution was walking, which accounted for 44% of all participants. It is clear that the problem of attention loss is common when working with computers, and that people are used to taking breaks to alleviate the problem of attention loss.

Health Problems While Working with Computers. All participants identified themselves as having mental, physical, or social problems. In the detection of mental health problems, 62% believed that using a computer office tends to lead to psychological problems of low well-being. Meanwhile, 54% and 16% felt anxious and lonely, respectively. In the detection of physical health problems, discomfort in different parts of the body dominated. Among them, 60% of people felt neck soreness. Fatigue and vision loss was also the main health problems, accounting for 46% and 44% respectively. In the detection of social problems, half of the people said that they tend to lose the ability to socialize offline after working long hours on the computer. This was followed by a perceived fear and fatigue of social interaction, which accounted for 46% of the respondents.

Acceptance of the Companion Robot. In the perception of safety question, the results were neutral mean (M = 0.12, SD = 0.746). Of these, 34% felt safe or very safe when the companion robot was working around them, 10% more than the number of people who felt unsafe. In the question on interactivity, the results were neutral mean (M = 0.24, SD = 0.942). Nearly half of them were willing or very willing to interact with the companion robot. In the perception question, the results were neutral (M = 0.06, SD = 0.005). 56% of people had a neutral view on "I think it is easy to interact with a companion robot". This shows that people have a neutral positive attitude towards the issue of safety and interactivity, while their perception of companion robots is still lacking.

The Appearance of the Companion Robot. We consulted the participants about their views on the shape of the companion robots. Among this group, 60% accepted that the companion robots were designed as more concrete images, such as animals and plants.

Companion Robot Functionality. When a companion robot is used as a relational peer, 32% said they want it to have the ability to play games. A close second feature is sharing life, accounting for 28%. When a companion robot is used as an intimate buddy, nearly half want it to have the ability to comfort negative emotions. When a companion robot acts as a personal assistant, 44% want to be able to use the companion robot to look up information. Collectively, people prefer companion robots to have the functions of sharing life, checking information, comforting negative emotions, and resting reminders.

3.3 Define

The target users of this design are workers who face the screen for a long time. According to the above-mentioned survey, long hours of work facing the screen will lead to high-frequency distractions, which will affect the mental health, physical health, and brain health of workers in the long run. When facing a computer, there are always inefficient behaviors and negative emotions. The design hopes that the robot can not only bring psychological comfort to the workers but also monitor the workers' work status in real time and remind them to return their attention to work.

One study identified companion robots as having three potential roles: personal assistant, relational companion, and intimate partner [17]. In this paper, we classify the functions of this companion robot in conjunction with questionnaire research, as in Table 2 below:

Table 2. Function Definition.

Personal assistant	Relational peer	Intimate buddy
Information Search	Play Mini Games	Comforting negative emotions
Timer	Casual Chat	Break reminders
Attention Monitoring	Share Life	Companion
Schedule reminder		

4 Results

4.1 Appearance Design and Modeling

Since the screen and camera need to be integrated into the robot, we used the head of the robot as the main functional and interactive area, and the torso part of the robot as the place for the Raspberry Pi, considering the overall aesthetic appearance and functional utility. To make the overall appearance of the robot cuter and more approachable, we deliberately exaggerated the size of the head, designed the screen in the shape of goggles, and hid the camera at the nose (see Fig. 1) after confirming the key appearance elements, we also added some body language elements, such as movable ears and hands on the screen, in order to increase the interaction variety.

Fig. 1. A figure Rendering of the robot's appearance.

4.2 Hardware

We will use Raspberry Pi 3 Model B (operating at 5V) as the main controller of the robot. The other structures are divided into four main parts: camera, display, ear driver, and power supply.

Camera Part. The TC410HD camera module is used for real-time communication with the USB connection of the Raspberry Pi to get the user's reaction in real time. The camera has a clarity of up to 1080P for high-definition face recognition.

Ear Driving Part. Two MG90S servo motors are used to connect with the GPIO interface of Raspberry Pi to make the ear achieve the effect of swinging left and right through the program responsible for interactive feedback. This servo motor has the features of large starting torque, high precision, and easy control, which is an excellent actuator for the robot control system.

Display Part. A 5-inch display is connected to the HDMI of the Raspberry Pi, which is used as a real-time display feedback to the system. At the same time, to achieve the visual effect of the goggle-type display, we assembled a black goggle-type transparent case on the base of the display.

Microphone Section. The Semmation S9 microphone module is used for real-time recording with the Raspberry Pi's USB connection. The microphone has an internal integrated noise reduction chip that effectively restores the human voice and runs the device to pick up speech at a range of 3 m.

Speaker Section. Use the Yahboom speaker module to connect to the Raspberry Pi's USB for sound playback.

Power Supply Part. LM2596 buck converter DC-DC step-down is used to connect four 3.7v Li-ion batteries (700mAh) to the power connector of Raspberry Pi to provide a stable 5V voltage to ensure the stable operation of the system.

4.3 Software

In order to enable the intended functionality, the software framework of the robot is designed in this paper (see Fig. 2). The framework considers multiple input possibilities in two input modes, video, and sound, and also preprocesses the input data with several preprocessing modules to filter and filter the valuable parts of the raw data. These parts are sent to Action Selection Engines for processing, and after preprocessing the output, the final result is a result that the user can feel and interact with.

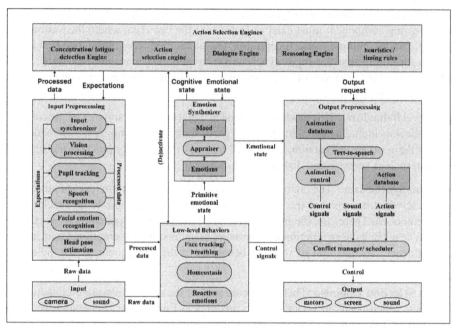

Fig. 2. Software framework diagram (square boxes represent data storage, capsule-shaped boxes represent processes, and oval-shaped boxes represent sensors/actuators).

The architecture is divided into seven functional components, which are Input, Input Reprocessing, Low-level Behaviors, Emotion Synthesizer, Action Selection Engines,

Output Preprocessing, and Output. Each functional component contains several functionally related modules. The main line of execution of the whole system is the five functional components Input, Input Reprocessing, Action Selection Engines, and Output Preprocessing. The Low-level Behaviors and Emotion Synthesizer components are only activated when an emotionally charged image or voice is detected and are used to analyze the emotions in these representations and reflect them in the Action Selection Engines and Output Preprocessing components. This process enables the robot's feedback to be emotionally based, which is an important component of the companion robot.

Each of these seven functional components and the modules they contain is briefly described below.

Input. This component is the most basic and critical part of the robot, which mainly consists of a camera and microphone. The clarity and recognizability of the raw data collected by the camera and microphone is the key to the normal operation of the whole program. They are responsible for receiving and transmitting the raw data to the subsequent Input Reprocessing and Low-level Behaviors functional components.

Input Reprocessing. For Action Selection Engines, it is impractical to directly input the raw data obtained by the Input component, which requires a huge amount of wasted computation and reduces the response time of the whole system. Therefore, the Input Reprocessing component must exist to preprocess the raw data, where the Vision processing, Pupil tracking, Speech recognition, Facial emotion recognition, and Head pose It is worth noting that the Input synchronizer, as the data manager, can create links between the different modes of processing data in order to pass them to another module as individual events.

Low-level Behaviors. This module is special in that it can detect some examples of low-level behaviors including facial tracking and gaze, blinking, breathing, robot homeostasis such as the need for interaction, sleep and "hunger" (low battery power), and reactive emotion such as surprise and disgust [18].

Emotion Synthesizer. The companion robot needs to have a certain level of emotional feedback, which means that the system needs to provide appropriate feedback to the user's emotions. Therefore, the main role of this functional component is to work with the Low-level Behaviors functional component to understand the emotional part, which will influence the selection of relevant behaviors in the subsequent Action Selection Engines.

Action Selection Engines. This is the core part of the entire software architecture of the robot, which needs to select specific modules in Engines for processing based on the incoming feature data. To output the results related to the user's concentration, voice text, robot interaction action selection, etc.

Output Preprocessing. Not every module in Action Selection Engines can output an action that can be directly executed. Therefore, these abstract actions require some preprocessing to convert them into low-level control signals that can be directly executed by the Output section of the robot.

Output.
This component is mainly composed of the motor, speaker, and screen that control the ear part, which needs to feed the final input of the system to the user.

4.4 Detection and Quantification of User Attention

Previous studies have shown that the pupil dilates in response to the cognitive demands of the task and that there is a task-induced pupillary response in various tasks in which the pupil exhibits dilation relative to baseline levels due to an increase in cognitive processing load [19]. Based on these phenomena Kahneman [20] and Beatty [21] showed that task-induced pupillary responses are psycho-physiological markers of cognitive load and attentional intensity with reliability and validity.

Therefore, the model used in this paper is shape_predictor_68_facelandmarks.dat. This is a face 68 key point detection model, as shown in Fig. 3, which uses 68 key points for face detection.

Firstly, the data are used to remove the regions with less than 100-pixel points in the skin color-like block using the open operation in image processing and segment the face region. Second, mark the 6 feature points of the eyes (see Fig. 4), each eye region is represented as 6 coordinates, and the key point range of the left and right eyes i.e. 36th–47th.

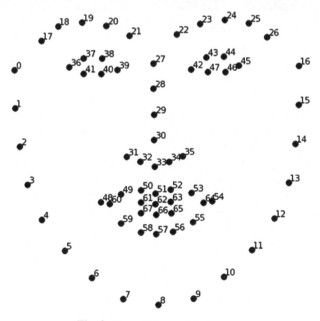

Fig. 3. Face 68 key point diagram.

To be able to obtain the user's concentration, we can derive the equation that reflects this relationship, called the eye aspect ratio (EAR), based on the work of Soukupová and Čech in mid-2016 [22]. When the EAR is greater than or equal to 0.25, we consider that the user is in a focused state. Conversely, when it is less than 0.25 we consider that the user appears to be wandering.

$$EAR = \frac{\|p_2 - p_6\| + \|p_3 - p_5\|}{2\|p_1 - p_4\|} \tag{1}$$

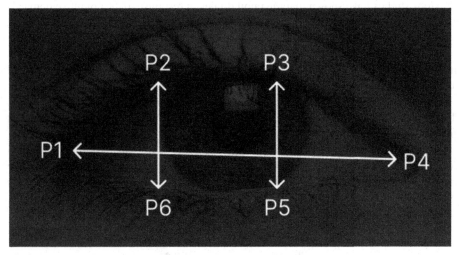

Fig. 4. Map of eye feature sites.

4.5 Interaction Methods

The robot is usually dormant in its daily work and needs to be activated by the user's voice to enter the attention detection mode. In this mode, the robot will face the user's face and obtain information about the user's pupils in real time for attention detection. Once inattention is detected, the robot's ears will swing from side to side and the head display will show an angry expression. The sound generated by the ear motors in motion will also be fed back to the user to remind him/her of the inattention. After the user refocuses, the robot will stop the movement and reenter the attention detection state until the user turns off the attention detection mode. After this, the user will receive a report of his or her current attention detection to review his or her work and study status.

4.6 Assessment of the Effect of Attentional Detection

In order to evaluate the effectiveness and accuracy of this robot for user attention detection, this section conducts an attention fluctuation test experiment for a group of school students.

Experimental Subjects. The subjects of this experiment were all undergraduate students from the South China University of Technology, and the study was aimed at the group with normal attention levels, i.e., the healthy group, so seven healthy subjects (four males and three females) were selected after scale screening. The main scales assessed were: the Adult ADHD Self-Assessment Scale (ASRS) [23], the MOSS Attention Rating Scale (MARS) [24], and the Schulte Squared Scale [25], which were applied as screening tools for attention.

Experimental Content. In visual tests, the total response time was significantly slower in the complex reaction time task compared to the single-stimulus reaction time task, which is the time required to respond in the presence of two or more stimuli and several possible responses, indicating that task complexity has higher demands on attentional abilities [26].The Stroop task has been widely used to study the limitations of the ability to suppress the influence of other information sources, and recent work supports that the attentional system for Stroop task performance is inherently transient and tends to fluctuate over time of time, and efficiency tends to fluctuate. This paradigm has also been frequently used in numerous studies of attention deficits as well as mind wandering in the literature, so it was ultimately chosen for the experiments in this paper [27].

In the Stroop experiment, a prompt is presented first to inform the subject of the task, i.e., the color of the response rather than the meaning of the word and how to press the key to correspond to the desired response color and possible attention detection problems, and the subject presses Enter when ready to start the experiment.

The experiment was divided into two parts, a test experiment and a formal experiment, with identical experimental setups in both parts, but only data from the formal experiment were analyzed. The stimuli of the experiments were words with color representing color, i.e., participants would see a word (red, green, or blue) presented in one of three different font colors (red, green, or blue), and on these trials, 67% were consistent, i.e., the word and font color matched (e.g., the word red was shown as red), and the other 33% were inconsistent (e.g., the word red was shown as green). The subject's task was to respond to the color rather than the meaning of the word, while the subject was required to click a key (red = left arrow key, green = down arrow key, blue = right arrow key) within a response time of 3000 ms to indicate the font color. Before each stimulus was displayed, there was a 2000 ms resting state of the baseline cycle, with a " + " appearing in the center of the screen to determine the baseline pupil diameter, and a stimulus response followed by another resting state for the next segment, as shown in Fig. 5 below.

During the test experiment, the subject observes the subject's actions and asks and prompts the subject when appropriate to ensure that the subject can respond correctly to the task and select the most appropriate state for him or her. After the test experiment, there is a "Ready to start the formal experiment" prompt screen, and the subject presses Enter to start the formal experiment when ready. The formal experiment consisted of 60 sessions of Stroop stimulus recognition.

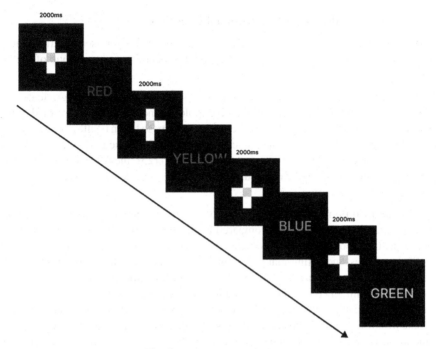

Fig. 5. Stroop Color Word Test.

During the duration of the experiment, the robot will continue to record the subject's concentration level. At the end of the experiment, we compare each of the 60 responses to the subject's concentration in the formal experiment. If the subject's answers are correct, we consider the user to be focused, and if the subject answers incorrectly or takes longer than the time limit to make a choice, we consider the subject to be unfocused. On this basis, we compare the results returned by the robot with the subject's responses and record the number of inconsistencies and count them.

Experimental Results. The overall experimental results are shown in Table 3, with an accuracy rate of 92.9% for male students and 95.0% for female students, for an overall accuracy rate of 93.3%.

Table 3. Statistical table of experimental results.

	Male				Female		
Consistent	57	55	58	53	59	57	55
Inconsistent	3	5	2	7	1	3	5
Accuracy rate	95.0%	91.7%	96.7%	88.3%	98.3%	95.0%	91.7%

5   Conclusion

In the field of companion robots, the elderly, children and patients are the main research targets, and there are fewer designs for the general public, while the existing companion robots for the general public are focused on giving the user a sense of pleasure and novelty. This design puts it into a work context and gives it a more practical function based on companionship. A literature review was conducted for this design and a survey of workers was conducted. According to the results, workers need a companion robot to alleviate their psychological problems, to remind them to take breaks to avoid physical pain from sedentary activities, and to monitor the workers' concentration and fatigue to improve their productivity. Therefore, we defined the function, appearance, and hardware of this robot, constructed its software framework diagram, and developed a minimalist attention and fatigue detection demo. To verify the detection accuracy of this system, we designed Stroop experiments and analyzed the results. Further work will explore the supervisory effectiveness of the robot and the user acceptance of the work supervision function.

Acknowledgements. This research was funded by "2022 Constructing Project of Teach-ing Quality and Teaching Reform Project for Undergraduate Uni-versities in Guangdong Province" Higher Education Teaching Reform Project (project No. 386), "Innovation and practice of teaching methods for information and interaction design in the context of new liberal arts" (project grant number x2sj-C9233001).

References

1. Bhat, S.K., Pande, N., Ahuja, V.: Virtual team effectiveness: an empirical study using SEM. Procedia Comput. Sci. **122**, 33–41 (2017). https://doi.org/10.1016/j.procs.2017.11.338
2. Skundžiasi darbu namuose, bet noru grįžti į biurus nedega: tyrimo rezultatai atskleidė priežastis, https://spinter.lt/site/lt/vidinis/menutop/9/home/publish/MTMwODs5Ozsw. Accessed 05 Feb 2023
3. Raišienė, A.G., Rapuano, V., Varkulevičiūtė, K., Stachová, K.: Working from home—who is happy? a survey of lithuania's employees during the COVID-19 quarantine period. Sustainability **12**, 5332 (2020). https://doi.org/10.3390/su12135332
4. Nakrošiene, A., Butkeviciene, E.: Telework in lithuania: the concept, bene-fits and challenges to the employees. Filosofija, Sociologija. **27**, 364–372 (2016)
5. Hegel, F., Muhl, C., Wrede, B., Hielscher-Fastabend, M., Sagerer, G.: Under-standing Social Robots. In: Proceedings of the 2009 Second International Conferences on Advances in Computer-Human Interactions. pp. 169–174. IEEE Computer Society, USA (2009). https://doi.org/10.1109/ACHI.2009.51
6. Pu, L., Moyle, W., Jones, C., Todorovic, M.: The Effectiveness of social robots for older adults: a systematic review and meta-analysis of randomized controlled studies. Gerontologist **59**, e37–e51 (2019). https://doi.org/10.1093/geront/gny046
7. Rydén, F., Nia Kosari, S., Chizeck, H.J.: Proxy method for fast haptic render-ing from time varying point clouds. In: 2011 IEEE/RSJ International Confer-ence on Intelligent Robots and Systems. pp. 2614–2619 (2011). https://doi.org/10.1109/IROS.2011.6094673

8. Gross, H.-M., et al.: Robot Companion for Domestic Health Assis-tance: Implementation, Test and Case Study under Everyday Conditions in Private Apartments. In: 2015 Ieee/Rsj International Conference on Intelligent Robots and Systems (iros). pp. 5992–5999. Ieee, New York (2015)

9. Casey, D., et al.: What People with Dementia Want: Designing MARIO an Acceptable Robot Companion. In: Miesenberger, K., Bühler, C., Penaz, P. (eds.) ICCHP 2016. LNCS, vol. 9758, pp. 318–325. Springer, Cham (2016). https://doi.org/10.1007/978-3-319-41264-1_44

10. Kory, J., Breazeal, C.: Storytelling with robots: learning companions for preschool children's language development. In: The 23rd IEEE International Symposium on Robot and Human Interactive Communication. pp. 643–648 (2014). https://doi.org/10.1109/ROMAN.2014.692 6325

11. Wei, C.-W., Hung, I.-C., Lee, L., Chen, N.-S.: A joyful classroom learning system with robot learning companion for children to learn mathematics multiplication. Turk. Online J. Educ. Technol. **10**, 11–23 (2011)

12. Lorenz, T., Weiss, A., Hirche, S.: Synchrony and reciprocity: key mechanisms for social companion robots in therapy and care. Int. J. Soc. Robot. **8**(1), 125–143 (2015). https://doi.org/10.1007/s12369-015-0325-8

13. Okita, S.Y.: Self-other's perspective taking: the use of therapeutic robot companions as social agents for reducing pain and anxiety in pediatric patientss. Cyberpsychology Behav. Soc. Netw. **16**, 436–441 (2013). https://doi.org/10.1089/cyber.2012.0513

14. Bavel, J.J.V., et al.: Using social and behavioural science to support COVID-19 pandemic response. Nat. Hum. Behav. **4**, 460–471 (2020). https://doi.org/10.1038/s41562-020-0884-z

15. de Graaf, M.M.A., Allouch, S.B.: Exploring influencing variables for the acceptance of social robots. Robotics and Autonomous Systems. 61, 1476–1486 (2013). https://doi.org/10.1016/j.robot.2013.07.007

16. Heerink, M., Kröse, B., Evers, V., Wielinga, B.: Assessing acceptance of assistive social agent technology by older adults: the almere model. Int. J. Soc. Robot. **2**, 361–375 (2010). https://doi.org/10.1007/s12369-010-0068-5

17. Odekerken-Schröder, G., Mele, C., Russo-Spena, T., Mahr, D., Ruggiero, A.: Mitigating loneliness with companion robots in the COVID-19 pandemic and beyond: an integrative framework and research agenda. J. Serv. Manag. **31**, 1149–1162 (2020). https://doi.org/10.1108/JOSM-05-2020-0148

18. Steunebrink, B.R., Vergunst, N.L., Mol, C.P., Dignum, F., Dastani, M.M., Meyer, J.-J.C.: A Generic Architecture for a Companion Robot. In: ICINCO-RA (2018)

19. Unsworth, N., Robison, M.K.: The importance of arousal for variation in working memory capacity and attention control: a latent variable pupillome-try study. J. Exp. Psychol. Learn. Mem. Cogn. **43**, 1962–1987 (2017). https://doi.org/10.1037/xlm0000421

20. Kahneman, D.: Attention and Effort. Presented at the (1973)

21. Beatty, J.: Task-evoked pupillary responses, processing load, and the struc-ture of processing resources. Psychol. Bull. **91**, 276–292 (1982). https://doi.org/10.1037/0033-2909.91.2.276

22. Soukupová, T., Cech, J.: Real-Time Eye Blink Detection using Facial Land-marks. Presented at the (2016)

23. Kessler, R.C., et al.: The world health organization adult ADHD self-report scale (ASRS): a short screen-ing scale for use in the general population. Psychol. Med. **35**, 245–256 (2005). https://doi.org/10.1017/s0033291704002892

24. Hart, T., et al.: Dimensions of disordered attention in traumatic brain injury: fur-ther validation of the moss attention rating scale. Arch. Phys. Med. Rehabil. **87**, 647–655 (2006). https://doi.org/10.1016/j.apmr.2006.01.016

25. Pavlenko, V., Lutsyuk, N.V., Borisova, M.: Correlation of the characteristics of evoked EEG potentials with individual peculiarities of attention in children. Neurophysiology (2005)

26. Martin, T.L., Solbeck, P.A.M., Mayers, D.J., Langille, R.M., Buczek, Y., Pelle-tier, M.R.: A review of alcohol-impaired driving: the role of blood alcohol concentration and complexity of the driving task. J. Forensic. Sci. **58**(5), 1238–1250 (2013). https://doi.org/10.1111/1556-4029.12227

27. West, R., Alain, C.: Effects of task context and fluctuations of attention on neural activity supporting performance of the Stroop task. Brain Res. **873**, 102–111 (2000). https://doi.org/10.1016/S0006-8993(00)02530-0

The Strategy of Sustainable Concepts in the Design of Digital Services for Broken Screen Insurance

Xiaotong Tian[(✉)] and Yichen Wu

China Academy of Art, Hangzhou, China
2221351279@caa.edu.cn

Abstract. The trend of the digital society leads to an increase in the number of digital services that users experience in their daily lives, and this poses new challenges for digital interaction design. The appearance of screen insurance services attached to mobile phones has raised the demand for digital insurance services, transcending geographical restrictions and integrating multiple services. However, the massive amount of electronic waste generated by users is not receiving enough attention, and it is necessary to introduce the concept of e-waste to more people and promote its importance in environmental remediation to reduce resource waste and environmental pollution. This article explores the strategies for sustainable design in digital service design, using screen insurance as a case study. It discusses how to convey the sustainable concept of e-waste recycling and environmental protection to users in screen insurance digital service design. The research shows that digital service design should be social, easy to understand, and have high retention rates while also increasing public attention to sustainable concepts, which can deepen users' environmental awareness.

Keywords: Digital service design · sustainable concept · digital insurance

1 Introduction

With the continuous development and popularization of digital technology, the digital society has become a part of modern society. The increase of digital services provides users with more convenient, fast, and efficient experiences, and offers businesses more commercial opportunities and profit margins. As the number of virtual digital products increases, users' demands for digital product experiences have become higher. Digital interaction designers need to continuously optimize the user interface, interaction methods, and usage details of digital products to improve the user experience and meet users' needs. At the same time, they also need to focus on the maintainability and upgradability of digital products to adapt to changing market demand and technological development. Therefore, the role of digital interaction design in sustainable design is increasingly prominent and needs to pay attention to sustainable concepts to achieve the sustainable development of digital services. Taking mobile phone screen insurance as an example, the appearance of mobile phone screen insurance services is an important case of digital

A. Marcus et al. (Eds.): HCII 2023, LNCS 14031, pp. 262–272, 2023.
https://doi.org/10.1007/978-3-031-35696-4_19

transformation, which promotes the development and popularization of digital insurance services, increases the demand of users for digital insurance services, and brings opportunities and challenges to the digital transformation of the insurance industry.

The commercial insurance of phone screen protection comes with an inevitable environmental issue. With continuous innovation and updates in technology, the lifespan of many electronic products is getting shorter. People tend to buy new models of electronic devices, which accelerates the obsolescence of old devices and leads to a large amount of electronic waste. The lack of environmental measures in the production process of electronic products contributes to the growing quantity of electronic waste. Therefore, handling electronic waste is not only an important part of sustainable development but also a necessary measure for human health and environmental protection. The emergence of screen protection insurance fully utilizes digital technology and innovatively solves the limitations of traditional insurance services, greatly improving user experience and satisfaction. At the same time, this is a successful case of digital transformation, which can provide reference and inspiration for the digital transformation of other industries.

It is noteworthy that the screen insurance service has integrated sustainable ideas into digital design, providing efficient and convenient services to users while also reducing unnecessary resource waste and environmental pollution. For the screen insurance digital service as the design subject, it is closely related to the resource chain of electronic waste and recycling. This will serve as the design entry point, combining with the core of sustainable ideas, and promoting and popularizing it through multimedia network platforms. Currently, there is a certain blank in the promotion of electronic waste on the Internet, and according to research, most people are not aware of the current and future environmental burden of electronic waste. Therefore, combining sustainable ideas in screen insurance digital services has certain significance and value.

2   An Overview of the Sustainability Concept

2.1   The Relationship Between Sustainability and Digital Services

The concept of sustainable development has been continuously proposed and gradually received attention since the 1970s. Its core is to meet current needs without destroying the natural ecosystem, while ensuring a sustainable development path for future generations to meet their own needs. With the rapid development of economic globalization and information technology, the digital economy has become a new growth point, and the concept of sustainable development has received widespread attention in the digital field. The integration of sustainable concepts into the design of digital services can promote sustainable development of society, environment, and economy, making digital services more closely aligned with users' needs and values, and improving the quality and competitiveness of digital services. **Sample Heading (Third Level).** Only two levels of headings should be numbered. Lower-level headings remain unnumbered; they are formatted as run-in headings.

In today's design and development of digital services, the integration of sustainable concepts has become an indispensable part. For example, in the design process of digital products, reducing energy consumption, optimizing logistics management, and improving product life cycle can achieve goals such as reducing carbon emissions, reducing production costs, and increasing product quality. At the same time, the development of digital services also needs to follow sustainable concepts, such as developing green data centers and using clean energy to minimize the impact of digital services on the environment. This sustainable development approach has received attention and practice from many scholars and companies. For example, the United Nations proposed "Sustainable Development Goals" (SDGs), which involve the important role of digital services in sustainable development. Some companies have also begun to integrate sustainable concepts into the design and development of digital services, such as Apple's efforts in sustainable development, where its supply chain has achieved 100% renewable energy, resulting in significant improvements in environmental protection in its digital services.

2.2 Digital Design Examples of Sustainable Concepts

Apple is committed to green and sustainable development in the field of electronics, reducing the impact of plastic waste on the global environment. The company uses sustainable forests and recycled materials for 99% of its product packaging. They design smaller packaging and maximize the use of recycled paper. Apple's electronic products use recycled aluminum, which eliminates direct greenhouse gas emissions in the aluminum smelting process and minimizes direct environmental pollution. This sustainable design embodies the optimization of material utilization in the production process. Apple is also creating a circular supply chain, which means only renewable resources or recycled materials are used to manufacture products, and old devices are recycled to collect copper, tin, and precious metals. The concept of sustainability is systemically integrated into Apple's overall goals, with a service-oriented design that transforms product design into service design. Service design that focuses on sustainability coordinates the entire system, transforming the traditional linear production chain into a circular one. Each link aims to break through tradition and achieve sustainable development with less resource consumption and higher resource utilization.

A food waste reduction application is designed to assist users in reducing food waste by providing features such as food preservation advice, recipes, and shopping lists. The application aims to encourage users to purchase and prepare reasonable quantities of food in order to reduce waste and save costs. Its primary design feature is user-centric, with a simple and easy-to-use interface to minimize the learning curve and usage costs, while also providing personalized recommendations and customization options to meet user needs.

The application employs eco-friendly materials and manufacturing processes, such as energy-efficient hardware used in the servers and devices, to minimize energy consumption. Sustainable services are also provided, such as food preservation advice and recipes, to help users better utilize leftover food and reduce waste. Additionally, the application provides community support and sharing features to encourage users to share food, reduce waste, and save costs.

The application has been widely adopted, with users reporting a reduction in the amount of wasted food and a decrease in food purchasing costs. Moreover, the application's use has resulted in environmental benefits, such as reduced energy consumption and waste. This successful case of digital service design demonstrates that sustainability can be achieved while providing high-quality services and reducing negative impacts on the environment and society.

3 Overview of e-Waste in the Context of Sustainability

3.1 The Current Situation of e-Waste

Electronic waste, or e-waste, has become a major environmental concern in recent years due to its significant negative impact on the environment and human health. As technology advances, electronic devices are becoming more affordable and accessible, leading to a sharp increase in the volume of e-waste generated worldwide. According to a report by the United Nations, approximately 53.6 million metric tons of e-waste were generated globally in 2019, and this number is expected to increase to 74.7 million metric tons by 2030 if no action is taken (Global E-waste Monitor 2020).

To address this issue, sustainable practices and the circular economy model have been proposed as potential solutions. The circular economy model emphasizes the reuse, repair, and recycling of products to reduce waste and conserve resources. By applying this model to e-waste, the recovery of valuable materials and components can be maximized, reducing the environmental impact of disposal, and conserving natural resources. As noted by Li et al. (2021), "the circular economy offers a new perspective and opportunity to address the e-waste problem in a more sustainable manner by enabling the sustainable use of resources and the reduction of environmental pollution."

In addition, it is important to consider the entire lifecycle of electronic products, from production to disposal. Sustainable design practices, such as reducing the use of hazardous materials, increasing energy efficiency, and designing for repair and recycling, can contribute to reducing e-waste and promoting a more sustainable electronics industry. As stated by Kusch and Zeng (2021), "sustainability should be integrated into the entire lifecycle of electronics, from product design to end-of-life management, to create a more sustainable and circular electronics industry."

It is widely acknowledged that people's understanding of environmental protection has been increasing since the 21st century. With the development of the times and the improvement of national quality, individuals have gradually taken action to protect the environment. For example, many people participate in Ant Forest by collecting energy online to plant trees, demonstrating their willingness to contribute to environmental protection in this way. While people can easily distinguish between wet and dry waste, their knowledge of e-waste is limited. Public awareness of e-waste's resource recovery value is insufficient, partly due to insufficient publicity and education on e-waste pollution prevention and control laws.

Taking mobile phones as an example, research shows that many users discard old phones with functional problems and let them become ordinary waste until they are scrapped after purchasing a new phone. They are unaware that electronic resources, such as circuit boards, still exist in these old phones and have not been completely used (see Fig. 1). Over time, these resources are wasted. To reduce waste at the source, the concept of e-waste should be introduced, and the importance of e-waste in future environmental governance should be popularized. In today's world of fast-consuming electronic

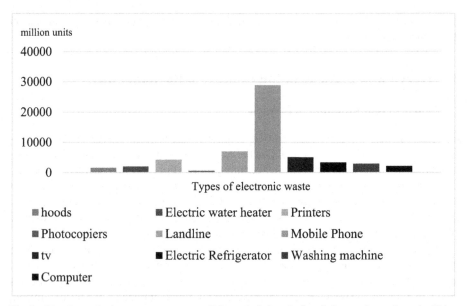

Fig. 1. The theoretical scrappage amount of discarded electrical and electronic products in China in 2019.

products, individuals can also increase resource recovery rates, reduce resource waste, and environmental pollution from a grassroots perspective.

Overall, the adoption of sustainable practices and the circular economy model can play a crucial role in mitigating the environmental impact of e-waste and promoting a more sustainable electronics industry.

3.2 Analysis of e-Waste Recycling System

The current electronic waste recycling system faces several issues. Firstly, the diverse and complex nature of electronic waste requires significant financial and technological investment for proper handling and disposal. Developing countries lack adequate support, resulting in incomplete recycling and persistent environmental pollution and health risks. Secondly, the absence of supportive policies in many countries has hindered effective electronic waste recycling. Additionally, some consumers lack sufficient awareness of the importance and impact of waste recycling, resulting in suboptimal results.

Moreover, the existing electronic waste recycling system presents some challenges. For instance, some companies and manufacturers fail to prioritize sustainable development and do not pay enough attention to environmental protection and sustainability in their products and production processes, leading to an increase in the amount of electronic waste. Furthermore, the management and supervision of the waste recycling system are inadequate, making it difficult to ensure compliance and transparency in the recycling process. The electronic waste recycling system requires more technological, financial, and policy support, as well as greater awareness and action from companies and consumers to promote sustainable development.

4 Sustainable-Based Digital Service Design Practices

4.1 Preliminary Research

Focusing on screen insurance, this study investigates the design of a multi-modal digital service for broken screen insurance in the context of the circular economy. We selected mobile phones as the research subject and analyzed data from a questionnaire completed by 544 consumers to understand how they handle and recycle their discarded phones. Results showed that most respondents (approximately 85%) considered their old phones as garbage and threw them into the trash. Only about 15% of the respondents said they would give their old phones to a specialized recycling center or waste collection service.

We further investigated the reasons why some respondents were unwilling to recycle their discarded phones. Results revealed that the most common reason was a lack of knowledge about how to recycle (approximately 30%), followed by inconvenience in recycling channels (approximately 25%), and a lack of motivation to recycle (approximately 20%). Additionally, a small portion of the respondents expressed concerns about personal information leakage, which deterred them from recycling their discarded phones (approximately 10%).

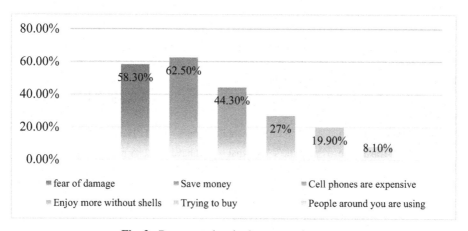

Fig. 2. Reasons to buy broken screen insurance

Analysis from this perspective of the masses, people who buy broken screen insurance also distrust the protection of good cell phone screens (see Fig. 2), so buy as a kind of insurance, and for broken screens or electronic waste, people for the new environmental protection propaganda trust value in the absence of general awareness does not improve so that people will question the brand propaganda of environmental protection, the back may not be simple The user's attitude towards a product or a new idea goes from ordinary to trust, and the process is built from three aspects: cognition, emotion, and attitude.

We also noted a correlation between age, education level, and whether or not respondents recycled their discarded phones. Specifically, older and more highly educated respondents were more likely to recycle their discarded phones. This may be because these individuals have greater environmental awareness, a better understanding of the importance of recycling, and more access to channels and opportunities for recycling their discarded phones.

These findings indicate a need for more education and awareness campaigns to increase people's understanding and motivation to recycle discarded phones. Additionally, greater convenience in recycling channels is necessary to encourage more people to recycle their discarded phones and reduce their negative impact on the environment.

4.2 Requirements Definition

The "Screen Damage Insurance Digital Service System" focuses on protecting users' phone screens and providing investment-based risk protection. However, user interviews and on-site research have found that original equipment manufacturers also replace other components when replacing screens, leading to a variety of electronic waste entering the company's resource recycling line. Therefore, we hope to expand this service into a screen damage insurance online operation system with environmental protection characteristics. We incorporate environmental concepts into the overall design and use emotional design to reflect the caring nature of screen damage insurance, as shown in Table 1.

Table 1. Definition of requirements for the three segments

E-waste	Emotional design	Environmental Philosophy
·Popularization & understanding	·Services & Processes	·Production & Promotion
1. Phone life (screen life)	1. The End of Mobile Phones	1. The use of green elements
2. The Life of Trash (The E-Waste Cycle)	2. (The screen that would have been garbage) gives value	2. A new type of environmental hazard that needs urgent attention
3. The value of recycling	3. Demonstrate the efficiency of the repair process	3. Youthful communication

The entire service and process design is full of emotional design concepts. For shattered screens, which should be waste, we give them unique meaning and nostalgic value. Each shattered screen carries its own reason for being produced and emotional memories, which is unique to everyone. Every phone has a better ending. As the most discarded electronic product, the number of discarded phones produced each year is astonishing. By more efficiently utilizing their residual value, we can increase resource utilization and achieve the goals of environmental protection and sustainable development.

The term "electronic waste" has been frequently mentioned in recent years. We hope that this term can be more widely popularized in our project design, so that the public can understand and promote its importance in protecting the environment, beyond household waste, construction waste, and industrial waste. By using professional factories and equipment to recycle electronic products, users can transparently understand through the screen damage insurance online operation system that their actions can have a positive impact on society.

Both emotional design and electronic waste are intertwined with environmental protection, and green elements are used in both to make users begin to pay attention to the new environmental hazards that may arise from electronic waste. By using screen damage insurance as a medium, we can spread this message through the Internet in a younger and more contemporary way.

4.3 Design Framework

Combining the attitudes and behaviors of people towards environmental protection and electronic waste from the previous research, as well as the needs defined in the three blocks of research, I propose my design concepts on sustainability and electronic waste throughout the entire service design process, by linearly connecting digital services and organizing the logic, achieving multimodal service design, as shown in Table 2.

01. Prior to purchasing insurance, I believe that the screen insurance service can be extended earlier in the process. "Reducing screen damage is also a form of environmental protection" allows users to learn about electronic waste on other platforms and media, reducing the use of phone cases or tempered glass films, and reducing the production of new waste. Users may not be interested in learning about screen insurance, but the small environmental slogan has already been imprinted in their minds, making them aware.

02. In the preliminary contact stage, we hope to attract users through social-like forms of communication, using the popular psychological test MBTI personality test as an innovative point of introduction on other platforms. Different people with different personalities have different ways of using their phones, and perhaps 16 different types of screen damages are unique as well. In this stage, we want to connect with the first stage, incorporating the ideas of electronic waste and sustainability.

03. Understanding screen insurance: When users become interested in screen insurance through the previous two steps, we aim to provide clear and explicit terms of service that describe the repair results for different types of screens when browsing the screen insurance interface. We want users to have the freedom to choose and, at the same time, promote the slogan 'reducing screen damage is a form of environmental protection.'

04. Purchasing insurance: After users purchase screen insurance, we hope to provide a friendly interface that evokes trust, rather than a cold feeling about insurance money. After purchasing, the "Repair Shop" page will display a guide to claims processing, allowing users to experience screen insurance claims in advance. We can provide services such as videos of repairers repairing mobile phones to prevent parts from being replaced, etc. Our emotional design includes the idea of leaving each person's "broken thoughts" to promote social interaction and to provide memories for each new piece of electronic waste.

Table 2. Definition of requirements for the three segments

	Reach (keyword)	Interaction (behavior)	Transformation (communication)
01 Before you buy insurance	" Perhaps reducing broken screens is also a form of environmental protection "	Animation guide	1. Advance implantation of environmental protection concept 2. Publicity of risk cases 3. The generation of plastic waste from cell phone cases 4. Whether the bare phone is an environmental protection
02 Initial Contact	MBTI's cell phone usage habits	Animation/Dialogue	1. Understand the broken screen insurance 2. Test for cracks and usage status
03 Understanding Broken Screen Insurance	Full-scene experience introducing broken screen insurance	Switching scenes	1. In-depth understanding of "my repair store" "broken thoughts" "broken screen museum"
04 Purchase Insurance	Owning a private repair store	Enter a scene	1. Have exclusive customer service, claims guidance, etc 2. Light up the memory property of e-waste
05 Claims Completion	Broken screen stories arise	Browse Shredding	1. Share to "Museum" 2. Browse through the fragmentation 3. Explain the environmental attributes of e-waste
06 Recycling	E-waste debris	Go to animation	1. Connect to recycling platforms 2. Communicate more sustainable ideas

05. Completion of claims: After using screen insurance once and experiencing a screen damage incident, the "Repair Shop" will become a memorial hall that promotes environmental protection ideas for electronic waste. Our program aims to achieve environmental protection actions, record environmental protection journeys, and convey environmental protection concepts to fulfill environmental protection missions.

06. Recycling: In our program's final stage and in our expectations for future development, we hope that not only screen damage but also outdated phones can be linked to related recycling platforms so that more electronic waste can be recycled and utilized with people's attention."

5 Conclusion

With the continuous advancement and popularization of technology, smartphones have become an indispensable part of our lives. However, the problem of broken screens also comes with it. To solve this problem, digital services for screen insurance have emerged. This study conducted field research and user interviews on screen insurance services and found that the electronic waste generated during the repair process is diverse and has significant recyclable value. However, there is still a knowledge gap among users regarding sustainable concepts related to e-waste, and there is a lack of related promotion in internet digital services. Therefore, we believe that expanding screen insurance to an online operation system with environmental properties is feasible. Through the application of emotional design concepts, the process of screen insurance service is redesigned to give unique meaning to broken screens that were once considered garbage, making each broken screen have a memory value. At the same time, the design process emphasizes the implementation of sustainable development concepts, improves the environmental friendliness of screen insurance services, utilizes their residual value, and increases resource utilization.

Through our exploratory research and practice, we have drawn the following conclusions: the application of sustainable concepts in the design of digital screen insurance services can not only effectively address the problem of electronic waste, but also deepen consumers' understanding of the importance of environmental protection and further raise their environmental awareness. At the same time, the application of emotional design can not only enhance the service's personalization and user experience, but also give new meaning to waste materials and improve their utilization. In the era of the internet, expressing sustainable concepts through digital services requires a balance between user-friendly social functions, easy-to-understand and practical features, and the achievement of improved user retention rates. Therefore, we recommend that in future screen insurance services, there should be a focus on the implementation of sustainable development concepts, the use of emotional design to give new value to waste materials, and an emphasis on improving resource utilization to promote the development of environmental protection.

References

1. Ulusoy, G., Özkan, F.G., Arslan, A.: Sustainable digital service design: an investigation of e-government services in Turkey. Sustain. Comput. Inform. Syst. **28**, 100382 (2020). https://doi.org/10.1016/j.suscom.2020.100382

2. Global E-waste Monitor: Global E-waste Monitor 2020. United Nations University (UNU), International Telecommunication Union (ITU), and International Solid Waste Association (ISWA) (2020)
3. Li, Y., Lu, B., Li, J., Li, K., Li, X., Li, X.: A review of the circular economy in electronic waste management: current research progress, challenges and future directions. Resour. Conserv. Recycl. **170**, 105638 (2021). https://doi.org/10.1016/j.resconrec.2021.105638
4. Kusch, M., Zeng, X.: Sustainability in the lifecycle of electronics: A review of contemporary research. Renew. Sustain. Energy Rev. **150**, 111461 (2021). https://doi.org/10.1016/j.rser.2021.111461

POLARISCOPE – A Platform
for the Co-creation and Visualization
of Collective Memories

Ana Velhinho$^{(\boxtimes)}$ ⓘ and Pedro Almeida ⓘ

Digimedia, Department of Communication and Arts, University of Aveiro, Aveiro, Portugal
{ana.velhinho,almeida}@ua.com

Abstract. POLARISCOPE is an R&D project supported by Digital Humanities and Participatory Media to develop an online platform to collect and share memories. The project aims to evaluate if a mobile-based technological solution, that eases multimedia data collection and generates correlated visualizations from resources shared by users, can enhance the experience and collective memory of events. Namely, aiming the social enrichment of documental archives and events that contribute to memory safeguarding and giving visibility to the cultural diversity of territories. To this end, the digital platform aims to facilitate the collection, cataloguing and sharing of multimedia records (images, videos, sounds, oral testimonials, etc.) and their integration into an aggregation system, which presents correlated visualizations of content shared by several participants. Focused on pilot trials on the territory of Aveiro (Portugal), the platform will document the natural landscape and the tangible heritage and urban fabric and also the social and intangible cultural practices of different communities that mingle in the region. As a tool for collecting and correlating multimedia records in mobility, it also aims to facilitate research field activities with communities, particularly to collect oral testimonies from the elderly with lower digital literacy. In summary, the POLARISCOPE project explores mixed methods to approach digital heritage and digital memories for generations to come, having as a differentiating value the potential of correlated visualizations to provide meaningful insights and trigger the discovery and storytelling possibilities through collective content remix and co-creation.

Keywords: Participatory Platform · Visualization · Digital Storytelling · Collective Memory

1 Introduction

POLARISCOPE is an R&D project resulting form a consortium between academia – University of Aveiro and Nova University Lisbon – and the Historical Archive of Aveiro, who joined efforts to develop and validate an online platform to collect and share multimedia memories. This platform intends to take advantage of already naturalized practices and behaviours in social media, directing them to the activation of historical and collaborative archives that, despite being digitized and structured in databases, do not prevent them from becoming "dead files". With that purpose in mind, the project proposes an open-access platform to work in synergy with face-to-face activities carried out by specialized teams or informal associations and groups working with communities. To this end, the project will develop and evaluate a digital platform to facilitate the collection, cataloguing and sharing of multimedia records (images, videos, sounds, oral testimonials, etc.) and their integration into an aggregation system, which presents correlated visualizations of content shared by several participants. These visualizations, generated from geographic, temporal, semantic and emotional metadata, intend to provide a multidimensional perspective and interactive exploration of those digital memories. The platform's exploratory features also encourage the continuous expansion of this living archive through social tagging and related content to foster the co-creation of new visual narratives from the combination of multiple records.

Departing from the territory of Aveiro, the platform proposes to give visibility to the natural landscape (rich in biodiversity around the river and the beaches in the region) and the tangible heritage and urban fabric (including monuments and municipal facilities). But also, to the social and cultural practices of several communities that mingle in the region (local population; immigrant communities that embed their cultural backgrounds; student communities that renew every year; and recurring or occasional visitors). To do so, it adopts a participatory design methodology involving stakeholders, local associations, and community representatives. Taking into account a set of annual cultural initiatives that already sign the identity of the city of Aveiro and generate mobilization of different audiences (Celebrations of Saint Gonçalinho; The Canals Festival; Criatech), the prototype will be tested in real events to cross historical records with new records that invigorate Culture, as a living instance in permanent negotiation, which will also be translated into the updated visualizations generated by the participation through the platform.

The document is divided into four sections: the first, introducing the context and goals of the project; the second, presenting the theoretical background; the third, regarding the methodology and conceptual model; and last section with the final considerations towards future work.

2 Co-creating Collective Memories Through Visualization and Participatory Approaches

Visualization and participatory approaches constitute relevant operative dimensions in contemporary culture sustained by platforms and devices that encourage interpersonal interaction around online content but also through locative media. Thus, the combination between visualization and participation is an opportunity for the development of cultural and creative projects, which rely on the active participation of people as *prosumers* who consume, produce, and disseminate content in their daily lives and when attending to cultural events. Currently, social dynamics among online communities are intrinsic to participatory societies, increasing possibilities for inclusion through User Generated Content (UGC) and life testimonials, which are gradually becoming relevant contributions. Additionally, the proliferation of interactive media gives users control and opens new possibilities for visual presentation, since the same data can be tailored to tell different stories [1–3]. In this way, participation and visualization coming together in exploratory interfaces [4, 5] may lead to more expressive representations to evoke memories as shared constructs, and also amplifying how experiences are enjoyed when they happened, through practices such as commenting, sharing and content appropriation and remix to convey group storytelling [6]. But these interfaces also open the opportunity to study shared content, user behaviour and cultural patterns [5, 7] while contributing to generate and expand communal archives supported by the self-organized crowd [8].

2.1   Visual Insight and Discovery in Digital Mediated Experiences

The ability to generate and store data has become more effective in the era of datafication. However, there is only value in such accumulation if the information is organized, contextualized and correlated, since no data is processed as an isolated phenomenon but rather in an encoded and contextualized way [9]. This transformation of data into knowledge presupposes a structuring effort to give meaning to disperse and disorganized stimuli that need to be gathered, processed and presented in the most appropriate way, depending on diverse objectives, contexts and audiences. Storytelling and visualization strategies are some approaches to organize and create meaning.

Visualizations can be designed for different purposes: to be explanatory, therefore dependent on quick conveying of information for task effectiveness; or to be exploratory, for discovery, contemplative or playful uses. Exploratory visualizations integrate the "casual visualizations" typology and comprise artistic, social and participatory expressions, allowing different types of insight (analytic; awareness; social; and reflective) [10]. Casual visualizations usually reach broader audiences, including non-specialists, and may incorporate personal stories that increase emotional connection, self-identification and memorability [11].

Donald Norman [12] emphasizes the importance of experience, associated with environments and contexts to trigger emotion and critical thinking, through the physical and cognitive interaction that we establish with the objects and people that surround us, highlighting the possibility of "discoverability" and to create "understanding" as the main elements for the "good design" of an experience or artefact. However, Elizabeth Sanders [13, 14] draws attention to the fact that the experience itself is not designable, only the conditions for the experience, defending co-design practices based on the collaboration between specialists and non-specialists, through participatory approaches supported by generative ideation tools.

Accordingly, the research group Social Spaces [14] proposes a hybrid participation-driven methodology based on collaborative dynamics of co-creation between citizens and specialists, to generate ideas and innovation within social and cultural contexts. Their hybrid model frames participatory projects as permanent negotiations oriented by the concepts of "hybridity" and "generativity", explored in different phases of the projects. "Hybridity" operates in the creation phase (project-time) with heterogeneous teams, through exploratory ideation methods, used to encourage discussion and sharing of knowledge and skills – namely through creative toolkits, using mapping techniques and collages that combine multiple perspectives open to interpretation. In turn, "generativity" is explored through open and self-regulated technological systems to mediate autonomous participation, assuring the sustainability of projects designed for future generations. In this sense, "generativity" implies a higher degree of planning and flexibility, to allow adapting projects to other contexts and attracting more participants, so it must follow "modularity", "deviationism" and "shareability" criteria [15]. Within this hybrid methodology, risk and uncertainty are embraced as qualitative dimensions of the project, which mirror the complexity and challenges of our current society. Thus, the creative discovery combined with ethical and social responsibilities should be in the forefront of contemporary participatory practices for designing the artefacts of the future.

In the context of participation in online platforms and communities, the type of user participation depends on different variables, such as the frequency of use (occasional or regular), the maturity of membership in the community (novice or experienced), the purpose, motivation and incentives to participate (administrator, moderator, contributor, visitor, etc.). The roles of leader, moderator and administrator are paramount to boost the activity of online communities, and to ensure respect for rules of conduct for participation in some communities and online groups. To this end, it is necessary for digital platforms to provide such interaction, socialization and collaboration features, as well as to implement strategies to reward and encourage participation and new memberships [16] insofar as the sustainability of any social platforms depends on the scale and intensity of participation. Some strategies can lead to the role of users evolving within communities, making them more active, namely through gamification mechanisms and challenges for granting scores, prizes and distinguishing badges to generate engagement and content sharing.

Regardless of the contexts, the motivations for online participation usually surpass remuneration and functional gratifications, in favour of affective and symbolic needs, valuing social and human capital, as well as cognitive, experiential and socio-communicative dimensions, which constitute the pillars of "emotional design" [17]. Tharon Howard [18] proposes the RIBS Model which orders the four essential motivational aspects for participation in online communities, placing at the top Significance, followed by the sense of Belonging, Influence and placing Remuneration at the bottom). In general, monetary rewards are mainly associated with mechanical tasks. While in cognitive and creative tasks, people value achievement and personal enrichment, namely the development of skills and participation in experiences, which allow them to be closed and establish a connection with others, despite valuing autonomy and some sense of control over the experience.

2.2 Digital Memories and Co-creation of Community Archives

Given the acceleration of the on-going process of culture digitization, the construction of collective memory is increasingly affected by the forms and technologies of capturing and accessing records of those memories [19, 20], which also impacts the internal workflow of memory institutions (archives, libraries and museums). In this context, we also witness the synergy between computing and the humanities, leading to emerging disciplines to study Culture, namely the Digital Humanities. This recent area of knowledge is strengthened by analytical and visualization computational tools (in particular the subarea of Cultural Analytics [7]), which allow the development of techniques for data encoding, in order to accelerate research and analysis, in addition to promoting open access standards and the balance between scientific and digital data processing in collaboration with people, to give back to the community with added value [21].

The recommendations for Open Science and best practices in Digital Humanities [21, 22], along with UNESCO's guidelines on cultural diversity, intangible cultural heritage and digital heritage – encouraging participatory practices with individuals, communities and groups [23] – led to participatory methodologies and projects becoming more frequent. Well-succeeded examples of participatory platforms that have endured in the long run – like *Museu da Pessoa* (1997), a collaborative museum in Brazil based on life testimonials, that invites people to share their stories and create collections with other testimonials; and *History Pin* (2010) born from a Google supported initiative as a collaborative archive for sharing stories and "pinning" content about places, also being adopted by libraries, museums and community groups – provide good hints on effective practices and strategies.

Simultaneously, social media and digital platforms increasingly explore the sense of nostalgia to celebrate memories. Such strategies induce the feeling of reliving the moments and the sense of belonging to a community, motivating social engagement. The mechanisms also amplify how experiences are enjoyed and remembered and motivate keeping affective records for the future. This phenomenon contributes to the process of collective memory [24], a construct resulting from a permanent dynamic of resignification of individual experiences modelled by social experiences, including communicative memories produced by the media [25]. In this sense, more relevant to collective memory than historical memory, often distant from people's daily lives, are the social experiences within groups, which is the core of POLARISCOPE project.

For this research particular methodologies are relevant, namely the constitution of community archives [26] and cultural mapping [27], having as a differentiating value compared to other projects the focus on the potential of correlated visualizations (hierarchical, relational, spatio-temporal, textual and hybrid models) to provide visual insights and trigger discovery and storytelling. Within the Participatory Culture, these living archives fed by multiple contributions constitute a "collective intelligence" [28] using networks of users to structure and expand meaning within user-generated content [29]. Based on the power of networks, the concept of "neogeography" [30] and "deep maps" [31] are some examples of collaborative cartographic annotation practices focused on people's interests that, beyond pinning landmarks, aim to get a deeper understanding of places through social participation. Hence, locative technologies constitute a surplus when exploring territories as catalysts of contextual information and location-based storytelling.

As to related work, we highlight some research prototypes, such as: *CLIO* project [32], a content sharing tool based on ubiquitous urban computing using a mobile app and outdoor/indoor displays in Finland; *CoShoPho* [33], a toolkit developed by museums and archives in Sweden, Denmark and Finland to create and engage with social photography archives; *QueryLab* [34], an *online* platform that aggregates content from multiple intangible culture heritage archives, through the stabilization of a minimal metadata structure; and the *Artfacts* prototype [35], developed with a two-speed architecture as an interoperable data model and an object-oriented user interface running on a fast-speed infrastructure, for customized interactive modules about museum digital collections to be explored by visitors, which work preserving the stability of the information system of the institutional online archives. Also, regarding the POLARISCOPE's team previous projects relevant for the current research, we highlight: *MixMyVisit*, a technologic solutions for automatic generation of videos based on the aggregation of content from several sources, within the context of museum visits [36] and *SOMA – Archive of Sounds and Memories of Aveiro*, a collaborative archive based on ethnomusicology research and creative patrimonies for social inclusion developed by members of the University of Aveiro; and the program *Memory for All* (MfA) [37] from the NOVA University Lisbon partner, that collect and share in an open access platform oral testimonies valuing life stories and oral History. Among other digital strategies, MfA organizes the Memory Days to collect face-to-face testimonials and records of personal objects and documents, and SOMA collaborates with local institutions and groups of retired citizens to develop cultural activities and create podcasts with the community.

3 Methodology and Conceptual Model

The POLARISCOPE project proposes the activation of a participatory dynamic involving stakeholders, local associations and community representatives mediated by a digital platform to collect, visualize, and co-create collective memories. To that purpose, the project aims to assess if an online-based participatory platform that eases multimedia data collection (combining historical documents with resources shared by multiple users) and generates correlated visualizations, can contribute significantly to enhancing the experience and collective memories of places and events. Namely by supporting content sharing, social tagging and practices of visual storytelling and content remix. Furthermore, beyond the use by broad audiences, it is intended that the platform may constitute a useful mediation tool for institutions and researchers working with communities, allowing the creation of new documental collections that preserve contemporary culture, as digital heritage.

To evaluate the potential of the prototype to generate engagement and relatability to contribute to the collective memory of the events being "polariscoped" the project team designed a collaborative framework involving potential users in all steps of the process. Thus, guided by the aforementioned research goals, the empirical study follows a participatory methodology for:

- *Data collection* – through in-depth analysis of standard and robust data models of the information systems of centralized archives (Historical Archive of Aveiro) and from community-based projects (Memory for All program), complemented with ethnographic fieldwork with stakeholders and potential users [23];
- *Data processing* - following best practices in the Digital Humanities field regarding open access standards and the balance between scientific and digital processing of data in collaboration with people to give back to the community with added value [21, 22];
- *Development* - adopting Participatory and User Centred Design approaches for the prototype development [15, 38];
- *Evaluation* - conducting quali-quantitative User Experience (UX) evaluations to assess usability and emotional reactions of the target audience. The UX assessment

of the platform will be focused on four dimensions – aesthetic, emotion, stimulation, and identification– using a triangulation of validated instruments (System Usability Scale; Self Assessment Manikin; and AttrackDiff) consolidated by the team in previous projects [39, 40].

Within an iterative process, the project comprises fieldwork through focus groups with stakeholders and potential end-users, including museums, cultural associations and community members to identify requirements for the prototype development. These participatory sessions will be followed by two evaluation cycles: laboratory testing with a medium-fidelity prototype and field trials using a high-fidelity prototype in Aveiro, but also in Lisbon, to assure the replicability of the prototype to different contexts. Additional to autonomous individual exploration through personal devices, other strategies like providing access to the platform through the outdoor interactive displays available in the public space for group dynamics, as well involving schools and day care facilities for elderly and retired people and the collaboration of local radios and outdoor kiosks to collect testimonials and promote intergenerational dynamics for digital and storytelling skills exchange will also be contemplated.

According to previous data collection through a qualitative study carried with experts to get their feedback about the concept of the platform [41], the study revealed receptivity for what they considered a useful and timely social tool. The sample included eleven experts, five male and six female, aged between 37 and 55 years-old, with relevant theoretical and practical work within the scientific domains of archives, museology, heritage, ethnography, community projects, cultural events, design, participatory media and digital platforms. The experts were prolific in suggesting different use contexts they considered more relevant to benefit from the proposed platform (mostly events, like concerts and exhibitions, intangible heritage and traditional celebrations, oral history and life stories testimonials). The systematization of the results allowed consolidating the concept and identifying relevant contexts and strategies. From all the suggestions, three emerged as possible distinguishing features for the platform, in parallel with the correlated visualizations focus: i) to ease the collection of testimonials from communities in loco (many at risk of being lost due to the advanced age of their beholders); ii) to automatize content organization and aggregation from several sources, namely regarding different typologies of cultural heritage; and iii) to provide social tools for documenting the work-in-process of events, including dimensions often invisible to the public (creative process, preparation, backstage, etc.).

The previous research [41, 42] (which included experts interviews; the case study of multiple participatory projects and apps for the identification of relevant interfaces and visualization models for the platform; and the evaluation of a medium-fidelity prototype of a digital community around music events to understand social and content sharing dynamics), culminated in the development of a conceptual model as a starting point for the POLARISCOPE prototype development (Fig. 1). The model is not a framework for designing a visual repository search engine but instead a mediation device that aims to represent multiple points of view on collective memories of experiences in their observable and sharable dimensions (digital multimedia records).

In this way, the model (Fig. 1) describes a multimedia documental system based on triggers of remembrance, through a cyclical and non-sequential participatory process,

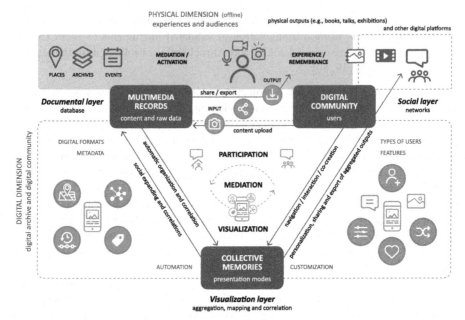

Fig. 1. Conceptual model for digital co-creation and visualization of collective memories based on a participatory platform

aiming at the exploration and discovery through association and recombination of content. The model is based simultaneously on a cognitive dimension of content curation and tagging along with an emotional dimension to motivate participation, namely the feeling of belonging to a community gathered around a shared experience. The model is built-on three operative components:

- The **documental layer** of resources evocative of experiences, shared by the various participants of the platform, thus consisting of the raw material, whose contextual information is structured in a database that allows correlated forms of presentation;
- The **aggregation and correlation layer** which automatically organizes the different records based on defined filters and semantic connections. These visualizations are reconfigurable and personalized based on social dynamics of content sharing and enrichment. Thus, the visualizations are the trigger for exploring the content, according to different criteria and representation models;
- The **social and emotional layer** composed by users that feed the system by interacting and sharing content. This digital community (of pre-existing communities around events and experiences or new digital communities that emerged through the platform that brought together users with common interests) includes different types of users whose motivation and degree of participation is variable (from institutions and event promoters that disseminate content and promote its activation through mediation

activities, to more passive and contemplative users, as opposed to others who are more active in contributing with their own content).

The model's components articulate according to three platform principles – *mediation, visualization* and *participation* – which are mutually interdependent. The *visualization* and *participation* mechanisms only exist due to the *mediation* mechanisms provided by the digital platform, and this *mediation* is focused on the operationalization of the other two mechanisms. Likewise, *visualization* mechanisms are inapplicable if they are not activated by *participation* mechanisms that feed the system with raw material and through social dynamics that enrich and contextualize it. Each principle unfolds in guidelines and good practices for the prototype development and to assure the sustainability of the platform in the long run:

Mediation Principle: *"The platform should support activities that encourage remembrance and social dynamics around the digital archive of records of experiences shared by various users, with the aim to better represent these collective memories and consolidate the community around them"*. The **mediation guidelines** comprise ethical and transparency standards regarding the open access to participants' content and suggestions for mediators to design content activation activities to foster participation. Also, comprises users' capacitation strategies so they can enjoy the platform autonomously and benefit from challenges and calls to action, exclusively digital or in synergy with face-to-face events. Complementary mediation activities may derive from the main event being "polariscoped" to allow further discussion and materialization of the records shared through the platform, namely trough talks, screenings, exhibitions, publications, etc.

Visualization Principle: *"The platform should offer automatic and customizable ways of aggregating, organizing and presenting shared resources with the aim of enhancing their critical and creative exploration from multiple perspectives"*. The **visualization guidelines** refer to the media formats that enhance storytelling and best evoke emotions of shared experiences. These records are inseparable from the contextual information added by their authors, and the metadata automatically extracted through computer vision and geolocation methods. So that semantic criteria, desirably based on archiving standards, can be used to aggregate and correlate records from multiple users, both to generate interactive and exploratory visualizations that update dynamically according to new contributions, and also allow curating and combining records that can be downloaded and shared in other social networks (contributing to disseminating and giving visibility to the platform).

Participation Principle: *"The platform should provide functional features for contribution, exploration, interaction and creation, with the aim of enhancing social dynamics of enrichment, recombination and co-creation, based on the content shared by multiple users"*. The **participation guidelines** concern the permissions granted to the platform users, based on their roles and motivations for participation, which materialize in the features they have access, namely exploring visualizations based on different filters, uploading their own content, and enriching the content already available. But also, the possibility of co-creating customized collections and remixed stories, which can be downloaded, saved in their personal profiles or shared publicly.

In summary, the participatory platform is the central element of the model, whose digital mediation enables the visualization and co-creation of collective memories, based on shared records. This social dynamic of content sharing and enrichment leads to the constitution of *digital archives* and the consolidation of *online communities*, around common interests and experiences, with the possibility of replication and adaptation to different contexts. User generated content and socially contextualized metadata may be of interest not only for exploratory purposes but also for integration with institutional archives, for historical, cultural or sociologic reasons. Therefore, it is crucial the system abides to Linked Open Data standards that allow interoperability with the state-of-the-art archiving systems to promote sustainability, usability and visibility of this on-going community archive.

4 Final Considerations

With the aim of evaluating if a digital platform that eases sharing multimedia records and generates correlated visualizations from multiple users' resources can enhance the experience and collective memory of events, this paper presented the theoretical and methodological framework to guide the process of a prototype development and assessment. It is expected through the POLARISCOPE research project to achieve a robust solution capable of supporting the participation of different audiences; to generate different visualization outputs according to metadata-based filters (location, time, categories, emotions); and to promote user engagement and content sharing instigated by common interests and location-based exploration of territories and events. In addition to a functional prototype validated by end-users, this project also aims to produce theoretical contributions to be discussed and transferred to the scientific community and the civil society through a final workshop, to promote the use of the platform among institutions and communities.

Beyond providing a practical tool to create and expand community archives, the digital platform based on users' contributions is not an isolated result, but rather an integral part of a broader social system, because it comprises the generation of different visualizations suggesting possible narratives and supporting social activities (digital and face-to-face), which together allow the study of the documented subjects and shared content, each preserving their intrinsic value as well as part of a collective. Hence, it is strategic to consider judicious management of these resources to assure interoperability with existing archiving standards and databases, aligned with the Open Science goals and recommendations from the Open Knowledge Foundation and the Open Archives Initiative. Therefore, the platform intends to deliver meaningful outputs for: *individual users* (being a social and content-sharing tool; generating compelling visualizations that correlate multiple contributions; providing content they can save and share); and for *researchers and institutions* (being a tool for collecting and organizing resources from users; supplying structured datasets about user content bearing in mind the data protection policies; contributing for expanding existing archives with social-driven information and media; and contributing to the enhancement of events).

Focusing on memory mediated by technology, a core paradigm in the current digitization of culture, this project has the opportunity to explore much-needed approaches to digital heritage and digital memory for generations to come. Also, the project allows to test mixed methods and flexible ways of working with communities towards a social empowerment tool that can be useful for institutions and people, since it refers to meaningful content they are emotionally attached. Therefore, it draws an opportunity not only for technological innovation but mostly to contribute with a useful social mediation tool that may bring inclusion, instigate creativity and meaningful experiences and knowledge transfer among different age groups, as well as bringing together the scientific community and the civil society.

Acknowledgments. The R&D project (grant agreement no. 2022.04424.PTDC) is funded by FCT - Fundação para a Ciência e a Tecnologia.

References

1. Segel, E., Heer, J.: Narrative visualization: telling stories with data. IEEE Trans. Visual. Computer Graph. **16.6**, 1139–1148 (2010)
2. Cairo, A.: The Functional Art – An Introduction to Information Graphics and Visualization. New Riders, USA (2013)
3. Meirelles, I.: Design for Information. An Introduction to the History, Theories, and Best Practices Behind Effective Information Visualizations. Rockport Publishers, Massachusetts (2013)
4. Shneiderman, B.: The eyes have it: a task by data type taxonomy for information visualizations. In: Proceedings of the 1996 IEEE Symposium on Visual Languages (VL 1996), pp. 336–343. IEEE Computer Society, USA (1996)
5. Whitelaw, M.: Generous interfaces for digital cultural collections. Digital Hum. Quar. **9**, 1 (2015). http://www.digitalhumanities.org/dhq/vol/9/1/000205/000205.html. Accessed 10 Feb 2023
6. Alexander, B.: The New Digital Storytelling - Creating Narratives with New Media. Praeger, Santa Barbara, California (2011)
7. Manovich, L.: Cultural Analytics. The MIT Press, Cambridge, London (2020)
8. Li, W., Huhns, M.N., Tsai, W.-T., Wu, W. (eds.): Crowdsourcing. PI, Springer, Heidelberg (2015). https://doi.org/10.1007/978-3-662-47011-4
9. Drucker, J.: Graphesis: Visual knowledge production and representation (2011). http://petera hall.com/mapping/Drucker_graphesis_2011.pdf. Accessed 10 Feb 2023
10. Pousman, Z., Stasko, J., Mateas, M.: Casual information visualization: depictions of data in everyday life. IEEE Trans. Visual. Comput. Graph. **13.6**, 1145–1152 (2007)
11. Kosara, R., Mackinlay, J.: Storytelling: the next step for visualization. Computer **46.5**, 44–50 (2013)
12. Norman, D.: Design of Everyday Things (Revised and Expanded Edition). Basic Books, New York (2013)
13. Sanders, E.: Generative tools for co-designing. In: Scrivener, S.A.R., Ball, L.J., Woodcock, A. (eds.) Collaborative Design, pp. 3–12. Springer, London (2000). https://doi.org/10.1007/978-1-4471-0779-8_1
14. Sanders, E.: Scaffolds for experiencing in the new design space. In: Information Design. Graphic-Sha Publishing, Tokyo (2002)

15. Huybrechts, L. (ed.): Participation is Risky – Approaches to Joint Creative Processes. Valiz, Amsterdam (2014)
16. Twente, U.: Uses and Gratifications Approach. In: Theorieënoverzicht TCW (2014). http://www.utwente.nl/cw/theorieenoverzicht/TheoryClusters/CommunicationandInformationTec hnology/Uses_and_Gratifications_Approach-1/. Accessed 10 Feb 2023
17. Norman, D.: Emotional Design: Why We Love (Or Hate) Everyday Things. Basic Books, New York (2004)
18. Howard, T.: Design to thrive: creating social networks and online communities that last. In: Analyzing Social Media Networks with NodeXL: Insights from a Connected World. Morgan Kaufmann, Burlington (2010)
19. Dijck, J.V.: Mediated Memories in the Digital Age. Stanford University Press, Stanford (2007)
20. Ernst, W.: Digital Memory and the Archive. University of Minnesota Press, Minneapolis, London (2013)
21. levenberg, I., Neilson, T., Rheams, D.: Research Methods for the Digital Humanities. Palgrave Macmillan (2018)
22. Rollo, M., Brandão, T., Queiroz, I.: Revising the institutionalization of science policies: historical contexts and competing models. Portuguese J. Soc. Sci. **17**(1) (2018)
23. Sousa, F.: The Participation in the Safeguarding of the Intangible Cultural Heritage. The role of Communities, Groups and Individuals. Memória Imaterial CRL, Alenquer (2018)
24. Halbwachs, M.: On Collective Memory. The University of Chicago Press, Chicago (1992)
25. Assmann, J.: Communicative and cultural memory. In: Cultural Memory Studies. An International and Interdisciplinary Handbook, pp. 109–118. Walter de Gruyter, Berlin (2008)
26. Bastian, J.A., Flinn, A. (eds.): Community Archives, Community Spaces: Heritage, Memory, and Identity. Facet Publishing, London (2020)
27. Duxbury, N., Garrett-Petts, W.F., MacLennan, D. (eds.): Cultural Mapping as Cultural Inquiry. Routledge, New York (2015)
28. Lévy, P.: Inteligência Coletiva: Para Uma Antropologia do Ciberespaço. Instituto Piaget, Lisboa (1994)
29. Jenkins, H.: Convergence Culture: Where Old and New Media Collide. New York University Press, New York (2008)
30. Turner, A.: Introduction to Neogeography. O'Reilly Media Inc, Massachusetts (2006)
31. Bodenhamer, D.J., Corrigan, J., Harris, T.M. (eds.): Deep Maps and Spatial Narratives. Indiana University Press (2015)
32. Ringas, D., Christopoulou, E.: Collective city memory: field experience on the effect of urban computing on community. In: Proceedings of the 6th International Conference on Communities and Technologies (C&T 2013), pp. 157–165. ACM (2013)
33. Boogh, E., Hartig, K., Jensen, B., Uimonen, P., Wallenius, A. (eds.): Connect to Collect. Approaches to Collecting Social Digital Photography in Museums and Archives. Stiftelsen Nordiska museet, Sweden (2020)
34. Artese, M.T., Gagliardi, I.: A platform for safeguarding cultural memory: the QueryLab prototype. In: MEMORIAMEDIA Rev. Intangible Cultural Heritage, vol. 4 (2019)
35. Araújo, L.M.: Hacking Cultural Heritage. The hackahton as a method for heritage interpretation [Doctoral thesis]. University of Bremen (2018)
36. Almeida, P., Beça, P., Soares, J., Soares, B.: MixMyVisit – a solution for the automatic creation of videos to enhance the visitors' experience. In: Abásolo, M.J., Olmedo Cifuentes, G.F. (eds.) Applications and Usability of Interactive TV. jAUTI 2021. CCIS, vol. 1597, pp. 105–118. Springer, Cham (2022). https://doi.org/10.1007/978-3-031-22210-8_7
37. Rollo, F.: Desafios e Responsabilidades das Humanidades Digitais: Preservar a Memória, Valorizar o Património, Promover e Disseminar o Conhecimento. O Programa Memória para Todos. In: Estudos Históricos (Rio de Janeiro) 33 69 (2020), pp. 19–44 (2020)

38. Lowdermilk, T.: User-Centered Design. A Developer's Guide to Building User-Friendly Applications. O'Reilly Media, USA (2013)

39. Almeida, P., et al.: Iterative user experience evaluation of a user interface for the unification of TV contents. In: Abásolo, M., Abreu, J., Almeida, P., Silva, T. (eds.) jAUTI 2017. CCIS, vol. 813, pp. 44–57. Springer, Cham (2018). https://doi.org/10.1007/978-3-319-90170-1_4

40. Velhinho, A., Fernandes, S., Abreu, J., Almeida, P., Silva, T.: Field trial of a new iTV approach: the potential of its UX among younger audiences. In: Abásolo, M., Silva, T., González, N. (eds.) jAUTI 2018. CCIS, vol. 1004, pp. 131–147. Springer, Cham (2019). https://doi.org/10.1007/978-3-030-23862-9_10

41. Velhinho, A., Almeida, P.: Sharing and visualizing collective memories – contexts and strategies for a participatory platform. In: Abásolo, M.J., Abreu, J., Almeida, P., Silva, T. (eds.) jAUTI 2020. CCIS, vol. 1433, pp. 3–14. Springer, Cham (2021). https://doi.org/10.1007/978-3-030-81996-5_1

42. Velhinho, A.: Sobre a Influência da Visualização e da Participação na Cultura Visual em Rede do Século XXI e na Cocriação Digital de Memórias Coletivas [Doctoral thesis]. Faculdade de Belas-Artes da Universidade de Lisboa (2023)

Applying UX Design Process for a Web-Documentary Development: A Project Development

Elisângela Vilar[1,2(✉)] ⓘ, Milena Monteiro[1], Sónia Rafael[2] ⓘ, Francisco Rebelo[1,2], and Paulo Noriega[1,2] ⓘ

[1] CIAUD, Faculdade de Arquitetura, Universidade de Lisboa, Rua Sá Nogueira, 1349-063 Lisboa, Portugal
{ebpvilar,pnoriega}@edu.ulisboa.pt, frebelo@fa.ulisboa.pt
[2] ITI- LARSyS, Universidade de Lisboa, Rua Sá Nogueira, 1349-063 Lisboa, Portugal
srafael@campus.ul.pt

Abstract. This paper aims to present the application of a User Experience (UX) design process in developing a web documentary based on promoting empathy among social groups, with the broader concern of contributing to the fight against prejudice and discrimination against immigrants in European countries. The Human-Centred Design methodology was used as the foundation for web-documentary development, comprising four main phases: discovering, defining, developing, and testing. This paper will explain the developing phase of this case study, and the final prototype will be presented. In the end, the results of this phase will be discussed, considering UX design. Usability tests were made, and the main results were applied to improve the solution. In this sense, this paper presents a case study of a web-documentary creation, from tools development and application to user testing.

Keywords: UX design · Ergodesign · Human-Centred Design · Interaction Design

1 Introduction

According to Xu [1], ergonomics and human factors have been developing human-centred approaches to deliver ergonomic products, namely the Human-Centred Design (HCD) methodology [2]. From Noman's [3] seminal book formally introducing the user in the centre of the design process to now, Human-centred Design (HCD) [2] has been established as a standard for the development of interactive products, systems and services that consider Human needs and expectations in the centre of the developmental process to meet Human requirements.

ISO 9241-210:2019 [2] presents the HCD methodology with its phases arranged in an iterative circle, in which all processes are traced by a research-develop-test cycle that ends when requirements are met. ISO 9241-210: 2019 [2] also define experience as the perceptions and responses that users have while using a system, product, or service,

A. Marcus et al. (Eds.): HCII 2023, LNCS 14031, pp. 286–295, 2023.
https://doi.org/10.1007/978-3-031-35696-4_21

including their emotions and beliefs. According to Bargas-Avila and Hornbaek [4], the User Experience (UX) term emerged to cover the new ways of studying the quality-in-use of an interactive product that is less task-oriented and more focused on hedonic qualities of use. Thus, UX is a broad range term that can be understood as a continuum from research to practice, focusing on the dynamics of the experience and on studying how all parts of a complex system - comprised of personal characteristics, products or services and context – can be modelled to work together shaping the experience of use [5]. According to Van Schaik and Ling [5], when researching and practising UX, the cognitive, socio-cognitive, and affective dimensions that influence users' interaction are considered core factors, together with usability.

Increasingly, people's needs or superior technical and functional capabilities are not exclusive mediators of people's intention of having a product, system, or service. Nowadays, they are interested in the whole experience products, systems, or services can provide, such as social integration, recognition, and freedom, among others [6]. The UX process approaches the emotional nature of the experience, and the experiences that products, systems or services elicit should align with the user's needs, beliefs, motivations, and expectations [7]. For this, a rich and empathic understanding of the user's desired experiences is needed to define requirements that truly reflect users and create empathy in designers, inspiring them to feel like the users [8].

In this context, this paper presents the case of a web-documentary creation developed considering a UX process approach [9]. The argument for the web-documentary development was based on promoting empathy among social groups, with the broader concern of contributing to the fight against prejudice and discrimination against immigrants in European countries.

2   Methodology

The Human-Centred Design (HCD) framework was set as the basis for the project development. The Double-Diamond Design Process [10] from the UK Design Council was adopted for the project development. This way, the four phases of the design process (i.e., Discover, Define, Develop and Deliver) were adapted to the project's main objective considering an HCD perspective resulting in a Discover, Define, Develop and Test cycle.

2.1   The Discover Phase

This phase comprises general research from a literature review to the systematic analysis of similar solutions (benchmarking). Benchmarking was made with the primary objective of knowing the best practices and weaknesses of already developed interactive systems focusing on empathy promotion among social groups. According to Lankford [11], this technique allows the improvement of existing ideas based on the use of the experience and knowledge from others, mainly through the analysis of the strengths and weaknesses of similar products, services, systems, or organisations.

For this project, twenty-one similar were selected with the main criteria of having a direct or indirect goal to contribute to increasing empathy among social groups and that, in some way, considered narratives to achieve their goals. The twenty-one projects can be categorised as websites, exhibitions, games, actions and organisational, video and others. Analysing these categories also contributed to the definition of the primary approach used for prototype development.

The analysis comprises four main topics: the use environment (i.e., in-person or online), the goals and methodologies, the strong and weak points, and general comments and perceptions.

The main results from this analysis were that authentic personal narratives have high importance. Despite being sad or not, they humanise the characters contributing to catching users' attention and interests. Another point is that the language barrier hinders the dissemination of the objectives. Some projects allow direct contact between users and narrators (or storytellers). Even if, at some point, this contact could benefit empathy development, it can also provoke problems related to adverse user reactions that could harm the narrators physically or psychologically. The online solutions were considered to have more impact as they can reach a higher number of users when compared to in-person solutions (such as physical exhibitions).

2.2 The Define Phase

Results from the literature review point to the university context as one of the challenging environments to tackle the problem of prejudice. Prejudice is a social phenomenon also reflected in university (e.g., [12, 13]). In this way, it was defined that the project's target is Europeans living in Europe, aged between 18 and 30 years old (average ages from graduation, master's, and PhD programs).

From the target definition, a questionnaire was developed, and three personas were created from acquired data [7]. From this, empathy maps were also developed to help prioritise users' needs, aiding the project team in decision-making [14].

Finally, the main project requirements were defined based on findings from the discovery phases and Personas (see Table 1).

2.3 The Develop Phase

This phase comprises ten main tasks that were accomplished to reach a functional prototype (task 10). As an iterative development cycle, the development and test work together to achieve the best results.

The first task was ideation (T1), in which two main concepts were delineated from data previously acquired. These concepts were hand drawn (see Fig. 1), and two main questions were answered: what and why.

Three experts on Communication Design (1), Ergonomics (1) and UX Design (1) evaluated the concepts against the requirements defined in the previous phase (Define Phase). The selected concept was Concept B. In this concept, the site, with a web-doc format, presents on its main page a skyline with buildings, some with lights turned on that can be seen through the windows. When passing the mouse cursor on these windows, the user can hear the voice of a character (immigrant) in the documentary. The user is invited to enter that home by clicking on the window. Like a friend who came for a visit, the user is received by a small welcome video in which the immigrant presents

Table 1. List of Mandatory and Desirable Requirements and Restrictions.

Mandatory	Desirable	Restrictions
Integrate expository and interactive elements	Inform data on the immigrant population	Avoid possible personal distress caused by emotional empathy
Humanising immigrants through narratives	Share external content on the subject (e.g., books, movies)	Avoid possible discussions between users
Use different forms of narratives	Be able to adapt the solution for use also in the physical world (interactive exhibition)	Avoid the possibility of offending the characters (immigrants)
Be fun		
Be light (avoid the possible personal suffering caused by emotional empathy)		
Have short interactions		

Concept A   Concept B

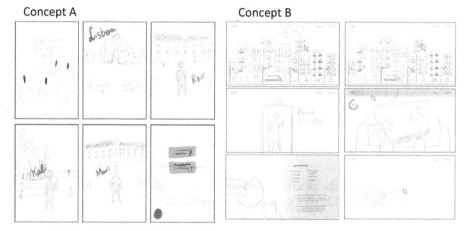

Fig. 1. Hand-drawn images from Concepts A and B.

him/herself. The interaction continues with short videos in a different part of the house in which the user deepens on immigrant's life history and culture.

The next task (T2) was Defining Context Scenarios that were defined following Cooper and colleagues' [15] definitions. Three context scenarios were developed, one for each persona, and they were used to develop the next task, the user journey map.

The user journey map (task 3 – T3) is a valuable tool to visualise how the user has his/her first contact with the solution and how he/she uses it, also making evident the touchpoints, the different types of media, subtasks that may occur and the user's feeling when interacting with the solution (being these feelings positive or negatives). According to Komninos and Briggs [16], the journey maps also can help other stakeholders explore what users think, feel, see, listen to, and do, helping them to speculate about possible "what if" and the possible solution to this question. Thus, the user journey map was made for the three defined personas. An example can be seen in Fig. 2.

The next task (T4) was the development of the site map in which the possibilities to present the theme "immigration" into the concept of a city were explored. The main approaches previously defined are also considered, mainly to potentialize empathy by sharing personal narratives and cultural information.

Fig. 2. The User Journey Map made for the primary persona.

The apartments are the central point of the concept of visiting an immigrant, and there, empathy is approached in three different ways:

Knowing: using personal narratives from real immigrants.

Learning: where the immigrant teaches something about his/her culture.

Sharing: where the user can contact the immigrant through a digital letter (that would be analysed before being delivered to the immigrant).

The user flow (task 5) was created based on these dynamics of using the city metaphor and setting the bases for the wireframes and prototype development.

The narratives were the next task to be done (task 6). The audio-visual modality was chosen because users seeing the immigrant's facial expressions and his/her voice tone while talking about a specific topic could be beneficial for empathy promotion. According to Leonard [17], when audio and visual modalities are together, information retention increases compared to only hearing or seeing information on a website. Thus, this web documentary is developed as a series. Each chapter presents the history of a character in the first person. The user can choose the character's narrative he/she wants to know, navigating through the history and making his/her own choices, such as the themes they want to listen about.

Based on the interpersonal empathy and social empathy concepts [18], the narratives for each character were developed planning to expand the capacity of absorbing information about others, including their different life situations, their life experiences, and the history of their social groups.

Thus, the interview guide for narratives creation should include components that evoke specific reactions, that are:

- Humanisation: realising that the other is human and has feelings like mine.
- Identification: realising that I and the other have things in common.
- The feeling of injustice: realising that the person is judged unfairly.
- Sympathy: realising that the person has left important things behind and that he/she admires the new culture in which he/she is inserted, as well as the local citizens.
- Welcoming: realising the person's desire to be inserted in the new context.

A filming guide was also developed with the interview guide, considering the concept of visiting a person. Thus, interview questions were linked to house locations to develop the narrative for the documentary.

A low-fidelity wireframe (task 7) was developed based on the user flow and interview questions (see Fig. 3). Low-fidelity wireframes are essential for the ideation process, enabling the creation of quick drafts for a more significant generation of ideas. The focus of these initial wireframes is to define, for example, the product's functionalities, its layout, the hierarchies, and the intended navigation.

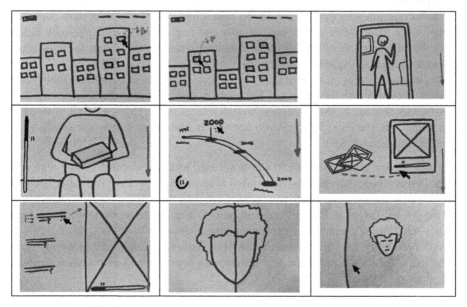

Fig. 3. The low-fidelity wireframe of the web documentary.

The Filming the Interview task (T8) was done with four immigrants living in Lisbon. The first two interviews (Welsh woman and English man) were made as pre-tests for the questions understanding, the audio capture and the positioning of the cameras and lights. After reviewing and correcting the problems that emerged from the pre-tests phase, two other interviews were conducted (a woman from Brazil and a woman from Cape Verde).

A medium-fidelity prototype was developed already considering the final line of narrative presentation that was defined as:

1. Reception - the character is at the front door of his house, welcoming the visitor (user).
2. Overview - the user can see a video that shows the character's house, where he quickly tells who he is.
3. Timeline - an audio timeline where the user drags the suitcases along the line to activate the character's audio talking about each phase of the line until he/she arrives in the country where he/she immigrated.
4. Happy/sad - in this part, the user sees an illustration of the character's face divided in half, with the left side coloured and smiling and the right side serious and no colours. When choosing the happy face, the user sees a video in which the character tells about his happiest moment and, in the sad face, talks about the saddest moment of his life.
5. Typical recipe - while watching a relaxed video of the character teaching a typical recipe from his home country and telling things about his culture and life, the user has access to the list of ingredients and the written step-by-step of that recipe.
6. Conversation - to simulate a conversation between the user and the character, questions are displayed on the screen, and as the user chooses one of them, the character responds.
7. Photos - as often happen on a visit, the host (character) shows important photos to the visitor (user) while describing the story and importance of each photo by audio. To start the narrative of each photo, the user must remove the photos from the stack and drag them to the indicated area.
8. Share - the last part of the character's page is dedicated to sharing his/her story and users' thoughts with the character. The user can share that character's story on social networks or share his/her thoughts through a letter to the character (it is advised in advance that the letter will undergo analysis before being sent to the character to prevent hate messages).

High fidelity wireframe (task 9) was developed to allow usability testing with real users. In this phase, only static images (taken from interview videos) were used without sound. The main objective was to test the user interface, mainly the planned interactions and the graphic language. So, during the usability test, the researcher explained the video content to allow the participant to understand the interaction context.

After usability tests (explained in the Test Phase), the identified problems were corrected, a functional prototype was developed (Task 10), and final tests with users were done.

2.4 The Test Phase

Usability tests were made with high-fidelity wireframes with the main objective of evaluating the human-system interaction. The specific objectives for this test were:

- Check if the user can complete the main task.
- Check how the user interacts with the prototype and if the interaction was as expected.
- Check the average time spent to complete the task.
- Identify interaction problems.
- Identify possible problem-solving opportunities.
- Improve the prototype.
- Improve user experience.

The tests were individually done with five participants during an online meeting with video through the Zoom platform. The researcher presented the test and the functional wireframe, giving instructions about the tests and monitoring the participant's performance when interacting with the prototype.

The usability test protocol comprised two phases, task accomplishment and structured interview.

For task accomplishment, two main tasks were given to the participant: i) know the history of an immigrant and ii) share this history on social networks or send a letter to the immigrant.

A thinking-aloud method was used to collect participants' impressions about the interface. Metrics about Participants' performance were also collected in the form of the number of errors and time to accomplish the task.

After accomplishing the tasks, participants were asked to answer some questions in a structured interview.

3 Results

The main results acquired from usability tests with the high-fidelity functional wireframe were used to make improvements during the development of the functional prototype.

According to usability test results, most of the participants feel enthusiasm about knowing the history of others in an interactive web-doc format. All of them felt that dividing the character history into parts, with different interaction types, helped to fix their attention from the beginning to the end of the narrative (some of them expressed that they thought it would be a YouTube video and that they would not have the patience to see until the end). A participant said, "the organisation of the story, how it is told, and the elements used to tell the story were very well done and generated genuine interest in getting to know the person involved and gave enough motivation to get to know the stories of the other immigrants."

Considering the primary constraints, most participants did not notice they could navigate through a menu at the top of the page. On the home page, most of the participants did not see the arrows that appeared on the right side to show the direction to move the screen (side scroll). They said that it appeared and disappeared very fast, and all of them suggested staying on the page until action was done. Two that saw the arrows tried to click on them, thinking they would allow them to see what was next.

Additionally, on the characters page, the indications about how to interact with the objects on the page also appeared and disappeared very fast and were not realised by the participants, causing confusion about how they should enable videos and audio.

Visual communication pleased the participants, being considered simple, fun, and jovial, with one of the participants saying: "the elements were not so salient as to draw attention (from the character), but they also kept me stuck there on the screen. I thought it was excellent.".

After the feedback was collected through the tests, the adjustments were applied to the functional prototype. In summary, the interaction indications that appeared and disappeared quickly from the screen had their times extended or remained on the screen until the first interaction with that part. After the first one, the indications disappeared as the user knew what to do. Arrows indicating page scrolling became clickable. Also, an explanation of how to scroll to explore the city in Home has been added. The functional prototype can be seen on: https://www.figma.com/proto/iO4mhAqgL6G460uRpAn9Nh/Site_pro-t%C3%B3t ipo?page–id0–3%1A&node-id225–3%21A&viewport-241%2C48%2C0.41&scaling-min–zoom&starting-point-node-id-225%3A21&show-proto-sidebar-1.

4   Conclusion

This study aimed to apply UX methodology used on a Human-Centered Design (HCD) framework to develop a web-based documentary to increase empathy among social groups. With the development of this project, three main points could be highlighted: i) the importance of the HCD that adapts the design answers to the individual human needs of a studied group; ii) the social design as a work area, using the same methodologies as more conventional areas of the design practice to solve social problems; and iii) using User Experience process as a methodological approach that allows the designer to empathise with users, making it the central point in the development of innovative and efficient solutions.

With this project, it was possible to conclude that not only the interaction design associated with the HCD has a significant impact on the development of effective and innovative design projects, but also that designers have the power to promote an improvement in the social well-being of their communities. In addition, the importance of empathy as a fundamental component of the human being and as a factor contributing to this improvement of society as a whole was highlighted and should be considered in design projects.

Acknowledgement. National funds finance this work through FCT - Fundação para a Ciência e a Tecnologia, I.P., under the Strategic Project with the references UIDB/04008/2020 and UIDP/04008/2020 and ITI -LARSyS-FCT Pluriannual funding's 2020–2023 (UIDB/50009/2020).

References

1. Xu, W.: Enhanced ergonomics approaches for product design: a user experience ecosystem perspective and case studies. Ergonomics **57**(1), 34–51 (2014). https://doi.org/10.1080/001 40139.2013.861023

2. International Organization for Standardization: ISO - ISO 9241-210:2019 - Ergonomics of human-system interaction—Part 210: Human-centred design for interactive systems, pp. 1–33 (2019). https://www.iso.org/standard/77520.html
3. Norman, D.A.: The Design of Everyday Things, 3rd edn. MIT Press (1998)
4. Bargas-Avila, J.A., Hornbæk, K.: Old wine in new bottles or novel chal-lenges? A critical analysis of empirical studies of User Experience. In: Conference on Human Factors in Computing Systems - Proceedings, pp. 2689–2698 (2011). https://doi.org/10.1145/1978942.197 9336
5. van Schaik, P., Ling, J.: An integrated model of interaction experience for information retrieval in a Web-based encyclopaedia. Interact. Comput. **23**(1), 18–32 (2011). https://doi.org/10. 1016/j.intcom.2010.07.002
6. Jetter, H.-C., Gerken, J.: A Simplified Model of User Experience for Practical Application. NordiCHI 2006 Oslo: The 2nd COST294-MAUSE International Open Workshop "User EXperience :Towards a Unified View". 106–111 (2007). http://nbn-resolving.de/urn:nbn:de: bsz:352-opus-31516
7. Vilar, E., Monteiro, M., Rafael, S., Rebelo, F., Noriega, P.: Developing personas in UX process: a case study for a web-documentary to increase empathy among social groups. In: Soares, M.M., Rosenzweig, E., Marcus, A. (eds.) Design, User Experience, and Usability: UX Research, Design, and Assessment. HCII 2022. LNCS, vol. 13321, pp. 93–107. Springer, Cham (2022). https://doi.org/10.1007/978-3-031-05897-4_7
8. Battarbee, K., Koskinen, I.: Co-experience: user experience as interaction. CoDesign, **1**(1), 5–18 (2010). https://doi.org/10.1080/15710880412331289917
9. Farrell, S.: UX Research Cheat Sheet. Nielsen Norman Group (2017). https://www.nngroup. com/articles/ux-research-cheat-sheet/
10. Ball, J.: The Double Diamond: A universally accepted depiction of the design process - Design Council. Design Council (2019). https://www.designcouncil.org.uk/our-work/news-opinion/ double-diamond-universally-accepted-depiction-design-process
11. Lankford, W.: Benchmarking: understanding the basics. Coast. Bus. J. **1**(1), 57–62 (2022). https://digitalcommons.coastal.edu/cbj/vol1/iss1/8
12. Equality and Human Rights Commission: Tackling racial harassment: Universities challenged Thank you (2019). https://www.equalityhumanrights.com/sites/default/files/tackling-racial-harassment-universities-challenged.pdf
13. van Laak, C.: Survey - Foreign students complain about difficulties | deutschland-funk.de. Deutschlandfunk (2014). https://www.deutschlandfunk.de/umfrage-auslaendische-studierende-klagen-ueber-100.html
14. Gibbons, S.: Empathy Mapping: The First Step in Design Thinking. Niel-sen Norman Group (2018). https://www.nngroup.com/articles/empathy-mapping/
15. Cooper, A., Reimann, R., Cronin, D., Noessel, C.: About Face: The Es-sentials of Interaction Design, 4th edn. Wiley (2014). https://www.wiley.com/en-us/About+Face%3A+The+Essent ials+of+Interaction+Design%2C+4th+Edition-p-9781118766576
16. Komninos, A., Briggs, C.: Customer Journey Maps—Walking a Mile in Your Customer's Shoes | IxDF. Interaction Design Foundation (2021). https://www.interaction-design.org/lit erature/article/customer-journey-maps-walking-a-mile-in-your-customer-s-shoes
17. Leonard, J.: The Importance of Using Visual Content in Social Media Marketing - Business 2 Community. Business Community (2022). https://www.business2community.com/social-media-articles/importance-using-visual-content-social-media-marketing-01980627
18. Segal, E.A.: Social Empathy: The Art of Understanding Others. Columbia University Press (2018)

IPlay: Towards Social Media for Community-Design Design

Min Wang, DanDan Yu[✉], Xin Li, and LiMin Wang

Art and Design Academy, Beijing City University, Beijing, China
961515176@qq.com

Abstract. Online social networks are now common place in day-to-day lives. They are also increasingly used to drive social action initiatives, either led by government or communities themselves. However, such initiatives are mainly used for crowd sourcing community views or coordinating activities. In this paper we present the iPlay platform that combines social media with toy sharing concepts to empower communities to discuss and realize community resource sharing. We designed the systems to assist people in communities to share locally relevant information. It mainly includes idle toys, public facilities, public spaces, children's activities, etc. It involves mobile app, to record, store and share media, and users can transfer media by their cell-phones. This system talks about the positive significance of social media in community design. By community design and information sharing widen information access, the approach drives a shift towards large-scale engagement of community stakeholders for community Involvement.

Keywords: Social Media · PlaceMaking · community interaction · resource sharing · social relationship

1 Introduction

Communities are an important basic unit in cities. They are living spaces that allow for neighborhood interactions among residents. As the pace of urban life quickens and community services and functions improve, residents are increasingly able to meet their basic needs without leaving their community. However, as a result, interactions among neighbors and emotional communication are decreasing in frequency [1]. At the same time, familiar connections based on the original geography and kinship relationships are beginning to weaken, with community residents becoming increasingly indifferent to each other, leading residents to shift from "enthusiastic interaction" to "nodding acquaintances" or even "familiar strangers."

In light of the above, cities are gradually implementing placemaking. Placemaking originated from multiple countries including Japan, the UK, and the US. The term refers to a social community within a specific geographic area working together to enhance the quality of life for residents and protect the community's cultural diversity through various interactions [2]. Its main aim is to coordinate relationships between people and between people and the environment, emphasizing the interactions between the community space and community residents. Placemaking can be carried out using various resources within the community to solve community problems together, improve the living environment, and revitalize the community [3].

In an era of networked interactions, the planning profession now has new digital technologies and applications that the planning profession can use to connect and engage with citizens, such as social media tools [4]. Such technologies have the potential to reshape the planning process, allowing communities to convey the meaning of places in their lives and actively shape the urban environments in which they live [5]. Social media has become a part of community communication, radically altering traditional community interaction patterns to promote group integration and implement community residents' actions, participate in interaction and communication between residents, build a platform and space for community residents' communication, and enrich community cultural activities. In light of this novel opportunity for development, this paper combines placemaking with social media to systematically explore the innovative community interaction patterns of community media construction and how social media helps people in the community share local information and promotes the harmonious development of community neighborhood relationships.

2 Research Context and Concepts

This project focuses on the positive role played by social media in community placemaking, with a particular emphasis on community toy-sharing programs for children. The project researches a series of problems relating to idle children's toys using questionnaire surveys and in-depth interviews, surveying 79 households from different communities in 17 cities with children aged 2 to 10. The majority of the survey respondents were mothers from families with one or two children; this group of respondents allows for a better understanding of the situation of idle children's toys in the community and the current status of communication and interaction between community neighbors.

2.1 Current Communication in the Community Neighbourhood

A community is a place where residents live. In communities, community neighborhood communication forms a key and inevitable part of community interactions. With the improvement of people's living environment, the relationship between community residents has evolved from the original "neighborhood style" to a "modern community system". At the same time, the community has gradually lost its function of promoting close communication among residents, with community residents lacking the motivation to participate in community activities. Most notably, the increasing role of the Internet in people's lives has led to a decrease in the depth of communication between residents, resulting in relationships premised on indifference. Moreover, mutual ignorance has become a common feature of current community information exchange. According to the survey results, most residents in the community do not engage in interactions very often, with most communication taking the form of a greeting. Seventy percent of the interviewees never visit their neighbors, feeling that they lack a sense of identification with interpersonal communication between neighbors in the same community. Even so, most of the interviewees agreed that good community interactions are important. Community interactions still form the foundation of harmonious neighborly relationships, with resident interactions being the optimal interpretation of neighborhood relationships. The lack of communication among community residents gives rise to a lack of liveliness and warmth in the community. In this context, social media communication constitutes good neighbor interaction, providing community residents with a sense of common community belonging and behavioral standards.

2.2 The Advantages of Social Media Application Use in Communities

A community can be understood as a collective connection, whereby people share social and cultural constructs relating to certain locations and traditions [6]. A growing number of residents in communities are active on social media closely related to their environment, including blogs, Facebook and Twitter [7]. Online Neighborhood Networks (ONNs) are online communities comprised of neighborhood residents, nested within larger communities. These self-organized ONNs can create a sense of community and foster neighborhood relationships by mobilizing individuals and engaging their online community awareness of and involvement in online neighborhood activities. Additionally, posting community and resident activities on social media platforms helps residents to share neighborhood information, exchange tools, provide informal care, and cultivate a rich online communication platform. This contributes to the formation of a common community culture and maximizes the use of social media to promote interaction among community residents.

Fundamentally, the application of social media in communities has the following advantages:

1. Rapid and widespread dissemination: Social media can rapidly and widely disseminate information, allowing community residents to stay informed of community issues and events in a timely manner.
2. Convenient means of interaction: Social media allows for convenient interaction, enabling community residents to discuss community issues and seek help where necessary.
3. Efficient Organization: Social media can assist community leaders and members in efficiently organize community events and action.
4. Enhancement of community awareness: Social media can help enhance the community awareness of residents and promote their participation in community affairs.
5. Providing feedback and suggestions: Social media can provide a forum in which community members can provide feedback and suggestions relating to community issues, thereby helping community leaders to better manage the community.

In general, building an online social media platform for community residents is a central means to realizing the psychological and emotional integration between people. Social media can help residents to better communicate, interact, collaborate, and solve problems in the community. However, it is important to note that social media cannot completely replace real-life interaction and communication.

2.3   The Current State of People's Everyday Unused Items

Due to updates in business strategy and consumer theory, households now possess a large number of unused items, particularly children's toys. As children get older and parenting styles are forced to change, families often purchase corresponding toys or aids during each stage of a child's development. According to the project survey data (see Fig. 1), children most favour sports toys, puzzles, and arts and crafts. However, children are only interested in a given toy for a relatively short period: 37% of children are interested in new toys for a week, whilst 25% are interested for just three days. Parents also have the dilemma of "keeping outdated toys at home, taking up space, and feeling sorry to throw them away". The possible solutions are to leave the toys idle at home, give them away to relatives and friends, donate them, or throw them away.

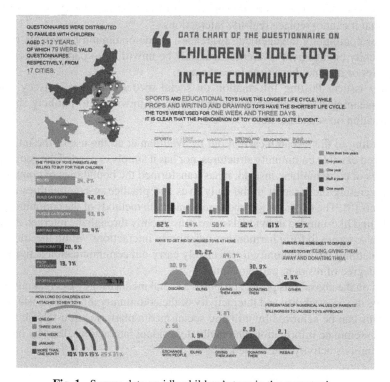

Fig. 1. Survey data on idle children's toys in the community

Additionally, through surveys, it was found that an increasing number of people hope to fully utilize idle resources through safe and reliable platforms that facilitate idle item transactions. Not only does exchanging these idle items in life optimize item utilization, but it also redresses and improves wasteful behavior to some extent, which is beneficial for environmental protection. What's more, idle item exchange can enhance interaction and communication among neighbors, assisting to break down the barriers between them and strengthening ties between residents.

3   Social Media Application Strategies in Community Creation

Establishing effective community resident relations can help improve the safety, stability, and quality of life in the community. However, at present, in a society where communication between residents is limited and neighbors are indifferent to each other, it is a challenge to establish positive relationships within communities. In light of this goal, our study was conducted based on the following questions:

1. Information overload: There is a large amount of information on social media, and community residents may not be able to effectively identify and extract information related to community relationship building.
2. Deceptive information: False or deceptive information is rife on social media, which can lead to misunderstandings and conflict among community residents.
3. Lack of real interaction: Interaction on social media inherently lacks a sense of reality, such that it cannot replace real-life interactions.
4. Lack of community engagement awareness: Some community residents may lack community engagement awareness and may be unwilling to partake in community activities or may not have time to participate.
5. Privacy issues: Posting information on social media may have privacy implications, meaning that community residents may be unwilling to publicly share their information on social media.

According to the research carried out by Wellman et al. the use of the internet has not replaced existing community structures, nor has it simply expanded the geographical boundaries of communities; instead, it has transformed the boundaries of communities, better integrating the Internet in the daily lives and practice of communities and their constituents [8]. The organization and communication methods of the community allow people to find like-minded individuals more conveniently through the internet. Additionally, it is also easier to form harmonious neighborly interactions within the community, thereby enabling the community to effectively carry out communication activities with a certain degree of resident participation.

Based on the above, this project proposes a social media usage placemaking strategy to enhance the accessibility and interactivity of the community through the use of social media. This can be achieved by utilizing social media platforms to establish the community, disseminate information, and facilitate resident interactions, thereby increasing the community's activity and influence.

3.1   Interactivity

Social media should be applied in the community in a highly interactive manner, such as sharing content, commenting, responding, and encouraging user participation and content creation. On community social media platforms, real-time and delayed communication methods should be designed in such a way as to facilitate communication among residents with different needs or who engage in different activities, allowing community residents to solve community problems or make suggestions. These platforms should adopt residents as the mainstay, based on interaction, and use media as the core of the platform. This is not only the essential aspect of community building, but also the foundation for effectively promoting community interaction, thereby deepening the emotional and relational ties among residents.

3.2 Personalization

Social media applications in the community should provide personalized content based on users' interests and preferences. Since its inception, social media has been a forum and gathering place for people and huge amounts of information. Accordingly, it is a time-consuming task for users to sift out the information they require. Therefore, social media in the community should focus on personalized needs and precisely design personalized social functions for different types of users based on their needs; doing so will avoid the problem of information overload and classify information correctly for easy access.

3.3 Social Relationships

Social media applications should enable users to establish and maintain social relationships in the community. For instance, a friend list may be built on relationships, like neighbors, similar interests, and shared needs. On the social media platform in the community, users can be grouped in different ways, such as location, interests, and activities. This saves more time searching for friends and allows community residents to readily connect with those who share common interests or live nearby.

3.4 Establish Online and Offline Relationships

In modern society, online social networking has become a daily (often primary) mode of communication for people, enabling them to easily communicate across regional boundaries and freely join groups based on common topics and shared interests. Despite their many benefits, online communication cannot achieve in-depth exchange; as such, offline activities need to be organized through social media to create new scenarios for community-style services, such as community gatherings, public service projects, and sporting activities. This allows community residents to directly interact offline and promotes interaction and individuality among the community residents as a group. Furthermore, community social media serves as a tool for information dissemination: by publishing information about offline activities, it facilitates online and offline social interactions between residents, thereby helping to build positive neighborhood relationships in communities.

4 The Sharing and Dissemination of Content

Social media applications should enable users to easily share, disseminate, and track the reach of content. Community residents can demonstrate their attention and contributions to the community, whilst at the same time establishing positive relationships with other community residents as a group. Additionally, community residents can use social media for interaction, communication, experience sharing, and selective content creation. In this way, users with common needs and interests can freely join together and exchange information with each other.

Social media has a positive impact on community communication and is of great value in promoting information access for community residents, which in turn is conducive to neighborhood communication and community services.

1. Improving community accessibility: Social media can easily expand the range of individuals participating in the community and attract new members.
2. Increasing interactivity: Social media can facilitate interaction and communication more easily, thus increasing community activity.
3. Enhance community impact: Social media can spread community information more efficiently, increasing the community's visibility and impact.
4. Collecting information: Social media can collect feedback and suggestions from community members to help community administrators better plan and improve their activities.

In summary, communities should create a positive social atmosphere, which can be achieved through social media; social media itself breaks traditional time and space restrictions. Due to these benefits, it shapes a new social interaction model and defines the social attributes of the community and its connection to other social media, allowing community residents to easily and quickly share content and expand the community's influence.

4.1 Social Media Application Cases: "IPlay"

"iPlay" is a service design project based on community toy sharing that is committed to solving the problems of toy accumulation and waste in households. In this project, children exchange toys and families interact, simultaneously meeting the recreational needs of children and increasing the frequency of interaction between community residents. At the same time, social media provides a convenient medium through which residents can participate in community interaction, enhances mutual understanding and harmony among residents, and forms a new community communication structure through effective and positive community actions.

This project incorporates the community social media use strategy proposed in the above placemaking and designs the "iPlay" community social platform in the service system to combine online and offline resident interaction. At the same time, a community children's play space is also designed for communities, with a storage place for unused or unwanted children's toys, providing a public communication space for community children and also a shared space for commonly used toys. "iPlay" fosters community cohesion through a combination of online organizing and offline activities, drawing in more community residents to actively participate in community building activities, whilst also establishing a sustainable community culture and friendly atmosphere (See Fig. 2).

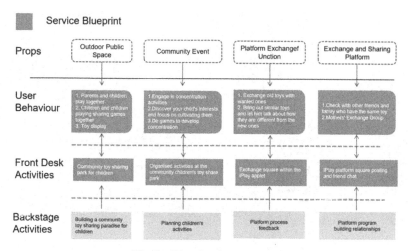

Fig. 2. iPlay Service Blueprint

4.2 "IPLay's" Real Time and Differential Social

The online communication community of "iPlay" (see Fig. 3) can be used to publish idle children's toys owned by oneself or to publish requests for toys. Users can also comment, collect and re-post toys on the platform, thus allowing community residents to communicate, connect, share, and express their personal wishes through differential communication. Residents with the intention of interacting can make appointments for a given time and place, or temporarily store toys by scanning the community's shared toy cabinet's QR code (see Fig. 4). This approach is both convenient for residents and provides users with a sense of physical and psychological safety and privacy. Crucially, iPlay can also facilitate real-time communication among residents during offline activities organized on the platform. For example, during performances, residents can vote, during contests they can support each other, and during games, they can be grouped together. This reinvigorates the community and increases resident participation in offline activities.

4.3 "iPlay" Personality Group

"iPlay" can set up personalized groups (see Fig. 5) and refine and label contacts using tags and groups, such as friends who are close by, friends who can lend things to each other, and friends who are free to play together. "iPlay" can also create chat groups based on children's interests, making it easier to form and join different community neighbor groups. Private chat and group chat directly reflect the different needs for interpersonal communication and group communication, effectively distinguishing between private and public spaces. iPlay can also proactively post suggestions for toys for children at a given age or stage of development in the appropriate groups based on big data analysis of user reviews of toys within the platform. By posting in social circles, both parties can meet the exposure needs of community interaction and access the required information.

Fig. 3. The "iPlay" shared toy cabinet

Fig. 4. The "iPlay" online communication community

Fig. 5. Personalised grouping of "iPlay"

4.4 "iPlay" Community Information Dissemination

"iPlay" can post toys for sale and loan, recommend and evaluate toys, and organize children's parties, games, and competitions. Through these features, iPlay makes socializing an important factor in promoting the formation and development of residents' self-organization, and online communication expands to include interaction between community residents. By drawing residents in to interact in these new ways, it mobilizes all types of members within the community to actively interact and involve more people in community building and integration. Through online interpersonal communication, residents cultivate trust and affection for each other, which in turn leads to the development of a moderate and rational public sphere of interaction in the community.

4.5 "IPlay" Online and Offline Event Integration

Embracing a grassroots approach towards activities and planning, "iPlay" is a way to facilitate community-run operations. Using the platform, residents can plan their own events and post "event boards" (see Fig. 6), which can then be booked by community members, such as 'one piece' scavenger hunts (Fig. 7), where reusable toys are hidden somewhere in the community and children and parents are asked to search for the treasure according to a scavenger hunt map. Community users can also organize and initiate

Fig. 6. The "iPlay" activity section

communication activities of interest, such as weekend performances, competitions, and usual games in the shared community space. These various features and provisions attract many residents and friends who are interested in the activities and steering the future direction of their community in a positive direction. There are also opportunities for small sponsorships or donations to individual projects. Its vision for events is to spark interest in ongoing events beyond exchanging idle items to create opportunities for action and promote a new way to interact with others.

Fig. 7. "iPlay" events in the community

5 Conclusion

Online social media have become a valuable source of information and insights regarding social problems that communities face. If the digital platform can be harnessed, it can provide communities with a tool that can empower community residents to become important role of life affecting themselves. This paper has described the social media in place making design strategy that brings communities more vitality. Our strategy uses a combination of social media and face to face active that takes information from online social media to create personalized online community, facilitate information sharing, and organize offline events. These are application in an toy sharing service design project that Encourage community residents to communicate and share toys, establish a friendly atmosphere among residents.

IPlay can also be used in general to improve resource sharing and social relationship by enhancing the interaction with community residents. Most significantly, however, iPlay offers a blueprint for next generation social media that are designed principally to provide opportunity residents to be at the heart of community.

Acknowledgments. Many thanks to my classmates SiMan Yang, Kui Ren, TianXiu Wang, members of the project. Their works are very essential for the paper.

References

1. Huang, W.: Research on Neighborhood Relations in Urban Communities from the Perspective of Stakeholder Theory. Nanchang University (12). 2018
2. Ge, Y.: Village over distribution and rural identity reconstruction. J. China Pudong Cadre Inst. (06) (2015)

3. Gong, H.: Research on the historic district of Fenghuang Town, Zhushui County, Shaanxi Province - National Research Center for Historic and Cultural Cities. Urban Plan (08) (2012)
4. Fredericks, Foth, M.: Augmenting public participation: enhancing planning outcomes through the use of social media and web 2.0. Austral. Plan. **50**, 3, 1–13 (2013)
5. Evans-Cowley, J.: Planning in the real-time city: the future of mobile technology. J. Plan. Literat. **25**(2), 136–149 (2011). https://doi.org/10.1177/0885412210394100
6. Aquilino, L., Harris, J., Wise, N.: A sense of rurality: events, placemaking and community participation in a small Welsh town. J. Rural Stud. **83**, 138–145 (2021). https://doi.org/10.1016/j.jrurstud.2021.02.013
7. De Lange, M., De Waal, M.: Owning the city: new media and citizen engagement in urban design. First Monday (2013). https://doi.org/10.5210/fm.v18i11.4954
8. Wellman, B., Boase, J., Chen, W.: The networked nature of community :Online and offline. IT Soc. **2002**(1), 151–165 (2002)
9. Avery: Social Value of Social Media in China under the Epidemic Research Report 2020. Ariadne Consulting Series Research Report (06) (2020)
10. Dabbagh, A., Kitsantas, A.: Personal Learning Environments, social media, and self-regulated learning: a natural formula for connecting formal and informal learning. Internet High. Educ. **15**, 3–8 (2012)
11. Dabbagh, N., Reo, R.: Impact of Web 2.0 on higher education. In: Surry, D.W., Stefurak, T., Gray, R. (eds.) Technology Integration In Higher Education: Social and Organizational Aspects, pp. 174–187. IGI Global, Hershey, PA (2011b)

Research on the Application of Clothing Elements of Ming Dynasty in Confucian Mansion Collection in Home Textile Design

Wei Wu[1]([⊠]), Beile Su[2]([⊠]), and Lili Zhang[2]([⊠])

[1] Jinan University, No. 336, Nanxinzhuang West Road, Jinan, Shandong, China
739893547@qq.com
[2] School of Art, Shandong Jianzhu University, No. 1000 Fengming Road, Licheng District, Jinan 250101, Shandong, China

Abstract. China is known as "the state of etiquette" and "the kingdom of clothing". The costumes of the Ming Dynasty in the old collection of the Confucian Mansion are the earliest surviving costumes handed down from generation to generation. These costumes are important cultural relics for the study of politics, economy, culture, etiquette, art and other aspects of the Ming Dynasty. They have unique aesthetic characteristics and high aesthetic value. This paper analyzes the styles, patterns, colors, techniques and fabrics of the Ming Dynasty costumes in the Confucian Mansion, and excavates the artistic features of the Ming Dynasty costumes in the Confucian Mansion. Then combined with modern aesthetic needs, it is directly or indirectly integrated into modern home textile design to create home textile design works that not only have national story heritage but also have modern technological civilization innovation. Demonstrate the important value of the clothing elements of the Ming Dynasty collected by the Confucian Mansion in modern home textile design, and promote the innovative development of home textile design.

Keywords: Old Collection of Confucian Mansion · Clothing Elements of Ming Dynasty · Home Textile Design · Application Research

1 Introduction

With the improvement of living standards and the improvement of living environment, people's demand for home textiles is no longer limited to basic functions, but more inclined to its artistic and cultural nature. Some home textile designs that permeate traditional art elements often contain profound national cultural heritage, especially the costume elements of the old Tibetan and Ming dynasties of Confucius, which have high aesthetic and artistic value and are favored by people. Due to the influence of historical, geographical, economic, humanistic and other factors, different countries present different cultural characteristics with different characteristics. Chinese traditional clothing culture is a characteristic culture accumulated by the 5,000-year history of the Chinese nation, with the unique imprint and cultural heritage of the Chinese nation. Traditional

A. Marcus et al. (Eds.): HCII 2023, LNCS 14031, pp. 309–325, 2023.
https://doi.org/10.1007/978-3-031-35696-4_23

clothing culture is a part of traditional Chinese culture, and traditional clothing elements not only reflect modern design concepts, but also embody the strong national spirit and cultural essence in home fabric design, and express the characteristic regional culture. On the basis of modern and contemporary aesthetics, designers should combine the needs of home textile design and the characteristics of traditional clothing elements, redesign traditional clothing elements, and integrate them into modern home textile design in a reasonable and orderly manner.

2 An Overview of Ming Dynasty Costumes in the Confucian Mansion Collection

Because of his special position in Chinese ideology and culture, Confucius was highly praised by successive dynasties. Because of their special relationship with Confucius, the descendants of Confucius also enjoy special preferential treatment in traditional society. They have a high social status, and at the same time, they do not forget to inherit their ancestral business and pass on poetry and rites. Therefore, the Kong family has become the longest-running aristocratic family in my country and even the world, and is also the most famous cultural family. The formation of this cultural family is the result of the gradual accumulation of the descendants of Confucius.

The old Tibetan costumes of Confucius are an important part of Confucius culture. The costumes handed down by Confucius include clothing, crowns, robes, shoes, accessories, etc. of the Yuan, Ming and Qing dynasties, among which the Ming Dynasty is the most precious, which involves political, economic, cultural, technical, aesthetic concepts and other aspects of social information, and has certain academic significance for understanding and studying the historical and artistic characteristics of the Ming Dynasty. At the same time, it has important historical and aesthetic value for inheriting and developing the research of traditional clothing culture in China, and also has a reference role for modern design. The old Tibetan costumes of Confucius show the political, economic and cultural colors of the upper class of the Ming Dynasty.

The artistic beauty of the old Tibetan costumes of Confucius is the aesthetic embodiment of the social, political and cultural perspectives of the upper classes of the Ming Dynasty, and the artistic beauty embodied through the conception, design, craftsmanship and science and technology of clothing, and the harmony and unity of modeling beauty, pattern beauty, color beauty, technical beauty and material beauty, and is a costume art boutique with a high degree of aesthetic awareness.

3 Analysis of Ming Dynasty Costume Elements in the Confucian Mansion Collection

3.1 Design of Pattern and Style

The main styles of men's clothing are clothes and clothes, robes, and accessories. Among them, the round neck robe and Taoist robe in the men's robe have the design of "hem", "hem" is also one of the most characteristic clothing structures, the "hem" of the round neck robe is a representative style detail of men's formal wear, it has the ceremonial function of covering the slit, and has the style of the robe with the belt, showing the majesty and solemnity of men. Therefore, the "hem" not only has the functional role of covering the slit of the robe, but also has the aesthetic needs of the upper class in the Ming Dynasty to pursue solemnity and majesty, and is a symbol of traditional clothing civilization (Fig. 1). The collar collar of the robe is embellished with a white collar, which is shorter than the collar, which is convenient for disassembly and washing, and has the effect of decorative beauty. The lower part of the Taoist robe is long to the feet, which can extend the figure of the Ming Dynasty man. The style of the Taoist robe shows the solemn and elegant shape of the man.

Fig. 1. Dahongsu gauze gown (Photo source: Shandong Museum "Clothes and Clothes - Ming Dynasty Costume Culture Exhibition" album)

The main styles of women's clothing are shirts, robes, bijia, and skirts. The length of women's shirts, jackets, and robes varies greatly, and when matched with skirts, the wearing ratio effect is also different. Shirts, jackets, robes and horse face skirts are called "shirt skirts" or "skirts", and the upper and lower skirts are also typical clothing matching for women in the Ming Dynasty. The horse face skirt is relatively wide and lengthy to the feet, highlighting the femininity of women (Fig. 2). Standing collars appear, which can completely cover a woman's neck than a collar, and wear a better fit. Women's dresses have a certain standardization, dignified and generous, with elegant beauty. The old Tibetan and Ming dynasty women's clothes of the Confucius House show the popular characteristics and artistic styles of the times.

The style beauty of traditional clothing is a collection of functionality and aesthetics, and the clothing shape not only conforms to the practicality and etiquette of wearing, but also produces artistry. Men's clothing is mainly robes, women's clothing is mainly robes, shirts and skirts, and the structure inherits China's traditional flat cut, with the characteristics of loose beauty.

3.2 Patterns and Emblazonry

The old Tibetan costumes of Confucius have a wealth of patterns, including animal patterns, flowers and plants, natural weather patterns, geometric patterns, etc. Most of

Fig. 2. Red Dark Satin Embroidered Cloud Python Skirt (Photo source: Shandong Museum "Clothes and Clothes - Ming Dynasty Costume Culture Exhibition" album)

the men's clothing uses the image of the beast as a pattern to show the power and power of men. Women's clothing mostly uses flowers and plants, rare birds as patterns, and also borrows the patterns of men's clothing or official clothes as clothing patterns.

Common animal patterns in the old Tibetan costumes of Confucius include: dragons, pythons, bullfights, flying fish, cranes, magpies, peacocks, mandarin ducks, etc., and the most common pattern is python. The highest level of clothing with python patterns was given by the emperor, and the Ming Dynasty also used the python pattern in the costume used on the auspicious costume worn during auspicious ceremonies. The blue ground makeup flower python clothes, dark green ground makeup flower python clothes, brown silk flat gold group python robes, pink gauze embroidered cloud python skirts and other costumes in the old Tibetan costumes of Confucius have different shapes of python patterns (Fig. 3).

Fig. 3. Dark green makeup flower gauze cloud shoulder sleeves knee-length boa gown (Photo source: Shandong Museum "Clothes and Clothes - Ming Dynasty Costume Culture Exhibition" album)

The plant patterns in the old Tibetan costumes of Confucius are small and realistic, mainly appearing in silk fabrics. The pattern image mainly includes folding flowers, tangled flowers, etc. Folded flowers are generally single-branched flowers, only inter-cepting the pattern pattern composed of plant heads, branches and leaves. The types of folding flowers cover peonies, chrysanthemums, plum blossoms, orchids, pomegranate flowers, etc. In the old Tibetan costumes of Confucius, the collar of the dark green makeup gauze python robe, the dark pattern of the green woven golden phoenix robe, and the dark green dark flower yarn single skirt all appear the same folded branches (Fig. 4). Developed from the Tang and Song dynasties, the tangle pattern had a fixed form in the Yuan dynasty, and was widely used in the Ming dynasty and was the main pattern in silk fabrics. The basic composition of the tangle pattern is composed of plant stems, leaves, flowers and fruits, and the stems and flowers are intertwined with each other, and the shape is wavy curve or circle. Entwined flowers, also known as string flowers and longevity vines, generally take flowers as the expression theme of entwined branches, and the stems and leaves are the structure and bones of the entwined branches.

Fig. 4. Part of dark green dark floral yarn single skirt (Photo source: Shandong Museum "Clothes and Clothes - Ming Dynasty Costume Culture Exhibition" album)

Moire is an important subject of traditional patterns. In the Ming Dynasty, moire and entwined patterns were the main patterns in traditional patterns. The moire patterns in the old Tibetan costumes of Confucius appear frequently, and the combination of appearance and other patterns is rich. The shape of the cloud pattern mainly includes pile cloud pattern, flowing cloud pattern, and four-in-one ruyi cloud pattern. Among the old Tibetan clothing patterns of Confucius, the four-in-one ruyi cloud pattern appears more frequently. Green dark flower yarn single robe, lake-colored cloud pattern dark flower robe, blue floor makeup flower yarn python robe and other clothing are woven with the dark pattern of the four-in-one ruyi cloud pattern, and the four-in-one ruyi cloud pattern also appears as a dark pattern in the python robe, which sets off the main pattern of the python pattern, highlighting the level and momentum of the clothing pattern (Fig. 5). The four ruyi cloud dark patterns in the plain robe fabric make the robe simple and gorgeous.

In the Ming Dynasty, the prototype of the seawater river cliff pattern has appeared, and the seawater river cliff pattern in the old Tibetan costume of Confucius is based on the theme of eight treasures standing stones and churning water waves, the tide is

Fig. 5. Part of the single gown in green dark floral yarn Photo source: Shandong Museum "Clothes and Clothes - Ming Dynasty Costume Culture Exhibition" album

undulating, and the "tide" is compared to "dynasty", which has the auspicious meaning of "the land is forever solid" and "the rivers and mountains of all generations". It generally appears on the chest, back, knees and hem of the skirt of the robe, and is decorated on the edge of the "persimmon pit" composed of pythons and flying fish, mainly in the form of collocation, making the main pattern richer (Fig. 6).

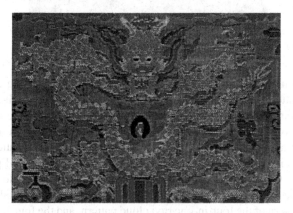

Fig. 6. Lush green ground makeup floral gauze python skirt (Photo source: Shandong Museum "Clothes and Clothes - Ming Dynasty Costume Culture Exhibition" album)

The back pattern is one of the most traditional geometric patterns in China, derived from the Neolithic swirl pattern, which is composed of thread splicing, and the shape is similar to the "back" character pattern. It uses a separate echo as the basic unit, and through repeated and overlapping design combinations, new geometric shapes are formed. In the Ming Dynasty, echo patterns mostly appeared in porcelain, furniture, clothing, and architecture, and their composition forms were simple and generous. Because of its repeated circulation of the composition form, it has the characteristics of dynamic and flowing, so people give it an auspicious meaning of continuous continuation and auspiciousness (Fig. 7).

Fig. 7. Part of the blue twig four seasons woven golden makeup damask skirt. Photo source: Shandong Museum "Clothes and Clothes - Ming Dynasty Costume Culture Exhibition" album

The old Tibetan costume pattern of Confucius not only pays attention to the beauty of the shape of the pattern pattern, but also has rich meaning, expressing the rich cultural connotation of clothing, which is also an important field of ancient art aesthetics. Through the ingenious design and combination of traditional craftsmen, natural things become more culturally meaningful, producing far-reaching aesthetic meaning, showing the perfect unity of man and nature, and becoming a higher level of beauty.

3.3 Color Type

The dyeing and weaving industry in the Ming Dynasty was unprecedentedly prosperous, and various dyeing and weaving techniques were improved and upgraded compared with previous generations. Because the costumes of the Ming Dynasty in the old collection of Confucius are cultural relics, they better retain the true color of the Ming Dynasty costumes. The word "chi" has long appeared in oracle bones, referring to people dancing by the fire, and the fire illuminates the human body red. The red color can be subdivided into many types, such as zhu, dai, red, etc., and in the official color of the Ming Dynasty, red color is widely used. The imperial uniform is the official service of the ancient monarchs and officials, and the occasions used are occasions such as court meetings and important festivals. According to the "Daming Canon", the Ming Dynasty was a red imperial costume, and the most complete set of Ming Dynasty imperial clothing in Shandong Museum is the old collection costume of the Confucius Mansion, Yansheng Gong Dynasty Costume. During important festivals such as the Great Worship, Qingcheng, Zhengdan, Winter Solstice, Entry Table and Transmission of the Ming Dynasty, civil and military officials would wear red imperial uniforms.

Among the colors of traditional clothing, there is a very distinctive color - moon white. The moon white, reminiscent of the color of the moon, is very poetic and has a beautiful artistic conception. The moon white Suluo single robe in the old Tibetan costume of Confucius is moon white, according to the contemporary color attribute, the color of this dress is light blue, not white, very elegant (Fig. 8).

Fig. 8. Moon white Suluo single gown (Photo source: Shandong Museum "Clothes and Clothes - Ming Dynasty Costume Culture Exhibition" album).

"White, enlightenment; like ice, the color of the season."[1] In ancient times, white was often considered an unlucky color, but this custom was not evident in the middle and late Ming dynasties. The old Tibetan costume of Confucius has a men's white plain gauze placket, its straight collar and right side, the collar and white silk protective collar, the color of the white collar and the plain clothes are suitable, and the left and right sides are swinging, which can set off the plain temperament of the dresser (Fig. 9). Pleats are often worn in robes or inside and out, while plain puffs are more suitable for matching with other clothing.

Fig. 9. White plain yarn Da Hu (Photo source: Shandong Museum "Clothes and Clothes - Ming Dynasty Costume Culture Exhibition" album)

---

[1] [Han] Liu Xi, Shi Ming, Volume 4, Shi Caibao No. 14, Compilation of Books.

3.4   Craft and Techniques

The old Tibetan costume craft of Confucius is a perfect combination of technology and art, and has the characteristics of artistic beauty. The craftsmanship techniques of the old Tibetan costumes of Confucius include jacquard, makeup, gold weaving, embroidery, etc., visually showing a colorful and imposing effect. The Ming Dynasty is the prosperous period of makeup flower technology, makeup flower is another name for digging shuttle technology, according to the ground organization of different fabrics, makeup flower fabric can be divided into makeup flower yarn, makeup flower luo, makeup satin and so on. There are many makeup and flower techniques used in the fabric weaving process of the old Tibetan costumes of Confucius, such as weaving gold makeup flower blue satin skirt, dark green floor makeup flower python clothing, blue floor makeup flower python clothing and other clothing fabrics.

"Weaving gold" process refers to weaving gold thread into the fabric, which can be divided into gold yarn, gold yarn, gold satin, gold weaving and so on. The gold thread of weaving gold is divided into a piece of gold thread and a round gold thread. Sheet gold thread, also known as flat gold thread, in the Ming Dynasty, sheet gold thread is generally lined up, and the material of the liner is animal skin or paper; Round gold wire, also known as twisted gold wire, is directly wound on the wire using thin gold bars or directly glued to the wire with metal powder. The obvious difference between round gold wire and sheet gold wire is the existence of core wire, and the overall shape of round gold wire is cylindrical because of the core wire inside, which is relatively three-dimensional. In the old Tibetan costumes of Confucius, there are woven gold woven into sheet gold thread, and there are woven gold woven into round gold thread. Among them, the gold thread used in the gold weaving of the green Luo woven gold phoenix women's robe is a piece of gold thread.

Embroidery is a method of regularly piercing the pattern formed by the fabric with needle and thread. The style, line, and texture of the embroidery are determined by stitching and threading. The stitch method refers to the method of needle movement and the organization of the line during embroidery, each stitch method has its own effect, and the texture of the embroidery pattern is also different. The embroidery costumes of the old Tibetan costumes of Confucius are all made by combining a variety of stitch methods, such as flat embroidery, pan gold embroidery, stitching embroidery, seed embroidery, etc., and the embroidery thread is mostly twisted double-stranded silk thread and twisted gold thread. The main embroidery methods of pythons in the blue compass gold embroidery python robe are flat gold embroidery, nail gold embroidery, flat embroidery, etc., of which the head and body of the python are flat gold embroidery process (Fig. 10). The so-called flat gold embroidery is to wind gold and silver platinum paper on the silk thread to form gold and silver threads, spread the gold or silver threads on the substrate, circle and fill the pattern according to the embroidered shape, and fix the silk thread short needle on the substrate. At the place of gold pan, the three gold wires are a group of nails and one needle, the distance between the nail threads is uniform and neat, and the stitches of the nail threads between the groups are staggered, the gold thread head is hidden, and the gold wire is tight. The characteristics of flat gold embroidery are that the embroidered objects are realistic, vivid and textured.

Fig. 10. Part of blue and gold embroidered python robe (Image source: Quoted from Xu Xiao's "Research on Clothing of the Ming Dynasty in the Old Collection of the Confucian Mansion")

3.5 Fabric Material

Silk is one of the precious traditional clothing fabrics, and the type of silk is like a pattern, which is the external expression of hierarchical culture. Most of the clothing fabrics in the old Tibetan costumes of Confucius are high-grade silk, covering the types of silk: yarn, luo, silk, silk, satin, etc. The selection and matching of fabrics are very exquisite, pay attention to the characteristics of the fabrics, and perfectly combine with the shape, function and wearing season of the clothing, so that the clothing materials are functionally suitable for different occasions, and the aesthetics are full of artistic charm. Thin silk fabrics such as yarn and luo are generally used in spring and summer, and thicker satin materials are used in autumn and winter.

Some clothing has a difference between the surface and the inside, that is, the face and the inside of the clothing, this combination generally uses soft and hard thick and thin fabrics to make the clothing more layered. Lizi can enhance the sense of shape of clothing, such as women's dresses, skirts hem, and inner lining, creating a flat and beautiful effect. The trim and inlaid gold thread at the edge of the garment are both beautiful and protect the edges of the collar, sleeves and skirt.

Confucius old Tibetan clothing in the style, fabric, technology, color, pattern and other aspects of strict, exquisite clothing requirements, craftsmen from the selection of materials, color embellishment, craftsmanship, matching decoration and other process process, rigorous production, serious production can meet the requirements, which plays an important role in the overall level of clothing production. The exquisite production skills of costumes contain the aesthetic ideas in the art of clothing.

4   The Application of Clothing Elements of the Ming Dynasty in the Collection of the Confucian Mansion in the Design of Home Textiles

4.1   Traditional Pattern Application

In modern home textile design, designers combine traditional pattern elements with modern aesthetic consciousness to adapt to the modern living environment and are welcomed by many consumers in the market. The entwined floral patterns that often appear in the old Tibetan clothing of Confucius are one of the patterns that are often used in home textile products. The tangle pattern in traditional clothing is a very popular form of decorative pattern because of its curved and long shape and lush flowers. Combined with the aesthetics of modern people, the tangle pattern has evolved into a fashionable and new tangle pattern in home textile design (Fig. 11)

Fig. 11. Design and Application of Chanzhi Pattern Home Textile Bedding (Image source: Xiaohongshu home textile pictures)

The cloud pattern in the old Tibetan costume of Confucius Mansion is one of people's favorite traditional patterns, which contains the cultural concept and aesthetic spirit of the Chinese nation. The moire pattern has smooth, curly and undulating lines, from which the ruyi shape is derived, and it is the carrier and symbol of beautiful meanings such as vitality, spirituality, spirituality, and auspicious rui. The cloud pattern has flowing, flowing curves and the wrong structure of the back and forth in the form, reflecting the general tendency of the aesthetic consciousness or aesthetic psychology of the Chinese nation, so the cloud pattern is often used in home textile products, forming a gorgeous, round, full, vivid and flowing aesthetic form (Fig. 12).

4.2   Clothing Color Application

Traditional clothing color is the customary color of a specific ethnic region, and has been closely linked with traditional folk customs, living habits and aesthetic awareness, which

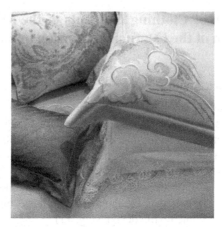

Fig. 12. Design and Application of Moire Home Textile Bedding (Image source: Xiaohongshu home textile pictures)

is the imprint of the nation and the symbol of emotion. However, with the change of social form and concept of life, the use of home textile color is gradually integrated with fashion and popular colors, and regional colors highlight their rich aesthetic connotations in popular combinations. This organic combination of traditional and popular colors has become a topic of joint research by international popular color institutions. Red is a color that Chinese people like very much, known as Chinese red, and is loved by designers in the home textile industry (Fig. 13).

Fig. 13. Red home textile bedding design and application (Image source: Xiaohongshu home textile pictures)

4.3 Clothing Accessories Application

Like the collar, button, knot, slit and other details in the old collection clothing of Confucius, although closely related to people's lives, when applied to modern home textile design, the practical function of these details will gradually decrease or disappear. In modern home textile design, combined with people's aesthetic needs, these details play a decorative role and meet the psychology of modern consumers, especially the pursuit of fashion young people. For example, as an important part of traditional clothing in the past, its decorative significance and practical significance are equally important, and it is used in cushions and pillows in home textile products as decorative details, and its practical function has been reduced and transformed into decorative details that meet the traditional cultural psychology of modern people (Fig. 14).

Fig. 14. Design and application of button home textile products (Image source: Xiaohongshu home textile pictures)

4.4 Apparel Technology Application

Traditional costume crafts include hand painting, tie-dyeing, batik, embroidery, etc. These traditional crafts demonstrate the profound national cultural heritage and the level of craftsmanship of traditional arts. Due to the advancement of science and technology, many products in modern life have the characteristics of patterning and commonality. Modern designers should combine the unique expression of traditional clothing crafts-manship with modern science and technology to design high-quality and culturally connotative home textile design products. However, traditional clothing technology is not simply copied in modern design, but extracts, mixes, splices, etc. of traditional clothing technology characteristics, and cleverly designs and integrates them into modern home textile design concepts, aesthetics and craftsmanship, and innovates home textile products that adapt to modern life and aesthetics.

Tie-dye is one of China's ancient folk traditional hand-printing and dyeing processes, using different tying auxiliary tools, seam methods, through the tightness, area, part control and change, produce different dyeing and osmotic effects, its pattern shape is abstract and changeable. Due to the unique craft expression of tie-dye art, the artistic image presented is changeable and the visual aesthetic is unique, which has become a fashion in pursuit of modern personality, and is widely used in the design and production of high-end home textile products at home and abroad (Fig. 15).

Fig. 15. Tie-dyeing Curtain Cushion Design Application (Image source: Xiaohongshu home textile pictures)

Due to the specific process of pulp dyeing, the pulp dyeing pattern is completely "the world of points", which is completely different from the batik pattern, without a single coherent line. This is the main graphic of blue printed cloth, and it is expressed in two forms, one is blue flowers on a white background and the other is white flowers on a blue background. Blue printed fabric home textile products, with national characteristics, simple and elegant, contain the unique aesthetics and lifestyle of the Chinese nation. With the passage of time and the development of technology, this traditional pulp dyeing process has been redesigned and more and more in line with the aesthetics and lifestyle of modern people (Fig. 16).

Traditional embroidery is one of China's traditional clothing crafts, produced in the Spring and Autumn period, China's four famous embroidery is Su embroidery, Xiang embroidery, Shu embroidery, Cantonese embroidery. Su embroidery pays attention to the thickness of the flower line, with eight characteristics: flat, qi, fine, dense, uniform, smooth, harmonious and light; Xiang embroidery emphasizes the realism of things,

Fig. 16. Application of Blue Calico Home Textile Design Products (Image source: Xiaohongshu home textile pictures)

and the image is vivid and beautiful; Shu embroidery is good at using a variety of stitch methods, staggered changes, thickness and thickness, embroidered things far and near, virtual and real combination, three-dimensional image; Cantonese embroidery composition is complex and orderly, needle steps are uniform and changeable, the texture is clear, the colors are rich, the use of color primary colors, there are light and shadow changes, and it has a Western painting style. The seawater river cliff pattern in the old Tibetan costumes of Confucius House is redesigned and applied to modern home textile products, which has strong traditional Chinese cultural characteristics (Fig. 17).

4.5 Traditional Fabric Application

Fabrics are the carriers of colors, patterns, and styles of home textile products and traditional clothing, and are important constituent elements that can directly affect their style and sales. Therefore, in the design of modern home textile products, designers should make full use of different textures of fabrics to shape different product style characteristics. Through the analysis of the fabrics of the old Tibetan clothing of Confucius, the fabrics of different textures give people different feelings in sight, touch and psychology. For example, cotton fabrics embody the characteristics of simplicity, comfort and nature; Silk fabrics give people a gorgeous, silky, soft and noble feeling; The hemp fabric gives a natural, rough and breathable feel. With the advancement of science and technology, there are more and more new fabrics, and traditional fabrics are still loved by consumers and designers by relying on their pure natural characteristics (Fig. 18).

Fig. 17. Embroidery home textile design and application (Image source: Xiaohongshu home textile pictures)

Fig. 18. Design and application of cotton and linen home textile bedding (Image source: Xiaohongshu home textile pictures)

5 Conclusion

In recent years, national styles have become popular in home textile design, and there is a broad consumer market for the application of traditional Chinese clothing elements to home textile products. However, how to use traditional clothing elements in modern home textile design is worth thinking about. Through the analysis of traditional clothing elements, combined with the characteristics of home textile products, the aesthetics of contemporary people, and the progress of science and technology, it is necessary to selectively inherit traditional clothing elements and innovate designs in inheritance. In terms of expression and cultural connotation, the traditional clothing elements of the old collection of Confucius can provide rich materials and beneficial enlightenment for modern home textile design.

References

1. Liu, X. (Han): Shi Ming, vol. 4, Shi Cai Bo, Cong Shu Ji Cheng Chu Bian (1960)
2. Li, J.(Ming), et al.: Ming Tai Zu Shi Lu. Academia Sinica, Taibei (1968)
3. Zhang, T.(Qing): Mingshi, Yu Fu Zhi. Zhonghua Book Company, Beijing (1974)
4. Wang, Q.(Ming), Wang, S.(Ming): San Cai Tu Hui, vol. 6. Shanhai Ancient Books Publishing House, Shanghai (1988)
5. Wu, Y.(Qing): Tian Shui Bing Shan Lu. Commercial Press (1937)
6. Liu, R.(Ming): Zhuo Zhong Zhi, vol. 5, p. 171. Beijing Ancient Books Publishing House, Beijing (1994)
7. Zhao, F.: General History of Chinese Silk, p. 11. Soochow University Press, Suzhou (2005)
8. Zhang, X.: Zhong Guo Gu Dai Ran Zhi Wen Yang Shi. Peking University Press, Beijing (2016)
9. Huang, N., Chen, J., Huang, G.: Costumes of China—Seven Thousand Years of Chinese Costumes. Tsinghua University Press, Beijing (2013)
10. Gao C.: Zhong Guo Gu Dai Fu Shi Da Ci Dian, vol. 12, p. 484. Shanghai Lexicographical Publishing House, Shanghai (1996)
11. Wu, S.: Zhong Guo Li Dai Fu Zhuang, Ran Zhi, Ci Xiu Ci Dian, vol. 6, p. 337. Nanjing: Jiangsu Fine Arts Publishing House (2011)
12. Dong, J.: Tu Shuo Ming Dai Gong Ting Fu Shi(Six)—Huang Di Bian Fu, Issue 03, p. 115. Forbidden City (2012)
13. Tian, Z., Wu, S., Tian, Q.: Zhong Guo Wen Yang Shi, p. 115. Shandong Fine Arts Publishing House, Jinan (2009)
14. Xu, X.: Kong Fu Jiu Cang Ming Dai Fu Shi Yan jiu, p. 5. Suzhou University, Jiangsu (2018)
15. Lu, J., Yu, Q.: Da Ming Hua Shang—Clothing handed down from the Ming Dynasty in Shandong Museum. Shandong Art, vol. 04, p. 64–75 (2020)

Visual Design for Predictive Display in Spatial Time-Delay Environments Considering Workload

Jiadai Yan$^{(\boxtimes)}$, Jiahao Sun, TianLe Tang, and Zhuohao Chen

School of Design Art, Changsha University of Science and Technology, Changsha, China
yaaaijd@163.com

Abstract. Time delay is an inherent technical feature that cannot be eliminated during space robot teleoperation and can significantly impact operator workload. In this paper, based on predictive display technology, we investigate the change of operator workload during teleoperation by image prediction graphical interface and virtual reality prediction graphical interface. By constructing a virtual simulation experiment platform for a remote operation system, 20 participants were tested and analyzed in a fetch-place experiment; TAM, NASA-TLX, and AB-directed questionnaires were distributed for subjective measurements to understand the personal perceptions and visual preferences of the participants on their workloads, and to investigate the applicability of the predictive display technology to reduce the operator's cognitive load. The results showed that the subjective and objective performance of the virtual reality predictive graphical interface (VR-PGI) was higher than that of the image predictive graphical interface (I-PGI) in the fetch-place operation scenario. It was found that the operator's workload did not change significantly with the increase of spatial time delay in the predictive graphical interface, which proved the practicality of applying the predictive graphical interface to the spatial teleoperation scenario.

Keywords: Predictive Graphics · Time Delay · Teleoperation · Workload

1 Introduction

In this paper, we analyze the extent to which the operator's body perception translates into workload at different time delays against the background of the significant time delay Human-robot collaboration is an effective means of increasing the productivity of human labor and improving the ergonomics of manual tasks.

As the complexity of human operations increases, robotic collaboration is also used in more remote scenarios that cross geographical limitations [1]. For example, it is used to assist humans in dangerous and extreme environments (battlefield, nuclear waste disposal, deep sea, space, etc.) with high accuracy requirements [2]. This kind of human instruction conveyed using information interaction to realize the fine-grained operation of one or more remote execution objects within a certain distance is called teleoperation. Teleoperation has primarily changed how robots operate and expanded their operational capabilities, allowing a closer connection between humans and robots. For the time being, the time delay is still an inherent technology that cannot be eliminated during space robot teleoperation. When an operator gives a command, the robot does not immediately execute it. It does not provide real-time feedback, and the time delay generated by remote space signal transmission can often be as high as 100 ms–10 s [3], which significantly hinders the work of space robots and can very negatively impact the operator's workload. Rated by the process of the master machine controlling the slave machine movement and re-feedback, evaluate the practicality of different visual interaction interfaces by workload.

The workload arises from the complexity of the interaction task in terms of representation or semantics [4]. It manifests itself in the space-time delay environment as the complexity arises from the difficulty in matching the instructions issued by the operator with the feedback quickly. Studies have shown that human performance is highly dependent on workload, and behaviors such as physical jitter and high psychological stress generated by an increased workload can cause operators to enter incorrect instructions. Depending on the operational task, it is essential to mitigate the negative impact of workload caused by time delay by optimizing the visual form in a virtual reality environment. Predictive display technology is currently the primary means to implement remote complex environment operations visually [5], which enables geometric and dynamical modeling of virtual reality environments of unknown environments based on multiple feedback information, enriching the human perception and behavioral capabilities of traditional operations [6] and improving the fluency of remote operations.

In this paper, based on predictive display technology, the remote interaction interface is divided into two forms of visual interaction: image-predictive graphical interface (I-PGI) and virtual reality-predictive graphical interface(VR-PGI). And we explore how the cognitive load under different predictive graphical interfaces varies with the degree of spatial time delay and seek a universal method of visual interaction to reduce the operator's workload. The results are used to optimize visual feedback to reduce the workload caused by spatial time delays and to respect the operator's work experience while maintaining actual work performance.

2   Related Work

As the complexity of human-operated machines increases, new technologies and means are needed to help human operators. As a result, researchers have been seeking to improve the fluency of human-machine systems in human factors and human-computer interaction. Here, we review related work and identify critical gaps in the literature that demonstrate the need for the experimental studies we present in this paper.

2.1   Predictive Display Techniques in Teleoperation

Predictive display techniques effectively address the problem of time delay, and their work focuses on developing computational methods that can generate solutions for predicting graphical interfaces using scene information collected from remote ends. Noyes and Sheridan collaborated to create the first predictive display system that overlays video images returned from remote ends with simulated wireframes of robot models generated from simulations at the local end to make predictions about the robot's Kim and Bejczy developed a display system based on a graphical prediction of environmental scene information [5]. Throughout the procedure, Kim and Bejczy used two approaches, i.e., wireframe and solid model, to display the real robot, overlaying the video image of the robot environment scene returned from the remote end with the graphics of the virtual simulation robot model with the help of camera calibration technique. Hirzinger et al. in Germany also used the prediction technique of graphical simulation based on the superimposition of graphics and images. They also used the prediction simulation technique of image superimposition in their experiments with the ROTEX space robot aboard the U.S. "Columbia" space shuttle. Their experiments also proved that the prediction display technique could overcome the time delay problem [8]. Freund and Rossmann et al. of the German Robotics Institute studied 3D reconstruction techniques, virtual reality, and joint operations and proposed the concept of projection-based virtual reality [9]. The method significantly improved teleoperation performance [10].

Most of the studies have been conducted from the technical level to mitigate the negative impact of time delay and limited space on teleoperation performance. However, in addition to hardware technology, human-related factors are equally important in teleoperation. One of the most fundamental issues in designing a predictive display system is achieving a compatible and harmonious relationship between the machine and its operator. To create scenarios in which operators work effectively, engineers need to understand how people perform operational tasks and how they monitor and control operations. To do this, we design a series of experiments to evaluate the effectiveness of operations. There needs to be more theory to guide engineers on these issues, and more in-depth research is required between the instincts and principles of human operation (Fig. 1).

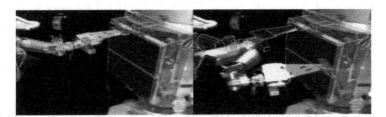

Fig. 1. JPL's graphical prediction display system

2.2 Human Impact of Workload

Workload allocation is a critical issue in human factors. Workload refers to the unique mental resources that can be used to solve a problem or complete a task at a given time [11]. It is not only involved in the storage of information, but also in the manipulation of information in various cognitive tasks [12]. When people receive more new information directly or indirectly than the capacity of working memory, it increases the burden on the cognitive system and creates a workload [13]. In previous studies it was shown that human performance is highly dependent on workload: too much or too little workload reduces performance [14, 15].

Many studies have shown that teleoperation performance is strongly correlated with human perception, cognition, and emotion [16]. Li et al. found that human skill level significantly affects teleoperation performance by collecting EEG signals from operators [17], and Schmidlin and Jones found that operator judgment was significantly correlated with performance on teleoperation tasks [18]. Loft et al. developed a model to predict the workload level of air traffic controllers and confirmed the results of previous work showing that brain load increases with task difficulty [19]. To help assess brain load, researchers have proposed various subjective and psychophysiological metrics [20–23]. The most well-known measure is the NASA Task Load Index: a unique, multivariate method for assessing perceived brain load [21]. Clarke, Schuetzler, and Windle et al. [21] used the NASA-TLX scale in conjunction with retrospective interviews to determine the previsit health load in hospital Personal Health Records (PHRs) systems. You Qian used the NASA-TLX scale for cognitive load measurement to propose and validate a usability model for a virtual reality interactive teaching interface [24].

Although the relationship between workload and job performance has been extensively explored in terms of human factors making an essential contribution to the advancement of human-computer interaction, we found in previous literature, but in the context of spatial time delay, that predictive graphical interfaces play an essential role in the actual work of remote operating systems remains unexplained. Although different predictive display interfaces have been developed, workloads have not been studied in human-computer collaboration of remote operating systems with predictive graphical interfaces. There is a need to fill these gaps in the literature.

In this paper, we analyze the extent to which the operator's body perception translates into workload at different time delays against the background of the significant time delay

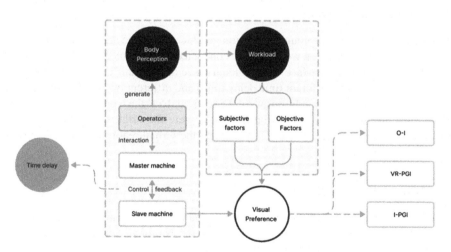

Fig. 2. Visual interaction interface research process

generated by the process of the master machine controlling the slave machine move-ment and re-feedback, and finally evaluate the practicality of different visual interaction interfaces by workload (see Fig. 2).

3 Experimental Design

3.1 Experimental Purpose

Previous literature has shown that operator workload increases with time delay and that predictive display techniques are an effective way to address sizeable spatial time delays. These studies have shown that visual interaction interfaces are effective in reducing operator workload and teams are able to complete assigned tasks more efficiently when they display a predictive model rather than a single real scene. However, this paper presents a new picture for this research. For example, would a realistic virtual reality prediction model have additional workload caused by overlapping with a real robot that is not easily distinguishable, or would an image prediction model be distorted to cause inaccurate discrimination in position. In addition, we do not understand how the predictive model affects the operator experience. Whether the workload increases with increasing latency when the operator is in the predictive graphical interface; the operator's preference between the two different predictive graphical interfaces when performing a grasp-and-place operation; and the tradeoff between the operator's visual preferences for workload during teleoperation.

The total number of participants in this experiment was 20, aged between 20 and 32 years, with a male to female ratio of 3:7 (6 males and 14 females). All participants had normal visual acuity (or corrected visual acuity), no color blindness or color weakness, and had not previously participated in this type of experiment.

3.2 Independent Variables

To investigate the effect of image prediction graphical interface and virtual reality pre-diction graphical interface on workload, we conducted an experiment with 3 (time delay) × 3 (visual interaction interface) for the fetch-place task. In this experiment, the inde-pendent variables were different time delay times and different two predicted graphical interfaces; the time delay conditions were 0.5 s, 1 s, and 5 s; the work task was the fetch-place task; and the visual interaction interfaces were the original interface(O-I), the image predicted graphical interface (I-PGI), and the virtual reality predicted graphical interface (VR-PGI).

3.3 Dependent Variables

The experiments were attributed by subjective and objective phenomena, measured by the Technology Acceptance Model (TAM) and the National Aeronautics and Space Administration Task Load Index (NASA-TLX) (see Fig. 3). In which the operator's behavioral intention is discerned by the technical TAM model, the NASA-TLA scale explores the subjective value of the operator, and the subjective preference of the operator is understood by the AB-directed test, and the subjective perception of his workload is explored tripartite; then the objective measure is conducted based on the experimental data feedback of the operational performance to assess the accuracy of the subject's workload perception of the predicted graphical interface. Subjective measures were paired with objective measures to ensure accurate results of the experiment.

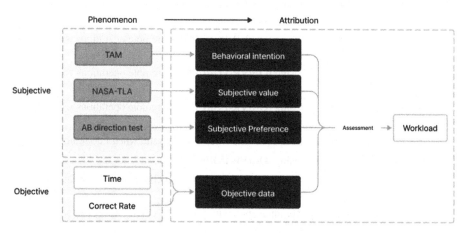

Fig. 3. Subjective questionnaire and objective data model

Perceived Usefulness. According to Davis' definition, perceived usefulness is the extent to which users subjectively perceive or believe that the use of a specific particular application system will improve their work performance [25]. When users feel that a particular technology can improve their work efficiency, such as saving time, better results, etc., then they are more inclined to accept the innovation. Drawing on Davis' definition, this paper defines perceived usefulness as the operator's workload for using a form of visual interaction that improves their job performance, faster and more flexible teleoperation tasks, and it has a significant correlation with behavioral intentions. That is, the lower the workload an individual perceives to receive from using a particular form of visual interaction, the higher the intention to use it. Based on previous related research, the author initially identified six question options to measure the perceived usefulness of visual interaction interfaces.

Perceived Ease of Use. Like perceived usefulness, perceived ease of use is also a core variable in TAM, and Davis defines perceived ease of use as the degree of difficulty and effort that users subjectively perceive in using an information system function [26]. In this paper, perceived ease of use is positioned in the context of real-world situations as the ease of performing the fetch-place task as perceived by the operator. The more convenient and easy to use a visually realistic interface is, the more positive the operator's attitude towards it will be. This paper initially identifies six questions to examine this variable (Table 1).

Six Dimensions of the NASA-TLX. The NASA-TLX scale uses six dimensions to assess mental load: mental demand (MD), physical demand (PD), time demand (TD),

Table 1. Post-test questionnaire-TAM

Factor	Number	Measurement issues
Perceived usefulness	PU1	Using [O-I/VR-PGI/I-PGI] in remote operations allows me to complete tasks faster
	PU2	Using [O-I/VR-PGI/I-PGI] in remote operations will improve my work performance
	PU3	Using [O-I/VR-PGI/I-PGI] in remote operations will increase my output
	PU4	Using [O-I/VR-PGI/I-PGI] in remote operations will improve my work efficiency
	PU5	Using [O-I/VR-PGI/I-PGI] in remote operations will make my job easier
	PU6	[O-I/VR-PGI/I-PGI] is very useful when I do remote work
Perceived ease of use	EU1	Using [O-I/VR-PGI/I-PGI] was easy for me
	EU2	I find it easy to get [O-I/VR-PGI/I-PGI] to do what I want to do
	EU3	My interaction with [O-I/VR-PGI/I-PGI] is clear and understandable
	EU4	[O-I/VR-PGI/I-PGI] is flexible in interaction
	EU5	Proficiency in using [O-I/VR-PGI/I-PGI] is easy for me
	EU6	I found [O-I/VR-PGI/I-PGI] very easy to use

performance (OP), effort (EF), and frustration (FL), with each dimension represented by a 21-point straight line. The score for each dimension determines the operator's workload at the time (Table 2).

3.4 Scheduling Mechanism

We set up the virtual simulation platform of fetching and placing tasks by Unity3D, (see Fig. 4). In the experimental simulation, the essential operation of the robot arm is realized by real-time manipulation of the angle of each joint of the robot arm. The critical binding in Input Manager can be set to achieve key customization, and the speed of each joint can be controlled by rotationSpeed. The delayed following algorithm of each model is implemented using a concurrent process, when the user operation will create a concurrent function to delay according to the delay time selected before the experiment, the main robotic arm will operate after the delay without affecting the user operation of the simulated model robotic arm to realize the whole placement experiment simulation. The simulation task part uses random numbers to assign the task, and each time after completing the operation of taking and placing the statistics, according to the name of the box taken and the table placed to compare and determine the correctness

Table 2. Post-test questionnaire-NASA-TLX

Number	Measurement issues
Mental Demand	The mental activity required to manipulate [O-I/VR-PGI/I-PGI] to complete a remote operation task, and whether the task is difficult?
Physical Demand	Manipulate [O-I/VR-PGI/I-PGI] to complete the physical demands required for remote operation tasks, whether to feel muscle tension?
Time Demand	Does the speed required to operate [O-I/VR-PGI/I-PGI] for remote operation tasks make people feel nervous or panicky?
Performance	The level of effort required to manipulate [O-I/VR-PGI/I-PGI] to complete remote operation tasks
Effort	Whether the performance level of manipulating [O-I/VR-PGI/I-PGI] to complete remote operation tasks is satisfactory?
Frustration Level	Do you feel frustrated and depressed when operating [O-I/VR-PGI/I-PGI] to complete remote operations?

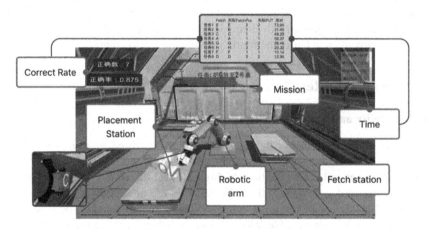

Fig. 4. Crawl placement task virtual simulation platform page

according to the string, and finally all tasks are completed to generate the results, the participants to record the correctness and completion time of objective data.

3.5 Experimental Flow

The experiment is divided into five steps (see Fig. 5). The experimental scenario includes two types of tasks: fetching and placing parts. The experimental environment includes one fetch station and two placement stations, and the extraction station is placed with 8 parts A, B, C, D, E, F, G, H. A set of fetching and placing tasks is 8 tasks, each task consists of a fetching and placing subtask. The pickup consists of moving the robot arm to the pickup station according to the task cues above, fetching the corresponding part, and bringing it to one of the two placement stations. Additional constraints were

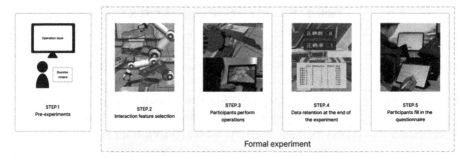

STEP.1
Pre-experiments

STEP.2
Interaction feature selection

STEP.3
Participants perform
operations

STEP.4
Data retention at the end of
the experiment

STEP.5
Participants fill in the
questionnaire

Formal experiment

Fig. 5. Flowchart of fetching and placing tasks

also imposed to better simulate the assembly manufacturing environment. A part can be picked and placed multiple times so that errors can be better corrected during the operation.

In all experiments, three different time delays were completed for each visual interaction interface, after a set of tasks for the visual interaction interface were performed. The researcher would tell the participants to complete a questionnaire, and after three questionnaires were completed, an AB-directed comparison questionnaire was administered, and the experiment ended after the fourth questionnaire was completed.

4 Experimental Results

4.1 Reliability and Validity Analysis

In this paper, the reliability of the questionnaire was verified by testing the internal consistency. The coefficients are between 0 and 1, with 0 representing the lowest point of reliability level and 1 representing the highest level of reliability. In this study, the coefficient standard was set at ≥ 0.7. The results were analyzed for reliability in the following table, almost all variables were above the standard, and the coefficient of the factor NASA-TLX scale variable VR-PGI was slightly lower than the standard coefficient, presumably due to the reason of small sample size, and the overall reliability of the questionnaire in this study was more satisfactory (Table 3).

In the actual analysis, the KMO statistic is better when it is above 0.7. The lower the net correlation coefficient between variables the more suitable for factor analysis. The results of the KMO and Bartlett's spherical test analysis for this study are shown in Table 4 below.

Table 3. Reliability analysis table

Factor	Variables	Cronbach a
Perceived usefulness	O-I	0.924
	VR-PGI	0.869
	I-PGI	0.894
Perceived ease of use	O-I	0.835
	VR-PGI	0.922
	I-PGI	0.929
NASA-TLX	O-I	0.726
	VR-PGI	0.677
	I-PGI	0.849

Table 4. KMO and Bartlett test

Factor	Variables	KMO	Bartlett Test		
			Chi-square	DF	Significance Level
Perceived usefulness	O-I	0.716	115.971	15.000	0.000
	VR-PGI	0.760	71.972	15.000	0.000
	I-PGI	0.841	78.895	15.000	0.000
Perceived ease of use	O-I	0.835	71.305	15.000	0.000
	VR-PGI	0.922	46.450	10.000	0.000
	I-PGI	0.929	99.718	15.000	0.000
NASA-TLX	O-I	0.726	95.060	15.000	0.000
	VR-PGI	0.711	66.883	15.000	0.000
	I-PGI	0.849	95.561	15.000	0.000

4.2 Objective Results Analysis

In this study, the objective performance indicators included two items: task completion time and correctness rate. For the authenticity of the experiment, when the workload caused by the delay on the user during the test of different groups is significant, resulting in the inability to complete the task, the group of experiments can be actively abandoned. A one-way ANOVA was conducted with visual interaction interface as the independent variable and task completion time as the dependent variable. As shown in Fig. 6, the correct rates of O-PGI and VR-PGI were significantly higher than those of O-I. The completion time of the experiments increased with the increase of time delay and leveled off with the change of different visual interaction interfaces, and the participants' operation time using the virtual reality prediction line graphical interface was slightly lower than that of the image display prediction interface. There was no significant difference in the task completion times of the three visual interaction interfaces at low time delays (0.5 s, 1 s), indicating that the workload effects of the three interfaces on the participants were similar at low time delays, while the task completion times at considerable time delays (5 s) of the original interface were significantly different with increasing time delays, and the task completion times increased significantly with increasing time delays. In contrast, the task completion time increased slowly with increasing time delay in the case of image and virtual reality prediction graphical interfaces, indicating that the prediction display technique is effective. In terms of correctness, the correctness rate of VR-PGI is greater than that of O-PGI than O-I. The correctness rate of users decreases significantly with increasing time delay on O-I, while the difference decreases significantly on VR-PGI. In addition, we also found an interesting fact that O-PGI was completely opposite in this performance, a phenomenon we speculate is because the more symbolic, flat O-PGI has a weaker sense of three-dimensionality, and requires more time to convert and adapt when applied in realistic three-dimensional scenes, during the operation, participants mostly showed the need to repeatedly try to test the fit between the claw and the grasping object, this phenomenon also objectively This phenomenon further confirms the applicability of VR-PGI in a significant time delay environment (Fig. 6).

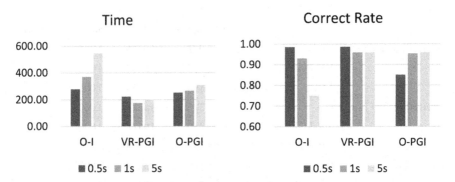

Fig. 6. Total time spent and correctness rate of participants testing the completion of each set of tasks

4.3 Analysis of Questionnaire Results

Data Analysis Based on the TAM Model. From the results of perceived usefulness, the original interface is concentrated between scores 1–3, the virtual reality prediction graphical interface is mainly concentrated between scores 6–7, and the image prediction graphical interface is mainly concentrated between 5–6. The mean value of perceived usefulness in the TAM questionnaire for the original interface is 1.88, while the mean values for the virtual reality prediction graphical interface and the image prediction graphical interface are 6.28 and 5.08, respectively.

In the topics related to perceived usefulness and perceived ease of use, the situation was statistically analyzed as follows (Fig. 7).

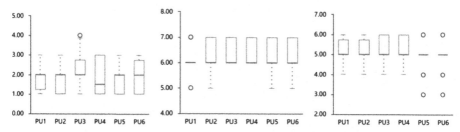

Fig. 7. Box line diagram of questions related to operator perceived usefulness questionnaire under O-I (left), VR-PGI (middle), and I-PGI (right)

From the results of perceived ease of use, the O-I (M = 2.49) was concentrated between scores 1–4, the VR-PGI (M = 6.01) was mainly concentrated between scores 5–7, and the I-PGI (M = 5.08) was mainly concentrated between scores 5–6. It can be seen that the perceived ease of use of the operator's VR-PGI and I-PGI is higher than that of the O-I, and the perceived ease of use score of the VR-PGI is higher than that of the I-PGI (Fig. 8).

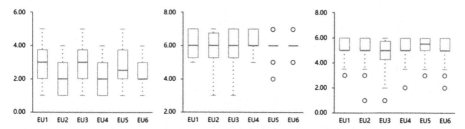

Fig. 8. Box line diagram of questions related to operator perceived ease of user questionnaire under O-I (left), VR-PGI (middle), and I-PGI (right)

Data Analysis Based on the NASA-TLA Scale. Among the questions related to perceived usefulness and perceived ease of use, the scores of mental demand (MD) (M = 16.80), physical demand (PD) (M = 16.05), time demand (TD) (M = 15.56), effort level (EF) (M = 16.75) and frustration level (FR) (M = 15.25) were positively correlated. Performance level (OP) (M = 5.15) scores were negatively correlated with the other terms. Under the O-I, operators generally rated their performance lower when the median scores of mental demand (MD), physical demand (PD), time demand (TD), effort level (EF), and frustration level (FR) were between 16–17, while the opposite was true for the VR-PGI and the I-PGI, and compared to the I-PGI, the VR-PGI required lower mental demand (MD), physical demand (PD), time demand (TD), effort level (EF), and frustration level (FR) and higher performance level (OP) than the I-PGI (Fig. 9).

Preference-Based Data Analysis. When participants made a forced preference for the prediction display interface, we found that all 20 participants preferred the VR-PGI over the I-PGI. However, a tiny percentage of participants verbally indicated that both interfaces were available during the process, but the preference for the VR-PGI was

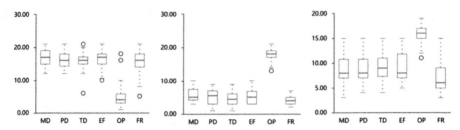

Fig. 9. Box line diagram of questions related to operatorNASA-TLX questionnaire under O-I (left), VR-PGI (middle), and I-PGI (right)

still evident from the selection. Based on this result, we propose that the participants' preference for the task type was a more tangible VR-PGI, which is also consistent with their previous two subjective questionnaire measures (Fig. 10).

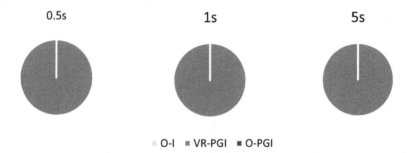

Fig. 10. AB to the questionnaire sectoral statistics chart

5   Conclusion

In this paper, we investigate the effects of VR-PGI and I-PGI on workload based on predictive display technology. By constructing a virtual simulation experimental platform for the remote operating system to test and analyze the grasp-placement experiment on 20 participants and distributing questionnaires for subjective measurements, we gain insight into the participants' subjective perceptions of their workloads. The results showed that the TAM scores and NASA-TLX scale scores of the VR-PGI and the I-PGI were higher than those of the O-I for the grasp-placement task, indicating that human-computer interaction through predictive display technology significantly reduced the cognitive load during the grasp-placement operation. In between, the VR-PGI scored slightly higher than the I-PGI, which is also broadly consistent with our hypothesis. Although there was little difference between the two in objective values, participants preferred the VR-PGI in terms of user preference, indicating that the realistic immersion of the VR-PGI was more acceptable to operators than the symbolic and simplistic I-PGI; and it was found that the presence or absence of the predictive display interface had little effect on participants in the low latency case, while it was more significant in the large latency environment. It was also found that the presence or absence of a predictive display had little effect on participants in low-latency situations, but was more significant in high-latency environments. In addition, with the predictive graphics model, the cognitive load of the operators did not change significantly with the increase of spatial latency, which proved the feasibility of applying the predictive graphics interface to spatial tele-operation scenarios. The above findings provide a framework for the predictive display visual interaction of remote operation systems in different remote operation scenarios.

Funding Information. The Funding Agency is CHINA VIDEO INDUSTRY ASSOCIATION (CVIA), and the grant number is ZSXKT2023002.

References

1. Wang, X., Cao, J.: Dual-arm collaborative robot technology. Autom. Panor. **328**(10), 84–90 (2020)
2. Chen, J., Huang, W., Song, A.: Dynamic model of human operator in force telepresence system based on virtual reality technology. J. Trans. Technol. **15**(1), 230–236 (2001)
3. Arcara, P., Melchiorri, C.: Control schemes for teleoperation with time delay: a comparative study. Robot. Auton. Syst. **38**(1), 49–64 (2002)
4. Sweller, J.: Cognitive load theory. Psychol. Learn. Motiv. **2011**(55), 37–76 (2011)
5. Bejczy, A.K., Kim, W.S., Venema, S.C.: The phantom robot: predictive displays for teleoperation with time delay. In: International Conference on Robotics and Automation, Cincinnati, OH, USA, pp. 546–551 (1990)
6. Chou, W., Meng, C., Chen, J., Li, S.: Robot-assisted remote operating system for space science experiments. China Space Sci. Technol. **2003**(06), 10–16 (2003)
7. Sheridan, T.B.: Human supervisory control of robot systems. In: 1986 IEEE International Conference, pp. 808–812 (1986)
8. Hirzinger, G., Landzettel, K., Dietrich, J.: Sensor-based space robotics - ROTEX and its telerobotic features. In: IEEE Transactions on Robotics and Automation, Graz, Austri, pp. 649–663 (1993)
9. Freund, E., Rossmann, J.: A new telepresence approach through the combination of virtual reality and robot control techniques. SPIE's Int. Tech. Gr. Newsl. (2001)
10. Dybvik, H., Loland, M., Gerstenberg, A., Slattsveen, K.B., Steinert, M.: A low-cost predictive display for teleoperation: investigating effects on human performance and workload. Int. J. Hum. Comput. Stud. **145**(1), 10–15 (2021)
11. Deying, G.: Optimization Management of Cognitive Load in Multimedia Learning. Southwest University, Chongqing (2009)
12. Kalyuga, S.: Expertise reversal effect and its implications for learner-tailored instruction. Educ. Psychol. Rev. **19**(4), 509–539 (2007)
13. Sweller, J.: Cognitive load during problem solving: effects on learning. Cogn. Sci. **12**(2), 257–285 (1988)
14. Gombolay, M., Bair, A., Huang, C., Shah, J.: Computational design of mixed-initiative human–robot teaming that considers human factors: situational awareness, workload, and workflow preferences. Int. J. Robot. Res. **36**, 597–617 (2017)
15. Parasuraman, R., Sheridan, T.B., Wickens, C.D.: Situation awareness, mental workload, and trust in automation: viable, empirically supported cognitive engineering constructs. J. Cognit. Eng. Decis. Mak. **2**(2), 140–160 (2008)

16. Jia, Y., Xi, N., Liu, S., et al.: Quality of teleoperator adaptive control for teleroboticoperations. Int. J. Robot. Res. **33**(14), 1765–1781 (2014)

17. Li, Y., Liu, S., Xi, N., et al.: A study of the relationship between brain states and skill level of teleoperator. In: 2013 IEEE International Conference on Robotics and Biomimetics (ROBIO), pp. 390–395 (2013)

18. Schmidlin, E.A., Jones, K.S.: Do tele-operators learn to better judge whether a robot can passthrough an aperture? Hum. Factors **58**(2), 360–369 (2016)

19. Loft, S., Sanderson, P., Neal, A., et al.: Modeling and predicting mental workload in en route air traffic control: critical review and broader implications. Hum. Factors **49**(3), 376–399 (2007)

20. Brookings, J.B., Wilson, G.F., Swain, C.R.: Psychophysiological responses to changes in workload during simulated air traffic control. Biol. Psychol. **42**(3), 361–377 (1996)

21. Hart, S.G., Staveland, L.E.: Development of NASA-TLX (task load index): results of empirical and theoretical research. Adv. Psychol. **52**, 139–183 (1988)

22. Kramer, A.F.: Physiological metrics of mental workload: a review of recent progress. Physiol. Metr. Ment. Workload Rev. Recent Prog. 279–328 (1991)

23. Steinfeld, A., Fong, T., Kaber, D., et al.: Common metrics for human-robot interaction. In: Proceedings of the 1st ACM SIGCHI/SIGART Conference on Human-Robot Interaction, New York, pp. 33–40 (2006)

24. Clarke, M.A., Schuetzler, R.M., Windle, J.R., et al.: Usability and cognitive load in the design of a personal health record. Health Policy Technol. **9**(2), 218–224 (2020)

25. You, Q.: Research and Application of Virtual Reality Oriented Digital Interface Usability. Guizhou University, Guiyang (2020)

26. Davis, F.D.: A technology Acceptance Model for Empirically Testing New end-User Information Systems: Theoryand Results. Sloan School of Management, Massachusetts Institute of Technology, Cambridge, MA, pp. 40–64 (1986)

Exploration of the Interactive Design of Interior Space Under the New Retail Mode – Based on the Case of "Cultural and Creative Space" in the Traditional Dong Villages

Guanyi Yu[1(✉)], Fang Jiang[2], and Baoyu Ling[1]

[1] School of Design, Guangxi Normal University, Guilin 541006, China
125232515@qq.com
[2] School of Foreign Studies, Guangxi Normal University, Guilin 541006, China

Abstract. With the constant improvement of people's living standards and the continuous development of social transformation, the concept of interactive design is increasingly valued in the new retail space. The interactive information in various spaces can more directly and effectively reflect the purchase behavior and psychology of consumers. Leveraging the information, interaction design can better realize the interaction between people, people and objects, and people and space, and can promote the consumption and dissemination of local cultural and creative products while serving consumers and meeting their needs. Through researching and analyzing online and offline data collection, relying on the application of artificial intelligence, augmented reality, big data and other technologies in space, following the ethics of behavioral science, social psychology, ergonomics and other ethics, and analyzing the type of interactive space in new rural retail stores, the article puts forward the concept of new retail and spatial interaction, presents the design schemes of spatial innovation, interactive innovation, product innovation and retail mode innovation, and provides a basis for the future design of traditional village retail store space.

Keywords: interactive design · new retail · cultural and creative products · space type · scene experience

1 Introduction

Guangxi Zhuang Autonomous Region is located in southeastern China, between 104°28′–112°04′ East longitude and 20°54′–26°23′ North latitude, east of the Pearl River estuary, west of Sichuan Province, south of the South China Sea, and north of Hunan Province. The Tropic of Cancer crosses Guangxi Province, and the area to the north is called Guibei. North Gui is a medium pressure tropical monsoon climate zone, humid and rainy, the region contains 462 traditional villages, including 60 national traditional villages and 60 villages with minority characteristics. Most of the villages are located in the outskirts of cities or mountainous areas, with closed information and inconvenient transportation, making it difficult to sell local traditional cultural output, agricultural products and traditional handicrafts. Although a large number of villages in recent years the rapid development of tourism, resulting in serious homogenization of villages. Second, the in-depth development of social transformation and the continuous promotion of urbanization process, urban population gathering [1]. Almost all the young and strong people of the villages have gone to the big cities to work, resulting in a large number of elderly people and children left behind, and the phenomenon of empty villages is serious. The gradual decay of traditional village culture, the absence of local customs, weak infrastructure, low-level repetition of villages, degradation of land production, loss of young and strong population, and the absence of new ideas and technologies are obvious features.

With the development of the Internet era, the applicability of offline physical stores continues to be iteratively upgraded, and traditional retail stores are insufficient to meet the needs of contemporary consumers. The new retail store has become a new driving force to expand the sales of mountainous agricultural products. The new terminal consumption method can expand the sales of mountain agricultural products and meet the needs of consumers in the new era. The addition of space design can better facilitate product trading and cultural heritage, thus promoting local economic development. The integration of interaction design can provide more direct and effective feedback on the behaviour trajectory of consumers. Therefore, more new terminal consumption methods need to be urgently explored, and the integration of new modes of interior space interaction design prompts local history and culture, lifestyle, behavioural customs, aesthetic sensibilities, and economic development. Therefore, this paper analyzes the behavioural characteristics of human and human, human and object, and human and space activities from the perspective of interior space interaction design in the new retail mode, and explores the interaction design of new retail "cultural space" suitable for all three to improve the quality of life in traditional villages.

2   Concept Definition

2.1   New Retail

The term retail means selling goods and linking customers with goods through venues. In our neighbourhood mostly in the form of brick-and-mortar stores, ground stalls, circle of friends sales, etc., selling goods in a variety of spaces and places, the ultimate goal is to find the target customers to sell their goods. But with the arrival of the Internet, traditional retail forms are also undergoing new changes. The emergence of new retail has broken the boundaries of traditional retailing, which is mainly based on advanced technology combined with new trendy ideas as a guide to selling products and goods to consumers' activities [2]. From a single offline consumer transaction, through the conversion of multi-media characteristics, customers have more possibilities at the level of human tactile perception, spatial framework design, and market business strategy, in addition to obtaining information flow from offline and completing capital flow and logistics online. By comparing the relationship between traditional retail stores and new retail stores in human-object-space and the difference between different levels (see Fig. 1).

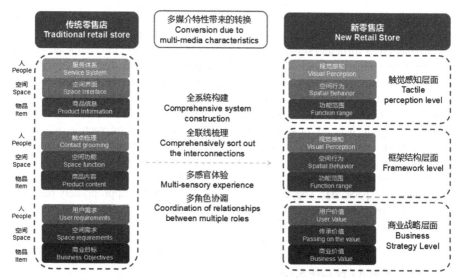

Fig. 1. Comparison chart between traditional retail and new retail

2.2 Spatial Interaction Design

Origin of Spatial Interaction Design. Generally speaking, interaction is the exchange of information between two or more people, and can also include the exchange of physical objects and services. Interaction design is also called "interaction design". The concept of interaction design was first introduced by Bill Mogridge, the originator of interaction design, at a conference in 1984. "Interaction" [3]. The origin of spatial interaction design is mainly derived from human-computer interaction technology and the human-centred design concept. It aims to make spaces more convenient, safe and comfortable through technical means, to improve people's work efficiency and quality of life. Until now, the expansion of the concept of spatial interaction can be the emotional communication between people, the touch communication between people and things, and the symbiosis between people and space.

The Meaning of Spatial Interaction Design. The significance of spatial interaction design is to improve user experience so that users can understand products or sell services more easily and effectively. At the same time, it can help users better understand the function of the product and adhere to the user as the core of the design so that our design can bring users a quality experience [4]. Spatial interaction design studies the value of human behaviour and psychological patterns, and users can better understand the sales of products through the shuttle and communication in the functional space. On this basis, different ways of interaction between people and things are designed to meet the users' psychological needs, security needs, social needs, respect needs, self-actualization needs, etc., and to provide users with control over the interaction between people and things and people and space.

The Realization Path of Spatial Interaction Design in Commercial Space. First, determine the goal of spatial interaction design and clarify the needs of customers. It should conform to the process of users' psychological activities when browsing products and receiving information. From the satisfaction of content and rational satisfaction to the satisfaction of form and sensual satisfaction. Second, analyze the characteristics of space and determine the function of space. People in space are a dynamic experience, so through the functional analysis of the space, set the dynamic line, find the interface between people and space, and finally integrate with the space. Furthermore, determine the technical scheme and architecture of space interaction design and implement space interaction design. It is not possible to interact for the sake of interaction, making it disconnected from the space and product content. Spatial interaction design gives the user to get pleasure while the proper interaction items are the features of in-depth information. Finally, test the spatial interaction design to ensure that it is correct. Good interactive items, location, space, size, shape, colour, sound, etc. should be appropriately reflected in the spatial environment, harmoniously symbiotic with the main content, and with their characteristics.

2.3 Cultural and Creative Space

Wagner states that when two objects and actions interact with each other, interactive behavior ensues, i.e., behavioral and psychological activities that produce mutual influence between people, people and objects, and people and space [5]. Culture is the spiritual core of a region, and we should preserve it and develop it at the same time. Traditional village culture is rich and colorful, and its application in commercial space can enhance the local residents' sense of identity with the local culture. The proposed new retail "cultural space" can strengthen the interaction between space - people - culture, enhance the development of local culture and make the commercial space more dynamic at the same time. The application of new retail "cultural space" interaction in traditional villages proposed in this paper should meet the following three characteristics: Firstly, Building a platform: Enriching the marketing content of traditional villages and preserving the elements of local culture in the overall space design is the key to reflecting the culture of villages. Secondly, Enriching social interaction: Customers' interaction with villagers, products and space in the new retail store will have a mutually reinforcing positive impact on their behavioral psychology. Thirdly, Comprehensive experience: While meeting the needs of outsiders, the elderly and children left behind, i.e., the living heritage of the traditional village, have a clearer space for their activities in the process, so as to develop diversified interactive behaviors of space, people and things.

3 The Value and Significance of Existing New Retail Spaces

3.1 Research Sample Extraction

In this paper, Pingtan Village in Chengyang Bazhai, Sanjiang County was selected as the research sample. As this village is a traditional Dong village, restricted by the traditional Dong culture and economy, the villagers' activity spaces are all traditional drum towers, fire pits and outdoor spaces, and the construction process is mainly to meet the traditional culture of the village. Although these traditional activity spaces can hardly meet the current needs of villagers, they still preserve the traditional Dong dry bar style architectural forms. The design is in line with the place characteristics of cultural and creative space construction, and the existing favorable features and problems need to be summarized (see Fig. 2).

Fig. 2. Architectural space research

The above table can summarize that in the public space the main space types are storm pavilion, theater, fire pit, etc., the semi-private space types are residents' hallway, kitchen, living room, chicken pen, etc., and the private space types are storage room, bedroom, stairwell, etc. And to summarize its spatial scope (Table 1).

By observing the activity time of the elderly, children and some villagers in the outdoor space of the village, the peak activity time of the elderly in the fire pit and the drum tower was 2:00–5:00 p.m., the children's outdoor activity was 4:00–6:00 p.m., and the fire pit in the drum tower was 6:00–7:00 p.m. The activity time of the young adults in the fire pit was 7:00–9:00 p.m. The elderly and young villagers did not spend much time outdoors. The period of the young adults in the Gulou fire pit is 7:00–9:00 p.m. The elderly and young villagers do not spend much time outdoors, so 3:00–6:00 p.m. is chosen as the main research period, which can maximize the in-depth observation of the behavioural characteristics of the elderly, children and villagers left behind and their needs for space for the new retail "cultural and creative space". The study of the spatial type of interaction behaviour of "cultural and creative spaces" yielded detailed and comprehensive data. In the research of 3 drum spaces and 4 fire pit spaces, it was found that there are mainly 3 types of behaviours when left-behind elderly and children's behaviours are separated and co-participated (e.g. co-participation, separate and independent when still talking about elderly and youth, elderly and children, and children and youth). When the elderly and children's behaviours are co-participating, the elderly mainly chat and chess; children mainly play, write homework and gossip, and young villagers mainly work for temporary water breaks and meetings. Older people in the drum and fire pits behaviour occurs most frequently, more than 85% of the behaviour

Table 1. Example of residential building space

名称 Name		面积范围 Area range	主要活动时间节点及 活动内容 Main activities Time and date and content
公共建筑 Public build-ings	戏台 Stage	28.4㎡-42㎡	闲聊、嬉戏、举办活动、棋牌 Gossiping, playing, holding activities, chess and cards
	风雨亭 Gloriette	8.4㎡-12.9㎡	休息、交流 Break, Networking
	火塘 A kind of Chinese fireplace	5.4㎡-7.3㎡	聚会、洽谈 Party, negotiation
民居 Residential	客厅 Living room	16㎡-24㎡	聚会、洽谈 Party, negotiation
	厨房 Kitchen	8.6㎡-12㎡	餐饮、接待客人 Catering, reception of guests
	火塘 A kind of Chinese fireplace	4.2㎡-6.8㎡	接待客人 Catering, reception of guests
	卧室 Bedroom	22.2㎡-27.5㎡	休息 Break
	储物间 Storage room	18㎡-36㎡	粮食储藏 Grain storage

is mainly chatting, resting, chess and cards, when the spatial scale is small or when the elderly and children use the same space, the minimum space area is 14 m^2 distance is 2 m. The elderly and young and strong villagers are in common use, forming a more obvious space division. When the elderly, children and young adults use the fire pits for activities at the same time, they have high requirements for the space, and the space available for their respective activities is insufficient in quantity and quality; therefore, in addition to retail stores selling local products, the new retail "cultural and creative space" also provides additional functions for the elderly, children and young adult labourers left behind in their communal activities to meet The traditional drums, fire pits, and national councils, ceremonies, welcoming, singing and dancing entertainment activities also enhance the close relationship between village folk and each other (see Fig. 3).

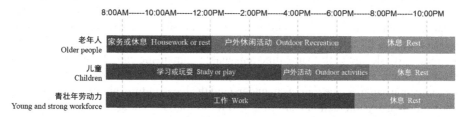

Fig. 3. The main activities of the day for the elderly, children and young adults

3.2 Study on the Value of the Form of "Cultural and Creative Space" Suitable for New Retail

Economic Value. From product to the industry is a long process. To create the unique Dong culture in Pingtan Village, it is necessary to build the whole system and sort out the whole linkage from the macro level, and to seize the multi-sensory experience and multi-role coordination at the operation level. At this stage, the new retail "cultural space" is designed to be a new cultural experience space, allowing consumers to experience the local culture first-hand. It will be a cultural space that integrates light catering, accompanying gift sales, and living heritage, allowing the traditional dry bar style building to show its richer value through creative use. Finally, the local specialties are concentrated to give self-created brands to create original ecology and an original atmosphere, driving the industry to enhance the happiness of residents.

Cultural Value. The starting and ending point of cultural creative products is "people's livelihood", meeting the people's needs for a better life. The local Dong culture has distinctive features, but due to geographical restrictions on economic development and difficulties in life, the local community has long diluted the inheritance and innovative development of national culture. The emergence of new retail "cultural and creative space" can not only bring economic development to the local area but also bring the original ecological products into the new era, change the residents' minds to accept and reasonably use the new things, and inject a new spring of fresh water into the local culture. Under the influence of local culture, the new retail "cultural and creative space" is created based on Dong elements, injected with cultural and creative products, spread Dong culture, and does a good job of telling stories to introduce the spirit, to improve the resident's sense of identity to the local culture. Technically, virtual projection technology can promote the local characteristics of architecture, products, people and stories, customs and habits, etc. to bring a strong minority flavour experience to foreign visitors, and also help the spread and development of local ethnic culture.

Service Value. The new retail "cultural and creative space" reflects a new concept, where culture and business complement each other. The service targets are mostly foreign tourists, local left-behind elderly, children and a few young and strong labourers, and for different groups of people to help the spread of culture in a way that they are happy to experience in-depth, and use the industry to drive the upgrading and development of the cultural industry. Second, injecting humanistic care emotions, in addition to shopping needs, can also provide the elderly with a rest and conversation area. For children there is a professional children's entertainment rest area, in the rest area can be clearly understood through big data supervision of children's whereabouts, to protect children's safety, design focus on the growth of children in physical and mental health, fully reflecting our interactive design at the same time reasonable humanistic care. In the treatment of tourists, the new retail "cultural and creative space" is convenient for tourists to buy and at the same time can meet the tourists to understand the local culture, high-tech technology and local industry interaction can bring novelty to tourists, but also can provide more quality services for tourists.

4 Analysis of the New Retail "Cultural and Creative Space" in Pingtan Village

4.1 Site Analysis of the New Retail "Cultural and Creative Space" in Pingtan Village

Research on the Site of the New Retail "Cultural and Creative Space" in Pingtan Village. Pingtan Village is one of the eight villages in Chengyang, located in the northeastern part of Sanjiang Dong Autonomous County in Guangxi, where the village is located on the outskirts of the city. It is about 180 kms from Guilin City and 18 kms from the local county. Chengyang Bazhai mainly takes tourism as the pillar of local industrial development, and different retail spaces appear one after another in the scenic spot, with different locations, scales and business industries, and the business objects are mainly local villagers and a few foreign merchants. According to the search of online websites such as "retail", "commercial" and "shopping", there are 164 retail spaces in Chengyang Bazhai and 18 commercial retail spaces in Pingtan Village. There are 18 retail spaces, and they are scattered. Most of the retail spaces are laid out in the main neighbourhoods of pedestrian streets, radiating to the surrounding area through several major pedestrian streets, with large population flow in the main streets of the scenic area, advantageous location and convenient transportation, which is the village commercial space with the longest history of retailing and the widest range of services at present. This research takes Pingtan Village, one of the eight villages in Chengyang, as the object of study. Because of its relatively remote location, it has not been affected by the tourism industry and has a strong Dong traditional style. Through the design of the new retail space, we hope to drive the development of the area and move the regional industrial output.

Design Characteristics of the New Retail "Cultural and Creative Space" in Pingtan Village. The new retail "cultural and creative space" breaks the traditional retail industry development boundaries, in constant innovation and use of exploration, to provide customers with a more new, comfortable and safe experience. In the site selection, the core area of Pingtan Village was chosen to serve the whole village and drive the tourists to visit the village at the same time. The area of Pingtan Village is about 1.48 km^2, with a total of 246 households and 1200 people. The site of the new retail "Creative Space" is near the square in front of the village drum tower, which is a gathering place for the Dong people and a representative building of the local culture and spirit. The design of the new retail "creative space" is based on indoor safety and fire safety issues, but also the integration of natural elements of the traditional village. While providing convenience to consumers in terms of infrastructure, the building materials are combined with the use of modern materials in the form of open skylights and glass curtain walls to connect with the outside world and improve the visibility of consumers. In this way, the interaction between people and the village environment, the interaction between people and space, and the interaction between people and people (villagers) are achieved.

Elements of New Retail "Cultural and Creative Space" Venue. As a new local marketing model, the new retail "cultural and creative space" includes a special product area, a living material area, a cultural and creative product area, a service area, a health area, a rest area, a children's area, etc. The interaction between people and people, people and things, and people and space is the main design means of this new retail "cultural and creative space". The main design means of "cultural and creative space" connects the whole space - people - culture through the ties of emotional interaction, cultural and creative products, artificial intelligence and digital media display. Firstly, the listed products, by focusing on localized presentation, package design and give a living space display to agricultural products, while giving full play to their functions such as cultural communication and material use. Secondly, the application of "cultural and creative space" interaction brings the spatial environment "alive" and allows environmental art to provide people with the experience of human-scene interaction and human-scene empathy.

Finally, the new retail "cultural and creative space" should pay more attention to the use of wisdom. Relying on the current artificial intelligence, virtual simulation and digital media as carriers, the simulation environment, visual system and simulation system are bundled into one during the interaction period, and users can easily obtain a variety of perceptions such as traditional Dong architectural and cultural space, local farming culture and traditional non-heritage handicraft through sensing devices. Relying on high-tech hardware and software to generate a virtual environment that simulates the real world, generating interactive and multi-perceptual experiences (See Fig. 4).

4.2 Embodiment of the New Retail "CUltural and Creative Space" in Pingtan Village

Based on the existing research of new retail space and the preliminary research of Pingtan Village, based on the functional needs of people and people, people and things, and people and space interaction, we conclude the "small square" integrated new retail "cultural and creative space" area classification, design governance The new retail "cultural and creative space" service system and the new retail "cultural and creative space" activities for the left-behind elderly and children under the perspective of design governance (See Fig. 5).

Fig. 4. Block Function

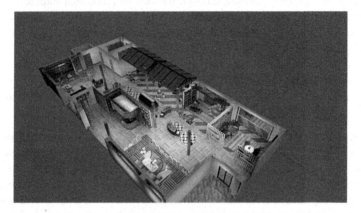

Fig. 5. Renderings

New Retail "Cultural and Creative Space" Area Classification Integrated by "Small Square". New retail "cultural and creative space" area classification integrated by "small square". This case mainly combines the current situation of the preliminary site study, summarizes the area range of 10 m²–25 m² adopts the idea of "small module" to design, and splices different functional spaces one by one. The sales space is divided into agricultural products sales area, non-foreign heritage cultural and creative experience area, left-behind elderly and children activities area and other functional distribution. The design principle of "small module" is: the square is flexible and universal, which is a key factor, taking the new retail "cultural and creative space" as the starting point, using the square to unite the strength of the village, activating the surface with the point, gradually activating the vitality of people and people, people and things, people and space and pick up the fireworks so that each "small module" will be cohesive in the overall environment of the new retail "cultural and creative space", and pick up the cohesion and sense of belonging among people, objects and space.

Service System of New Retail "Cultural and Creative Space" Under the Design Governance Perspective. The marketing mode of the new retail "cultural and creative space" is a governance strategy, and the form of sales service is to achieve governance through the design of the movement line of the space and the provisions of style, color and function. From the customer shopping experience, offline shopping can bring a more intuitive experience to customers. Therefore, we try to meet the various needs of customers in the space design, from large to small, from small to micro to achieve the ultimate. First of all, we entered the new retail "Culture Space" as the attraction system, and the distinctive color attracts customers to understand the layout of the space and want to arrive and purchase instructions. Secondly, the sales space contains a physical display and store cloud screen system, whose main purpose is to channel sales. Interaction design based on user shopping experience in practice to meet the needs of customers in various aspects such as visual, tactile and aesthetic. A clear product partition and shopping guide can be used in the visual interaction design, and the overall shopping space is full of items but also regular and feasible. The non-heritage cultural and creative experience area then promotes each other with the sales space and provides participation in membership-based online shopping in the rest area. Based on the principle of target-oriented, customer recognition and trust mentality of agricultural products, different types of experience trigger multiple services. Technical means can be used to enhance customer shopping online experience by means of horizontal scrolling interaction mode and establishing 3D entities and spaces. It enables users to devote themselves to the virtual visual space of the shopping webpage and facilitates customers' online shopping. Establishing 3D entities and spaces mainly for products and product information online to establish virtual three-dimensional products and product-related scene simulation, mainly through the three-dimensional entities can make users a better all-round understanding of product information, product information scene simulation, so that customers more clearly and directly understand the story behind the product and the product production process, etc.. Through this means, we can guarantee the uniformity and simplicity of the customer shopping experience and maximize the human-computer interaction between the shopping page and the user.

Participation in the New Retail "Cultural and Creative Space" for the Elderly and Children Left Behind. A village is a living environment and a gathering place for cultural exchange. Most of the permanent residents of Pingtan Village are left-behind elderly and children, and the group of left-behind elderly in the village has a deep memory of the development history of the village and a deep affection for its culture, which is the inheritance of the living cultural lineage itself. A healthy village environment, physical and psychological care and education for children, and a sense of belonging for children, are the focus of social attention. The design of the new retail "cultural and creative space" allows the elderly and children to participate in the space together, so the space is designed for the elderly as a static pile-up type, while the children are dynamic scattered type for functional settings. The space for the elderly retains their traditional lifestyle, sitting on low stools and sitting around each other to chat, play cards, embroider and other static activities; the space for children is designed to meet the three points of group, inquiry, initiative and concentration. Fresh things can stimulate children's curiosity and create an area space that meets their physiological and psychological characteristics.

5   Conclusion

The development of the village has experienced generations of people constantly pushing the boundaries, rather than innovation it is still inheritance. In today's Internet era, the design of new retail space for village business is a new inheritance situation for traditional culture. The main purpose of the design of the new retail "cultural and creative space" is to serve the people and facilitate the people. The use of interactive design in space local village culture dissemination and inheritance has a self-evident positive effect, and also promotes the villagers and nature, and social development trend of deep communication and harmonious coexistence. On the one hand, the concept of new retail "cultural and creative space" and interactive design also makes us notice that the current prospect of rural development is the inheritance and innovation of the history, culture and characteristics of less traditional villages. On the other hand, the development of our society needs to pay attention to the elderly and children left behind today and always insist on people-oriented and functional and aesthetic innovation in design.

Funding. Research topics of philosophy and social science planning of Guangxi Zhuang Autonomous Region, "Research on Heritage Protection and Innovation of Ethnic Traditional Villages under the Perspective of" Design Governance (Serial number: 21FMZ036).

References

1. Tang, T.: Comparative Study on the Spatial Aesthetics of Traditional Village Landscapes in Northern Gui. Guangxi University (2019)
2. Wen, J., Cai, J.: Exploration of terminal interaction design in new retail model–a case study based on "Yueyi". J. Econ. Res. (27), 24–26 (2022)
3. Zhihu. https://zhuanlan.zhihu.com/p/77035344. Accessed 09 Feb 2023
4. Wen, J., Cai, J.: Exploration of terminal interaction design in new retailing model–a case study of "Yueyi". Econ. Res. Guide (27), 24–26 (2022)
5. Wagner, E.D.: In support of a functional definition of interaction. Am. J. Distance Educ. **8**(2), 6–26 (1994)

Cooking Experience Design for Generation Z in the Digital Age

Yuting Yuan, Wa An$^{(\boxtimes)}$, Jinze Li, Haiyu Tang, and Jiamei Lin

Guangzhou Academy of Fine Arts, Guangzhou 510006, China
anwa_design@163.com

Abstract. Generation Z who live alone face the problems of poor cooking ability, dining alone and weak emotional connection with others. This study analyzes the behavioral characteristics of eating and socializing among Generation Z. By combining quantitative and qualitative methods to analyze the behavior and experience of target users, and with the help of the Fogg behavior model and the PCI model of life experience composition, summarized the strategy of sharing-based kitchen product and experience design. Under the guidance of this strategy, the design of sharing-oriented kitchen products is carried out from three aspects: enhancing user motivation, improving user ability, and adding trigger factors, so as to bring users the new meaning of cooking that is more convenient, efficient and interesting.

Keywords: Cooking Experience · Lifestyle · Behavior · Product Design · Generation Z

1 Introduction

The need for cooking has been changing since the birth of the kitchen, but socializing has always been a very important part of culinary life and is still relevant to explore and design today. In the 21st century, the social function of the cooking space is becoming more and more prominent, with work and play coming into the space, and people starting to enjoy more diverse forms of cooking and a better dining atmosphere. With 260 million people living in China, these young people, who have been brought up in a multicultural society, have a growing need for a better life as China moves towards a moderately affluent society. Generation Z have various living patterns, such as living with family members, living alone, and sharing a room. Among them, living alone is becoming a common way of life. This group has been eating alone for a long time and has weaker emotional ties with friends and relatives due to time and distance, which means more "demand scenarios" will be generated in the cooking and eating space of this group. This paper analyzes and designs behavioral experiences in cooking and eating socially for Generation Z, including guidance and documentation of cooking behaviors and facilitating sharing of daily meals with friends and family to enhance emotional connections, in order to provide a better cooking and eating social experience for this population.

2 Research Objects and Methods

2.1 Research Object

Generation Z refers to those born between 1995 and 2009. There are a large number of Generation Z in China, about 260 million people. These young people, known as "Internet natives", have been influenced by all-around multiculturalism and have a unique way of life. Through desktop research, the author analyzed the Internet research report [1–6], and summarized the understanding of the meaning of social and cooking, and the keywords of emotional connection (offline gathering and remote social networking) among the Generation Z group, see Fig. 1. The upper part is the keywords recognized by Generation Z that can represent social and culinary aspects. For them, social can enable them to obtain real and rich emotional links in interpersonal communication, making it easier for people to discover the beauty of life. The lower part represents the common emotional connection keywords among Generation Z people. Most of them choose to use online platforms for remote socializing, dinner parties, and other offline gatherings to maintain emotional connections with others. At the same time, they believe that cooking is also an act of emotional connection. They value the sense of ritual in the cooking process, which can guide them to eat mindfully and obtain spiritual relaxation and satisfaction. To sum up, in the lives of Generation Z, cooking has a strong correlation with emotional connection, and cooking is a part of their social life. For the scene of Generation Z living alone, the significance of social cooking is more prominent.

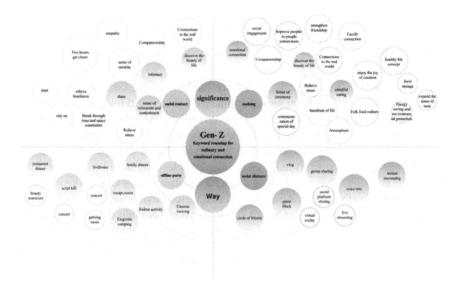

Fig. 1. Keywords of cooking and emotional connection behavior of Generation Z

2.2 Model Reference

This research combines the Fogg behavior model and life experience to form PCI (Past Current Ideal) model for design practice. The Fogg behavior model is mainly used in the user research and design phase, designing questionnaires and interview outlines from motivation, ability, and triggers, understanding the key elements behind user cooking and social interaction, and guiding the design phase. The lifestyle experience composition PCI model is mainly used in the analysis of the survey results to understand the user's past and ideal cooking lifestyle, organize the user's past and ideal cooking life experience in the form of keywords and thus deduce that it is currently targeting the Generation Z. The design direction, and put forward the concept of eating and living for the Generation Z people who live alone.

The Fogg behavior model is the most typical model among many persuasive models. The core of the theory is "B = MAP", that is, only sufficient motivation, ability and trigger mechanism can guide the Generation Z of behavior. Among them, B refers to the user's behavior, M represents the user's motivation, and P represents the trigger point. Only when the three are combined, the user will implement a certain behavior [7] (see Fig. 2). Lifestyle experience composition PCI model, which believes that people's current life experience is not only the state at this moment, but also affected by past experience and ideal life [8]. People's past experience and abilities will affect their current behavior and experience, providing a reference for ideals. People's ideals guide their current life, and their current behavior and experience will change with the happiness and pain in the ideal. At the same time, people can also achieve an ideal life through reflection on their current life (see Fig. 3).

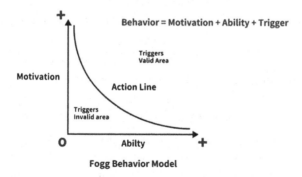

Fig. 2. Fogg Behavior Model

2.3 Research Methods

In order to understand the dietary and social behavior characteristics of Generation Z, a combination of online questionnaire survey and offline interviews was adopted,

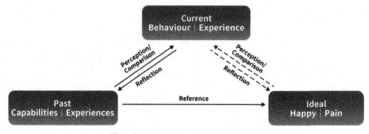

Lifestyle experience composition PCI model

Fig. 3. Lifestyle experience composition PCI model

combined with the Fogg behavior model, and a more universal design strategy was obtained based on the analysis of user survey results.

Quantitative Research. In order to understand the target users' initial views on cooking-related life experience and remote eating socialization, a questionnaire outline was developed. The four parts of the outline, basic information, cooking information, dinner party information, and remote social interaction, are mainly formulated according to the behavioral triggers in the Fogg behavior model, as shown in Table 1.

Table 1. Questionnaire Outline.

Module	Insight point	Questionnaire questions
Basic Information		What is your age?
		What is your average monthly income?
		What is your profession?
		What is your current living situation?
Cooking information	Frequency	How often do you cook every month?
	Trigger	May I ask why you choose to cook by yourself?
		What cooking method do you usually use?
	Motivation	What do you think cooking means to you?
	Ability	What special behavior do you have during cooking?
	Pain points	What parts of the cooking process bother you the most?
	Chance	What are your expectations and suggestions for the cooking experience?
Dinner information	Ability	Have you ever been to a dinner party with friends?
		What are you responsible for when you are involved in cooking for a gathering of friends?

(continued)

Table 1. (*continued*)

Module	Insight point	Questionnaire questions
social distance	Ability	Do you often socialize online with your friends?
		How do you connect with your friends online?
	Trigger	What do you typically involve when you connect with friends online?
		What do you talk about food when you connect with friends online?
	Motivation	In what form will you share your cooking process?
		What stage of cooking would you like to share with your friends?
	Pain points	What troubles do you encounter when sharing food with friends online?
	Chance	If there is a product that allows you to interact online, what form do you want?

Qualitative Research. In order to gain a deeper understanding of the behavioral experience and emotional needs of the target user's diet and social interaction, an interview outline was developed. The interview outline focused more on cooking and social situations, and formulated more open and in-depth questions based on the behavior triggers of the Fogg behavior model, as shown in Table 2.

Table 2. Interview Outline.

Module	Insight point	Interview questions
Basic Information		Do you live by yourself or with family and friends?
Cooking information	Ability	Do you have cooking experience?
	Frequency	How often do you cook about a few times a month? In what way?
	Trigger	What made you choose to cook for yourself?
	Motivation	What is your happiest moment while cooking or eating?
	Ability, Pain point	What troubles you most during cooking or dining? What issues will be considered in the cooking process?
	Motivation, Pain Points	Besides the product, what bothers you most about cooking and eating, respectively?

(continued)

Table 2. (*continued*)

Module	Insight point	Interview questions
	Motivation	What does cooking for yourself mean to you? Or how has it affected your life?
	Chance point	Do you usually share the delicious food after you make it? In what form? How do you feel after sharing?
		If possible, what forms of cooking do you expect to share, and who are you looking forward to sharing with?
		Do you have any special habits in the process of cooking and eating? For example, arranging plates, taking pictures, sharing with friends, etc.?
	Motivation	Why did these behavior occur, and what emotional value did these behavior bring to you for you?
social distance		Do you have friends you haven't seen for a long time, or friends you keep in touch with often?
	Trigger	When do you usually contact them? How often do you contact me?
	Motivation, trigger	What do you usually talk about with your friends?
	Motivation	What is the biggest feeling you get when you connect with friends? Why?
	Trigger	Do you usually do something online together? Such as playing games, voice mic and so on?
	Pain point, Ability	What are the obstacles that keep you from meeting each other?
	Opportunity, Expectation	What if there was a product that would allow you to interact and connect online? What form do you want?
	Chance point	What is the best way to share food with friends when you can't meet each other? What can we talk about food?
		Is there anything that you find difficult to convey when sharing your daily cooking life? Or is there anything more difficult?

3   User Behavior Analysis

3.1   Analysis of Questionnaire Research Results

A total of 168 copies of the Generation Z Kitchen Lifestyle Questionnaire were distributed and 135 valid questionnaires were returned. According to the results of the questionnaire, basic information about the Generation Z population was obtained: more than 50% of the respondents live alone or semi-alone. Nearly half of the respondents cook frequently and consider cooking to be a healthy and sophisticated way of life. In the process of cooking, most respondents search for recipes in advance and look forward to recipe recommendations and guidance, fun experience, recording and sharing. It is clear that cooking means a sophisticated lifestyle experience and a way to connect emotionally for the Generation Z demographic. In terms of remote social habits, food socializing is very popular among Gen Z. The majority of respondents use online social networking to connect with friends and family, with discussions about food focusing on tastes, dish recommendations and cooking methods. Most sharing occurs during the cooking and eating stages, but the experience is affected by the inability to visualize the state of the food and to share and communicate in real-time while cooking. The results of the questionnaire are shown in Fig. 4.

Analysis of the questionnaire results shows that cooking and eating socially has become an important part of the lives of Generation Z. In addition to satisfying basic physical needs, emotional connections are becoming a motivating factor in their cooking and eating lifestyles, but the limited time, space and interaction methods have an impact on the cooking and eating social experience.

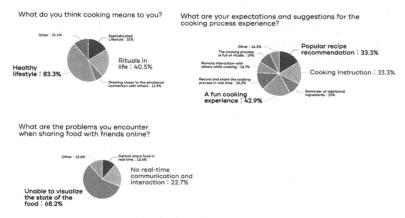

Fig. 4. Questionnaire results

3.2   Analysis of User Interview Results

Through in-depth interviews with 18 people from Generation Z who have a habit of cooking, the content of the interviews was collated and distilled into relevant descriptions reflecting the needs of Generation Z in terms of cooking and food life.

1) Cooking brings spiritual satisfaction to the respondents. For respondents, cooking is not only a daily chore or leisure activity, but the ritualistic handling of cooking, such as plating and photographing to record, can provide positive emotional feedback to respondents.
2) Sharing cooking in a remote social way can compensate for the loneliness of eating alone. Due to time and space constraints, respondents spend a lot of time eating alone. This can lead to a lack of happiness over time, which can stimulate the desire to share. The positive feedback received from sharing a meal with others amplifies the positive emotions and taste experience of the respondents, which in turn leads to a sense of well-being.
3) Respondents want a more authentic sensory experience when they use telesocial to share their food. Respondents' triggers for remote communication behavior were divided into two categories: daily habits and opportunities to share recent events in their daily lives. However, the majority of respondents felt that when communicating online, they lacked the sensory experience of a closer, more realistic interactive experience and clearer delivery of their cuisine.

3.3   Analysis of User Interview Results

Based on the relevant results of the questionnaire research and user interviews, it was clear that the users are young people of Generation Z who live alone and have cooking habits. The user journey map was used to organize the respondents' cooking and eating social behavior according to two stages: cooking and eating, and the three dimensions of motivation, ability and trigger in the scene, contact, place, behavior, need, distress, and the Fogg behavior model were used as the analysis dimensions of the user journey map, see Fig. 5.

1) Motivation dimension. The user journey diagram shows that the needs of Gen Z people for cooking and eating socially include access to cooking information, a rich and convenient social experience and a simple and fun cooking experience.
2) Ability level. Respondents' cooking ability mainly includes the time, physical strength, brain power and money spent on cooking. Busy workloads fragment respondents' time for eating and socializing. Living alone makes them often connect emotionally by socializing online, and they are more interested in accessing cooking information and cooking guidance.
3) Trigger level. Respondents' cooking triggers mainly come from access to information, for example, seeing friends' recommended recipes, food presentation, etc., can trigger users to cook.

Fig. 5. Analysis of the cooking journey map of Generation Z people living alone

4 Design Strategy

4.1 New Kitchen Lifestyle Defined

Based on the results of the preliminary quantitative and qualitative research, the keywords for emotional needs in cooking and socializing among Generation Z people who live alone were extracted and combined with the three latitudes of past, present and ideal in the PCI model of life experience to derive the keywords, see Fig. 6. The emotional needs of Generation Z in cooking and socializing are influenced by both their past experience and their ideal life, resulting in "present" emotional needs keywords, such as sharing, emotional connection and rituals. The words "sharing" and "emotional connection" cover social attributes and are high-frequency words in the pre-survey and qualitative research results. The new concept of life for Generation Z regarding cooking and eating socially - "sharing adds to the taste, connecting keeps the emotion fresh" - is proposed through the keywords obtained. The result is a feasible design direction: firstly, to allow users to complete the cooking process smoothly; secondly, to increase the emotional connection of users in the kitchen life through various forms of interaction.

4.2 A Subsection Sample

Based on the above research summary and the definition of the new kitchen lifestyle, this study proposes a shared kitchen product and experience design strategy based on the three elements of motivation, ability and trigger of the Fogg behavior model, in terms of enhancing user motivation, improving user ability and increasing the trigger mechanism, see Fig. 7.

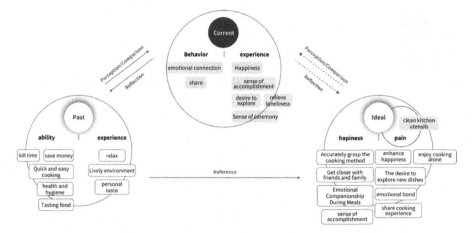

Fig. 6. Keywords Analysis of the PCI Model of the Kitchen Experience of Generation Z

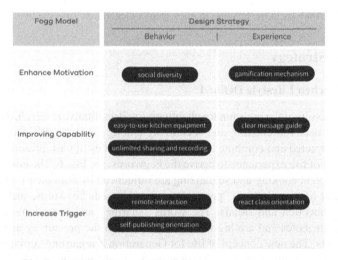

Fig. 7. Shared kitchen product and experience design strategy

Enhanced User Motivation. Users' motivation to cook and eat socially comes from both internal motivation and external conditions [9]. Enhancing users' motivation to cook and eat socially can be based on both intrinsic and extrinsic conditions, with intrinsic conditions including the sense of cooking achievement and satisfaction from social-emotional connections gained by users, and extrinsic conditions enhancing users' cooking experience and diversifying their social interaction in the following ways.

1) Gamification of the cooking experience. The user's cooking process is dismantled and combined with videos and graphics to create a clear form of cooking instruction and incentive mechanism, allowing the user to receive corresponding ratings and medals upon completion of cooking to motivate the user to cook.

2) Diversified social approach. To enhance the sense of atmosphere and ritual when users cook and eat, interactive forms such as buddy recipe search, buddy pop-up interaction, live cooking video, virtual character interaction and remote toasting are added to bring users closer to their friends and relatives and enhance their motivation to cook and eat socially.

Enhanced User Capabilities. The user's ability to cook and eat remotely and socially can be enhanced by clear guidance on cooking information, easy-to-use kitchen products, and easy and quick recording and sharing of the time and brain power spent cooking and eating socially by.

1) Clear information guidance. The user's preferences will be pushed to the recipe, thus reducing the user's time to select the dishes; there will be a clear cooking tutorial to ensure that the user's cooking process goes smoothly; voice announcement, gesture control, panel touch and other control methods will be used to reduce the user's operational confusion and reduce the difficulty of cooking.
2) Easy-to-use kitchen products. With a modular design approach, users can choose the combination of kitchen appliances according to their needs, improving space and product utilization. The interaction between the products is clear and simple, with key buttons easy to reach, reducing the user's mental effort.
3) Easy and quick recording and sharing

The rotatable and liftable camera is ready to record the cooking process and share life, and the voice communication method can send sharing commands quickly, enhancing the user's ability to share during the cooking process.

Adding a Trigger Mechanism. Cooking and eating social behavior require certain triggers to help users sustain the target behavior. Triggers can be designed in three ways: interactive experience, information reminders, and incentives.

1) Interactive experience. Emphasis on interactive experience during cooking and eating, in the form of live video streaming, remote group photos, virtual character interaction, and the vibrating sensation of a toast, to enhance the sense of remote companionship.
2) Information alerts. Provide a community platform for sharing food, increase cooking communication topics, add interactive buttons for "want to dine" and "ask for tutorials", show recipes to friends, etc., to increase the frequency of users sharing their cooking lives with friends and relatives, and bring users closer to their friends and relatives.
3) Incentive mechanism. This can be achieved by introducing gamified medal rewards, which are published on personal homepages and in the circle of friends and family, to satisfy users' sense of achievement and motivate them to cook and share their food again.

5   Cooklink Shared Kitchen Product Design Solutions

Based on the resulting product and experience design strategy, the functional content of the shared kitchen product was defined and divided into software and hardware functional modules. Based on the functional planning and conceptualization of the shared kitchen product, the product was named "Cooklink", a shared kitchen that meets the cooking and emotional connection needs of Generation Z. Cooklink consists of a mobile modular cooking station and a mobile app that together form a service system. The relationship between the products is illustrated in Fig. 8. Where the Cooklink shared kitchen product combines hardware and software to form a complete cooking-sharing service, enabling the ongoing social act of sharing cooking life.

In the process of user cooking and remote social interaction, the modular combination of intelligent mobile cooking stations can break the space constraints of users, improve the ability to cook, and enhance the motivation of users to cook on their own. At key points when users share their cooking lives and learn about their friends and family, the app and smart screen are designed to trigger interactive functions that guide users to share their cooking lives, increase common cooking topics and enhance the satisfaction and enjoyment of the interactive experience. This completes the user's behavioral persuasion towards cooking and sharing, encouraging the user to make a continuous emotional connection and achieve a sharing experience with a sense of happiness in their cooking life.

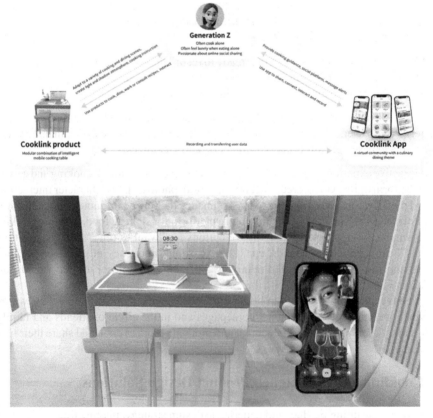

Fig. 8. The relationship between Cooklink shared kitchen products

5.1 Modular Kitchen Products

In order to adapt to different living spaces, the modular design of this product provides a range of cooking essential modules for the user to customize the combination, including pull-out tabletops, storage units, cooking units and cooking units. The modular combination is well suited to single-person cooking and multi-person dining scenarios, see Fig. 9, where the pull-out tabletop can be combined as a casual bar or work table during non-cooking times. When cooking, the pull-out tabletop can be used as a preparation table, the built-in electronic hob at the bottom as a hot food handling surface, and the custom-installed oven, fridge and other appliances and storage space together provide a complete cooking function area. For multi-person meals, each side of the product has a different function, allowing multiple people to use the cooker and access the utensils in a small area without interfering with each other, see Fig. 10. During meals, the hob and tabletop together form a large worktop that can accommodate multiple people. The auto-sensing ambient lighting adds a sense of ambiance to the meal and makes for a memorable photo opportunity. With the universal wheels on the bottom of the unit, it can be moved to the living room or terrace for cooking and other activities such as watching TV or barbecuing outdoors, meeting the needs of multiple scenarios.

Fig. 9. Cooklink shared kitchen hardware product application scenario

5.2 Cooking and Interactive Guidelines

The shared kitchen software product provides clear cooking and interactive guidance to enhance the user's cooking skills. The Cooklink software provides two types of cooking guides, video and graphic cards, for users to choose from. Taking into account the fact that the user's hands are busy when cooking, VUI human-computer voice interaction is provided to enable multiple information input, output, feedback and response operations, giving the user a more fluid experience. See Fig. 11 for the detailed interface.

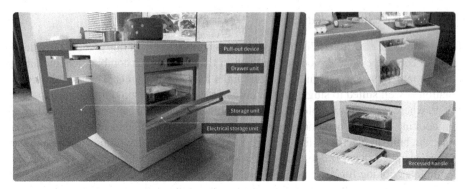

Fig. 10. Cooklink shared kitchen hardware product application scenario

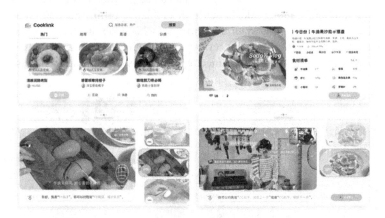

Fig. 11. Cooklink shared kitchen product lift screen interface design

5.3 Remote Socialization

The sharing kitchen product combines user cooking and sharing behaviors in the context of cooking and eating to meet the basic functional needs of cooking food and to provide remote social functions that satisfy the need for emotional connection [10]. This product introduces gamified incentives and provides a food community platform and diverse social approaches to increase user motivation and ability while adding trigger conditions to purposefully guide users through the act of cooking and eating socially.

During the cooking process, users can interact with friends and family on the elevated screen with video cooking, fun pop-ups and emoticons, as well as communicate with each other through the "Want to dine" and "Request a tutorial" interactive buttons, bringing them closer together and exchanging feelings during long cooking sessions. During the meal, the product provides a realistic interactive experience, allowing users to choose toast and take photos together while instant messaging. These functions can increase the immersion of the embodied cognition during the meal. After cooking and eating, the software product provides incentivized gamification to visualize the user's achievements in cooking and social interaction. The dishes created by the user are rated on the Taste Value Index from the system. When a certain amount of cooking and social interaction is accumulated, the user will receive an achievement badge from the system and the title and badge will be displayed on the user's social display page. See Fig. 12 for details.

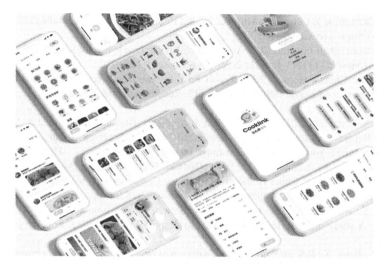

Fig. 12. High-fidelity prototype of Cooklink's shared kitchen software product

6   Concluding Remarks

Generation Z, born in the Internet era, have a new understanding of food and social life, which has led to a lifestyle that combines cooking and emotional connection, and they pay more attention to the experience of the cooking process, which poses new requirements for designing kitchen products. This paper explores the behavioral and experiential issues of Generation Z in cooking, eating and eating socially from the perspective of user behavior experience, explores design opportunities, and proposes design strategies based on the PCI model of life experience composition and the Fogg behavior model, to create an innovative design for a shared mobile kitchen product that combines virtual social interaction with cooking to bring users an experience that satisfies their emotional connection. However, due to limited conditions, further research on the technical implementation and experiential effects of the product is lacking, and the concrete practical effects are yet to be further verified.

Acknowledgements. The authors acknowledge the Key Area Special Project of Guangdong Provincial Department of Education: Application of Artificial Intelligence Big Data in Intelligent Unmanned Hotel and Data Visualization Research (Grant: 2019KZDZX2033); The Education research Project of Guangdong Province: Research on the Development of Interaction Design Education in the Era of Intelligent Internet of Things (Grant: 2021GXJK320); The

Project Guangzhou Academy of Fine Arts: Design Method of Transformation and Upgrading of Traditional Manufacturing Industry under AIoT Ecological Construction, (Grant: 21XSB20).

References

1. 2020 Generation Z Consumer Attitudes Insight Report. https://www.digitaling.com/articles/336657.html. Accessed 07 Jan 2023
2. DT Finance, Shell Institute: 2022 Youth Home Living Trends Insight Report. https://mp.weixin.qq.com/s/9cT11TN3_fonoHu-2qYPyg. Accessed 07 Jan 2023
3. CBNData: China's Home - 2021 Report on Lifestyle Trends Impacting China's Habitat. https://www.cbndata.com/report/2502/detail?isReading=report&page=2. Accessed 16 Jan 2023
4. China National Grid: 2022 China Kitchen & Appliance Built-in & Integrated & All-in-One Trend Report. https://www.fxbaogao.com/detail/3457977. Accessed 16 Jan 2023
5. Crowley: 2022 Young People's Consumer Insights Research Series - Home Furnishings. https://max.book118.com/html/2022/1011/7024146022005002.shtm. Accessed 16 Jan 2023
6. Mob Research: 2022 China Household Appliance Consumer Insights Report. https://baijiahao.baidu.com/s?id=1746114954414998112&wfr=spider&for=pc. Accessed 16 Jan 2023
7. Wang, S.: A review of research on persuasive design. Packag. Eng. **43**(22), 32–46 (2022)
8. Anwa: A study of lifestyles from contexts to design objects. Packag. Eng. **40**(20), 15–21 (2019)
9. Tan, Z., Jiang, X.: Research on interaction design of online learning platform based on FBM behavioral model. Packag. Eng. **41**(04), 189–194 (2020)
10. Li, J., Liu, S.: Research on intelligent kitchen design based on scenario analysis. Packag. Eng. **37**(24), 51–56 (2016)

Creativity and Design Education

Industrial Design Education and Immersive Virtual Reality: Perceptions on Utility and Integration

Nuno Bernardo[1,2(✉)] 📓 and Emília Duarte[2] 📓

[1] Xi'an Jiaotong-Liverpool University, Jiangsu, Suzhou, China
nuno.bernardo@xjtlu.edu.cn
[2] IADE Universidade Europeia, Lisboa, Portugal

Abstract. The use of Immersive Virtual Reality (IVR) in collaborative and co-design contexts has proven valuable to product or industrial design specializations, yet integration has been notoriously slow within Higher Education (HE). This work sheds some light on the "why?" based on primary data sourced from two groups of design educators, through a mixed-methods design. The first group confirms the importance of digital and connected technologies in today's design-centered learning environment and depict current stances regarding the use IVR as a tool for teaching and learning. The second, composed solely of educators operating in an industrial design HE program, add specificity by offering qualitative insight into aspects concerning IVR utility and integration into this particular specialization. Results foresee the technology furthering learning both on-campus and from afar, with richer virtual interactions, digital re-enactment of experiential learning, or using simulation to create new or replicate existing contexts virtually. However, the envisioned benefits appear to hinge on a series of factors, including critics over an already exceeding amount of technology in the learning environment, personal competence, skepticism over the technology merits, and other more concrete such as time, resources, familiarization or lack of technical support. Overall, participants envisage a more virtually interactive educational experience with IVR, though its reputed complexity or lack of a solid and pressing need seems to be keeping integration at bay.

Keywords: Design Education · Industrial Design · Virtual Reality

1 Introduction

1.1 Context

Traditionally, design is a studio-based discipline taught in Higher Education (HE) design-centered programs using a signature pedagogy that mimics professional practice [1, 2]. Learning design is conditioned by numerous factors, ranging from the methods and modalities employed to the socio-cultural contexts in which they occur or the experiences these may afford. Prior to the COVID-19 pandemic, and for the more conservative, bringing online technologies into design pedagogy was seen as a loss [3]. Concerns related to how the integration could alter the learning environment, the overall context-based studio culture, and subsequent pedagogy. To others, more progressive, integrating online tools was a sign of the times. It reflected a shifting paradigm in design education, attesting to its permutable nature and the increased need for accessibility and flexibility while developing competencies required in today's information-driven global environment [4]. The need to keep education uninterrupted during the pandemic would fast-track online tools' development and integration and fortify the distance learning modality.

In this increasingly technology-enabled educational context, the study authors reached out to the academic design community seeking answers to the following research questions:

1. Do online technologies play a central role in today's design-centered pedagogies?
2. What are design educators general perception on the use of Immersive Virtual Reality (IVR) as a tool for the teaching and learning?
3. What are the critical factors surrounding IVR integration to a HE industrial design context?

The first, more general, meant to depict the relationship between design educators, online technology and pedagogy. The second places emphasis on the perceptions surrounding IVR as a tool for the teaching and learning of design competencies. The last dives into the particular and explores the arguments surrounding IVR integration into an HE industrial design specialization. To answer these, the investigation relied on a mixed-methods approach where primary data derives from two consecutive and complementary studies conducted between March and June 2021. Their combined analysis and synthesis illustrate the critical role technology has within todays' learning environment and frame internal and external factors hindering IVR adoption.

Overall, findings contribute to the intersecting fields of design, education and pedagogy by mapping, presenting and discussing design educators' perceptions about the general need, use and interaction with online tools but also opportunities and entry barriers facing IVR. From a practical standpoint, this study volunteers guidance and perspective to those currently navigating or strategizing IVR integrations into their curriculums or looking to develop more effective practices in a rapidly evolving digital landscape.

2 Literature Review

2.1 Online Technology in Design Education

Innovations of the 1990s in interactive technology, the explosion of the internet, and the rapid development of technology in general, created new opportunities for the teaching and learning of design in the digital age [5]. At the turn of the century, this leap forward supported the development of new teaching and learning modalities and the digital expansion of the learning environment online [6]. It rallied design educators to research and explore the opportunities afforded, evaluate prospective worth as a tool and, subsequently, its receptiveness among participants [7–10].

Recurrent explorations often involved social media networks, image sharing and participatory platforms. For instance, Schnabel and Ham [11] looked into using Facebook for community building and information exchange, exploiting the platform as a medium for project discussion and resource sharing. Güler [12] went further, leveraging it for studio critiques, noting positive results in communication, broader exposure to peer progress and archiving and backtracking capabilities. Oygür and Ülkebaş [13] integrated Facebook groups into their industrial design course, exploring the different cohorts' ability to leverage it to exchange knowledge, concluding that the latter years show more effective use of the tool than first-year students and partly sophomores. Lapolla [14] resorted to Pinterest to connect fashion design students with young urban professionals and the wider community. Fleischmann [3] turned to the collaborative platforms ConceptBoard and GoVisually to supplement face-to-face interaction and prompt stronger connections between team members and projects. The use of digital tools within the online modality rose to prominence amidst the COVID-19 pandemic when teaching and learning activities that foresaw face-to-face interaction ceased during its critical stages. Synchronous and asynchronous forms dominated where the technological infrastructure and internet connectivity allowed it, enabling ways for participants to engage with each other and content, and effectively keep education going uninterrupted [15].

2.2 Developing Design Competencies Through Virtual Environments

Less common but growing frequent are integrations involving different types of Virtual Reality (VR). In 2015, Sakalli and Chung [16] reviewed the affordances of a desktop-based non-Immersive form of VR (n-IVR) known as Multi-User Virtual Environment (MUVE). MUVEs are a computer-mediated three dimensional (3D) virtual environments accessible online using a web browser where a user, visually represented as an avatar, can interact with other users, the environment or digital artefacts, carry on individual tasks or take part in collaborative activities [17, 18]. From a design perspective, Sakalli and Chung indicated a range of suitable applications, such as distant collaboration, role-playing simulations, sensitivity training, or empathy practice. These were enabled by attributes they identified as accessibility, availability of design visualization and communication tools, and fostering of student engagement.

Greenwald, Corning and Maes [19], Häkkilä, Colley, Väyrynen and Yliharju [20], and later Roberts, Page and Richardson [21] explored the immersive form. The first researched the tangibility of digital interactions within a custom-built shared 3D virtual space dubbed "CoCoVerse." Research goals included the appraisal of co-creation and collaborative experiences between multiple users. From an educational perspective, their results hint at a broad set of educational interactions such as educators' ability to develop 3D content and present it to students, learning from interaction with dynamic systems, or "by exploring and annotating environments, models, and datasets." Their conclusions about learning find support in Häkkilä et al. [20] and Roberts et al. [21] work, who independently explored integrations into a range of teaching and learning activities related to design processes. Both note a wide applicability and multiple benefits towards design learning, ranging from increased student motivation and interest, creative outputs and lateral thinking, among others, as summarized in Bernardo and Duarte's [22] literature review.

3   Study One

3.1 Methodology

Questionnaire

Study one resorted to an online questionnaire to answer the first two research questions using a combination of quantitative and qualitative data. It comprised three sections totaling 24 questions varying from multiple-choice, opinion scale, Likert scale, and open-ended. The first section (A) focused on participants' relationship with digital technology and the learning environment, while the second (B) enquired about perception and first-hand experiences with IVR, and the third (C) recorded participants' demographics.

Participants

A total of 47 participants (n = 47), spread across 16 countries and five continents, answered the questionnaire. All were academics within the broad field of design, recruited through the JISCMail mailing list "[PhD-DESIGN]" and by email to a professional contact network of design educators. Participants consisted of 23 females (49%) and 24 males (51%), most between the age interval of 35–44 (32%), followed by 45–54 with 30%, and 25–34 with 19%. 26% have between 15 to 19 years of professional practice, 23% have "20 or more", and 21% between 5 and 9. Regarding the number of years actively teaching in a HE design-related program, the 5–9 threshold is the most frequent, with 34%, followed by "20 or more" with 19%, and the 10–14 accounting for 17%. A doctoral degree is the most common academic qualification (49%), closely followed by a master's (47%).

3.2   Results

Section A: Technology in the Design-Centered Learning Environment

When asked to assess the amount of digital technology currently present in the learning environment and available to them, 49% agree there is a good compromise or variety, while 40% note it as insufficient without elaborating further. Its use in teaching and learning activities varies (see Table 1); the most common form (rated on a 1–6 scale) is to have students use the internet as part of the lesson (5.6), followed by the creation of multimedia presentations (5.0) or accessing and reviewing online content (4.8). The least popular uses are having students cooperate online via online third-party applications (3.3) or using the computer lab (3.2).

On the use of the school computer labs (item G), and looking at the extremes, 28% noted regular use of the computer labs against 43% who indicated "never." A sub-question aimed to substantiate the results, which appear to relate to students' preference in using their own devices (53%) or the taught subject not requiring its use (21%).

Next, participants were asked to evaluate a series of statements using a four-point Likert scale (Table 2). Some related to their confidence using digital technology, while others offered perspectives concerning the curriculum and needs of the profession. Three statements rise to the top with an equal value of 3.4 points: "A. I feel technology enables

Table 1. Frequency in which educators integrate digital technology into instruction or teaching activities, ranked in a six point scale

Question 3. How often do you integrate digital technology into your instruction or teaching activities? Please rate the actions below.	(1)	(2)	(3)	(4)	(5)	(6)	Weighted Avg.
A. Have students use the Internet as part of their lesson	4%	0%	0%	2%	19%	74%	**5.6**
B. Have students create multimedia presentations (e.g., PowerPoint, Prezi)	2%	0%	9%	13%	43%	34%	**5.0**
C. Have students access and review online content (e.g., YouTube, GitHub, Vimeo)	2%	2%	15%	17%	19%	45%	**4.8**
D. Have students use content specific software for teaching or skill reinforcement (e.g., CAD, Lynda.com, Grammarly)	21%	6%	2%	17%	19%	34%	**4.1**
E. Have students take assessment online (e.g., Exam.net, Moodle, Google Forms)	30%	6%	1%	15%	21%	17%	**3.4**
F. Have students cooperate online via third-party digital applications (e.g., Slack, GoVisually, Trello)	38%	6%	6%	13%	13%	23%	**3.3**
G. Have students use the computer lab	43%	4%	6%	11%	9%	28%	**3.2**

(1) Never: Never use it (2) Rarely: At least once per year (3) Seldom: At least once per semester (4) Occasionally: At least once per quarter (5) Frequently: At least once per month (6) Regularly: At least once per week

Central tendency

Mean: 4.2   Median: 4.1   Mode: 5.60, 5, 4.80, 4.10, 3.40, 3.30, 3.20

Variability

Distribution Range: 3.2 — 5.6	Interquartile range: 1.77	Standard Deviation: 0.95044	Variance: 0.90333

me to explore additional teaching and learning opportunities", "B. I believe students should have access, experience, or become acquainted with, a diverse range of digital technology", and lastly, "C. I believe that integrating digital technology into my curriculum is important for student success". These were followed by "D. I have a good variety of ideas and lessons for integrating technology into my teaching" (3.1) and "E. I feel confident in my ability to integrate multiple digital; technologies into my teaching and learning plan" (3.0). In contrast, statements such as "I. I lack the technical skill to support students when they use technology in a design project" or "J. Integrating digital technology is not pertinent to my curriculum" are the most disagreed with, each with 2.0 and 1.7, respectively. The low results in the latter (Table 2, items J. and I.) illustrate well participants' acknowledgement over the role technology plays in design curriculums. In contrast, the top results show their aptitude or confidence in leveraging it.

Table 2. Views towards the use of digital technology in the learning environment

Question 5. *Please rate the statements below.*	(1)	(2)	(3)	(4)	Weighted Avg.
A. *I feel digital technology enables me to explore additional teaching and learning opportunities*	0%	4%	49%	47%	**3.4**
B. *I believe students should have access, experience, or become acquainted with, a diverse range of digital technology*	0%	4%	49%	47%	**3.4**
C. *I believe that integrating digital technology into my curriculum is important for student success, both academically and professionally*	2%	2%	53%	43%	**3.4**
D. *I have a good variety of ideas and lessons for integrating digital technology into my teaching*	0%	21%	51%	28%	**3.1**
E. *I feel confident in my ability to integrate multiple digital technologies into my teaching and learning plan*	2%	21%	49%	28%	**3.0**
F. *I can easily access any type of digital technology at my the school when I need it*	9%	38%	36%	17%	**2.6**
G. *The amount of time needed to prepare technology-based or enhanced lessons deters me from creating them*	13%	38%	40%	9%	**2.4**
H. *I feel digital technology is a distraction from critical design studio skills*	19%	51%	26%	4%	**2.1**
I. *I lack the technical skill to support students when they use technology in a design project*	30%	43%	28%	0%	**2.0**
J. *Integrating digital technology is not pertinent to my curriculum*	45%	47%	6%	2%	**1.7**

(1) Strongly Disagree (2) Disagree (3) Agree (4) Strongly Agree

Central tendency

Mean: 2.71   Median: 2.8   Mode: 3.4

Variability

Distribution Range: 1.7 — 3.4	Interquartile range: 1.29	Standard Deviation: 0.63848	Variance: 0.40766

Next, the questionnaire offered three new statements on aptitude and asked participants to self-assess. Each point of the 1–5 scale listed a skill level (1-Unable, 2-Basic, 3-Developing, 4-Proficient, and 5-Advanced: can teach others). Statements referred to their ability to: "A. Plan and integrate digital technology-based learning activities that promote student engagement in higher-order thinking skills", "B. Plan and teach student-centered learning activities in which students make use of digital tools or resources", and lastly, the "C. Use of content-specific tools (e.g., software, simulation, web-based tools) to support learning and research." Participants scored above average across all three, bordering proficiency, with results ranging between 3.5 and 3.7.

This self-assessment was followed with an open question about the number one factor preventing the integration of more digital technology into their frameworks. Coding each answer and grouping the former by type revealed three main categories. "Time" is first with 13 codes, acknowledging that picking up new skills requires time and dedication that many find hard to insert into their schedules. The second is attributed to the need for "Licenses or Access" (7), which relates to software, equipment or facilities. "Training and Support" (6) ranks third, noting that even if the two initial causes were not an impediment, they would still need some level of guidance, support, or instruction to mitigate the learning curve.

Section A of the questionnaire concluded by asking participants which digital technology they would be more enthusiastic about bringing into their design studio modules (Table 3). The multiple-choice question listed nine not mutually exclusive answers and an open-answer field. With an equal percentage, both "Programming/coding (e.g., Arduino, Raspberry Pi)" and "Augmented Reality (AR)" come out on top with 47% each. These were followed by "CAD (2D/3D Digital Design, Finite Element Analysis)" with 43% and "Virtual Reality" with 30%. The least desirable share an equal 15% and pertain to "Video-conferencing", "Multi-User Virtual Environments (MUVEs)", and "Learning Management Systems (LMSs)."

Section B: Perspectives and Expectations About IVR

The concept of IVR has different degrees of familiarity across the group. Looking at the extremes, 13% are unfamiliar, while 17% have practical experience. The remaining 70% are familiarized but lack practical experience, which they attribute to: lack of access to VR equipment (21%), lack of interest or curiosity (19%), or opportunity (15%). Nearly half (49%) see it as a potential high-value tool to use in the design studio, but various factors prevent integration (see Table 4).

When asked to choose which type of IVR application was deemed the most pertinent from a list of ten non-mutual exclusive options (Table 5), 42% of participants converged on "A. Engage in graphic expression, form-finding exercises, product in-context visualization, 2D/3D modelling, or similar." This result was followed by "B. Develop experiential learning activities based on simulation (e.g., role-play, physics simulation, service design)" with 38%, then "C. Situate learning according to specific contexts or hypothetical scenarios (e.g., user-journey, user scenarios)" (33%), and lastly "D. Conduct usability tests (e.g., user interface testing, ergonomics evaluation)" with 31%. The least desirable use is to conduct "tutorials or attend meetings" (2%).

The last four questions enquired participants about encouraging and discouraging factors related to IVR. They were open-ended; the first two asked them to consider it from an on-campus perspective, while the other two enquired from a distance-learning modality. Qualitative data was made quantifiable through coding, and the resulting codes were grouped under categories based on affinity.

Table 3. Technologies design educators are interested to explore in a design studio context

Question 8	
Given the time and opportunity, which digital technology would you be interested to explore or integrate in a design studio context? Please select three	
A. *Programming/coding (e.g., Arduino, Raspberry Pi)*	47%
B. *Augmented Reality (AR)*	47%
C. *CAD (2D/3D Digital Design, Finite Element Analysis)*	43%
D. *Virtual Reality (VR)*	30%
E. *Artificial Intelligence (AI) and Machine Learning*	28%
F. *Internet of Things (IoT)*	28%
G. *Social Media*	26%
H. *Video conferencing*	15%
I. *Multi-User Virtual Environments (e.g., Second Life, OpenSimulator)*	15%
J. *Learning Management Systems (e.g., Learning Mall, Blackboard, Moodle)*	15%
K. *Other(s) (Please specify):* *(1) Lucidboard* *(1) Collaboration software like Miró* *(1) Photorealistic rendering* *(1) Creative use of technology: product hacking, circuit bending*	9%

Two main categories emerge: "Simulation" (of product or context) with 31 codes and "User-Experience" with 19. The first refers to the technology's ability to change context or surroundings instantly, demonstrate end-products in scale and proportion, test and iterate. It transpires from participants' verbatim quotations such as "enhancing the learning experience by simulating situations", "context-based simulations that facilitate experiential learning, to compliment and in parallel to 'on-campus' physical learning experiences", or "create an experience that otherwise is out of reach." The second category, User-Experience, refers to the technology affordances in providing a new medium to experiment in, being for concept development, experiments with form and surrounding space, or widening the classroom to a new range of activities or possibilities. They derive from quotations such as "I imagine being able to demonstrate something in an embodied manner", "experience environments and actions that are not physically present", "experimentation/futurism", or "concept experience."

When asked about the opposite—factors discouraging IVR integration, responses lead to five categories, from which "Apprehension or Doubt" (19) and "Resources" (16) emerge as the most significant. The former captures participants' aversion, doubt or skepticism towards the technology. Codes in this category come from verbatim quotations such as "unlikely to improve teaching and learning practice", "lacks strong need", "pushback from design community", "lack of precedents", "over sensing", or "I see no need for it." The category "Resources" relates to the lack of equipment or access, cost, space or infrastructure. Codes derive from quotations such as "not have a dedicated space

Table 4. Factors thwarting IVR integration into teaching and learning processes

Question 15	
I believe the main difficulties to integrate IVR in the teaching and learning process may be related to: *Please select three*	
A. *Equipment availability or limited amount*	34%
B. *Learning curve for both staff and students*	30%
C. *Knowledgeable technical team/support*	28%
D. *Equipment cost*	26%
E. *Unclear or unproven benefits towards learning*	23%
F. *Workload prep: time required for planning and execution*	21%
G. *VR sickness (e.g., headache, dizziness, disorientation, nausea, sweating, etc.)*	19%
H. *Limited or unsuitable physical space*	17%
I. *Lack of a strong reason, need, or motive to implement*	17%
J. *The VR experience and my ability to manage it in class*	15%
J. *Heavy computer system requirements*	13%
J. *Limited software applications*	11%
J. *Other (please specify):* *(1) Bureaucracy* *(2) I'm not convinced that attempts to make a simulacra of being in-person would come with the same benefits of actually being there. Diminishing returns*	4%
J. *Maintenance*	2%
K. *I'm not entirely sure*	2%

for it and the equipment already set up", "the absence of equipment", "the quantity and the equipment are still fairly bulky", or "do not have access."

Lastly, two final questions shift the perspective to distance learning. Encouraging factors divide into two main categories: "Teaching and Learning Dynamics" (21) and "Simulation" (14). The former suggests IVR technology opens opportunities for collaborative work or group activities and higher levels of interaction, partly improved by participants' embodiment in virtual spaces. The "Simulation" category refers to the ability to reproduce on-campus experiences virtually, the added tangibility that virtual experiences enable through 3D simulation, and the effect of digital presence. Codes in this category derive from verbatim quotations such as "virtual spaces like a design studio", the "ability to visualize ideas into tangible 3D", "collaboration", or "participants, including the instructors and the students, could digitally present in the same room/space", or "active learning/teaching sessions." On the negative side, participants' lack of knowledge and experience with the technology is the prime convergence point. Other discouraging factors include "gamification and loss of attention", "bandwidth and

Table 5. Most pertinent uses of IVR in a design studio context

Question 16	
From the range of possible IVR applications listed below, which ones do you consider most pertinent to the design studio. Please select three	
A. Engage in graphic expression, form-finding exercises, product in-context visualization, 2D/3D modelling, or similar	42%
B. Develop experiential learning activities based on simulation (e.g., role-play, physics simulation, service design)	38%
C. Situate learning according to specific contexts or hypothetical scenarios (e.g., user-journey, user scenarios)	33%
D. Conduct usability tests (e.g., user interface testing, ergonomics evaluation)	31%
E. Develop empathy (e.g., visually impaired users, repetitive work conditions)	27%
F. Conduct or engage in co-design or collaboration projects	27%
G. Problem-solving: design activities that require students to come up with solutions	24%
H. Practice certain skills in a safe environment (e.g., operating machinery)	13%
I. Enrich specific lectures, seminars, or workshops	13%
J. Case-study simulations (e.g., equipment malfunction leading to car accident)	13%
K. Other (please specify): (1) Designing in context - i.e. a bench for a park but you can be in the park (2) see the space from within and move in it (3) as a prototyping material	9%
L. Conduct tutorials or attend meetings	2%

stable connection", "VR technology for collaboration work is not mature", "brings burden to students if they need to prepare the equipment and space by themselves", or "addiction to the virtual world." Fig. 1 summarizes the key findings.

	In STUDIO	REMOTELY
ENCOURAGING	SIMULATION (31) USER–EXPERIENCE (19)	TEACHING AND LEARNING DYNAMICS (21) SIMULATION (14)
DISCOURAGING	APPREHENSION OR DOUBT (19) RESOURCES (16) COORDINATION (5) TIME (5) KNOWLEDGE OR EXPERIENCE (4)	KNOWLEDGE OR EXPERIENCE (21) APPREHENSION OR DOUBT (14) RESOURCES (5) TIME (3) CONNECTIVITY AND ACCESS (2)

Fig. 1. Encouraging and discouraging factors surrounding IVR integrated in the on-campus design studio and distance learning modality

4   Study Two

4.1   Methodology

Study two addressed the third research question using an empathy map. The map was available through Lucidspark.com for two weeks, and participants gained access to it via an URL received by email, which also described the study's aim, timeframe, and activity. Any interaction and resulting input were anonymous, strictly voluntary, and unrestrained by any metric. These were critical elements intended to minimize participant bias towards the study derived from knowing one of the researchers.

Participants
Fourteen (n = 14) participants contributed to study two. They were part of a convenience sample composed of full-time academic staff members belonging to the department of Industrial Design of the Xi'an Jiaotong-Liverpool University (XJTLU) in Suzhou, China. They are native to nine countries and three continents and share three aspects deemed crucial: a background in a design specialization, active within a HE industrial design program, and involvement in at least one design studio module. The group consisted of five females (36%) and nine males (64%), most between the age interval of 25–34 (43%), followed by the 45–54 and 55–64, each with 21%. 50% of the participants had at least 5–9 years of professional practice, and 43% had the same years teaching in a HE design-related program. A master's degree is the most common academic qualification (71%), followed by a doctoral (29%). Specializations include information design experience (1), product design (2), industrial design (6), graphic design (1), architecture (1), history of design (1), multimedia and telecommunication (1), and research and education (1).

Empathy Map
The central area of the map comprises four quadrants (Says, Thinks, Does, Feels), with two additional areas (Gains, Pains) to the right (see Fig. 2). Built-in instructions asked participants to use digital post-its to record their predictable reactions (vocal, cognitive, actionable, and emotional) and perspectives (benefits and drawbacks) to the following hypothetical scenario: "The university has just told you that you will need to integrate Immersive Virtual Reality into your teaching and learning plan for the next semester." The description aimed to trigger a multi-dimension reaction within participants, which they were asked to annotate using a post-it and place within the appropriate quadrant. The activity resulted in 98 unique interactions, as portrayed in Fig. 2.

4.2   Results

This part of the study took an inductive approach to qualitative data analysis. The writing on each post-it was transcribed and coded on the MAXQDA software by assigning tags to data segments; initial code building involved both open and in vivo. Subsequent codes are more interpretative and have a degree of inference beyond the data; these take the role of categories. A third-level coding nests categories under concepts (codes > categories > concepts) [23].

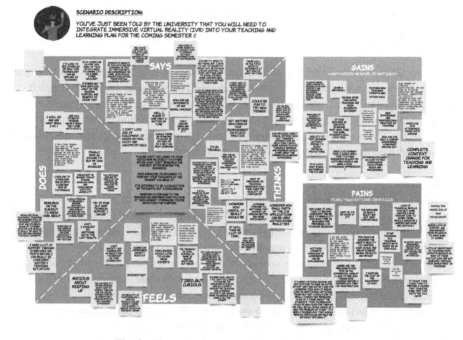

Fig. 2. The empathy map at the end of the activity

Figure 3 summarizes all coded data rendered in MAXQDA's code matrix browser. The matrix illustrates the distribution of coded segments among the different quadrants. Quadrants are represented in the columns, while the rows list the categories nested under each central concept. The calculation of node size refers to the column. The size and color of the node clusters in the matrix represent the number of segments coded inside each category in the respective quadrant they were identified in. The larger the cluster, the greater the number of segments assigned to the category. The entire code system comprises 144 codes distributed between three main concepts. "Teaching and Learning" is the largest, with 94 coded segments, followed by "Feelings or Emotions" (27) and "Attitude" (23). The most relevant findings are analyzed and interpreted next.

Under the first concept, three categories stand out: "Tangibility with the Real-world" with 16 codes, followed by both "Training and Support" and "New Possibilities", each with 15. The first speaks to a general concern over losing a sense of materiality and context and how these could harm the design process. This concern is experience-based and includes model-making, workshop know-how, or similar "tangible experiences" with a tactile or practice-based dimension. However, chunks of code are also positive in the opposite sense. These note that IVR technology "gives a material level to digital and online teaching" and allows "virtual scenarios for product testing without recurring to materials", avoiding disposal and waste generation.

In the "Training and Support" category, concerns focus on the level of support participants would receive from their employer. Expectations assume some level of online assistance, face-to-face training, or workshops where field professionals demonstrate

Code System	GAINS	PAINS	DOES	SAYS	FEELS	THINKS	SUM
EMPATHY MAP							
∨ ⊙ Teaching & Learning							
> ⊙ New possibilities	●	•		•	●		15
> ⊙ Distance learning	•			•		•	3
> ⊙ Class management		•					2
> ⊙ Tangibility with real–world	●			•	●	●	16
> ⊙ Time or workload		●		•		●	8
> ⊙ Training or support		●	•	•	●	•	15
> ⊙ Equipment		•		•			2
> ⊙ Application (how to?)			•	●		•	8
> ⊙ Validation or proof		●		●		•	7
> ⊙ Comfort and usability		•	•	●		•	6
> ⊙ Cost		●		•			4
> ⊙ Student engagement	●	•		•			8
∨ ⊙ Feelings or Emotions							
> ⊙ Insecurity or inadequacy		•					1
> ⊙ Doubt or uncertainty		•			●		5
> ⊙ Curiosity					•	•	2
> ⊙ Anxiety			●		●		4
> ⊙ Competency		•			●		4
> ⊙ Tireness					●		2
> ⊙ Challenged					•		1
> ⊙ Fear or scared					●		2
> ⊙ Excitement					●		2
∨ ⊙ Attitude							
> ⊙ Negative				•	●	•	6
> ⊙ Positive	•		●	●	•	●	21
SUM	28	26	16	28	27	19	**144**

Fig. 3. Distribution of coded segments, belonging to each category, in the different quadrants

IVR uses in design education. Although some participants illustrate a level of confidence or pro-activeness in tackling the subject head-on, the overall sense is that they need assurances from their employer. A commitment ensuring suitable means and support would be available throughout each stage of the skill acquisition process.

The third category, "New Possibilities", represents the range of foreseen experiences available in the learning environment, its influence over class dynamics, and the enthusiasm it may generate. Participants mention "huge amounts of creative opportunities", "students' experience of the given task beyond the boundaries of physical space", "testing new teaching formats and potentials", or "ability to test designs without having to build physical prototypes." All are perceived to bring more variety and possibilities to how design is taught and learnt.

Under the second concept, "Feelings or Emotions", the category "Doubt or Uncertainty" comes out on top with a total of 5 codes, followed by "Anxiety" (4) and questions related to "Competency" (4). The first captures participants' doubts about integrating the technology into pedagogy, educators' ability to accomplish it, or the benefits it may bring. Feelings of anxiety transpire in statements demonstrating a lack of confidence or self-assurance in achieving what the scenario description proposes in a relatively short amount of time, especially when outside their comfort zone. This also relates to a sense of competency with new forms of technology, particularly an inability self-awareness to pick up new skills fast and the additional impact it would add to the workload. Even though these three categories hold the most considerable amount of codes, within this umbrella concept, none rises considerably above others.

Regarding "Attitude", the overall perception is positive (21 to 6). Although there is a degree of skepticism about the technology itself, most responses reflect a high level of openness and desire for self-improvement, further supported by a pro-active mindset. These are noted in the "Does" quadrant in comments such as: "research on the subject to know more about it", "would buy VR headset for my iPhone, download apps, and familiarize with its usability", "I would propose to organize a seminar inviting colleagues that have already introduced IVR in their modules" or "learn how VR can improve the design process, especially prototyping and testing."

Coding each statement allowed the identification of the most pressing concerns, perspectives, and triggers related to the rendered scenario. The balance between the "Gains" and "Pains" columns is offset only by a small margin towards the former. The advantages it may bring to the learning environment still come at a high cost in the form of complexity. Nevertheless, although IVR's current state of maturation is far from being perceived as ideal, most participants show a positive attitude about it if told to incorporate—some by their initiative and drive, but more preferably with technical support. The range of feelings or emotions is broad and hard to attribute to a particular scenario instance—if they relate solely to the technology, the technology and the timeframe, or just the timeframe. However, one thing is clear, IVR is still very much detached from their roles as educators and their personal life outside of work. This unfamiliarity, in any aspect, makes it harder to imagine possibilities or to dispel perceived complexity or disutility.

5   Conclusions

Although the role of digital or online technology in design teaching and learning has grown and evolved in the last decades, its ongoing relationship with design educators and the design studio context has not been sufficiently examined. This study aimed to contribute to design pedagogy by investigating the community's perceptions about the use of and interaction with technology in the learning environment and exploring the attractiveness of IVR solutions. The outcomes glance over various perceptions, uses and near-future applications, and the tug-of-war argumentation surrounding a future integration in design-centered learning environments.

Study One results show design educators as confident and competent with various digital technologies and aware of their positive and significant role in the learning process, not only by enabling new opportunities but also by retaining or nurturing student motivation and engagement. When asked what technologies they would be more inclined to bring into their design studio modules nowadays, programming/coding and AR rise to the top. The preference hints at how design is evolving and the additional tools or skills educators believe students need to be equipped with to face an ever-more technology-inclined job market. From this perspective, VR is not considered as pertinent or as fundamental as others, or at least not presently. However, this may also connect with the fact that a majority sees VR as a tool to predominantly "engage in graphic expression, form-finding exercises, product in-context visualization, 2D/3D modelling, or similar" (Table 5), which the authors consider somewhat unexpected. Certainly, immersive creation and visualization would be interesting to explore but unlikely to be a crucial enough reason to integrate, particularly when considering the price of equipment, and learning curve, among others (see Table 4). Hence, the result raises questions about how well the design educator community is aware of IVR affordances.

In Study Two, industrial design educators are quick to imagine IVR opening new pathways for digital learning, bringing more variety and possibilities to the learning environment, including product and context simulation, collaboration, creative opportunities, new teaching formats, or more dynamic and engaging teaching and learning experiences. These could help broaden the educational horizon by enabling the development of new teaching and learning formats or bring some sense of physical tangibility to the online modality, allowing a more "present" experience through richer interactions between participants or the latter with virtual objects. However, this forward-thinking idealization is not without fear or concerns as they also wonder what may be lost when more technology is taken on board. For instance, some voice concern over the falling out of touch with materials and product materiality, while others fear the diminished amount of person-to-person interaction. Common to both groups of participants is that the discouraging factors outweigh the technology's potential advantages in either modality. Critical factors such as time, access to equipment, lack of knowledge, experience, or purchasing cost are consistent across studies and deemed consequential to an overall lack of rapport with the technology.

This was a small-scale exploratory research study with relatively few participants whose results and conclusions are inevitably limited in scope and generalizability. However, two things seem apparent: the need for opportunities for design educators to develop familiarity with IVR and better communication of its affordances past the visual experience. Lacking this awareness and knowledge makes it difficult for educators to realize its potential for design pedagogy. The authors interpret these as factors slowing IVR dissemination, adoption and use and believe that institutions will require a more proactive and supporting role if the technology is to flourish within design contexts.

6 Closing Remarks and Suggestions for Future Studies

Overall, even if design educators see potential value in IVR, this form of technology is not their first choice for the design studio. The reasons extend past the technology specifics per se. They may latch to others, such as personal affinity, views towards design futures, particular module needs, specialization, or professional pathways. Unfortunately, the study needed more broadness to explore the different variables that participants consider when considering integrating a specific technology into the design studio. The lack of foresight ultimately made it unable to frame a more comprehensive depiction. However, the line of enquiry is worth exploring. Understanding the personal motivations that lead design educators to favor a specific technology over others, e.g., the considerations behind and how it ties to context, what specific pedagogical needs it addresses, and how it will contribute to developing design competence, among others, are all worth exploring and mapping. At a time when technology populates nearly every instance of daily life, awareness of the potential benefits and drawbacks behind specific forms, their contribution to developing design competency, and the ramifications could serve as a compass leading to better-informed decisions.

Acknowledgments. This study was conducted at the UNIDCOM, supported by the Fundação para a Ciência e Tecnologia, (FCT), under Grant No. UID/DES/00711/2019 attributed to UNID-COM – Unidade de Investigação em Design e Comunicação, Lisbon, Portugal. The authors would like to thank the academic staff of Department of Industrial Design of Xi'an Jiaotong-Liverpool University for their willingness to participate and contribute to this study.

References

1. Shulman, L.: Signature Pedagogies in the Professions. Daedalus **134**(3), 52–59 (2005)
2. Davis, M.: Teaching Design: A Guide to Curriculum and Pedagogy for College Design Faculty and Teachers Who Use Design in Their Classrooms. Allworth Press, New York (2017)
3. Fleischmann, K.: From Studio Practice to Online Design Education: Can we Teach Design Online? Canadian Journal of Learning and Technology 45(1), (2019)
4. Souleles, N.: E-learning in Art and Design: Perceptions and Practices of Lecturers in Undergraduate Studio-based Disciplines and the Rhetoric of Innovative Practices. In: Proceedings 5th International Technology, Education and Development Conference INTED2011, pp. 4492–4501. IATED, Valencia (2011)
5. Cross, N., Holden, G.: Design education in the open. Open Arts J. **9**(10), 149–161 (2020)
6. Prensky, M.: The Games Generations: How Learners Have Changed. McGraw-Hill, New York (2001)
7. Maher, M., Simoff, S.: Variations on the Virtual Design Studio. In: Proceedings of the 4th International Workshop on CSCW in Design, Universite de Technologie de Compiegne, pp. 159–165. Compiegne (1999)
8. Saghafi, M., Franz, J., Crowther, P.: Perceptions of physical versus virtual design studio education. Int. J. Architectural Res.**6**(1), 6–22 (2012)
9. Masdéu, M., Fuses, J.: Reconceptualizing the design studio in architectural education: distance learning and blended learning as transformation factors. Int. J. Architectural Res.**11**(2), 6–23 (2017)
10. Iranmanesh, A., Onur, Z.: Mandatory virtual design studio for all: exploring the transformations of architectural education amidst the global pandemic. Int. J. Art Design Educ. **40**(1), 251–267 (2021)
11. Schnabel, M., Ham, J.: Virtual design studio within a social network. J. Inf. Technol. Construct. **17**, 397–415 (2012)
12. Güler, K.: Social media-based learning in the design studio: a comparative study. Comput. Educ. **87**, 192–203 (2015)
13. Oygür, I., Ülkebaş, S.: Facebook as a boundary object in industrial design studio. A SoTL Study Design J. **20**(sup1), S1037–S1047 (2017)

14. Lapolla, K.: The pinterest project: using social media in an undergraduate second year fashion design course at a United States University. Art Des. Commun. High. Educ. **13**(2), 175–187 (2014)
15. Bernardo, N., Duarte, E.: Design, Education, and the Online Tech-Pandemic. Strateg. Design Res. J. **13**(3), 577–585 (2020)
16. Sakalli, I., Chung, W.: Design on the MUVE: synergizing online design education with multi-user virtual environments (MUVE). Turkish Online J. Educ. Technol. **14**(3), 20–31 (2015)
17. Codier, E.: Teaching Health Care in Virtual Space: Best Practices for Educators in Multi-User Virtual Environments. University of Hawai'i Press, Honolulu (2016)
18. Leung, T., Zulkernine, F., Isah, H.: The use of virtual reality in enhancing interdisciplinary eesearch and education. J. Syst. Cybern. Inf. **16**(6), 4–9 (2018)
19. MIT Media Lab: Fluid Interfaces, https://www.media.mit.edu/projects/cocoverse/overview/. Accessed 09 Feb 2023
20. Häkkilä, J., Colley, A., Väyrynen, J., Yliharju, A.: Introducing virtual reality technologies to design education. Int. J. Media Technol. Lifelong Learn. **14**(1), 1–12 (2018)
21. Roberts, S., Page, R., Richardson, M.: Designing in Virtual Environments: The Integration of Virtual Reality Tools into Industrial Design Research and Education. In Boess, S., Cheung, M., and Cain, R. (eds.) DRS2020 International Conference, vol. 4, pp. 1628–1643. Design Research Society, held online (2020)
22. Bernardo, N., Duarte, E.: Immersive virtual reality in an industrial design education context: what the future looks like according to its educators. Comput. Aided Design Appl. **19**(2), 238–255 (2021)
23. Charmaz, K.: Constructing Grounded Theory. Sage Publications, London (2006)

Presenting a Digital Toolkit for Training Hyper-Observant Experience Design Researchers

Dennis Cheatham[✉] [iD]

Miami University, Oxford, OH 45056, USA
`dennis.cheatham@miamioh.edu`

Abstract. This article describes *Aspects of Experiences for Design* (AoE4D), a framework supported by an online toolkit that expands undergraduate and graduate students' perceptions when conducting observational field research necessary for designing useful, usable, desirable, and memorable experiences. Three examples of the digital toolkit are presented, including two custom-built web applications and an online whiteboard activity that develops early-career designers' skills for coding and analyzing qualitative data. This piece presents how the framework develops students' design research skills by guiding them through scaffolded critical thinking—focusing their attention on one or two aspects of an experience at a time to enable thoughtful consideration of how the alignment or misalignment of these aspects affects a user experience. The AoE4D framework's core principles and theoretical underpinnings that shaped its development are presented, as well as an overview of experience design as an emerging design practice. I propose in this article that observation skills and the ability to make connections between those observations are crucial competencies for designing meaningful, relevant products, services, and systems.

Keywords: experience design · design research education · evidence-based design · qualitative research methods · field research · interpreting experiences

1 Introduction

Experience Design is an approach to creating products, services, and systems that produce positive experiences. These outcomes are useful, usable, desirable, and intensely personal because they seamlessly align with user makeup and preferences. With this approach, designers strive for their creations to produce an emotional response from users instead of simply improving logistical matters like efficiency or ease of use. The ultimate goal for an experience design outcome is for users to be engaged participants who take a meaningful memory away from the time they used the product [1]. When people repeatedly visit a restaurant whose staff gives them a sense of belonging or feel that a car's features are so intuitive that it must have been made just for them, the designed *experience* is why.

A. Marcus et al. (Eds.): HCII 2023, LNCS 14031, pp. 388–400, 2023.
https://doi.org/10.1007/978-3-031-35696-4_28

Organizations, including Best Buy, General Motors, and an increasing number of colleges and universities, identify their experiences as critical brand differentiators—even establishing customer experience leadership positions at their highest administrative levels [2–5]. When designing for experiences, teams consider concerns like participants' emotional moods, physical sensations, socio-cultural makeup, and actual and perceived environmental factors. In experience-centered organizations, this approach blends product design and customer experience, integrating the two over the entire timeline with an organization's product—from before the interaction with a product to a person's feelings and memories after use.

The holistic and ill-defined nature of designing for experiences makes this approach a daunting subject for early-career designers in undergraduate design programs and those new to experience-centered design, including graduate students. When concepts like memorics, time, and systems are elements of design research and production akin to accessible web design or brand consistency, the list of skills students in design programs must possess expands exponentially. Students learning to design for experiences must develop a perceptive ability to recognize and apply this expanded set of real and perceived factors in their work. To effectively integrate these concepts into their designs, experience designers formulate problems, conduct research, and create. They mix concepts from psychology, design, engineering, and theatre to produce omnichannel outcomes, integrating products, services, and systems into a unified experience. Through primary and secondary research, they identify behaviors, touchpoints, and pain points to uncover what kinds of experiences to design [6]. When students can become hyper-observant design researchers, they perceive a full spectrum of participants' behaviors to produce insights that turn into design decisions that form valuable experiences.

This article describes *Aspects of Experiences for Design* (AoE4D), a framework supported by an online toolkit that expands designers' perceptions when conducting observational field research and provides a vocabulary for designing experiences. It is used in eight different interaction design and experience design courses in the Communication Design Bachelor of Fine Arts program and the Master of Fine Arts Experience Design program at Miami University in Oxford, Ohio, in the United States. These courses are facilitated in various ways, including asynchronously online, face-to-face, hybrid online, and domestic study abroad. The content of this article articulates how different delivery formats incorporating AoE4D enhance and detract from teaching observational research skills.

2   Observation Skills for High-Fidelity Design Research

Experience designers are problem formulators, storytellers, researchers, and creators all in one. Designing for experiences requires high-fidelity observation skills via field research to decipher what users value, their makeup, and their background, so designed outcomes match user makeup [7, 8]. Soft skills, observation techniques, critical thinking, and emotional intelligence can seem amorphous and impossible to quantify, much less teach. However, participant observation skills can be learned like any other skill [9–12]. Researching for experiences challenges practitioners to become astute observers, skilled in methods that encourage participants to share their feelings and desires—an approach blending psychographic and demographic information that Disney Institute refers to as *Guestology* [13].

The ill-formed nature of experiences requires problem formulation as an essential component of the design process. Namely, design teams conduct research to identify what potential users value and how their makeup informs what product, service, or system (channels or a combination of channels) would best align with users. Observations are only sometimes visual. Sounds, such as honking and screeching traffic outside a library, could be at fault for disturbing readers, or pleasant weather at an outdoor funeral could reduce the emotional impact of a family's loss—setting their mind on hope. Calibration is necessary for qualitative researchers to sense details like these. With training, students can develop a high degree of sensory perception—learning what to observe and record in their field notes.

However, many undergraduate and graduate students in the United States enrolled in visual communication design or user experience design programs have limited experience formulating, operating, and analyzing data gleaned from qualitative research methods such as interviews and observations. Early in the semester in my undergraduate and graduate level Design Research Methods courses, students produce imprecise field notes—often omitting information essential for designing at the experience level. For example, field notes describe people as "a group of people" or "a person sitting in a chair" instead of describing details about these individuals, like their dress, posture, skin tone, or conditions in the environment that surrounds them. Experiential learning [14, 15] was integrated into coursework to improve observational skills with assignments that required students to practice these skills off campus as they would in the profession when completing a site visit.

3 Aspects of Experiences for Design: A Vocabulary for Complete Design Experiences

The concept of an "experience" is difficult to describe because of its phenomenological characteristics [16–18]. To teach and research designing for experiences, I studied concepts essential for this design approach—an effort that produced the *Aspects of Experiences for Design* framework. Because designing is goal-driven—creating interventions that people use to accomplish tasks—Don Norman's definition of *Activity-Centered Design* became AoE4D's theoretical core, and the adage of useful, usable, and desirable outcomes measured the measure of a successful experience [19, 20]. Works by researchers and practitioners writing on interaction design to dissect the user experience were invaluable for establishing the framework's main components. A review of the literature of the most highly cited works in experience-centered design revealed experience design concepts that overlapped across disparate sources. Of note are works by Richard Buchanan, [7] Nigel Cross, [21] Peter Desmet and Paul Hekkert, [22] Susan Fiske and Shelley Taylor, [23] Jodi Forlizzi and Shannon Ford, [24] Marc Hassenzahl, [25] Lars-Erik Janlert and Eric Stolterman, [26] Vesa Jääskö, Tuuli Mattelmäki, and Salu Ylirisku, [27] Harold Nelson and Erik Stolterman, [28] Don Norman, [29] Joseph Pine II and James Gilmore, [30] Liz Sanders and Peter Stappers, [31] and Herbert Simon, [32].

Following this review, three components of an *Activity-Centered Design* scenario emerged: Context, People, and Design. Whenever someone (People) completes an activity where a human-made product, service, or system (Design) is involved, it takes place in a setting (Context) and produces an experience. These components comprised an *Experience Design Scene*—the scope of interaction from when a person begins an activity to its conclusion and the resulting experience (Robert Rossman and Matthew Duerden use "Experiencescape" in their 2019 book *Designing Experiences* [1], which confirmed components identified in *AoE4D's Experience Design Scenes*.) The word "scene" positions that experiences—everyday or extraordinary—take place over time, like a moment in a play, theatre production, or film. By defining the *Scene* concept, the framework gained boundaries that guided the process of defining aspects of each component to include in the framework. When students conduct observational research, directing them to decode what is happening in a scene guides their inquiry and focuses their observations on a sequence, a place, and those in the scene.

Theories related to each *Scene* component were then selected from a literature review. Four theories serve as AoE4D's theoretical underpinnings: *Soft Systems Methodology*, [33] *Self-Determination Theory*, [34] *The Theory of Planned Behavior* [35], and *Semiotics* [36–38]. Each theory established a theme for the AoE4D framework.

Soft Systems Methodology: Actual and perceived aspects, such as climate conditions and worldview (weltanschauung), can influence people and organizational decisions in a setting.

Theme: *Experience Design Scenes* occur in settings that constrain and impact experiences.

Self-determination Theory: People are more likely to be intrinsically motivated when basic needs such as relatedness, competency, and autonomy are met. A person's self-concept heavily influences their perception and understanding of the world around them.

Theme: People's identities shape the way they make meaning of the world.

The Theory of Planned Behavior: A person's intention to perform a behavior is determined by their attitude about the activity, if they believe they can do it, and what they think others will feel about them when performing it.

Theme: People's relationships with other people steer their motivations.

Semiotics: Symbols and signs are inherent in any interaction with design and can enhance or damage the accuracy of messages. The quality of signifiers for communication shapes the message.

Theme: The characteristics and functionality of products, services, and systems impact their use and what they mean to users.

An expanded literature review driven by concepts within each theory produced the remaining aspects in the framework until salient concepts were exhausted. Sources in this tertiary literature review included work by Patricia Hill Collins, [39] James J. Gibson, [40] Erving Goffman, [41] Martin Heidegger, [42] LeCompte and Schensul, [43] and Donella Meadows [44].

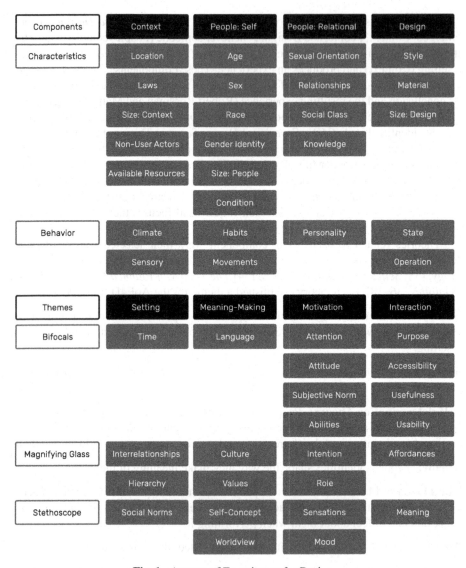

Fig. 1. Aspects of Experiences for Design.

This review produced a final set of 48 aspects (see Fig. 1) that impact experiences that design researchers can study and that designers can account for when creating products, services, and systems. The *AoE4D* framework vocabulary makes *Experience Design Scenes* more manageable for students and experienced designers alike because it allows users to focus on one aspect at a time to drive inquiry into a scene and identify its impact on the scene. When students conduct observational research, they can consider one aspect as a theoretical framework to guide inquiry. For example, observing a family with small children attending a puppet show through the *social class* aspect can help researchers become more sensitive to ways the family's buying power may impact their experience. Observing a room of people attending a political rally through the *personality* aspect may produce insights into ways the event alienates people with more reserved tendencies and prioritizes those with outgoing personalities. Not all aspects are directly observable and may require research methods other than observation to study.

4 The AoE4D Evaluation Equation

When alone, aspects guide highly-detailed observations. When paired, *AoE4D* aspects are a tool for identifying pain points that damage experiences or alignments that enhance them. The more severe the misalignment between aspects, the worse the experience. The more serendipitous the alignment, the more appealing the experience.[1] Using this tool, students can extrapolate where to implement design interventions to improve usefulness, usability, desirability, and the overall experience. The following equation demonstrates how the *Aspects of Experiences for Design* framework helps users determine how and which aspects impact the quality of an experience.

(an aspect of one component)
Compared with
(an aspect of another component)
Reveals
(the degree of alignment between the aspects)
Which indicates
(the quality of the experience)
Prompting action
(how and where a design intervention can align the aspects)
To produce a more desirable experience

The equation is applied in a scenario below to demonstrate usage:
Context: Social Norms -> People: Language

(context aspect: social norms)
French is the only language spoken in a shop in the Paris, France banlieue of Clichy-sous-Bois.
(people aspect: language)
A person who visits the shop can only speak and read Hindi.
(degree of alignment)
The social norms in this context do not align with the person's language.
(the quality of the experience)
A negative experience occurs because the person cannot easily order a sandwich. The social norms in the shop damage the person's experience because of the severe misalignment between the aspects.

---

[1] "Ideal" alignments can produce sad or sorrowful experiences. It is important not to assume that delight is ideal. For example, healing often comes at memorial services through tears and mourning. An event that provides a safe space for difficult emotions is the desirable design outcome.

(how and where a design intervention can align the aspects)
A product, service, or system that assists communication via language as a focus would likely produce a more desirable experience.

The *AoE4D Evaluation Equation* helps students focus on one aspect pair at a time, reducing the chance of being overwhelmed by the seemingly infinite number of variables in an experience design scene. It systematizes the analysis of usefulness, usability, and desirability. Once students complete a full analysis of an experience design scene, the aspect pairs most out of alignment represent crucial pain points where design interventions could affect the most significant improvement. In contrast, the aspect pairs that align most harmoniously reveal what makes the experience special, ideal, intuitive, exemplary, or even inspiring and memory-making.

5   Digital Tools for Developing Observation Skills

Starting in 2019, I built digital tools to develop students' observation skills, including web applications and online whiteboard activities. Some of these tools are used in the field, such as when I assigned students to conduct observations on their own or when on study away *Destination Weekend* trips with Miami University graduate students in the MFA in Experience Design. Other tools strengthen students' qualitative coding and analysis skills—an activity that applies critical thinking skills. I have assigned all the following tools to undergraduate and graduate students in my interaction and experience design courses.

5.1   The AoE4D Field Evaluation Tool Web Application

The *AoE4D Field Evaluation Tool*[2] puts the AoE4D framework into practice by placing it in students' hands. With this tool, students can document every aspect of the experience design scene they choose to observe. The *AoE4D Field Evaluation Tool* was designed responsively to function on mobile devices and computers. Students document all scene components using this tool by completing a web form.

As the user scrolls down the screen, the web application focuses the user's attention on each aspect pair. Students can tap an aspect button, and a brief description of the aspect will appear. For each pairing, students can select if the aspect enhances, supports, damages, or has no effect on the experience (see Fig. 2). Once completed, users can send their responses to themselves via e-mail.

I created the *AoE4D Field Evaluation Tool* in 2019, and since then, students who have used it have shared that the tool challenged them to observe particular parts of the scene in front of them. Between 2019 and 2022, I led study away trips for graduate students in the MFA in Experience Design to Montréal, Quebec, Canada; Santa Fe, New Mexico, USA; and New Orleans, Louisiana, USA. In the summer of 2022, I taught Applied Experience Design: Walt Disney World, a six-week course that featured one week on-site at the Walt Disney World Resort in Orlando, Florida, USA. During each

---

[2] The *AoE4D Field Evaluation Tool* is located at https://www.aoe4d.com/tools/field-evaluation-tool/

Fig. 2. Three screens from the *AoE4D Field Evaluation Tool* web application.

trip, I assigned students to use their travel experience as the subject for developing their observational sensitivity. Each time students were on-site or in transit, I challenged them to observe and record their findings in extreme detail to reveal pain points and challenges in their environment. Students who used the *AoE4D Field Evaluation Tool* used its aspect words in our class discussions—mentioning how the size of a ride vehicle or a person's health condition contributed to an unpleasant experience. Astute observations about the impact of "self-concept" and "affordances" drove our class discussions when none of these words were part of our early trip discussions.

Students have also used the *AoE4D Field Evaluation Tool* to assist their non-trip coursework. A group of three graduate students in Miami University's online MFA in experience design used the tool for all of their semester project field observations—observing the same service design multiple times in three different cities. Though the students in the group did not live in the same cities, the tool standardized their observations across 48 aspects yet left enough openness in their responses where each student could select which aspect pairs they felt were most relevant to their observations.

5.2   Seeing in Detail: Coding Data with AoE4D

Every semester, undergraduate and graduate students in my Design Research Methods courses complain that coding data is confusing. The most common complaints are that they do not know *what* to code and are unsure of what codes to generate. I developed the *Seeing in Detail* assignment built with the Miro online whiteboard tool to help students learn how to code while also introducing them to the aspects of the framework. Miro allows all students in my class to participate simultaneously. Typically, about 22 students are in my undergraduate Design Research Methods course, whose delivery mode is face-to-face. Students begin by opening the assigned Miro board and selecting one of my vacation photos from a grid (see Fig. 3).

Fig. 3. A grid of vacation photos in Miro for students to code.

Students then use pre-built labels of all 48 *Aspects of Experiences for Design* aspects to label instances on their selected photograph (see Fig. 4).

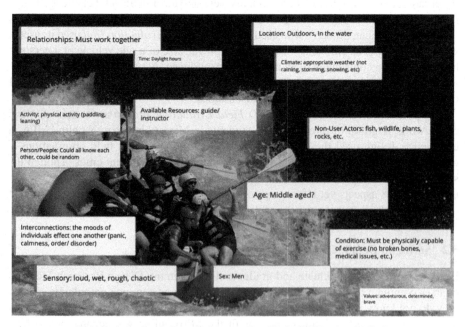

Fig. 4. A *Seeing in Detail* photograph with AoE4D codes applied.

During the *Seeing in Detail* activity, I project the class's activity on a screen at the front of the classroom to offer comments about students' work. Because the activity is simultaneous and all on the same Miro board, students can see each other's work. Those unsure about their coding can compare their work to others and often begin adding more codes to their photograph once they see the process in action. The *AoE4D* aspects are a coding primer in the *Seeing in Detail* activity. Students do not have to generate codes, which is very difficult for first-time design researchers. At the same time, some AoE4D aspects are concepts that students may otherwise not consider because of their limited life experience and as early-career designers.

Seeing in Detail instilled confidence in students that appeared later in the semester when they had to code qualitative data independently. The first year I taught *Seeing in Detail*, the number of codes on final project coding at the end of the semester doubled. It improved my students' skills with detailed, descriptive coding and was a fun way to get to know their instructor through the vacation photos.

5.3 Self-awareness: The Sensory Fieldwork Tool

When conducting field research, students utilize their senses to gather data. Isolating the senses is an effective way to heighten one's perception of their other senses. For example, when someone closes their eyes or walks into a pitch-black room, they often report that they become more aware of their hearing and touch. Though it is debatable that humans have only five senses [47], the *Sensory Fieldwork Tool*[3] calls students' attention to the five most prevalent senses to challenge them to develop each one within sensory-rich experiences.

Fig. 5. Three screens from the *Sensory Fieldwork Tool* web application.

Like the *AoE4D Field Evaluation Tool*, the *Sensory Fieldwork Tool* has a feature where users can email their responses to each prompt to themselves. This tool heightens the user's perception of their surroundings and how their senses record stimuli (see Fig. 5). When using this tool, students record the activity they are completing and the environment in which it takes place. The tool asks the user to respond to two prompts that

---

[3] The *Sensory Fieldwork Tool* is located at https://www.aoe4d.com/tools/sensory-fieldwork-tool/

highlight how the state of the experiencer can impact their perception. The two prompts are:

Intention: What is your intent while having this experience? What are you focused on doing?
Role: What role are you playing while having this experience?

These prompts are essential for framing the conditions that affect sensory observation. If a student's intention or role does not align with the activity, their attention will be divided, and their entire perception will be compromised.

Following the two pre-sensory questions, users are prompted to enter the sight, touch, smell, taste, and sound stimuli they experience into the tool. The last prompt asks users, "What emotions are you feeling from this experience and beyond it?" directing them to consider how a sensory experience can produce emotions in the experiencer.

I designed this tool in the Spring of 2022 for graduate students in my Experience Design Studio course for the MFA in Experience Design during an on-site "Destination Weekend" class trip to New Orleans, Louisiana, USA, where the weekend's topic was multisensory design. Students used the tool during various experiences as they explored the city together and individually, from attending a jazz concert to visiting an art gallery. Students used highly descriptive words to share their experiences during our final on-site class discussion and in the work they submitted upon returning home after the trip. These reports described the tinkle of glasses in a small jazz club, the glow of neon on puddles in the streets, and the smell of garbage in open trash cans on deserted alleyways. These detailed accounts suggested that students' perceptions and ability to record findings had developed through using the field tool.

6 Conclusion

Designing for experiences can be overwhelming, especially for students just learning this approach. Experience design requires the imagination and craft of a well-trained designer, familiarity with narrative and sequence like a storyteller, and the perceptiveness of a seasoned researcher. As people in our societies value experiences over amassing products and expect useful, usable, and desirable interactions regardless of the service, the demand for experience design will only grow. Our duty as design educators is to equip students with the knowledge, thinking, and skills necessary to design memorable experiences. Like learning a new language, the vocabulary of experiences is new to most students in our design programs. By scaffolding learning through specially designed tools, it is possible to help students speak the language of experiences and become more observant of the world around them.

References

1. Rossman, R.J., Duerden, M.D.: Designing Experiences. Columbia University Press, New York City (2019)
2. Deighton, K.: Some Chief Experience Officers Want to Make Their Jobs Disappear. https://www.wsj.com/articles/some-chief-experience-officers-want-to-make-their-jobs-disappear-11624456801

3. Omale, G.: Gartner Says Nearly 90% of Organizations Now Have a Chief Experience Officer or Chief Customer Officer or Equivalents. https://www.gartner.com/en/newsroom/press-rel eases/2020-02-10-gartner-says-nearly-90--of-organizations-now-have-a-c

4. Schybergson, O.: The CXO Title May Be Temporary, But The Role Will Be Perma-nent. https://www.forbes.com/sites/forbesagencycouncil/2021/08/23/the-cxo-title-may-be-temporary-but-the-role-will-be-permanent/?sh=1888835c109b

5. Zahneis, M.: A New Job Comes to the College Cabinet: Chief Experience Officer. https://www.chronicle.com/article/a-new-job-comes-to-the-college-cabinet-chief-experience-officer

6. Mumford, M.D., Reiter-Palmon, R., Redmond, M.R.: Problem construction and cognition: applying problem representations in ill-defined domains. In: Runco, M.A. (ed.) Problem finding, problem solving, and creativity, pp. 3–39. Ablex Publishing Corporation, Westport (1994)

7. Buchanan, R.: Design research and the new learning. Des. Issues **17**, 3–23 (2001)

8. Gjoko, M.: Research for Designers: A Guide to Methods and Practice. SAGE Publications, Thousand Oaks (2016)

9. Elkins, J.: How to Use Your Eyes. Routledge, Palo Alto (2000)

10. Gilmore, J.H.: Look: A Practical Guide for Improving Your Observational Skills. Greenleaf Book Group, Austin (2016)

11. Haury, D.L.: Fundamental skills in science: observation. ERIC Clearinghouse for Science Mathematics and Environmental Education, Columbus, OH (2002)

12. Levine, H.G., Gallimore, R., Weisner, T.S., Turner, J.L.: Teaching participant-observation research methods: a skills-building approach. Anthropol. Educ. Q. **11**, 38–54 (1980)

13. The Disney Institute, Kinni, T.: Be Our Guest: Revised and Updated Edition: Perfecting the Art of Customer Service. Disney Electronic Content, New York (2011)

14. Knight, J.: High-Impact Instruction: A Framework for Great Teaching. Corwin Press, Thousand Oaks (2012)

15. Kolb, D.A.: Experiential Learning: Experience as the Source of Learning and Development. FT Press, Upper Saddle River (2014)

16. Coxon, I.: Fundamental aspects of human experience: a phenomeno (logical) explanation. In: Benz, P. (ed.) Experience design: concepts and case studies, pp. 11–22. Bloomsbury Academic, London (2015)

17. Dewey, J.: Art as Experience. Penguin, London (2005)

18. Gendlin, E.T.: Experiencing and the Creation of Meaning: A Philosophical and Psychological Approach to the Subjective. Northwestern University Press, Evanston (1997)

19. Norman, D.: Human-Centered Design Considered Harmful. Interactions **12**, 14–19, July, August 2005

20. Sanders, E.B.-N.: converging perspectives: product development research for the 1990s. Des. Manag. Rev. **3**, 49–54 (2010). https://doi.org/10.1111/j.1948-7169.1992.tb00604.x

21. Cross, N.: Designerly Ways of Knowing. Springer, New York City (2006)

22. Desmet, P., Hekkert, P.: Framework of Product Experience. Int. J. Des. **1**, 57–66 (2007)

23. Fiske, S.T., Taylor, S.E.: Social Cognition: From Brains to Culture. SAGE Publications Ltd., Los Angeles (2017)

24. Forlizzi, J., Ford, S.: The building blocks of experience: an early framework for interaction designers. In: Proceedings of the 3rd Conference on Designing Interactive Systems: Processes, Practices, Methods, and Techniques, pp. 419–423. Association for Computing Machinery, New York (2000)

25. Hassenzahl, M.: Experience Design: Technology for All the Right Reasons. Morgan and Claypool Publishers, San Rafael (2010)

26. Janlert, L.-E., Stolterman, E.: Things that keep us busy: the elements of interaction. MIT Press, Cambridge (2017)

27. Jääskö, V., Mattelmäki, T., Ylirisku, S.: The scene of experiences. In: Proceedings of the Good the Bad and the Irrelevant Conference, pp. 341–345. Media Lab at the University of Art and Design Helsinki (2003)
28. Nelson, H.G., Stolterman, E.: The Design Way. Intentional Change in An Unpredictable World. The MIT Press, Cambridge (2012)
29. Norman, D.: The Design of Everyday Things: Revised and Expanded Edition. Basic Books, New York City (2013)
30. Pine, J.B., II., Gilmore, J.H.: The Experience Economy, With a New Preface by the Authors: Competing for Customer Time, Attention, and Money. Harvard Business Press, Boston (2019)
31. Sanders, E.B.-N., Stappers, P.J.: Convivial Toolbox: Generative Research for the Front End of Design. BIS Publishers, Amsterdam (2012)
32. Simon, H.A.: The Sciences of the Artificial. MIT Press, Cambridge (1996)
33. Checkland, P., Scholes, J.: Soft Systems Methodology in Action. Wiley, Hoboken (1999)
34. Ryan, R.M., Deci, E.L.: Self-determination theory and the facilitation of intrinsic motivation, social development, and well-being. Am. Psychol. **55**, 68–78 (2000). https://doi.org/10.1037/0003-066x.55.1.68
35. Ajzen, I.: The theory of planned behavior. Organ. Behav. Hum. Decis. Process. **50**, 179–211 (1991)
36. Deely, J.N.: Basics of Semiotics. Indiana University Press, Bloomington (1990)
37. Peirce, C.S.: Collected Papers of Charles Sanders Peirce. Harvard University Press, Cambridge (1974)
38. de Saussure, F., Baskin, W., Meisel, P., Saussy, H.: Course in General Linguistics. Columbia University Press, New York (2011)
39. Hill Collins, P.: Black Feminist Thought: Knowledge, Consciousness, and the Politics of Empowerment. Routledge, New York (2000)
40. Gibson, J.J.: The Ecological Approach to Visual Perception: Classic Edition. Psychology Press, London (2014)
41. Goffman, E.: The Presentation of Self in Everyday Life. Anchor Books, New York (1959)
42. Heidegger, M.: Being and Time. SUNY Press, Albany (2010)
43. LeCompte, M.D., Schensul, J.J.: Designing and Conducting Ethnographic Research: An Introduction. Rowman Altamira, Lanham (2010)
44. Meadows, D.H.: Thinking in Systems: A Primer. Chelsea Green Publishing, Chelsea (2008)
45. Stone, M.J., Petrick, J.F.: The educational benefits of travel experiences: a literature review. J. Travel Res. **52**, 731–744 (2013). https://doi.org/10.1177/0047287513500588
46. Kolb, A.Y., Kolb, D.A.: Learning styles and learning spaces: enhancing experiential learning in higher education. Acad. Manag. Learn. Educ. **4**, 193–212 (2005). https://doi.org/10.5465/amle.2005.17268566
47. Bruno, N., Pavani, F.: Perception: A Multisensory Perspective. Oxford University Press, Oxford (2018)

Embodied Virtuality: A Method on the Exploration of Sound-Based Virtual Jewellery

Zhilu Cheng[1], Jing Zhao[2(✉)], and Canhe Yang[1]

[1] Beijing Institute of Fashion Technology, Beijing 100029, China
[2] Beijing University of Technology, Beijing 100000, China
zhaojing_milan@163.com

Abstract. Over the past few years, jewellery designers have gotten significantly more skilled at employing digital technology as a method of production. Virtual jewellery has steadily become more prominent across a variety of platforms, serving as a hub for fashion and a design harbinger. The paper investigates the possibility of creating a connection between virtual jewellery and physical space on the embodiment by applying existing digital technology, combining with the study on the sound-based design method of interactively virtual jewellery, and proposing the design methodology model on Data Collection, Technology Construction, Sculpture Generation, Interactive Verification, and System Imposition. The paper provides a verification and iteration process based on the three-tier evaluation value of aesthetics, interaction, and sustainability, which confirms the efficacy of the design results. The study establishes the jewellery space co-created by designers and users to investigate the feasibility of designing jewellery in a digital environment, adhering to the design methodology.

Keywords: Virtual embodiment · Sound-based Technology · Design Methodology

1 Introduction

As more and more jewellery designers use digital technology to create, virtual jewellery has gradually appeared on various fashion platforms. Since the global COVID-19 in the year 2020, jewellers and relevant practitioners have begun to reevaluate the future of jewellery, which has assisted the transition of the jewellery industry to digital. In addition, the jewellery industry has benefited from this transition. Virtual jewellery has gradually developed into the current design trend. It serves as a leading signal of future development because mixed reality has driven design into an essential manner of production. It is common practice for contemporary designers to begin innovating the form and shape of virtual jewellery by beginning with a single technology or method. These designers need to pay more attention to the connection between the body field and the digital space, which disconnects the jewellery from its primary purpose of being worn and makes it challenging to develop a genuinely interactive experience between the work and the viewer.

Therefore, the paper attempts to establish a sound-based virtual jewellery design method based on the existing digital technology, to explore interactive virtual jewellery, trying to connect virtual jewellery and physical space in the embodiment. *Embodiment* is the term that refers to the sense of one's own body and is intimately related to the sense of self [1]. A general framework of an embodiment is provided by the dissociation between body representations [1]. This is done to correct the flaw that digital jewellery has not been directly connected with physical space and improve the development of virtual jewellery.

2   Overview of Virtual Jewellery

2.1   Virtual Technology and Jewellery: Theoretical Research Needs to Expend

Since the 1990s, with the emergence of Internet-based network art and remote communication technology, virtual reality technology (VR) has emerged as the times require, a computer simulation technology that can create and experience a virtual digital world with a strong sense of immersive experience. Augmented reality technology (AR) is derived from virtual reality technology. The term augmented reality (AR) originates from the English term "Augmented Reality", which is a technical means to superimpose virtual content on real space. Subsequently, augmented reality (AR) began to develop rapidly, and its impact on the game and film industry was gradually significant.

Jewellery comes in many variations: reaching from skillfully crafted pieces in extraordinary materials to experimental wearable pieces of art and from emotionally charged heirlooms to mass-produced accessories matching one's outfit. [2] Most definitions contain at least the notion that jewellery is a physical object worn on the human body. Digital jewellery is broadly understood as referring to physical personal adornments and related decorative on-body items that incorporate electronics [3]. Terms such as Computational Jewelry, Smart Jewelry, and Interactive Jewelry are also used, often interchangeably to describe the design space of combining tangible jewellery with physical computing [3]. However, from a theoretical point of view, "Virtual Jewellery" is a new term that has emerged in recent years. There are not nearly enough scholarly articles or research findings on the topics connected to "Virtual Jewelry" because a new phrase has only very recently come into existence. In another word, Virtual jewellery will be the future development trend in fashion and jewellery, but its theoretical research is still in its infancy and needs to be expanded.

2.2   Augmented Reality and Jewelry: Practice Transformation Needs to Deepen

Technology has provided new ways for participants in cultural fields to connect and consume. In fashion, technology and social media platforms such as Instagram play an increasingly central role in the industry, facilitating the literal and figurative consumption of fashion on a newly wide-ranging scale [4]. Augmented reality technology brings new visual experiences and application potential for wearing and provides more possibilities for exploring fashion aesthetics and clothing functions. For example, in May 2011, fashion retailer Topshop demonstrated virtual wearable technology based on Kinect devices to the public. Dress X/Replicant, the world's first digital fashion retail platform, has been studying virtual clothing since 2016. During the epidemic in 2020, luxury brands tried to turn virtual games into fashion display platforms. By 2021, digital fashion will be linked with NFT (Non-homogeneous Token), which is popular in the digital art world. Social media platforms such as Snapchat, Tiktok and Instagram are all closely linked to the development of digital fashion. They have launched AR creation platforms that the public can participate in January 2018, September 2018 and August 2019. The research of augmented reality technology is in the initial stage, but systematic research with an empirical basis and practical value still need improvement.

2.3 Purpose

This paper aims to investigate a novel and exciting creative way of developing original jewellery designs developed by the interaction between humans and computers. There will be accomplished through a practical investigation based on virtual technology and interactive jewellery to broaden the understanding of different body-wearing disciplines and to provide creative methods and research ideas for the academic development of this topic. Jewellery is supplementary to humans; to be more precise: the function of jewellery can be defined as the meaning it adds to the person wearing it and therefore to people in general who recognise its meaning and who can use this for their own benefit or purpose [5]. This endeavour aims to broaden the understanding of different disciplines on the body wearing. The salient feature of digital media is considered a unique form of aesthetics: it is interactive, participatory, dynamic and customizable [6]. The application of digital technology as a medium means that works from production to presentation use entirely digital to display and explore the inherent possibilities of this platform.

The purpose of this paper is to establish a virtual jewellery design method in order to produce output results that include both physical and virtual attributes. These results will be used to provide an aesthetic experience for the design of future jewellery. This is accomplished by constructing a methodology for jewellery within the context of digital sound technology. The design method is based on integrated manufacturing that progresses from low technology to high technology. There is a good chance that in the not-too-distant future, our reality will be described as having "dematerialized." Our body may engage in strategic and physical interaction with the outside environment by utilizing the concept of "Cyborg," which refers to the merger of the human body with technological systems. Because it possesses the attributes of creative exploration, natural adaptation, playful curiosity, and interactive, participatory co-creation, virtual jewellery was selected for the experimental research component of the study. For this reason, the study of jewellery has a relevance that extends beyond simply making improvements to its beauty or functionality. Additionally, it is a form of cognition that can be utilized to construct new material and spiritual ties with other individuals.

The following objectives of the paper are intended to be attained through the investigation of the design process for interactive virtual jewellery:

(1) To investigate the connection between virtual jewellery and actual wearing through virtual technology.
(2) To construct a sound-based virtual jewellery design and evaluation model, as well as perform case analysis.

(3) To discuss how to conduct collaborative innovation through virtual jewellery research and multidisciplinary.

3 Interactive Experiment with Sound

In this experiment, Python is used as the logical language, Open Source Code is used for data transmission, and the programming software Tianwen, Arduino and Blender are used for data transmission. A program is designed to generate jewellery shapes triggered by sound automatically. The work triggers the generation of virtual jewellery through the accurate data generated by the audience's voice interaction in the real space and realizes the virtual wearing and scene display.

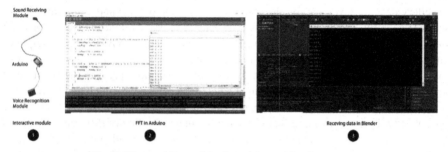

Fig. 1. The workflow of the Sound Interaction Experiment

Tools: Sound Receiving Module, Arduino.

Technology: Fast Fourier Transform, Parametrically generated.

Content: The term 'embodiment' has significant implications for human-computer interaction design, science, and engineering. This perspective of the embodied mind implies that an interface is adequate to the degree that it engages the broad spectrum of the human interactor's embodied cognition and perception resources [7]. According to the understanding of 'embodiment', as seen in Fig. 1, the sound intervention experiment can obtain the parameters of decibel, frequency, and duration, save these data in real time, and upload them to the virtual space to create sound sculptures. This is done based on designers' creation and exploration through the analysis of sound parameters and combining the analysis with the sound from the human body.

Method: The first step is to establish the permissible sound frequency range, which is set between 100 Hz and 10,000 Hz, by connecting the sound receiving module, the sound identification module, and the single-chip microcontroller Arduino (as shown in Fig. 1-1). The frequency can then be adjusted to various ranges, such as 100 Hz–3,000 Hz, 3,000 Hz–7,000 Hz, and 7,000 Hz–10,000 Hz. The collected data can then be transferred to Blender for receiving and bound in the parameters (as shown in Fig. 1-2). The sound receiver can create a sound sculpture as information support for design development using the various behavioral sounds that users emit in front of the device. The sound receiver can store the sound, analyze it in real-time, upload the sound parameters to the three-dimensional space and upload the proper parameters (as shown in Fig. 1-3).

Development: After analyzing the sound sculptures, the experiment will undertake varying degrees of manual intervention to develop product materialization or virtual apparel. Updates will be made synchronously in the interim to improve the virtual space. In order to expand new design concepts and application possibilities, the visual sculpture model display is finally made possible in the virtual environment. In such a scene, the viewer becomes the creator. The number of spatial models will rise as audience interactions increase, generating a virtual and accurate field of interactive co-creation.

4   Interaction Jewelry Integrated with Digital Technology

To begin, as shown in Fig. 2-1, the case use of MSP and Arduino in order to carry out analysis experiments. The following step involves connecting with 3D software compatible with parametric modelling. Next, it performs a functional assessment and a software screening during the sound reception and analysis stage, as illustrated in Fig. 2-2. In Fig. 2-3, the study defined the working mode of connection between Arduino and Blender to ensure that the interactive goal of sound analysis, 3D production, and real-time display can be achieved. The data obtained from the Arduino analyzer is then transferred to the 3D modelling program Blender through the OSC communication protocol. The received data is tied to a node at the Blender port, and the generation can only occur once the essential processes have been completed.

After then, the voice recognition process is carried out. When the audience member speaks the instructions in front of the device, the node function is realized in the programming software, which activates the rapid Fourier transform algorithm to generate the design form in real-time in the three-dimensional software. It occurs when the audience member speaks the instructions. In order to extend the method of inspiring creative ideas based on human-computer interaction, the experimental process conducts the free generation of forms from the path of "Data Collection - Technical Construction - Sculpture Generation." It represents the application of real-time data triggered by sound to generate an infinite number of design forms. It expands the method of inspiring creative ideas based on human-computer interaction. However, the visual 3D model built up to this point is still in its infancy, and more evaluation methods need to be developed so that the data model may be further refined.

Following the acquisition of the model of the sound-generated sculpture, as shown in Fig. 2-4, the complete network will be optimized, the parameters of each node will be bound to the experiment, and the clarification may be executed by the model's size, dimensions, and qualities. The partial node parameters in the three-dimensional model are then organized to be appropriate for the state of the objects, and the proper parameters that are enabled by this technology are bound to other controllable nodes. The design and improvement are derived from "Interactive Verification - Mixing Virtual Reality" through semi-manual intervention, which indicates that the new form generated by the sculpture is evaluated, the infinite design form is generated by real-time data, and the evaluation and optimization methods are established, and the comprehensive creation

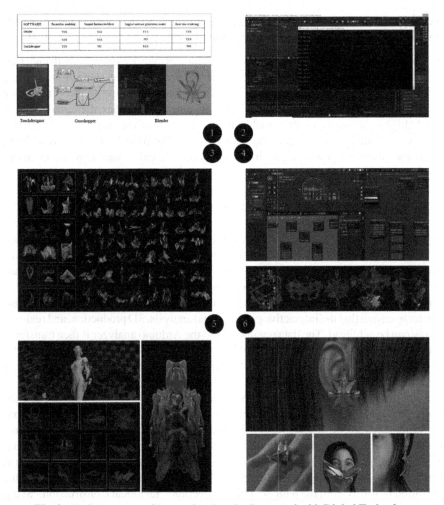

Fig. 2. Design process of Interaction Jewelry Integrated with Digital Technology

from "Object" to "Field" is stimulated. This means that the design and improvement is a semi-manual process.

After that, as illustrated in Fig. 2-5 and Fig. 2-6, the project hosted a co-design workshop in the public area that was physically available. 20 audiences were allowed to participate in interactive behaviour tests, and 100 three-dimensional models were developed based on sound interaction. The database developed in the project's early stages consisted of one hundred sound sculptures. Because of the hand simulation algorithm utilized to construct the form, the sound sculpture created is ideally suited for application in jewellery items. The project also designs a scene in the virtual realm, produces a genuine interaction between reality and virtuality, and allows the audience to try virtual reality by integrating VR goggles as part of the show's props.

In this stage of the experiment, the building of a complete jewellery interaction system based on the "Sound Sculpture-Virtual Field" was brought to a successful conclusion. This system enabled the audience and the device to interact dynamically through sound in the physical space. The outcomes of the interaction, which include the sound sculpture and virtual space created as a result of human-computer interaction, can be seen in real-time through the screen to the free generation of jewellery shapes. Other outcomes of the interaction include the creation of jewellery shapes. Enhanced realism lends the simulation closer to the actual thing regarding sensory authenticity. Enhanced reality is a brand-new interactive technology that embeds virtual jewellery into the physical world to integrate it into the real world seamlessly. Producing a "Super Reality" by inverting the sequence in which digital virtual things and physical objects are formed has produced an experience that integrates virtuality and reality in real-time.

The design project establishes a new method for creating jewellery that is interactive and co-creative. Additionally, through design practice, the project broadens the relationship between virtual jewellery and the actual wearing of the jewellery. It diverges from the traditional labour model for jewellery creation, progressing from "Hand-painted" to "Production". It integrates the gathering and analysis of acoustic data, technical construction, sculptural generation, interactive verification, and the integration of virtuality and reality. According to Honeywell, Advanced Technology Lab states, 'Our preliminary findings from the survey indicate that virtual worlds can positively impact the users' behaviour. Overall, users' engagement during the virtual tour could contribute to learning and the development of lasting positive behaviours within the virtual world, which can, in turn, translate into real-world behaviours [7]'.

When the information contained within the virtual world has become sufficiently rich, the knowledge humans obtain while interacting within the virtual world will affect particular behaviours that occur within the real world. The relationship between real space and virtual space can be thought of as being intricately intertwined. Because the virtual environment is an analogue computer-generated digital context, the audience can engage with the sound, vision, and touch produced by the computer. Information connection is developed due to the data trails left behind by the interactive behaviour of viewers in virtual space, both among viewers and between viewers and designers. The audience's data in the virtual space will be used to establish the design principle of "virtual space to assist people in living better in the real space". The virtual space will establish this principle as a continuation of the natural world and map the audience's real life with appropriate behaviours.

5 Design Method and Evaluation Model

Vision and hearing are just two of the many senses that are part of the body's complex sensory system, which allows us to detect shifts in our surroundings and take in information from the world around us. This perception, which may operate independently, can give a virtual interpretation of the outside environment. A time node, a period, or even real-time can affect people's perceptions of the presented information. In order to include a significant amount of information, it is necessary to develop an effective, virtually interactive jewellery design model structure. Ultimately, the project will generate a creative model basis by utilizing a particular procedure for evaluation and optimization.

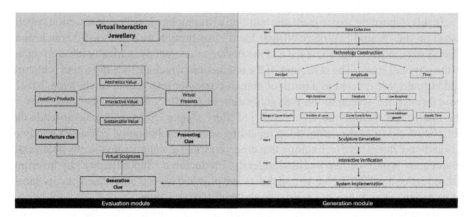

Fig. 3. Design method and evaluation model of Interaction Jewelry

The sound-based virtual jewellery design method and evaluation model is a circular interaction system. This model takes virtual interaction as the technical core, uses sound triggering to generate jewellery forms, and finally completes from physical space (data collection) to virtual space (modelling) and finally back to physical space (manufacturing and display). The design method model consists of two modules, the first part is the generation module, and the second part is the evaluation module. The core process of the generation module is five steps, as shown in Fig. 3, which are "data collection-technology construction-sculpture generation-interactive verification-mixed virtual and real".

After the five steps, the design and application can be divided into "sound sculpture" and "virtual field" corresponding to the entity and virtual through the verification link. The design results are returned to the virtual and real space in the form of jewellery entity and virtual wear, respectively, to form a sound-triggered jewellery form database. Finally, in the evaluation module, the generated models are selected and optimized by three evaluation criteria of "aesthetic value", "interactive value", and "sustainable value", and finally, the model library of solid modelling and virtual modelling is formed.

5.1 Generation Module

In the design generation module of virtual jewellery interaction, as shown in Fig. 3, **the first step** is Sound Data collection, which collects the sound of the audience in the real space through the accessible workshop as the primary database for digital model construction. **The second step** is technology construction; digital generation logic is constructed through the integration and analysis of decibels, amplitude, and time of sound. **The third step** is sculpture generation, that is, free-form generation based on programming language and computer parameters. **The fourth step** is interactive verification, which gives the audience the right to decide on the proper form and encourages them to leave their own "sound sculpture" in a virtual space. **The fifth step** is to mix virtual and accurate, that is, to integrate the mixed virtual and real interactive experience from digital generation, physical manufacturing, and virtual wearing.

5.2 Evaluation Module

In the evaluation module, as shown in Fig. 3, our evaluation of the model is divided into three clues, which are summarized as Generating clue, Manufacturing clue and Presenting clue. The generated model's processing under different natural and virtual space requirements is evaluated and verified. **In Generation clue**, the sound sculpture generated by the audience through interactive behaviour is presented in the virtual space, and the model is presented in the original form of free generation at the design end, which does not have the conditions of the physical product. As a data sculpture, it is stored in the virtual space for the audience to browse during the virtual reality experience. When the audience thinks that the generated shape is consistent with their intentions in **manufacturing clues,** they could choose to produce the model. The sketching, model supplement and 3D printing workflow are used to produce data sculpture. **In the Presenting clue**, the models in the virtual space database are collected, and the valuable content has been presented. The sound sculptures produced by similar sound contents are produced and presented, but not the physical outputs.

In addition, in the evaluation module, the valuable feedback of the generated entity and virtual model is carried out, and finally, the level of the generated model is divided into three values: aesthetic, interactive and sustainable. **The first value corresponds to the aesthetic**, which means that jewellery products bring users an instinctive and intuitive perception of the five senses through shape, colour, material, and other aspects. Jewellery products generated based on sound data can arouse users' aesthetic experience and perception through shape, pattern, colour, and material texture. **The second is interactive value**, which refers to the pleasure virtual jewellery conveys to users through an interactive experience in virtual wearing, interaction, and vision. Its connotation includes creating a virtual wearing experience and arousing sensory perception. **The third value is sustainable**, meaning that virtual jewellery fits people's expectations of life, perception and reflection of materials and time, and sustainable design identity. Through the above three layers of value evaluation, users can select the generated design modelling to a certain extent to select the design modelling in line with their value recognition. The above overall construction is the essential path and creative ideas of the virtual interactive jewellery design method, which is different from the traditional linear design steps.

6   Implementation

The whole process is a circular path, starting from the integrity of the design, from technology introduction to verification output, and then back to the path for technical iteration. Finally, the design application needs to enter the "Jewellery Products" and "Virtual Presents" corresponding to the physical and virtual space through the functional verification link and return the design results to the virtual and real space virtually and materially, respectively. Formation, generation, and performance are the motivating forces in the new design. They, as concepts and processes, begin to condition new design procedures that are uniquely conceptual. To some extent, these conceptual stages - in the establishment of an appropriate morphology for the design- are also non-contextual [8]. The development of digital technology provides a diversity of output results for design. "Virtual Sculpture" means the jewellery entity constructed by material and data in physical space and the virtual form automatically generated by interactive experience in virtual space; "Virtual Presents" refers to the spatial form generated by algorithms in virtual space. The jewellery gradually transforms from the research and application of "known form" to the exploration and innovation of "unknown form", and the virtual jewellery interaction model is the core methodology of its transformation.

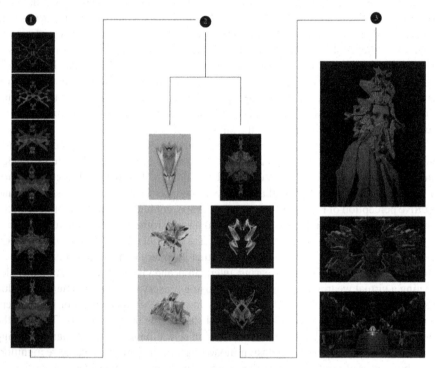

Fig. 4. Design implementation of Virtually Interactive Jewelry

To verify the model, this study invited 20 audiences to use sound to generate the shape through the design method. Finally, it verified the generated design through aesthetic, interactive, and sustainable value. Among them, five viewers chose to produce the generated data sculpture, and six chose to have the static picture of the data sculpture in the grid file of the model. Seven viewers chose to leave the data sculpture in the virtual space and not act on it outside the generation step.

Figure 4 shows that Aesthetic Value refers to the parameterized interactive jewellery. The consequences include mirror image growth, which is subsequently shown in a decorative shape interwoven with intricate lines. According to the feedback, 4 audiences thought the modelling was scientific and technological, and 8 audiences thought the completed sculpture had a visual effect at a high level.

Interactive Value: Interactive parametric jewellery solves the problem that most virtual jewellery cannot interact with the body all the time and breaks the phenomenon that designers occupy the dominant position in determining the jewellery shape in traditional jewellery design. The generation right of modelling is transferred to the audience during the interactive parametric jewellery modelling generation process. This enables the audience to participate in the jewellery design process and experience the conceptual significance of creation while the process is in progress. 8 audiences think that this participatory way of creation is exciting and willing to experience, and 6 audiences think that they can more clearly understand the ideas that the creator wants to express.

Sustainable Value: The generative jewellery design that users can participate in can give the audience a faster and more efficient production experience. Although the process has been simplified in the real-life jewellery creation experience, the audience still needs to carry out the traditional jewellery workflow of sketching, sawing metal, quenching, modelling, and welding, which takes time. It is also easy to appear that the audience's aesthetic ability is different; occasionally, they need help to satisfy themselves and rework the production. Virtual interactive jewellery enables the audience to complete the generation, virtual wearing and display of a single piece of jewellery within one minute. Due to the non-entity and rapid generation of virtual jewellery, the waste of materials and time can be avoided. The audience can repeatedly interact with the device to generate a jewellery shape that can satisfy them. In this process, only part of the electricity and computer power is used, which is more sustainable than the traditional jewellery-making experience. According to statistics, 12 audiences prefer online jewellery creation, believing it is more efficient and aesthetic to create works in this way. Seeing the creation in the virtual space is very meaningful for other audiences. At the same time, it will be a good use of resources.

7 Conclusion

The concept of virtual jewellery is generating a significant amount of interest and has room for development. As a result of the proliferation of science and technology, international collaboration in developing new technologies has been growing steadily. Combining jewellery with virtual interaction technologies unquestionably broadens the scope of a new aesthetic between virtuality and reality. This paper aims to broaden the depth and breadth of the combination of digital art and fashion in the modern digital era by investigating the interdisciplinary nature of digital technology in fashion and the diversity of design methods through practical cases. The investigation combines virtual technology and jewellery and examines other design methods. The study focuses more on the theoretical debate surrounding the use of augmented reality in digital fashion, investigates the construction of virtual reality, and develops a digital style with a unique level of realism. This is done from the standpoint of technology's influence on artistic production. The research also combines theory and practice, which is beneficial for conducting research and producing new products and technologies within interconnected sectors. Additionally, it has value in terms of aesthetics, collaboration, and sustainability. The worldwide COVID-19 will likely lead to the development of new business models in addition to bringing about potential social and economic benefits.

The methodological model, based on the verification of the actual case study results, focuses on researching and exploring the fusion of virtual interaction technology and jewellery design to focus better on the body itself. The model is based on the verification of the results of the actual case study. Whether it was made digitally or through an immersive wearing experience in a virtual space, virtual jewellery should always present a variety of attitudes to the public. This would be the case even if the jewellery were created digitally. The "Dialogue" between the body and the outside world will eventually be served by a return of digital technology to the tactile and kinesthetic senses, which will benefit individuals in their day-to-day lives. In addition, this study combines theory and practice. It provides beneficial help for the research and development of emerging products and new technologies in related fields, which have aesthetic, interactive, and sustainable value. The hope is that it will trigger a new business model in the context of the global pandemic and generate potential socio-economic benefits.

References

1. Longo, M.R., Schuur, F., Kammers, M.P.M., Tsakiris, M., Haggard, P.: What is embodiment? A psychometric approach. Cognition **107**, 3, 978–998 (2008)
2. Versteeg, M., van den Hoven, E., Hummels. C.: Interactive jewellery: a design exploration. In: Proceedings of the TEI 2016: Tenth International Conference on Tangible, Embedded, and Embodied Interaction, pp. 44–52 (2016). https://doi.org/10.1145/2839462.2839504
3. Paul, C.: Digital Art, 3rd edn. (2015) Thames & Hudson Ltd., London
4. Tuite, A.: Communicating material characteristics in a digital age: three case studies in independent fashion. Stud. Commun. Sci. **18**(2), 411–423 (2018). https://doi.org/10.24434/j.scoms.2018.02.014
5. den Besten, L.: On Jewellery: A Compendium of International Contemporary Art Jewellery. Arnoldsche Art Publishers, Stuttgart (2012)
6. Quek, F.: Embodiment and multimodality. In: ICMI 2006: Proceedings of the 8th International Conference on Multimodal Interfaces, pp. 388–390 (2006). https://doi.org/10.1145/1180995.1181067
7. Thiruvengada, H., Derby, P., Foslien, W., Beane, J., Tharanathan, A.: The influence of virtual world interactions toward driving real world behaviors. In: Shumaker, R. (ed.) VMR 2011. LNCS, vol. 6774, pp. 100–109. Springer, Heidelberg (2011). https://doi.org/10.1007/978-3-642-22024-1_12
8. Oxman, R.: Re-thinking digital design. In: Ali, A., Brebbia, C.A. (eds.) Digital Architecture and Construction, pp. 239–247. WIT Press, UK (2006).https://doi.org/10.2495/DARC060241

M-term Architectonic Context and Meditation Practitioners: A Concept to Be Implemented in an Informatic Application to Help Architects

Mário Bruno Cruz[1]([✉]) [iD], Francisco Rebelo[1,2] [iD], and Jorge Cruz Pinto[1]

[1] CIAUD, Research Centre for Architecture, Urbanism and Design, Lisbon School of
Architecture, Universidade de Lisboa, Lisboa, Portugal
mariobrunocruz@yahoo.com
[2] ITI/LARSyS, Universidade de Lisboa, Lisboa, Portugal

Abstract. In the cities of industrialized countries, long-term stress with effects on physical and mental health is considered a problem. Meditation shows effective therapeutic benefits to physical, and in some cases, mental health. There is some neuroscientific evidence, and traditional belief, that certain buildings may induce contemplative experiences. The creation of these buildings by architects might be mainly based in cultural, aesthetic and even poetic assumptions. Assumptions that some-times might be in contradiction to the real needs of its users. We verify the necessity of an approach to determine how medium-term meditation practitioners' behavior could be influenced by the architectural context. Our main objective is to propose the development of a concept for an informatic application that supports architects in planning decisions concerning architectonic contexts for meditation in urban environments. A concept that should allow architects to know which visual, haptic, and other architectonic context features influence medium-term practitioners' meditation. We will meet with the research team to define the variables to study; we will also use an experts' survey and finally search in the literature for architectonic contexts prone to be manipulated. This problem will be addressed in three stages: 1. Understanding the interaction context; 2. Defining the architectonic context variables to be manipulated; 3. Defining the body-mind reactions related with meditation of medium-term practitioners; 4. Proposal for the informatic application. To conclude, we will discuss the positive and negative aspects of this decision sup-port tool, the variables selection, the subtleties of meditation and this model acceptance amongst architects.

Keywords: Creativity · Architecture · meditation · expert systems

1 Introduction

In urban environments of industrialized countries, social and psychological events may cause long-term stress with effects on physical and mental health [29]. Contemplative practices, namely meditation, may show effective therapeutic benefits to physical, and in some cases, mental health. Studies reveal meditation contribution to affective regula-tion, immunologic response, anxiety and stress reduction, better pain tolerance, amongst others [5, 7, 9, 11, 15, 18, 25, 27, 30, 31]. There is some neuro-scientific evidence and traditional belief that certain buildings (e.g. temples and churches) may induce contemplative experiences [1, 2, 6, 8, 12, 14, 17, 22]. The creation of these buildings by architects might be mainly based in cultural, aesthetic and even poetic assumptions. These assumptions are sometimes in contradiction with the real needs of its users. Therefore, we verify the need of a scientific approach to determine how meditation practitioners' behavior is influenced by the architectural context.

Our main objective is to develop an application that would support architects on such planning decisions. This application is an expert system that helps architects to know which visual, auditory, haptic, and other architectonic context features, influence medium-term practitioners' meditation.

This expert system is supported by the *Kansei* method [19–21] to create a predictive model that combines previous architectural variables and user behavior reactions.

2 Methods

Meeting with architects, and meditation and human factors experts, to determine the architectonic context's variables that can affect meditation favorably or unfavorably.

Make use of the 1st part of a survey with experts in meditation done in 2021. It was an online questionnaire with open and closed multiple choice questions to eight experts out of twelve asked to participate. The average age of the participants was 52,25 years old (between 41 and 70 years old); 37,5% were woman and 62,5% were man; with an average of 20 years of meditation practice experience; with diversified kinds of meditation practice (e.g., *Śamatha*, *Vipaśyanā*, Catholic); 87,5% with high education level; from several nationalities (Portuguese, Italian and Spanish). The purpose of this survey was to inquire the characterizes, in meditation rooms, conducive to *Śamatha* practice in Buddhism as practiced in Tibet.

The bibliographic reference related to architecture and meditation where we will search is A Guide to Locations for Cultivating *Samādhi* [24] by Longchen Rabjam Drimé Özer (ཀློང་ཆེན་རབ་འབྱམས་པ་དྲི་མེད་འོད་ཟེར།, 1308–1364). This reference is a quiet stable one, as meditation and its dwellings are seen by this author in very detailed way drawing from his experience as an important meditator in the Tibetan plateau. There are other bibliographic references not used in this article which are pertinent. They were not used to avoid confusing this study. Such references are Julio Bermudez, Externally-induced [sic] meditative states: an exploratory fMRI study of architects' responses to contemplative architecture (2017) [2]; Jeffery S. Poss, Spaces of Serenity: Small Projects for Meditation & Contemplation (2015) [23]; Jose M. Cabeza-Lainez, Lighting Features in Japanese Traditional Architecture (2006) [4]; Jun'ichirō Tanizaki (谷崎 潤一郎, 1886–1965), In Praise of the Shadows (1977) [26].

3 Results

The results will be presented in four stages:

1. Understanding the interaction context.
2. Defining the architectonic context variables to be manipulated.
3. Defining the body-mind reactions related with meditation of medium-term practitioners.
4. Proposal for the informatic application.

3.1 Understanding the Interaction Context

The architectures which might shelter meditation practice in urban contexts are very much still, churches, temples, parks. There has been a crescent interest, in the West, for the eastern meditation techniques. And, as the long-term stress in cities seems to increase, it is possible an emergence of a necessity for urban architectures to practice meditation. Furthermore, we see that the traditional facilities named above, sometimes are not prepared, nor are adequate or even well accepted by non-secular meditation practitioners.

Although we are proposing an expert system to plan architectures for meditation in an urban context (cabins, backyards' huts, and others), we draw our architectonic variables from ideal contexts, like chosen contexts by experts in architecture and meditation or the Tibetan plateau. This idealization of context is expected to be productive and in a sense it is utopic. Like the idealization of cities (Ebenezer Howard, Garden Cities of Tomorrow (1898) [10]) in the end of XIX century, we expect that it might "force" solutions to an ideal perfection.

3.2 Defining the Architectonic Context Variables to Be Manipulated

Table 1 shows the results from the meetings with the investigation team (architects, mediation and human factors experts). In this table, we see the architectonic variables from the research team whose concept is explained by us (column 1); we see the favorable way of planning these characteristics (column 2); and finally, in we see the unfavorable way of conceiving them (column 3). Some ways of building the characteristics are repeated in the second and third column because they are still undetermined and are just hypothetic.

Table 2 shows the results from the 1st part of the survey to architecture and meditation experts. These results correspond the architectonic context's characteristics reported by the study participants (column 1); the way of planning them in a favorable way (column 2); and finally, there were no related unfavorable ways of conceiving them.

Table 1. Variables reported by the research team, and favorable and unfavorable ways of planning them.

Variables from the Research Team	Favorable	Unfavorable
openings to the exterior *openings that frame the exterior landscape*	• wide or small • transparent or opaque	• wide or small • transparent or opaque
proportion *the balance of measures*	• low right foot or high right foot	• low right foot or high right foot
materiality *material elements that constitute form*	• natural	• artificial
landscape views *what we can see framed by the openings to the exterior*	• countryside or sea • sky or vegetation	• countryside or sea • sky or vegetation
sound *what we can hear inside the architectonic form*	• nature or music	• nature or music
smell *what we can smell inside the architectonic form*	• soft or intense	• soft or intense

Table 3 shows the results from the literature search on the variable characteristics that might favor, or not, meditation according to way they are planned. These results correspond the characteristics of the architectonic context found in the literature (column 1); the way of planning them in a favorable way to meditation (column 2); and finally, the unfavorable of conceiving them (column 3).

3.3 Defining the Body-Mind Reactions Related with Meditation of Medium-Term Practitioners

The negative body-mind reactions related with meditation [16] are dullness and excitement. Being dullness, "a dimming or blurring of the object" and excitement, which is distraction, would arise when "the intensity of the focus causes one to be hyper aroused."

Table 4 shows the positive body-mind reactions related with meditation taken from the experts' survey.

Table 5 shows the positive (column 1) and negative (column 2) body-mind reactions taken from the literature.

Table 2. Variables taken from the expert's survey, and favorable ways of planning them.

Variables from the 1st part of the Experts' Survey	Favorable
form *material elements that confine and delimit architectonic space*	• minimal (empty with few objects) • ornamented (some plant)
materiality	• natural (wood, stone)
landscape views	• sky • nature (sea) • any other view
light *what lights up the interior of architectonic form*	• natural • dim
sound	• silence
function *activity that is sheltered by the architectonic form*	• cult or blessed (throughout centuries by great meditators or where masters meditated) temples (or merely temples) • churches • meditation practice room (consecrated or not) • airports • sacred places • any place
context *place where the architectonic form is located*	• natural isolated beautiful places (mountain tops or headlands) • nature

3.4 Proposal for the Informatic Application

The variables corresponding to the properties of the architectural context that can be manipulated, depending on the body-mind's reactions that are intended to be created in meditation practitioners, can be worked on using the *Kansei* method to develop an inference model (references).

The inference engine developed by *Kansei* can be used for the development of expert systems that allow the help of architecture students or professionals in the development of architectural contexts. The above variables can be implemented in computer solutions that can be integrated into two types of solutions, teaching and training of architecture students and support in architectural design.

In the first case, in a computer application that can be used for teaching and training architecture students, during the development of an exercise that involves a project for the practice of meditation. Depending on the type of reaction (body-mind's) that the student intends to provoke in meditation practitioners, the application presents ideas for solutions for architectural contexts that can be developed.

Table 3. Variables taken from the literature, and favorable and unfavorable ways of planning them.

Variables from Longchen Rabjam	Favorable	Unfavorable
form	• simple dwellings • a circular 'dark house' (night-time yoga)	
openings to the exterior	• rocky cave • hollow in the earth • dwelling open at the sides and with a clear view • should have an entrance (yoga of light)	–
materiality	• dwellings made out of [sic] reeds, bamboo or straw (summer) • a building made of stone (autumn)	–
landscape views	• with a broad, unobstructed view onto glaciers, waterfalls, forests or valleys, and the vast and open sky • a clear, inspiring view	–
frequency *the architectonic space's attendance*	• secluded • empty houses, solitary trees [sic] and the like, which are frequented by humans and non-human demons (stable practitioners) • the lands of outcastes, nagas, *nyen*, and local spirits • in (…) a peaceful place, the meditation dwelling should be in solitude • a solitary hut surrounded by a fence	• empt houses, solitary trees [sic] and the like, which are frequented by humans and non-human demons (beginners) • temples and shrines, inhabited by *gyalpo* and *gongpo* spirits • caverns in the earth and such places, haunted by the *senmo* demonesses • solitary trees and other places, which are inhabited by mamos and dakinis • the lands of outcastes, nagas, *nyen*, and local spirits,
temperature *the architectonics' space temperature*	• cooler dwellings and cooler locations (summer) • a region and residence of moderate temperature (autumn) • somewhere warmer at a lower altitude (winter) • buildings with mild and even temperature (spring) • mild in temperature (yoga of light)	–

(*continued*)

Table 3. (*continued*)

Variables from Longchen Rabjam	Favorable	Unfavorable
context	• places which are agreeable to the mind and well suited to the season • the location must be one that is secluded and agreeable, somewhere conducive to spiritual practice in the different seasons • places near to glaciers or on mountaintops and the like • a forest or a mountainside (autumn) • a forest (winter) • the mountains or on the edges of a forest or desert island (spring) • inspiring (…) places which you find uplifting • high among the mountains • snowy regions • forests • below rocky cliffs • on the banks of a river • charnel grounds • by the lakeside, or in meadows, forests [sic] and such places, adorned with beautiful flowers, plants and trees • those which seem frightening and unpleasant at first, but prove agreeable once you have grown accustomed to them • peaceful places are the best • in a high place, and in the middle of the central chamber, • with your pillow to the north, lying down in the posture of nirvana • low-lying and shaded areas, such as forests and ravines • higher regions, such as among snowy mountains • equal of the sacred site of the heart of awakening (*Bodhgaya*, a. n.)	• villages, markets • by the lakeside, or in meadows, forests [sic] and such places, adorned with beautiful flowers, plants and trees • all the areas and dwelling places that seem agreeable at first, but not so once you come to know them • any place in which virtues decline, mental afflictions increase

In a second case, the inference engine developed by *Kansei*, could be integrated into a BIM (Building Information Modelling) module for CAD (Computer Aided Design) tool. The architect involved in the design of a space for meditation can, from body-mind reactions, receive information from the BIM about aspects related to the architectural context (e.g., if the architect wanted to create an environment suitable for a certain combination of body-mind, the openings to the exterior should be of the type small).

Table 4. Positive body-mind's reactions taken from the expert's survey.

Experts' Survey Positive Body-Mind's Expected Reactions
simply to understand better the situations in which I am involved
sometimes to relax
return to present time
tranquility that arises from knowledge of being/consciousness
become aware of my humanity
mental calm
attain liberation
deep insight
intensification of the state of consciousness
be mentally present
to attain liberation
to attain a high level of consciousness and well-being
eradicate fear
remove ignorance veils and see things as they are

Table 5. Positive and negative body-mind's reactions taken from the literature.

Longchen Rabjam Body-Mind's Expected Reactions	
Positive	Negative
[on mountaintops, in secluded forests and on islands and the like, places which are agreeable to the mind and well suited to the season,] cultivate a tranquil samadhi, which is single-pointed and unwavering – clear light, which is free from the slightest conceptual elaboration	[villages, markets, empty houses, solitary trees [sic] and the like, which are frequented by humans and non-human demons,] are distracting for beginners and can bring many obstacles
[high among the mountains] the mind becomes clear and expansive, ideal for refreshing mental dullness and for practicing the generation phase	[temples and shrines, inhabited by *gyalpo* and *gongpo* spirits, can] disturb the mind and incite thoughts of anger and aversion
[snowy regions help] to make samadhi clear and awareness bright and lucid, so for cultivating *Vipaśyanā* they make ideal places with the fewest obstacles	[caverns in the earth and such places, haunted by the *senmo* demonesses, cause] passionate desire to arise and bring excessive dullness and agitation

(*continued*)

Table 5. (*continued*)

Longchen Rabjam Body-Mind's Expected Reactions	
Positive	Negative
[forests bring] stillness of mind and help us to develop mental stability, so they are ideal places for cultivating *Śamatha* with a sense of ease	[solitary trees and other places, which are inhabited by mamos and dakinis, contribute, it is believed, to] mental turmoil and bring all manner of obstacles
[below rocky cliffs we can] feel a vivid sense of impermanence and disenchantment, clear and inspired, helping us to achieve the union of *Śamatha* and *Vipaśyanā*	[the lands of outcastes, nagas, *nyen*, and local spirits, by the lakeside, or in meadows, forests and such places, adorned with beautiful flowers, plants and trees, (…),] but later prove disruptive
[on the banks of a river,] our attention becomes well focused, and the wish to escape samsara comes rapidly and afresh	[all the areas and dwelling places that seem agreeable at first, but not so once you come to know them, are sites of] lesser accomplishment
[charnel grounds are powerful places for] swift accomplishment, ideal for the generation or completion phases	[magnetizing places, where] mind feels captivated and develops attachment
[villages, markets, empty houses, solitary trees and the like, which are frequented by humans and non-human demons, (…) for stable practitioners,] they are a support, regarded as supreme	[wrathful places, where] mind is disturbed by feelings of fear and dread
[the lands of outcastes, nagas, *nyen*, and local spirits, by the lakeside, or in meadows, forests and such places, adorned with beautiful flowers, plants and trees, are] pleasant enough at first	[any place in which] virtues decline, mental afflictions increase, and one is overcome by distractions and the affairs of this life, is a demonic haunt of evil actions
[those (places) which seem frightening and unpleasant at first, but prove] agreeable once you have grown accustomed to them, are powerfully transformative, bringing great accomplishments without obstacle	
[peaceful places, where] mind naturally becomes focused and still	
[expansive places,] delighting the mind, which are awesome and inspiring	
for samadhi, [peaceful places are the best]	
[in (…) a peaceful place, the meditation dwelling should be in solitude, as this will suit] the development of concentration in the mind. [The ideal dwelling is one that is open at the sides and has a clear view]	

(*continued*)

Table 5. (*continued*)

Longchen Rabjam Body-Mind's Expected Reactions	
Positive	Negative
[the location for practicing the yoga of light during the daytime, should be mild in temperature and should have an entrance with a broad, unobstructed view onto glaciers, waterfalls, forests or valleys, and the vast and open sky, so that] mind becomes clear and bright	
[when cultivating *Śamatha*, a solitary hut surrounded by a fence is the ideal place for] stillness of mind naturally to arise	
for *Vipaśyanā*, [it is important to have a clear, inspiring view, and to be constantly cheerful and well attuned to the seasons]	
[low-lying and shaded areas, such as forests and ravines, are ideal for] practising *Śamatha*	
[higher regions, such as among snowy mountains, are] ideal for *Vipaśyanā*	
[any region or actual dwelling place for retreat, in which] renunciation and disenchantment arise, attention is well focused, and samadhi grows in strength – any such place of virtuous activity – is said to be the equal of the sacred site of the heart of awakening (*Bodhgaya*, a. n.)	

4 Conclusions

To conclude, we will discuss the positive and negative aspects of this decision support tool, the problems of the variable's selection, the subtleties of meditation and this model acceptance.

Positive aspects would be to allow the integration of data about the real users of meditation spaces in an efficient way; to turn architects decisions more efficient, as spending a lot of time gathering information and studying about how to plan these facilities would not be necessary; to help to justify planning options to the client and finally it might be an interesting tool for architecture students. On the other way, this tool negative aspects or limitations might be its dependence from the *Kansei* survey volunteers who answer the question, as if they do not have any experience of meditation, the answers will not be the most adequate; the choice of the variables (characteristics of the architectural context), as if it will not be well done and justified, we might get irrelevant results; the difficulty of choice of the *Kansei* words that are related to body-mind reactions associated with meditation.

Moreover, we must take into account that what would inspire us today might do the opposite tomorrow, as our humor is very instable and dependent, from a Buddhist point of view [13]. So that what we choose to build might result today but not function so well tomorrow. On our favor we have the conviction with Alain de Botton [3], that a great part of the world is against our most cherished comfort zone. And we need a refuge to shelter our states of mind and our visions of happiness.

Another aspect to consider is that long term practitioners might not be so affected by the architectonic context [16–28], as medium-term practitioners. And short-term practitioners might be prone to not be yet able to sustain a stable state of mind.

We will conduct a survey amongst the architects' population to explore this expert system acceptance, to know better its viability for commercial use.

Glossary

Śamatha from Sanskrit समाधान (samādhāna) (śamatha) meaning "tranquility" and "concentration" (referring to Buddhist meditation) or "equality". (Source Wiktionary)

Vipaśyanā (Sanskrit, vipashyana) is commonly translated as "insight," and this is a good fit for both its literal and general meanings. (Source Tricycle)

Samādhi (Sanskrit: "total self-collectedness") in Indian philosophy and religion, and particularly in Hinduism and Buddhism, the highest state of mental concentration that people can achieve while still bound to the body and which unites them with the highest reality. (Source Britannica)

nagas (in Indian mythology) a member of a semi-divine race, part human, part cobra in form, associated with water and sometimes with mystical initiation. (Source Oxford Languages)

nyen the spirits that reside in rocks and trees are called nyen (gnyan); they are often malicious, and Tibetans associate them with sickness and death. (Source Google) *gyalpo* is also the name for a certain type of 'arrogant king-like spirit', who are often associated with a particular area or even a particular family; they may function as protectors, or they may be harmful. (Source Rigpawiki)

gongpo are male, female ('gong mo'), and children ('gong phrug'). They are said to be hostile to the rulers of Tibet, and their evil influence has to be regularly transferred to substitute offerings (glud). (Source Google)

senmo the above-mentioned demoness is referred to as "she-demon" ("罗刹女"), or senmo (srin mo སྲིན་མོ) in Tibetan. (Source Google)

mamos are unenlightened aspects of the feminine principle. In Tibetan Buddhism the insight or prajna possessed by both men and women is seen as an aspect of the feminine principle. Mamos become enraged when people lose touch with their own intelligence, and therefore with reality. (Source Google)

dakinis means "sky dweller" or "sky dancer," and is the most sacred aspect of the feminine principle in Tibetan Buddhism, embodying both humanity and divinity in feminine form. (Source Google)

Final note and acknowledgement. This work is financed by national funds through FCT – Fundação para a Ciência e a Tecnologia, I.P., under the Strategic Project with the references UIDB/04008/2020 and UIDP/04008/2020.

TI-LARSyS FCT Pluriannual fundings 2020–2023 (UIDB/50009/2020).

References

1. Bergmann, S.: Theology in Built Environments. Transaction Publishers, New Brunswick, NJ (2012)
2. Bermudez, J., et al.: Externally-induced [sic] meditative states: an exploratory fMRI study of architects' responses to contemplative architecture. Front. Architect. Res. **6**(2), 123–136 (2017). https://doi.org/10.1016/j.foar.2017.02.002
3. de Botton, A.: A Arquitetura da felicidade. Lisbon, D. Quixote (2009)
4. Cabeza-Lainez, J.M., Saiki, T., Almodovar-Melendo J.M., Jiménez-Verdejo, J.R.: Lighting features in Japanese traditional architecture. In: PLEA2006 – The 23rd Conference on Passive and Low Energy Architecture, Geneva, Switzerland (2006)
5. Carlson, L.E., Ursuliak, Z., Goodey, E., Angen, M., Speca, M.: The effects of a mindfulness meditation-based stress reduction program on mood and symptoms of stress in cancer out-patients: 6-month follow-up. Support. Care Cancer **9**(2), 112–123 (2000). https://doi.org/10.1007/s005200000206
6. Eliade, M.: The Sacred and The Profane – The Nature of Religion. Harcourt Brace and World, New York (1959)
7. Grant, J.A., Courtemanche, J., Rainville, P.: A non-elaborative mental stance and decoupling of executive and pain-related cortices predicts low pain sensitivity in Zen meditators. Pain **152**(1), 150–156 (2011). https://doi.org/10.1016/j.pain.2010.10.006
8. Hejduk, R., Williamson, J.: The Religious Imagination in Modern and Contemporary Architecture: A Reader. Taylor & Francis, New York (2011)
9. Hölzel, B.K., et al.: Mindfulness practice leads to increases in regional brain gray matter density. Psychiatry Res. **191**(1), 36–43 (2011). https://doi.org/10.1016/j.pscychresns.2010.08.006
10. Howard, E.: Garden Cities of Tomorrow. Swan Sonnenschein & Co., Lda, London (1902)
11. Jacobs, T.L., et al.: Intensive meditation training, immune cell telomerase activity, and psychological mediators. Psychoneuroendocrinology **36**(5), 664–681 (2011). https://doi.org/10.1016/j.psyneuen.2010.09.010
12. Jones, L.: The Hermeneutics of Sacred Architecture. Kazi Publications, Chicago (2016)
13. Khyentse, D.J.: Não é para a felicidade: Um guia para as chamadas práticas preliminares. Padmakara, Lisbon (2021)
14. Kieckhefer, R.: Theology in Stone: Church Architecture from Byzantium to Berkeley. Oxford University Press, New York (2004)
15. Lutz, A., Brefczynski-Lewis, J., Johnstone, T., Davidson, R.J.: Regulation of the neural circuitry of emotion by compassion meditation: effects of meditative expertise. PLoS ONE **3**(3), e1897 (2008). https://doi.org/10.1371/journal.pone.0001897
16. Lutz, A., Dunne, J.D., Davidson, R.J.: Meditation and the Neuroscience of Consciousness: An Introduction. The Cambridge Book of Consciousness. Cambridge University Press, Cambridge (2012)
17. Mann, A.T.: Sacred Architecture. Element Books, Rockport, MA (1993)
18. Moore, A., Malinowski, P.: Meditation, mindfulness [sic] and cognitive flexibility. Conscious. Cogn. **18**(1), 176–186 (2009). https://doi.org/10.1016/j.concog.2008.12.008
19. Nagamachi, M., Lokman, A.M.: Innovations of Kansei Engineering. CRC Press, Taylor & Francis Group, Milton Park, Oxfordshire (2011)
20. Nagamachi, M. (ed.): Kansei/Affective Engineering. CRC Press, Taylor & Francis Group, Milton Park, Oxfordshire (2011)
21. Nagamachi, M.: Home applications of Kansei engineering in Japan: an overview. Gerontechnology **15**(4), 209–215 (2016). https://doi.org/10.4017/gt.2016.15.4.005.00
22. Norberg-Schulz, C.: Meaning in Western Architecture. Rizzoli, New York (1974)

23. Poss, J.S.: Spaces of Serenity: Small Projects for Meditation & Contemplation. ORO Editions, China (2015)
24. Rabjam, L.: A Guide to Locations for Cultivating *Samādhi*. Lotsawa House Homepage. https://www.lotsawahouse.org/tibetan-masters/longchen-rabjam/locations-cultivating-samadhi. Accessed 24 Jan 2023
25. Tang, Y.-Y., Hölzel, B.K., Posner, M.I.: The neuroscience of mindfulness meditation. Nat. Rev. Neurosci. **16**, 312 (2015). https://doi.org/10.1038/nrn3916
26. Tanizaki, J.: In Praise of the Shadows. Leete's Island Books, USA (1977)
27. Thompson, R.W., Arnkoff, D.B., Glass, C.R.: Conceptualizing mindfulness and acceptance as components of psychological resilience to trauma. Trauma Violence Abuse **12**(4), 220–235 (2011). https://doi.org/10.1177/1524838011416375
28. Wallace, B.A.: The Buddhist tradition of Samatha: methods for refining and examining consciousness. J. Conscious. Stud. **6**(2–3), 175–187 (1999)
29. Wilkinson, R., Marmot, M.: Social Determinants of Health: The Solid Facts, 2nd edn. World Health Organization (2003)
30. Williams, K.A., Kolar, M.M., Reger, B.E., Pearson, J.C.: Evaluation of a wellness-based mindfulness stress reduction intervention: a controlled trial. Am. J. Health Promot. **15**(6), 422–432 (2001). https://doi.org/10.4278/0890-1171-15.6.422
31. Zeidan, F., et al.: Mindfulness meditation-based pain relief employs different neural mechanisms than placebo and sham mindfulness meditation-induced analgesia. J. Neurosci. **35**(46), 15307–15325 (2015). https://doi.org/10.1523/JNEUROSCI.2542-15.2015

Construction and Practice of "Lean" Teaching Mode
Take Fashion Design Course as an Example

RuiTong Gao[1,2(✉)]

[1] Shandong University of Arts and Design, No. 1255, College Road, Changqing District, Jinan, China
31808866@qq.com

[2] Sejong University, 209, Neungdong-ro, Gwangjin-gu, Seoul, Gunja-dong, South Korea

Abstract. Lean thinking originated from the lean production mode of Toyota Motor Company in Japan. Now, as a concept and thinking mode, lean thinking has been applied to many industries. This paper studies and draws on the concept of "lean", and puts forward a results-oriented "lean" teaching mode in view of the problems existing in the current teaching mode of fashion design courses, such as the low utilization rate of teaching resources, the inaccurate measurement of learning achievement, the lack of systematic setting of curriculum system, and the difficulty of integrating innovative design with real life. This teaching model is based on the concept of "lean", takes the curriculum system, curriculum content, teaching form, and curriculum evaluation as the four basic elements of curriculum construction, and reversely designs the curriculum system based on results. The current design curriculum has been systematically planned, integrated and restructured, breaking the traditional curriculum content framework of division and separation, and building a "lean" teaching model with the characteristics of simplified model, high resource utilization, strong relevance, and accurate evaluation. Through the construction and implementation of the "lean" teaching mode of fashion design course, it is verified that the "lean" teaching mode can effectively improve the efficiency of innovative practice teaching. The practice shows that the "lean" teaching mode can meet the needs of talent training of fashion design specialty, improve the setting of professional curriculum system, reduce the waste of teaching resources, improve the degree of achievement of students' learning, and improve the quality of talent training, with a view to providing theoretical framework, empirical model and paradigm guidance for the reform of undergraduate teaching mode of fashion design specialty in art colleges.

Keywords: Lean Thinking · Teaching Mode · Fashion Design Course · Construction

1 Introduction

On April 4, 2019, the Ministry of Education issued the Notice on the Implementation of the "Double Ten Thousand Plan" for the Construction of First-class Undergraduate Majors [1], which planned the target orientation and focus of the development of higher education in the new era. On October 30, 2019, the Ministry of Education issued the Implementation Opinions on the Construction of First-class Undergraduate Courses [2], pointing out that courses are the core elements of talent cultivation, and the quality of courses directly determines the quality of talent cultivation. We must deepen the reform of education and teaching, and implement the results of the reform into curriculum construction [3]. On January 11, 2023, the People's Daily issued an article that pointed out that China's higher education has entered the popularization stage, the construction of new agricultural, medical and liberal arts has continued to deepen, the organizational model of talent training has continued to innovate, and innovation and entrepreneurship education has led the world [4]. As an important way to cultivate fashion talents, the course teaching of fashion design specialty has become an important topic in the teaching reform. In general, the curriculum exploration of fashion design has initially formed a diversified teaching system:

1.1 Curriculum Construction Mode of School-Enterprise Joint Training

The fashion design specialty has always attached importance to the practical teaching mode of school-enterprise combination, and established the practice base and flexible school-enterprise combination talent training mode according to its own professional characteristics and advantages. Many scholars have discussed this kind of curriculum construction mode, such as "Research on Teaching Mode under the Background of School-Enterprise Cooperative Education – Taking the Course of Molding Knitwear Design as an Example" [5], "Teaching Reform of Fashion Design Course Based on the Practical Teaching of School-Enterprise Cooperative Studio Project" [6], etc. However, most of them are based on case studies of school-enterprise courses, and the theme of the demonstration has not yet broken through the barriers of traditional teaching models. In the form of teaching, the emphasis is on indoctrination and the light is on guidance, and students are basically in a passive acceptance position.

1.2 Multi-disciplinary and Multi-disciplinary Curriculum Design Mode

In order to meet the needs of the cultivation of compound applied talents and improve the innovative thinking and ability of students, some achievements, such as "Teaching Research on the Combination of College Aesthetic Education and Excellent Traditional Culture – Taking the Course of Fashion Design as an Example" [7], integrate traditional culture into professional courses. At the same time, the fashion design specialty began to establish a joint training platform with other professional teachers to explore cross-professional and interdisciplinary knowledge. These cross-integration achievements have initially touched the connotation of the construction of "first-class specialty", and have a certain guiding role for the research of this topic.

1.3 Special Research on the Practical Course of Fashion Design

Fashion design is an important specialty leading the social fashion and cultural trend, and its particularity determines its strong practicality. The academic circles discussed the necessity, principle and path of the practical course of fashion design. According to the Exploration of Educational Reform Path of Fashion Design Practice Course [8], the fashion design practice course is divided into basic, professional and subject practice courses. Based on the training of students' practical ability, the Research on the Innovation-Driven Practical Teaching Model of Art and Design Courses by Innovation-driven has constructed a teaching model combining theory with social practice [9]. In addition, there are also scholars who discuss and analyze the standards and effects of fashion design curriculum reform.

Looking at the above studies, we can find that although these studies have initially abandoned the ideas and methods of traditional curriculum concepts, there are still problems. For example, we can only see a single element of the curriculum, but not the multi-dimensional, pluralistic and two-way curriculum paradigm. There are still many gaps between this and the first-class curriculum construction standards, and the future curriculum construction needs to work on "accurate teaching". Therefore, this study focuses on the classroom teaching of fashion design, aiming to explore the effective way of all-round and multi-dimensional "lean" classroom teaching, and then construct the "lean" teaching mode to achieve the goal of curriculum construction.

2 Construction of "Lean" Teaching Mode

Lean thinking originated from the lean production mode of Toyota Motor Company in Japan [10]. Now, as a concept and thinking mode, lean thinking has been applied to many industries. This paper studies and draws on the concept of "lean", based on the current situation of design education and design industry development in China's colleges and universities, in view of the problems existing in the current teaching mode of art fashion design courses, such as the low utilization rate of teaching resources, the inaccurate measurement of learning achievement, the lack of systematic setting of curriculum system, and the difficulty in integrating innovative design with real life, a results-oriented "lean" teaching model with the characteristics of simplification, high resource utilization, strong relevance, and accurate evaluation is proposed, which focuses on promoting "quality construction", takes industrial demand as the orientation, and aims at cultivating application-oriented and compound innovative design talents.

The core of the "lean" teaching mode is to transform the traditional "flooding" teaching mode into a "lean curriculum" teaching mode with student-centered, problem-oriented, quality-centered, school-enterprise inter-school linkage and collaborative innovation, at the same time, we should continue to improve and innovate in the teaching process, explore the connection mechanism between college design talent training and social needs, let design education burst into vitality, and effectively improve the quality of talent training. Through the research on the curriculum subject, curriculum content, curriculum link design, and curriculum evaluation during the implementation of curriculum construction, the "lean" education model is constructed (see Fig. 1).

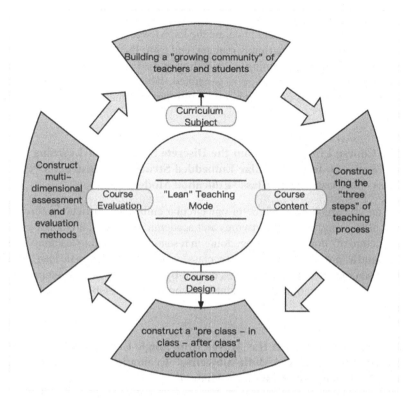

Fig. 1. Construction of "lean" teaching mode

2.1 The Main Body of the Curriculum Changes from Single to Multiple, and Constructs the "Growth Community" of Teachers and Students

The "lean" education teaching model tries to break the barriers of region, time and space, discipline and specialty, and build a multi-dimensional learning and research community, by establishing the dialogue relationship between students and teachers in different dimensions, we can build the multiple subjects of the curriculum structure. The subjects are the driving force and source of growth for each other. The multi-agent curriculum structure takes curriculum as the platform and innovation as the driving force. Teachers and students realize energy exchange and circular interaction in a diversified, multi-dimensional and multi-level coordination relationship, to obtain inexhaustible growth impetus and source, thus forming a "growth community".

2.2 The Content of the Course Changes from Fragmentation to Comprehensiveness, and Constructs a "Three-Step" of the Teaching Process

Systematically sort out the curriculum knowledge system, understand the discipline classification and existing form of the knowledge system, and then explore the relationship between the scientific nature and value of knowledge in the implementation of classroom teaching. In particular, we should integrate the knowledge of the new proposition of the development of the times in a timely manner, and form the three stages of "knowledge reserve – expansion and deepening – innovation and advancement", finally, a curriculum paradigm with universal value is generated, which provides a logical approach to reconstruct a first-class curriculum with multi-dimensional and dynamic knowledge system.

2.3 The Course Links Move from the Discrete Structure of Learning and Research to the Circular Embedded Structure, Construct a "Pre Class – in Class – After Class" Education Model

Through the construction of a three-in-one circular embedded curriculum ecosystem of "theoretical learning, practical activities and academic research", a circular communication structure of "doing in learning, doing in research, and feeding teaching" has been formed. Build a "pre class – in class – after class" whole process heuristic lean "education model to overcome a series of problems caused by the closed-loop development of the curriculum, fundamentally cultivate students' comprehensive ability to solve complex problems.

2.4 Curriculum Evaluation Has Moved from Single Evaluation to "Multiple, Multi-dimensional and Multi-subjective" Evaluation, and Constructed a Multi-dimensional Evaluation Method

Pay attention to the characteristics and benefits of evaluation, and build a process-based evaluation method of mutual evaluation, self-evaluation, expert evaluation and project enterprise evaluation, at the same time, the Internet-based social evaluation is introduced to encourage personality development, allow continuous improvement, further expand and deepen the curriculum structure, and promote the effectiveness of the dissemination of curriculum knowledge.

In short, the construction of the "lean" teaching model focuses on the goal of educating people, and takes curriculum system, curriculum content, teaching form and curriculum evaluation as the basic elements of curriculum construction, focus on the improvement of teaching quality and explore diversified "lean" teaching mode.

3 Implementation and Effect of "Lean" Teaching Mode in Fashion Design Course Teaching

3.1 Project Background of Teaching Mode Implementation

It is pointed out in the Guiding Opinions on the Development of China's Clothing Industry during the "Fourteenth Five-Year Plan" and the Vision for 2035 [11]. "Focusing on the construction of a powerful fashion country, we should improve the talent training mechanism, promote the construction of a cross-industry, cross-industry and cross-field talent team, focus on cultivating fashion design masters who represent Chinese fashion, have distinctive style and have market influence, and vigorously promote the cultivation of a large and innovative high-skilled talent team." The clothing industry has entered a new era of comprehensive transformation, upgrading and development, a large number of garment enterprises have gradually shifted from simple processing to an integrated business model of product design, production and sales, more and more garment enterprises focus on cultural creativity, scientific and technological progress and innovative development of business models, and have higher requirements for talents' innovative ability and comprehensive quality. Based on this, the College of Fashion, Shandong Academy of Arts and Crafts revised the "Undergraduate Clothing and Fashion Design Professional Credit System Talent Training Program" in 2022, which clarified the training objectives, teaching direction and curriculum of fashion design talents in the new era, training high-quality application-oriented clothing professionals has become the core purpose of the current teaching system. Taking the course of fashion design as an example, this paper explores the construction and practice of teaching mode under the concept of "lean" education.

3.2 Specific Implementation Plan

The implementation of the "lean" teaching mode of fashion design course is results-oriented, and the teaching links and curriculum system are reversely designed according to the teaching objectives and the direction of school-enterprise cooperation, design teaching process with Feynman learning method, carry out systematic planning, integration and reorganization, arrangement and implementation, monitoring and evaluation of the current design curriculum, the specific implementation is carried out in three stages (knowledge reserve stage, expansion and deepening stage, and innovation and upgrading stage). Taking a professional course of fashion design in 2022 as an example, this paper expounds the specific implementation plan of "lean" teaching from four aspects: course subject, course content, course link design, and course evaluation (see Fig. 2).

Construct the Curriculum Subject. In terms of building the curriculum subject, this semester's course cooperates with Shandong Fushan Group, a school uniform enterprise, and introduces corporate tutors, at the same time, it breaks the limitation of separate teaching for clothing engineering and design majors, with teachers from different professional backgrounds and professional titles working together to teach and discuss, students from two professional backgrounds work together to complete the course tasks, break the barriers of region, time and space, and specialty, and build a multi-dimensional learning and research community. To enable teachers and students, schools and enterprises, students and students to realize communication and cooperation in a diversified, multi-dimensional and multi-level coordination relationship, the teacher-student community aims to solve the contradiction between the professional structure and individual limitations of teachers and the cultivation of compound and innovative talents by achieving the mutual benefit of teaching and learning while acquiring knowledge.

Build Course Content. In the construction of course content, due to the phased characteristics of the curriculum, the content of the previous courses was characterized by fragments, the "lean" teaching model reversely designs the course content based on the course results, through school-enterprise cooperation and practical project training, the course content is from fragmentation to integrity and comprehensiveness. At the same time, the training project focuses on the needs of industrial development and social development in the new era, in the specific implementation, teachers and students formed three stages of "knowledge reserve – expansion and deepening – innovation and upgrading" around the proposition through research, data collation, discussion, grouping, direction determination, continuous deepening and multi-party collaborative innovation, and continued to evolve to generate the final plan, which was incubated by enterprises. The teaching content designed in the reverse direction from the project training aims to form a multi-dimensional and dynamic knowledge system and curriculum paradigm with universal value by combing and constructing the "three steps" of the teaching process.

Course Design. In the design of curriculum links, according to the three stages of the course content ("knowledge reserve – expansion and deepening – innovation and advancement"), the learning list is listed separately, and each stage takes "theoretical study, practical activities and academic research" as the trinity of the course discussion method, according to the accurate course schedule and the task list of "pre class – during class – after class", build a linked education model. It is intended to fundamentally cultivate students' comprehensive ability to actively explore knowledge, solve complex problems and carry out innovative design, the specific design of course links at each stage is as follows:

Lean Drip Irrigation in Knowledge Storage Stage: Problem-Oriented. Before class: the teacher should make a list of questions and tasks, and attach high-quality online teaching resources and reference books to guide students to self-study, self-inspection and self-inspection; students should make a list of questions and points of interest according to the self-study content, and expand the reading of the points of interest at the same time.

In class: teachers change into tutors, and classes change into lecture halls. Students will talk about themselves, discuss in groups, and teachers and students will discuss and check problems together.

After class: the teacher makes a list of tasks to guide students to expand and deepen their knowledge and interest points.

Lean Drip Irrigation in the Expansion and Deepening Stage: Guided by Actual Projects. Before class: the teacher and the industry tutor are connected to discuss the project proposition; Students conduct market research and industry analysis.

In the class: the industry tutor enters the class, and the students report the survey in groups, and propose the project design plan. The three parties jointly discuss industry problems, guide students to find problems and propose different solutions.

After class: students deepen the design scheme, find out the feasibility basis of the scheme, and discuss the design method and expression form through interdisciplinary combination.

Lean Drip Irrigation in the Advanced Stage of Innovation: Provide Classified Guidance for Design Creativity and Encourage Individual Development. Before class: teachers and students use the Internet, new media and other tools to achieve real-time communication, real-time discussion, and help and guide students to complete the design scheme.

In class: students report the project plan, the inter-school experts come into the classroom, and "five in one" with industry tutors, course teachers, students of this major, and cross-major students, to discuss together, collide with each other in thinking, and innovate cooperatively.

After class: through social practice, project service, innovation and entrepreneurship and other independent activities, achieve the purpose of applying what is learned and making use of what is learned.

Course Evaluation. In terms of curriculum evaluation, we should reform the traditional performance evaluation system, according to the teaching links of the course, the learning tasks are classified and commented, discussed and feedback, problem diagnosis and continuous improvement are carried out in stages, and a diversified and multi-agent evaluation model is constructed. The final score proportion is: mutual evaluation of students and students accounts for 20% of the total score, self-evaluation accounts for 10%, expert evaluation accounts for 20%, project enterprise evaluation accounts for 30%, and teacher evaluation accounts for 10%, the introduction of Internet-based social evaluation accounts for 10%, while allowing continuous improvement and focusing on gainful evaluation. The specific implementation of the curriculum review is intended to effectively supervise and evaluate the learning effect, thus promoting the learning quality, further expanding and deepening the curriculum structure, and promoting the dissemination of curriculum knowledge and teaching results.

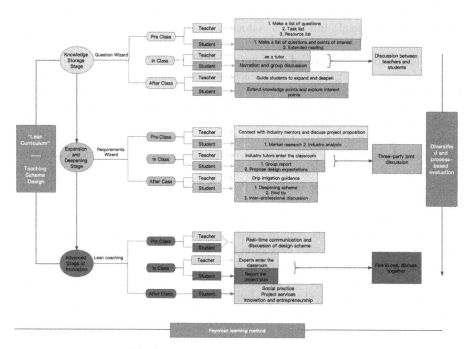

Fig. 2. "Lean" teaching implementation plan

3.3 Practical Effect

"Lean" course construction and cooperation with Hongguan Qipao (Suzhou Congran Clothing Co., Ltd.), Shandong Fushan Group and Yantai Tianhong Needle Textile Co., Ltd, the student team and the tutor team jointly participate in the research and development of new products of fashion design, and the school-enterprise cooperation carries out the incubation, promotion and operation of online brands. The "lean" concept teaching model, which is results-oriented and accurately meets the needs of the industry, has achieved remarkable results in the implementation process.

The student-centered "lean" teaching model has awakened students' subjective consciousness and greatly improved students' practical ability, creative ability and comprehensive application ability. Relying on the course results, 20 of the 46 students in the class were shortlisted in the 2022 "Xianxia Cup" National College Student Fashion Design Competition, in the final competition, 17 people won the prize, including one first prize and one second prize in the professional clothing category, and one first prize of network popularity; Two first prizes and one second prize for uniforms; The first prize of the school uniform category is 10, and the second prize is 1. Four instructors of the course won the Best Instructor Award, and the course partner "Tianhong Needle Textile Co., Ltd." won the first prize. In addition, the course work "Qi Yun", developed in cooperation with Suzhou Congran Clothing, won the excellent prize in the first "Revitalizing Traditional Crafts – Luban Cup" competition; The works of 7 students were included in the 2022 Yearbook of Contemporary Chinese College Students' Art Works; The works of three students won the provincial first prize of the 16th College Student Scientific and Technological Academic Innovation Achievement of Shandong University of Arts & Design.

The "growth community" of teachers and students built under the "lean" teaching mode aims at improving the quality of teaching and learning, and effectively meets the needs of the industry, while enhancing the employment and entrepreneurship abilities of students majoring in fashion design, the teaching and scientific research abilities of teachers have been comprehensively improved. Three projects of the teaching team have been approved for the provincial educational reform project; Two international invention patents were approved; The team teacher won the provincial excellent instructor award; The works of teachers and students were exhibited at the "Third China International Tourism Expo" in 2022; The textbook "Procedures and Methods of Fashion Design" was approved by China Textile Press.

In short, during the implementation of the "lean" teaching mode, a new mode of fashion design education with the core of improving teaching quality has been established; A new model of fashion design education has been established, in which schools and enterprises, teachers and students, and students cooperate to educate people; Establish a new teaching evaluation method of mutual promotion between teachers and students. Make teaching closely related to the industry, the quality of design teaching meet the needs of social development, and help the fashion design industry to cultivate complex and innovative high-quality talents.

4   Conclusion

The construction of the "lean" teaching model has broken the traditional teaching-centered "flooding", focus on the improvement of student-centered learning quality, Pay attention to the improvement of students' cognitive ability, emotion, behavior, etc., and stimulating their learning ability and innovation ability. It is conducive to exploring and establishing a training mechanism for complex and innovative fashion design talents in line with China's national conditions.

The construction of "lean" teaching content, combined with the requirements of "first-class curriculum" construction and the needs of China's higher design education for the development of design theory, through a series of curriculum reforms such as practical exploration, curriculum group construction, project-based training, and so on, has connected the fragmented knowledge of previous courses, solved the problems caused by the fragmentation, repetition, and disconnection between theory and practice of professional curriculum content, and made students clear the value orientation in this process, it provides an optimized path for the construction of first-class courses, and provides a reference for the theoretical framework and knowledge system of fashion design education in the new era.

The construction of the "growth community" of teachers and students under the "lean" teaching mode has transformed teachers and students from the traditional relationship between teaching and learning into a community of teaching and research. Teaching and learning complement each other and promote each other. Students in the teaching team are no longer simply receiving knowledge, but in the main position of design research, this state makes students deeply aware of the lack of their own knowledge storage and the lack of methods, and then take the initiative to learn to more effectively promote the co-frequency resonance of the new community; in the teaching team, teachers can break the limitations of personal vision, knowledge structure, professional background, and regional environment, connect with the academic frontier and industrial needs, and update their knowledge structure in time. The project draws on the teaching experience of first-class universities in the same field, builds a cross-regional curriculum research and exchange platform, and adopts the multi-frequency interactive teaching mode of joint discussion, academic lectures, investigation and exchange, art salon, etc., so that students have a broader vision and cutting-edge ideas, resolve the contradiction between talent training and social needs in colleges and universities, and better serve the economic and cultural development.

In short, the reform of "lean" teaching method aims to improve the teaching quality and build a new ecological system of fashion design education, aiming at promoting the development of connotative characteristics of fashion design specialty, consolidating the basic position of undergraduate education, and promoting the construction of high-quality and high-level new paradigm of fashion design teaching.

Acknowledgements. This work was supported by a grant from the Shandong Undergraduate Teaching Reform Research Project (No. M2021072), and the New Liberal Arts Research and Reform Practice Project of Shandong University of Arts & Design (2021–2023).

References

1. Ministry of Education issued the Notice on the Implementation of the "Double Ten Thousand Plan" for the Construction of First-class Undergraduate Majors (2019). http://www.moe.gov.cn/srcsite/A08/s7056/201904/t20190409_377216.html?from=timeline&isappinstalled=0
2. Ministry of Education issued the Implementation Opinions on the Construction of First-Class(2019)
3. Implementation Opinions of the Ministry of Education on the Construction of First-class Undergraduate Courses (2019). http://www.moe.gov.cn/srcsite/A08/s7056/201910/t20191031_406269.html
4. China's Higher Education has entered the Popularization Stage (2023). http://www.moe.gov.cn/jyb_xwfb/s5147/202301/t20230111_1038961.html
5. Wang, L., Yu, S.P.: Research on teaching mode under the background of school-enterprise collaborative education – taking the course of shaped knitted fashion design as an example. West. Leather. **43**(16), 132–133 (2021)
6. Chen, S.C., Wang, B.: Teaching reform of fashion design course in practical teaching of school-enterprise cooperative studio project. Design **33**(23), 106–108 (2020)
7. Li, H.C.: Teaching research on the combination of college aesthetic education and excellent traditional culture – taking the course of fashion design as an example. Art Educ. **370**(6), 276–279 (2021)
8. Yan, F.: Exploration of educational reform path of fashion design practice course. Chin. Handicraft **173**(3), 179–180 (2021)
9. Zhou, M.Y., Li, M.: Research on the innovation-driven practical teaching model of art and design courses. Ind. Technol. Forum **20**(1), 155–156 (2021)
10. Cao, X.F.: Henry Ford's lean thinking. Enterprise Manage. **474**(2), 30–32 (2021)
11. Guiding Opinions on the Development of China's Clothing Industry during the "Fourteenth Five-Year Plan" and the Vision for 2035 (2021). https://mp.weixin.qq.com/s?__biz=MjM5ODI0NDA5Nw==&mid=2651365120&idx=1&sn=8d57d70b79a99cf4389b8ff37c8c8a01&chksm=bd31856e8a460c78442b1427c6c69213632463f0a846188953fa4060d9c5e06217f4a7cfb60d&scene=27

Virtual Reality in the Teaching of History of Architecture and Urbanism: A Literature Review

Emerson Gomes[1,3](✉), Francisco Rebelo[1,2], Naylor Vilas Boas[3], Paulo Noriega[1,2], and Elisângela Vilar[1,2]

[1] CIAUD, Research Centre for Architecture, Urbanism and Design, Lisbon School of Architecture, University of Lisbon, Lisbon, Portugal
b.emersongomes@gmail.com

[2] ITI/LARSys, University of Lisbon, Lisbon, Portugal

[3] PROURB, Postgraduate Program in Urbanism of the Faculty of Architecture and Urbanism of the Federal University of Rio de Janeiro, Rio de Janeiro, Brazil

Abstract. Virtual reality has become popular recently, and many Colleges now have immersive labs. However, the application of this tool still needs to be widely consolidated, mainly in teaching theoretical subjects related to the field of design, such as the History of Architecture and Urbanism. In addition, only some publications still discuss the advantages of using VR on this theme. The objective of this research is to map the scientific articles published in the last 25 years related to the use of virtual reality in teaching the history of architecture and urbanism.

The scientific research sites ScienceDirect.com, CuminCad.org and GoogleScholar.com were chosen to perform data collection. The keywords "history of architecture", "virtual reality" and "learning" were used in the advanced search of each of the three sites mentioned. Subsequently, a two-stage filtering was carried out, the first related to reading the titles and the second aimed at reading the abstracts. Finally, the works found were all classified according to their own methodology, as well as their main contributions were identified.

The main conclusion from this study is that, although VR is not yet consolidated in most architecture courses, especially in history teaching, the studies showed several benefits of applying the tool. However, the ways to do so still require further investigation, especially considering the emergence of new applications that are increasingly easy to use.

Keywords: history of architecture · Virtual reality · Learning

1 Introduction

1.1 Context

The discipline history of architecture and urbanism is considered fundamental in teaching the profession by many authors. It is present in the most diverse faculties focused on design and construction [1–4]. It seeks, among other things, to study and interpret the forms, purposes, and evolutions of the constructed spaces, considering the social, economic, technological, and cultural context of each epoch and place.

Conventionally, in the subject matter classes, it is common for teachers to use a wide variety of photos, maps, drawings, and in some cases, even physical maquettes to transmit to students the three-dimensional spatial content of the place to be taught [5, 6]. In a complementary way, whenever possible, some colleges add to the teaching methodology the realization of field trips so that students can have a more complete and efficient learning experience about a given space.

1.2 Justification

Although photographs, drawings and perspectives are of enormous help in learning, occasionally there is a gap in which students are led to learn about a given building or urban space, visualizing it only through the photos, leaving all the rest of the space, that is, the area not shown in the images, depending on the abstraction exercise of each student, which can vary considerably and not reflect what is actually built [5, 6].

For the above reasons, many architecture schools schedule field trips for their students, including them in their curriculum [7], so that, at least in certain subjects, knowledge can be understood in a more complete, face-to-face, and interactive way and, by analogy, more efficient and desirable. This method, however, is quite limited due to high financial costs, limitations of public access, and sanitary restrictions, among others [5, 8].

Furthermore, when it comes to disciplines such as the history of architecture and urbanism, depending on the space and time that one intends to investigate, the place may already have undergone drastic changes over decades, centuries, or even millennia. In cases where this happened, even field trips may need to be increased, limiting the transfer of knowledge [9].

Another variable that interests the topic in question is student engagement, especially nowadays when digital technologies are part of everyday life. Considering the ease of access to a smartphone, even within the classroom, more traditional teaching methods, for example, a long PowerPoint full of images and texts [10], maybe unattractive for those watching, resulting in the difficulty that many teachers have keeping students focused on the subject being taught.

For this reason, and often faced with the impossibility of carrying out a visit to the site (whether due to the high financial costs, sanitary reasons, or simply because it is inaccessible), many teachers saw in virtual reality a way of offering the student the experience of entering the place and observe it from the angles of your choice, walking and interacting in real scale, as if you were there, thus obtaining two great advantages that are usually present in field trips: 1) a more complete spatial perception due to the freedom of exploration and interaction, and 2) having the professor himself as a tour guide, being able to walk around the buildings and explain the details and elements he considers relevant.

In addition, contrary to what happens with works of art (which can be transported from one city to another), buildings are immovable, which results in a great limitation in the practice of architectural teaching or even in the dissemination of an architectural culture [11], In this sense, VR has shown a high potential to change this paradigm [12], since given the due limits, it makes it possible for users, for example, students and teachers, to collectively enter (virtual) buildings and walk through them, allowing interaction through avatars, which replicate human movements and reactions in real-time, as if everyone were there [2].

1.3 Research Problem

Although virtual reality has become popular in recent years and several colleges already have immersive laboratories, the practical application of VR in teaching the history of architecture and urbanism is not yet widely consolidated, as well as, so far, few publications discuss the advantages and disadvantages of using VR for the purpose discussed here.

In this sense, it is not uncommon for professors of predominantly theoretical disciplines, such as the history of architecture and urbanism, to encounter situations in which, during class, they need to make a considerable effort to keep students' attention [10]. Mainly in view of the ease of losing focus that today is amplified, for example, due to the banality of access to cell phones in classrooms. This problem can become even more emphatic if the teaching is of the remote type, when students often turn off their cameras and the teacher must teach the content just by looking at the computer screen, that is, without getting immediate feedback on how the message was transmitted.

Thus, with the popularization of virtual reality equipment in recent years and its potential use in teaching, it is not uncommon for professors of disciplines such as the history of architecture to be interested in the application of technology. But due to the frequent lack of familiarity with immersive environments and the low number of articles reporting teaching practices [13–15] makes implementation difficult. Thus, the doubts of architecture professors about the real benefits, the difficulties of use and the paths to be taken form, sometimes, an abyss between the intention of use and the effective practice.

In addition, the application of VR, whether in teaching history or other disciplines, needs to occur in a planned and structured way, so that the content is transmitted efficiently, enhancing the use of the tool. Applications without due care on the part of the teacher can bring negative results, even causing disinterest and even nausea in students [16].

For this reason, the present work carries out a literature review that aims to find scientific investigations that have applied immersive technology in teaching history of architecture and urbanism, seeking to bring to light the advantages, limitations, and relevant knowledge for its implementation in said classes.

2 Objectives

The general objective of this work is to map the scientific articles published in the last 25 years, related to the use of virtual reality in teaching the history of architecture and urbanism. This research encompasses works that portray different ways of using immersive environments in the didactics of the discipline in question. It is intended to list the methodologies used, the contributions, as well as the problems and limitations reported.

3 VR – Basic Concepts

Before analyzing the investigated works, it is considered relevant to clarify some concepts necessary to understand the application of VR in teaching architecture and urbanism. Several terms are frequently mentioned when discussing virtual reality, for example, presence, immersion, interaction, imagination, involvement, engagement, and incorporation, among others [17–19]. Although there is no current, we will adopt lines from authors frequently cited in scientific papers in this article. We will explore three specific expressions: presence, immersion, and virtual reality.

3.1 Presence

A consensus among many researchers is that 'presence' is the key to defining virtual reality [20]. In general terms, presence can be described as a psychological state in which the user feels and acts as if he were in a different place than he is physically [18, 21, 22].

In this sense, it is a sensation that can occur at different levels of depth, due to factors such as: the type of experiment; the quality of the equipment or even the psychological condition of the user. For example, if two people carry out the same experience in VR, but only the second is having serious personal problems, it is possible that this person will dedicate little focus to the experiment, and consequently will tend to feel the presence with less depth than the first.

Within this context, we can mention the example of a user who enters a virtual environment where he sees himself on the edge of a precipice. Even though he is fully aware that he is in a physical room (a college laboratory, for example), his reactions are like those of someone who moves under the imminent threat of falling, sometimes with a racing heart and even anxiety [23]. By reacting to the digital space as if it were there, the participant demonstrates heightened sensations of presence.

3.2 Immersion

There are several concepts on this topic, but similarly to the item above, a consensus among authors is that immersion should be distinct from presence [17, 18, 24]. In the context in question, the term is related to the illusion of perceiving yourself as inserted in the digital space, that is, to feel inside it. This is a variable in which the user can also have more or less deep levels, depending mainly on the type of hardware used [21]. For example, a person who, sitting in his chair, plays a video game through a common screen, may even feel psychologically very involved with the events, but he will hardly perceive himself within the game environment. A conventional computer screen tends to offer low levels of immersion, even if the experience offers high levels of involvement and interaction. On the other hand, if the game takes place on a relatively large display, of the wide (ultrawide) and curved type (reaching a viewing angle close to 180°), there will certainly be greater sensations of immersion than in the case of the simple conventional screen.

In this sense, the more advanced the hardware, such as the high resolution of the screen, wide viewing angle, real-time response to human movements, and good auditory and tactile feedback, among others, the greater the user's perception of being immersed. For this reason, virtual reality is typically associated with high levels of immersion [23].

It should be noted that immersion and presence can be related, but high levels of immersion do not necessarily imply high levels of presence. For example, if an experience was performed with very advanced immersive technology, but the virtual environment needed to be more complete, the user probably felt immersed but hardly had high levels of presence. It is added that, for some authors, for example Brown [25] and Paes [26], if the virtual world was created through a computer, it can be considered a type of virtual reality. For this reason, it is not uncommon to come across the expression Immersive Virtual Reality – RVI, used when researchers want to ensure that the digital world they are referring to is, without a doubt, one that offers high immersive levels.

3.3 Virtual Reality

The first scientific publications on immersive equipment appeared in the 1960s, by Ivan Sutherland [27, 28], while the term virtual reality was coined in the 1980s by Jaron Lanier [29, 30] and evolved considerably until today. In a broad concept, virtual reality can be considered a way to experience presence. In it, one or more users immerse themselves in an environment produced by a computer, and in it they feel as if they were there, often reacting in a natural way, even knowing that physically they are in another place [19, 22].

4   Method

The present work is a literature review that investigates scientific research based on the use of the keywords "history of architecture", "virtual reality" and "learning", applied on the sites ScienceDirect.com, CuminCad.org and GoogleAcademico.com.

The articles were selected considering the insertion of all keywords in the advanced search of the three sites. Then, two filters were adopted: a) reading the titles and b) reading the abstracts. After these steps, the works that effectively discuss the immersive tool in on-screen teaching were segregated. The results culminate in the selection of 17 investigations dated from 1999 to 2023.

The first search site was ScienceDirect.com, which displays the Scopus database, one of the most relevant in scientific research. He listed 31 works and, after reading the titles and abstracts, resulted in the selection of 7 texts effectively linked to virtual reality and history of teaching architecture and urbanism.

The second site was CuminCad.org, a repository of scientific articles containing research published in six international conferences, distributed in five continents, and focused on research on computer-aided architecture. In the search engine, after filling in the keywords in the advanced search, 29 articles related to the topic were listed, and after reading the abstracts, 6 research remained highlighted.

The third and last site was Google Scholar, one of the most complete search engines for scientific research. The initial result was 1,210 works, a number considerably higher than that presented in the two previous sites. For this reason, it was decided to start reading the titles according to the list presented by the search engine, separating the works that seemed most related to the theme in question.

Each displayed page contained a list of 10 jobs. As the pages advanced, the content of the investigations moved away from the theme, until in the twentieth sequence (after 200 works) it was decided to end the search because the listed titles no longer demonstrated any relationship with the desired content. So, discarding the titles already found in the two previous searches, therefore repeated, 31 articles remained, and finally, after reading the abstracts, 5 were related to this research.

Among the articles selected in the three search engines, we chose to include the contribution from the literature reviews. To this end, two criteria were considered: a) VR reviews applied to teaching (various areas) and b) VR reviews applied to architecture and urbanism teaching. In both cases, only revisions whose findings contained research related to the teaching of the history of architecture and urbanism were considered.

5 Results

The table below is a summary of the 17 selected investigations. These studies were classified by year and methodology, with the description of the contribution of each research to the theme discussed here being clarified in the last column. The four approached methodologies, their results, and their limitations are presented in the following topics (Table 1).

Most works used experimental methodology, often comparing, among other things, the performance of students who used VR with that of students who used conventional

Table 1. Classification of selected articles.

Author	Year	Methodology	Contribution
Won, Mihye [31]	2023	Literary review	It analysed 219 empirical studies concerning learning activity with immersive Virtual Reality, including virtual trips to historic cities
Gomes, Emerson [2]	2022	Workflow	It presents a collaborative virtual reality application workflow, where teachers and students interact simultaneously within an immersive environment, through avatars. The discipline history of architecture is used as an example

(continued)

Table 1. (*continued*)

Author	Year	Methodology	Contribution
Gomes, Emerson [32]	2022	Literary review	The article discusses the benefits of using immersive virtual environments in the routine of architects and students. Professional practice, teaching design and historic buildings are discussed here
Carrasco-Walburg [33]	2022	Experimental	The article evaluates the impact of VR on the observation task and development of spatial thinking. Teaching design and history of architecture used as a research discipline
Chan, Chiu-Shui [14]	2022	Experimental	Explores the use of virtual reality technologies in teaching architectural history
Gaafar, Ashraf A [34]	2021	Workflow	Proposes the use of a metaverse in the teaching of architectural history. A pharaonic tomb was used as an example
Puggioni, Mariapaola [16]	2021	VR tool prototype	It proposes ScoolAR, an easy-to-use didactic VR tool, including in disciplines such as the history of architecture
Ibrahim, Anwar [15]	2021	Experimental	Examines the effect of using VR technology on students' learning skills in the history discipline of architecture

(*continued*)

Table 1. (*continued*)

Author	Year	Methodology	Contribution
Kowalski, Szymon [35]	2020	Experimental	It examines the impact of virtual reality and remote education on the history and conservation of architecture. It concludes that VR can positively affect the transfer of knowledge in the discipline under the
Ge, Yanru [36]	2020	Experimental	Examines how immersive technologies can influence the development of students' technical skills and their logical reasoning skills
Ghida, Djamil Ben [10]	2020	Literary review	Describe the importance of using virtual reality and augmented reality tools in architecture teaching, especially architecture history
Gomes, Emerson [40]	2018	Workflow	The article presents a workflow for modelling historic urban spaces optimized for virtual reality applications
Wendell, Augustus [6]	2017	Experimental	The article comes on traditional teaching of architectural history, through photos and drawings, with the use of VR in the classroom. The results indicate that VR has proposed high gains in learning
Moloney, Jules [37]	2017	Immersive tool prototype	Propose two VR applications, based on Unity, intended for virtual immersion for architectural historical interpretations of buildings that have not been built

(*continued*)

Table 1. (*continued*)

Author	Year	Methodology	Contribution
Agirachman, Fauzan Alfi [38]	2017	Workflow	Features a workflow for historic city modelling, optimized for virtual reality applications
De Freitas, M Regina [39]	2013	Literary review	Conducts a survey of research activities in Virtual and Augmented Reality applied to architecture. 200 articles were researched, of which 23% deal with the history of architecture
Chan, Chiu-Shui [5]	1999	Experimental	The work proposed a digital library of buildings relevant to the teaching of architecture history, for use in virtual reality

(non-immersive) systems. In general, groups that had VR as a tool available in most surveys did better, especially in recent years.

Exceptions occasionally occurred, for example, with students who had some type of nausea and, in these cases, preferred conventional classes.

5.1 Experimental Works

The work by Chan et al. [5] discusses the importance of the on-screen tool from several points of view, including:

a) the fact that field visits (made by teachers and students) often do not allow an accurate reading of the original building, either because time and lack of maintenance have caused severe wear, or because the site has already undergone several remodelling.
b) when the space taught by the teacher is currently inaccessible, or where the value of the visit is too expensive.
c) when changes throughout history are relevant for teaching, VR can be programmed to allow students to observe the passage of time.
d) when geographically very distant buildings are relevant to be studied in sequence, for example, European baroque churches, immersive environments can allow you to easily jump from one place to another with a simple button.

In all cases, VR is proposed as a tool that can help broaden the student's perception of works often taught mainly through photos and PowerPoint drawings.

More than 20 years later Chan published again on the subject [14], now seeking to compare experiments that allow to better clarify the benefits of the use of VR in the history teaching of architecture. The work was attended by 123 students. The Pantheon of Rome was the building chosen as the theme of the lesson. Among the results, 74% of the participants considered that VR helped to understand the architecture of the historic environment. It was also observed that more detailed virtual models with audio-guided scripts received almost 50% more votes in user opinion about the best learning experience.

Although not making a direct comparison between immersive and conventional classes (with little or no immersion), the authors asked the participants what their preference would be, and only 17% said that the lecture format was more efficient in learning. This number, despite not being as expressive, corroborates the idea that the application of VR in the classroom does not refer to a replacement of previous tools, but to a complementation [2, 33].

Another relevant work was that of Ibrahim et al. [15], which examined the effect of VR technology on students' learning skills in architectural history. They conducted two experiments, the first based on the BLOOM taxonomy and the second aimed at testing the participants' skills. In both, the group that used VR obtained better knowledge gains compared to traditional methods. Participants also reported a high level of satisfaction with technology use. Among the limitations pointed out, it is reported that the research focused only on a subject of a certain time and other works should investigate different contents. It is also described that the research did not consider the effects of VR in a group class, that is, the investigations took place with a single student at a time within the virtual environment.

Other experimental works also proved to be quite relevant in examining the benefits of VR in teaching architectural history, such as Wendell [6] and Kowalski [35], who identified gains related to the use of the tool.

5.2 Literary Review Works

An argument present in several of the investigated works was about the scarcity of publications on the subject in this article, which is why the present literature review is, so far, the first specifically intended for works that applied the RV in the field of education of history of the architecture and urbanism.

Three of the four selected reviews surveyed articles on the use of VR in teaching historical places [31, 32, 39]. Won et al. analysed 219 studies (in various areas of knowledge) on learning using immersive environments. They noted that resources about physical presence were investigated more than pedagogical resources. Among the findings, although numerous studies report positive results from the use of VR in teaching, it was not clear to the authors what specifically makes VR efficient for learning. It was also mentioned that the pedagogical characteristics related to engagement were rarely reported.

Among the limiting is the difficulties with the variations of the expressions used in the search, for example: "virtual reality", which sometimes writes "immersive virtual reality" or even "VR". Another example was "Head Mounted Display" which is sometimes called "headset" or "HMD". As a result, other relevant studies may have been left out of the literary review.

From Freitas and Ruschel [39] reviewed 200 articles extracted from the database of international congresses ACADIA, ECAADE, CAAD, CAADRIA, ASCAAD e SIGRADI. The authors classified 23% of the findings to be related to the history of architecture, and only 9% fell into architecture education. Both virtual reality and augmented reality were part of the study. In the end it was observed that the technologies discussed showed a shy incorporation in both architectural practice and teaching.

Gomes et al. [32], in turn analysed 67 articles extracted from the ScienceDirect and Cumincad database. Among the investigated works, there are research that reports the use of VR in the profession, teaching of architecture and in historical heritage. Part of the findings were incorporated into this research, for example Wendel and Altin [6].

Ghida's work [10], on the other hand, discusses the practice of architectural history teaching, pointing out with considerable wealth the difficulties of teachers in the discipline and the potential of RV to improve the learning system. The author reports his personal teaching experience on architecture history, including attempts to prevent the class from becoming a memorization course, or the display of a long sequence of images that eventually make the class boring. Among the obstacles described, it is mentioned that teaching about buildings through photos and drawings can fall to the loss of much geometric information. Then VR is pointed out to minimize problems, reducing the existing gap between teaching architecture using photos and drawings, and performing with the class a face-to-face visit to the works.

5.3 Workflows

With the exception of the few cases in which the teacher can gain access to some digitized models of historic buildings, for example on the free sites described by Gomes [2, p. 454], the other situations will require that a group of people get together to investigate and model the architectural or urban environments that will be explained in the classes, seeking to make them as faithful as possible to their existence in the past [9]. In this sense, research that indicates workflows on the subject can help to shorten such paths.

Of the four selected workflows, two specifically address historic building modelling and VR experimentation [38, 40]. The other two discuss flows aimed at the collaborative use of the immersive system in learning the history of architecture.

The first job [40] presents a path aimed at recreating the facades of historic buildings in urban areas. The researchers reconstructed a stretch of the city of Belém, Brazil, from around 100 years ago. A step-by-step guide includes, among others: a) crossing maps of the past with old photographs, b) guidelines on modelling facades, c) modelling characters, and d) exporting to Unity software, in which lighting treatments and basic VR programming were carried out. Finally, the package was exported in an executable format, making it possible to use it in virtual reality. Experiments were carried out with students and professors from the Architecture and Urbanism course at the University of Amazônia, who were able to experience the place in real scale, textured, shaded, and with small animations of the characters.

Among the limitations of this research, it is reported that there was not a considerable number of students who experienced the place in a controlled way. As a distant past was modelled, users had few references to locate themselves and make their own comparisons with the present day. Finally, as the focus of the research was the reconstruction and experimentation of the historic space, despite having involved students and teachers, no practical application in teaching architectural history was reported.

The second workflow [38] depicts the reconstruction of a historic stretch of Braga, in Bandung, Indonesia. A research group worked on the modelling, carrying out field visits (for measurements and capturing photographs), using maps and georeferenced satellite images, among others. Next, a step-by-step guide on editing the photos, preparing the modelling, and applying textures was described. Subsequently, the data were exported to the Unity software where, similarly to the previous workflow, the lighting procedures and basic VR programming were carried out. Finally, after these steps, the product could be used in immersive mode. The results indicated that users were enthusiastic about the potential of the system, although part of the responses indicated the need for several improvements in modelling. No limitations were reported by the authors.

The two workflows below discuss methods of implementing collaborative virtual reality[1] in architecture teaching, especially in the case of the discipline history of architecture. In both research's, the idea of the metaverse seems to be at the heart of the author's intentions, but only in the second work are practical ways presented for the implementation of online systems using VR in architecture teaching.

Gaafar's work [34] refers to the teaching of architectural history in a college in Egypt. As an example of an environment to be virtually reconstructed, the author chose Pashedu's tomb, located in the West Bank. Like other modelling workflows, the research focused on how to develop virtual buildings step-by-step. Field visits, photograph treatment, modelling, exports to the Unity software and basic programming for VR are steps that are present in the article. The research makes references to the use of the metaverse in the teaching of the history of architecture, however, there is little clarification about which paths should be followed for this purpose.

Among the limitations, the research did not carry out controlled experiments using the virtual environment in the teaching context. Also, the work did not explore the use of the Metaverse in practice, it only recommended and indicated some resources for such.

Gomes et al. [2] proposed the work that comes closest to a workflow for the metaverse in the teaching at hand. The authors deal with the implementation of multiplayer virtual reality in architecture teaching, where several users can simultaneously access the same virtual environment, on a 1:1 scale, interacting with each other through avatars. The authors present a brief description of basic concepts related to virtual reality, followed by a step-by-step guide that explains how to collectively implement immersive technology in the classroom.

Among the reported problems, teleportation[2] is cited, which when used in groups, led some students to easily get lost from the rest of the class. The online chat (by audio) also presented considerable delays, making dialogue between those present in the same room difficult.

---

[1] When several users (for example, teachers and students) can simultaneously access the same virtual environment, and in it they can observe and communicate, interacting through avatars.

[2] Allows users to move quickly in long distances in the immersive virtual world.

5.4 Prototypes

Two studies were selected that developed prototypes related to the use of virtual reality in teaching. In the first, Moloney et al. [37] proposed the use of non-realistic immersive virtual environments intended for historical architectural interpretations. This idea seems to corroborate one of the findings by Slater [41], which suggests that environments with a high degree of realism are not necessary to achieve high levels of presence. In this sense, if we bring Moloney's proposal and Slater's discovery into the context of teaching architectural history, this union may indicate that teachers do not need to spend a lot of time with the realism of the environment.

Furthermore, the author also considers that even buildings that were never built have didactic relevance and can collaborate in enriching discussions in the classroom and in the students' repertoire.

Moloney's work, therefore, brings, among other things, two relevant contributions to the topic at hand, the first, as already mentioned, is the proposal that realistic finishes are not necessary for a good VR experience; and the second is that walking, in full scale, through projects that were never built can bring new interpretations about the evolution of cities and, consequently, new lessons or reflections for classes in the history of architecture and urbanism.

The second work listed was that of Puggioni et al. [16], who noted that the various software programs today aimed at creating new experiences in VR (for example, a history of architecture class) are usually not intended for non-programmers, often requiring the user to have a minimum level of knowledge about 3D modelling, programming, among others, something that is not common among architecture history professors. Faced with this bottleneck, the author proposed ScoolAR, a tool that allows the creation of VR/AR applications for users without programming skills.

The author described a fast workflow for using the platform, then presented an experiment with 50 students to test the effectiveness of the proposed program in teaching the history of architecture. The results indicated high satisfaction for the group that used the new system. In addition, the percentage of correct answers for those using the virtual platform was around 20% higher than for those using traditional methods. In the same line of Puggioni's article, there are other applications available on the market that also facilitate the creation of visits in virtual reality, provided that the buildings have already been modelled, as exemplified by Gomes et al. [2]. However, in all cases there is some kind of benefit and limitation, for example, the @VRSketch and @Arkio software offer visits in collaborative mode (multiplayer type) and real-scale modelling, in addition, their use is considerably facilitated, not requiring any knowledge in programming, but its graphics are not realistic. In another sense, renderers like Enscape and Twinmotion are realistic and easy to use, allowing access to VR with a single click, but the visit to the immersive space is only individual.

6 Limitations

As in Won's work [31], the various existing denominations for the keywords used may have masked some works that ended up being left out of the searched list. For example, the term virtual reality, in some cases it was observed as immersive environments or virtual environments.

In the same sense, in the Google Scholar search engine, despite observing that there were no longer works related to the search objectives from a given sequence of pages, it is possible that the engine has left some relevant research in the last pages. This possibility is small, but it exists, and if it occurred, such research might have been left out of the list.

7 Considerations

Most of the selected articles contain some argument that supports the idea that VR can efficiently integrate conventional techniques for teaching the history of architecture and urbanism. There are also recurrent claims that VR can considerably alleviate the impossibility of visiting the study sites, and is therefore a cheaper and safer way to carry out field trips, something highly desirable in the context of teaching the history of architecture, despite considering the due limitations as it is a virtual system.

In addition, it is understood that the objectives of mapping the scientific works that associate VR with the teaching in question were achieved, as well as the methods, contributions and problems/limitations presented were discussed.

It should be noted that only two works were dedicated to the use of VR cooperatively (multiplayer) and, in both cases, it is believed to be a promising teaching method.

The results reflect two relevant points; the first is that almost all the findings suggest a positive or very positive relationship with implementing virtual reality in the teaching purposes discussed here. Second is verifying a reasonable scarcity of scientific works aimed directly at, for that matter.

Finally, although VR is not yet consolidated in most architecture courses, especially in history teaching, the studies showed several benefits of applying the tool. However, the ways to do so still require further investigation, especially considering the emergence of new applications that are increasingly easy to use.

Acknowledgments. The authors would like to acknowledge the Portuguese National funds finance this work through FCT – Fundação para a Ciência e a Tecnologia, I.P., under the Strategic Project with the references UIDB/04008/2020 and UIDP/04008/2020 and ITI-LARSyS FCT Pluriannual fundings 2020–2023 (UIDB/50009/2020).

References

1. Brandão, C.A.L.: Porque estudar história da arquitetura? (2012). https://doi.org/10.11606/issn.2317-2762.v19i32p26-36

2. de Gomes, E.B.O., Rebelo, F., Vilas Boas, N., Noriega, P., Vilar, E.: A workflow for multi-user VR application within the physical classrooms of architecture and urbanism courses. Ergon. Des. **47** (2022). https://doi.org/10.54941/ahfe1001969

3. Hein, C., van Dooren, E.: Teaching history for design at TU Delft: exploring types of student learning and perceived relevance of history for the architecture profession. Int. J. Technol. Des. Educ. **30**(5), 849–865 (2019). https://doi.org/10.1007/s10798-019-09533-5

4. Nofal, E.: Virtual 3D modelling of built heritage in history of architecture course: digital didactic activities. In: International Conference of Cultural Heritage among the Present Challenges and Future Prospects (2013). https://www.researchgate.net/publication/258510 256_Virtual_3D_Modeling_of_Built_Heritage_in_History_of_Architecture_Course_Dig ital_Didactic_Activities

5. Chan, C.-S., Maves, J., Cruz-Neira, C.: An electronic library for teaching architectural history. In: Proceedings of the 4th Conference on Computer Aided Architectural Design Research in Asia (CAADRIA), pp. 335–344 (1999). https://doi.org/10.52842/conf.caadria.1999.335

6. Wendell, A., Altin, E.: Learning space – incorporating spatial simulations in design history coursework. In: eCAADe 35, vol. 1, pp. 261–266 (2017)

7. Universidade Federal de Minas Gerais. Ementa do Curso de Arquitetura e Urbanismo da Universidade Federal de Minas Gerais (2023). https://ufmg.br/cursos/graduacao/2372/91203/ 61618. Accessed 09 Feb 2023

8. De Farias, T.C.: As viagens de estudo como prática educativa no curso de graduação em Arquitetura e Urbanismo (2013)

9. de Gomes, E.B.O., Araujo, T.S.L., Ferraz, A.S.P., Aflalo, A.-B.B.: Mapa de confiabilidade: um método quantitativo para análise do grau de confiança nas reconstruções digitais de patrimônios históricos demolidos ou fortemente modificados. Gestão Tecnologia de Projetos **17**(1), 219–237 (2021). https://doi.org/10.11606/gtp.v17i1.183924

10. Ben Ghida, D.: Augmented reality and virtual reality: a 360° immersion into western history of architecture. Int. J. Emerg. Trends Eng. Res. **8**(9), 6051–6055 (2020). https://doi.org/10. 30534/ijeter/2020/187892020

11. Zevi, B.: Saber ver arquitetura, 5th edn. Martins Fontes, São Paulo (1996)

12. Esteves, J.C., Falcoski, L.A.N.: gestão do processo de projetos em universidades públicas: estudos de caso. Gestão Tecnologia de Projetos **8**(2), 67 (2013). https://doi.org/10.11606/gtp. v8i2.80950

13. Leal, B.M.F.: Propostas para o ensino dos conteúdos de arquitetura e urbanismo através de ferramentas digitais. UFRJ (2018).https://doi.org/10.13140/RG.2.2.27891.22564

14. Chan, C.-S., Bogdanovic, J., Kalivarapu, V.: Applying immersive virtual reality for remote teaching architectural history. Educ. Inf. Technol. **27**(3), 4365–4397 (2021). https://doi.org/ 10.1007/s10639-021-10786-8

15. Ibrahim, A., Al-Rababah, A.I., Baker, Q.B.: Integrating virtual reality technology into architecture education: the case of architectural history courses. Open House Int. **46**(4), 498–509 (2021). https://doi.org/10.1108/OHI-12-2020-0190

16. Puggioni, M., Frontoni, E., Paolanti, M., Pierdicca, R.: ScoolAR: an educational platform to improve students' learning through virtual reality. IEEE Access **9**, 21059–21070 (2021). https://doi.org/10.1109/ACCESS.2021.3051275

17. Murphy, D., Skarbez, R.: What do we mean when we say "presence"? Presence Virtual Augment. Reality **29**, 171–190 (2022). https://doi.org/10.1162/pres_a_00360

18. Witmer, B.G., Singer, M.J.: Measuring presence in virtual environments: a presence questionnaire. Presence Teleoper. Virtual Environ. **7**(3), 225–240 (1998). https://doi.org/10.1162/ 105474698565686

19. Rebelo, F., Noriega, P., Duarte, E., Soares, M.: Using virtual reality to assess user experience. Hum. Fact. **54**(6), 964–982 (2012). https://doi.org/10.1177/0018720812465006

20. Steuer, J.: Defining virtual reality: dimensions determining telepresence. J. Commun. **42**(4), 73–93 (1992). https://doi.org/10.1111/j.1460-2466.1992.tb00812.x

21. Slater, M., Linakis, V., Usoh, M., Kooper, R.: Immersion, presence, and performance in virtual environments: an experiment with tri-dimensional chess. In: Proceedings of the 3rd ACM Symposium on Virtual Reality Software and Technology (VRST 1996), Hong Kong, China, pp. 163–172 (1996). 10.1.1.34.6594

22. Slater, M.: Presence, Virtual Characters and Immersion (2013)

23. Slater, M.: Immersion and the illusion of presence in virtual reality. Br. J. Psychol. **109**(3), 431–433 (2018). https://doi.org/10.1111/bjop.12305

24. Bystrom, K.-E., Barfield, W., Hendrix, C.: A conceptual model of the sense of presence in virtual environments. Presence Teleoper. Virtual Environ. **8**(2), 241–244 (1999). https://doi.org/10.1162/105474699566107

25. Brown, E., Cairns, P.: A grounded investigation of game immersion. In: Conference on Human Factors in Computing Systems – Proceedings, pp. 1297–1300 (2004). https://doi.org/10.1145/985921.986048

26. Paes, D., Arantes, E., Irizarry, J.: Immersive environment for improving the understanding of architectural 3D models: comparing user spatial perception between immersive and traditional virtual reality systems. Autom. Construct. **84**, 292–303 (2017). https://doi.org/10.1016/j.autcon.2017.09.016

27. Sutherland, I.E.: A head-mounted three dimensional display. In: Proceedings of the December 9–11, 1968, Fall Joint Computer Conference, Part I on – AFIPS 1968 (Fall, Part I), p. 757 (1968). https://doi.org/10.1145/1476589.1476686

28. Sutherland, I.E.: The ultimate display. In: Proceedings of the Congress of the International Federation of Information Processing (IFIP), pp. 506–508 (1965). https://doi.org/10.1109/MC.2005.274

29. Machover, C., Tice, S.E.: Virtual reality. IEEE Comput. Graph. Appl. **4**(3) (1994). https://doi.org/10.1109/38.250913

30. Lanier, J., Heilbrun, A.: A Protrait of the Young Visionary (1988). http://www.jaronlanier.com/vrint.html. Accessed 20 Apr 2018

31. Won, M., et al.: Diverse approaches to learning with immersive virtual reality identified from a systematic review. Comput. Educ. **195**, 104701 (2023). https://doi.org/10.1016/j.compedu.2022.104701

32. de Gomes, E.B.O., et al.: Architecture, virtual reality, and user experience. In: Vilar, E., Filgueiras, E., Rebelo, F. (eds.) The Wiley Handbook of Human Computer Interaction Set, 1st ed., vol. 1, pp. 191–206 (2022). https://doi.org/10.1002/9781118976005.ch10

33. Carrasco-Walburg, C., Valenzuela-Astudillo, E., Maino-Ansaldo, S., Correa-Díaz, M., Zapata-Torres, D.: Experiential Teaching-Learning Tools: Critical Study of Representational Media and Immersion in Architecture, pp. 475–488 (2022). https://doi.org/10.5151/sigradi2021-359

34. Gaafar, A.A.: Use of Fully Immersive Virtual Reality Techniques to Generate Scale 1:1 Interactive Models of Pharaonic Tombs, vol. 6, pp. 66–86 (2021)

35. Kowalski, S., Samól, P., Hirsch, R.: Virtual reality tools in teaching the conservation and history of Polish architecture. World Trans. Eng. Technol. Educ. **18**(4), 399–404 (2020)

36. Ge, Y.: Teaching research on 'experience' architecture history with VR technology. Front. High. Educ. **1**(1), 5–9 (2020). https://doi.org/10.36012/fhe.v1i1.569

37. Moloney, J., Twose, S., Jenner, R., Globa, A., Wang, R.: Lines from the past – non-photorealistic immersive virtual environments for the historical interpretation of unbuilt architectural drawings. In: eCAADe 35, vol. 2, Evans 1995, pp. 711–721 (2017)

38. Agirachman, F.A., et al.: REIMAGINING BRAGA remodeling Bandung's historical colonial streetscape in virtual reality. In: CAADRIA, pp. 23–33 (2017)

39. De Freitas, M.R., Ruschel, R.C.: What is happening to virtual and augmented reality applied to architecture? In: Open Systems – Proceedings of the 18th International Conference on Computer-Aided Architectural Design Research in Asia, CAADRIA 2013, pp. 407–416 (2013)

40. de Gomes, E.B.O., da Machado, R.C.S., Gomes, C.M., de Xavier, L.G.S.: The Virtual Reality as a tool to analyze modifications in the architecture of the city. Case study: the historical center of the city of Belém-Pará. In: Blucher Design Proceedings, pp. 860–865 (2018). https://doi.org/10.5151/sigradi2018-1412

41. Slater, M., Lotto, B., Arnold, M.M., Sanchez-Vives, M.V.: How we experience immersive virtual environments: the concept of presence and its measurement. Anuario de Psicologia **40**(2), 193–210 (2009)

The Comparison of Slider and Somatosensory Interfaces in Parametric Modeling for Chair Shape Manipulation

Yu-Hsu Lee🆔 and Wen-Jui Tsai⁽⊠⁾ 🆔

National Yunlin University of Science and Technology, Yunlin 64002, Taiwan, ROC
jameslee@yuntech.edu.tw, m11031005@gemail.yuntech.edu.tw

Abstract. This research parametric design programs to create a simple and effective way for products to interact with users, and through the interactions and models generated compared to traditional parametric models, documents and summarizes the models and processes, and then makes recommendations for future interactive customization systems.

In experiment phase, chairs were classified into block, column and surface shapes, and based on these three categories, the Swan Chair, The Red and Blue Chair and the Panton Chair were used as reference models. Six participants (two experienced and four novice designers) were invited to modify three chairs and create a shape of their choice for each of the two models, comparing the user experience of body-controlled modelling with that of the traditional parametric programmed, and collecting suggestions and feedback through semi-structured retrospective interview after the experiments.

According to the analysis of the results, the novice designers consider the somatosensory system to be new, fast and easy to use, more intuitive and easier to understand than the traditional interface, and through the somatosensory system they could quickly see if the shape was reasonable and comfortable. However, novices also felt that somatosensory was limited by the body's inability to make too many gestures and that the accuracy of the capture could be improved. Experienced designer felt that the somatosensory system possesses the intuitive nature of body sensing and shape decision can be done quickly, but that it is inconvenient and uncontrollable when it comes to accurately controlling the arbitrary parameters of the model, and that the development of the model is limited by the limitations of the body.

Keywords: Parametric Modeling · Somatosensory Interface · Furniture Design · Grasshopper Programming

1 Research Background

In recent years, the increasing use of digital manufacturing technology has made it easier to create customized or even home-made products, and there has been a greater emphasis on creating or designing products with a more personal style. The use of furniture in public and private spaces, whether in businesses or schools, is increasing every day and users have different needs for furniture in their homes and public spaces. However, there is a huge gap between designers, manufacturers and consumers, with traditional design and manufacturing relying on designers and manufacturers using computer graphics to create designs that are then production and sale by manufacturers. It is extremely time-consuming and inefficient for designers to redraw input information from different users into computer graphics software and then send it back to the manufacturer for re-prototyping and re-testing. This research introduces a somatosensory interface combing with grasshopper program for designer and user to adjust product shape through their posture.

1.1 Motivation

Furniture is a product related to human scale and the products that consumers currently choose are often those produced by the largest convention on the market, leaving them to settle for the closest ergonomic size of mass-production. When a customer needs a customized product, this process can be time consuming and costly. One of the easier ways to create a digital model by users themselves is using Grasshopper in Rhino 3D. By asking users what they want or measuring their body information, the data is translated into appropriate parameters and the shape is modified through parametric design to create a product that fits the consumer. Parametric design in the pre-design phase still relies mainly on visual adjustment of parameters one by one to select shapes. This research uses the Kinect sensor to capture multiple body sensory data simultaneously as an input method to control the styling design. Moreover, to investigate whether it is more user-friendly than traditional parametric adjustment input as a control option, and whether the variables are more user-friendly when it comes to styling changes and selection.

2 Literature Review

2.1 Body Sensing Applications

Lee et al. (2016) proposed a user-centered experimental approach and participant was asked to gesture and move as input, and the input data is used to customize the furniture. The method includes the use of body parts by the participant and the use of simple verbal commands to specify dimensions. For example, "this wide" or "from here to here", where the size is indicated the size by the distance of the arms. For viewing, a head-mounted display is used. (A head-mounted display is used for viewing.) Provide users with real-time, true-to-scale feedback so that test participants can experience and evaluate their designs. Through formative and evaluative studies, Bokyung demonstrates that this approach allows ordinary users to participate in the iterative design process of customized products, Bokyung's research also shows that user involvement in the design process helps to improve the relationship between the designed product and the user's use, body and environment. Our research also uses physical sensing as an input to seat size and uses Rhino and Grasshopper as test platforms. The different part is in terms of operation, product generation and construction method. The operation is mainly based on capturing the angle of the participant's hands and feet, with only forearm position information for the seat handle height, and the seat height is calculated from the distance between the feet and the buttocks. The TouchOSC software is employed when the size of the shape is confirmed by user. In addition, three different types of personal chairs were used as the products generated in this research, the three chairs are among the more recognizable pieces in the history of design, and are made up of block, column and surface shapes.

Young and Smith (2016) presents an augmented reality furniture customization system, introducing Kinect to capture real-world information in their experiments. And by combining the two types of image information and calculating them. In this way, the problem of the obscuration of the movements of the participant during the experiment is solved. In the follow-up experiment, participants were asked to place the furniture in the virtual reality in the correct position and interact with it. Participants were also asked to complete a questionnaire for comparison with the original system. The results show that increasing the realism of the AR environment helps to improve participants' experience of moving virtual objects. The previous article demonstrated that the use of Kinect helps to improve the user's intuition. Our research uses Kinect to control the shape of furniture and the effect of the participant's use of body control. Quickly adjust the seat shape by adjusting the angle of the participant's body, after the test, qualitative interviews were conducted to summaries the perceptions of novices and experienced.

2.2 Parametric Furniture

Hamza & Husein (2020) used verbal analysis, reviewed literature, and developed a standardized scale for evaluating the scores of parametric furniture compared to geometric models. Thirty subjects, all of whom were architects with experience in furniture design, were invited to conduct the test. 65.38% of the subjects used parametric tools, while 34.62% did not use parametric tools. The results of the study showed that 92.31% of the respondents believed that parametric design could improve creativity. The above research shows that using parametric models allows designers to be more creative, but parametric models have a certain threshold. This research uses a pre-written Grasshopper as a platform to study parametric design and compares two different models in terms of control and ease of usage. Grasshopper's plug-in and built-in features was used to derive two ways of operating. The first way is to use the mouse to adjust the parameters and confirm the modeling. In this research, we use Kinect to capture the skeletal data of the real subject and use this data to influence the modeling style in the modeling software. The participant can describe the overall feeling and experience of the operation then organize and summarize the advantages and disadvantages of the two modes.

Felek (2022) points out that CAD is widely used in the design and modeling process in the furniture design industry. Using Rhino and Grasshopper to parameterize the cabinet products and Microsoft Excel as data input. The paper concludes that there is a way to make the shape change quickly and advantageously for production. It will be an advantageous for future factories to manufacture quickly and respond customers' needs effectively. In this research, we use the data from the real space to calculate the angle and position of the back and legs of the chair and use the calculation function in Grasshopper to calculate the angle and position of the real data. The calculated data is used to change the shape of the furniture so that in the future the user can select the shape of the chair and then make a customized chair according to his or her riding experience.

2.3 The Difference Between Experienced and Novice

Chen (2020) collected data by using the think-aloud method and compared the sequence of execution, time spent, and the number of occurrences in each design phase between experienced and novice designer. They used verbal analysis to examine the qualitative and quantitative data of five experienced and five novice designers. The experimental results show that there are indeed differences between experienced and novice designers, and there are many reasons for the differences such as in ability, experience, thinking, and even self-confidence. However, this repetitiveness is presented in a different way, i.e., the experts define the design early in the process, so their performance in the later stages may be more stable than that of the novices. Novice designers, on the other hand, often jump back to the previous two stages to re-explore or redefine their designs when they reach the later stages. In this research, we took the parametric design feature to allow the participants to change the design shape quickly, let the design experienced and novice adjust three different shapes of chairs respectively, and use the traditional and somatosensory mode to test in the experiment. Considering the novice's ability to operate and design at the same time, the design behavior and think-aloud were summarized by means of retrospective interviews, and the data was consolidated to understand whether the two systems could influence the design process.

Lee (2018) uses parametric software to reduce the obstacles and problems that novice and experienced designers encounter when modeling, and to help designers have more ideas in modeling through 3D software so that designers can focus more on design. The experimental design was first, the expert group interview was used to distinguish the strengths and weaknesses of the stylistic design ability and to obtain the experts' opinions. Finally, the experiments were conducted to test the difference in the transformation of the students' modeling skills after using pictures and CGDM when they had no modeling ideas or had ideas but could not draw them, and to summarize the recommendations of the expert group. Since the program is not always written in the same way as the actual user, the pilot study showed that when the number of adjustable parameters is larger than 15, novices are prone to make false connections between the parameters and the corresponding shape changes. The design experienced also needs time to get used to the logic of the generative designer's parameters. Therefore, the flexibility of the interface, i.e., the visualization of effective parameter adjustment and shape change, needs to be enhanced in the future. This research hopes to free users from the dilemma of having to use both hands to adjust the mouse through Kinect motion capture. The body waving was employed to quickly change the shape compared to the previous mouse-keyboard adjustment lever adjustment system. This research refers to the previous research which suggested that the controllable parameters of are within 15 parameters. This experiment can be used to find out whether fewer device adjustment parameters can have a more positive effect on the participant's change of shape, and to learn about the different perspectives of experienced and novice designers.

3 Method

3.1 Experimental Steps

This research conducted two design experiments to test the different operating modes of experienced and novice designers. There are two experienced and four novice designers after grouping by participant's modeling and sketch ability. In the experiment, three different types of design chairs were tested in traditional GH and somatosensory interfaces, totaling six chairs. Then the participants were asked to adjust the chair shape to the participants' mind that the comfortable or ideal shape. During the test period, the researcher will time each chair operation and conduct a semi-structured interview with the participant after the experiment.

3.2 Parametric Design

This research was conducted to test the difference between the somatosensory control interface and derive the parametric programming interface. Through three famous design chairs as a model in the program. These three chairs are distinguished by different generation methods, with the block-shaped Swan chair, the column-shaped the Red and Blue chair and the surface-shaped Panton chair as models in the generative program by grasshopper. Through the Grasshopper plug-in Firefly in order to capture the skeleton information in the Kinect to the Grasshopper as the parameters of the three chairs (Fig. 1). The information between skeleton of the waist, thighs, calves, arms was treated as two points and translated to x, y, z parameters to calculate the angle and length (Fig. 2). By using these parameters, user is able to control the three chairs' shape. The OSC Listener function in Firefly was used to connect to the Touch OSC in the mobile phone to stop the data transfer while user decide the chair shape. A button was created in TouchOSC to control the toggling of the 0 and 1 values in the program. Finally, the data from TouchOSC was transferred back to Rhino.

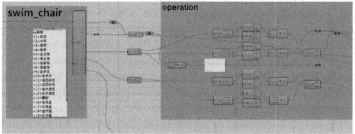

Fig. 1. Schematic diagram of the program

Fig. 2. Skeleton information used in the program.

In the traditional way, a starting point is used to connect the skeleton of chair for controlling the shape through increasing and decreasing the value of parameter. The information is transferred to Rhino to connect Grasshopper as an interface for user to control and edit through extra window in Rhino (Fig. 3).

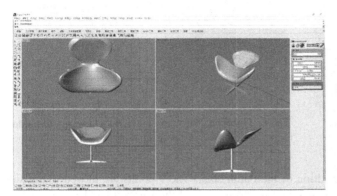

Fig. 3. User Interface.

Fig. 4. Traditional Model Skeleton.

The three chairs are based on the basic skeleton in the traditional model and transplant to somatosensory mode (Fig. 4). The structure of Swan Chair is block modeled by dividing the skeleton from the data into sections, generating straight lines from these sections, bending these straight lines to the sides, offsetting the bent lines to form polygons, and converting the polygons to blocks using the loft function, and then transforming the blocks to a mesh surface (Fig. 5), and the mesh to a SUBD fast smoothing surface (Fig. 6).

Fig. 5. Offset the curve and loft the sample.

Fig. 6. Convert face to SUBD.

The Red and Blue chairs is structured by using the seat and back of the chair as the starting point to structure the program, through the data in the skeleton to generate the back of the chair, the seat cushion line, offset it to form the thickness (Fig. 7), offset the line to the sides to form the width of the chair. The chair legs are based on the edge line of the width of the chair and the chair is divided into paragraphs and then extend it up and down (Fig. 8). The height of the seat is treated as the starting point of the handle to higher or lower the position. Finally, the model is mirrored after all parts are completed (Fig. 9).

The structure of Panton chair is deformed based on the most basic skeleton, a single surface, the skeleton line is divided into 9 points (Fig. 10), and the 9 points are moved

Fig.7. Generate chair board with straight line.

Fig. 8. Generate chair legs according to the chair board.

Fig. 9. Mirroring the model.

to the relative curved position of the Paton chair. The 9 points are moved to the side according to the curved position of the front view of the Paton chair. These points are connected by interpolated curves (Fig. 11), and the curves are connected as sections to build up a surface through loft function (Fig. 12).

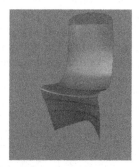

Fig. 10. Create straight lines with dots.

Fig. 11. Derivation through the line segment to both sides.

Fig. 12. The line segment is loft into the surface.

Before the participant executes the experiment, the researcher will verbally explain the shape structure and the connection with GH program parameter adjustment so that the participant can make manipulate the parameters conveniently during the test.

3.3 Participants

The above description of the composition and adjustment of the generative program is verbally explained by the researcher before the participant undergoes the experiment, so that the participant can easily make adjustments during the test. The researcher also explains the detail of the experimental steps and the purpose and methods of this research before the participant executes the experiment. This involved asking the participants to change the parameters in the computer by adjusting their posture in the office chair and using the computer at the research site to change the parameters (Figs. 13 and 14), and then collecting feedback from the participants through semi structured retrospective interviews. The participants were fully informed the content before experiment, consented document was also given to sign up. The researcher who conducts the interview and collects data is finished IRB training and sign a consent form. All information provided by the participants will be fully protected by the researcher and will be represented by participants 1, 2 and 3 in the subsequent paper. This research is currently a pilot study, so only six participants have been invited. Any expansion of the number of participants in further studies will be submitted to the Ethics Review Board for review in accordance with the regulations.

Fig. 13. Traditional mouse keyboard method to adjust parameters.

Fig. 14. Input by Somatosensory mode.

4 Research Results

4.1 Tested Results

This research takes three classic chairs as typical types of three category to construct generative program. The human data and control parameters were captured by Kinect and TouchOSC devices to build up a somatosensory system. An industrial design graduate student who familiar with computer-aided design was invited to conduct pre-tests to confirm the program's usability. There are five participants, one is familiar with computer aided design and the other four are not, were invited after confirming the usability of the program. The five participants were asked to perform experiments on three chairs in traditional and somatosensory modes, adjusting their preferred shapes.

The experiment was videotaped and the time of each shape was timed. After the experiment, semi-structured and retrospective interviews were conducted with the participants to describe each shape and its purpose, as well as their preference for the two systems and the reasons why.

This research invites participants to execute experiment with three types of chairs in body-sensory mode and traditional mode. The experiment demands each participant to generate six chairs in total. The researcher records the time when participants start to adjust until press the stop button to determine each chair shape. The overall efficiency of body-sensory mode is faster than the traditional mode. In addition, novice designers

	Swan Chair Traditional mode	Swan Chair Somatosensory mode	The Red and Blue Chair Traditional mode	The Red and Blue Chair somatosensory mode	PANTON Chair Traditional mode	PANTON Chair somatosensory mode
participant 1	1min12sec 	23sec. 	1min1sec 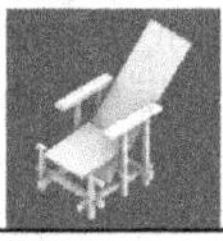	20sec. 	1min13sec 	35sec. 
participant 2	1min10sec 	20sec. 	55sec. 	22sec. 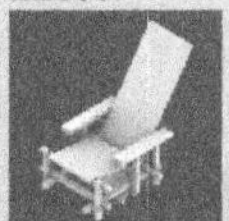	1min11sec 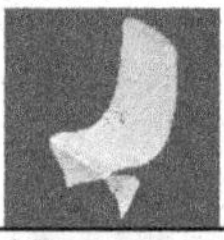	50sec. 
participant 3	1min02sec 	32sec. 	35sec. 	12sec. 	32sec. 	11sec. 
participant 4	1min24sec 	20sec. 	51sec. 	50sec. 	1min 24 sec 	1min27sec 
participant 5	45 sec. 	37sec. 	42sec. 	27sec. 	1min 02 sec 	13sec. 
participant 6	3min26sec 	2min27sec 	2min34sec 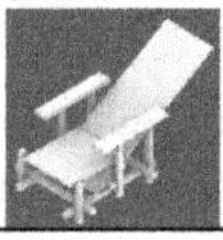	1min54sec 	2min38 sec 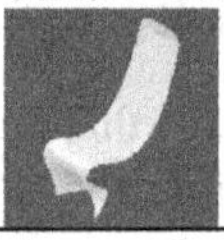	1min 44 sec 

Fig. 15. Chart of test results. The red word is the preference of the participant, red background is t faster time (Color figure online).

(participants 2–5) prefer Swan chair and PANTON chair to make adjustment in body-sensory mode. There is only one novice designer prefer body-sensory mode than the traditional in the red and blue chair. In general, novice designers prefer the body mode. The experienced designer think that only PANTON chair is relatively good in adjustment for the body-sensory mode, the traditional mode is better than the body-sensory mode for that other two chairs (Fig. 15).

4.2 Summary of Experimental Results and Recommendations for Novice Designers

The four novice designers were all master of design students (1 male and 3 females, ages 23–28) with 2–4 years of training, and all four completed the entire experiment.

Most of the novice designers thought that the advantages of the somatosensory mode were newer and more interesting than the traditional mode (participant 5), and that the somatosensory mode was faster and more convenient for motion capture than the traditional mode, and that it was more intuitive to use (participant 2). In addition, the somatosensory mode allows the participants to feel the real situation and consider the comfort of the user's sitting posture (participant 4), most novice designers said that in the somatosensory mode you can feel the comfort of the chair by changing the body's posture (participant 3), and through the somatosensory mode you can obviously feel the body controlling the model in the computer (participant 3), they said that in the traditional mode, it is difficult to imagine the shape of the chair in reality, but in the somatosensory mode you can clearly feel the thighs, knees, buttocks and others have an impact on the shape of the change (participant 2). In the traditional mode, it is necessary to adjust the lever without knowing what is the most comfortable posture (participant 3), the sensitivity of the sensory capture is very accurate, the model will move with the participant's body when he changes the posture (participant 3), compared with the traditional adjustment method, by adjusting the body posture can quickly adjust the model (participant 3), and the sensory detection and model change is very obvious (participant 5), in addition, some of the more difficult to adjust the model in the traditional mode, but in the use of the somatosensory mode is good to adjust (participant 5).

The disadvantage of the somatosensory mode is that it cannot be adjusted one scale at a time like the traditional mode, which makes the somatosensory mode relatively less accurate than the traditional mode (participant 3), and sometimes the content displayed by the body sensing detection and the real movement of the participant may not be one to the other (participant 2), and some of the motion capture and the actual feeling are not the same (participant 4), and it requires a large swing to make the shape change (participant 5), and sometimes it needs to be reset to make the program accurate (participant 4). In some cases in the somatosensory mode, the shape and posture of the upper body were consistent, but the posture and shape of the lower body were inconsistent (Participant 2), the program of the somatosensory mode put the real position of the buttocks together with the virtual position of the seat cushion, which made the participants confused about the shape during operation (Participant 3), In addition, the participant said that when the shape was fully adjusted to the preferred look, the whole body would exert muscles in order to maintain the shape, resulting in a stiff rather than relaxed sitting posture, and thus the focus would become on the presentation of the shape rather than on comfort (Participant 4).The somatosensory mode would be affected by the chair the participant was sitting in, and the participant would need to be in a semi-squatting position to adjust a shorter shape (Participant 4), and it would be more difficult to fix the shape when the participant was in a semi-squatting or out-of-chair position (Participant 5).

The advantage of the traditional mode is that it can be called to focus on the performance of the shape (participant 4), the traditional mode can make the most preferred shape for each chair (participant 2), the adjustment options in the traditional mode correspond to the shape of the chair from top to bottom, which is clear to the participant (participant 4), and participant said that the data in the traditional mode does not affect the participant's view of the shape, the participant said that only the maximum and minimum values are paid attention to (participant 5), and the furniture shape can be adjusted in the traditional mode to focus on a single detail to make adjustments (participant 3).

The disadvantage of the traditional model is that it is not possible to intuitively know the parameters corresponding to the shape (participant 4), it needs to be adjusted repeatedly to know the parameters corresponding to the shape (participant 3). Some of the shapes in the traditional mode required more parameter changes to know which part was changed (participant 5). The traditional mode requires frequent adjustments to the shape to make it realistic (participant 5). The traditional mode can only adjust one part at a time and requires repeated adjustments between different parameters (participant 5). It takes more time to adjust to different chair shapes (participant 3), and adjusting the parameters does not give a true sense of whether the shape is comfortable for the user, and sometimes the shape is considered uncomfortable after adjustment (participant 2).

4.3 Summary of Experimental Results and Recommendations for Design Veterans

The two experienced designers have gone through 2–4 years of training in design master students and are good at computer aided design and modeling ability (2 males, age 23). Both of them completed the whole experiment, and the design experienced were interviewed at the end of the experiment to understand each form and the overall feeling and details of the experiment. The advantage of the somatosensory mode is the ability to adjust the shape through body movements, which makes the process of shape adjustment more intuitive (participant 1), the somatosensory mode is easier to interpret than traditional parameters, and the sensitivity of capturing body movements is sufficient (participant 1). The somatosensory mode allows multiple parameters to be changed at the same time, providing a quicker way to experience the overall look than the traditional mode with a single parameter adjustment (Participant 1). The skeletal information of the human body allows a quick change of shape in some chairs where the shape is difficult to adjust (participant 1). The somatosensory mode allows the participant to quickly calculate the desired shape (participant 1). In addition, the movements are very consistent with the model changes when adjusting the shape (participant 1).

The disadvantages of the somatosensory mode are that there is no obvious feedback, so the participant cannot immediately know whether the OK button has been pressed (participant 6), the detection is not always very stable, so the skeleton runs away and the participant feels uncertain (participant 6), and the parameters of the skeleton captured by the somatosensory mode keep changing as the participant fixes the posture, so the participant cannot complete the desired shape (participant 6). In addition, somatosensory detection does not know the maximum and minimum values of the shape as in the traditional mode, which makes the participant feel uncertain (participant 6). Some participants said that after adjusting the shape of one part, they did not necessarily want to change another part (participant 6), so they did not want the parameters to keep changing, which would confuse the participants (participant 6). Participants also felt that their posture did not match the shape produced by the somatosensory model (participant 6).

In the somatosensory mode, the modeling was limited by the limits of body movements, and the chairs provided at the experimental environment made it impossible to make different models (participant 1).

The advantage of the traditional mode is the adjustment, the experienced designers are very familiar with the use of the computer, and think that the traditional mode can be controlled and precise compared to the somatosensory mode (Participant 1). In terms of parameters, the traditional mode is also better understood, as experienced designers are used to picking the whole shape by the numbers in the computer (Participant 6). The first point is that the list of parameters is completely listed on the left side for easy understanding by the participants, and the second point is that using the traditional mode is very stable and all parameters do not change all the time (participant 6).

The disadvantage of the traditional model is that the participant needs to repeatedly check the shape and parameters. When the participant adjusts one part of the parameters and then adjusts the next part, it may lead to changes in shape and scale (participant 1), and each parameter needs to be understood one by one, requiring multiple iterations to check the shape (participant 6).

5   Conclusion

5.1   Novice and Experienced Users Use the Physical Sense of Difference

According to the analysis of the experimental results, novice designers find the somatosensory mode fresh, fast and very convenient. In terms of operation, it is more intuitive and easier to understand compared to the traditional interface. Through the somatosensory mode, novice designers can quickly understand whether the shape is reasonable and comfortable. This system allows the novice designer to consider whether the sitting position is comfortable for the human body. However, novice designers also feel limited by the body's inability to make too many gestures and are restricted in their styling. Furthermore, the accuracy of the capture needed to be improved. Experienced designer feels that body sensing is intuitive and quick, but less comfortable and controllable. The parameters model is required when precise control. Experienced designer indicates that the physical limitations also limit the development of modelling.

The researcher believes that the future development of the somatosensory mode can be used for novice designers to create programs with parametric designers when they are unsure of the shape, and to express actual ideas through body movements with somatosensory devices such as KINECT, which has the advantage of allowing novice designers to quickly generate models and communicate with others without the limitations of modelling and hand-drawing. Experienced designers can use the body-sensing mode to generate some models that they would not normally think of, and use them as a reference for later, more detailed models.

5.2 Customized Furniture Applications

Through this research, we understand that novice designers consider the somatosensory mode to be new, fast and convenient. Therefore, in the future, in addition to the traditional measurement, verbal and purely graphical communication, we can use this method to create products for customized furniture. This allows consumers to quickly control the shape of the product through their bodies when expressing their customized products, and to communicate with designers through the results generated and as a reference for designers in the subsequent production of products. In this way, it can reduce the time and errors in communication between consumers and designers.

5.3 Research Limitations

In this research, due to the limitations of the field and the chair equipment, the participants could not have a better experience, so the motion capture did not translate all the information into the shape of the chair. The viewing method only used the computer screen as a viewing window therefore virtual object was to be integrated with the real object later. In addition, this research only refers to testing a single motion capture method, so it is not certain whether all devices can effectively adjust the shape by motion capture.

6   Suggestions

6.1 Future Recommendations

This rehash is based on qualitative interviews, and it is now known that there is a difference in the preference of novice and experienced designers between the somatosensory mode and the traditional mode, and that the somatosensory mode has better performance in terms of operational efficiency. However, the number of participants is relatively small, so future research can collect more data by quantifying the specific user groups to make a more accurate analysis. In terms of products, this research uses three different types of chairs with different shapes and structures as modelling stimuli, suggesting that in the future research can test whether different types of products have different results in the same mode of operation and can capture skeletal information through different devices.

References

Chen, Y.T.: A Study on Comparing Design Behavior of Novice and Expert in Design Process (2020). https://hdl.handle.net/11296/m9w65h

Felek, S.Ö.: Parametric modelling in furniture design, a case study: two door wardrobe. Euras. J. Sci. Eng. **2**(2), 62–74 (2022)

Hamza, S., Husein, H.A.: The influence of parametric design tools on increasing creativity in the furniture design process. Euras. J. Sci. Eng. **6**(1), 199–211 (2020)

Hou, Z.: Experience research on application of computer parameterization technology in modern office furniture design. J. Phys. Conf. Ser. **1992**(3), 1–6 (2021). https://doi.org/10.1088/1742-6596/1992/3/032052

Lee, B., Cho, M., Min, J., Saakes, D.: Posing and acting as input for personalizing furniture. In: NordiCHI 2016, vol. 44, pp. 1–10 (2016)

Lee, C.L.: Studies on Cooperative Generative Design Method for Product Shapes Development (2018). https://hdl.handle.net/11296/cd44jj

Tang, X.B., Zhao, J.C., Li, W.B., Feng, B.: Design and implementation of smart home cloud system based on kinect. In: Shi, Z.Z., Mercier-Laurent, E., Li, J.Y. (eds.) IIP 2018. IAICT, vol. 538, pp. 120–126. Springer, Cham (2018). https://doi.org/10.1007/978-3-030-00828-4_13

Young, T.C., Smith, S.: An interactive augmented reality furniture customization system. Virtual Augment. Mixed Reality **9740**(8), 662–668 (2016)

The Feasibility Study Using Geometric Objects Constructed by Grasshopper (GH) as Shape Thinking Stimulation

Yu-Hsu Lee🆔 and Hsin-Min Hsu⁽✉⁾ 🆔

National Yunlin University of Science and Technology, Yunlin 64002, Taiwan, ROC
jameslee@yuntech.edu.tw, m11031026@gemail.yuntech.edu.tw

Abstract. This study investigates the feasibility of using geometric objects constructed by grasshopper (GH) as shape thinking stimulation. The final sketch was made to create six kinds of animal-shaped speaker, and the final evaluation of the shape was conducted by design experts. In the first stage of the experiment, the experimental participants (5 Master of Design students) were asked to select one of the three GH programs composed of different geometric elements provided by this study to change the shape by adjusting the parameters in order to obtain six different kinds of animal head shapes. The other five design master students, control groups, were asked to search the Internet for images as stylistic stimulation. After that, 10 participants were asked to sketch six kinds of animal-shaped computer speaker cases in the Second stage.

The experimental result shows that the experimental group using GH program can adjust the parameters of the program to effectively adjust the details of the animal shape features, such as ears or nose and mouth. They can also adjust six animal models in about 1 h, and could convert the adjusted models into product proposals within 40 min. While the control group was told to search for animal-shape products and to Although the control group had been told to search for animal-shaped products and convert them, it took more time to search and think about drawing six kinds of animals (more than 1 h).

Keywords: Product Shape Thinking · Parametric Modeling · Grasshopper · Hand Drawing Sketch

1 Research Background

In the process of product shape designing, designers often need to think about the reference objects (stimuli) of the shape based on the design task. Generally, designers will reach a consensus on the shape from the appearance of existing products or by making an image board with customers, and then confirm the direction of the shape or generate special ideas before designing the appearance of the product. During the process, they often search for images on the internet, focusing on specific shape themes or features, which designers then transform into product details. From the perspective of corporate development, customers usually hope to develop a common product language for a series of consistent products in order to establish product recognition in the minds of consumers. At this time, using specific elements as the main shape to develop product appearance is also a common design skill used by designers. Computer speakers are often used as design tasks for students in design departments to train the ability of product shape because they contain speaker units and basic functions such as switches and volume adjustment. This study aims to explore the feasibility of using Grasshopper (GH) as shape thinking stimuli. Therefore, different animal shapes were chosen as the design theme, and polygon and sphere were used as basic elements. Three GH programs were written to adjust the shape of design elements by changing parameters, allowing participants to easily select design elements and adjust the shape to create different animal heads. This study focuses on the breadth of thinking through stimuli, so six different animal shapes are designated and make participants to think about the characteristics of different animals during the adjustment process, and then adjust the parameters, or in the adjustment process discover the characteristics of different animals to achieve the purpose of encouraging creative thinking. To avoid limiting the participants' creation due to the different shapes of a single animal. The purpose of this study is to understand the feasibility of GH as shape thinking stimulation, and the following research projects will be carried out:

1. To compare the differences between different participants when using GH and Internet search pictures as stimuli for product shape ideas.
2. To compare the continuity and commonality of the efficiency and design elements in the process of sketch from six animal-shaped computer speaker and sketches.
3. To understand the thought process of different participants during the series product design by retrospective interviews.
4. To compare and evaluate the design results by experts to understand the effectiveness differences of using different stimuli to perform design tasks.

2   Literature Review

The study compares the effectiveness of GH parametric program and internet search pictures as stimuli for product shape thinking. The literature review including: 2.1 Use parametric design tool to understand the timing and scope of parametric design tools in the design process; 2.2 Review literature related to design thinking stimuli to understand the various ways that stimuli affects designers during the design process and how to evaluate design outcomes; 2.3 Discuss how designers utilize sketch for design thinking to understand the functionality and significance of sketches in different situations for designers.

2.1   Parametric Design Tool

Krish (2011) found that the 5 steps of parametric generative design, 1. Creating the genetic model 2. Setting the initial envelope 3. Generating designs 4. Filtering phenotypes 5. Selection & fine tuning. The process can explore changes in form within a specific solution space with the assistance of a program that calculates a large number of forms within the specified parameter range, or loosen the solution space to obtain an infinite number of solutions. Lee (2018) observed that using the high degree of freedom of the Grasshopper visualization program can provide open solutions within the defined solution space, instead of the traditional CAID that only provides a single solution. Three kinds of geometric shapes are used as the basic elements of animal heads. Sophomores in the second group (49 and 48 people) are asked to perform sketch task first, and then use the GH program to adjust the heads of 6 animals (the control group searches for pictures on the Internet), and then invites students draw 6 animal-shaped computer speakers. This experiment is mainly to find the differences of computer tools in design novice modeling thinking in a quantitative way. The result showed that the GH program could stimulate students to carry out more shape transformations from the original idea than the Internet search, and the novice designers could be divided into three groups: have the idea and can draw it, have the idea but can't draw it, and have no idea. However, this experiment did not discuss in depth the participants' feedback on GH and whether this phenomenon also exists when expert designers think about product shape. Based on above experiment, this study discusses the differences between expert designers using GH program and Internet search pictures as stimuli. At the same time, retrospective interviews are used to understand the thinking mode of expert designers when they think about series product shape.

2.2 Visual Stimuli

Humans are visual creatures and designers are no exception. Unlike ordinary people, designers often use shapes and forms in their thoughts rather than just verbal thoughts. Therefore, stimuli, the 'consumption' of external visual representations is a crucial aspect of visual representation in design (Goldschmidt and Smolkov, 2006). In most experiments, drawings and pictures or 3D objects are used as visual stimuli commonly, and the results show that visual stimuli can enhance the creativity of designers in solving design problems. For example, in Malaga's experiment in 2000, three stimulus patterns were used which are pictures, words, and both pictures and words. Participants were asked to use stimuli complete the experimental tasks. The experimental results showed that picture stimuli were more creative than the other two stimulus patterns. In Goldschmidt and Smolkov's experiment in 2006, the test participants were divided into three groups. The first group was not given any stimuli, the second group was given rich stimuli, and the third group was given abstract sketches. Participants were asked to complete a design task and then their design solution evaluated by experts from originality, practicality, and quality with a score from 1 to 5. The purpose of the experiment was to observe the influence of visual stimuli on participants' design performances and the result showed that there is a high positive correlation between visual stimuli and creativity in design. This study refers to the above two studies and asks the participants to search for pictures that match the design goal according to the design task as visual stimuli.

2.3 Sketches and Design Thinking

In the design process, sketch can help designers to develop ideas and creative extension. Sketch is part of the early stage of the design process, which can be further divided into two parts. The first part is exploration, and the second part is development. The former is a conceptual idea of visual thinking and contains uncertainty and differences. The latter is a process of modifying and concrete sketches of the former and is clear and with small differences (Tsai and Tseng, 2010). In the stage of ideation, designers often draw a large number of sketches, which designers can gradually concretize the design concept. Goldschmidt (1992) found that in the early stages of creation, artists and designers do not draw a single sketch, but a series of sketches in a very short period of time, sometimes even within minutes. And this way of drawing sketches is a great tool. Through this tool, in the process of finding solutions to design problems, we can transform and improve design concepts that have not yet completed. A large number of sketches will provide designers visual cues, and these visual cues will stimulate designers to think, and use relevant knowledge in memory to interact with visual cues, which can help designers produce more solutions of design problem (Fish and Scrivener, 1990). Tseng and Ball's experiment in 2010 found that the ambiguity in concept sketches can cause designers' uncertainty, which is beneficial to produce more design concepts. The following two points are the reasons why uncertainty appears in the process of design thinking, (1) the designer lacks relevant design experience or knowledge to complete the design task; (2) the design stimuli or design clue is vague and insufficient clarity. In both cases, the designers produce more new solutions to the design problem in order to reduce the uncertainty. In order to prevent participants from encountering this situation in the design thinking process, so this study clearly informed participants the design task goals, and also asked participants to search for pictures related to the design goals as visual stimuli.

3 Method

This study compares the process and effectiveness of sketch between the experimental group and the control group by using an practical experiment. Five participants in each group went through two kinds of stimuli which are GH objects and internet pictures. Using the observation method, the researchers explained the task and recorded the process with a video, while observing the participants. Finally, with a semi-structured questionnaire, retrospective interviews were used to understand how the participants adjusted the GH program or searched for pictures on the Internet, as well as the sketch process. The results were then organized, and the design results were evaluated by two design experts who have more than 10 years of design teaching experience.

Topics for the semi-structured interview included:

- How many years of design experience do you have?
- What are the difficulties you have in learning sketch and CAID?
- Do you use sketch or interact with CAID when doing thematic design, and Why?
- Could you express it completely by sketch when inventing a new shape?
- During the product design process, how many hours do you spend on product shape ideas, and how many sketches do you draw?
- Please talk about your impressive design thinking process in your experience.
- Do you usually go back and modify the design when you enter the CAID program?
- What kind of workflow do sketch and CAID represent for you? Think-draw-model it, think-draw-model it and then correct it.

- When you think about the product shape, the more common situations you encounter are: 1. You can't draw what you want, 2 You can't think of a new shape, 3. It doesn't look good when you draw it.
- Have you ever tried referring to similar products or specific shape and then modifying them as a design method? Do you believe that this method is beneficial for training shape thinking?
- Please describe your own habitual way of thinking about shape (movies, books or activities)
- Which animal-shaped speaker did you spend the longest time thinking about?
- Which parts of the stimuli did you refer to as the creative elements of the animal-shaped speakers?

3.1 Experimental Steps

The study was divided into two groups, the experimental group and the control group. The experiment was divided into three stages. In stage one, five participants from the experimental group were asked to choose one of the three different geometric element based GH programs provided by the study, and adjust the parameters to obtain six different animal heads as stimuli for sketch in stage two. The control group was asked to find six different animal shape stimuli through online searches of suitable images. In stage two, ten participants from both groups used the stimuli obtained in stage one as inspiration and drew six animal-shaped speaker proposals with pen and paper. In stage three, semi-structured interviews were conducted to gain a deeper understanding of the design behaviour of participants in the experimental group and control group and the design problems encountered during the experiment. Finally, ten participants' design inspiration stimuli and sketches were summarized, and two design experts evaluated the effect of different stimuli on design outcomes.

3.2 Stimuli

This study investigates the effects of two stimuli on different participants' shape ideas. The stimuli in the experimental group were three symmetrical GH programs. The shape change rule of the GH program is to use the three parts of the head, nose and ears as the main variables to distinguish the animal shapes, and let the participants adjust the parameters to change the details. They do not need to define a clear value. The three elements are a regular dodecahedron, a hexagonal pyramid, and two connected spheres (as shown in Fig. 1). The components of the regular dodecahedron and the double spheres are reduced and moved to the top of the head to become the animal's ears, and they can be adjusted independently to change their shape and angle. There is a vertex on the left and right sides of the back of the a hexagonal pyramid that can move forwards, backwards, left, right, up or down, serving as the ears. The front nose part of all three modeling elements can be moved forward, backward, up, down, or enlarged or reduced.

The control group uses Pinterest and Google to search for images as design stimuli. Participants can decide whether or not to search for design references online or directly sketch the design. All images searched online by the control group participants are saved by the researchers for later comparison. During the sketching process, the participants

Fig. 1. The three kinds of animal heads GH programs as stimulation in this research.

Table 1. Basic information of participants in this study

Experimental group	Learning design experience	Control group	Learning design experience
A	7 years of sketch ability and using Rhino experience	a	7 years of sketch ability and using Rhino experience
B	8 years of using Creo and Rhino experience	b	5 years of sketch and using Creo and Alias experience
C	7 years of sketch ability and using Rhino experience	c	6 years of sketch ability and using Rhino experience
D	6 years of sketch ability and using Creo and Rhino experience	d	4 years of high school advertising design/6 years of sketch ability and using AI, Solidworks and Keyshot experience
E	7 years of sketch ability and using Rhino experience	e	4 years of multimedia design in high school/6 years of sketch ability and using Solidworks experience/1 year of using VR experience

use pencil and paper to draw their design ideas. They are allowed to access visual stimuli while sketching. The entire experiment is recorded on an iPad, and the interview phase is recorded on an iPhone 11. The hardware equipment used in the experimental group of this study was an ASUS TUF Dash F15 laptop and an external monitor, allowing participants to adjust GH parameters and view the changes in the modeling on another screen. The software used was Rhino 6 and Grasshopper. In addition, OBS studio software was used for screen recording. The equipment used in the control group was a desktop computer and unlimited A4 paper, along with the participant's preferred ballpoint pen or pencil. The retrospective interview was recorded using an iPhone 11.

3.3 Participants

In this study, the participants were 10 male graduate students from the design department. This study was not aimed at exploring gender issues, but rather the experiment task of product shape and rapid design. The participants were recruited as design department graduate students who have received training in sketch and 3D modeling (industrial design group), with no gender restrictions. However, since all participants were male, the results of this study did not include female participants. The ages of the participants ranged from 23 to 26, and they have all received more than 4 years of training in sketch or CAID. Two of the participants received training in advertising and multimedia during high school (Table 1).

4 Results

At this stage, the experimental results of the experimental group and the control group were sorted out, as well as the overall opinions of the retrospective interviews. Finally, two designers with more than 10 years of design teaching experience evaluated the effectiveness of the two groups of sketch results.

4.1 Experimental Group Results

Overall, among the 5 participants in the experimental group, except for participant A, the other 4 completed the adjustment of the GH program and the sketch within 40 min. Participant A used three GH programs for shape ideas, double sphere for cats, mice, and pigs, hexagonal pyramid for dogs, and dodecahedron for rabbits and horses. Participant B chose hexagonal pyramid as the main shape element and adjusted six animal heads, while participants C and D chose dodecahedron as the main shape element. Participant E chose double sphere as the shape element (as shown in Fig. 2). In the retrospective interview, participant A mentioned that because they were uncertain about the dog and cat shapes, they felt that the mouse (with a sharp mouth) and pig (fat) were easier to grasp, so they switched to adjusting with hexagonal pyramid. Moreover, when using hexagonal pyramid to adjust the rabbit and horse, they felt that it was not similar, so they changed to use dodecahedron. Participant B used GH to adjust 6 kinds of animals within 5 min, but it took a lot of time (35 min) in the sketch stage. During the retrospective interview, participant B said that because he wanted to draw more animals' details (such as dogs and horses) based on the shape of GH, so it took more time to think. Participant E was the fastest among the five and took about 5 min to adjust 6 animals with double sphere and finished sketching the speakers of 6 animals in 15 min. In the retrospective interview, participant E mentioned that because he already had basic ideas about the 6 animal shapes, so he chose the closest sphere to adjust.

In the sketch, participant A referred to the GH model that he adjusted for the design of the computer speaker. For the dog and pig parts, during the retrospective interview, participant A stated that because he was not familiar with animals, he drew the shape based on the sound function of the computer speaker as a consistent design language. For the cat, in order to distinguish it from the dog, he added a body. For the mouse, to emphasize the long nose (combined with sound), but without a body it looked strange, so he added a body as well. The pig was designed to emphasize the fun of being plump by using its body, while the rabbit ears and horse mouth were added to emphasize the part of the speaker that outputs sound. Participant B said that because he wanted to use folded lines and folded surfaces as a unified shape, he spent a lot of time drawing front and side views. Although the rough shape was already established in GH program, he wanted to draw more details, such as the longer mouth of a dog compared to a cat, the elongated face of a horse, and the ears of a rabbit can be bent. C and D had a similar process, they stated in the retrospective interview that they had already planned the design elements of the computer speaker before adjusting the GH program. The adjustment was only a test of the program to see if it could produce sharp noses or big ears, etc., and they didn't have any specific design in mind. Participant C stated that the sketch elements were based on a flattened sphere that was cut, and the cat's tail and hands were its features. The dog's long nose, the mouse's small head and big ears, the pig's round face and big nose, the rabbit's flat face and long ears, and the horse's long face and mane were all features that were transformed into the design. Participant D uses a half-cut sphere as the main element of the shape and combines it with another element as the ear or nose to make a sound component, becoming a series of shape elements. Participant D said that horses are animals that people rarely interact with, so he was thinking about how to present a long face. But then, he came up with an idea and cut the main element into an elongated droplet-shaped section with a larger inclined angle and added small ears as a distinctive feature of the horse's shape. Participant E's sketches refer to the GH program's modeling, quickly drawing the main shape after elongating or cutting the ball, and adding a cone-shaped ear and thin cylindrical nose to complete five animal shapes. He also spent a lot of time thinking about the horse's shape. Finally, he used a column with a large R angle as the main body to show an feature of elongation.

4.2 Control Group Results

The control group invited five industrial design students with more than five years of design experience to search for pictures on the Internet as design stimuli for animal-shaped speakers. Except for participant c, other participants all searched for pictures as stimuli. Both participants a and b searched for pictures on the Internet when they had no ideas during the design process, and participants d and e searched for pictures before designing. The five participant sketch for about 30 to 50 min, and participant e spent the longest time (about 53 min). It is speculated that this was due to his design having more details, being more complex, and drawing two to three shapes for each animal. Participant A paid more attention to customer needs, considering that the speakers were designed for the same company. Therefore, he designed a consistent switch for the six animal-shaped speakers, but his design thinking was more jumping. When designing the pig, rabbit, and mouse speakers, he was based on the animal's appearance to give a feeling of design. But when designing the cat and dog speakers, he even thought of the dog house and cat bed. Participant A stated that the horse-shaped speaker was the most difficult to convert and he ultimately modified it based on the chess in the reference picture. On the other hand, participant B's design behavior was logical because he analyzed the characteristics of the six animal's appearance before designing the speakers, such as

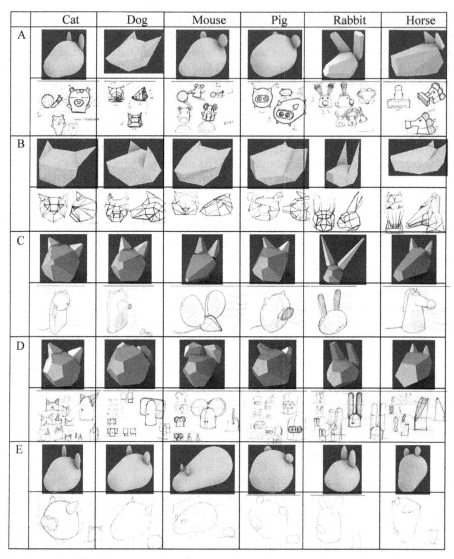

Fig. 2. The 6 animal shapes by adjusting the GH program and sketches by the 5 participants in the experimental group.

the cat, dog, and rabbit were designed based on the head and face as the main feature, the cat also has a nimble image feeling; the pig and mouse were designed based on the round body, with the pig's nose shape as the design feature; finally, the horse focused on the lines of muscle. According to the pre-design analysis, the final computer speakers of participant b also corresponds to his original setting, making his computer speakers clearer and more complete. Participant b stated that when designing, he would do product positioning before sketch, and then he would adjust during design but would not go against the original direction. Participant d had similar design behavior to participant

b. From participant d's design sketch, it could be seen that the speaker shape designs were more rounded. Among all the participants, participant d's design was the most systematic. However, participant d stated that before designing, there was no specific geometric shape in mind. Instead, he thought that if a geometric shape with sharp angles and corners, it would become too technological and lose the feeling that animals bring to people. Therefore, during design, he used the rounded shape more often. The reference that he searched before design were mostly rounded products, which showed that even though participant d did not write down the product design setting like participant b, there was already a subconscious direction for the product design. As a result, participant d's sketch was also clearer like participant b.

Participant c's design behavior was more special, because his CAID ability was greater than his sketch ability. Therefore, when conceiving the shape, he often thought about the steps of CAID while drawing, and consider the function before designing the shape. He followed the principle of "shape follows function". When designing the speakers, participant c first decomposed the shape of the animal and then eliminate unnecessary elements to emphasize a specific feature of the design. For example, when drawing the horse-shaped speaker, the head of the horse was deleted and only the body was left, and the characteristic of the horse's thin legs was emphasized as the product's feature (Fig. 3).

During the design process, participant c did not refer to any pictures and designed based on his impression of the animals and the speakers. This was a big difference from participant e, who mainly modified the design from references and mostly searched for pictures that had already transformed the animal image into products. Participant e said that due to this experiment was a rapid design experiment, so he decided to present the design in a more concrete way. Because it would take more time to transform the design and search for more pictures for abstract designs. It's noteworthy that participant e tried different switch modes to increase the uniqueness of the speaker design, such as buttons, panel control, or rotating switch. This is less common in other participant's sketches.

4.3 Evaluation Results of Design Experts

Stimuli and sketches of 10 participants were coded and organized, and then two experts with more than 10 years of design teaching experience, one specializing in sketch and the other in CAID were asked to evaluate the effectiveness of different stimuli on the design idea. Both experts agreed that visual stimuli are helpful in generating design conceptions when lacking ideas, but it is also possible to start drawing or modeling directly if there is already a design idea in mind. This opinion is consistent with the operation mode of participants C and D and the feedback from participant c.

However, the two experts have different opinions on the GH as stimuli. The sketch expert stated that the sketch process was a divergent design behavior aimed at seeking various possibilities of different shapes. Designating a certain element as the main shape usually happened after divergent thinking when there was already a shape idea for convergence (similar to the opinion of participant a), or it would be too limiting. The sketch expert also stated that this study provided the basic elements of three stimuli and maintains a certain range of shape divergence (participant A's mode of operation). The CAID expert said that GH as a visual stimuli for product shape was more in line with the

	Rabbit	Dog	Cat	Pig	Mouse	Horse
a			No	No		
b		No		No		
c	No	No	No	No	No	No
d					No	
e					No	

Fig. 3. The 6 animal stimuli searched on the Internet and sketches by the 5 participants in the control group.

design behavior in CAID. Usually, there would be a basic shape and then different product appearances would be developed based on this shape using different modeling methods (similar to the opinions of participants B, E, and a). The CAID expert also agreed that the current computer modeling tools are more suitable for small-scale shaping divergence within a specific solution space. To make large-scale structural changes, the range of parameters may need to be expanded and unreasonable shapes allowed to occur in order to have unexpected shapes appear (similar to the opinions of participants e).

Both experts believe that using GH as a stimuli and then drawing a sketch, can see the thought of the participants, or they want to use the GH program to test the modeling characteristics of certain animals, such as participant B's folded surface composition, participant C's adjustment of the proportion of the animal's nose and ears, and participant D's concern for the position and shape of the main body and details. Searching for pictures on the Internet can reveal which parts of the sketches have been transformed, such as participant a's horse, participant b's cat, participant d's pig, and participant e's rabbit and cat. Unless the participants have previously decided on a certain form direction (such as participants c and d), it is difficult to see the overall product language of the series of products. Both experts also stated that because it was a fast design with sketch, the familiarity of sketch skills would affect the result of product shape idea presentation. Some creative ideas or details required more precise rendering or modeling to see the effect, such as the common interface of the participant a, which can instead show the same family shape features on different basic elements. Design experts rated the experimental group highly, saying that they were able to effectively capture the spirit of the animal's shape and translate it into a product that could also correspond to the product's function, while some of the control group's performance was also favoured by experts. Experts indicate that such results may be due to the different l hand-drawing ability of the test subjects. The present study suggests that subsequent screening of hand-drawing ability should be conducted to investigate more deeply with a larger number of participants.

5 Conclusion

In this study, the feasibility of using the GH program and Internet search pictures as stimuli for shape ideas was compared through the sketch and design task of the experimental group and the control group, and then design experts evaluated the design effectiveness. Overall, the experimental group thinks that the GH program can be used to test the proportion of shape details, or to develop and modify the details of a series of product shape when designers have the idea. If there is no idea about the shape of the product, designers can also adjust the parameters and refer to the characteristics of the product shape proposal from GH. In the control group, if designers have ideas, they don't need to search for pictures on the Internet. Most of the pictures found on the Internet are used as references for a single shape or product details. If designers want to develop a series of product shapes with the same product language, they need to transform by themself. The following discusses the experimental results of the experts and the two groups.

5.1 Differences Between GH and Visual Stimuli—The Application of GH to Shape Thinking

Design experts believe that the GH program is more suitable for changes in a limited range of a specific shape (explore the solution space). Therefore, when the design proposal is to be carried out in the direction of a certain shape, the designer can pre-write the program for adjustment, or use the random calculation of different parameters, which can generate dozens or hundreds of different shapes, and then selected by the designer. The parameters are not necessarily adjusted by the designer, so that the shape convergence can be done with more efficiency in a state of small-scale shape convergent development. Searching for pictures on the Internet still depends on the designer's own shape transformation, which belongs to the design behavior of divergent shape thinking, because the searched pictures may stimulate the designer to think again or transform into a different shape.

5.2   Conclusion of the Experimental Group

From the process of adjusting the GH program, it can be found that the familiarity of participants with different animals will affect the adjustment results. For example, participants A and B do not know the characteristics of cats and dogs very well, so participant A tried three different programs also took more time to understand the corresponding relationship between the structure of the program and the parameters. In a similar situation, participant B chose the same program to adjust 6 shapes, but because the program could not fully achieve the shape he wanted, so a lot of time was spent on sketch. Participant B also said that it would be more efficient to do it directly with CAID. Participants C and D already had ideas about the shape of the series of products before adjusting the GH program, so they deliberately chose the element (dodecahedron) that was different from their idea, in order to understand whether there is any possibility of other shape development. Participant D stated that he had already planned the features of six animal shapes to be composed of another component, but after adjusting the dodecahedron, he came up with another GH program's spherical structure. Therefore, he decided to use the upright cylindrical shape as the main element of the animal head. Although participant E had a preliminary understanding of the features of animals, he did not have any ideas when transforming them into products, so he referred to the GH shape and draw the sketch after adjusting the GH program of the sphere. Overall, the 5 participants in the experimental group showed three types of shape thinking. Participants A and B were unfamiliar with animal characteristics, and the GH program could help them develop a series of shape features or adjust details; participants C and D had the product shape ideas before sketch, the GH program can help them adjust and think about the details of the shape; participant E also had the idea of animal features, but had no idea how to transform it into a product, and the GH program can help him think about the product elements and details when it is productized.

5.3   Conclusion of the Control Group

Many participants said that they thought of the computer mouse when drawing the animal-shaped speaker of the mouse, so they used the shape of the computer mouse to create the product shape idea. It can be seen that most designers will refer to the common products around them as the design references. Out of the five participants, four of them stated that horses are more difficult to come up with designs for compared to other animals. The reasons include: 1) the elements of horse-shaped design are harder to extract, 2) the association between horses and speaker is difficult to link, and 3) horses are less common compared to other animals and therefore harder to form a deeper impression, making it harder to design. However, participant e believes that because horses are less common, there is more imagination, whereas animals like cats and dogs are more common so harder to break away from their preconceived images. During the interview with the participants, they all said that they had used the design method of referring to similar products and modifying them. But participants a and c both expressed that they did not like to use this method for design and thought that it was not helpful for the training of product shape thinking, because that design method was difficult for them to transform and modify the references into their own designs. If they weren't careful, the design might become to imitation or plagiarism. Participant c thought that the design method of referring to similar products and modifying them was more suitable for novices. Because novices didn't have much design experience, it is a good way to learn from copying. But as an experienced designer, it was a better way to design by himself/herself first, then learned from other people's good design details, and then added them to his/her own design. However, the rest of the participants thought that the design method of referring to similar products and modifying them could help to train the product shape ability and they also used this method to design. Participants b said that usually he would not only refer to one product picture, because it would be too similar to the original design. Therefore, he would search for multiple product picture references, and take some elements from each picture, then integrate them into his own design. Participant b said it was a model learning method that refer to other designers' product shape to transform it into your own design, and he used this way to train shape ability. Participants d and e both said that when they had no ideas in the design and could not think of a new shape, they would use the method of referring to similar products and modifying them. For participants d and e, this design method can be trained the product shape ability, because looking at different design shapes can establish different product concepts and transform good design elements into your own design style.

5.4 Suggestions

According to the opinions of the two groups of participants and design experts, the GH program is more effective for specific shape directions or product details than searching for pictures on the Internet. In the future, researchers can use the GH program to test the feasibility of developing a series of product languages for specific products, such as furniture or electronic products.

Although the experimental group and the control group have different ways and opinions on the use of stimuli, for example, participant A and B in the experimental group have different opinions from C and E on the cognition of animal characteristics and the ability to transform into a series of products, participant a and c in the control group have different views on the design method of referring similar products and modifying them from participant b, d, and e. However, participant a, b, c, d and e all think that collecting and reading more product pictures on weekdays will internalize good elements into their own design materials, and these materials can be transformed into the design when designing. To sum up, the participants can be divided into two categories, one is to think about the design direction before designing, and then draw the design; the other is to start the design without prior plan and then draw while thinking. The final design sketch of the former is relatively clear and complete, while the sketch of the latter is more messy and jumpy in shape. It is suggested that in the future researchers can conduct more further purposive sampling for participants in different situations, and propose design aids in different situations.

References

Fish, J., Scrivener, S.A.R.: Amplifying the mind's eye: sketching and visual cognition. Leonardo **23**, 117–126 (1990)

Goldschmidt, G.: Serial sketching: visual problem solving in designing. Cybern. Syst. **23**(2), 191–219 (1992)

Goldschmidt, G., Smolkov, M.: Variances in the impact of visual stimuli on design problem solving performance. Des. Stud. **27**(5), 549–569 (2006)

Krish, S.: A practical generative design method. Comput. Aided Des. **43**(1), 88–100 (2011)

Lee, L.C.: Studies on Cooperative Generative Design Method for Product Shapes Development (2018)

Tsai, Y.C., Tseng, S.W.: Uncertainty for the difference in creative between experts and novices. Ind. Des. **123**, 150–155 (2010)

Cultivating Researcher-Sensibility in Novice Designers: Exploring Genre-Specific Heuristics for Game Evaluation in a Design Studio

Xueliang Li[1](✉) and Haian Xue[2]

[1] School of Design, Southern University of Science and Technology, Chuangyuan Bldg. 6, 1088 Xueyuan Avenue, Shenzhen, Guangdong, People's Republic of China
`lix16@sustech.edu.cn`
[2] Faculty of Industrial Design Engineering, Delft University of Technology, Landbergstraat 15, 2628 CE Delft, The Netherlands
`h.xue@tudelft.nl`

Abstract. This paper presents an eight-day design studio that teaches heuristic evaluation of games to third-year bachelor students at the School of Design, Southern University of Science and Technology. Through this course, students gain the first-hand experiences of developing heuristics for games through online survey and using them in idea generation and game evaluation. 13 students (working in groups of two or individually) developed 88 heuristics for 8 game genres by analyzing 349 quotes of game reviews collected from online. The heuristics were further developed into questionnaires and tested with invited 51 game players, followed up by post-interviews. The heuristics were also used as inspirational tools to help the students generate design ideas in an ideation exercise. Results of the students' work indicate usefulness of the heuristics as evaluative and inspirational tools. In the discussion, we reflected on the challenges encountered by the students over the course and how dealing with these challenges could reveal further directions of teaching research methods in HCI studios.

Keywords: Design Education · Studio · Design Research Methodology · Design Evaluation

1 Introduction

As the field of design develops, there have been continuous efforts to investigate, reflect on and add to pedagogical approaches in HCI curriculum. A solid body of literature has provided us knowledge on how to teach design in the creative context (Cross, 2007; Davis, 2017). The purposes and formats of design education have vastly changed since the focus of design education moved from artefacts to interactions (Wilcox et al., 2019). Researchers, educators, and design practitioners have reached the shared understanding that design is a fast-evolving and multidisciplinary subject that responds to the emerging technologies, product types and users' needs and contexts (Churchill et al., 2014; Grandhi, 2015). This ever-changing nature of design and its close relationship to current social-technical systems bring forward the complexity to teaching complicated design skills of crafting computational things while guiding students to base their design rationale on real users' needs. Design educators face the challenge of finding suitable approaches to teaching design in classrooms. Compared to the major efforts made to guide students in making activities, less emphasis is put on the prelogical approaches to teaching research methods in studios.

This course takes the form of an eight-day studio aimed at teaching students to develop and evaluate genre-specific heuristics for game design. Over the course, students collected game reviews from various online platforms and websites which reflected design problems of specific genres of games. Based on analysis of the shared problems, students propose a set of design principles, i.e. heuristics, which indicate the good qualities of games of those genres. Students then conducted user tests of existing games using the heuristics developed by themselves. The heuristics were also used as inspirational tools in an ideation exercise to generate design ideas across different genres. As a result, students developed 88 heuristics for 8 game genres by analyzing 349 quotes of game reviews. The findings from the user tests and ideation exercise indicate potential usefulness of the heuristics as evaluative and inspirational tools. Through reflecting on students' learning experiences during the courses, we discussed the main challenges encountered by the students while adopting and practicing research methods in the studio. Our contribution to the HCI community is twofold. First, we provide an initial model of teaching research methods in a HCI studio. Second, we call for closer attention to the key elements that shape students' experiences of learning and practicing research methods in the contexts of studio-based course, opening up future discussions on how to introduce and integrate research methods as part of design practice.

2   Related Work

2.1   Teaching Design in Studios

Studio-based courses (also known as project-based courses) have emerged as the main format of teaching HCI in classrooms. The studio-based pedagogy, long established in product and architecture design, provides an active and focused learning environment—oftentimes lasting several hours each session–in which the students apply newly gained knowledge and skills to address real-world problems while instructors provide formative feedback given each student' or groups' progress (Reimer & Douglas, 2003; Schön, 1985, 1987). The studio-based teaching emphasizes the philosophy of leaning by doing: the process of gaining knowledge is closely integrated with the act of creating artefacts. Its malleability also allows for integration of other classroom activities such as lectures, classroom exercises, students' presentation, and peer review. However, introduction of the studio-based pedagogy to HCI education (or computer science curriculum) also raises other concerns and critiques. While research methods in HCI are well established–including methods on how to conduct investigative activities in formative, iterative and evaluative stages of the design process–these methods are often taught through textbooks or lectures spread over the semester, and less emphasized as the key learning objectives in design education (Wilcox et al., 2019).

2.2 Teaching Research Methodology to Design Students

Teaching design practice and teaching research methodology seem intrinsically conflicting. This has been mentioned by design educators who recognize design as a creative process, which can be hindered by provision of prescriptive methods. Some researchers (e.g., Rivard & Faste, 2012) even hold that assumptions borrowed from traditional "call-and-response or memorization-based methods" might be *irrelevant* or even *harmful* to students in the context of design education. Such a lack of attention to teaching research methodology can be due to the limited time and teaching resources over the course. While many universities do not restrict resources that can be integrated in studio courses, students are often encouraged to work independently to grasp knowledge across disciplines such as psychology, software engineering and design (oftentimes outside classrooms) (Plimmer & Amor, 2006). In the model of studio-based pedagogy, instructors' roles are often described as advisors or coaches who provide tailored consultancy to individuals. Finally, it is acknowledged that the learning objectives of studio-based courses are not necessarily in line with the pursuit of the knowledge contribution to the filed. To this point, Rivard and Faste (2012) proposed the notion of "learning reflexivity" which is the students' ability to reach a deep awareness of learning objectives and to impose critical reflection on their progress to reach such goals. According to them, the learning of knowledge by the students should not be judged by the *depth*, but the *interconnectedness* of different aspects of the knowledge.

2.3 From Design Practitioners to Design Researchers

Introducing research methodology to designers mechanically or uncritically could be problematic as well. This was noticed in 1980 by Jones, who shared the concern that overemphasis on the procedural knowledge on design might instead constrain creativity of designers:

> *"I can see, very readily, from my experience with design methods, that, when one attempts to introduce a new idea of how something should be done, it is either ignored… or, worse than that, is misunderstood and applied in a way that contradicts the original reasons for seeking a new method… Rationality, originality seen as the means to open the intuition to aspects of life outside the designer's experience, became, almost overnight, a toolkit of rigid methods that obliged designers and planners to act like machines, deaf to every human cry and incapable of laughter."* (Jones, 1980, p. 173)

Regardless of the debate on whether design should be taught with methodological approaches, we see the type of knowledge obtained by the students through hands-on creative practice, critique and reflection in the studio differ from that preprogrammed by design researchers or methodologists. This can be explained by the three types of knowledge proposed by Nagel (2014). What studio instructors can provide to the students include *propositional knowledge* (knowledge of facts), which might include concepts and frameworks explaining the phenomena from theoretical perspectives, and *procedural knowledge* (knowledge on how to do something), which can refer to the procedural guidance provided to the students on how to create artefacts and how to investigate users' needs and impacts of the design. In studios, students might first acquire *personal knowledge* (knowledge by acquaintance) which is informed by their previous life experiences and self-discovery while confronting previously unfamiliar real-world problems. The gaining of personal knowledge forms the starting point for the students to master procedural knowledge and understand the propositional knowledge relevant to their design practices. From our point of view, it seems that the current studio-based pedagogy mainly focuses on training of design practitioners who are masters of *knowing-how*, but lacks attention to the cultivation of design researchers who not only know *how to design* but also *why design* and *what* their designs could bring about.

A new flavor needs to be added to the teaching of studios to promote the transformation for the students from a technically *skillful* designer (being able to create things) to a *sensible* design researcher (being able to perceive and articulate real-world problems and come up with design ideas to address them). To follow up on this argument, in this paper we present a case of teaching research methods to undergraduate students in studios. The design rationale and procedure of the course are explained below.

3 Methods

3.1 Heuristic Evaluation in Game Design

The course's structure is informed by the application of heuristic evaluation in games, and research on playful experiences within and beyond game design. Heuristic evaluation is an (informal) inspection technique where expert evaluators find the usability problems in an interface by referring to a set of predefined usability principles, called heuristics (Nielsen, 1995). In game design, heuristic evaluation provides a flexible and low-cost method to identify usability problems that do not necessarily require fully functional prototypes and procedural task references (Pinelle et al., 2008; Rajanen & Rajanen, 2018; Strååt et al., 2014; Vieira et al., 2019). Note that usability of games might indicate different meanings as in typical product usability. Some researchers (e.g., Desurvire et al., 2004; Pinelle et al., 2008) tend to define game usability as independent issues that are separate from entertainment, engagement and storyline. For example, Pinelle et al. (2008) described game usability as "as the degree to which a player is able to learn, control, and understand a game," which is additional to artistic issues (e.g., voice acting and visual styles) and technical issues (e.g., graphic quality and performance issues). Other researchers proposed heuristics for games oriented around engagement, fun and pleasure, which can be observed on top of functionality issues (see Korhonen et al., 2009 for a review of these works). Building on Korhonen et al.'s (2009) work, Lucero and colleagues (Lucero et al., 2013, 2014; Lucero & Arrasvuori, 2010) made the effort of developing a set of design principles to promote playful experiences that apply within and beyond the game design. In this paper, we take a broader understanding of game usability that covers any aspect that might promote or hinder positive playful experiences in games.

We choose heuristic evaluation as the research method to be taught in the studio because: (1) it serves as an introductory method to a broader range of product evaluation methods; (2) it is easy to understand and does not require too much resource beyond the classrooms. The main structure of the course is inspired by Pinelle et al. (2008) who engaged with a bottom-up approach to develop game evaluation heuristics by analyzing game reviews from online. Inspired by this work, we encouraged students to develop their heuristics on their own by collecting and analyzing players' and game reviewers' comments from online. By doing so, we aim to keep the students updated with the latest development of games and the online community, the understanding of which could form the basis of the categorization of the heuristics. The specific agenda of the course is introduced below.

3.2   Procedure of the Workshop

At the beginning of the course, 13 students (third-year bachelor students) teamed up in 2 or work individually on eight game genres that cover the most games available on the market, i.e., RPG Games, Puzzle Games, Construction & Management Simulation Games, Board Games, Platform Games, Rouge-like Games, Party Games, and Grand Strategy Games. During the eight days of the course, the students are guided through six stages (illustrated in Fig. 1):

1. **Problem identification:** students search online for game reviews and players' comments that reflect shared "design problems" of those genres;
2. **Developing game heuristics:** students propose genre-specific heuristics by "reversing" the identified "design problems" into "design principles";
3. **Self/Pilot-test of the heuristics:** students improve their heuristics by self-testing (writing game reviews using the heuristics as outlines) and pilot-tests within the classroom;
4. **Evaluation of the heuristics:** students invite game players to evaluate a target game using the heuristics (taking the form of a 5-point scale) and interview them afterwards;
5. **Heuristics in idea generation:** students engage in an ideation exercise using the *heuristic cards* as sources of inspiration;

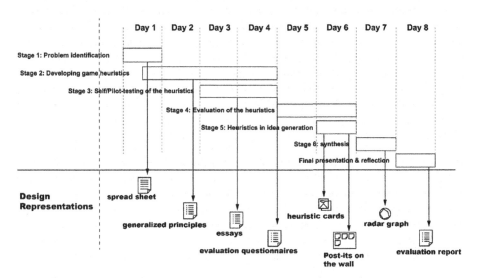

Fig. 1. Timeline of the course and the design representations used in the course.

6. **Synthesis/reflection on the results:** students summarize results of the user test and the ideation exercise and reflect on the strength and weakness of their heuristics. Students also write a piece of reflection on their learning experiences throughout the course.

3.3 Strategies to Motivate Active Learning

During the course, certain strategies were implemented to motivate active learning of the students.

Multi-modality of Representations. With representation, we refer to the design tools and methods and production of their use in the design process, with which designers externalize their design rationales, specific design ideas and vision of the future use scenarios (Bodker, 1998). Representations reflect expectations and experience of designers as they are working through design problems in the present towards solutions in the future. Note that some representations are rather descriptive which are mainly used in communication within design teams and with other collaborators (such as analysis of design problems); others are oriented towards future use of the technology and efficient to share with users and other stakeholders in the system (e.g., prototypes, mock-ups and visualization of use scenarios). In this studio, the students have engaged with different modalities of representations including spreadsheet (data sheet using Excel), generalized principles (text), heuristic cards (visualization with description), essays (game reviews), evaluation questionnaires, post-its on the wall, radar graph and evaluation report. Both textual and visual methods are used to help students to investigate and analyze the situations and to present their design ideas. How these representations are implemented along the process of the course is also illustrated in Fig. 1.

Learning by Playing. At the stage of "heuristics in idea generation" (Day 6), *heuristic cards* were created by the students, each composed of a brief explanation and a visualization of the design principle. See Fig. 2 for some examples of the cards. These cards were used as sources of inspiration in an idea-generation game. Inspired by the "PLEX Brainstorming technique" (Lucero & Arrasvuori, 2010), this game asks each player to take turns to add one card on top of each other's in the pool and try to create a narrative based on their connections (which is noted down on the post-it). The player can skip their turn if he or she is stuck. The one who empty their hands first will win. The students were asked to take the cards created by different groups. Figure 3 shows the scenarios of the students playing the game and sharing their design ideas on the wall.

Peer Observation and Discussion. In the final presentation, students tried the "peer observation & post-presentation discussion" (Fig. 4). Each group of the students was assigned as the observer of another group while they are presenting. The observer group were re-invited back to the stage together with the observed group after the final presentation and gave their comments on how well the observed group has presented their work. By doing so, each group took both the roles of presenters and observers and might gain different perspectives while reflecting on their own work and presentation skills.

Fig. 2. Examples of the heuristic cards made by the students. Left to right: the design principles that are visualized are Cause and Effect (Puzzle Games), Friendly Conflict (Board Games) and Good Storytelling (Platform Games).

Fig. 3. Scenarios of the ideation exercise using the heuristic cards as sources of inspiration (left) and sharing the ideas through post-its on the wall (right).

Fig. 4. Students sharing comments on their observation on another group's work.

4 Results

4.1 Genre-Specific Heuristics

As a result, the students proposed 88 genre-specific heuristics generated from the analysis of 349 online reviews and comments collected from online. Table 1 shows an overview of these heuristics. These heuristics were tested with 51 game players on eight games selected as representatives of these genres. Both quantitative data (scores of the scales) and qualitative data (quotations of players from the follow-up interviews) are reported by the students. In the ideation exercise, students generated 70 initial design ideas.

4.2 Usefulness of the Heuristics

Findings from the user tests of the games using the heuristics indicated the usefulness of these heuristics to identify potential design problems and elicit insights on the experiences of games. For example, students on the group of Puzzle Games learned how unmatching background music could disrupt the experience of the game while investigating the principle of "Atmosphere and Vibe" on a puzzle-solving game with a horror style (Paper Wedding Gown 4™), to which point they shared a comment from a player

Table 1. Summary of the genre-specific heuristics for game evaluation.

Genres	Functionality	Non-functionality
RPG games	• Appearance • Action • Interaction • Sound effect • Operation • 3D view comfortability • Matching level between devices and game	• Immersive engagement • Community harmony • Task system • Achievement • Pleasure
Puzzle games	• Difficulty and complexity • Cause and effect • Guidance and feedback • Friendly operation process • Network and server technology	• Fun of puzzles • Theme expression efficiency • Reality meaning • Atmosphere or vibe • Built-in charges and Ads • Quick save and quit
Construction & Management Simulation Games	• Programming accomplishment [richness of gameplay] • Randomness control • Miscellaneous control • Inflation control and purchasing experience • Complexity balance	• Reward system • Information richness • Interaction richness • Socialization sustainability • Aesthetics, vision, and acoustics E • thical problems

(*continued*)

Table 1. (*continued*)

Genres	Functionality	Non-functionality
Board Games	• Uncertainty • Diversity of gameplay • Portability • Learnability • Reasonable duration • Good quality [of making] • Clear process • Proper visual style • [Appropriate] Level of Challenge	• Friendly vibe • Immersion of background story • Engagement • Positive emotion • Value guidance
Platform Games	• Good guidance • Proper difficulty • Good sense of manipulation • Immersive feedback	• Good story telling • Good game art • Rich game content • Diversified gameplay • Motivated exploration • Possibilities for expansion
Rouge-like Games	• Variety • Appropriate inheritance • Beauty of game pictures • Effects of striking response • Incentive frequency • Compatibility between the narrative and the game [gameplay]	• Sense of achievements • Affection fading • Proper frustration • Consolation for mistakes
Party Games	• Narrative • Virous playing mechanism • Difficulty • Participants [participation] • Content • Single-player • Balance of different players • Visual effect • Software infrastructure	• Involvement • Atmosphere • Friendship
Grand Strategy Games	• System compatibility • Game mechanics • PvE experience • PvP experience	• Learning effort • Memes [icons] in the game • Historical representation • Goal setting

in the interview: "it [the background music] does no good to its horror atmosphere, on the contrary [it] makes it quite funny." Group of Board Games discovered how the principle of "Friendly Conflict" could help identify the potential of the game to stimulate the tension among players in a positive way. They shared a quote from a player who participated the heuristic evaluation of a board game (Love Letter™): "I think it always causes conflict, for the five other players were having fun from me, but I was happy that they were having fun."

We also see the potential of these heuristics to be used as inspirational tool to generate design ideas across game genres. In the brainstorming exercise, the groups of Board Games and Rogue-like Games came up with the idea of a moral system in the game by combining the principles of "Value Guidance" and "Appropriate Inheritance":

"The player can take inheritance from his character' previous life for doing good. If his character does a lot morally good behavior before the character die, then he will serendipitously find his new character stronger than the previous one and get a sense of achievement."

Students also learned about the directions to improve the heuristics and how to better use the heuristics to inspect usability issues of games. Students saw the opportunities to reorganize the structure of the heuristics, like Group of Board Games who realized that some of principles (e.g., Diversity of Gameplay and Appropriate Level of Challenge) could be grouped into a higher-level class. Many students mentioned that they need better approaches to introduce the heuristics to the players. For example, a student from Group of Platform Games shared her observation that "some participants would have his or her own understanding of the principle after just reading the title, and this led to misunderstanding... [and] some interviewees didn't know which principle they [the problems] belong to and may have different opinions." Some students were also aware that the order of going through the heuristics could affect the players' understanding of the set of heuristics. To this point, one student from Group of Puzzle Games mentioned that the principle of "Atmosphere or Vibe" could confuse people if asked at the beginning, which should be based on a general understanding of the game.

5 Discussion

Below, we reflect on students' learning experiences based on the instructor's (the first author) observation notes, the students' self-reflection by the end of the course, and collaborative reflection with colleagues. We discuss the challenges that students have encountered when developing and evaluating the heuristics, and how these challenges could inform some initial insights on how to promote active learning of research methods in design studios.

5.1 Tension Between Creation and Documentation

We recognize how the students' mindsets differ when engaged in design representations with the intention of creation and documentation. Bodker (1998) explained the dilemma regarding the use of design representations: design representations should be *sketchy* and *incomplete* to allow for open interpretation and flexible use here and now; they need to be *complete* and *rigid* for designers to hold on to when moving towards the design implementation. As in the context of design education, similar situations are observed when students try to use methods of representations as ways to explore design ideas and at the same to document their work-in-progresses (e.g., sketching).

Through our course, we see how the design representations were adopted by the students differently due to their orientation to creation or documentation. The students seemed more enthusiastic when involved in creation, for example design of the *heuristic cards* for games. As for assignments that are to be done with strict procedures (e.g., collecting reviews and comments from online, summarizing shared design problems), some students expressed their concern about how this work could link to design. One student (Construction & Management Simulation Games) mentioned that "learning something about game survey and evaluation might not be so interesting as designing something." Making the transformation from description of design problems to creation of design is also difficult for the students. Frustration was observed among students when they were to generate new ideas from analysis of the data. We see their instinct of recognizing potential opportunities did not always end up with explicit rationale leading to specific designs.

5.2 Switch Between the First-Person, Second-Person and Third-Person Perspectives

In this course, students engaged in different perspectives to identify the design problems, investigate existing games, and come up with initial design ideas.

While analyzing design problems collected from online and reflecting on insights gained from the investigation of existing games using the heuristics, students took a third-person perspective to make sure their interpretations were based on solid evidence and justifiable. In the interviews with players after evaluation of the games, students were encouraged to follow a second-person perspective, to resonate or empathize with the player through paying close attention to the interviewees' singular experiences and asking follow-up questions, to elicit *fine grained descriptions* and *rich narratives* from the interviewees (Petitmengin, 2006). The students were also asked to write an autobiographical game review–from a first-person perspective–using the heuristics developed by themselves.

We see how integration of these three interrelated perspectives could help the students gain the sense of the dynamic characteristics of a design researcher as being *sensitive* (to their own life experiences), empathic (to the other's experiences) and *objective* (to the general audience or academic community) in different contexts. For example, the student working on Rogue-like Games reflected on his notes taken in the interviews and regretted that he was too polite and should have asked more follow-up questions. To this point, we see how the second-person perspective could get in the way when trying to collect useful data from an objective view. One student of the Board Games Group appreciated the practice of writing a game review themselves and comparing it to the results of the interview with others: "it is important not to accept the knowledge instilled by others without thinking at all. It is important to have your own ideas, and learn actively." Hereby we see the importance of the training of introspection ability of designers. As suggested by Xue and Desmet (2019), the starting point for a designer to conduct design research should be defining the experiential distance between the designer's own life experience and that of the target users.

5.3 Dealing with Generalization and Specification

Students also faced the challenge of managing design knowledge at different levels of abstraction. Höök and Löwgren (2012) discussed how the knowledge generated from the design-oriented HCI research might vary on different levels of abstraction, ranging from specific design instances to general theories that apply across different contexts and over time. According to them, a design researcher should not only focus on present novel design work, but also engage in the reflection and articulation of the design knowledge that connects design examples to general insights or rules that can be beneficial to other designers. In the context of design education, this requires the instructors to not only involve the students in design exploration and implementation, but also familiarize them with the process of knowledge construction, i.e., how the knowledge is generated, communicated, and contested.

In our studio, students worked on both specific design examples (e.g., reviews and comments on specific games) and general design heuristics, which according to Höök and Löwgren (2012) is a typical *intermediate level knowledge* as the other evaluative tools. We recognize how the students experienced difficulties in both making abstract categorization and keeping their insights relevant to the specific context. Some students regretted that they had not made the full use of the data collected from online. One student (Party Games) admitted that he was too "subjective" when making the principles and "didn't get good use of the collected data." On the other hand, some students also found it difficult to articulate commonalities shared by the problems while at the same time making the heuristics pertain to the specific genres. For example, the group of Board Games shared the concern that their heuristics were both too detailed that they could not cover all the aspects and at the same time too vague that they were not clear to the users. Another student of RPG Games mentioned that "our design principles were too detailed and didn't highlight the key design principles of RPGS."

While reflecting on these difficulties encountered by the students, we realize that mastering the ability to manage different levels of abstraction in design research might take further individual development that goes beyond a studio course. This individual growth requires not only deep familiarity with the original contexts, but also rich understanding of the common senses and shared languages in the knowledge domain. This is especially seen in students who struggled to find the right terms that could accurately elaborate their insights, as said by a student (Platform Games): "when we were confused, we just thought and thought, but didn't try to read more to find out the solution."

5.4 Research Methods in Design as Informative Processes or Backwards Reasoning?

Last but not the least, we would like to address the point that whether research methods are needed to produce good quality design. Many researchers (e.g., Bodker, 1998; Button & Sharrock, 1994) noticed in design practice methods are not *followed*, but *made working* in specific contexts, or even in the backward fashion in designers' minds. To this point, we find an explanation from Horst Rittel who talked about *design reasoning* in 1987:

> *"[F]rom the beginning, the designer has an idea of the 'whole' resolution of his problem which changes with increasing understanding of the problem, and the image of its resolution develops from blurry to sharp and back again, frequently being revised, altered, detailed and modified."* (Rittel, 1987, p. 2)

Following Rittel's words, we see the value of teaching research methods to design students, who might not appreciate the logic of research or even find it redundant while learning. However, introduction of research methodology to novice designers provides an anchor point in the back-and-forth between the designers' intuition and how their designs could make a difference in the real world. Such cultivation would benefit the students in the long run whether they would one day engage in design as design practitioners or design researchers.

6 Conclusion

While work exists that aims to provide step-by-step guidance to students in design studios, less attention is paid to the cultivation of researcher-sensibility that fills the gap between the education of design practitioners and design researchers. In this paper, we present a studio course in which students were guided to develop and evaluate heuristics for games of different genres. Through reflecting on the students' work and observation from the instructor's perspective, we revealed the potential issues faced by the students when learning and practicing research methods in design studios. We highlighted how, by paying close attention to the tension between the act of creation and documentation, switching between different perspectives (as the first person, second person and third person in the situation), and acceptance of design knowledge at different levels of abstraction, the design instructors could guide the students to achieve deeper learning experiences in learning research methods in studios. Our work provides some initial insights for broader discussions on how to teach research methodology to novice designers.

References

Bodker, S.: Understanding representation in design. Hum. Comput. Interact. **13**(2), 107–125 (1998)

Button, G., Sharrock, W.: Occasioned practices in the work of software engineers. In: Requirements Engineering: Social and Technical Issues, pp. 217–240 (1994)

Churchill, E., Preece, J., Bowser, A.: Developing a living HCI curriculum to support a global community. In: CHI 2014 Extended Abstracts on Human Factors in Computing Systems, pp. 135–138 (2014)

Cross, N.: From a design science to a design discipline: understanding designerly ways of knowing and thinking. In: Design Research Now, pp. 41–54. Springer (2007). https://doi.org/10.1007/978-3-7643-8472-2_3

Davis, M.: Teaching design: a guide to curriculum and pedagogy for college design faculty and teachers who use design in their classrooms. Simon and Schuster (2017)

Desurvire, H., Caplan, M., Toth, J. A.: Using heuristics to evaluate the playability of games. In: CHI 2004 Extended Abstracts on Human Factors in Computing Systems, pp. 1509–1512 (2004)

Grandhi, S.: Educating ourselves on HCI education. Interactions **22**(6), 69–71 (2015)

Höök, K., Löwgren, J.: Strong concepts: Intermediate-level knowledge in interaction design research. ACM Trans. Comput. Hum. Interact. (TOCHI) **19**(3), 1–18 (2012)

Jones, J.C.: … in the dimension of time: thoughts about the context of designing. Des. Stud. **1**(3), 172–176 (1980). https://doi.org/10.1016/0142-694X(80)90025-3

Korhonen, H., Montola, M., Arrasvuori, J. (2009). Understanding playful user experience through digital games. In: International Conference on Designing Pleasurable Products and Interfaces, pp. 13–16 (2009)

Lucero, A., Arrasvuori, J.: PLEX Cards: a source of inspiration when designing for playfulness. In: Proceedings of the 3rd International Conference on Fun and Games, pp. 28–37 (2010)

Lucero, A., Holopainen, J., Ollila, E., Suomela, R., Karapanos, E.: The playful experiences (PLEX) framework as a guide for expert evaluation. In: Proceedings of the 6th International Conference on Designing Pleasurable Products and Interfaces, pp. 221–230 (2013)

Lucero, A., Karapanos, E., Arrasvuori, J., Korhonen, H.: Playful or gameful? Creating delightful user experiences. Interactions **21**(3), 35–39 (2014). https://doi.org/10.1145/2590973

Nagel, J.: Knowledge: A Very Short Introduction. OUP Oxford (2014)

Nielsen, J.: How to conduct a heuristic evaluation. Nielsen Norman Group **1**(1), 8 (1995)

Petitmengin, C.: Describing one's subjective experience in the second person: an interview method for the science of consciousness. Phenomenol. Cogn. Sci. **5**(3–4), 229–269 (2006)

Pinelle, D., Wong, N., Stach, T.: Heuristic evaluation for games: usability principles for video game design. In: Proceedings of the SIGCHI Conference on Human Factors in Computing Systems, pp. 1453–1462 (2008)

Plimmer, B., Amor, R.: Peer teaching extends HCI learning. In: Proceedings of the 11th Annual SIGCSE Conference on Innovation and Technology in Computer Science Education, pp. 53–57 (2006)

Rajanen, M., Rajanen, D.: Heuristic evaluation in game and gamification development. GamiFIN, pp. 159–168 (2018)

Reimer, Y.J., Douglas, S.A.: Teaching HCI design with the studio approach. Comput. Sci. Educ. **13**(3), 191–205 (2003)

Rittel, H.: The reasoning of designers: delivered at the international congress on planning and design theory. IGP (1987)

Rivard, K., Faste, H.: How learning works in design education: educating for creative awareness through formative reflexivity. In: Proceedings of the Designing Interactive Systems Conference, pp. 298–307 (2012)

Schön, D.A.: The design studio: an exploration of its traditions and potentials. International Specialized Book Service Incorporated (1985)

Schön, D.A.: Educating the Reflective Practitioner: Toward a New Design for Teaching and Learning in the Professions. Jossey-Bass (1987)

Strååt, B., Rutz, F., Johansson, M.: Does game quality reflect heuristic evaluation?: Heuristic evaluation of games in different quality strata. Int. J. Gaming Comput. Mediated Simul. (IJGCMS) **6**(4), 45–58 (2014)

Vieira, E.A.O., da Silveira, A.C., Martins, R.X.: Heuristic evaluation on usability of educational games: a systematic review. Inform. Educ. **18**(2), 427–442 (2019)

Wilcox, L., DiSalvo, B., Henneman, D., Wang, Q.: Design in the HCI classroom: setting a research agenda. In: Proceedings of the 2019 on Designing Interactive Systems Conference, pp. 871–883 (2019)

Xue, H., Desmet, P.M.A.: Researcher introspection for experience-driven design research. Des. Stud. **63**, 37–64 (2019)

Optimizing the Design Process of 3D Printing Services for Personal Customization

Miao Liu$^{(\boxtimes)}$ ⬡ and Wenjing Yang

East China University of Science and Technology, Shanghai 200237, People's Republic of China
183787975@qq.com

Abstract. Based on the demand for service design process optimization in the field of 3D printing technology for private customization, a complete concept and procedure of the service design process of 3D printing technology applied to customized products are proposed to provide a reference for enterprises and designers. First, the literature research method is used in this study to summarize and arrange the associated research in the field of 3D printing technology and service design, and then the general process of 3D printing service design is summarized. Following that, user research and statistical analysis are employed to investigate the service requirements of user groups that favor personalized goods and to construct an integrated service process of "model-process-manufacturing-logistics" with users at the center. Finally, using the customized product client design as an example, the customized product service design system is obtained. The method and procedure of the 3D printing service design process for private customization can meet the public's demand for personalized and diverse product services while also completing the service mode transformation from product to experience, which reflects an important direction of future manufacturing mode evolution.

Keywords: 3D Printing Technology · Customized Products · Service Design · User Experience

1 Introduction

1.1 Research Background

With the growing popularity of human-centered concepts and rising market demand in the service industry, the field of service design is progressively displaying its enormous potential. To react to the demand of "Made in China 2025," additive manufacturing and product design have become significant areas of promotion with the growth of society and the economy. 3D printing technology, with its technical advantages such as digitalization of workflow, no need for machining and molds, and no increase in cost for manufacturing complex items, has broken through the original industrial design method and the existing traditional pattern of manufacturing industry, characterized by personalized customization and socialized manufacturing, has become an advanced manufacturing model in the development of manufacturing industry in the new era, and is gradually widely used in the field of industrial design, especially in the field of customized product design. Customized products are those that are made to satisfy the individual demands of clients and differ from conventional, large-scale manufacturing in a variety of ways, including specification index, quantity, color, odor, packaging, and branding. 3D printing technology can easily convert digital models to 3D models, modify and adapt product shapes flexibly, and give more precise service for customized items. Nowadays, the industry's development is more mature, and product design is more uniform. In the face of strong market rivalry, differentiation has emerged as the key to overcoming the homogeneity challenge. Consumers in the purchase of a product have not only generated the desire for product functioning, but more is the confession of self-emotion. As a result, precisely understanding the user's particular emotional demands and improving the service design process of customized products is the key to attaining industrial design value and winning the market. The 5G digital mobile Internet era is changing people's lifestyles, and at a time when information is becoming popular, consumers are looking for and experiencing services and needs that meet their personalities, and even directly or indirectly participate in the design, production, and manufacturing of products, resulting in products with individual characteristics [1]. Private customization through 3D printing may efficiently connect users' emotional links with product shapes. In the face of the high cost and low efficiency of customized items for the people, as well as other impediments, 3D printing technology offers clear benefits. With the advancement of technology, the maturity of business models, and the formation of big data in the context of the Internet, designers fully use and analyze users' real data for research and insight into their behavior, psychology, and needs, in order to better improve the existing service ecology [2].

1.2   Research Purpose and Significance

The purpose of this study is to confront the field of 3D printing technology for private customization, based on the demand for service design process optimization, emphasizing the perfect integration of products and services, attempting to integrate design resources and manufacturing resources from all over the world through a shared network, and proposing a complete concept and procedure of 3D printing technology service design process applied to customized products. The significance of this research may be seen in both theoretical and practical dimensions. The method and procedure of the 3D printing service design process for private customization can realize the user-oriented 3D printing customization service process, meet the public demand for personalized and diverse product services, optimize the user's use and customization experience, achieve design sharing and demand sharing, improve the efficiency of research, design, production, and other links, save the cost of mold opening, storage, logistics, and other processes, and save the cost of mold opening, storage, logistics, and other processes.

1.3   Current Status of Research

The Current State of Research on 3D Printed Customized Products. In the last three years, researchers both at home and abroad have produced impressive accomplishments in the field of 3D printing. Researchers in the United States and elsewhere are delving deeper into the topic of customization, particularly bespoke design mixed with 3D printing technology. Yang Yanhua classified 3D printing technology into material type, morphology, heat source, and process combination, and summarized the 3D printing trend toward diversity, efficiency, stability, and inclusion [4]. Using hydrogel material as an example, Li, Jinhua, et al. demonstrated the applicability of 3D printing in the medical industry and wearable electrical devices, among other things [5]. The combination of parametric modeling technology with 3D printing technology, according to Song, J. et al., will become a key design and manufacturing paradigm, particularly in the realm of personalized bespoke design and production [6]. With the advancement of 3D printing technology, Oliveira et al. proposed that users require the ability to completely change the process parameters of the product, and the authors studied the effect of 3D printing process parameters on manufacturing quality and material properties and guided how to modify the parameters to achieve specific design goals for a given product [7]. Yuan Mingjie et al. proposed that as 3D printing technology becomes more widespread, the identity and function of consumers in the customization business are reconfigured, and consumers may be involved in the custom design process [8]. According to Elkasabgy et al., 3D printing technology is projected to transform medication delivery methods by allowing for the customization of drug compositions [9]. 3D printer productivity is nearly identical for regular and bespoke goods. Because the whole manufacturing process is automated, the yield of printed items may be ensured by providing precise model files, matching equipment, and high-quality materials [3]. Using CiteSpace software to assess 3D printing research at home and abroad, current research successes in 3D printing are mostly represented in three aspects: technological innovation, material expansion, and application fields. The study in this article focuses on applications, such as research on customized organs, customization, product design, and industrial design. The key is in user demands, customization, personalization, service design, optimization design, user experience, and so on, when combined with the design field to study research hotspots and trends.

The Current State of Research on 3D Printing Service Design for Private Customization. The development of the customization industry also pulls the progress of the service industry, and in recent years, domestic and foreign scholars have conducted research on the field of service design. Wang Ke et al. proposed that the demand for customized products is increasing day by day and has reached a stage that cannot be ignored and should be vigorously researched to meet. With the continuous progress of 3D printing materials and technologies, the service design innovation combined with the concept of setting services from the user's perspective will promote the development of customized products in various industries [3]. Zhiyong Wang et al. proposed that in 3D printing technology, the four main components of target, screening, realization, and matching constitute the basic resources of the personalized customization service platform, as well as the future resources of the platform [10]. Dongming Chen et al. proposed that since only 3D digital model files are needed to complete printing by 3D printers, the accurate and fast creation, and maintenance of 3D models becomes an important factor affecting the product design cycle in the face of customization needs [11]. According to Lu et al., the service process of 3D printing customized products is user-oriented, and the user is "empowered" through a design solution generation system based on parametric technology [12]. In other words, the user's wants are translated into unique design solutions, and the goods are then made using 3D printing technology, which may enhance the efficiency of research, design, mold making, and manufacturing while reducing mold making and storage costs [3]. For example, Ying Liu claimed that 3D printing technology may play an active part in the whole life cycle of cultural and creative goods [13], which is one of the strong qualities of 3D printing technology in the information era. Using children's creative workstations as an example, Xiang Li et al. analyzed the characteristics and shortcomings of the service platform and proposed a 3D printing technology-based personalized customization service platform with the basic resource composition of "target-screening-realization-feedback" and the future resource composition of "logistics-management-innovation". Based on 3D printing technology, the fundamental foundation of a customized modification service platform for children's toys was presented [14]. Li Wanzuan et al. concentrated on Chengdu shadow head stubble symbols, created a symbol library and a personalized shadow image generation program, and combined user needs with intelligent 3D model application services to create a 3D printing-based self-customization system for Chengdu shadow cultural and creative products [15].

2   Research Methods

2.1   Literature Research Method

To understand the existing research ideas and methods, we collected 3D printing, customized products, and service design-related literature through various channels such as CNKI and the web of science, and by sorting out the concepts and practices in related fields at home and abroad, using a scientific analysis framework to discover their existing desirability and shortcomings, and clarify the research hotspots. This study serves as a reasonable beginning point for subsequent research by providing a theoretical foundation for an in-depth analysis of the optimization of the design process of 3D printing services for individual customization.

2.2   KANO Model Analysis Method

The KANO model is a two-dimensional cognitive model proposed in the 1980s by the famous Japanese quality management master Noriaki Kano, primarily used to classify and prioritize user requirements based on an analysis of the impact of user requirements on user satisfaction, reflecting the non-linear relationship between product performance and user satisfaction. Must-be Quality, One-dimensional Quality, Attractive Quality, Indifferent Quality, and Reverse Quality are the five sorts of factors that influence contentment (see Fig. 1).

The KANO model analysis method is a collection of structured questionnaires and analysis methods based on the KANO model's principle for customer demand segmentation, primarily through standardized questionnaires for research, categorizing each factor

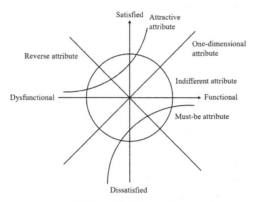

Fig. 1. KANO model

attribute based on the research results, and solving the problem of product attribute positioning to improve customer satisfaction. First, the product or service needs are identified from the user's perspective; second, the questionnaire is designed and effectively implemented to categorize the obtained user satisfaction into five levels and to generate a KANO model evaluation criteria table for the secondary demand attributes based on the user's two-way satisfaction evaluation of the service provision or not (see Table.1).

Table 1. KANO model evaluation criteria table

		Dysfunctional				
		Like	Must-be	Neutral	Live-with	Dislike
Functional	Like	Q	A	A	A	O
	Must-be	R	I	I	I	M
	Neutral	R	I	I	I	M
	Live-with	R	I	I	I	M
	Dislike	R	R	R	R	Q

M, O, A, I, and R are the initials of the 5 levels of needs, and Q is the suspicious result. The positive problem data and the negative problem data are counted out and substituted into the following calculation formula.

$$Better\ coefficient = \frac{A + O}{A + O + M + I} \tag{1}$$

$$Worse\ coefficient = \frac{O + M}{A + O + M + I} * (-1) \tag{2}$$

Better coefficient refers to user satisfaction, and its value is usually positive, the larger the value, the higher the user satisfaction; Worse coefficient refers to user dissatisfaction, and its value is usually negative, the smaller the value, the lower the user satisfaction. According to the Better coefficient and Worse index, four quadrants are drawn, which are the expected attribute, charm attribute, undifferentiated attribute, and essential attribute. Desired attribute means that user satisfaction will increase when an attribute falls into this quadrant; charming attribute means that user satisfaction will not decrease when an attribute does not fall into this quadrant; non-differentiated attribute means that user satisfaction will not change whether an attribute falls into this quadrant or not; essential attribute means that user satisfaction will not increase when an attribute falls into this quadrant.

The KANO model analysis approach is used in this study to correctly examine user demands. Customer demands may be more accurately defined by evaluating the questionnaire findings, allowing a 3D printing bespoke product service method geared at meeting user wants to be built.

3 KANO Model User Requirements Study

3.1 Subjects

The subjects of this research are primarily 3D printer website service personnel, suppliers, 3D printing technicians, 3D printing users, and potential users, who comprise the panel data. A total of 176 people participated in this study (age: $M = 29.72$, $SD = 2.238$; gender: 51% female), resulting in a valid sample size of 142 after removing outliers and invalid data.

3.2 Experimental Procedure

The 3D printing service process research questionnaire was designed by asking positive and negative questions to investigate users' responses when faced with the existence or non-existence of a certain link characteristic, and the subjects could choose between "Like", "Must-be", "Neutral", "Live-with", and "Dislike". The questionnaire is very reliable (Cronbach's alpha = 0.905). According to the questionnaire results, 48.86% of respondents were between the ages of 18 and 25, while just 14.2% were 46 or older. 42.61% were students, whereas 36.93% were professionals. 80% of research participants stated a preference/willingness to use 3D printing to personalize their items, with 89.16% being young individuals. These findings suggest that young people in this study are more fond of and responsive to 3D printing technology for customizing items than older people, and that groups such as students and professionals are more interested in 3D printing technology used to personalized products.

3.3 Results

After collecting the questionnaires, the survey data was totaled and entered into Eqs. (1)(2) to get the values of the Better and Worse coefficients (see Table 2.).

A Better-Worse quadrant diagram is constructed based on the values of the Better and Worse coefficients in the preceding table (see Fig. 2).

Table 2. Better coefficient and Worse coefficient

Function	Better coefficient	Worse coefficient
5. Users provide their own model files	26.43%	−72.14%
10. Service platform to manufacture products and assume logistics	64.29%	−60.71%
7. The service platform provides a library of product models	60.71%	−61.43%
6. Service platform designers provide design solutions for users	42.86%	−66.43%
9. Shop for 3D printing materials on the service platform	55%	−15.71%
8. Service platform provides 3D printing material configuration solutions	53.57%	−20%
11. Service platform provides turnkey services from design to manufacturing projects	15.71%	−7.86%

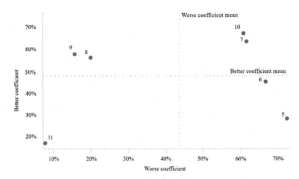

Fig. 2. Better-Worse quadrant diagram

In the quadrant of Better-Worse, "5. Users provide their model files" is located in the fourth quadrant and is a Must-be Quality, indicating that this service must be present in the design. "10. The service platform manufactures the product and takes care of the logistics", "7. The service platform provides a library of product models", and "6. The service platform designer provides design solutions for the user" are One-dimensional Quality, and the satisfaction ranking of each function is 10 > 7 > 6, indicating that when these three functions are provided, user satisfaction will increase, and the comprehensive expectation of "the service platform manufactures products and undertakes logistics" is the highest. The second quadrant, where "9. 3D printing materials are available on the service platform" and "8. 3D printing material configuration is available on the service platform", is Attractive Quality, indicating that, while removing these two functions has no significant impact on user satisfaction, these two services must still be designed in. These two services still need to be taken into account in the design. The "11. Service platform provides turnkey services from design to manufacturing" is located in the third quadrant, which is of Indifferent Quality, and so can be reduced in the design.

3.4 KANO Model Data Conclusion

It can be seen from the above Better-Worse quadrant and analysis that 3D printing users place more emphasis on the service platform to manufacture products and undertake logistics, provide product model libraries, and designers to provide users with design solutions and other services, indicating that users hope the platform can provide services and help in the more critical nodes of the 3D printing process. Users may be more satisfied if the platform offers material configuration and purchasing services. Users are less worried about the platform's capacity to deliver all-inclusive services from design to production, showing that users prefer to be directly involved in all stages of the 3D printing customized process.

4   The Process of 3D Printing Services for Private Customization

4.1   Situational Analysis Method Application to User Behavior Journey Exploration

The scenario analysis technique of the 3D printing service process for private customization is summarized according to the general step rule of the scenario analysis method to investigate and summarize the user behavior trip. First, determining the user's target behavioral needs is a combination of user self-awareness and designer awareness to develop product design; second, because different users have different needs, the design should also take a diverse docking mode to produce direct communication on the platform, accurate control of product positioning and design details, as well as different service models for different categories of users.

4.2   3D Printing Customized Product Service System Construction

The 3D printing service procedure for private customization is summarized by a study of the user behavior path. The model link, process connection, production link, and logistics link are the four key linkages.

Users in the model sector have three options for providing models. First, the user can provide and upload the model himself; second, the user can provide only the design plan, and then choose to select the appropriate model from the model library or customize or improve the model through the designer; third, the user can provide only the design demand, and the designer will customize the design plan and provide the model. The user picks the manufacturing process first, followed by the material, in the process link. The materials are designed in such a manner that customers may immediately purchase the platform-configured material solutions, or professional users can pick the corresponding materials themselves. The platform may provide online manufacturing product services in the manufacturing link, and customers can also acquire materials in the preceding stage to finish 3D printing at home. The platform may provide delivery service of materials and 3D printing items ordered by users via the logistics connection (see Fig. 3).

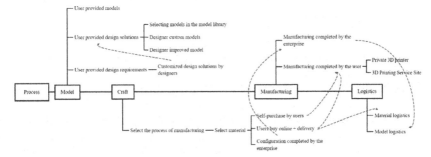

Fig. 3. Flowchart of 3D printing services for customization

5   Design Practice

5.1   Private Customized 3D Printing Service Platform

The 3D printing service platform for private customization is created via the investigation of the 3D printing customized product service process and the development of a service system. Determine the user's behavioral aim and finish the framework building of the personalized customization platform based on the user's demand. The 3D printing customized product service platform's personalized demand service is based on the service demand of various users for customized goods, and it delivers an effective service mode in a targeted manner. This service platform's possible customers include both professional and non-professional 3D printing users, designers, modelers, and other users with diverse identities; hence, the platform should create login channels for different types of users to adapt to the purpose and demands of different users. The platform interface should incorporate the whole process of private customization while expanding platform functionalities (see Fig. 4).

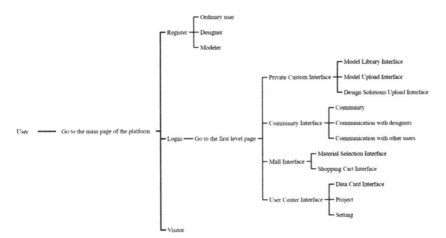

Fig. 4. 3D printing service platform framework for private customization

5.2   Illustration of a Design Effect

The design practice was carried out in accordance with the suggested framework of the 3D printing custom product service design platform, and the interface design was carried out using the "3D CUSTOMIZATION" app as an example. This study had 142 participants, with a valid sample size of 134. The questionnaire was meant to assess the app's interface and operation, and the participants were asked the following questions: (1) "Do you want this software's interface to be simple?" (2) "Do you want the colors in this app to be consistent?" (3) "Do you want the software to have a lot of features?" (4) "Do you wish to use this program to socialize with other users?" (5) "Do you desire a range of interaction techniques in the software? (For example, voice interaction, gesture interaction, button interaction, and so on.)". The average score for concise software interface is 4.53, the average score for uniform color is 4, the average score for rich software function is 4.2, the average score for socializing with other users is 3.33, and the average score for having various interaction methods is 3.31, according to the questionnaire data. These findings indicate that, in this study, consumers choose a simple and uniform color interface of the service app for 3D printing personalized items, with comprehensive functionality, the ability to network with other users at their leisure, and a reduction in the range of interaction techniques. As a result, the theoretical framework is coupled with the user demands in the specific design, and the interface as a whole uses blue color, with consistent lines for the interface layout. The program supports several registration and login methods, and users may log in with different identities. The main function of the app "private customization" is placed in the middle and prominent position when designing the functional partition, while the community information, shopping mall, chat interface, user home page, and other functional interfaces are evenly distributed in the navigation bar at the bottom of the interface based on most people's usage habits (see Fig. 5).

(a)

(b)

Fig. 5. 3D printing service app design for private customization

(c)

(d)

Fig. 5. (*continued*)

(e)

(f)

Fig. 5. (*continued*)

(g)

(h)

Fig. 5. (*continued*)

Fig. 5. (*continued*)

(k)

(l)

Fig. 5. (*continued*)

6 Discussion

In recent years, 3D printing technology has advanced fast, and consumer product needs have become increasingly diverse. This research begins with the demands of 3D printing users and potential users and then use the KANO model analysis approach to discover the qualities of those needs for the following building of the 3D printing customized product service system. User requirements are utilized as the foundation for identifying important influencing elements, building logical scenarios, constructing user journeys, and reasoning about service models in the scenario analysis method. The research on 3D printing custom product service design optimization is carried out in this work, and some useful findings are achieved, but there is still much space for future research owing to restricted personal awareness and research time, among other factors. At this point, the 3D printing service design process for private customization can only fulfill the general need for the service platform, and with the advancement of technology and diverse demands, this system will need to be developed further.

References

1. Zhang, H.: Study on customization service of 3D printing for cultural and creative product design. Packag. Eng. **40**(14), 1–6 (2019)
2. Luo, S., Zou, W.: Status and progress of service design research. Packag. Eng. **39**(24), 43–53 (2018)
3. Wang, K., Liu, Y.: Design of 3D printing services for customized products. Packag. Eng. **40**(14), 25–30 (2019)
4. Yang, Y.: Classification and research progress of additive manufacturing (3D printing). Adv. Aerosp. Eng. **10**(03), 309–318 (2019)
5. Li, J., Wu, C., Chu, P.K., Gelinsky, M.: 3D printing of hydrogels: Rational design strategies and emerging biomedical applications. Mater. Sci. Eng. R Rep. **140**, 100543 (2020)
6. Song, J., Chen, Q.M., Chen, L., Guo, Q., Zhang, J.Q.: Research on furniture design based on parameterization and additive manufacturing technology. For. Ind. **59**(06), 52–56 (2022)
7. Wang, Z., Li, Y.: The application of rationalized design concept in product innovation design. Packag. Eng. **35**(24), 27–3034 (2014)
8. Li, X., Wang, Z.J.: Design of a customized platform for children's toys based on 3D printing technology. Packag. Eng. **39**(08), 211–216 (2018)
9. Elkasabgy, N.A., Mahmoud, A.A., Maged, A.: 3D printing: an appealing route for customized drug delivery systems. Int. J. Pharm. **588**, 119732 (2020)
10. Oliveira, J.P., LaLonde, A., Ma, J.: Processing parameters in laser powder bed fusion metal additive manufacturing. Mater. Des. **193**, 108762 (2020)
11. Chen, D.M., Xi, P., Tang, J.P.: Application of associative design techniques in rapid modeling of wing box segments. J. Graphology **36**(05), 730–733 (2015)
12. Lv, W.T., Gong, M.: A study of service design and its empowerment in LEGO. Design (06), 130–131 (2015)
13. Liu, Y.: Exploring the path of 3D printing to help the development of cultural and creative industries in the information age. Packag. Eng. **40**(14), 31–34 (2019)
14. Yuan, M.J., Wang, L.W.: Innovative design of jewelry products based on 3D printing technology. In: Proceedings of the 2nd International Symposium on Bionic Design and Technology. Dalian University of Technology: School of Art and Design, Dalian University of Technology, pp. 274–278 (2021)
15. Li, W., Wang, C.: 3D printing-based self-customization system design for Chengdu shadow culture and creative products. Ind. Des. **188**(03), 112–114 (2022)

The 'Three Creative' Talent Characteristics Model

Zhen Liu[1]([✉]), Jinze Yang[2], Yali Chen[1], and Jia Cui[1]

[1] School of Design, South China University of Technology, Guangzhou 510006, People's Republic of China
liuzjames@scut.edu.cn
[2] School of Mathematics, South China University of Technology, Guangzhou 510640, People's Republic of China

Abstract. With the development of China economy, talents have become core element of development. Nowadays, the transformation of national industrial technology innovation is imminent. More and more national-level strategies have put emphasis on the training of students from universities. The three-creative talents in colleges and universities specifically refer to innovation, creation, and entrepreneurial talents. From the perspective of experience of technological innovation, innovation and creation is the foundation of entrepreneurship, but few studies have explored the experience relationship between the three creative and student entrepreneurial characteristics. Hence, this paper aims to explore the potential 'Three Creative' talent characteristics experience model in relation with entrepreneurial characteristics and experiences of the university students, which investigates potential influence of three creativity experience in university students' characteristics (background, personality, and entrepreneurial traits) regarding innovation, creativity, and entrepreneurship, and entrepreneurial potential, and establishes the relationship between them. This paper sums up the relevant traits that affect the performance of university students in the field of entrepreneurship (abbreviated to entrepreneurial traits), the evaluation index of university students in the field of entrepreneurship, such as entrepreneurial willingness, entrepreneurial potential, and entrepreneurial success rate, and the evaluation mechanism of the relationship between students' traits and the field of entrepreneurship, which is what methods are used to learn from university students. As such, the relationship between the quality of students and the evaluation indexes in the field of entrepreneurship can be established. Subsequently, the paper puts forward the mechanism of association of innovation, which connects the personality and background traits of university students with the entrepreneurial potential.

Keywords: Student Characteristics · Three Creative · Model · Personality · Background · Creativity Experience · Innovation · Entrepreneurship · Entrepreneurial Potential

1 Introduction

At present, with the rapid development of science and technology, talents are deemed to be the core power for innovation in terms of human resource. How to identify, train and foster excellent talents' experience for the 'three creative', i.e., creation, innovation and entrepreneurship, has become a hot topic in the field across the world.

There have been a number of researches on the entrepreneurial behavior of university student world widely. Schumpeter and Backhaus [1] believe that thinking and social behavior affect creative response of entrepreneurs. At the same time, the entrepreneurs' personality will affect their overall quality for the success of innovation. Therefore, if a person wants to be a successful entrepreneur, the person should better to be aware of the decisive personality traits in the process of starting business. Drucker [2] and Fleming [3] put forward similar views, emphasizing that the personality traits such as innovation, and technology driven, will affect the success of an entrepreneur in the future. For those start-ups with technology as the core, there have been a number of studies on the factors of success or failure of entrepreneurship, such as the gender, age and management experience of entrepreneurs. There are some correlations between the individual traits and entrepreneurial performance of entrepreneurs.

In view of its economic and social impact, the exploration and cultivation of innovative and entrepreneurial talents towards the 'three creative' have become one of the fastest growing research fields in universities across the world. Since the end of the 20th century, many experts and scholars in varies fields, including sociology, anthropology, business, and engineering, have begun to study entrepreneurship and entrepreneurial traits. Al-Habib [4] studies the relationship between the four personality traits of innovation, adventure, control source and energy, and the possibility of entrepreneurship in identifying the traits of entrepreneurs in a university setting, and points out that there are systematic differences in the personality traits of entrepreneurs and non-entrepreneurs. For entrepreneurial related traits of undergraduate students, Louw et al. [5] investigate whether these traits are related to each other, and tried to determine the impact of demographic variables on these entrepreneurial related traits. Hence, it is clear that the best entrepreneurial related traits are observed, and there is a significant statistical relationship between demographic variables and entrepreneurial related traits.

Business Development Bank of Canada (BDC) [6] puts forward a set of evaluation questionnaire for entrepreneurs' potential, which identifies the scores of candidate in three directions: motivation, aptitude and attitude. By comparing with the average level, the entrepreneurial potential of candidate can be evaluated. There are topics that have been studied in the past:

Can entrepreneurship project affect students' relevant personality traits [7]?

Whether there is significant difference in the related personality traits between the students in the entrepreneurial class and the students in the non-entrepreneurial class [8].

Whether there are significant differences in the related personality traits of different students [8–10].

The relationship between students' related personality traits and entrepreneurial possibility [4].

The relationship between students' related personality traits and entrepreneurial success potential [11].

The relationship between students' related personality traits and entrepreneurial willingness [12].

However, at present, there is a lack of research and method on evaluating the students' background and personality for entrepreneurship potential towards innovation and in China. From the perspective of experience of technological innovation, innovation and creation is the foundation of entrepreneurship, but few studies have explored the experience relationship between the three creative and student entrepreneurial characteristics. Hence, this paper aims to explore the potential 'Three Creative' talent characteristics experience model in relation with entrepreneurial characteristics and experiences of the university students, which investigates potential influence of three creativity experience in university students' characteristics (background, personality, and entrepreneurial traits) regarding innovation, creativity, and entrepreneurship, and entrepreneurial potential, and establishes the relationship between them.

2   Research Framework

As illustrated in Fig. 1, this paper sums up the relevant traits that affect the performance of university students in the field of entrepreneurship (abbreviated to entrepreneurial traits), the evaluation index of university students in the field of entrepreneurship, such as entrepreneurial willingness, entrepreneurial potential, and entrepreneurial success rate, and the evaluation mechanism of the relationship between students' traits and the field of entrepreneurship, which is what methods are used to learn from university students.

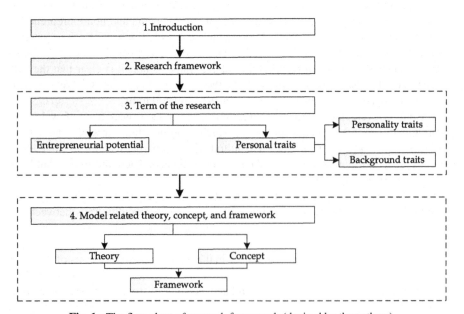

Fig. 1. The flow chart of research framework (devised by the authors).

Hence, the relationship between the quality of students and the evaluation indexes in the field of entrepreneurship can be established. Subsequently, the paper puts forward the mechanism of association of innovation, which connects the personality and background traits of university students with the entrepreneurial potential.

3 Terms of the Research

3.1 Three Creative Experience Regarding Entrepreneurial Potential

The term 'three creative' has different meanings in different fields, and this paper only considers the narrow concept of the three creatives in the university environment. Since China's requirements for the spirit of the 'three creative' of university students in the new era, the 'three creative' refers to "innovation", "creation" and "entrepreneurship", which are complementary to each other and closely related. In general, entrepreneurship includes innovation and creation. Therefore, this paper focuses on the concept of entrepreneurship when exploring the concept of the 'three creative'.

The term of entrepreneurship is more familiar to people than the 'three creative'. People can always hear inspiring stories of entrepreneurs who have created great value for themselves and society through their own efforts. Entrepreneurship is the process of creating greater economic and social value by optimizing and integrating the resources that entrepreneurs have or can have through their efforts. In addition, entrepreneurship is an act that requires the entrepreneur to be able to organize and manage resources effectively, use technological tools, services, and tools of thinking, reasoning, and judgment. According to the definition of New Venture Creation, the classic textbook in the field of entrepreneurship written by Timmons [26], the entrepreneurship is a way of thinking, character and quality, excellent behavior that requires a holistic approach and the possession of harmonious leadership skills.

3.2 Three Creative Student

Three creative students refer to contemporary university students who have the awareness of innovation, creativity and entrepreneurship, who have not only achieved certain achievements in the field of innovation, creativity and entrepreneurship, but also include all the students who have the will, interest and action in the three creative fields.

3.3 Entrepreneurial Potential

The definition of entrepreneurial potential in this paper refers to a self-assessment model on identifying candidates' entrepreneurial potential published by BDC [6] that is an investment bank dedicated to providing financial, investment and consulting services for small and medium-sized enterprises. Thus, the model has an important practical value. When the people complete 50 assessment scales and submits the questionnaire, the model will automatically calculate the candidate's entrepreneurial potential score. The results include one first-class index, i.e. total score, and three second-class indexes, such as motivation, aptitude and attitude. All of the above four indexes have reference values for candidates' entrepreneurial potential. The three second-indexes contain two to four, totally 10 third-class evaluation indexes. For example, the attitude indexes also include "views on luck and effort" and "views on action orientation". In addition, when candidates complete and submit questionnaires, the model will automatically calculate the scores of all indexes, and compare the scores of candidates with the average scores of all candidates, so as to objectively reflect the entrepreneurial potential of candidates. Therefore, this paper takes these indexes as the reference to reflect the entrepreneurial potential of candidates.

3.4 Personal Trait Related Terms

Personality Trait. According to the China Science Communication [14], personality traits is a kind of psychological structure that can make people's behavior tendency show a lasting, stable and consistent, and is the basic factor of personality composition. Everyone has his own personality, that is to say, everyone has personality traits. At the same time, over the years, there have been many different theories of personality traits in the world. These theories all have a basic hypothesis that one can judge a person's personality traits through the integrated analysis of some factors. Among them, there are representative theories of personality traits, including Eysenck's three factor theory [15], Cattell and Gibbons' 16-factors theory [16], and five factors theory improved and associated with the 16-factors theory [17]. From the perspective of the reference value of these theories of personality traits to this study, the common point of these theories of personality traits is that they all believe that each personality trait is a dimension of personality, which reflects that there is a certain consistency and regularity in human behavior, and these personality traits are relatively stable over time. It is precisely because of this theoretical background that this paper can use the personality traits of university students to infer the entrepreneurial performance of university students.

The personality analysis model adopted in this study comes from the evaluation model of NERIS [13] analysis company in the UK, who has authoritative and professional research results in the field of personality evaluation. Through 60 simple and easy to understand scales, the model divides the personality of candidates into four categories, i.e. analysts, diplomats, sentinels, and explorers, and 16 sub categories, such as architect, logician, commander, and so on, which is similar to the personality structure of the classic personality trait theory - the 16-factors theory [16]. Five groups of personality traits play a supporting role in these 16 kinds of personality, such as the first group: extroversion and introversion, the second group: intuitive, observant, the third group: thinking and perceptual. It is worth mentioning that these five groups of personality traits will not only be presented as output results of people, but also the internal proportion of each group of traits will be calculated by percentage formation.

Personal Background Trait. The traits of personal background in this paper are close to demographic traits, which is a concept defined for the convenience of studying the influence of University Students' background on entrepreneurship related indexes.

Personality Trait on Entrepreneurship and Innovation. In last decade, researchers across the world have conducted in-depth research and discussed on the impact of different traits on the field of entrepreneurship. Schumpeter and Backhaus [1] highlight that entrepreneurs' thinking level and social behavior decision-making affect their innovation response, and personality will affect the overall quality of entrepreneurs, as such a successful entrepreneur should have a certain personality. Drucker [2] and Fleming [3] respectively put forward the idea of making entrepreneurs successful, but they both emphasized the two traits of 'innovation' and 'technology driven', which indicates that potential entrepreneurs should have the specific personality traits needed to establish and lead innovative enterprises. There have been a number of studies on the success or failure factors of entrepreneurial traits, especially on the demographic traits of founders, such as gender, management experience and age. Say [18] reveals that because entrepreneurs are the ultimate decision makers, a successful entrepreneur should have many traits. These traits can be drawn from the theories most commonly used in the study of entrepreneurship. Wadhwa et al. [19] stress that entrepreneurs must have the ability to effectively deal with various uncertainties when creating new enterprises. Risk taking spirit is an important part of personal growth, which is very helpful for business activities. Ward [20] proposes that entrepreneurs must also be innovative, so as to burst out some new ideas about products, processes and services. All these indicate that personality traits do have a profound impact on entrepreneurial behavior, and the influencing factors are diverse.

3.5 Term of Personal Trait on Entrepreneurship and Innovation

Wong et al. [11] show that specific personality traits, including innovation ability, external control source, demand for success, risk-taking tendency, entrepreneurial willingness, and attitude towards entrepreneurs, can predict different inspiration factors that are proposed by Goldenberg et al. [21], while different inspiration factors can predict the possibility of entrepreneurial success. Thus, it indirectly indicates specific personality traits that can predict the possibility of success. The findings of the study can serve as a self-assessment of entrepreneurs, which means that the company may have a higher success rate.

Moreover, in a study of Saudi Arabian university students, Al-Habib [4] takes 600 university students as the sample, and finds that there are significant differences in some specific traits between entrepreneur students and non-entrepreneur students. Compared with non-entrepreneurs, student entrepreneurs have a higher level of innovation, risk-taking, energy, and self-control.

Furthermore, Kume et al. [12] reveal that entrepreneurship education, gender, work experience and parents' occupation will have an impact on students' entrepreneurial attitude in the process of studying the entrepreneurial traits of Albanian university students ($n = 519$). Entrepreneurial attitude defines how motivated a person is to become an entrepreneur and what motivates the person to develop business. A student with a high level of entrepreneurial attitude has higher innovation, independence, and entrepreneurial self-efficacy. It indicates that students' personal traits will affect their entrepreneurial traits, thus showing different entrepreneurial tendencies.

4 Model Related Theory, Concept, and Framework

4.1 Theory

The Entrepreneurial Traits of University Students Have an Impact on Their Entrepreneurial Potential. Wong et al. [11] support the hypothesis in the study of 215 students majoring in manufacturing engineering that at least among the students majoring in engineering. There is a close relationship between the entrepreneurial traits of the students' majoring in engineering and the six idea factors proposed by Goldenberg et al. [21], which can predict the possibility of product success in the future. Therefore, it can be indirectly considered that the enterprises of the students majoring in engineering. The traits of entrepreneurs have a significant impact on the potential of entrepreneurial success. Similarly, Al-Habib [4] takes 600 students from three universities in Saudi Arabia as samples to study the relationship between innovation, risk-taking, control source, energy level and entrepreneurial possibility. The results show that, compared with the non-entrepreneurs, the students with entrepreneurial intention show a higher level in the four personality traits.

The Influence of University Students' Background on Entrepreneurial Tendency. Kume et al. [12] compare the 519 students of the University of Albania who had entrepreneurial tendencies, i.e. answered "I want to start a business" in the questionnaire, with the students who had no entrepreneurial tendencies, i.e. answered "I don't want to start a business" in the questionnaire, found that university courses, entrepreneurial projects, gender, work experience and mother's occupation had entrepreneurial influence on the university students. The tendency is statistically significant. Therefore, it shows that the background of students has a certain impact on their entrepreneurial willingness. In addition, Salamzadeh et al. [9] study 422 university students from three universities in Iran and find that the study field of university students has significant relevance to some entrepreneurial traits. Further, Setiawan [7] discusses whether students' entrepreneurial traits would be affected after they participated in entrepreneurial projects, and the results are positive. Holienka et al. [10] further analyze the entrepreneurial potential of 370 university students in four different majors, such as Business Administration, Applied Information, Psychology, and Pedagogy, of which the results show that there are significant differences in the overall entrepreneurial tendency of students in different majors.

However, there are three main limitations of existing studies for helping with forming the theory of this paper:

Lack of Research on University Students in China. The research on university students outside of China accounts for the vast majority, on the contrary, the research on China domestic university students is few.

Lack of Objective and Accurate Evaluation Mechanism of Entrepreneurial Potential for University Students. Reviewing the previous research on the entrepreneurial potential of university students, it indicates that in order to study the relationship between personal entrepreneurial traits and entrepreneurial potential, an appropriate evaluation mechanism of entrepreneurial potential has to be established first for evaluating the entrepreneurial potential of different students. Due to the complexity of evaluating students' entrepreneurial potential, previous studies generally focus on the level of entrepreneurial willingness, entrepreneurial tendency and entrepreneurial attitude. A few studies have mentioned the entrepreneurial potential of university students. For example, in the study of Kume et al. [12], if a student answers "I want to start my own business", then the researcher will think that the student has entrepreneurial tendency and is a potential entrepreneur. Similarly, Holienka et al. [10] used a similar method to judge the entrepreneurial tendency and potential of 370 university students. In fact, students' willingness to start a business can be judged by their personal answers, but it is not accurate or quantitative to measure their entrepreneurial potential. In order to evaluate the entrepreneurial potential of the university students more objectively, accurately and measurably, this study makes a systematic evaluation of the entrepreneurial potential of the sampling students associating with the BDC's entrepreneurial potential evaluation model and the professional research results of authoritative institutions, which improves the objectivity and accuracy of the research.

Personality Traits are Limited to Some Specific Traits. The existing researches on the traits of university students and entrepreneurial tendency, potential, possibility and success rate are mostly focused on specific entrepreneurial traits. For example, Hian [22] studies six traits in his research on the entrepreneurial tendency of Hong Kong MBA students, namely, sense of achievement, desire to control, risk-taking tendency, tolerance of ambiguity, self-confidence and innovation. Aghazamani and Roozikhah [23] focus on five personality traits, including sense of achievement, self-confidence, risk-taking ability, market knowledge and creativity. In their study, Ürü et al. [24] investigate six entrepreneurial traits, including risk orientation, achievement needs, control sources, optimism, competitiveness and innovation. However, these specific entrepreneurial traits cannot be used to describe a complete personality. This study is trying to find a series of personality traits, which can not only describe a complete and sound personality, but also map the entrepreneurial potential under the personality through the measurement of different personality traits. As such, the evaluation model will have better extension to the universality students' personality traits.

4.2 Concept

Wong et al. [11] use the method of expert method to explore the relationship between 'six idea factors' and the possibility of product success. Then, through empirical analysis, this paper investigates the relationship between entrepreneurial traits and 'six idea factors', and indirectly studies the relationship between entrepreneurial traits and entrepreneurial success potential. The results show that there is a significant relationship between entrepreneurial traits and entrepreneurial success potential of students. Hence, this research lies in the use of 'six idea factors' as an intermediate variable, connecting the relationship between entrepreneurial traits and entrepreneurial potential, which as shown in Fig. 2 for the conceptual idea.

Additionally, Salamzadeh et al. [9] study the relationship between the entrepreneurial traits and professional subject fields of Iranian university students. Among them, the

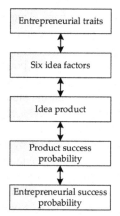

Fig. 2. The conceptual idea from entrepreneurial traits to entrepreneurial success probability (devised by the authors based on the literature).

entrepreneurial traits include openness, achievement needs, and pragmatism. Professional subject fields are divided into six categories, namely, humanities, basic science, engineering, art, psychology, and medicine. The results show that the differences in entrepreneurial traits and professional fields of university students are enlightening. Thus, this research uses similar method for entrepreneurial traits and professional subject fields.

Further, He [25] investigates the influence of university students' entrepreneurial attitude, personality traits, personal background and environment on entrepreneurial tendency. In short, personality traits, background and environment affect entrepreneurial attitude, which indirectly affects entrepreneurial tendency. The results show that personality trait, personal background and entrepreneurial attitude of university students will have a positive or negative impact on entrepreneurial tendency.

4.3 Model Framework

Based on previous theory and concept, this paper divides research into the following parts: personality traits, background traits, entrepreneurial traits, and entrepreneurial potential, and establishes the relationship between them by collecting the personality data, background data and entrepreneur data of the university students. As such, the conceptual 'Three Creative' talent characteristics model framework is shown in Fig. 3.

The personality traits are from the personality assessment model provided by NERIS [13], which contain 10 different traits in five groups, i.e., Mind (extraverted and introverted traits), Energy (intuitive and observant traits), Nature (thinking and feeling traits), Tactics (judging and prospecting traits), and Indentity (assertive and turbulent traits). In addition, the background traits are major, gender, academic degree, and work experience of the students, of which the impact on entrepreneurial potential can be explored. Further, for the assessment model of entrepreneurial potential of the university students, the entrepreneurial potential assessment model introduced by BDC National Business

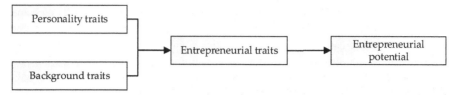

Fig. 3. The conceptual model framework of 'Three Creative' Talent Characteristics Model based on personality and background to entrepreneurial potential (devised by the authors based on the literature).

Development Bank of Canada [6] can be used, which is based on the principle of obtaining the results of filling out 50 scales of candidates and calculating the candidate's observations in 10 different dimensions of entrepreneurial traits with the help of the official authoritative model, through which the candidate's entrepreneurial motivation, entrepreneurial attitude and entrepreneurial talent are reflected and aggregated to obtain the candidate's overall entrepreneurial potential score.

5 Discussion and Conclusion

From the previous analysis, it is clear that the reason for studying the correlation between personal characteristics and entrepreneurial performance of university students is due to the following reasons: 1) Entrepreneurial projects play an increasingly critical role in today's economy. Currently, many graduates from higher education institutions are under pressure to find employment, and good entrepreneurial projects can bring value to them and to society at large by solving a large number of employment problems. Studying the relationship between university student traits and entrepreneurship-related traits can help companies, schools and teams better identify and cultivate those talents who are suitable for entrepreneurship, which can help improve the overall strength of project teams and promote team development; and 2) Research in the field of entrepreneurship by domestic scholars in China is still in its infancy, and the existing theoretical foundation is not yet able to provide effective guidance for social enterprises, universities and teams. In order to better help universities, teams train, and manage talents to improve the success rate of entrepreneurship, as well as to provide theoretical support for research on the relationship between personality traits and entrepreneurship-related evaluations of university students, it is particularly important to study the traits and entrepreneurial performance of students in higher education institutions.

This paper introduces the background of 'three creative' and 'three creative' education of university students in China, and then elaborates the theoretical basis and research value of studying the relationship between student traits and entrepreneurship evaluation in colleges and universities, taking into account the literature. In addition, this paper presents past research on the evaluation of traits and entrepreneurship related to university students, explaining the meaning of personality traits and listing the specifics. The paper also introduces the entrepreneurship evaluation directions of existing studies, including entrepreneurial intention, entrepreneurial possibility, and entrepreneurial potential, as well as specific research methods. Further, this paper makes a detailed analysis and comparison of student traits and entrepreneurial potential in universities, and proposes the 'three creative' talent characteristics model. At present, the research results on the evaluation of students' personality and entrepreneurial potential in China universities are relatively scarce, especially the research on the entrepreneurial potential of Chinese university students is relatively rare. As such, this paper contributes a proposed the 'three creative' talent characteristics model to fill this gap by conducting research on personality traits and entrepreneurial potential of Chinese university students with the help of personality traits and entrepreneurial potential evaluation models regarding three creativity experience (Innovation, Creativity, and Entrepreneurship). Further research will focus on the validation of hypothesis of the model for quantification of the model content.

Acknowledgements. This research was funded by "2022 Constructing Project of Teaching Quality and Teaching Reform Project for Undergraduate Universities in Guangdong Province" Higher Education Teaching Reform Project (project No. 386), 'Innovation and practice of teaching methods for information and interaction design in the context of new liberal arts' (project grant number x2sj-C9233001).

References

1. Schumpeter, J., Backhaus, U.: The theory of economic development. In: Schumpeter, J., Backhaus, J. (eds.), pp. 61–116. Springer, Boston, MA (2003). https://doi.org/10.1007/0-306-48082-4_3
2. Drucker, P.F.: Innovation and entrepreneurship: practice and principles. Harper & Row, New York (1986)
3. Fleming, P.: Entrepreneurship education in Ireland: a longitudinal study. Acad. Entrepreneurship J. **2**(1), 94–118 (2016)
4. Al-Habib, M.: Identifying the traits of entrepreneurs in a university setting: an empirical examination of Saudi Arabian university students. Int. Bus. Econ. Res. J. (IBER) **11**(9), 1019–1028 (2012)
5. Louw, L., van Eeden, S.M., Bosch, J.K., Venter, D.J.L.: Entrepreneurial traits of undergraduate students at selected South African tertiary institutions. Int. J. Entrep. Behav. Res. **9**(1), 5–26 (2003)
6. BDC Self-assessment, test your entrepreneurial potential. https://www.bdc.ca/en/articles-tools/entrepreneur-toolkit/business-assessments/pages/self-assessment-test-your-entrepreneurial-potential.aspx. Accessed 08 Feb 2023
7. Setiawan, J.L.: Entrepreneurship program assessment by students outcome on their perceived entrepreneurial characteristics. In: Proceedings of the 4th Indonesia International Conference on Innovation, Entrepreneurship, & Small Business IICIES 2012, pp. 1–6. Surabaya, Indonesia (2012)
8. Hayes, D., Richmond, W.: Using an online assessment to examine entrepreneurship student traits and to measure and improve the impact of entrepreneurship education. J. Entrepreneurship Educ. **20**(1), 88–107 (2017)
9. Salamzadeh, A., Farjadian, A.A., Amirabadi, M., Modarresi, M.: Entrepreneurial characteristics: insights from undergraduate students in Iran. Int. J. Entrep. Small Bus. **21**(2), 165–182 (2014)

10. Holienka, M., Holienková, J., Gál, P.: Entrepreneurial characteristics of students in different fields of study: a view from entrepreneurship education perspective. Acta Universitatis Agriculturae et Silviculturae Mendelianae Brunensis **63**(6), 1879–1889 (2015)

11. Wong, W.K., Cheung, H.M., Venuvinod, P.K.: Individual entrepreneurial characteristics and entrepreneurial success potential. Int. J. Innov. Technol. Manag. **2**(3), 277–292 (2005)

12. Kume, A., Kume, V., Shahini, B.: Entrepreneurial characteristics amongst university students in Albania. Eur. Sci. J. **9**(16), 206–225 (2013)

13. Free personality test, type descriptions, relationship and career advice_16Personalities. https://www.16personalities.com. Accessed 08 Feb 2023

14. China science communication. https://www.kepuchina.cn. Accessed 08 Feb 2023

15. Eysenck, S.B., Eysenck, H.J.: Crime and personality: an empirical study of the three-factor theory. Br. J. Criminol. **10**(3), 225–239 (1970)

16. Cattell, R.B., Gibbons, B.D.: Personality factor structure of the combined Guilford and Cattell personality questionnaires. J. Pers. Soc. Psychol. **9**(1), 107 (1968)

17. Noller, P., Law, H., Comrey, A.L.: Cattell, Comrey, and Eysenck personality factors compared: more evidence for the five robust factors? J. Pers. Soc. Psychol. **53**(4), 775 (1987)

18. Say, J.B.: A Treatise on Political Economy: Or the Production, Distribution, and Consumption of Wealth. Grigg & Elliot (1836)

19. Wadhwa, R.K., Davar, J., Rao, P.B.: Entrepreneur and Enterprise Management. Kanishka Publishers, New Delhi (1998)

20. Ward, T.B.: Cognition, creativity, and entrepreneurship. J. Bus. Ventur. **19**(2), 173–188 (2004)

21. Goldenberg, J., Lehmann, D.R., Mazursky, D.: The primacy of the idea itself as a predictor of new product success. Marketing Science Institute, pp. 99–110 (1999)

22. Hian, C.K.: Testing hypotheses of entrepreneurial characteristics: a study of Hong Kong MBA students. J. Manag. Psychol. **11**(3), 12–25 (1996)

23. Aghazamani, A., Roozikhah, E.: Entrepreneurial characteristics among university students: a comparative study between Iranian and Swedish University students. Eur. J. Soc. Sci. **18**(2), 304–310 (2010)

24. Ürü, F.O., Çalıskan, S.C., Atan, Ö., Aksu, M.: How much entrepreneurial characteristics matter in strategic decision-making? Procedia Soc. Behav. Sci. **24**, 538–562 (2011)

25. He, D.: Analysis of factors influencing university students' entrepreneurial tendency (in Chinese). Doctoral Thesis, Zhejiang University, Hangzhou, China (2006)

26. Timmons, J.A.: New Venture Creation: Entrepreneurship for the 21st Century. McGraw-Hill, American (2008)

Metadesign Tool for PBL-Based Design Masters Program

André Neves[1], Helda Barros[2], Walter Correia[1], and Marcello Bressan[2(✉)]

[1] UFPE, Recife, Brazil
{Andre.neves,walter.franklin}@ufpe.br
[2] CESAR School, Recife, Brazil
{helda,Mcb2}@cesar.school

Abstract. This paper examines the application of the metadesign tool Strateegia on the context of the Professional Masters Design Program that follows a Problem-Based Learning (PBL) approach. In this program, students formed three research units called Studios and are invited to take part on challenges provided by real organizations and must deliver a Proof of Concept following the entire design process within six months. This provided challenges for both tutors and students as on how to conduct the studios without compromising the design process or the learning process. As hybrid and asynchronous collaboration tools gained pervasiveness after the pandemic, the opportunity to adopt a more effective approach emerged, thus the Strateegia tool was incorporated in the process.

By thoroughly documenting and analyzing the process and evaluating feedbacks from students, faculty members and clients, this case tudy provides findings that will contribute with the improvement of the program and student learning journey.

The three Studios utilized the tool for the main process, but also experimented on it by applying different methods and processes to improve their performance and overall designs.

Keywords: Metadesign · Strateegia · PBL · Professional Education · Design · Process · Research

1 Introduction

The COVID-19 pandemic has had a significant impact on education, forcing educators who were used to the traditional learning models to adopt emerging online solutions. As both students and educators adjusted to what the media referred to as the "New Normal", new, innovative approaches that can improve student learning outcomes began to gain terrain in the Academy. This paper will explore the potential for a metadesign tool for a Problem-Based Learning (PBL) [1] master's program as a means to conduct their students' projects after the pandemic. As PBL is acknowledged for its student-centered approach to learning, the Strateegia Metadesign presented itself as a suitable alternative to the traditional methods of supervising the projects.

A. Marcus et al. (Eds.): HCII 2023, LNCS 14031, pp. 526–534, 2023.
https://doi.org/10.1007/978-3-031-35696-4_38

CESAR School is a Superior Education institution that uses PBL in the context of the Professional Masters Program in Design, in which students are divided in groups called Studios. Each Studio is presented to a client, who presents them with a real challenge and invites them to conduct a design-based intervention to the issue on a six-month period.

This paper will consider the evidence for the effectiveness of Strateegia for this use case scenario, learnings about the process, usability issues and potential challenges to overcome in order to ensure successful implementation of Metadesign-based approaches on PBL-based superior education programs post-pandemic. The research will draw on both theoretical and empirical sources, with a focus on studies conducted in the new context of superior education, transformed by the COVID-19 pandemic. By considering the evidence, this paper will provide insights into the potential of Metadesign [2] to improve education post-pandemic.

2 Context

When students begin the Professional Masters' Program in Design at CESAR School, they are introduced to a four-stage framework based on the classical design process and British Council's Double Diamond Framework [3]. The lectures and modules of the program are aligned with the framework, so that students can be trained in the proper tools and concepts just in time for the application throughout the research process. On the first stage, the class is divided in three Studios and are assigned a client with a specific challenge. The three design Studios are conducted throughout the semester by the students under the guidance of the professors and each team also have a professional designer as a tutor. Such tutors are employees of CESAR, the Innovation Center that owns CESAR School. As the classes happen on a twice-a-month basis, students come from different regions of the country, making the hybrid and asynchronous aspects of the program a necessity, especially after the Pandemic. As the critical stage of the Pandemic appears to have passed and displacement restrictions tend to loosen up, the operational gains and learnings from the use of digital tools came to stay. To promote a fluid and efficient educational process, the institution is constantly experimenting on new solutions and approaches to empower and enrich the educational experience, for both educators and students.

For the Class of 2022.2, the integration of Strateegia [4] has been implemented and is currently under use until the end of the semester of 2023.

Although we do not have the final results by the time this article is written, there are preliminary results and learnings from the implementation and kickoff of the Studios that are worthy of investigation.

3 The Design Studios Framework

The previous Studios drawn from the Double-Diamond framework and was divided in four stages that culminated in four Status Reports, each being associated with one of the stages of the design process.

It is also important to note that each module from the master's Program happen on the appropriate stage, giving the students the right tools to operate their research as they progress.

This alignment between learning and practicing is part of the PBL approach and shows accelerated returns on the learning curve of the students.

Fig. 1. Design Studios Process

As depicted on Fig. 1, on the Planning stage, students go through an integration process for teambuilding and organizing for working in four different teams, each one assigned to a Client.

Throughout the Operation stage, they have to:

- Understand, deepen and validate the problem and/or opportunity (research and field study);
- Define a solution for the problem worked that considers the deadline, the user/consumer, the complexity of development and feasibility;
- Prototype, develop and validate the proof of concept for the chosen solution.

On the Delivery stage, Students must produce a Pitch for their solution to the clients, professors and professionals form the local innovation ecosystem.

They also need to write a paper about their process and submit it for publication on design journals or journals from related fields according to the nature of their project.

To accelerate the students learning process, each team counts on the support of a professional designer as a tutor, whose task is to provide the teams with tools and insights, filling the gaps between the classroom and workplace practices.

4   Strateegia as an Education Platform

Strateegia is a cutting-edge platform for education and learning dedicated to providing an unique and innovative experience that takes learning to the next level. Its philosophy is based on the belief that learning is a strategic action where individuals can achieve their aspirations by building their capacities through the collective exploration and discussion of various topics.

To achieve this, the platform provides students with flexible and convenient access to information in multiple formats, and it also enables structured debates around students' areas of interest, which are then analyzed by advanced artificial intelligence to help students deepen their understanding of the topics.

In addition to supporting students, Strateegia also provides teachers with powerful tools to prepare their lessons and assess the performance of their students, both collectively and individually. This helps teachers to better understand their students' needs and tailor their teaching methods accordingly.

Learning is a means of empowering individuals and supporting them in their educational journey, thus this platform is designed to provide a dynamic and engaging experience that enables students to learn at their own pace and on their own schedule.

5   Metadesigning the Framework Within Strateegia

A metadesign can be described as a set of tools, parameters, and operating conditions that enable the end-user to take control of the final design by choosing among many available options [2]. This aspect is instrumental for a PBL-based program, as students need this flexibility and adaptability provided by the digital platform to be able to deal with the complexity of real-life challenges [5].

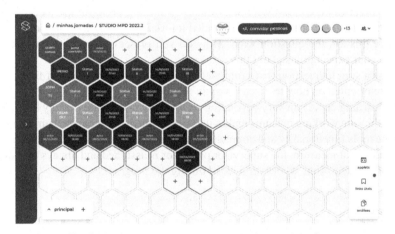

Fig. 2. Studio Journey Map on Strateegia User Interface

Breaking the process down to fundamental prompts and questions was essential for the supervisors to convert each step in to a "Divergence Kit" and distribute those along a "Journey" within Strateegia as depicted in Fig. 2.

Each team was assigned a color and had to follow the stages of the process by pursuing the questions on each divergence kit.

The first Kit for each team was named after the Client and had a single question: "Why are you interested in this problem? Explain the reason."

This single question works as a provocation and allows for deeper discussion on the presented challenges.

Entering the Operation stage, the design process is broken down in three main stages as seen in Fig. 1 on the previous section of this paper.

The questions on the Status I, II & III divergence kits, as seen in Fig. 3, are the structure for the research reports they must build in each step.

Fig. 3. Status Reports I, II & III Divergence Kits

5.1 Onboarding

The adoption of a new educational journey can be overwhelming due to the amount of information and instructions on a relatively short time.

Students were briefed with the entire process and presented with the challenges they would work on during the Studios.

With that in mind, the facilitation of the onboarding process was designed to be as light and as straightforward as possible. Students were conducted step-by-step to the generation of their accounts and were trained in how to use the platform.

A divergence kit called "Who are we" is the starting point on the journey map. It worked both as an icebreaker and as a guided tutorial on how to use the tool.

Inside this kit, the question was: "How do you present yourself to our group and what are your expectations about this course?".

It was a simple question that prompted discussions, more verbally at first, but then they were oriented on how to discuss within the tool.

The learning curve can vary depending on the student's digital literacy level, but the fact that they are working in teams makes it easier for them to exchange their understanding of the tools functionality and compensate for each other's deficiencies in that matter. As an additional measure, the supervisor professor is assigned and always available for them to make questions whenever needed during the program.

5.2 Status I

The first Status Report has the purpose of deepening the understanding of the context and the particularities of the issue, as well as of its stakeholders.

The students must investigate in the field and the academy to answer the following questions within the divergence kit Status I in Strateegia:

- Describe the initial research process.
- Which tools were utilized? To what purpose?
- Which tools does your team plan to use? To what end?
- Which hypothesis can you formulate about this challenge?

They must be able to justify every answer and provide evidence for their claims and build a presentation for discussing with their peers, tutors, and professors.

5.3 Status II

Moving forward to the next step of the design process, students now must present the evolution of what they planned on the previous status report and their findings.

There are six questions in this divergence kit, assessing the methodology and planning of the research.

- Describe the research process with the evolution from Status Report I.
- Which tools were utilized? To what purpose?
- Which tools does your team plan to use? To what end?
- What is your proposed approach to the research problem?
- Describe the Prototyping Planning.
- Which research findings can be linked to the identified hypothesis?

  In this step, the research must be linked with any hypothesis previously generated, or the students must reiterate the research as in any design process.

5.4 Status III

The final step of the design investigation requires the students to present their entire process and detail the validation of their proof of concept.

They must do so by following the structuring questions inside the Status III divergence kit:

- Research process with evolution of previous Reports;
- Tools used, their purpose and application;
- Hypotheses: Which were validated or discarded;
- What is the proposed approach to the problem? Is there any evolution or modification in comparison to the previous Status Report?
- Depiction of their field validation experiments and new findings;
- Lessons Learned.

The "lessons learned" question is an essential point of their learning journey that might not be present on the written reports afterwards, as it is a more personal account of their time working together as a team.

This may be the final opportunity for them to discuss and share with the entire class about their experience before they deliver their research papers.

5.5 Delivery

The Delivery stage consists on the writing of a research paper based on the entire production of each group. Students must gather all required contents and references throughout the previous steps, and properly register each advance, so the culmination of the process should naturally be structured as a research document.

The masters program contains methodology lectures that are in synchrony with the research stage, so the production of their research paper for the studios works as a preparation for the writing of their individual dissertations in the future.

6 Preliminary Results

The process has been initiated with the students and the learning curve on the use of the tool and the design research process is building, as the level of digital literacy or experience with design processes is not the same for every participant.

As this paper is being written, the students have reached the first Status Report and have used the questions as guidance for their work.

So far, the administrator tool shows a rate of active people in the journey of 24%, which could mean that group leaders may be in charge of most of the writing.

However, the engagement rate in the divergence kits has reached 58.83% on this step of the journey.

As they are on the "Understanding and Validation of the Problem" stage, one may assume that it is natural that their contributions do not diverge more and there is still a moderate number of discussions within the platform.

We can also attribute this to the overall lack of experience in design research process within a significant part of the research teams.

Nevertheless, it is expected that this number should increase on the following stages, that are more discussive by nature, like the ideation stages for example.

To follow-up on the progress of each group might need additional efforts should they significantly increase their textual inputs on the platform.

The "Resume" tool as in the example seen in Fig. 4 has proven itself quite helpful for the supervisor professor in that matter, as it allowed for a brief and concise overview of the current advancements on the discussion on Strateegia.

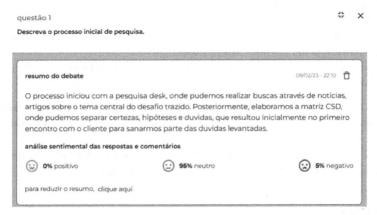

Fig. 4. Resume of the debate on question 1 "Describe the initial process of the research."

Another helpful feature was the "Conversation Point", as seen in Fig. 5, represented by black hexagons on the journey maps. These kits marked the dates for all relevant encounters, mentorship sessions and meetings. It allowed for a clear communication about deadlines, events, and the capacity for registering comments and discussions about every occurrence.

Fig. 5. "Conversation Point"

One of the teams used the "conversation Points" kits as a meetup backlog and research journal, helping them keep track of their progress, making it easier for the writing of the research paper afterwards and to keep track of events.

Red hexagons called "Notice Points" as seen in Fig. 6, served as a cognitive reinforcement to the deadlines, once again making it as clear as possible when the students had to deliver for each step.

Fig. 6. "Notice Point"

Every participant of the journey received an e-mail with the content of the notice point, so they would have the information even if they were eventually deprived of access to Strateegia.

This is important in this context, as most students in this segment tend to be professionals with different timetables and often live in different cities, making interstate travels for every class or whenever possible for the research execution.

7 Discussion

Through metadesign, we can map and act intentionally on complexity, making it visible and understandable, allowing us to form relationships in the environment and at the cognitive level [6].

It is then noticeable how Metadesign tools are being used in educational programs to create effective and engaging learning experiences. Learning environments can be tailor-made for students by utilizing metadesign, allowing for individual and differentiated instruction, which makes this kind of approach increasingly popular.

One aspect that is particularly appealing to educators is that it allows for them to create learning experiences that are interactive and engaging, which can help foster student engagement and motivation.

The anonymity provided by Strateegia in the incognito mode also helps educators to create learning environments that are more equitable and accessible to individuals with disabilities, as well as other marginalized groups. Additionally, it can be used to create learning experiences that are culturally sensitive, helping to ensure that all learners feel included and respected.

This is a relevant step towards using metadesign to transform superior education in a more positive direction and enabling social change [7] on the long run.

8   Conclusion

Strateegia has, so far, proven itself to be a promising tool on the context of the supervision of the development of educational design projects with design masters' students. The projects will be followed closely as to ascertain the performance of Strateegia in this complex educational setting.

The asynchronous work mediated by the tool combined with the live facilitations in presential encounters is expected to cover for different learning styles, making sure that every student has the opportunity to evolve.

In addition to that, the faculty will be constantly seeking feedback to adjust the process or to provide them with guidance whenever needed.

References

1. Klamen, D., Suh, B., Tischkau, S.: Problem-based learning. In: Huggett, K.N., Quesnelle, K.M., Jeffries, W.B. (eds.) An Introduction to Medical Teaching. ICPE, vol. 20, pp. 115–131. Springer, Cham (2022). https://doi.org/10.1007/978-3-030-85524-6_9
2. Giaccardi, E.: Metadesign as an emergent design culture. Leonardo **38**(4), 342–349 (2005). https://doi.org/10.1162/0024094054762098
3. Gustafsson, D.: Analysing the double diamond design process through research & implementation (2019)
4. Neves, A., et al.: Strateegia: a framework that assumes design as a strategic tool. In: Rebelo, F., Soares, M. (eds.) AHFE 2020. AISC, vol. 1203, pp. 90–95. Springer, Cham (2020). https://doi.org/10.1007/978-3-030-51038-1_13
5. Zaharova, A.A., Podvesovskiy, A.G., Krylov, R.A., Silchenko, N.S.: Applying the principles of metadesign in the educational platform development. Ergodesign **4**(2021), 250–259 (2023). https://doi.org/10.30987/2658-4026-2021-4-250-259
6. Vassão, C.A.: Metadesign: ferramentas, estratégias e ética para a complexidade. Editora Blucher (2021)
7. Vassão, C.A.: Design and politics: metadesign for social change. Strateg. Des. Res. J. **10**(2): 144–155 (2017). Unisinos. https://doi.org/10.4013/sdrj.2017.102.07

Connected: How Virtual Experiences Are Redefining Margins by Expanding Opportunities for Students at Historically Black Colleges and Universities

Kaleena Sales[(✉)]

Tennessee State University, Nashville, TN 37209, USA
ktucker2@tnstate.edu

Abstract. According to the American Council on Education, HBCUs (Historically Black Colleges and Universities) are historically underfunded, and often have lower alumni contributions and endowments when compared to predominantly White institutions. [1] This disparity of funding directly and indirectly impacts institutional budgets for academic units, resulting in many departments of art and design receiving little yearly support for visiting artists, designers, gallery programming, operational supplies, and facility maintenance. In this paper, I consider how art and design students from Tennessee State University–an HBCU in Nashville, TN, USA–benefit from utilizing virtual platforms as a means to facilitate new knowledge and expand their network. This is examined through four cases. The first examines the use of Zoom as a learning tool, where artists and designers share time and connect with students. The second explores virtual reality as digital placemaking. The third case examines how Zoom was used in an industry-to-student exchange as students participated in a global brand scoping project. The fourth case explores how Zoom was used as amplification, allowing student voices to be shared during a national design conference. The essential question that guides this inquiry is "how has virtual programming opened the door for equitable learning?".

Keywords: Virtual Platform · Historically Black Colleges and Universities · Equitable Learning

1 Introduction

It is important to consider the ways in which access to technology is linked to socio-economic privilege, and how lack of access contributes to underrepresentation of marginalized populations in creative spaces and learning environments. Equity in art and design education requires more careful and critical attention to the creation and allocation of resources to help level the playing field, especially on behalf of those who have traditionally been denied access to it. Beyond providing physical materials like laptops and textbooks, students from marginalized communities and those who attend low-funded institutions of higher learning require non-tangible access to experiential learning as well if they are to be afforded viable opportunities to discover and construct the knowledge they'll need to sustain viable career paths in the arts and design. The use of virtual platforms and virtual reality software has proven useful in removing some of the barriers that have long inhibited learning among these groups of students. This paper will explore how using these toolkits and tools can be effectively utilized to enhance their educational experiences so as to help them launch viable arts and design-based career paths.

2   Learning from Visiting Artists and Designers

Like many institutions, Tennessee State University (TSU) utilized online platforms like Zoom to allow for some measure of live engagement between students, faculty, staff and administration to continue as the evolution of the COVID-19 pandemic forced an end to in-person events. However, as faculty working within a small art and design department at an American HBCU, with very little budget to support robust programming, the shift to a fully virtual space opened doors for facilitating and learning that we had not anticipated. Suddenly, critical input from a diverse array of accomplished artists and designers was accessible to us and our students without the barriers of time and expenses related to having them travel to Nashville to share their experience with us. American design leaders like Michael Bierut, Cheryl D. Miller, Bobby C. Martin, and Forest Young critically engaged with our students and faculty about the development and effects of their work. Our students, nearly 100% Black, excitedly had front row seats to a diverse group of creative leaders who talked to them about issues pertaining to cultural identity, systemic exclusion, and design.

2.1   Lessons from the Field

The virtual platform allowed art and design students to hear and learn from textile and fiber artist, Bisa Butler, whose work has been met with international acclaim, as she shared insights about her time attending Howard University in the early 1990s. During her talk with students, Butler said, "Going to an HBCU gave me a sensibility and an aesthetic that was outside of the typical European aesthetic… While they [art students studying in many other American art programs] were looking to Ancient Greece, our heroes were Romare Bearden and Jacob Lawrence." Bearden and Lawrence are heralded as two of the most influential Black American artists of the 20th century, as their work centered the Black lived experience through bold and expressive stylings. [2] DEI (diversity, equity, and inclusion) practitioners often discuss the need to de-center white and male-dominant narratives in language, media, historical accounts, and more in order to challenge Eurocentrism. "*Eurocentrism* is generally defined as a cultural phenomenon that views the histories and cultures of non-Western societies from a European or Western perspective." [3] For students studying at an HBCU, learning from Bisa Butler about the intentionality behind her work (using Black imagery and Black cultural symbols) could have a life-long impact on their understanding of what's possible. Hearing her discuss her influences helps students to understand how to use authentic cultural expression that deviates from *canonical* views of high-art. The art *canon* is defined as "The conventional timeline of artists who are sometimes considered as 'Old Masters' or 'Great Artists'. Today's art history attempts to question these rules of 'greatness', considering issues of gender, race, class, and geography among others." [4].

Below is a selection of lessons from other visiting artists and designers to TSU's Department of Art & Design virtual speaker series:

On October 15th, 2021, Cuban American designer, Elaine Lopez, visited with students via Zoom and shared her thoughts on cultural assimilation, saying, "People arrive here [in the U.S.] and are expected to fit in… There is so much we can share about ourselves through design."

On November 9th, 2021, Black American lighting and furniture designer, Lani Adeoye, visited with students via Zoom and offered the following sentiments, "… every culture has something to add to the global design conversation." In discussing her furniture work that incorporates *Yoruba* principles, she added, "Unfortunately, people had a hard time saying elegant and African in the same sentence." *Yoruba* is a West African ethnic group.

On April 9th, 2021, Black American designer and letterpress printer, Rick Griffith, visited with students via Zoom to share his insights on culture and identity within design. Speaking of his upbringing in Washington, D.C., he said, "The D.C. punk scene taught me about social justice and acts of civil disobedience."

On February 5th, 2021, Black American designer, Bobby C. Martin, offered the following considerations for our students, "There's a struggle in the Black community around modernism." He added, "There's a tension between our (Black) history and where we are today. How do we move forward?".

When a professional artist or designer visits with our students at Tennessee State University, they share insights into and about their practices, their academic journeys, and often their creative processes and methodologies. This tends to be impactful for any student but can be particularly life-changing for a first-generation college student from a marginalized community, especially those with little access to the visual arts, much less visual arts education.

3 Digital Placemaking

"As the relationship between physical and digital landscapes grows, digital placemaking allows us to symbolically place ourselves in a virtual environment through digitally immersive or enhanced experiences using a variety of digital media such as augmented reality or virtual reality." [5].

Students enrolled in Art Appreciation at Tennessee State University concentrate on the visual arts by exploring why certain art works are historically important. They learn to evaluate art and develop an appreciation of various media, artists and styles represented through Western and multicultural traditions. When studying Michelangelo's work from the Renaissance period, students are encouraged to "visit" the famous work through virtual reality software. Below details our classroom experience facilitated by an online virtual tour.

Virtually walking through the doors of the Sistine Chapel in Rome was one of the most breathtaking experiences I've ever had. The virtual reality software removed the crowds of people that would undoubtedly exist in a real-world visit and allowed unobstructed views of the meticulously painted floor-to-ceiling artwork. Having a group of 20 first-generation college students with me made the moment even more meaningful as their faces lit up at the incredible frescoes by Botticelli and Perugino that lined the walls and those by Michelangelo that adorned the ceiling. Critically analyzing his famous depictions of the story of Genesis generated deep discussions among all of us about the famous artists' life. Seeing and moving about the space using online-facilitated, digital technology allowed my students to get a sense of its scale, and the level of commitment and time it took to complete a project of that magnitude. Many of my students are from urban American cities like Memphis, Atlanta, and Chicago, and had never traveled internationally. This virtual experience allowed them to explore a part of the world far from home with just a click of a button. Once we were done engaging with the work of these three Renaissance painters, I closed the tab on the browser, and left the virtual tour–a fully 3D, immersive experience. Suddenly, we were back in Nashville, TN, in a classroom on the campus of Tennessee State University. Opportunities to travel internationally are often limited to those with resources to do so. Due to this, many college students from Historically Black Colleges and Universities don't get to benefit from exposure to international cultures. "Almost 300,000 students choose to engage in study abroad experiences every year. In the 2012-13 academic year, for example, 289,404 students engaged in study abroad experiences. Yet, of these students, only around 10,000 (3.6%) hailed from Minority Serving Institutions (MSIs)." [6] Virtual reality software can be used to navigate international experiences and help provide access to the arts for students and institutions who are under resourced and underrepresented.

4   Equitable Learning

In the right hands, virtual platforms like zoom become more than a meeting space, it supports equitable learning by allowing members from marginalized communities to become stakeholders engaged in the planning of a national project.

Arts and Social Practice is a cross-disciplinary course offered to students at Tennessee State University in the Departments of Art & Design, Music, and Communications who seek to use *design thinking* methodologies to address social issues. *Design thinking* is "a human-centered approach to innovation that draws from the designer's toolkit to integrate the needs of people, the possibilities of technology, and the requirements for business success." [7] During the Spring 2022 semester, enrolled students were invited by Design for America (DFA) to engage in a national scoping workshop with global household product brand, Unilever. DFA, a non-profit organization that partners with universities throughout the United States, facilitates collaborative, inclusive design projects with the help of community and brand partners. As DFA's 2022 brand partner, Unilever's newest skincare brand, MELE (designed for melanin-rich skin) offered an opportunity for DFA to expand their university network to include minority-serving institutions. Representatives from Unilever and DFA joined Tennessee State University students via zoom to discuss skincare routines, family histories, and challenges specific to African American skin (Fig. 1).

Fig. 1. PowerPoint slide from Design for America (DFA) / Unilever Scoping Workshop with Tennessee State University. Slide illustrates DFA's workshop goals. Image courtesy of DFA and the Watson Foundation (a charitable trust that supports DFA).

During this scoping workshop, students were introduced to the following:

1. DFA's six-step design thinking process: Identify, Immerse, Reframe, Ideate, Build, and Test.
2. Mind-setting: Empathy, Humility, Collaboration, and Imagination
3. The differences between human-centered design, co-design, and community-created design (created by Equity Meets Design, adapted by Beytna Design)
4. How to identify parts of a design problem's context: Culture, Economics, Environment, and Politics
5. How to recognize problem spaces (i.e. transportation, hygiene, etc.) (Fig. 2).

This workshop set the foundation for a larger summer workshop where students worked in teams with undergraduate college students from other universities and learned more about the design process. In addition to the aforementioned design building skills, the project offered other critical benefits:

1. Historically Black Colleges and Universities "...disproportionately enroll low-income, first-generation and academically underprepared college students..." [8] Being a first-generation college student (FGCS) often has implications beyond the obvious. When immediate family members don't have college experience, professional networks may be small, if they exist at all. In these situations, students rely heavily on blind applications to internships and entry-level positions to get hired, vs assistance by friends and family. When opportunities arise that introduce FGCS to professional networks and provide insight into industry processes, there is a marked investment into their potential for success.

   Students in Arts and Social Practice who participated in workshops with DFA representatives provided feedback after the scoping session using DFA's "I like... I

Fig. 2. PowerPoint slide from Design for America (DFA) / Unilever Scoping Workshop with Tennessee State University. Slide illustrates DFA's Design Process. Image courtesy of DFA and the Watson Foundation (a charitable trust that supports DFA).

wish... I wonder..." format. This format was introduced as a reflection exercise after working in breakout rooms.

In their feedback about their overall experience working with DFA, student A wrote: "*I like* how they had us engaged and how interactive we were. *I wish* the PowerPoint that was used could be sent to us. Only for it to be a referral we can use later. *I wonder* if it's possible for leadership and mentorship opportunities." Student B wrote: "*I like* the communication practices and the critical thinking assignment at the end." Student C wrote: "*I like* how interactive everything was despite it being on Zoom. *I wish* that we had small groups so we could [have] more individualized convos. *I wonder* if they care about potentially talking some of us on as interns."

2. HBCU design programs are often smaller than those at Predominantly White Institutions (PWIs) in the United States. [9] This creates a challenge when attempting to establish student chapters of national organizations on HBCU campuses as there are usually required membership numbers to qualify as a student organization. In the DFA-led virtual meetings with TSU students, there were usually less than 10 student participants. Because of the virtual format, the small number of participants did not prevent representatives from DFA or Unilever from participating, as travel time and financial resources aren't factored in as losses.

Hosting a workshop via Zoom on topics that are meant to engage humans might seem counterproductive as distance learning doesn't require the physical sharing of space. Educators who are interested in using this technology as a learning tool might have the following questions: 1. *How do I know if students are paying attention if they have disabled their cameras?* 2. *How can I prevent students from online distractions while working?* These questions are valid, and point to the traditional use of a controlled setting (i.e. classrooms) to facilitate engagement. When teaching in the virtual space, educators might be best to accept the loss of certain behavioral controls and focus more on the benefits of virtual facilitation over in-person learning.

Below are some noted benefits specific to facilitating instruction via Zoom or other similar platforms:

1. Breakout rooms: Unlike group work held in a traditional classroom setting, virtual breakout rooms allow students true separation from other students in class. This intimate environment might be of additional interest to students who are less prone to speak up in large group settings.
2. Interactive components: Virtual platforms allow instructors to use polls, videos, and digital collaborative workspaces. The ability to seamlessly navigate between various teaching tools contributes to a lively and engaging learning environment (Fig. 3).

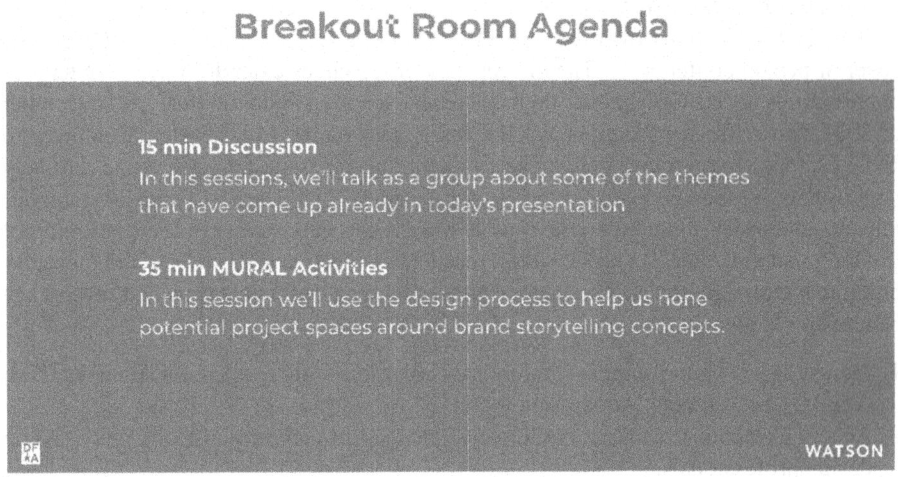

Fig. 3. PowerPoint slide from Design for America (DFA) / Unilever Scoping Workshop with Tennessee State University. Slide illustrates DFA's Zoom breakout room agenda. Image courtesy of DFA and the Watson Foundation (a charitable trust that supports DFA).

5   Amplification

The State of Black Design is a North American conference and career fair that centers conversations around the lack of diversity within the design industry, while also providing opportunities for professionals and students to connect with recruiters, educators, and activists. According to the conference website, more than 4,000 people live streamed the 2021 conference, which was offered virtually, via zoom. During the 2022 conference, Black design industry leaders presented on a range of topics, including design for social good, ways to amplify accessibility, redesigning higher education for equity and social justice, and design history. One conference session explored the rich history of Historically Black Colleges and Universities and featured an accomplished panel of design educators, including: Dr. D'Wayne Edwards (footwear designer and founder of Pensole Lewis College), Jennifer White-Johnson (disabled artist, designer, and activist), and Dr. Perry Sweeper (professor at Morehouse College). Tennessee State University design students, Synia Malbrough and Jonathan Digss, were invited to join this esteemed panel to discuss their experiences attending an HBCU.

Many industry conferences are not accessible for students due to the cost of registration and expenses related to travel. Students at HBCUs and other minority-serving institutions are often less financially equipped to handle the fees associated with in-person conferences than those attending Predominantly White Institutions (PWIs). "More than 75% of students at HBCUs rely on Pell Grants and nearly 13% rely on PLUS Loans to meet their college expenses. HBCUs have 1/8 of the average size of endowments than historically white colleges and universities." [8] *Pell Grants* are granted based on extreme financial need. *Plus Loans* are granted to parents of college students to cover tuition and related expenses. When it comes to institutional resources, students attending large, well-funded institutions of higher learning are more likely to have travel budgets to cover in-person conferences. The discrepancy of resources extends beyond conference opportunities, as HBCU funding deficiencies have a long and cruel history. In October of 2021, Nashville news station, WKRN ran a story on the over $500 million owed to TSU. "A bipartisan group of lawmakers meeting on the issue found the state routinely underfunded Tennessee State University for decades." [10] Lack of financial resources impact student learning experiences as it widens the gap in access to a multitude of teaching materials like 3D printers, letterpress labs, creative workspaces, and more. By utilizing a virtual platform, The State of Black Design Conference provided several key benefits for students:

1. Access to job opportunities: Conference career fair with symposium sponsors IBM, Agility, Citi Ventures, Adobe, and more.
2. Access to mentors: Student participants engaged in panel discussions with leading design professionals.
3. National visibility: Unlike traditional in-person conferences, the presentations weren't restricted to the four walls of a conference room, allowing HBCU students and other participants an opportunity to be seen by a large network of designers and design adjacent professionals.

Hybrid and virtual conferences create equitable opportunities for students that are underrepresented in art and design fields by removing the financial barrier of entry.

6 Key Takeaways

As creative industries work to diversify their respective fields, opportunities to connect with and engage students from marginalized communities may exist in virtual spaces. Used as a learning tool, platforms like Zoom and virtual reality technologies erase the distance between underrepresented students and the professional design world, contributing to access and equity in creative spaces.

References

1. 29 April 2019. https://www.acenet.edu/Documents/Public-and-Private-Investments-and-Div
   estments-in-HBCUs.pdf. Accessed 1 Feb 2023
2. https://www.metmuseum.org/toah/hd/most/hd_most.htm. Accessed 8 Feb 2023
3. Pokhrel: Eurocentrism. SpringerLink. https://doi.org/10.1007/978-1-4020-9160-5_25.
   Accessed 20 Jan 2023
4. Gallery, The National: Canon of art history. National Gallery, London. https://www.nationalg
   allery.org.uk/paintings/glossary/canon-of-art-history. Accessed 9 Feb 2023
5. AMT Lab @ CMU. AMT Lab @ CMU. 10 August 2023. https://amt-lab.org/blog/
   2022/11/draft-preliminary-research-on-digital-equity-and-placemaking-in-the-united-states.
   Accessed 2 Feb 2023
6. 25 March 2016. https://cmsi.gse.rutgers.edu/sites/default/files/MSI_StdyAbrdRprt_R4fin.
   pdf. Accessed 10 Feb 2023
7. IDEO Design Thinking. Design Thinking. https://designthinking.ideo.com/. Accessed 11 Feb
   2023
8. About HBCUs. Thurgood Marshall College Fund. https://www.tmcf.org/about-us/member-
   schools/about-hbcus/. Accessed 20 Jan 2023
9. What are the Largest HBCUs?. OnlineU, 2 March 2022. https://www.onlineu.com/magazine/
   largest-hbcus-by-enrollment-size. Accessed 11 Feb 2023
10. Harris, G.: TN still owes Tennessee State University over $500 million. WKRN News 2, 22
    October 2021. https://www.wkrn.com/news/tn-still-owes-tsu-over-500-million/. Accessed 8
    Feb 2023

Development of a Co-Creation Toolkit for Designing Smart Product–Service Systems: A Health Device–Related Case Study

Fang-Wu Tung[✉] and Chueh-Yu Lai

National Taiwan University of Science and Technology, No.43, Keelung Rd., Sec. 4, Da'an District, Taipei City 10607, Taiwan
fwtung@gmail.coom

Abstract. Smart product–service systems (PSSs) present massive opportunities for information technology–based enterprises to upgrade or transform their products and develop new revenue streams. The development of smart PSSs poses challenges to designers who must consider multiple criteria to meet the needs of customers. The effective involvement of customers in the design process requires a deliberate design approach that facilitates customer engagement in cocreation activities to generate ideas and determine customer needs and expectations. In this study, which focused on smart health systems, a card-based toolkit, namely SmartKit, was developed, and a workshop technique was used to involve designers and nondesigners in idea generation for smart health products and services. The results of this study indicated that the developed toolkit helped inform and guide idea generation and uncovered the participants' needs and expectations. According to the developed design concepts, we conducted means-end chain analysis to construct each participant's value model for smart health systems and analyze their attitudes toward and preference for products and services. The insights obtained in this study provide a basis for developing smart health systems that meet customer requirements.

Keywords: Co-Creation · Card-Based Tool · Smart Health System · Design Process

1 Introduction

Technological advancements are enabling the transformation of traditional products. Smart product–service systems (PSSs) are systems that integrate several digital technologies, such as the Internet of Things, artificial intelligence, and cloud computing [1]. The integration of these technologies improves products and provides customers with real-time information and services, such as performance monitoring, predictive maintenance, and personalized usage recommendations. Smart PSSs are closed-loop systems that connect products, services, and customer feedback for periodically improving the customer experience and driving business growth. Smart PSSs are more convenient, efficient, and personalized than are traditional products. Moreover, these systems provide a better experience than do traditional products.

A. Marcus et al. (Eds.): HCII 2023, LNCS 14031, pp. 544–554, 2023.
https://doi.org/10.1007/978-3-031-35696-4_40

Smart PSSs are becoming increasingly common in consumer markets. Examples of smart PSSs include smart home devices, wearable devices, health-care products, and smart appliances. An increasing number of companies are adopting PSSs; however, PSSs pose a challenge to product designers. The development of products that seamlessly integrate with technology and meet customer needs requires a deep understanding of technology and customer behavior. Furthermore, smart PSSs are driving a shift from product-dominant logic toward service-dominant logic, which requires designers to extend their focus beyond tangible products to service-based solutions [2]. With smart PSSs, value is cocreated by customers and service providers, and customers play an active role in creating value. Cocreating value with customers involves actively engaging them in the development of products and services [3, 4]. The involvement of customers in new product development allows for the collection of diverse perspectives and insights, which assist designers in better understanding customers' needs and creating products and services that meet customer expectations [2]. Customer involvement in new product development can be achieved through several methods, including workshops, focus groups, and ideation sessions [5]. Considering that smart PSSs are relatively novel to customers and designers, new methods and tools should be explored to help designers cocreate value with customers. With a focus on smart health systems, this study developed a set of toolkits that promote collaboration among designers, customers, and other stakeholders. Designers may use these toolkits for better understanding customer expectations, experiences, and ideas.

Smart health systems for consumers include wearable fitness trackers, smart scales, sleep monitors, air quality monitors, and smart mirrors [6]. These systems provide individuals with personalized insights and recommendations for managing their health and wellness. By providing real-time data and personalized recommendations, smart health systems can help individuals make more informed decisions about their health and wellness [7]. The increasing number of consumers who use smart health systems to manage their health and wellness suggests that these systems have become a key part of their lifestyle [8]. Individuals are becoming more aware of their health and are seeking to make positive changes in their lives. The increasing health consciousness of consumers has presented new opportunities for companies to create innovative solutions and products that address the changing needs of their customers. The demand for innovative, intuitive, user-friendly, and accessible health systems that ultimately lead to better health outcomes is increasing among consumers. Adopting a user-centered design approach is essential for designers who wish to unearth new possibilities for creating smart health systems. By actively collaborating with customers, designers can better understand their needs. The toolkits developed in this study are expected to enable designers and developers to cocreate value with customers and stakeholders and create innovative solutions that truly deliver real value.

2 Literature Review

2.1 Smart Health Systems

According to Valencia et al. [9], smart PSSs are *"the integration of smart products and e-services into single solutions delivered to the market to satisfy the needs of individual consumers."* Smart PSSs augment the value of products by providing new and improved services to customers. Furthermore, smart PSSs enable companies to capture new streams of revenue and reduce operational costs. These systems have been widely used in health-related products. Smart PSSs offer a wide range of benefits and opportunities for improving health-care delivery and outcomes. Several companies have been developing health-focused smart PSSs in the form of digital devices, mobile applications, and services. Examples of PSSs are Apple Watch and Fitbit [10], which are wearable devices that collect and transmit data about the wearer's health, as well as digital platforms, such as Omron's eHealth management platform [11], which provides users with personalized health insights and feedback.

Smart health systems and devices allow users to track their physical activity, nutrition, and sleep and to manage chronic conditions, such as diabetes and high blood pressure [12]. These systems collect and analyze health-related data and provide customized recommendations to help users better monitor their health and identify areas for improvement. Smart health systems also motivate users to maintain healthy exercise habits by providing personalized recommendations and real-time feedback. These systems enable users to set achievable goals and track their progress, thereby motivating them to stay on track with their exercise routines. The increasing demand for the self-monitoring of health promotion is driving the development of smart health devices, and the potential for growth and innovation in this field is high.

Smart health devices help users proactively manage their health and empower users to make changes that positively affect their well-being. Despite advances in technology and the increasing number of available smart health systems, opportunities still exist for developers to create innovative and effective solutions that meet the changing needs of consumers. A growing demand for smart health systems that are personalized, accessible, and effective has been identified [13]. Creating a PSS that is closely integrated with real-life scenarios can make it easier for people to attain their health-related goals. Identifying consumer needs by evaluating real-world scenarios is a crucial step in the development of smart health systems. With a deep understanding of consumers, designers can create solutions that are relevant, useful, and popular. Cocreation with customers, which involves obtaining feedback, insights, and information, is an effective method for designers to make more informed design decisions.

2.2 Card-Based Tools for Co-creation Workshops

Cocreation with customers refers to involving customers in the creation process of a product, service, or experience. The cocreation process is democratic. Users and customers have a voice in shaping the design of the product or service. The design mindset changes from "design for users" to "design with users." Design for users assumes that designers are the experts and know what is best for users, whereas design with users involves close collaboration between designers and users throughout the design process to gain a deep understanding of user needs and create tailored solutions. This shift recognizes that users can bring valuable insights and knowledge to the design process and can contribute to better design outcomes. Methods for cocreation with customers include focus groups, prototyping and testing, surveys, questionnaires, and cocreation workshops. Cocreation workshops are useful because they allow designers and customers to collaborate simultaneously, and they help designers understand end users from different perspectives.

A cocreation workshop is a structured event in which designers and stakeholders cocreate new solutions or ideas. Typically, a cocreation workshop includes activities such as brainstorming, prototyping, testing, and structured discussions and presentations. In a cocreation workshop, various visual aids, such as canvases, scenario images, or brainstorming cards, are used to guide the participants through the process. Roy and Warren [14] highlighted the importance of the use of card-based tools and physical artifacts in the design process. They classified card-based tools into three main categories: systematic design methods and procedures, human-centered design, and domain-specific design. Each category serves a different purpose, such as organizing information, generating ideas, making decisions, creating visual representations, providing a structured process framework, and facilitating reflection. The versatility and simplicity of card-based tools help facilitate collaboration and cocreation in many different contexts.

In general, card-based tools are not necessarily developed specifically for certain domains. However, the use of card-based tools for specific domains that address certain challenges or needs in these domains is increasing. LayeredCARD is a collaborative tool developed at Lotus Corporation that helps groups organize and visualize complex information [15]. It consists of a set of cards divided into several layers, and each card represents a different level of detail or abstraction. Participants use the cards to capture and organize their ideas, thoughts, and opinions for creating a visual representation of the information. Carneiro, Barros, and Costa [16] developed ilo cards as a tool for developing interactive digital artifacts. These ilo cards provide a visual representation of different aspects of digital product design and help designers communicate and understand complex design concepts. The Tiles IoT Inventor Toolkit [17] is a set of cards that support the ideation and design process for Internet of Things devices. This toolkit provides a structured approach to exploring and brainstorming ideas for Internet of Things products and services. Each card represents a different aspect of an Internet of Things product or service, such as its function, form, or user experience. By combining and rearranging the cards, designers can generate new ideas and explore different possibilities for their Internet of Things designs.

The emerging card-based tools for certain industries are a response to the increasing complexity of PSSs and the requirement for more structured and visual approaches to delivering innovative ideas. With the rise of smart, connected products and services, the design process has become increasingly interdisciplinary, thereby requiring the integration of technical, cultural, and social factors. This phenomenon has created a need for new and innovative design tools that can help designers and organizations explore and develop ideas in a structured and visual manner. Card-based tools are well-suited to this requirement. By breaking down complex problems into smaller, manageable components, card-based tools can help to simplify the design process and support the cocreation and collaboration of ideas among stakeholders, which can lead to the development of more innovative and successful PSSs.

3 Methodology

In this study, we adopted the research through design approach, which involves using the design process as a means to explore research questions and generate new knowledge [18]. The design process is considered a form of inquiry, and the resulting artifacts are used as a means of communicating and testing research findings. The design of a card-based tool for smart health systems may serve as a means of exploring research questions related to design issues. The resulting tool may also serve as a method for tangibly communicating and testing research findings. In this study, an iterative design process was conducted to develop a card-based tool. This process involved conducting research, developing initial design concepts, testing and collecting feedback, refining the design, retesting, developing a high-fidelity prototype, and launching the tool. We started the process by analyzing market trends and the current state of related products and services to obtain a better understanding of the industry landscape. Several prototypes were created and tested with potential users and then refined on the basis of user feedback. The iterative design process was repeated to make improvements to the tool, and a card-based tool, namely SmartKit, was created through repeated testing and refinement.

4 Result

4.1 Smartkit

This study developed a card-based tool called SmartKit, which comprises a cocreation canvas, three scenario images, and 77 brainstorming cards. This tool provides designers and nondesigners with a structured approach to generate ideas about smart health systems. The brainstorming cards, scenario images, and canvas are described as follows.

Brainstorming Cards
As descriptive and inspirational tools, the brainstorming cards of SmartKit facilitate collaborative and divergent thinking. The front side of each card explains its role and the deck to which it belongs. The back side provides content specific to each card (Fig. 1).

Each of the brainstorming cards belongs to one of seven decks, which are users, desired health statuses, devices, services, human actions, device feedback, and service data. The cards in the users and desired health statuses decks allow participants to express their brief profile. The cards in the other five decks allow designs to be developed for the combination of components of smart health systems, including devices, user interface elements, sensors, and services. Participants work together to consider how these components can be combined or modified in new and innovative ways to meet their needs.

Fig. 1. Brainstorming cards of SmartKit.

Scenario Images

The scenario images of SmartKit (Fig. 2) represent three environment types: home, workplace, and places where people work out. The scenario images were designed to engage participants by showing them real-life situations and encourage them to share their experiences. The images encourage participants to consider what actions they would take and what health-related products and services they might need in each environment.

Fig. 2. Three scenario images of SmartKit.

SmartKit Canvas

In a cocreation workshop, the use of well-designed canvases can provide a structured framework for capturing and organizing information and help facilitate a focused discussion among participants. The SmartKit canvas offers a means of visualization and is used in workshops to structure the design process. As shown in Fig. 3, the canvas structures the use of the cards by providing step-by-step instructions and complements the use of the cards with design and thinking techniques.

4.2   Smartkit Workshop

We implemented SmartKit in four workshops with 16 participants (Fig. 4). The 16 participants, who were recruited through online questionnaire screening, were divided into

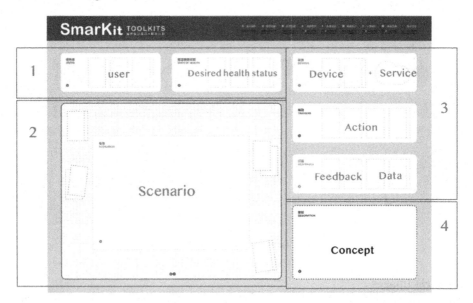

Fig. 3. SmartKit canvas

four groups according to their attitudes toward health. The implementation of SmartKit involved three stages: the preworkshop, workshop, and postworkshop stages.

Preworkshop Stage
Considering that the participants might not have been familiar with smart health systems, we sent the participants a briefing that provided fundamental and digestible information. The briefing contained aggregated information explaining what smart health systems are and how they work. Some examples of existing smart health systems were cited to provide participants a better understanding of these systems. Figure 4 displays some pages of the briefing.

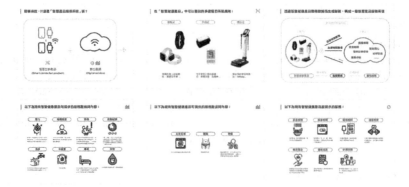

Fig. 4. Part of the preworkshop briefing.

During-workshop Stage

During the workshop, we led participants through the following activities (see Fig. 5).

1. User profile: Participant was asked to select a user and a desired health status related to the themselves. This helped define the boundaries of the design space by identifying user demographics and goals of using the smart health system. The facilitator could also use these cards to guide the participants towards specific health objectives, and to encourage more focused and meaningful conversations.
2. Usage scenario: Discuss in which environment (at home, at work, or work-out) participants tend to use smart health products or service, and place the scenario image on the co-creation canvas. Based on the selected environment, facilitators would lead participants to share their experiences in the real-life setting, and encouraged them to describe or envision their needs and expectations of using smart health systems.
3. Idea generation: Participants were asked to browse the service cards and pick the services that fit their needs or expectation in the scenarios. Then, they selected device cards to define the tangible products that can embody the services. The brainstorming cards enables participants to generating ideas drawing on their experiences and expectation.

   Human Actions cards illustrated various actions that trigger the devices. The cards allowed participants to envision the interaction between users and tangible products. Then participants browsed Feedback and Service data cards and decide how the selected device/service communicates back to the user, either via device feedback or via sending information over a data channel.
4. Flesh out ideas in the concept section. Each participant focuses on one or two ideas and visualizes the idea(s) through sketching or making prototypes.

Fig. 5. SmarKit workshops

Post-Workshop

After the workshop, we conducted interviews with the participants to assess the effectiveness of the workshops and SmartKit. The participants were asked questions about SmartKit and their experience participating in the workshop. The interviews allowed us to evaluate the results of the cocreation workshop and the SmartKit tool.

To evaluate cocreation outcomes, we conducted means-end chain analysis to construct each participant's value model for a smart health system. The means-end approach is used to understand the underlying motivations and values that drive consumer decision-making processes [19]. This approach involves identifying the means (i.e., the product or service) that a consumer uses to achieve a desired end (i.e., the ultimate goal or value that they are seeking). The approach adopted in this study was based on the assumption that the participants generated ideas related to smart health systems according to their health goals and that the ideas created by them would help them achieve these goals.

5   Discussion and Conclusion

According to the postworkshop interviews, the preworkshop briefing helped the participants grasp information about smart health systems and enabled them to better participate in the cocreation activities. According to our observations during the workshops and the participant feedback. The brainstorming cards, scenario images, and canvas of SmartKit enhanced the cocreation workshop process by fostering creativity and collaboration and providing a structured and guided approach to the cocreation process. The brainstorming cards, which divided smart health systems into several components, made it easier for the participants to communicate with each other and generate ideas. The brainstorming cards helped to simplify the design of smart health systems and supported the cocreation of ideas among designers and nondesigners. The scenario images visually illustrated potential usage environments and thus evoked the participants' real-life experiences, which prompted them to think about their experiences and encouraged them to envision what PSSs they required to enhance or maintain their health. The scenario images also facilitated communication and collaboration among the participants by providing them a shared visual reference point for better understanding and relating to others' perspectives. The canvas provided a structured and guided approach to the entire cocreation process.

The results of our means-end chain analysis revealed insights into the development of smart health systems. In general, the outcomes created by the participants showed that data recording and sensory cue attributes were fundamental. These attributes allow participants to make decisions most relevant to their health status and goals and to use health systems intuitively, thereby enabling them to achieve happiness, freedom, and self-understanding. In addition, some differences were found in the participants' degree of perceived control over their health. Participants with high perceived control preferred wearable health systems because they wanted a seamless user experience when managing their health behaviors. Moreover, participants with low perceived control preferred health systems embedded in daily objects that can detect their biological data without additional effort because such systems would provide them an accessible method to maintain their health.

Smart health systems are becoming increasingly complex because of advances in technology, demands for personalized health care, integration with other systems, and user expectations. Although this complexity can pose challenges to designers and developers, smart health systems must meet the needs and expectations of users. Customers are the best source of information about their needs. Their involvement in cocreation workshops can provide valuable insights. To enable more effective cocreation workshops, this study developed a card-based toolkit, namely SmartKit, to provide designers with an inclusive method to engage nondesigners in the cocreation process. By cocreating with customers, designers can gain insights into customers' needs, behaviors, and expectations, which can inform the design of smart health systems that are more likely to be used and adopted by the target audience.

Acknowledgments. This material is based upon work supported by the National Science and Technology Council of the Republic of China under grant MOST 110–2410-H-011–027-MY2.

References

1. Zheng, P., et al.: A survey of smart product-service systems: key aspects, challenges and future perspectives. Adv. Eng. Inform. **42**, 100973 (2019)
2. West, S., et al.: Value Co-creation in digitally-Enabled Product-Service Systems. The Palgrave Handbook of Servitization, pp. 403–417 (2021)
3. Tung, F.-W.: Co-creation with crowdfunding backers for new products and entrepreneurial development: a longitudinal study on design entrepreneurs in Taiwan. Des. J. **25**(5), 768–788 (2022)
4. Tung, F.-W., Chou, Y.-H.: Crowdfunding for design entrepreneurship and co-creation. In: International Association of Societies of Design Research Conference; Manchester School of Art, Manchester Metropolitan University: Manchester, UK (2019)
5. Witell, L., et al.: Idea generation: customer co-creation versus traditional market research techniques. J. Serv. Manag. (2011)
6. Piwek, L., et al.: The rise of consumer health wearables: promises and barriers. PLoS Med. **13**(2), e1001953 (2016)
7. Zeadally, S., Bello, O.: Harnessing the power of Internet of Things based connectivity to improve healthcare. Internet of Things **14**, 100074 (2021)
8. Khan, N., et al.: Digital health technologies to promote lifestyle change and adherence. Curr. Treat. Options Cardiovasc. Med. **19**, 1–12 (2017)
9. Valencia, A., et al.: The design of smart product-service systems (PSSs): an exploration of design characteristics. Int. J. Des. **9**(1) (2015)
10. Foster, K.R., Torous, J.: The opportunity and obstacles for smartwatches and wearable sensors. IEEE Pulse **10**(1), 22–25 (2019)
11. Papa, A., et al.: E-health and wellbeing monitoring using smart healthcare devices: an empirical investigation. Technol. Forecast. Soc. Chang. **153**, 119226 (2020)
12. Vashist, S.K., Schneider, E.M., Luong, J.H.: Commercial smartphone-based devices and smart applications for personalized healthcare monitoring and management. Diagnostics **4**(3), 104–128 (2014)
13. Cancela, J., et al.: Digital health in the era of personalized healthcare: opportunities and challenges for bringing research and patient care to a new level. Digit. Health, 7–31 (2021)
14. Roy, R., Warren, J.P.: Card-based design tools: a review and analysis of 155 card decks for designers and designing. Des. Stud. **63**, 125–154 (2019)
15. Muller, M.J.: Layered participatory analysis: new developments in the CARD technique. In: Proceedings of the SIGCHI Conference on Human Factors in Computing Systems, pp. 90–97 (2001)
16. Carneiro, G., Barros, G., Costa, C.Z.: ilo Cards: a tool to support the design of interactive artifacts (2012)
17. Mora, S., Gianni, F., Divitini, M.: Tiles: a card-based ideation toolkit for the Internet of Things. In: Proceedings of the 2017 Conference on Designing Interactive Systems, pp. 587–598 (2017)

18. Tung, F.-W.: Rediscovering herb lane: application of design thinking to enhance visitor experience in a traditional market. Sustainability **13**(7), 4033 (2021)
19. Reynolds, T.J., Olson, J.C.: Understanding Consumer Decision Making: The Means-End Approach to Marketing and Advertising Strategy. Psychology Press (2001)

Research on Evaluation Elements of Design Works for Design Education

Junyu Yang, Jiayi Jia, and Tianjiao Zhao[✉]

Tianjin University, Tianjin, China
zhaotianjiao@tju.edu.cn

Abstract. Design evaluation plays an important role in design education. The existing product design evaluation index system has problems on inconsistent standards and subjective evaluation. In order to establish a clearer evaluation index system of students' product design, this study uses factor analysis and analytic hierarchy process to establish an evaluation index of students' product design and the weight of the index. Based on the evaluation index, this study collects a large number of product design pictures and uses deep learning to construct the automatic evaluation model of students' product design. Product design works can be evaluate intelligently by this model. The research shows that VGG16 can classify and predict product design works well, and the evaluation accuracy reaches 70%. It provides a theoretical basis for product design evaluation in design education. At the same time, this study establishes the prototype of the design evaluation system based on the algorithm, explores the application mode of the evaluation of intelligent design works in the era of mass data, and establishes an automatic evaluation model for students' product design.

Keywords: Design Education · Design Evaluation · Deep learing

1 Introduction

Design is changing the way of life of human beings, and good design promotes the progress of society. Countries around the world are constantly strengthening their emphasis on design. Yan summarized the three-in-one design education model for today's society by exploring the Bauhaus educational philosophy [1]. Universities, as an important force to cultivate talents for the future design field, are also constantly improving the ability of design education. With the rise of project-based curriculum, students can learn new design knowledge and strengthen design thinking while completing a complete design. At the same time, design education increasingly concerned about the connection with real society, and introducing the concept of universal design and sustainable design [2]. Therefore, the traditional design evaluation index system may not meet the current needs of design education. Subsequent paragraphs, however, are indented.

However, the traditional product design evaluation oriented to design education still has the following two problems. Firstly, the evaluation indexes are not uniform. Different design teachers have different evaluation indexes, and the weight of each index in the total score is not clear. The subjective impression of the evaluator has a greater proportion, and the fluctuation is more obvious. In terms of feedback, students get the total score for the most time rather than sub-item scoring, which is disadvantage for students to improve their design specifically according to their score. Secondly, the basis for evaluation scoring is unstable. Standard of evaluation is affected by factors such as viewing sequence or evaluator's preferences, so the scoring standards for the same indicator are not uniform.

Therefore, this study establishes a specific evaluation index system for students' design evaluation through two data analysis methods of factor analysis and AHP. Design pictures are collected based on the evaluation index system. Finally, based on mass data, a deep learning-based automatic product evaluation model was established. Combining teachers' subjective evaluation and deep learning automatic evaluation, design an evaluation system for design education. The research content promotes the intelligence and objectivity of design education evaluation.

2 Literature Review

Nowadays, there are many researches on design evaluation, which can be roughly divided into two aspects: the establishment of design evaluation models and automatic evaluation using the internet and deep learning technology.

2.1 Traditional Design Evaluation

In the design evaluation process, manual scoring has always been the mainstream method. Compared with automatic evaluation based on Internet and deep learning, traditional evaluation methods focus more on evaluation indicators and weights.

Wang used a multimodal fusion to research for design decision. The authors used eye tracking and EEG response data as input dataset and ask subjects to rate the products as extremely positive, positive, neutral and negative. According to the experiment results, the performance of the fusion strategy combining EEG and eye movement features can fitting the expert decision making results well. Physiological signals can also reflect a person's subjective evaluation [3]. Miyeon Kim tried to establish a set of evaluation indicators for mobile phone universal design to quantitatively analyze whether product design meets the requirements of universal design [4]. Li Puhong and Shang Ka research the needs and characteristics of consumers, designers and manufacturers. And explored the basic principles of design evaluation, integrated the needs of the three subjects and Combining with the dynamic development of product, the author makes a scientific reasonable and practical set of evaluation index for cabinet air-conditioning design [5]. However, the research is more generalized, mostly qualitative analysis, without specific quantitative analysis and data research. Qiu Bian-bian establish a design evaluation system for the whole product life cycle of tractors. The whole product life cycle contains introduction stage, Growth stage and Maturity stage. The study uses the Delphi surveys method to establish indicators at first and then uses the analytic hierarchy process to determine the weight of each index. But this article only evaluates the specific product part of the tractor rather than propose the design evaluation index.

2.2 Intelligent Design Evaluation

Intelligent evaluation of design is a major area of interest within the field of design at present, and many researchers are exploring it, which researchers are more concerned with researching algorithms, improving models to improving evaluation accuracy.

Fan proposed a multi-objective creative design evaluation method for industrial design cloud service platform in 2019. Introduce customers into the decision-making process of design, and cooperate with algorithms to make decisions on design. Finally, the feasibility of this evaluation method is verified by taking yacht design as an example [7]. Dou proposed a method for automatically calculating web page aesthetics based on deep learning [8]. The existing body of research on it suggests that deep learning can extract representative features from web pages to quantify their aesthetics, providing designers with an objective aesthetic evaluation dimension.

Previous studies of design evaluation, less evaluation indicators are available for students' product design works, while more for enterprises or a specific product. And this field is still blank.

3 Materials and Method

This study collects design evaluation generalization index through literature collection, and streamlines them through expert interviews. Then the evaluation index is further established through factor analysis, and use the analytic hierarchy process to establish the weight of each index. Collect competition award-winning pictures based on evaluation index system, and use deep learning to intelligent evaluate students' product design. The research method of this paper is shown in Fig. 1.

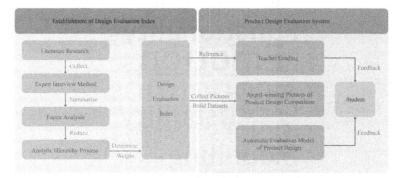

Fig. 1. The research method of this paper

3.1 A Subsection Sample

In recent years, more and more studies on the design of evaluation indicators have been conducted, and different experts and scholars have performed studies on various design indicators. In 2012, Shih-Wen Hsiao published a paper in which they described an affordance evaluation model for product design [9]. 10 evaluation indicators were sorted out through the literature, and then used MSD and cluster analysis to obtain the typical characteristics; next analyzed the evaluation results by using the AHP to determine the relative weights between indexes, so as to establish the available sexual evaluation model. In addition, an online affordance evaluation model was designed and tested on PHILPS steam iron GC2510. According to the evaluation results, some parts of GC2510 steam iron were redesigned, performed to verify the effect of the model by comparing the two designs.

Product service systems formed the central focus of a study by Min Qu in which the author analyze around tradeoffs between customer value, sustainability, and tradeoffs between perspectives [10]. The concrete contents of the three are elaborated and analyzed in detail.

Yue, H. improved the evaluation method of household medical product design for the elderly by using analytic Hierarchy process [12]. Firstly, the previous research results are sorted out and summarized, and the first-level index are established as aesthetic, functional, practical and second-level index. Secondly, the design elements of household medical products for the elderly are summarized by issuing questionnaires to the elderly, scientific researchers and medical personnel, and a hierarchical analysis model is established to determine its weight. Finally, a case study with the three examples of geriatric household blood glucose meters is performed to verify the effect of this model.

In this study, a large number of literature studies were carried out, and the design evaluation indicators were extracted for word frequency analysis. Word frequency analysis word cloud as shown in Fig. 2.

Fig. 2. Word frequency analysis word cloud

It can be seen from the figure that evaluation indexes such as Emotion, Functionality, Economice, Usability appear more frequently. Because in the existing studies, less evaluation indicators are available for students' product design homework, while more for enterprises or a specific product. In order to obtain more accurate design evaluation indicators, we interviewed industrial design teachers. Finally, obtaining ten indexes suitable for students' product design evaluation: colors for matching, shape, visual effect, product coordination, functionality, practicality, developability, product sociality, product creativity, design integrity.

3.2 Dimension-Reduction Analysis on Evaluation Indicators by Means of Factor Analysis

After the investigation in the early stage, dimension-reduction analysis on evaluation indicators is carried out by means of factor analysis. Factor analysis method was first proposed by Charles Spearman in 1904, and has been widely used in various fields such as psychology and medicine.

Formula and Theory. The specific calculation steps of factor analysis are Standardization of the data, Calculation of the data's correlation coefficient matrix, and analysis of the correlation between variables, Calculation of the initial common factor and factor loading matrix, rotation of factors and Calculation of factor score. Specific steps are as follows.

Step1 Standardization of the data. In order to eliminate the data deviation caused by huge differences in different dimensions and orders of magnitude, the data should be standardized to ensure the accuracy and rationality of the final analysis.

Step2 Calculation of the data's correlation coefficient matrix, and analysis of the correlation between variables. If most of the correlation coefficients in the data's correlation coefficient matrix are less than 0.3, then these variables are not suitable for factor analysis.

Step3 Calculation of the initial common factor and factor loading matrix. In this study, the factor loading is estimated by the principal component method. First, write the sample data matrix

$$\tilde{X} = \left(a_{ij}\right)_{p \times m} = \begin{bmatrix} X_{11} & \cdots & X_p \\ \vdots & \ddots & \vdots \\ X_{n1} & \cdots & X_{np} \end{bmatrix}_{n \times p} \tag{1}$$

Correlation matrix $R = \left(\gamma_{ij}\right)$. Subsequently, calculate R eigenvalue $\lambda_1 \geq \lambda_2 \geq \cdots \geq \lambda_p \geq 0$ and the corresponding unit orthogonal eigenvector $\mu_1, \mu_2, \cdots, \mu_p$, and the principle of determining the number of principal components is adopted when determining the number of common factors.

$$\frac{\lambda_1 + \lambda_2 + \ldots + \lambda_m}{\sum_{i=1} \lambda_i} = \frac{\lambda_1 + \lambda_2 + \ldots + \lambda_m}{P} \geq 0.7 \tag{2}$$

And the principle of determining the number of principal components is adopted when determining the number of common factors. Generally, it is more than 70%.

Set $a_i = \sqrt{\lambda_i}u_i, i = 1, \cdots, m$ so $A = (a_1, \cdots, a_m)$ refers to the factor loading matrix. The variance of the special factors is solved. Finally, combine professional knowledge to make a reasonable explanation for the m common factors is made.

Step4 Rotation of factors. If the practical significance of the obtained common factors is not obvious, need to rotation of factors to make the variable more explanatory. In order to polarize the square of each element in each column of A to 0 or 1 by column, orthogonal rotation of A is needed to be conducted. methods of factor analysis include orthogonal rotation method and oblique rotation method. In this study, orthogonal ro-tation method is adopted. The orthogonal rotation is obtained by multiplying the initial load matrix A right by an orthogonal matrix by the common method of varimax.

Step 5 Explain the factor and rename. To explain the m common factors after rotation reasonably requires professional knowledge.

Step 6 Calculation of factor score.

Research Object and Data Collection. Data for this study were collected using dis-tribute Data scale questionnaires. All the subjects were students and teachers of design major. Totally recover 46 sample data, and 4 samples that did not meet the requirements were removed (non-design-related majors). There are 44 valid data in total, among which 34 are from industrial design and product design, accounting for 73% of the total data. The questionnaire adopts the ten-point scale method. The subjects rated the 10 design evaluation indexes mentioned in Sect. 3.1 on a scale of 0 (very unimportant) to 10 (very important). Factor analysis was performed using IBM SPSS Statistics 26.

3.3 Analytic Hierarchy Process

In the 1970s, American management professor Thomas L. Saaty pointed to Analytic Hierarchy Process (AHP) which is a commonly used subjective evaluation method.

Formula and Theory. Analytic Hierarchy Process (AHP) divides complex problems into several hierarchical structures. Its Steps include Determination of the indicator system and establishment of the hierarchical evaluation model, Construction of judgment matrix, calculate the weight vector and Analysis result. In this study, AHP is mainly used to calculate the weight vector. The calculation process of analytic hierarchy process is shown in Fig. 3.

Establishment of the Hierarchical Evaluation Model. In this study, the goal layer is stu-dent product design evaluation. The criteria layer is five evaluation indexes after factor analysis, there are product visual effect, product function, product sociality, product cre-ativity, design integrity. The alternative layer is students' design works. The hierarchical evaluation model of this study is shown in Fig. 4.

Construction of Judgment Matrix. Construction of judgment matrix is to compare the elements of the criteria layer with each other, and finally determine the weight of each criteria layer to the goal layer. In general, Saaty's Scale of Relative Importance is used, that is, in the paired comparison, the numbers from 1 to 9 and their reciprocal are used to indicate the relative importance of the evaluation factors. Saaty's Scale of Relative Importance is shown in Table 1.

Construction of judgment matrix for criteria layer A

$$A = \begin{bmatrix} a_{11} & a_{12} & \cdots & a_{1n} \\ a_{21} & a_{22} & \cdots & a_{2n} \\ \cdots & \cdots & \cdots & \cdots \\ a_{n1} & a_{n2} & \cdots & a_{nn} \end{bmatrix} \tag{3}$$

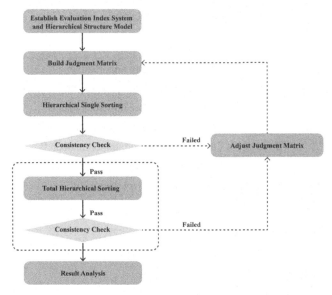

Fig. 3. The calculation process of analytic hierarchy process

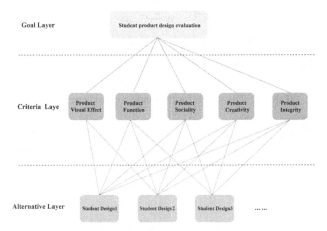

Fig. 4. The hierarchical evaluation model

Single Hierarchical Arrangement. Single hierarchical arrangement refers to the arrangement of important orders by comparing all elements in this layer with each other for an element in the previous layer. $w_1, w_2, \cdots, w_n$ refers to the weight value corresponding to each element.

Consistency Check of Matrix. The purpose of consistency check is to determine whether there is a logical problem in the constructed judgment matrix. For example, A is more important than B, B is more important than C, but C is more important than A. First

Table 1. Saaty's Scale of Relative Importance

Number	Indication
1	A and B is equally important
3	A is moderately more important than B
5	A is strongly more important than B
7	A is very strong more important than B
9	A is extremely more important than B
2, 4, 6, 8	Intermediate value
1/3, 1/5, 1/7, 1/9	B is more important than A

calculate the consistency index (CI).

$$CI = \frac{\lambda_{max} - n}{n - 1} \tag{4}$$

The formula for calculating the largest eigenvalue λ_{max} is.

$$\lambda_{max} = \frac{1}{n} \sum_{i=1}^{n} \frac{(Aw)_i}{w_i} \tag{5}$$

The values for the random consistency index R.I. obtained by 1,000 times of Satty's simulations are shown in Table 2.

Table 2. The values for the random consistency index

Order of matrix **n**	1	2	3	4	5	6	7	8	9	10	11
RI	0	0	0.58	0.90	1.12	1.24	1.32	1.41	1.45	1.49	1.52

Consistency ratio (CR)

$$CR = \frac{CI}{RI} \tag{6}$$

When CR is less than 0.1, the consistency of judgment matrix A is considered acceptable.

Research Object and Data Collection. Data for this study were collected using online questionnaires. All the subjects were students and teachers of design major. Totally recover 44 sample data, and 2 samples that did not meet the requirements were removed (non-design-related majors). There are 42 valid data in total, among which 34 are from industrial design and product design, accounting for 77% of the total data. After calculation, 3 pieces of data that failed Consistency check of matrix were eliminated, and 39 pieces of data were finally valid. AHP was performed using SPSSAU.

Table 3. Basic description of data

	The average value	standard deviation
Colors	7.45	2.027
Shape	7.81	1.941
Visual effect	7.81	1.966
Coordination	8.07	2.041
Creativity	7.26	2.198
Integrity	8.19	1.928
Functionality	8.38	1.780
Practicability	7.71	2.028
Developability	6.83	2.575
Sociality	6.52	2.671

4 Results

4.1 Factor Analysis

Basic Description of Data. 44 sample data will be collected for statistics, and their mean and their average value and standard deviation are shown in Table 3.

It can be seen from the table that the average value of functionality is the highest, 8.38; The social lowest is 6.52. This reflected that the participants generally believe that functionality is more important. The maximum social standard deviation was 2.67; The minimum functional standard deviation is 1.78.

Explained Variance Ratio. Total Variance Explained shown in Table 5. The higher the Variance Explained rate, the rawer data the factor contains. Generally, the extracted factor's total Variance Explained should be above 85. Therefore, a total of 5 factors were extracted in this study, and the variance interpretation rates of these 5 factors after rotation are25.574%, 23.434%, 14.203%, 11.824%, 11.229% respectively. The rotated Variance is 86.264%. Total Variance Explained shown in Table 4. The higher the Variance Explained rate, the rawer data the factor contains. Generally, the extracted factor's total Variance Explained should be above 85. Therefore, a total of 5 factors were extracted in this study, and the variance interpretation rates of these 5 factors after rotation are25.574%, 23.434%, 14.203%, 11.824%, 11.229% respectively. The rotated Variance is 86.264%.

Table of Factor Loading Factor After Rotation. The data in this study were rotated by means of varimax, so as to find out the corresponding relationship between factors and research items. Table 6 shows information extraction of research items, as well as the corresponding relationship between factors and research items, it can be seen that the commonality value of all research items is higher than 0.4. This means that there is a strong correlation between research items and factors, and factors can effectively extract information. Factor I include colors, shape, visual effect and product coordination, which is renamed as product visual effect. Factor II includes functionality, practicality and developability, which is renamed as product function. Factor III is product sociality. Factor IV is product creativity. Factor V is design integrity.

Test of Reliability and Validity. Cronbach's Alpha value is used to test the reliability of the questionnaire. Generally, Cronbach's alpha value is between 0 and 1. If it does not exceed 0.6, it will be generally considered that the internal consistency reliability is insufficient. If it reaches 0.7–0.8, it indicates that the scale has considerable reliability; if it reaches 0.8–0.9, it indicates that the scale has very good reliability. Cronbach's Alpha value of the factor analysis questionnaire in this study is .710, which proved good reliability. The reliability table is shown in Table 4.

Table 4. Cronbach's Alpha

Cronbach's Alpha	Frequency
.710	10

The validity of the questionnaire is tested by means of KMO test statistics and Bartlett's test. Like Table 5 shows that KMO measure of samping adequacy is 0.657, between 0.6 and 0.7. The research data is suitable for information extraction. Bartlett's Test of Sphericity is 0.000, Sig. < 0.05, Suitable for factor analysis (Tables 6 and 7).

Table 5. KMO and Bartlett's Test

KMO Measure of Samping Adequacy		.657
Bartlett's Test of Sphericity	Approx. Chi-Square	182.821
	df	45
	Sig	.000

4.2 AHP

Result. We calculated 39 valid data by analytic hierarchy process, and got the index weight value of each sample data. The average weight of all indicators is calculated, and the final weight of evaluation indicators is 12.48% product visual effect, 37.81% product function, 10.78% product sociality, 21.80% product creativity and 17.13% design integrity. The pie chart of specific results is shown in Fig. 5.

Reliability Test. Generally, the smaller the CR value is, the better the consistency of the judgment matrix is. If the CR value is less than 0.1, the judgment matrix meets the consistency test. If the CR value is greater than 0.1, it will indicate that there is no

Table 6. Total Variance Explained

Factor	Eigen			% of Variance(Unrotated)			% of Variance(Rotated)		
	Eigen Value	% of Variance	Cumulative % of Variance	Eigen Value	% of Variance	Cumulative % of Variance	Eigen Value	% of Variance	Cumulative % of Variance
1	3.331	33.313	33.313	3.331	33.313	33.313	2.557	25.574	25.574
2	2.428	24.284	57.597	2.428	24.284	57.597	2.343	23.434	49.007
3	1.169	11.686	69.283	1.169	11.686	69.283	1.420	14.203	63.210
4	0.897	8.965	78.249	0.897	8.965	78.249	1.182	11.824	75.035
5	0.802	8.015	86.264	0.802	8.015	86.264	1.123	11.229	86.264
6	0.457	4.566	90.830	-	-	-	-	-	-
7	0.335	3.347	94.177	-	-	-	-	-	-
8	0.258	2.584	96.761	-	-	-	-	-	-
9	0.175	1.753	98.514	-	-	-	-	-	-
10	0.149	1.486	100.000	-	-	-	-	-	-

consistency. The judgment matrix should be re-analyzed after being adjusted properly. Before calculation, the data that does not meet the consistency test of judgment matrix is removed to ensure the reliability of analytic hierarchy process data.

5 Design of Design Education-Oriented Product Evaluation System

5.1 Intelligent Evaluation Method for Product Design

After the design evaluation indicators was studied, it was found that most of the current competition evaluation systems are consistent with the evaluation indicator system we have developed. The evaluation criteria of IF student award are shown in Fig. 6. The problem-solving include the creative, refinement, uniqueness, use value and usability. Consequently, we have gathered a large number of award-winning pictures and hope that the automatic evaluation of product design works can be realized by using the technical means of deep learning.

Deep learning was conducted on the award-winning pictures in the design competition by using a 16-layer VGG network. As shown in Fig. 7, there are 13 Convolutional layers and 3 full-link layers in the VGG-16 network structure. We feed $224 \times 224 \times 3$ color images into the VGG network.

Specific Work Flow of VGG16

Step 1. The size of the input image is $224 \times 224 \times 3$. After 64 3×3 convolution kernels with the channel of 3, the step size of 1, padding = same, and twice convolutions, these pictures are activated by ReLU, and then the size of the output image is $224 \times 224 \times 264$.

Step 2. Max pooling is performed with a filter size of 2×2, the step size of 2, and the image size is halved. The pooled size becomes $112 \times 112 \times 64$.

Table 7. Factor loading (Rotated)

Name	Factor loading					Communality
	Factor1	Factor2	Factor3	Factor4	Factor5	
Colors	0.740	-0.191	0.341	0.219	-0.094	0.758
Shape	0.542	0.018	0.541	0.401	-0.298	0.836
Visual effect	0.876	0.083	0.111	0.208	0.068	0.834
Coordination	0.908	0.031	0.062	-0.032	0.091	0.838
Creativity	0.196	-0.049	0.014	0.959	0.006	0.961
Integrity	0.058	0.096	0.103	-0.006	0.961	0.947
Functionality	0.082	0.921	-0.007	0.015	-0.102	0.865
Practicability	-0.018	0.862	-0.244	-0.020	0.142	0.823
Developability	-0.106	0.834	0.396	-0.094	0.170	0.902
Sociality	0.254	-0.001	0.876	-0.017	0.172	0.863

Step 3. The image after 128 3 × 3 convolution kernels, and twice convolutions, these pictures are activated by ReLU, and then the size of the output image is 112 × 112 × 128.

Step 4. Max pooling, and then the size of the output image is 56 × 56 × 2128.

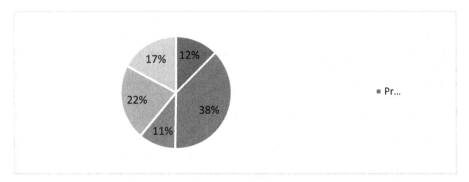

Fig. 5. Index weight

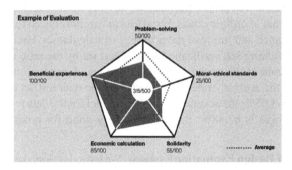

Fig. 6. IF design competition evaluation criteria

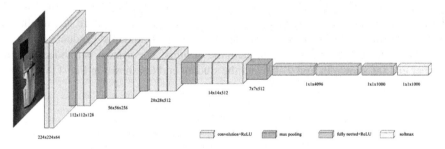

Fig. 7. Structure of the VGG-16 network

Step 5. The image after 256 3 × 3 convolution kernels, and thrice convolutions, these pictures are activated by ReLU, and then the size of the output image is 56 × 56 × 256.
Step 6. Max pooling, and then the size of the output image is 28 × 28 × 2256.
Step 7. The image after 512 3 × 3 convolution kernels, and thrice convolutions, these pictures are activated by ReLU, and then the size of the output image is 28 × 28 × 512.
Step 8. Max pooling, and then the size of the output image is 14 × 14 × 2512
Step 9. The image after 512 3 × 3 convolution kernels, and thrice convolutions, these pictures are activated by ReLU, and then the size of the output image is 14 × 14 × 512.
Step 10. Max pooling, and then the size of the output image is 7 × 7 × 2512

Step 11. Then Flatten(), flattening the data into vectors to become one-dimensional $512 \cdot 7 \cdot 7$ = 25088.

Step 12. After two layers of $1 \times 1 \times 4096$, one layer of $1 \times 1 \times 1000$ fully connected layer (a total of three layers), are activated by ReLU

Step 13. Finally, 1000 prediction results are output through softmax

5.2 Prototype Design of Evaluation System

Deep Learning Evaluation Model. We collected a total of 33,745 pieces of data from design competitions including IF, Reddot and others, including 29,178 images from international competitions, 2515 images from national competitions, and 2,052 images from provincial and municipal competitions. And in each layer, according to the award level, it is divided into excellent (special prize, gold prize, silver prize) and ordinary (bronze prize and excellent prize). Because the number of the excellent award-winning works is less than that of ordinary ones, Focal loss to was introduced to solve the problem of category imbalance and improve the accuracy of calculation. Each layer of data set was divided into training set, verification set and test set by the ratio of 8:1:1.

The accuracy rate of the model for the data test set of international award-winning works is 72.96%; the accuracy rate of the model for the data test set of national award-winning works is 68.65%; the accuracy rate of the model for the data test set of provincial award-winning works is 67.48%. Basic can be very good for product design picture evaluation.

Design of Product Design Evaluation System. We have developed a design education-oriented product design evaluation system for the product design evaluation indicators system and the intelligent evaluation model based on deep learning technology. The specific application process is shown in Fig. 8. Teacher can evaluate students' home-work in the system according to a clear indicator system. Furthermore, the intelligent evaluation model will also provide evaluation feedback on students' product designs, so as to facilitate students to better complete the designs. The system is divided into the teacher end (as shown in Fig. 9–10) and the student end (as shown in Fig. 11).

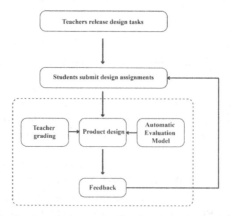

Fig. 8. Product design evaluation system operation process

Fig. 9. Teacher interface 1   **Fig. 10.** Teacher interface 2

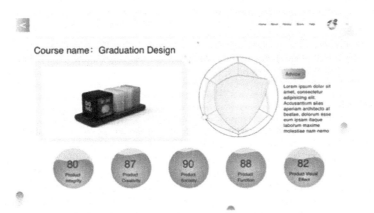

Fig. 11. Student interface

6 Conclusion

In this study, we systematically studied the design evaluation index to establish a more specific student product design evaluation index system. At the same time, deep learning was introduced to form an automatic evaluation model of product design. In the study, there are still some limitations. For example, the size of the samples found when establishing the design indicators was small, only 40 people, and the correlation between the automatic evaluation model and the indicators was relatively weak. But some useful findings.

1. According to the Literature and expert interview obtaining ten indexes suitable for students' product design evaluation: colors for matching, shape, visual effect, product coordination, functionality, practicality, developability, product sociality, product creativity, design integrity.
2. established the evaluation index system of student product design Through factor analysis and analytic hierarchy process: 12.48% product visual effect, 37.81% product function, 10.78% product sociality, 21.80% product creativity and 17.13% design integrity
3. VGG16 can classify and predict design product images effectively, and can be used to evaluate product design works automatically

4. Based on the above research, a design education-oriented product design evaluation system is designed. The system combines teacher scoring with intelligent evaluation based on deep learning algorithm model to better provide students with feedback on their product designs and help students improve design skills.

In the future, we can further explore design evaluation and introduce physiological signals such as EEG and eye movement to explore the relationship between design evaluation and subjective evaluation. The automatic evaluation model is further improved to improve the prediction accuracy, and corresponding to the sub-item design evaluation index system. It provides further exploration for automatic evaluation and automatic feedback in the future. To improve the quality of students' design and improve the evaluation system of design education.

Acknowledgments. This work is supported by the National Natural Science Foundation of China (Grant No. 62277038). We thank all the participants for carrying out the experiments.

References

1. Yan-hui, Y., Li-yong, Y., Lai-wen, L.U.O.: On the Bauhaus design education and training mode. Packaging Eng. **30**, 195–197 (2009)
2. Zhang, T., Lu, G., Wu, Y.: A conceptual framework for integrating inclusive design into design education. In: Antona, M., Stephanidis, C. (eds.) UAHCI 2017. LNCS, vol. 10277, pp. 123–131. Springer, Cham (2017). https://doi.org/10.1007/978-3-319-58706-6_10
3. Wang, Y.H., et al.: Prediction of product design decision making: an investigation of eye movements and EEG features. Adv. Eng. Inform. **45**, 101095 (2020)
4. Kim, M., Jung, E.S., Park, S., Nam, J., Choe, J.: Application of a universal design evaluation index to mobile phones. In: Jacko, J.A. (ed.) HCI 2007. LNCS, vol. 4551, pp. 364–373. Springer, Heidelberg (2007). https://doi.org/10.1007/978-3-540-73107-8_41
5. Li, P.H., Shang, K.: IEEE research on the evaluation index of product design based on consumer, designer and manufacturer. In: 2nd International Conference on Applied Robotics for the Power Industry (CARPI), pp. 481–483 (2012)
6. Bian-bian, Q., Ji-ping, Z., Zai-xiang, Z., Hui, S.: Establishing a dynamic ergonomic evaluation index system for complex product designs based on the theory of product life cycle. Int. J. Ind. Ergon. **69**, 153–162 (2019)
7. Fan, J.S., Yu, S.H., Chu, J.J., et al.: Multi-objective creative de-sign evaluation method for industrial design cloud service platform. Comput. Integr. Manuf. Syst. **25**, 9 (2019)
8. Dou, Q., Zheng, X.S., Sun, T., Heng, P.-A.: Webthetics: quantifying webpage aesthetics with deep learning. Int. J. Hum Comput Stud. **124**, 56–66 (2019)
9. Hsiao, S.W., Hsu, C.F., Lee, Y.T.: An online affordance evaluation model for product design. Des. Stud. **33**, 126–159 (2012)
10. Qu, M., Yu, S.H., Chen, D.K., Chu, J.J., Tian, B.Z.: State-of-the-art of design, evaluation, and operation methodologies in product service systems. Comput. Ind. **77**, 1–14 (2016)
11. Yue, H., Zhu, T.L., Zhou, Z.J., Zhou, T.: Improvement of evaluation method of elderly family medical product design based on AHP. Math. Prob. Eng. (2022)
12. Flora, D., LaBrish, C., Chalmers, R.: Old and new ideas for data screening and assumption testing for exploratory and confirmatory factor analysis. Front. Psychol. **3**, 55 (2012)
13. Saaty, T.L.: A scaling method for priorities in hierarchical structures. J. Math. Psychol. **15**, 234–281 (1977)
14. https://ifdesign.com/en/if-design-student-award. Accessed 22 Feb 2023

CTM Design Thinking Tool Stimulates Creative α and β Brain Activities

Chao Yang Yang[1](✉), Ding Hau Huang[2], Chin-Sheng Chou[1], and Yi Chi Fu[3]

[1] Department of Industrial Design, Tatung University, 40 Chungshan N. Rd., Sec. 3, Taipei 104, Taiwan
dillon.yang@gmail.com

[2] Institute of Creative Design and Management, National Taipei University of Business, 321 Sec. 1, Jinan Rd., Zhongzheng District, Taipei 100, Taiwan

[3] The Graduate Institute of Design Science, Tatung University, 40 Chungshan N. Rd., Sec. 3, Taipei 104, Taiwan

Abstract. The Concept Triangulation Map (CTM) was designed to enable the identification of the thinking of individual team members and the convergence of this thinking to produce common and creative concept combinations for innovation. This research examined the effects of the produced word combinations on creative brain activities. In total, 20 Taiwanese university students were recruited for an electroencephalogram (EEG) experiment with a baseline Chinese Word Remote Associates Test (CWRAT). The EEG results were compared by the CWRAT score, higher (scored over 18 points), middle (scored 13–17 points) and lower (scored under 12 points).

The α and β brainwaves were stimulated the most by combinations 5–8 (c5–8) from each CTM group and some combinations of common concepts. Participants with low CWRAT scores did not generally exhibit the stimulation α and β brainwaves in response to common combinations, and they seldom exhibited responses to creative combinations. Participants with higher scores generally exhibited sudden brainwave stimulation at high amplitudes. The results provide novel insights into creativity quality assessed using the CTM, in which common concepts are critical to calibrating optimised thinking performance.

Keywords: EEG · creative thinking · CWRAT · Concept Triangulation Map · innovation

1 Introduction

The Taiwanese government promotes the concept of multidisciplinary collaboration in higher education. Years of multidisciplinary education have demonstrated that students and teachers tend to think according to their own discipline rather than that of others. This is because of differences in the understanding and application of concepts. Teaching tools providing a communication platform that enables innovation on the basis of team capabilities, user experience, and user needs are lacking. To encourage the multidisciplinary integration of concepts, we developed the Concept Triangulation Map (CTM) (Fig. 1) [1] as an teaching tool for the conceptual stage of innovation projects.

A. Marcus et al. (Eds.): HCII 2023, LNCS 14031, pp. 571–578, 2023.
https://doi.org/10.1007/978-3-031-35696-4_42

Innovation depends on differences from other solutions/creations and abilities that the team could execute. The CTM systematically incorporates group and individual thinking activities in 'team knowledge' (A), 'life perception' (B), and 'future benefit expectations' (C) domains. Giving obligations to different phases for team member to think and communicate in preset discussion sections appointed to innovative values. CTM helps team to nominate the highest creative concept of team capability, user observations and user's needs aspects for creative combination (A2B2C2, also shown as c2) and the most common idea of each aspect for most common combination (A1B1C1, also shown as c1). The teams were encouraged to design an innovation by combining concepts from each of the three CTM aspects. The usefulness of the CTM as a tool for the generation of new ideas by a team has been demonstrated; however, the concept formation stage is considered difficult by students.

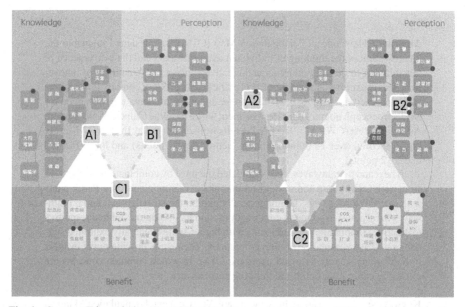

Fig. 1. Concept Triangulation Map (CTM) [1]. Common combination (left); creative combination (right).

The creation of new ideas by combining concepts from the three aspects depends on students' association abilities, which are an important component of creativity. This research evaluated whether the association of the three concepts triggered brain activities (EEG) and whether these activities were related to association ability in the Chinese Word Remote Associates Test (CWRAT) [2].

CWRAT

Remote Associates Test (RAT) [3] is a tool for testing convergent thinking ability based on Mednick [4]'s associative theory. Creativity is a thinking ability involving associating components in novel manners in a designated context. The RAT involves 30 word-association questions and requires no professional knowledge. To assess the Taiwanese university students, we used the CWRAT [2] in which three provided words must be associated. Correct answers are predetermined. For example, the prompts 'Newton', 'wax', and 'red' require the tester to think of the word 'apple'. A correct answer is worth 1 point.

Common and creative three-key-concept combinations were produced during the CTM process for different innovation topics. The CTM was designed to help multi-disciplinary team members to merge concepts or ideas in areas such as team member skills, life experience, and desires for the future into common and creative individual key concepts; three common key concepts or words and three creative concepts or words are produced in one CTM process. This study measured the brainwaves stimulated by associating the six common and creative concepts produced during previous CTM processes and compared the differences associated with individual CWRAT score.

2 Electroencephalogram (EEG)

EEGs record continuous brain electrical discharges during cognitive activities. Generally, the human brain processes in a stimulus–response order, with electrical discharge frequencies classified as $\alpha(8-14\,Hz)$, $\beta(14-30\,Hz)$, $\theta(4-8\,Hz)$, $\delta(<4\,Hz)$. As shown in Fig. 2, EEG electrodes are distributed according to cerebral cortex sections, including the frontal lobe, central sulcus, parietal lobe, temporal lobe, and occipital lobe. Increased α and β activities occur in the right frontal lobe and central sulcus during divergent thinking [5, 6]; therefore, α and β frequencies at the C4-P4 channel are used to measure creative association stimulation.

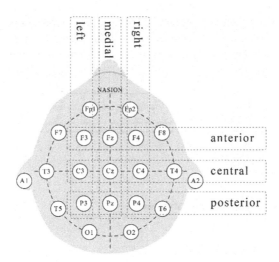

Fig. 2. 19 channels + 2 references (A1 & A2) EEG cap

3   Research Method

The experiment consisted of the completion of the CWRAT and brainwave monitoring during the association of three words. For the CWRAT, participants were asked to complete 30 questions in which they associated the three provided Chinese words to produce another word. Participants received 1 point for a correct association. In the EEG test, we recorded participants' brainwaves during the association of the three-word combinations produced during a previous CTM workshop and measured creativity-related brain activities by observing sudden increases in α and β brainwaves.

3.1   Experiment Design

In total, 20 Tatung University students (10 women and 10 men) with an average age of 22 years and normal vision who had not taken any medication within 24 h participated in this study. Participants provided informed consent regarding the experiment, method, process, and health risks. They first completed the CWRAT and then participated in the EEG test after a short rest interval. The stimuli (word combinations) in the EEG experiment were 14 CTM outcome groups. All words were confirmed individually to be understandable, and assessment using sample combinations was first undertaken to ensure the participant understood the association task. As shown at the bottom left of Fig. 3, each group contains common and creative combinations (c1 & c2) formed from six concepts in six combinations (c3–c8). The order of the combinations used in the test was random within each group. During the EEG test (Fig. 3), before each word combination was introduced, a "+" symbol was shown to the participant for 1000 ms to refresh their thinking process. The word combination was then displayed to the participant for 4000 ms, and the participant was encouraged to say a word representing the combination within 3000 ms. In total, 8 × 14 subtests were conducted for 16 min and 8 s. Following a 1000-ms white screen gap, the subsequent combination was displayed.

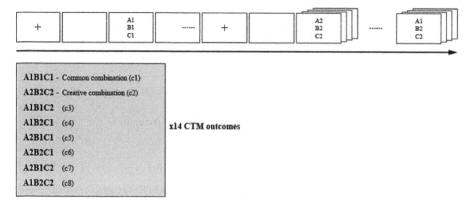

Fig. 3. EEG experiment process

3.2   Research Environment and Apparatus

The experimental environment was a quiet, empty room (Fig. 4). A 19-channel EEG device (Mindmedia NeXus-32), including two references and a ground, was employed to collect brain activity [7]. Eye movement [8] exceeding 80 μV and frontal facial muscle [9] noise exceeding 20 Hz was filtered by BioTrace + software. α and β brainwave data were analysed using WinEEG 2.124.95. Sudden increases of at least 30% in the amplitude of α (8–12 Hz) and β (12–30 Hz) waves in the central (C3 and C4) brain areas during the entire process were recognised as creative brain activities [6].

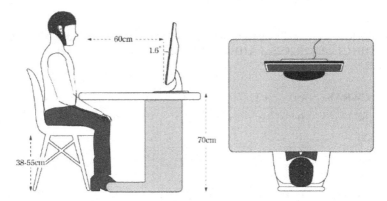

Fig. 4. Experiment environment

4   Results

Because of participant unfamiliarity with the association process and the tiring effect of the test, the first three and last four group results were discarded. The results of seven groups remained for further analysis. Generally, associating the CTM word combinations stimulated α and β brainwaves, and male participants exhibited more stimulations and higher CWRAT scores. Sudden brainwave increases of more than 30% were marked as one creative stimulation [6]. Examples of brain reactions to the association activities are shown in Fig. 5.

As shown in Table 1, c1 of each CTM outcomes are common combinations which are rarely (24 times) stimulated brainwaves whereas c5 ~ c8 has shown higher chance compare the other combinations. Combination c8 consists of common knowledge concept (A1), creative perception (B2) and benefit concepts(C2) had shown highest chance (85 times) to stimulate creative thinking. Combination c5, consists of only one creative word A2 also showed higher chance (62 times) provoking α and β. Although c2 is combined by all creative concepts A2B2C2, it had a relatively lower chance of stimulating brainwaves (44 times). Creative words produced using the CTM method are normally more conceptually irrelevant than common ones and are more likely to trigger brain association activities.

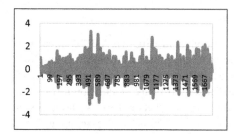 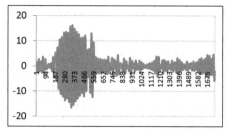

Fig. 5. Brainwaves when reacting to association: left figure is from participant with lower CWRAT score whereas right figure is from higher score.

Table 1. CWRAT score, and combinations of seven CTM groups with increased α and β stimulations. c1:A1B1C1; c2:A2B2C2; c3:A1B1C2; c4:A1B2C1; c5:A2B1C1; c6:A2B2C1; c7:A2B1C2; c8:A1B2C2

	CWRAT	c1	c2	c3	c4	c5	c6	c7	c8	total
F1	14	0	1	0	1	3	3	1	4	13
F2	20	1	5	3	0	6	3	4	7	29
F3	9	0	1	0	1	1	3	2	5	13
F4	15	1	3	2	1	2	2	4	3	18
F5	16	0	0	2	2	4	3	1	4	16
F6	9	4	1	1	2	3	3	1	2	17
F7	10	1	4	2	2	3	2	0	2	16
F8	10	3	3	2	2	3	1	0	4	18
F9	6	3	0	2	3	2	1	1	5	17
F10	21	3	3	1	2	4	3	3	5	24
M1	18	0	4	2	7	3	3	2	4	25
M2	17	5	2	3	2	3	5	5	3	28
M3	15	0	2	3	5	4	2	3	2	21
M4	14	0	2	0	2	2	4	4	6	20
M5	23	1	5	2	2	2	3	4	7	26
M6	20	0	2	3	2	3	3	5	4	22
M7	22	0	2	5	1	4	4	2	5	23
M8	17	1	0	4	1	3	5	3	4	21
M9	21	0	3	1	3	4	2	3	3	19
M10	19	3	1	3	2	3	3	5	6	26
		26	**44**	**41**	**43**	**62**	**58**	**53**	**85**	**412**

As shown in Table 2, participants with higher CWRAT scores tended to exhibit brain-waves with higher amplitudes during association. All groups exhibited higher stimulation frequencies in the c5, c6, and c8 test portions, whereas these frequencies differed during the c1, c2, and c7 sections for the CWRAT score groups. In the low score group, common combinations (c1) (mean = 2.20) were associated with more stimulations than were creative combinations (c2) (mean = 1.80). c7 elicited the lowest (mean = 0.80) response level, and c8 elicited the highest (mean = 3.60). Middle group performed lower stimulations in both c1 (mean = 1.00) and c2 (mean = 1.43) whereas the c3 ~ c7 performed averagely and c8 performed slightly higher. High group performed c1 in low stimulation (mean = 1.00) where c2 performed well (mean = 3.13) and c8 performed much higher than others (mean = 5.13).

The waveforms of different score groups also differed. As shown in Fig. 5, most of the stimulated waveforms of the middle group were steady, long, and high (as shown in the left figure), whereas the waveforms of some of the high group participants demonstrated 1000–2000-ms reactions at 500%–1000% amplitude, as shown on the right side of the figure. The waveforms of the low group exhibited an amplitude of just over 30% for long periods, in which α discharge was higher on average than β discharge.

Table 2. Comparison between CWRAT score groups and stimulation frequency of combinations

CWRAT score groups	c1	c2	c3	c4	c5	c6	c7	c8
>18 high	1.00	3.13	2.50	2.38	3.63	3.00	3.50	5.13
13−17 middle	1.00	1.43	2.00	2.00	3.00	2.43	3.00	3.71
<13 low	2.20	1.80	1.40	2.00	2.40	2.00	0.80	3.60

5 Conclusion

CTM is designed for multidisciplinary innovation team in exploring stage. The tool progressively leads the team to inventory the team experience and strength. Under the preset innovation context, common and creative concept combinations are converged for the final innovation definition. This research examined the usefulness of the combinations for team member associating the possible creative innovation ideas.

Overall, high group performed under CTM's expectation in which creative combination contains stronger concept for creative association. Without stimulation to the associations may mean that the task was not understandable of associable for them to initiate their creative thinking process. Creative words are important ingredient to stimulate association activities. Combining two creative words and one common word is the best to encourage α and β. Common words are the things/events people experience most. The commonness could be the reason of not being stimulated while associating. The creative words are more difficult to be related into an idea where the brainwave react severely, and the outcomes tend to be more valuable.

CWRAT score relates to the chance of increased amplitude stimulations. Higher score participants also perform sudden highly increased amplitude whereas lower score participants performed in steady, longer lower amplitude waveform. This may imply that high association ability depends on the α and β wave to be initiated in short period with high amplitude. Higher score participants also were better in express their associated words in time whereas lower score participants had more chance to give up or felt asleep.

In the future, the strength difference of creative words from CTM can be evaluated to further prove the CTM effects in innovation as well as the creative waveform reacting to the association task may be trained. The most stimulated combinations can be collected as a database for association training practice and the effects can be examined.

References

1. Yang, C.Y., Fu, Y.C.: Innovative Concept Blending - Progressive Design Thinking. Tatung University, Taipei, Taiwan (2022)
2. Wu, C.-L., Chen, P.-Z., Chen, H.-C.: Measuring conceptual associations via the development of the Chinese visual remote associates test. Front. Psychol. **13** (2022)
3. Mednick, M.T.: Relationship of the ammons quick test of intelligence to other ability measures. Psychol. Rep. **20**(2), 523–526 (1967)
4. Mednick, S.: The associative basis of the creative process. Psychol. Rev. **69**(3), 220–232 (1962)
5. Zhang, Y., Zhou, M., Wang, Q.: Interactions of stimulus quality and frequency on N400 in Chinese character recognition: evidence for cascaded processing. Neurosci. Lett. **715**, 134614 (2020)
6. Agnoli, S., Zanon, M., Mastria, S., Avenanti, A., Corazza, G.E.: Enhancing creative cognition with a rapid right-parietal neurofeedback procedure. Neuropsychologia **118**, 99–106 (2018)
7. Mantini, D., Perrucci, M.G., Del Gratta, C., Romani, G.L., Corbetta, M.: Electrophysiological signatures of resting state networks in the human brain. Proc. Natl. Acad. Sci. **104**(32), 13170–13175 (2007)
8. Onton, J., Westerfield, M., Townsend, J., Makeig, S.: Imaging human EEG dynamics using independent component analysis. Neurosci. Biobehav. Rev. **30**(6), 808–822 (2006)
9. Shackman, A.J., McMenamin, B.W., Maxwell, J.S., Greischar, L.L., Davidson, R.J.: Right dorsolateral prefrontal cortical activity and behavioral inhibition. Psychol. Sci. **20**(12), 1500–1506 (2009)

Research on R&D Strategy of Cultural Creativity Publishing in Beijing from the Perspective of Cultural Symbiosis

Fumei Zhang(✉) and Sun Yiran

Beijing Institute of Graphic Communication, Xinghua Street 1, Beijing 102600, China
82728339@qq.com

Abstract. Cultural creativity publishing is an emerging section in the development of cultural creativity industry in recent years. The combination of publishing industry and cultural creativity industry provides an important way for the publishing industry to seek media integration and diversified development, as well as broadens a new idea for the cultural creativity industry to explore cultural resources and creative research and development. This paper carries out a survey on the cultural creativity publishing in Beijing, discusses the transformation and innovation of cultural creativity publishing to cultural resources from the perspective of cultural symbiosis, and builds an interactive system of cultural connotation, cultural creativity and cultural value, so as to improve the research and development strategy of cultural creativity publishing.

Keywords: Cultural creativity publishing · Cultural symbiosis · Creative research and development · Resources transformation · Value promotion

1 Introduction

For the past few years, the cultural creativity industry around our country has shown a vigorous and updated development trend along with our increasing attention and positive guidance to the construction of cultural industry, and has become a newly-developing energy to boost the development of national economy, of which economic value-added ratio to GDP continues to rise. As an emerging section in the development of cultural creativity industry in recent years, cultural creativity publishing industry is not only an important way for the publishing industry to explore media integration and diversified development, but also provides a model for the cultural creativity industry to seek new space and new ideas in the process of exploring and transforming cultural resources, as well as provides method reference and idea guidance for the cultural creativity industry to develop in other sub-sections.

Since 2015, the State Administration of Press, Publication, Radio, Film and Television and the Ministry of Finance jointly issued the *Guiding Opinions on Promoting the Integrated Development of Traditional Publishing and Emerging Publishing*, which further defined the basic tasks and objectives of promoting the development of publishing integration, adhered to the complementary advantages and integrated development of traditional publishing and emerging publishing, and developed and applied the new technologies, new products and new types in the publishing industry.[1] In early 2019, Xi Jinping, the General Secretary, put forward the important instruction of "accelerating the development of media integration and building the pattern of all-media communication", which has practical guiding significance for media integration and transformation of our publishing industry.

The capital of Beijing has long implemented the urban development strategy guided by the thought of "four centers", among which the construction of "cultural center" is an important basis for the development of cultural creativity industry. Beijing is an important publishing city since ancient times, and also a benchmark city for the development of cultural industry in the new era and a core city to carry out cultural radiation and demonstration influence to the whole country. Currently, the traditional publishing industry is facing fierce competition, and the publishing industry has ushered in an important opportunity for transformation and upgrading under the background of information age. Publishing enterprises and relevant institutions in Beijing have taken the lead in exploring the development path of publishing integration, and conducted many innovative attempts in the field of cultural creativity publishing. This paper tries to evaluate the current R&D situation of cultural creativity publishing in Beijing, and puts forward the deepening concept and R&D ideas of cultural creativity publishing from the perspective of cultural symbiosis.

2   Current Development Situation and Existing Problems of Cultural Creativity Publishing in Beijing

2.1   The Extension of Traditional Publishing Industry Chain

At the time of proposing the concept of "cultural creativity publishing", it has already pointed to the dimension extension of traditional publishing industry chain. Cultural creativity publishing is "generated in the context of cross-border integration and emerging technology development to develop the cultural creative products and services based on published content, which is the extension of publishing industry chain and a new type of cultural creativity industry"[2]. In the meantime, cultural creativity publishing as an emerging type in the field of cultural creativity has formed a benefit growth point of the link between cultural creativity publishing industries besides the mainstream publishing form of traditional publications. From the comparison between the process of traditional publishing and the R&D process of cultural creativity publishing (see Fig. 1), it clearly reflects that the cultural creativity publishing industry chain has formed the linkage and connection of multiple industry chains, such as art collection, daily articles, leisure and entertainment, and film and television works, in addition to the main books.

The development of cultural creativity publishing in Beijing reflects the overall tendency, mainstream measures and development trend of the construction of domestic cultural creativity publishing industry chain. The publishing agencies, such as People's Literature Publishing House, Palace Museum Publishing House and Wuzhou Communication Publishing House, have all established cultural creativity publishing brands, and taken the lead in extending the distribution from the traditional publishing industry

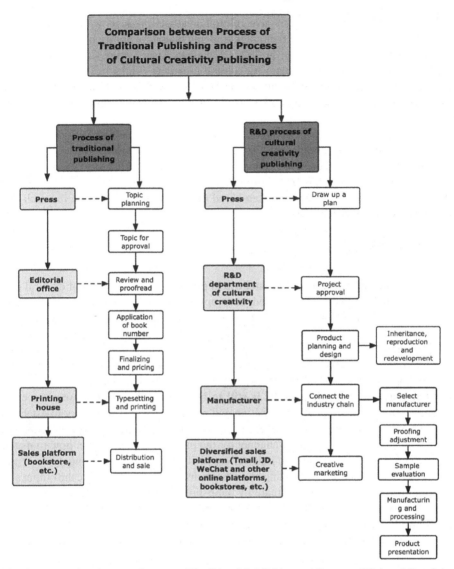

Fig. 1. Comparison between Process of Traditional Publishing and Process of Cultural Creativity Publishing (prepared by the author)

chain to the cultural creativity publishing industry chain. For example, People's Literature Publishing House, the largest literary and art publishing house in China, has established its official cultural creativity brand of "Treasure of Humanity" since 2019, which focused on Chinese and foreign classics, famous translations and other qualified publications to create the theme and content IP of cultural creativity publishing, such as China's four great classic novels, Lu Xun and *The Old Man and the Sea*, launched the book atlas gift box and book derivative cultural creativity products with the main function of collection, and reflected the integration and operation ability of industrial chain of cultural creativity publishing; in 2022, "Zhaohua Xishi·Coffee Cultural Creativity Agency" opened, which is featured by cultural creativity drinks including American-style coffee with Hemingway's theme of "The Old Man and the Sea" and jujube tea with Lu Xun's theme of "jujube badger", so as to open up the new form of offline cultural creativity.

However, the development of the whole cultural creativity publishing industry chain is still in the initial stage compared with the relatively mature museum cultural creativity industry chain. Although there have been many wonderful cases in recent years, there are also many problems that can't be ignored because most institutions have not established the procedures and hardware guarantee based on industrial chain for the research and development of cultural creativity.

Existing Problems

(1) **Ownership of copyright.** The intellectual property rights on R&D of cultural creativity publishing can't be ignored, and copyright disputes may be caused by carelessness. The publications of publishing house are subject to explicit author copyright according to the publishing contract. For the development of cultural creativity publishing, it is necessary to communicate with the author about copyright income. Additionally, whether the cultural creativity publishing in the form of books has a book number involves different related policies and operation system.

(2) **The business operation model is still to be improved.** Due to close connection between cultural creativity publishing and publications, it is necessary to establish a sound business operation model, form a gradually mature R&D mechanism, and set up an effective marketing channel for the problems, for example, how to match the publishing cycle with the cultural creativity R&D and marketing cycle of the book, the pre-sale, crowdfunding and other marketing models involve the output and production costs of cultural creativity publishing, and the multi-category derivative gift boxes involve warehouse storage, assembly and distribution.

(3) **Team building.** At present, because most publishing institutions don't have a clear organizational structure and continuous investment in cultural creativity team, few cultural creativity publishing can form its own brand culture and influence, and the workload of cultural creativity research and development doesn't match the number of staff. Only sustainable team maintenance can guarantee the talent supply of cultural creativity research and development, create the market demand, and ensure the product quality.

2.2 Local Conditions: Overall Appearance and Development Bottleneck of Publishing and Cultural Creativity in Beijing

According to the "2021 Cultural Industry Development Index of Provinces and Cities in China" resealed by the Institute of Cultural Industry Development of Renmin University of China, Beijing has been ranked first in the comprehensive index of cultural industry development of provinces and cities in China for six consecutive years [3]. As an emerging section in the positive development trend of cultural creativity industry, publishing and cultural creativity in Beijing has shown the overall advantages to adapt to local conditions, which benefits from the capital's unique political and cultural geography and the rich accumulation of publishing resources. First, Beijing is positioned as the capital of the country, so its publishing and cultural creativity have a stable dominant position in the national political, economic and cultural construction map; second, Beijing has a rich accumulation of publishing resources, so its R&D progress of publishing and cultural creativity could be effectively promoted by the combination of urban advantages and industry advantages, and a number of representative and exemplary masterpieces have emerged in the industry.

Taking the Palace Museum Publishing House as an example, its cultural resources is fully integrated with the artistic resources of the Palace Museum. *The Palace Museum Calendar* was launched in 2009, and has become a very influential paradigm of calendar publishing and cultural creativity after13 years of improvement; *Mi Gong · Ruyi Linlang Atlas* introduced in 2018, as well as the subsequent *Mi Gong · Jin Bang Ti Ming* (2020) and *Mi Gong · Yongle Mystery* (2022) became the annual hits in cultural creativity, which achieved commercial success through the way of crowdfunding marketing. (see Fig. 2).

Fig. 2. Publishing and Cultural Creativity Development of *Mi Gong* Series by the Palace Museum Publishing House (prepared by the author) Source: Palace Museum Publishing Flagship Store on Tmall official website

For the People's Literature Publishing House, the above-mentioned cultural creativity development aims at the linkage of the whole industrial chain with the complete categories. The IP development of "China's Four Great Classic Novels" are most representative, covering four types of publications, daily articles, leisure and entertainment, and art collection, with a total of more than 20 kinds of publishing and cultural creativity products. (see Fig. 3).

Nevertheless, although the publishing and cultural creativity development based on the classic content IP by the above well-known publishing houses enjoys exceptional advantages, there are still many specific problems. Moreover, other publishing units are

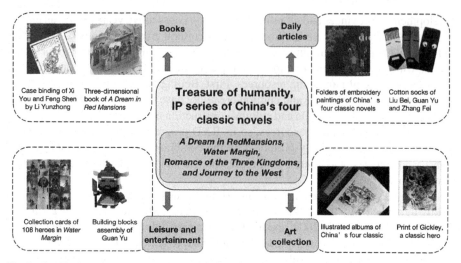

Fig. 3. Publishing and Cultural Creativity Development Diagram of "China's Four Classic Novels" Series by the People's Literature Publishing House (prepared by the author)

also prone to fall into the trap of product homogeneity and low-end imitation in the process of following up.

Existing Problems

(1) **The main categories of cultural creativity publishing are relatively single.** In addition to personalized classic research and development, the mainstream products of cultural creativity publishing are still handbooks, calendars, recycle bags, mugs, postcards, etc., with a single main category, a relatively common homogenization, and a lack of keen insight into the needs of the target market. As more and more products are independently developed and sold by publishing agencies, there are problems such as uneven quality and insufficient quality control in the research and development of multi categories of cultural creativity.

(2) **Research and development of cultural creativity publishing has not deeply explored the humanistic connotation.** In terms of R&D level, most cultural creativity publishing is still in a superficial state, and lacks in-depth exploration of humanistic spirit and cultural connotation. For example, the most homogenized products such as canvas bags and handbooks often simply integrate the existing elements and mechanically transplant the patterns, which is difficult to truly reflect the humanistic spirit behind the classic book IP.

(3) **The target audience of cultural creativity publishing is not clear.** The homogenization of cultural creativity publishing is also related to the lack of clear survey and judgement on the positioning and needs of target audience in the process of research and development. Different audiences differ greatly in their cognition and needs for cultural creativity publishing. For example, young people like cultural creativity publishing with entertainment and novelty creativity, while people in the cultural circle like products with certain collection value and cultural implication.

3   Cultural Symbiosis: R&D Strategy of Cultural Creativity Publishing

"Cultural Symbiosis" in the field of cultural research is borrowed and extended from the concept of "symbiosis" in the field of biology. In this paper, it means that different industrial fields are connected based on the core elements and spiritual values of specific cultures to form a close relationship of mutual influence, interdependence and common promotion. The integrated development of publishing industry and cultural creativity industry naturally shows the relationship of cultural symbiosis. The cultural creativity publishing is an important direction of industrial integration, which certainly has a profound cultural background. On the one hand, cultural creativity publishing takes cultural symbiosis as the premise of research and development, which fully reflects the industrialization R&D goals formed by the interaction between publishing culture and innovation culture; on the other hand, cultural creativity publishing is also the final result of cultural symbiosis, and the specifically-developed products of cultural creativity publishing will be market-oriented and become an important object to test the cultural transmission and value recognition.

The *Guiding Opinions on Promoting the Integrated Development of Traditional Publishing and Emerging Publishing* (2015) mentioned above not only provides an important basis for the construction of the whole industry chain of our publishing media, but also provides ideas for the content innovation, technological innovation and form innovation of cultural creativity publishing. "The six key tasks to innovate the content production and service, strengthen the construction of key platform, extend the content communication channels, expand new technologies and new types, improve the operation and management mechanism and play the role of market mechanism, which may promote the integrated development, specially emphasize that it is necessary to extend the advantages of professional editing and content resources of traditional publishing to the emerging publishing, so as to rely on advanced technologies and channels to promote the integrated development of publishing, establish and improve a production and operation mode with one content and multiple creativity, one creativity and multiple developments, one development and multiple products, one product and multiple forms, one sale and multiple channels, one input and multiple output, one output and multiple value added, and stimulate the vitality and creativity of the integrated development of publishing."[4] How to deal with the relationship between "one" and "multiple"? We can consider and take actions from the perspective of cultural symbiosis. Therefore, R&D strategy of cultural creativity publishing shall attach importance to the linkage effect of its cultural connotation, cultural creativity and cultural value, and take cultural symbiosis as the action version and important basis throughout the R&D process. (see Fig. 4).

3.1   Deepening of Cultural Connotation

Cultural connotation is the "soul" of cultural creativity publishing, and the spiritual core of its cultural taste and cultural attribute. The cultural connotation of cultural creativity publishing is closely related to the classical publishing form it relies on. Classic publications and characteristic publishing activities often present unique high-qualify

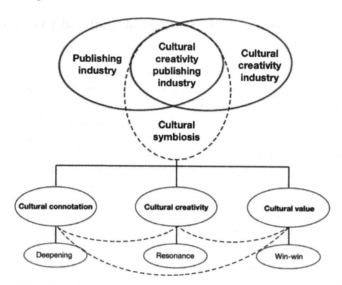

Fig. 4. Cultural Symbiosis Strategy of Cultural Creativity Publishing Research and Development (prepared by the author)

content, bear rich historical and cultural information, knowledge, experience and skills and precious humanistic spirit, and highly reflect the publishing behavior and activity itself as an important carrier of human spiritual civilization. The cultural connotation of cultural creativity publishing is the core cultural element that supports the development of the whole industry chain and the exploration of diversified forms, and also the knowledge basis and inspiration source of creative design. In the view of current situation, the research and development of cultural creativity publishing that attach importance to cultural connotation are often more convincing in the presentation of cultural concept, and can more fully arouse the deep cultural identity of target audience.

The time-honored Rong Bao Zhai is a Chinese historical brand, known for its printing and publishing culture and its skills. As early as the 1950s, it began to use the woodblock watermarking skill, a national intangible cultural heritage skill, to reproduce the famous works of contemporary artists such as Qi Baishi. In the era without the concept of "cultural creativity", Rong Bao Zhai has started the output of cultural connotations of publishing with unique Chinese characteristics through these artistic replicas. In 2021, Rong Bao Zhai, together with HEYTEA and Digiway, a Dutch-Chinese artist, created an "inspiration gift box" with the carrier of *The Night Revels of Han Xizai*. While maintaining the composition and displayed items of original painting, modern items such as fashion shoes and skateboards are added to make the classics collide with fashion, which skillfully integrated the traditional Chinese artistic atmosphere and fashion culture, and can be regarded as a contemporary case of activating the cultural connotation of publishing culture [5].

In the context of relatively impetuous market environment due to contemporary emphasis on economic efficiency, there are a few numbers of cultural creativity publishing cases that deeply study and deduce the cultural connotation. In the cultural creativity development for high-quality publishing cultural resources, it is common to see a superficial cultural output and homogeneous development. The industry should promote the deep exploration of cultural connotation, so that the cultural creativity publishing could realize the dimensional expansion of cultural concept transmission.

3.2 Resonance of Cultural Creativity

As the finishing touch of cultural creativity publishing, cultural creativity provides unique highlights and market-selling points for cultural creativity publishing through artistic thinking and creative design. Cultural creativity is an important bridge to communicate the cultural connotation of publishing and the form of cultural creativity products. In the process of transforming the cultural resources of publishing to modern design, the productization and joint experience of cultural creativity are the key links. Excellent cultural creativity is the foundation of cultural creativity publishing, the cornerstone to win practical audience recognition and economic returns, and an important way to achieve cultural popularization and cultural transmission.

Relying on cultural connotation, the cultural creativity of cultural creativity publishing ingeniously promotes the publishing cultural content to expand to the whole industry chain. Today, Chinese traditional culture is increasingly valued. Han-style clothing, as the representative of traditional Chinese costumes, has aroused the interest of cross-border cooperation in publishing industry due to continuous "broken circle" transmission in recent years. In 2021, the brand of "Treasure of Humanity" from People's Fine Arts Publishing House, together with "Zhi Yu Ji", a famous brand of Han-style clothing, jointly launched "Jinling Old Dream" series Han element clothing, which takes the "scenery in four seasons of the Red Mansion" as the creative inspiration to show the spring, summer, autumn and winter of the Grand View Garden through Han-style clothing with modern elements. It is a creative presentation of *A Dream in Red Mansions*, a Chinese classic, in the field of clothing.

Creative practice of cultural creativity publishing should be based on the transformation and realization of products at the level of daily life, so as to realize the deep cultivation of cultural connotation and the expansion of cultural value. Cultural creativity publishing shall have the ability to implement the humanistic spirit through creative design, realize the mutual care between literature and daily life, integrate the aesthetic characteristics of the times in the process of inheriting publishing culture, generate new aesthetic consensus among contemporary people, especially young people, and obtain emotional and spiritual resonance from it.

3.3 Win-Win of Cultural Value

Cultural property is the core value orientation of cultural creativity publishing. Cultural value is a light of culture retained by cultural phenomena and culture activities after a long river of time, and an important basis for publishing activity planning and cultural creativity research and development. Whether the cultural creativity publishing could withstand the test of the times and the judgement of public opinion depends on the cultural value which is a key evaluation standard. Cultural value of cultural creativity publishing is often positively related to its economic value.

For the shaping of publishing brands and publishing IP, the important evaluation standard is the cultural value contained in them. The establishment of a cultural creativity publishing value chain with cultural value as the core, the satisfaction of audiences' needs and the realization of economic value is an important basis for realizing the intrinsic value of publishing resources and forming the linkage development of the whole industry chain.

SinoMaps Press Group entered the map cultural creativity industry in 2010, and began to take shape in 2013, which has fully explored the cultural value of maps, and constantly strengthened the collation and development of map culture by means of cultural creativity and technology. It has successively published map calendar series, western ancient map decorative painting series, Beijing archaic tea set and other products of cultural creativity publishing, and obtained full market recognition and economic benefits. Monkey King is the childhood memory of several generations of Chinese people, and also an important symbol of our cultural spirit. In 2021, Blossom Press established the Rongchuang Center, of which the core publishing task is to dig and sort out the *Monkey King Series Books*, and to this day, it has realized the linkage development in various fields from book to electronic game, film and television, animation, garage kit and offline exploration hall, and also tried to combine high and new technology to create a cross-media experience of Monkey King's metaverse world, so that the contemporary teenagers have more opportunities to get in touch with the Monkey King and the core cultural value of traditional Chinese culture.

This shows the necessity of "high aspirations". When the realization of cultural value is the important goal of cultural creativity publishing research and development, the construction of industrial chain based on cultural value identification will help to create a benign industrial environment, thus realizing the effective transformation of economic benefits and finally achieving the public recognition of cultural value.

At present, China has become one of the cultural consumption markets in the world, which has the largest scale and fastest growth rate, but at the starting point of new era, the problem of unbalanced and inadequate development of China's cultural market is more and more prominent. The President Xi Jinping pointed out in the report of the 20th National Congress of the Communist Party of China that, "the main problems in our economic and social development include insufficient supply of high-quality cultural services and products, and the international communication power and influence of Chinese culture are not commensurate with our international standing" [6]. As a result, our cultural creativity industry should shift from high-speed development to high-quality development, undertake the important mission to promote the international influence and competitiveness of Chinese culture, and realize the innovation and transmission of traditional Chinese culture, thus providing strong support for the economic market. For the observation and strategic thinking on the current situation of cultural creativity publishing research and development, this paper not only aims at the case study of specific projects, but also expects to take cultural symbiosis as the starting point to urge the publishing industry and cultural creativity industry to focus on the cultural value promotion from quantity to quality in the process of industrial chain integration and expansion of cultural creativity publishing, and implement the connotation construction of cultural creativity, thus enriching the practice form of excellent Chinese culture.

Acknowledgements. This research is financial supported by Art Discipline Project of the Youth Project of Philosophy and Social Science Foundation of Beijing (No. 19YTC035) and the BIGC Project (No. Eb202310) .

References

1. The two departments issued the Guiding Opinions on Promoting the Integrated Development of Traditional Publishing and Emerging Publishing, 9 April 2015. Source: Portal Website of Central Government, website: http://www.gov.cn/xinwen/2015-04/09/content_2844294.htm
2. Luo, X., Wangqing. Discussion on publishing of cultural creativity: connotation and extension. View on Publishing, **22**, 13–15 (2017)
3. The result of 2021 Cultural Industry Development Index of Provinces and Cities in China is released, 16 April 2022. Website: http://cncci.ruc.edu.cn/sy/xwdt/18bc678499234d758ad6f 2fb58747719.htm
4. The two departments issued the Guiding Opinions on Promoting the Integrated Development of Traditional Publishing and Emerging Publishing, April 9, 2015. Source: Portal Website of Central Government, website: http://www.gov.cn/xinwen/2015-04/09/content_2844294.htm
5. Source: Rong Bao Zhai Online, WeChat official account
6. Xi, J.: Hold high the great banner of socialism with Chinese characteristics, and work together to build a socialist modern country in an all-round way-A report of the 20th National Congress of the Communist Party of China, 15 October 2022. Source: website of the Central People's Government, website: http://www.gov.cn/xinwen/2022-10/25/content_5721685.htm

Author Index

Printed in the United States
by Baker & Taylor Publisher Services